SIXTH EDITION

The European Union
Economics and Policies

Ali M. El-Agraa

with edited contributions

FINANCIAL TIMES

Prentice Hall

An imprint of **Pearson Education**

Harlow, England · London · New York · Reading, Massachusetts · San Francisco · Toronto · Don Mills, Ontario · Sydney
Tokyo · Singapore · Hong Kong · Seoul · Taipei · Cape Town · Madrid · Mexico City · Amsterdam · Munich · Paris · M

Pearson Education Limited

Edinburgh Gate
Harlow
Essex CM20 2JE
England

and Associated Companies around the world

Visit us on the World Wide Web at
www.pearsoneduc.com

First edition published in Great Britain under the Philip Allan imprint in 1980
Second edition 1983
Third edition 1990
Fourth edition published under the Harvester Wheatsheaf imprint in 1994
Fifth edition published under the Prentice Hall Europe imprint in 1998
Sixth edition published in 2001

© Ali M. El-Agraa 1980, 2001

The right of Ali M. El-Agraa to be identified as author of
this work has been asserted by him in accordance with
the Copyright, Designs and Patents Act 1988.

ISBN 0 273 64641 9

British Library Cataloguing-in-Publication Data
A CIP catalogue record for this book can be obtained from the British Library.

Library of Congress Cataloguing-in-Publication Data
A catalog record for this book can be obtained from the Library of Congress.

10 9 8 7 6 5 4 3 2 1
06 05 04 03 02 01

Typeset by 3 in Stone Serif
Produced by Pearson Education Asia Pte Ltd.
Printed in Singapore

To Diana, Mark and Frances

Lest it be forgotten, the European Union stands for the harmonized integration of some of the oldest countries in the world with very diverse cultures and extremely complicated economic systems. The European Union is about unity within diversity.

Contents

Contents

List of figures

List of tables

List of contributors

Mr Harvey W. Armstrong is Professor of Economic Geography, Department of Geography, University of Sheffield, UK.

Dr Marius Brülhart is Assistant Professor of Economics, Ecole des HEC, University of Lausanne, Switzerland.

Dr Kenneth Button is Professor of Public Policy, School of Public Policy, George Mason University, USA.

Dr Damian Chalmers is Senior Lecturer in Law, London School of Economics and Political Science, University of London, UK.

Dr C. Doreen E. Collins was Senior Lecturer in Social Policy and Administration, University of Leeds, UK, before taking early retirement in 1985.

Dr Victoria Curzon Price is Professor of Economics, University of Geneva, Switzerland, and Director of the same university's European Institute.

Dr Enzo Grilli is Professor of Economics, Johns Hopkins University, USA, and was previously Executive Director for Italy, IMF and the World Bank.

Dr Dermot McAleese is Whately Professor of Political Economy and Dean of the Faculty of Business, Economics and Social Studies, Trinity College, Dublin, Ireland.

Mr Francis McGowan is Senior Lecturer in Politics, Sussex European Institute, University of Sussex, UK.

Mr Alan Marin is Senior Lecturer in Economics, London School of Economics and Political Science, University of London, UK.

Dr David G. Mayes is Adviser to the Board of the Bank of Finland.

Dr Wolf Sauter is Professor of Economic Law, Groningen University, The Netherlands, Policy Advisor to the Independent Authority for Telecommunications and Posts (OPTA), The Hague, and National Expert with the EU's Directorate General for Competition.

Preface

The Economics of the European Community, first published in 1980, has undergone many changes. This is not the place to go through all of them, but three warrant particular mention. First, new policy areas have been added, either because they were non-existent at the beginning or have gained importance in later years. Second, fresh contributors have joined my team, some replacing those who, for one reason or another, could no longer be with me. Finally, the fifth edition, published in 1998, had a new title to reflect the changes that have taken place within the Community itself as well as in the general nature of the book. This edition maintains this tradition and in all three respects. There is a completely new chapter on the legal dimension of European Union integration by Dr Damian Chalmers of the LSE, who is a fresh addition to the team. Professor Victoria Curzon Price returns to relieve Mr Francis McGowan of the responsibility for EU industrial policy. Professor Enzo Grilli takes over from Mr Alan Marin the contribution on EU policy towards the developing world. Professor Wolf Sauter replaces Mr Francis McGowan on EU competition policy. Also, the 'History, Institutions' part of the subtitle has been dropped in the title of this edition since many users felt that the overall balance of the book weighed more heavily on economics and policies.

These changes provide adequate justification for a new edition. However, since the publication of the fifth edition, there have been major changes in the Union itself. For the first time, the entire Commission had to resign to assume responsibility for unbecoming conduct by at least one Commissioner, and the new President, Romano Prodi of Italy, has stated that he would ask any Commissioner to resign if proven guilty. Moreover, for the first time, a Commisssioner, Neil Kinnock, has been given responsibility for Administrative Reform. Furthermore, institutional reform has become a priority and at a time when there have been major changes in the governments of the member nations, most important of which are the swing towards neosocialism and the departure of German Chancellor Kohl, one of the driving forces behind European integration. Thus, much has been happening to the legal and institutional pillars of the Union. Also, the EU has gone beyond its *Agenda 2000* by allowing another six central and eastern European nations to join in the quest for membership, doubling the number of aspirants. Moreover, for the first time, Turkey has been deemed 'European' and allowed to join the queue and to negotiate membership when it is in a position to do so, i.e. when it is able to meet the criteria set out in *Agenda 2000*. Such a development would not have been possible without the reconciliatory gestures of Greece since new membership requires unanimous agreement. Furthermore, the EU has entered into 'Euro-land'. Eleven of the 15 EU member nations adopted the new currency on 1 January 1999, forfeiting the right to conduct their own monetary policies by transferring this right to the European Central Bank in Frankfurt. Although Denmark, Sweden and the United Kingdom were not expected to be on the first train to Euro-land, and Greece failed the test, Greece has been trying hard ever since to qualify, Sweden is expected to make a move soon and the Labour Government in Britain has decided to run a referendum on the matter after the next general election, expected sometime in 2002. Needless to add, an established euro will no doubt compete vigorously with the dollar and transform the EU into a major world economic power. One could go on, but covering these matters as well as updating the chapters in terms of both developments and data is enough justification for a new edition. Indeed, it could be argued that simple updating alone justifies biennial editions; that is what we shall aim for.

Let me add that the book continues to retain its original flavour: historical development is enshrined in its approach. This may make it appear outdated in some respects, but without an understanding of the development of European unity, many new initiatives would be very baffling.

A word about the style of the book is in order. The book is written in such a way that the pure theory and measurement techniques are confined to some chapters. This means that the policy chapters should be accessible to all educated laypersons. But it also means that those who seek rigorous background about economic integration can find it handy in the same book. Moreover, as my contributors will no doubt confirm, my editing style has been to ensure that the book reads as a complete whole, not as a collection of pieces, each contributed for its own sake. This has been ensured through cross-referencing, allowing repetition only where absolutely necessary.

Finally, let me thank all my contributors not only for their excellent chapters, but also for working with me under the strict conditions just mentioned. Also, many thanks to all those who continue to use the book and send me comments on it.

Ali M. El-Agraa
Fukuoka University
Japan
March 2000

Acknowledgements

The publishers wish to thank the following for permission to reproduce material:

Table 4.18: *Average tariffs (%), 1958* reprinted from *Political and Economic Planning*, Atlantic Tariffs and Trade, © Allen and Unwin 1962 with permission from Routledge.

Figure 6.5: *Public debt and budget deficits, 1996 forecast*, © European Communities, reprinted with permission from the European Communities.

Figure 7.1: *Predictions of trade creation and diversion in the EC* reprinted from Mayes, D., 'The effects of economic integration on trade', *Journal of Common Market Studies*, vol 17, no 1, p. 6, © Blackwell Publishers Limited 1978, with permission from Blackwell Publishers Limited.

Table 7.1: *Alternative estimates of aggregate effects of EFTA, 1965* reprinted from Mayes, D., 'The effects of economic integration on trade', *Journal of Common Market Studies*, vol 17, no 1, p. 8, © Blackwell Publishers Limited 1978, with permission from Blackwell Publishers Limited.

Table 7.2: *Resnick and Truman's (1974) estimates (R&T) of trade creation and trade diversion in the EC and EFTA compared with those of Verdoorn and Schwartz* reprinted from Mayes, D., 'The effects of economic integration on trade', *Journal of Common Market Studies*, vol 17, no 1, p. 12, © Blackwell Publishers Limited 1978, with permission from Blackwell Publishers Limited.

Table 7.3: *A comparison of the effects of different anti-mondes on the imports of the EC and EFTA in 1969* reprinted from Mayes, D., 'The effects of economic integration on trade', *Journal of Common Market Studies*, vol 17, no 1, p. 13, © Blackwell Publishers Limited 1978, with permission from Blackwell Publishers Limited.

Table 7.4: *A comparison of ex ante predictions of the effects of economic integration on trade for an Atlantic free trade area* reprinted from Mayes, D., 'The effects of economic integration on trade', *Journal of Common Market Studies*, vol 17, no 1, p. 18, © Blackwell Publishers Limited 1978, with permission from Blackwell Publishers Limited.

Table 10.5: *'Ad-hoc' aid to individual enterprises* reprinted from *Sixth Survey of State Aid*, © European Communities 1998, with permission from the European Communities.

Table 10.6: *'Ad-hoc' aid to individual enterprises: country breakdown* reprinted from *Sixth Survey of State Aid*, © European Communities 1998, with permission from the European Communities.

Table 10.7: *State subsidy decisions by member states, 1997* reprinted from *27th Report on Competition Policy*, © European Communities, with permission from the European Communities.

Table 10.8: *Reimbursements demanded by the Commission 1982–1993* reprinted from *23rd Report on Competition Policy*, © European Communities 1993, with permission from the European Communities.

Table 10.9: *R&TD programmes to be integrated into the multiannual framework programmes* reprinted from Peterson, J. and Sharp, M., *Technology Policy in the EU*, pp.74–75, © St Martin's Press 1998, with permission from St Martin's Press.

Table 10.11: *Aims of EU R&TD: Multiannual Framework programmes IV and V* reprinted from *Annual Report on Research and Technological Development Activities of the European Union 1999*, © COM 1999 with permission from the European Communities.

Table 10.12: *Annual R&TD expenditures at Community Level, 1984–2002* (Table 10) reprinted from *Annual Report on R&TD Activities of the European Union 1999*, © COM 1999, with permission from the European Communities.

Table 11.4: *Average unweighted ad valorem bound tariff rates, post-Uruguay Round for 10 agricultural products in 20 countries*, © World Trade Organisation, reprinted with permission from the World Trade Organisation.

Table 11.5: *Agricultural policy transfers by country, 1986–96* reprinted from *Environmental Taxes and Green Reform*, © OECD 1997, with permission from the OECD.

Figure 11.9: *Share of the EU, USA and Canada in total world export – subsidy quantity commitments for selected agricultural products for 2000*, © GATT 1994, reprinted with permission from the World Trade Organisation.

Figure 11.10: *Book value of products in public storage with intervention agencies* reprinted from *The Agricultural Situation in the European Union 1998*, © European Communities 1999, with permission from the European Communities.

Table 12.2: *EC funds to assist the fisheries sector, 1983–1986* reprinted from *Official Journal of the European Communities*, 26, C28, 3 February, © European Communities 1983, with permission from the European Communities.

Table 15.1: *Percentage composition of tax receipts and tax burdens in the EC, 1955* reprinted from Balassa, B., *The Theory of Economic Integration*, © Allen and Unwin, 1961, with permission from Routledge.

Table 15.5: *Excise duty application in each member state as a percentage of EU average* reprinted from *Bulletin of the European Communities*, Supplement 1/80, © European Communities 1980, with permission from the European Communities.

Table 15.6: *Excise duties, proposed and current in 1985* reprinted from *Europe without Frontiers* (Information 1987, p. 51), © COM 1987, with permission from the European Communities.

Table 15.8: *EU taxes on company earnings in 1996* reproduced with permission of the International Bureau of Fiscal Documentation, Amsterdam, the Netherlands. Source: *Guides to European Taxation*, Volume 2, The Taxation of Companies in Europe.

Table 16.5: *EC changes in milk production, 1984* reprinted from *18th General Report on the Activities of the European Communities*, © European Communities 1984, with permission from the European Communities.

Table 16.6: *Price changes for the 1984–1985 farm year* reprinted from *18th General Report on the Activities of the European Communities*, © European Communities 1984, with permission from the European Communities.

Table 16.9: *Financing an EC budget equal to 2.5% of the EC GDP in 1980* reprinted from *14th General Report of the Activities of the European Communities*, p. 57, © European Communities 1981, with permission from the European Communities.

Table 17.3: *Exchange rate variability against ERM currencies, 1974–85* reprinted from Ungerer, H. *et al*, *The European Monetary System and recent developments*, Occasional Paper No 148, Table 7, p. 35, © International Monetary Fund 1986, reprinted with permission from the International Monetary Fund.

Table 17.4: *Inflation and the 'sacrifice ratio'* reprinted from *Economic Outlook*, © OECD December 1996, with permission from the OECD.

Figure 18.1: *Regional Gross Domestic Product per Head, at Purchasing Power Parities, 1996* reprinted from *Sixth Periodic Report on the Social and Economic Situation in the Regions in the Community*, Map 1, © European Communities 1999, with permission from the European Communities.

Table 18.2: *EU Budget commitments, 2000–2006* reprinted from *Presidency Conclusions: Berlin European Council, 24–25 March 1999*, © Council of the European Union 1999, with permission from the European Communities.

Figure 18.2: *Regional Unemployment Rates, 1997* reprinted from European *Sixth Periodic Report on the Social and Economic Situation in the Regions in the Community*, Map 5, © European Communities 1999, with permission from the European Communities.

Figure 18.3: *Convergence of USA state personal incomes per capita, 1880–1992* reprinted from Sala-i-Martin, X., 'Regional cohesion: evidence and theories of regional growth and convergence', *European Economic Review*, vol. 40, Fig 2, pp. 1325–1352, 1996 with the permission of Elsevier Science.

Figure 18.4: *Structural Funds 1994–99: Eligible Regions Under Priority Objectives 1, 2, 5b and 6*, © European Communities, reprinted with permission from the European Communities.

Figure 18.5: *Gross Domestic Product per Capita in the Regions of Central and Eastern Europe, 1996* reprinted from *Sixth Periodic Report on the Social and Economic Situation in the Regions in the Community*, Map 47, © European Communities 1999, with permission from the European Communities.

Figure 18.6: *Eligible Areas for the Structural Funds: Objective 1, 2000–2006* reprinted from *Inforegio News*, Newsletter no. 66, © European Communities July 1999, with permission from the European Communities.

Table 20.1: *Greenhouse gas emission changes from 1990 to 2010* (Source: EU press document 9402/98), © European Communities 1998, with permission from the European Communities.

Table 21.8: *Foreign employees in the EC, 1976* reprinted from Emerson, M., 'The EMS in the broader setting of the Community's economic and political development', from Trezise, P. H. (ed), *The EMS: Its promises and prospects*, © The Brookings Institution, 1979, with permission from The Brookings Institution.

Table 22.3: *The EU in world merchandise trade, 1998* reprinted from WTO *Focus*, © World Trade Organisation April 1999, with permission from the World Trade Organisation.

Table 23.2: *Growth per capita income in developing regions* reprinted from Grilli, E. and Salvatore, D. (eds), *Economic Development*, © Greenwood Press 1994, with the permission of Greenwood Press.

Table 23.5: *Sector distribution of total Community aid to the ACPs* reprinted from Cox, A. and Chapman, J., *The EC External Co-operation Programmes*, © European Communities 1999, with permission from the European Communities.

Table 24.1: *Basic data for applicant CEECs and EU member states, 1998* reprinted from Eurostat, © European Communities 1998, with permission from the European Communities.

Table 25.1: *EC intra-area tariff reductions* reprinted from *First General Report on the Activities of the Communities*, p. 34, © European Communities 1957, with permission from the European Communities.

Table 25.2: *The establishment of the CET* reprinted from *First General Report on the Activities of the Communities*, p. 34, © European Communities 1957, with permission from the European Communities.

Table 25.3: *New members' intra-tariff reductions* reprinted from *Bulletin of the European Communities*, no. 8, © European Communities 1978, with permission from the European Communities.

Table 25.4: Approaching the CET reprinted from *Bulletin of the European Communities*, no. 8, © European Communities 1978, with permission from the European Communities.

Although every effort has been made to trace the owners of copyright material, in a few cases this has proved impossible and we take this opportunity to apologise to any copyright holders whose rights may have been unwittingly infringed.

List of abbreviations

AAMS	Association of African and Malagasy States
AAU	Arab African Union
ACC	Arab Cooperation Council
ACM	Arab Common Market
ACP	African, Caribbean and Pacific countries party to the Lomé Convention
ADAPT	Community initiative concerning the adaptation of the workforce to industrial change
AEC	Arab Economic Council
AIM	Advanced informatics in medicine
AL	Arab League
ALADI	Association for Latin American Integration
Altener	Specific actions to promote greater penetration of renewable energy sources
AMU	Arab Maghreb Union
ANZCERTA	Australia and New Zealand Closer Economic Relations and Trade Agreement
ARION	Programme of study visits for decision-makers in education
ASEAN	Association of South-East Asian Nations
ASEM	Asia–Europe meeting
BAP	Biotechnology action programme
BATNEEC	Best available technology not entailing excessive cost
BC-NET	Business Cooperation Network
BCR	Community Bureau of References
BEP	Biomolecular engineering programme
BEST	Business Environment Simplification Task Force
BENELUX	Belgium, the Netherlands and Luxembourg Economic Union
BRAIN	Basic research in adaptive intelligence and neurocomputing
BRIDGE	Biotechnological Research for Innovation, Development and Growth in Europe
BRITE/EURAM	Basic research in industrial technologies for Europe/raw materials and advanced materials
BSE	Bovine spongiform encephalopathy
BU	Benin Union
CAA	Civil Aviation Authority
CACM	Central American Common Market
CADDIA	Cooperation in automation of data and documentation for imports/exports and agriculture
CAEU	Council for Arab Economic Unity
CAP	Common Agricultural Policy

CARICOM	Caribbean Community
CARIFTA	Caribbean Free Trade Association
CCP	Common Commercial Policy
CCT	Common Customs Tariff
CEAO	Communauté Economique de l'Afrique de l'Ouest
CEC	Commission of the European Communities
CEDB	Component event data bank
CEDEFOP	European Centre for Development of Vocational Training
CEEC	Countries of Central and Eastern Europe
CEEP	European Centre for Population Studies
CEN	European Committee for Standardization
CENELEC	European Committee for Electrotechnical Standardization
CEP	Common energy policy
CEPGL	Economic Community of the Countries of the Great Lakes
CER	Closer Economic Relations
CERN	European Organization for Nuclear Research
CET	Common external tariff
CFP	Common Fisheries Policy
CFSP	Common Foreign and Security Policy
CI	Community Initiative
CIS	Commonwealth of Independent States
CM	Common market
CMEA	Council for Mutual Economic Assistance
CN	Combined Nomenclature
CODEST	Committee for the European Development of Science and Technology
COMECON	see CMEA
COMETT	Community programme in education and training for technology
CORDIS	Community research and development information service
COREPER	Committee of Permanent Representatives
CORINE	Coordination of information on the environment in Europe
COSINE	Cooperation for open systems interconnection networking in Europe
COST	European cooperation on scientific and technical research
CREST	Scientific and Technical Research Committee
CRS	Computerised Reservation System
CSCE	Conference on Security and Cooperation in Europe
CSF	Community support framework
CSTID	Committee for Scientific and Technical Information and Documentation
CTP	Common Transport Policy
CTS	Conformance testing services
CU	Customs union
DAC	Development Assistance Committee (OECD)
DDR	German Democratic Republic (now part of Germany)
DELTA	Developing European learning through technological advance
DG4	Directorate General Four
DI	Divergence indicator

DRIVE	Dedicated road infrastructure for vehicle safety in Europe
DV	Dummy variable
EAC	East African Community
EAGGF	European Agricultural Guidance and Guarantee Fund
EBRD	European Bank for Reconstruction and Development
EC	European Community
ECB	European Central Bank
ECHO	European Community Humanitarian Office
ECIP	European Community Investment Partners
ECJ	European Court of Justice
ECLAIR	European collaborative linkage of agriculture and industry through research
ECMT	European Conference of Ministers of Transport
ECOFIN	European Council of Ministers for Financial Affairs
ECOSOC	Economic and Social Committee
ECOWAS	Economic Community of West African States
ECSC	European Coal and Steel Community
ECU	European currency unit
EDC	European Defence Community
EDF	European Development Fund
EDIFACT	Electronic data interchange for administration, commerce and transport
EEA	European Economic Area
EEC	European Economic Community
EFTA	European Free Trade Association
EGE	European Group on Ethics in Science and New Technologies
EIB	European Investment Bank
EIF	European Investment Fund
EMCF	European Monetary Cooperation Fund
EMF	European Monetary Fund
EMI	European Monetary Institute
EMS	European Monetary System
EMU	European monetary union or economic and monetary union
EP	European Parliament
EPC	European political cooperation
EPOCH	European programme on climatology and natural hazards
EQS	Environmental quality standard
Erasmus	European Community action scheme for the mobility of university students
ERDF	European Regional Development Fund
ERM	Exchange-rate mechanism
ESA	European Space Agency
ESCB	European System of Central Banks
ESF	European Social Fund
ESI	Electricity supply industry
ESPRIT	European strategic programme for research and development in information technology
ETUC	European Trade Union Confederation
EU	European Union

EUA	European Unit of Account
Euratom	European Atomic Energy Commission
EUREKA	European Research Co-ordinating Agency
EURES	European Employment Services
EUROCONTROL	European Organization for the safety of Air Navigation
EURONET-DIANE	Direct information access network for Europe
EUROSTAT	Statistical office of the EC/EU
EVCA	European Venture Capital Association
FADN	EEC farm accountancy data network
FAO	Food and Agriculture Organization of the United Nations
FAST	Forecasting and assessment in the field of science and technology
FCO	Foreign and Commonwealth Office
FEER	Fundamental Equilibrium Exchange Rate
FEOGA	European Agricultural Guidance and Guarantee Fund
FIFG	Financial Instrument for Fisheries Guidance
FLAIR	Food-linked agro-industrial research
FSU	Former Soviet Union
FTA	Free trade area
GATS	General Agreement on Trade in Services
GATT	General Agreement on Tariffs and Trade (UN)
GCC	Gulf Cooperation Council
GDP	Gross domestic product
GFCM	General Fisheries Council for the Mediterranean
GNP	Gross national product
GSP	Generalized system of preferences
HDTV	High-definition television
HELIOS	Action programme to promote social and economic integration and an independent way of life for disabled people
HS	Harmonized Commodity Description and Coding System
IAEA	International Atomic Energy Agency (UN)
IATA	International Air Transport Association
IBRD	International Bank for Reconstruction and Development (World Bank) (UN)
ICONE	Comparative index of national and European standards
IDA	International Development Association (UN)
IDB	Inter-American Development Bank
IDO	Integrated development operation
IEA	International Energy Agency (OECD)
IEM	Internal energy market
IGC	Intergovernmental conference
IIT	Intra-industry trade
ILO	International Labour Organization
IMF	International Monetary Fund (UN)
IMP	Integrated Mediterranean programme
IMPACT	Information market policy actions
INSIS	Inter-institutional system of integrated services
INTERREG	Community initiative concerning border areas
IRCC	International Radio Consultative Committee

IRIS	Network of demonstration projects on vocational training for women
IRTE	Integrated road transport environment
IPR	Intellectual Property Rights
ISIS	Integrated standards information system
ISPA	Instrument for structural policies for pre-accession
ITA	Information technology agreement
ITER	International thermonuclear experimental reactor
JESSI	Joint European Submieron Silicon Initiative
JET	Joint European Torus
JHA	Judicial and home affairs
JOP	Joint venture programme PHARE-TACIS
JOULE	Joint opportunities for unconventional or long-term energy supply
JRC	Joint Research Centre
KALEIDOSCOPE	Programme to support artistic and cultural activities having a European dimension
LAFTA	Latin American Free Trade Area
LDC	Less-developed country
LEDA	Local employment development action programme
LIFE	Financial Instrument for the Environment
LLDC	Least-developed country
MAGP	Multi-annual guidance programme
MARIE	Mass transit rail initiative for Europe
MAST	Marine science and technology
MB	Marginal benefit
MC	Marginal cost
MCA	Monetary compensatory amount
MEDIA	Measures to encourage the development of the audio-visual industry
MEP	Member of the European Parliament
MERCUSOR	Southern Cone Common Market
MERM	Multilateral exchange rate model
MFA	Multifibre Arrangement (arrangement regarding international trade in textiles)
MFN	Most-favoured nation
MFP	Multiannual framework programme
MFT	Multilateral free trade
MISEP	Mutual information system on employment policies
MONITOR	Research programme on strategic analysis, forecasting and assessment in research and technology
MP	Marginal productivity
MRU	Mano River Union
NAFTA	North Atlantic Free Trade Agreement; New Zealand Australia Free Trade Area
NAIRU	Non-accelerating inflation rate of unemployment
NATO	North Atlantic Treaty Organisation
NCB	National Central Bank
NCI	New Community Instrument
NEAFC	North-East Atlantic Fisheries Commission

NET	Next European Torus
NETT	Network for environmental technology transfer
NGO	Non-governmental organisation
NIC	Newly industrializing country
NIE	Newly industrializing economy
NIEO	New International Economic Order
NIS	Newly Independent States (of the former USSR)
NOHA	Network on Humanitarian Assistance
NPCI	National programme of Community interest
NPT	Treaty on Non-proliferation of Nuclear Weapons
NTB	Non-tariff barrier
NTM	Non-tariff measure
NUTS	Nomenclature of Territorial Units for Statistics
OAPEC	Organisation of Arab Petroleum Exporting Countries
OAU	Organisation for African Unity
OCTs	Overseas countries and territories
ODA	Overseas Development Aid
OECD	Organisation for Economic Cooperation and Development
OEEC	Organisation for European Economic Cooperation
OPEC	Organisation of Petroleum Exporting Countries
OSCE	Organization for Security and Cooperation in Europe
OSI	Open systems interconnection
PAFTAD	Pacific Trade and Development Conference
PBEC	Pacific Basin Economic Council
PECC	Pacific Economic Cooperation Conference
PEDIP	Programme to modernize Portuguese industry
PETRA	Action programme for the vocational training of young people and their preparation for adult and working life
PHARE	Programme of community aid for central and eastern European countries
POSEIDOM	Programme of options specific to the remote and insular nature of the overseas departments
PPP	Polluter pays principle
PTA	Preferential trade area
PTC	Pacific Telecommunications Conference
PTT	Posts, Telegraphs and Telecommunications
QMV	Qualified Majority Voting
RACE	Research and development in advanced communication technologies for Europe
RARE	Réseaux associés pour la recherche européenne
R&TD	Research and technological development
RCD	Regional Cooperation for Development
REGIS	Community initiative concerning the most remote regions
REIMEP	Regular European interlaboratory measurements evaluation programme
RENAVAL	Programme to assist the conversion of shipbuilding areas
RESIDER	Programme to assist the conversion of steel areas
RIA	Regional impact assessment
RTA	Regional trade agreement
RTD	Research and Technological Development

SACU	Southern African Customs Union
SAP	Social action programme
SAST	Strategic analysis in the field of science and technology
SAVE	Specific Actions for Vigorous Energy efficiency
SCENT	System for a customs enforcement network
SCIENCE	Plan to stimulate the international cooperation and interchange necessary for European researchers
SDR	Special drawing rights
SEA	Single European Act
SEDOC	Inter-state notification of job vacancies
SEM	Single European Market
SEM 2000	Sound and efficient management
SFOR	Multinational stabilization force
SLIM	Simpler Legislation for the Internal Market
SMEs	Small- and medium-sized Enterprises
SPD	Single Programme Documents
SPEAR	Support programme for a European assessment of research
SPES	Stimulation plan for economic science
SPRINT	Strategic programme for innovation and technology transfer
STABEX	System for the stabilization of ACP and OCT export earnings
STAR	Community programme for the development of certain less-favoured regions of the Community by improving access to advanced telecommunications services
STEP	Science and technology for environmental protection
SYNERGY	Multinational programme to promote international co-operation in the energy sector
SYSMIN	Special financing facility for ACP and OCT mining products
TAC	Total allowable catch
TARIC	Integrated Community tariff
TEDIS	Trade electronic data interchange systems
TELEMAN	Research and training programme on remote handling in nuclear hazardous and disordered environments
TEMPUS	Trans-European cooperation scheme for higher education
TENs	Trans-European Networks
TESS	Modernization of the exchange of information between national social security institutions
TEU	Treaty on European Union
TRIPs	Trade-related aspects of intellectual property rights
TSEs	Transmissible spongiform encephalopathies
t/t	Terms of trade
TVA	Tax sur la valeur ajoutée
TUC	Trades Union Congress
UDEAC	Union Douanière et Economique de l'Afrique Centrale
UEMOA	West African Economic and Monetary Union
UES	Uniform emission standards
UN	United Nations
UNCLOS	United Nations Conference on the Law of the Sea
UNCTAD	United Nations Conference on Trade and Development
UNECA	United Nations Economic Commission for Africa

List of abbreviations

UNEP	United Nations Environment Programme
UNESCO	United Nations Educational, Scientific and Cultural Organization
UNHCR	United Nations High Commissioner for Refugees
UNICE	Union of Industries of the European Community
UNIDO	United Nations Industrial Development Organization
UNRWA	United Nations Relief and Works Agency for Palestine Refugees in the Near East
URAA	Uruguay Round Agreement on Agriculture
URBAN	Community initiative for urban areas
UTR	Unilateral tariff reduction
VALOREN	Community programme for the development of certain less-favoured regions of the Community by exploiting endogenous energy potential
VALUE	Programme for the dissemination and utilization of research results
VAT	Value-added tax
VER	Voluntary export restraint
VSTF	Very short-term financing facility
WEU	Western European Union
WFC	World Food Council (UN)
WFP	World Food Programme (UN)
WIPO	World Intellectual Property Organization (UN)
WTO	World Trade Organization
YES	'Youth for Europe' programme (youth exchange scheme)

1 General introduction

A. M. EL-AGRAA

1.1 What is economic integration?

'International economic integration' (hereafter, simply economic integration) is one aspect of 'international economics' which has been growing in importance for almost five decades. The term itself has a rather short history; indeed, Machlup (1977a) was unable to find a single instance of its use prior to 1942. Since then the term has been used at various times to refer to practically any area of international economic relations. By 1950, however, the term had been given a specific definition by economists specializing in international trade to denote a state of affairs or a process which involves the amalgamation of separate economies into larger free trading regions. It is in this more limited sense that the term is used today. However, one should hasten to add that economists not familiar with this branch of international economics have for quite a while been using the term to mean simply increasing economic interdependence between nations.

More specifically, economic integration (also referred to as 'regional integration') is concerned with the discriminatory removal of all trade impediments between at least two participating nations and with the establishment of certain elements of co-operation and co-ordination between them. The latter depends entirely on the actual form that integration takes. Different forms of economic integration can be envisaged and many have actually been implemented (see Table 1.1 for schematic presentation).

1. *Free trade areas*, where the member nations remove all trade impediments among themselves but retain their freedom with regard to the determination of their own policies *vis-à-vis* the outside world (the non-participants – for example, the European Free Trade Association (EFTA), the defunct Latin American Free Trade Area (LAFTA), and the North American Free Trade Agreement (NAFTA) but which also covers investment).

2. *Customs unions*, which are very similar to free trade areas except that member nations must conduct and pursue common external commercial relations – for instance, they must adopt common external tariffs (CETs) on imports from the non-participants as is the case in, *inter alia*, the European Union (EU, which is in this particular sense a customs union, but, as we shall presently see, it is more than that), the Central American Common Market (CACM) and the Caribbean Community and Common Market (CARICOM).

3. *Common markets*, which are custom unions that allow also for free factor mobility across national member frontiers, i.e. capital, labour, technology and

enterprises should move unhindered between the participating countries – for example, the EU (but again it is more complex).

4. *Complete economic unions*, which are common markets that ask for complete unification of monetary and fiscal policies, i.e. the participants must introduce a central authority to exercise control over these matters so that member nations effectively become regions of the same nation – the EU is heading in this direction.

5. *Complete political unions*, where the participating countries become literally one nation, i.e. the central authority needed in complete economic unions should be paralleled by a common parliament and other necessary institutions needed to guarantee the sovereignty of one state – an example of this is the unification of the two Germanies in 1990.

Table 1.1 Schematic presentation of economic integration schemes

Scheme	Free Intrascheme trade	Common commercial policy	Free factor mobility	Common monetary and fiscal policy	One government
Free trade area	Yes	No	No	No	No
Customs union	Yes	Yes	No	No	No
Common market	Yes	Yes	Yes	No	No
Economic union	Yes	Yes	Yes	Yes	No
Political union	Yes	Yes	Yes	Yes	Yes

However, one should hasten to add that political integration need not be, and in the majority of cases will never be, part of this list. Nevertheless, it can of course be introduced as a form of unity and for no economic reason whatsoever, as was the case with the two Germanies and as is the case with the pursuit of the unification of the Korean Peninsula, although one should naturally be interested in its economic consequences (see below). More generally, one should indeed stress that each of these forms of economic integration can be introduced in its own right; hence they should not be confused with *stages* in a *process* which eventually leads to either complete economic or political union.

It should also be noted that there may be *sectoral* integration, as distinct from general across-the-board integration, in particular areas of the economy as was the case with the European Coal and Steel Community (ECSC, see Chapter 2), created in 1951, but sectoral integration is a form of co-operation not only because it is inconsistent with the accepted definition of economic integration but also because it may contravene the rules of the General Agreement on Tariffs and Trade (GATT), now called the World Trade Organization (WTO) – see below. Sectoral integration may also occur within any of the mentioned schemes, as is the case with the EU's Common Agricultural Policy (CAP, see Chapter 11), but then it is nothing more than a 'policy'.

One should further point out that it has been claimed that economic integration can be *negative* or *positive*. The term negative integration was coined by Tinbergen (1954) to refer to the simple act of the removal of impediments on trade between the participating nations or to the elimination of any restrictions on the process of trade liberalization. The term positive integration relates to the modification of existing instruments and institutions and, more importantly, to the creation of new ones so as to enable the market of the integrated area to function properly and effectively and also to promote other broader policy aims of the scheme. Hence, at the risk of oversimplification, according to this classification, it can be stated that sectoral integration and free trade areas are forms of economic integration which require only negative integration, while the remaining types require positive integration, since, as a minimum, they need the positive act of adopting common relations. However, in reality this distinction is oversimplistic not only because practically all existing types of economic integration have found it essential to introduce some elements of positive integration, but also because theoretical considerations clearly indicate that no scheme of economic integration is viable without certain elements of positive integration; for example, even the ECSC deemed it necessary to establish new institutions to tackle its specified tasks – see below and Chapter 2.

1.2 Economic integration and WTO rules

The rules of WTO, GATT's successor, allow the formation of economic integration schemes on the understanding that, although free trade areas, customs unions, etc. are discriminatory associations, they may not pursue policies which increase the level of their discrimination beyond that which existed prior to their formation, and that tariffs and other trade restrictions (with some exceptions) are removed on *substantially* (increasingly interpreted to mean at least 90% of intra-members' trade) all the trade among the participants. Hence, once allowance was made for the proviso regarding the external trade relations of the economic integration scheme (the CET level, or the common level of discrimination against extra-area trade, in a customs union, and the average tariff or trade discrimination level in a free trade area), it seemed to the drafters of Article XXIV (see Appendix to this chapter) that economic integration did not contradict the basic principles of WTO – trade *liberalization* on a most-favoured-nation (MFN) basis, *non-discrimination*, *transparency* of instruments used to restrict trade and the promotion of *growth and stability* of the world economy – or more generally the principles of *non-discrimination*, *transparency* and *reciprocity*.

There are more serious arguments suggesting that Article XXIV is in direct contradiction to the spirit of WTO – see Chapter 5 and, *inter alia*, Dam (1970). However, Wolf (1983, p. 156) argues that if nations decide to treat one another as if they are part of a single economy, nothing can be done to prevent them, and that economic integration schemes, particularly like the EU at the time of its formation in 1957, have a strong impulse towards liberalization; in the case of the EU at the time mentioned, the setting of the CETs happened to coincide with GATT's Kennedy Round of tariff reductions. However, recent experience, especially in the case of the EU, has proved otherwise since there has been a proliferation of non-tariff barriers, but the point about WTO not being able to deter countries from pursuing economic integration has general validity: WTO has no means for enforcing its rules; it has no coercion powers.

Of course, these considerations are more complicated than is suggested here, particularly since there are those who would argue that nothing could be more discriminatory than for a group of nations to remove all tariffs and trade impediments on their mutual trade while *at the same time* maintaining the initial levels against outsiders. Indeed, it would be difficult to find 'clubs' which extend equal privileges to non-subscribers, although the Asia Pacific Economic Cooperation (APEC) forum aspires to 'open regionalism', one interpretation of which is the extending of the removals of restrictions on trade and investment to all countries, not just the members. Moreover, as we shall see in Chapter 5, economic integration schemes may lead to resource reallocation effects which are economically undesirable. However, to have denied nations the right to form such associations, particularly when the main driving force may be political rather than economic, would have been a major setback for the world community. Hence, all that needs to be stated here is that as much as Article XXIV raises serious problems regarding how it fits in with the general spirit of WTO, it also reflects its drafters' deep understanding of the future development of the world economy.

1.3 The global experience

Although this book is concerned with the EU alone, it is important to view the EU within the context of the global experience of economic integration. This section provides a brief summary of this experience – see El-Agraa (1997) for a full and detailed coverage.

Since the end of the Second World War various forms of economic integration have been proposed and numerous schemes have actually been implemented. Even though some of those introduced were later discontinued or completely reformulated, the number adopted during the decade commencing in 1957 was so great as to prompt Haberler in 1964 to describe that period as the 'age of integration'. After 1964, however, there has been such a proliferation of integration schemes that Haberler's description may be more apt for the post-1964 era.

The EU is the most significant and influential of these arrangements since it comprises some of the most advanced nations of Western Europe: Austria, Belgium, Denmark, Finland, France, Germany, Greece, Ireland, Italy, Luxembourg, the Netherlands, Portugal, Spain, Sweden and the United Kingdom (UK) – see Table 1.2 for a tabulation of integration arrangements (note that Tables 1.2–1.5 include arrangements not specified in the text but which are self-explanatory. The EU was founded by six (not quite, since Germany was then not yet united) of these nations (Belgium, France, West Germany, Italy, Luxembourg and the Netherlands, usually referred to as the *Original Six*, simply the Six hereafter) by two treaties, signed in Rome on the same day in 1957, creating the *European Economic Community* (EEC) and the *European Atomic Energy Community* (Euratom). However, the Six had then been members of the *European Coal and Steel Community* (ECSC) which was established by the Treaty of Paris in 1951. Thus, in 1957 the Six belonged to three communities, but in 1965 it was deemed sensible to merge the three entities into one and to call it the *European Communities* (EC). Three of the remaining nine (Denmark, Ireland and the UK) joined later, in 1973. Greece became a full member in January 1981, Portugal and Spain in 1986, and Austria, Finland and Sweden in 1995.

At present, the EU recognizes 13 candidates for membership. Six began full accession negotiations in 1988 and if all goes well, they may join in 2004: Cyprus, the Czech Republic, Estonia, Hungary, Poland and Slovenia. Also, the Helsinki summit

Table 1.2 Economic integration in Europe

EU/	Existing schemes and arrangements									Prospective arrangements		
	EU 1957 CM[a]	EFTA[b] 1960 FTA[a]	EEA CU[a]	EFTA/East Europe[c] FTA[a]	EU/Czech R. FTA[a]	EU Slovakia FTA[a]	EU/ Hungary FTA[a]	EU/ Poland FTA[a]	Israel[d]	EU/ Bulgaria FTA[a]	EU/ Israel[e] FTA[a]	EFTA/ GCC[f] FTA[a]
Aim												
Austria	x		x		x	x	x	x	x	x		x
Belgium	x		x		x	x	x	x	x	x		x
Denmark	x		x		x	x	x	x	x	x		x
Finland	x		x		x	x	x	x	x	x		x
France	x		x		x	x	x	x	x	x		x
Germany	x		x		x	x	x	x	x	x		x
Greece	x		x		x	x	x	x	x	x		x
Ireland	x		x		x	x	x	x	x	x		x
Italy	x		x		x	x	x	x	x	x		x
Luxembourg	x		x		x	x	x	x	x	x		x
Netherlands	x		x		x	x	x	x	x	x		x
Portugal	x		x		x	x	x	x	x	x		x
Spain	x		x		x	x	x	x	x	x		x
Sweden	x		x		x	x	x	x	x	x		x
UK	x		x		x	x	x	x	x	x		x
Iceland		x	x	x							x	
Norway		x	x	x							x	
Switzerland		x		x							x	
Bulgaria				x						x		
Czech Rep.				x	x							
Hungary				x			x					
Poland				x				x				
Romania				x								
Slovakia				x		x						
GCC												x
Israel									x		x	

[a] FTA = free trade area; CU = customs union; CM = common market.
[b] Finland was an associate member until its accession in 1986, and Liechtenstein became a full member in 1991.
[c] The countries involved have agreed to examine conditions for the gradual establishment of an FTA.
[d] The EU and Israel reached an agreement similar to the EEA in 1995.
[e] Currently being negotiated.
[f] See Table 1.5 for members of the Gulf Cooperation Council (GCC).

of December 1999 ruled that six more could commence full negotiations from February 2000, each at its own pace: Bulgaria, Latvia, Lithuania, Malta, Romania and Slovakia. Moreover, after 36 years of temporizing, it was also agreed at the same summit that Turkey is a recognized candidate, but negotiations are unlikely to start for a long time since the EU wants to see big improvements in Turkey's political and human rights behaviour, including the rights of Kurds and other minorities and the constitutional role of the army in political life, which might require changes in its constitution. The EU also wants the country to resolve territorial squabbles with Greece in the Aegean Sea and to help end the division of Cyprus, where a Turkish-backed regime has occupied the north of the island since 1974. However, one should add that these conditions are not new since they are consistent with those in *Agenda 2000*, the EU's official document on enlargement (CEUa, 1997). Note that most of these Central and Eastern European nations (CEECs), had already signed *Agreements of Association* with the EU. Furthermore, the EU, Iceland, Liechtenstein and Norway belong to the *European Economic Area* (EEA), a scheme which provides Iceland and Norway with virtual membership of the EU, but without having a say in EU decisions; indeed the EEA is seen as a stepping-stone in the direction of full EU membership. Thus, if all goes according to plan, the EU is set to comprise the whole of Europe since Switzerland has not withdrawn the application it lodged several years ago.

Although the EEC Treaty relates simply to the formation of a customs union and provides the basis for a common market in terms of free factor mobility, many of the originators of the EEC saw it as a phase in a process culminating in complete economic and political union. Thus the *Treaty on European Union* (the Maastricht Treaty, later ratified and extended by the Treaty of Amsterdam – see Chapter 2), which transformed the EC into the EU in 1994 and which provides the EU with, *inter alia*, a single central bank, a single currency, and common foreign and defence policies by the end of the twentieth century, should be seen as a positive step towards the attainment of the founding fathers' desired goal.

EFTA is the other major scheme of economic integration in Europe. To understand its membership one has to know something about its history. In the mid-1950s when an EEC of the Six plus the UK was being contemplated, the UK was unprepared to commit itself to some of the economic and political aims envisaged for that community. For example, the adoption of a common agricultural policy and the eventual political unity of Western Europe were seen as aims which were in direct conflict with the UK's powerful position in the world and its interests in the Commonwealth, particularly with regard to 'Commonwealth preference' which granted special access to the markets of the Commonwealth. Hence the UK favoured the idea of a Western Europe which adopted free trade in industrial products only, thus securing for itself the advantages offered by the Commonwealth as well as opening up Western Europe as a free market for its industrial goods. In short, the UK sought to achieve the best of both worlds for itself, which is of course quite understandable. However, it is equally understandable that such an arrangement was not acceptable to those seriously contemplating the formation of the EEC, especially France which stood to lose in an arrangement excluding a common policy for agriculture. As a result the UK approached those Western European nations which had similar interests with the purpose of forming an alternative scheme of economic integration to counteract any possible damage due to the formation of the EEC. The outcome was EFTA, which was established in 1960 by the Stockholm Convention with the object of creating a free market for industrial products only; there were some agreements on non-manufactures but these were relatively unimportant.

The membership of EFTA consisted of Austria, Denmark, Norway, Portugal, Sweden, Switzerland (and Liechtenstein) and the UK. Finland became an associate member in 1961, and Iceland joined in 1970 as a full member. But, as already stated, Denmark and the UK (together with Ireland) joined the EC in 1973; Portugal (together with Spain) joined in 1986; Austria, Finland and Sweden joined the EU in 1995. This left EFTA with a membership consisting mainly of a few and relatively smaller nations of Western Europe – see Table 1.2.

Until recently, economic integration schemes in Europe were not confined to the

EU and EFTA. Indeed, before the dramatic events of 1989–90, the socialist planned economies of Eastern Europe had their own arrangement which operated under the CMEA, or COMECON as it was generally known in the West. The CMEA was formed in 1949 by Bulgaria, Czechoslovakia, the German Democratic Republic, Hungary, Poland, Romania and the USSR; they were later joined by three non-European countries: Mongolia (1962), Cuba (1972) and Vietnam (1978). In its earlier days, before the death of Stalin, the activities of the CMEA were confined to the collation of the plans of the member states, the development of a uniform system of reporting statistical data and the recording of foreign trade statistics. However, during the 1970s a series of measures was adopted by the CMEA to implement their 'Comprehensive Programme of Socialist Integration', hence indicating that the organization was moving towards a form of integration based principally on methods of plan co-ordination and joint planning activity, rather than on market levers (Smith, 1977). Finally, attention should be drawn to the fact that the CMEA comprised a group of relatively small countries and one 'super power' and that the long-term aim of the association was to achieve a highly organized and integrated bloc, without any agreement ever having been made on how or when that was to be accomplished.

The dramatic changes that have recently taken place in Eastern Europe and the former USSR have inevitably led to the demise of the CMEA. This, together with the fact that the CMEA did not really achieve much in the nature of economic integration – indeed some analysts have argued that the entire organization was simply an instrument for the USSR to dictate its wishes to the rest – are the reasons why El-Agraa's (1997) book does not contain a chapter on the CMEA; the interested reader will find a chapter in El-Agraa (1988b). However, one should hasten to add that soon after the demise of the USSR, Russia and 17 former USSR republics formed the Commonwealth of Independent States (CIS) which makes them effectively one nation.

Before leaving Europe it should be mentioned that another scheme exists in the form of a regional bloc between the five Nordic countries (the Nordic Community): Denmark, Finland, Iceland, Norway and Sweden. However, in spite of claims to the contrary (Sundelius and Wiklund, 1979), the Nordic scheme is one of co-operation rather than economic integration since its members belong to either the EU or EFTA, and, as we have seen, the EU and EFTA are closely linked through the EEA.

In Africa, there are numerous schemes of economic integration – see Table 1.3. The *Union Douanière et Economique de l'Afrique Centrale* (UDEAC), a free trade area, comprises the People's republic of the Congo, Gabon, Cameroon and the Central African Republic. Member nations of UDEAC plus Chad, a former member, constitute a monetary union. The *Communauté Economique de l'Afrique de l'Ouest* (CEAO), which was formed under the Treaty of Abidjan in 1973, is a free trade area consisting of the Ivory Coast (Côte d'Ivoire), Mali, Mauritania, Niger, Senegal and Upper Volta (now Burkina Faso); Benin joined in 1984. Member countries of the CEAO, except for Mauritania, plus Benin and Togo, have replaced the CEAO by an Act constituting an economic and monetary union. In 1973 the *Mano River Union* (MRU) was established between Liberia and Sierra Leone; they were joined by Guinea in 1980. The MRU is a customs union which involves a certain degree of co-operation, particularly in the industrial sector. The *Economic Community of West African States* (ECOWAS) was formed in 1975 with 15 signatories: its membership consists of all those countries participating in UDEAC, CEAO and MRU plus some other West

Table 1.3 Regional trade arrangements in Africa

	CEAO[a]	CEPGL	EAC[b]	ECOWAS	MRU[a]	COMESA[c]	SACU	UDEAC[d]	Sene/ Gambia	Lagos Plan of Action
Founded	1972	1976	1967	1975	1973	1981	1969	1964	1981	1980
Aim	FTA	FTA	EU	FTA	CU	FTA	CU	FTA	CON[e]	EU
Angola						x				x
Benin	x			x						x
Botswana						x	x			x
Burkina Faso	x			x						x
Burundi		x				x				x
Cameroon								x		x
Cape Verde				x						
CAR								x		x
Chad								x		x
Comros						x				x
Congo								x		x
Côte d'Ivoire	x			x						x
Djibouti						x				x
Eq. Guinea								x		x
Ethiopia						x				x
Gabon				x				x		x
Gambia				x					x	x
Ghana				x						x
Guinea				x	x[f]					x
Guinea-Bissau				x						x
Kenya			x			x				x
Lesotho						x	x			x
Liberia				x	x					x
Madagascar						x				x
Malawi						x				x
Mali	x			x						x
Mauritania	x			x						x
Mauritius						x				x
Mozambique						x				x
Namibia							x			x
Niger	x			x						x
Nigeria				x						x
Rwanda		x				x				x
Senegal	x			x					x	x
Seychelles										x
Sierra Leone				x	x					x
Somalia						x				x
South Africa							x			x
Sudan						x				x
Swaziland						x	x			x
Tanzania			x			x				x
Togo				x						x
Uganda			x			x				x
Zaire		x								x
Zambia						x				x
Zimbabwe						x				x

[a] In effect since 1974.
[b] Dismantled in 1978.
[c] The Common Market for Eastern and Southern Africa is an ambitious recent replacement of the PTA which was in effect from 1984.
[d] In effect since 1966.
[e] CON = confederation.
[f] Joined in 1980.

African states. Despite its name, ECOWAS is a free trade area. Its total membership today is 17.

In 1969 the *Southern African Customs Union* (SACU) was established between Botswana, Lesotho, Swaziland and the Republic of South Africa; they were later joined by Namibia. The *Economic Community of the Countries of the Great Lakes* (CEPGL), a free trade area, was created in 1976 by Rwanda, Burundi and Zaire. Until its collapse in 1978, there was the *East African Community* (EAC) between Kenya, Tanzania and Uganda. In 1981 the *Preferential Trade Area* (PTA), a free trade area, was created by fifteen nations from Eastern and Southern Africa: Angola, Botswana, the Comoros, Djibouti, Ethiopia, Kenya, Lesotho, Malawi, Mauritius, Mozambique, Swaziland, Tanzania, Uganda, Zambia and Zimbabwe; they were later joined by another five nations. The PTA has been replaced by the much more ambitious *Common Market for Eastern and Southern Africa* (COMESA). In 1983 the *Economic Community of Central African States* (EEAC, the acronym is from French) was created by eleven nations in Equatorial and Central Africa. In 1985 the *Benin Union* (BU) was formed by Benin, Ghana, Nigeria and Togo. In 1980, the *Lagos Plan of Action* was inaugurated with a membership which included practically the whole of Africa. There are also many smaller subregional groupings such as the Kagera River Basin organization (KBO), the Lake Tanganyika and Kivu Basin organization (LTKBC) and the Southern African Development Coordination Council (SADCC).

Moreover, there are schemes involving the Northern African nations, but which also figure in Middle Eastern arrangements – see Table 1.5. In August 1984 a Treaty was signed by Libya and Morocco to establish the *Arab–African Union*, whose main aim is to tackle their political conflicts in the Sahara Desert. In 1989 the *Arab Maghreb Union* (AMU), a common market, was created by Algeria, Libya, Morocco and Tunisia. Egypt participates in the *Arab Cooperation Council* (ACC) which was formed in 1990 (see below).

Hence, a unique characteristic of economic integration in Africa is the multiplicity and overlapping of its schemes. For example, in the West alone, there was a total of 33 schemes and intergovernmental co-operation organizations, which is why the United Nations Economic Commission for Africa (UNECA) recommended in 1984 that there should be some rationalization in the economic co-operation attempts in West Africa. However, the diversity and overlapping are not confined to West Africa alone. Needless to add, the Lagos Plan of Action is no solution since, apart from encompassing the whole of Africa and being a weaker association, it exists on top of the other schemes. When this uniqueness is combined with proliferation in schemes, one cannot disagree with Robson (1997) when he declares that:

> *Reculer pour mieux sauter* is not a dictum that seems to carry much weight among African governments involved in regional integration. On the contrary, if a certain level of integration cannot be made to work, the reaction of policy makers has typically been to embark on something more elaborate, more advanced and more demanding in terms of administrative requirements and political commitment.

Economic integration in Latin America has been too volatile to describe in simple terms, since the post-1985 experience has been very different from that in the 1960s and 1970s. At the risk of misleading, one can state that there are four schemes of economic integration in this region – see Table 1.4. Under the 1960 Treaty of Montevideo, the *Latin American Free Trade Association* (LAFTA) was formed between Mexico and all the countries of South America except for Guyana and

Table 1.4 Regional trade arrangements in the western hemisphere[a]

	Existing arrangements												Prospective arrangements					
	NA-FTA	CACM[b]	LAFTA-LAIA	CARICOM[c]	Andean Pact[d]	US-Canada	MER-COSUR[e]	OECS[f]	US-Israel	Argentina-Brazil	Chile-Mexico	El Salvador-Guatemala[g]	EAI (US)[h]	Mexico-Central America[i]	Chile-Colombia-Venezuela	Colombia-Mexico-Venezuela[j]	Venezuela-Central America[k]	RIO Group
Founded	1993	1961	1960/80	1973	1969	1988	1991	1991	1989	1990	1991	1991	1991	1991				
Aim	FTA	FTA	FTA	CU	FTA	FTA	FTA	CI	FTA	FTA	FTA	FTA	FTA					
Canada	×					×												
Mexico	×		×								×			×		×		×
USA	×					×			×									
Belize													×					
Costa Rica		×											×	×			×	
El Salvador		×										×	×	×			×	
Guatemala		×										×	×	×			×	
Honduras		×											×	×			×	
Nicaragua		×											×	×			×	
Panama[l]													×	×			×	
Antigua/Bermuda				×				×					×					
Bahamas				×									×					
Barbados				×									×					
Dominica				×				×					×					
Grenada				×				×					×					
Jamaica				×									×					
Montserrat				×				×					×					
St Kitts/Nevis				×				×					×					
St Lucia				×				×					×					
St Vincent				×				×					×					
Trinidad/Tobago				×									×					
Argentina			×				×			×			×					×
Bolivia			×		×								×					
Brazil			×				×			×			×					×
Chile			×		×						×		×		×			×
Colombia			×		×								×		×	×		×
Ecuador			×		×								×					
Guyana				×									×					
Paraguay			×				×						×					
Peru			×		×								×					×
Uruguay			×				×						×					×
Venezuela			×		×								×		×	×	×	×
Israel									×									

a Does not include unilateral trade preferences and exclusive countries with no arrangements.
b Revived in 1990; aimed to establish a common market by 1992.
c Aimed to achieve a common external tariff by 1994.
d Efforts were being made to revive the AP and to create a common market by 1994.
e Aims to achieve a common market by 1995.
f Organization of East Caribbean States.
g Effective in October 1991.

h The Enterprise of the Americas Initiative aims to achieve a hemisphere free trade zone. By October 1991, the USA had signed framework agreements with 29 countries, including: the 13 CARICOM nations; the 4 MERCOSUR states, Chile, Colombia, Costa Rica, Ecuador, El Salvador, Honduras, Panama, Peru, Nicaragua and Venezuela.
i These countries aim to form a Central America–Mexican free trade zone by 1996.
j Signature of the trade and investment agreement occurred in 1991 and trilateral limited free trade was supposed to happen by the end of 1993.
k The agreement aims to phase out tariffs on trade in the area.
l Panama participates in summits but is not ready to participate fully in regional integration.

Surinam. LAFTA came to an end in the late 1970s but was promptly succeeded by the *Association for Latin American Integration* (ALADI or LAIA) in 1980. The Managua Treaty of 1960 established the *Central American Common Market* (CACM) between Costa Rica, El Salvador, Guatemala, Honduras and Nicaragua. In 1969 the *Andean Pact* (AP) was established under the Cartegena Agreement between Bolivia, Chile, Colombia, Ecuador, Peru and Venezuela; the AP forms a closer link between some of the least developed nations of LAFTA, now LAIA.

Since the debt crisis in the 1980s, economic integration in Latin America has taken a new turn with Mexico joining Canada and the US (see below) and Argentina, Brazil, Paraguay and Uruguay, the more developed nations of LAIA, creating MERCOSUR in 1991. MERCOSUR became a customs union by 1 January 1995 but aimed to become a common market by 1995. Bolivia and Chile became associate members in mid-1995, a move which Brazil sees as merely a first step towards the creation of a *South American Free Trade Area* (SAFTA), a counterweight to the efforts in the north (see below). In June 1999 MERCOSUR reached agreement with the EU to start negotiations in November 1999 on an arrangement for free trade and investment between them.

There is one scheme of economic integration in the Caribbean. In 1973 the *Caribbean Community* (CARICOM) was formed between Antigua, Barbados, Belize, Dominica, Grenada, Guyana, Jamaica, Montserrat, St Kitts–Nevis–Anguila, St Lucia, St Vincent, and Trinidad and Tobago. CARICOM replaced the *Caribbean Free Trade Association* (CARIFTA) which was established in 1968.

In 1988 Canada and the United States established the *Canada–US Free Trade Agreement* (CUFTA), and, together with Mexico, they formed the *North American Free Trade Agreement* (NAFTA) in 1993 which started to operate from 1 January 1994. Despite its name, NAFTA also covers investment. The enlargement of NAFTA to include the rest of the western hemisphere was suggested by George Bush while US President. He hoped to construct what is now referred to as the *Free Trade Area of the Americas* (FTAA) which is under negotiation, aiming for a conclusion by 2005. Chile has been negotiating membership of NAFTA.

Asia does not figure prominently in the league of economic integration schemes, but this is not surprising given the existence of such large (if only in terms of population) countries as China and India. *The Regional Cooperation for Development* (RCD) was a very limited arrangement for sectoral integration between Iran, Pakistan and Turkey. The Association for *South-East Asian Nations* (ASEAN) comprises 10 nations: Brunei, Cambodia, Indonesia, Laos, Malaysia, Myanmar, the Philippines, Singapore, Thailand and Vietnam. ASEAN was founded in 1967 by seven of these countries. Brunei joined in 1984, Vietnam in July 1995, Laos and Myanmar in July 1997 and Cambodia in December 1998. After almost a decade of inactivity ASEAN 'was galvanized into renewed vigour in 1976 by the security problems which the reunification of Vietnam seemed to present to its membership' (Arndt and Garnaut, 1979). The drive for the establishment of ASEAN and for its vigorous reactivation in 1976 was both political and strategic. However, right from the start, economic co-operation was one of the most important aims of ASEAN, indeed most of the vigorous activities of the group since 1976 have been predominantly in the economic field, and the admission of Vietnam in 1995 is a clear manifestation of this. Moreover, ASEAN has recently been discussing proposals to accelerate its own plan for a free trade area to the year 2000 from 2003, itself an advance on the original target of 2008.

In 1965 Australia and New Zealand entered into a free trade arrangement called the *New Zealand Australia Free Trade Area*. This was replaced in 1983 by the more important *Australia New Zealand Closer Economic Relations and Trade Agreement* (CER, for short): not only have major trade barriers been removed, but significant effects on the New Zealand economy have been experienced as a result.

A scheme for the Pacific Basin integration-cum-co-operation was being hotly discussed during the 1980s. In the late 1980s I (El-Agraa, 1988a, 1988b) argued that 'given the diversity of countries within the Pacific region, it would seem highly unlikely that a very involved scheme of integration would evolve over the next decade or so'. This was in spite of the fact that there already existed:

1. the *Pacific Economic Cooperation Conference* (PECC) which is a tripartite structured organization with representatives from governments, business and academic circles and with the secretariat work being handled between general meetings by the country next hosting a meeting;

2. the *Pacific Trade and Development Centre* (PAFTAD) which is an academically oriented organization;

3. the *Pacific Basin Economic Council* (PBEC) which is a private-sector business organization for regional co-operation; and

4. the *Pacific Telecommunications Conference* (PTC)) which is a specialized organization for regional co-operation in this particular field.

The reason for the pessimism was that the:

> region under consideration covers the whole of North America and Southeast Asia, with Pacific South America, the People's Republic of China and the USSR all claiming interest since they are all on the Pacific. Even if one were to exclude this latter group, there still remains the cultural diversity of such countries as Australia, Canada, Japan, New Zealand and the USA, plus the diversity that already exists within ASEAN. It would seem that unless the group of participants is severely limited, Pacific Basin *cooperation* will be the logical outcome. (El-Agraa, 1988a, p. 8)

However, in an attempt to provide a rational basis for resolving Japan's trade frictions, I may appear to have contradicted myself:

> it may be concluded that . . . Pacific Basin cooperation-cum-integration is the only genuine solution to the problems of Japan and the USA (as well as the other nations in this area). Given what is stated above about the nature of the nations of the Pacific Basin, that would be a broad generalisation: what is needed is a very strong relationship between Japan and the USA within a much looser association with the rest of SE Asia. Hence, what is being advocated is a form of involved economic integration between Japan and the USA (and Canada, if the present negotiations for a free trade area of Canada and the USA lead to that outcome), within the broad context of 'Pacific Basin Cooperation', or, more likely, within a free trade area with the most advanced nations of SE Asia: Australia, New Zealand, South Korea, the nations of ASEAN, etc. (El-Agraa, 1988b, pp. 203–4)

I added that the proposed scheme should not be a protectionist one. Members of such a scheme should promote co-operation with the rest of the world through their membership of GATT (now WTO) and should co-ordinate their policies with regard to overseas development assistance, both financially and in terms of the transfer of technology, for the benefit not only of the poorer nations of SE Asia, but also for the whole developing world.

Thus the *Asia Pacific Economic Cooperation* (APEC) forum can be considered as the

Table 1.5 Regional trade arrangements in Asia-Pacific and the Middle East

	Existing arrangements							Prospective arrangement
Founded Aim	CER 1983 FTA	ASEAN 1967 FTA	ACM 1964 CU	ECO[a] 1985	GCC 1981 CU	AFTA[b]	APEC[c]	EAEC[d]
Australia	x						x	
Brunei		x				x	x	x
Cambodia		x						
Chile							x	
China							x	x
Hong Kong							x	x
Indonesia		x				x	x	x
Japan							x	x
Laos		x						
Malaysia		x				x	x	x
Myanmar		x						
New Zealand	x						x	
Papua New Guinea							x	
Philippines		x				x	x	x
Singapore		x				x	x	x
South Korea							x	x
Taiwan							x	x
Thailand		x				x	x	x
Vietnam		x					x	
Bahrain					x			
Egypt			x					
Iran				x				
Iraq			x					
Jordan			x					
Kuwait					x			
Libya			x					
Oman					x			
Qatar					x			
Saudi Arabia					x			
Syria			x					
UAE					x			
Yemen			x					
Canada							x	
Mauritania					x			
Mexico							x	
Pakistan						x		
Peru							x	
Russia							x	
Turkey						x		
USA							x	

[a] The purpose of this group is bilateral trade promotion and co-operation in industrial planning.
[b] Thailand proposal endorsed by ASEAN Ministers in 1991.
[c] Originally a regional grouping to represent members' views in multilateral negotiating fora, now committed to freeing trade and investment among its richer members by 2010 and by 2020 by the rest.
[d] This grouping was initially proposed by Malaysia in 1990.

appropriate response to my suggestion. It was established in 1989 by ASEAN plus Australia, Canada, Japan, New Zealand, South Korea, the USA. These were joined by China, Hong Kong and Taiwan in 1991. In 1993 President Clinton galvanized it into its present form and increased its membership to 18 nations. In Bogor, Indonesia, in 1994 APEC declared its intention (vision) to create a free trade and investment area by the year 2010 embracing its advanced members, with the rest to follow suit ten years later. APEC tried to chart the route for realizing this vision in Osaka, Japan, in November 1995, and came up with the interesting resolution that each member nation should unilaterally declare its own measures for freeing trade and investment, with agriculture completely left out of the reckoning. In November 1998 Peru, Russia and Vietnam joined the APEC forum, increasing its total membership to 21 nations – see Table 1.5.

There are several schemes in the Middle East, but some of them extend beyond the geographical area traditionally designated as such. This is natural since there are nations with Middle Eastern characteristics in parts of Africa. The *Arab League* (AL) clearly demonstrates this reality since it comprises 22 nations, extending from the Gulf in the East to Mauritania and Morocco in the West. Hence the geographical area covered by the scheme includes the whole of North Africa, a large part of the Middle East, plus Djibouti and Somalia. The purpose of the AL is to strengthen the close ties linking Arab states, to co-ordinate their policies and activities and to direct them to their common good and to mediate in disputes between them. These may seem like vague terms of reference, but the *Arab Economic Council*, whose membership consists of all Arab Ministers of Economic Affairs, was entrusted with suggesting ways for economic development, co-operation, organization and co-ordination. The *Council for Arab Economic Unity* (CAEU), which was formed in 1957, had the aim of establishing an integrated economy of all AL states. Moreover, in 1964 the *Arab Common Market* was formed (but practically never got off the ground) between Egypt, Iraq, Jordan and Syria, and in 1981 the *Gulf Cooperation Council* (GCC) was established between Bahrain, Kuwait, Oman, Qatar, Saudi Arabia and United Arab Emirates to bring together the Gulf states and to prepare the ground for them to join forces in the economic, political and military spheres.

The latest schemes of economic integration in the Middle East have already been mentioned, but only in passing in the context of Africa. The ACC was founded on 16 February 1989 by Egypt, Iraq, Jordan and the Arab Yemen Republic with the aim of boosting Arab solidarity and acting as 'yet another link in the chain of Arab efforts towards integration'. Moreover, on 18 February 1989 the AMU was formed by Algeria, Libya, Mauritania, Morocco and Tunisia. The AMU aims to create an organization similar to the EU.

There are two schemes of sectoral economic integration which are not based on geographical proximity. The first is the *Organization for Petroleum Exporting Countries* (OPEC), founded in 1960 with a truly international membership. Its aim was to protect the main interest of its member nations: petroleum. After verging close to liquidation, OPEC seems to have been revived, but it has lost some of its political clout. The second is the *Organization for Arab Petroleum Exporting Countries* (OAPEC), established in January 1968 by Kuwait, Libya and Saudi Arabia. These were joined in May 1970 by Algeria, and the four Arab Gulf Emirates: Abu Dhabi, Bahrain, Dubai and Qatar. In March 1972 Egypt, Iraq and Syria became members. OAPEC was temporarily liquidated in June 1971 and Dubai is no longer a member. The agreement establishing OAPEC states that the:

principal objective of the Organization is the cooperation of the members in various forms of economic activity . . . the realization of the closest ties among them . . . the determination of ways and means of safeguarding the legitimate interests of its members . . . the unification of efforts to ensure the flow of petroleum to its consumption markets on equitable and reasonable terms and the creation of a suitable climate for the capital and expertise invested in the petroleum industry in the member countries. (*Middle East Economic Survey*, 1968)

However, in the late 1960s OAPEC flexed its muscles within OPEC to force the latter to use petroleum as a weapon against Israeli occupation of certain Arab areas. Many analysts would argue that the tactic was to no avail; indeed many believe that it accomplished no more than to undermine OAPEC's reputation, especially since there is nothing in the aims quoted above to vindicate such action. Since then, OAPEC has undertaken a number of projects both within and outside the organization – see, for example, Mingst (1977/78).

Finally, there are also the *Organization for African Unity* (OAU), *Organization for Economic Cooperation and Development* (OECD) and the *World Trade Organization* (WTO). However, these and the above are schemes for intergovernmental co-operation rather than for economic integration. Therefore, except where appropriate, nothing more shall be said about them.

1.4 The EU

Since this book is devoted to the EU, it is important to establish the nature of the EU within the context of the different types of economic integration discussed at the beginning of the chapter – readers interested in the other schemes will find a full discussion of them in El-Agraa (1997).

Article 2 of the treaty establishing the EEC pronounces that:

The Community shall have as its task, by setting up a common market and progressively approximating the economic policies of Member States, to promote throughout the Community an harmonious development of economic activities, a continuous and balanced expansion, an increase in stability, an accelerated raising of the standard of living and closer relations between the Member States belonging to it. (Treaty of Rome, Article 2, p. 3)

Article 3 then states that for the purposes set out in Article 2:

The activities of the Community shall include, on the conditions and in accordance with the time-table provided in this Treaty:
(a) the elimination, as between Member States, of customs duties and of quantitative restrictions in regard to the import and export of goods, as well as of all other measures having equivalent effect;
(b) the establishment of a common customs tariff and a common commercial policy towards third countries;
(c) the abolition, as between Member States, of obstacles to the freedom of movement for persons, services and capital;
(d) the establishment of a common policy in the sphere of agriculture;
(e) the adoption of a common policy in the sphere of transport;
(f) the establishment of a system ensuring that competition in the common market is not distorted;
(g) the application of procedures by which the economic policies of Member States can be co-ordinated and disequilibria in their balances of payments can be remedied;

(h) the approximation of the laws of Member States to the extent required for proper functioning of the common market;

(i) the creation of a European Social Fund in order to improve the possibilities of employment for workers and to contribute to the raising of their standard of living;

(j) the establishment of a European Investment Bank to facilitate the economic expansion of the Community by opening up fresh resources; and

(k) the association of overseas countries and territories with a view to increasing trade and to promoting jointly economic and social development. (Treaty of Rome, pp. 3–4)

These elements are stated more elaborately in later articles. For instance, Article 9(1) states:

The Community shall be based upon a customs union which shall cover all trade in goods and which shall involve the prohibition between Member States of customs duties on imports and exports and of all charges having equivalent effect, and the adoption of a common customs tariff in their relation with third countries. (Treaty of Rome, p. 6)

Articles 35–7 elaborate on the common agricultural policy (CAP), Articles 48–73 on the conditions for freedom of movement of factors of production, Articles 74–84 on the common transport policy (CTP) and Articles 99 and 100 on the harmonization of certain taxes.

The Treaty of Rome provisions should, however, be considered in conjunction with later developments. These have been incorporated into the Single European Act (SEA) which includes the European Monetary System (EMS), the creation of a true single market by the end of 1992 and the Maastricht Treaty which, when fully implemented by all the member countries, will realize the 'European Union', with a single currency (the Euro), a common central bank, a common monetary policy, a common defence policy and a common foreign policy by the beginning of 1999 – these are fully discussed in Chapter 2. Here, it can be categorically stated that the EU is at present more than a common market but falls short of being a complete economic union, but it is aspiring to achieve the latter as well as political union.

1.5 The possible gains from economic integration

We shall see in Chapters 2 and 6 that the driving force behind the formation of the EU, the earliest and most influential of all existing integration schemes, was the political unity of Europe with the aim of realizing eternal peace in the Continent. Some analysts would also argue that the recent attempts by the EU for more intensive economic integration can be cast in the same vein, especially since they are accompanied by one currency, the Euro, and by common foreign and defence policies. At the same time, during the late 1950s and early 1960s economic integration among developing nations was perceived as the only viable way for them to make some real economic progress; indeed that was the rationale behind the United Nations' encouragement and support of such efforts. More recently, frustrations with the GATT's slowness in reaching agreement, due to its many participants and their variable interests, have led some to the conclusion that economic integration would result in a quicker pace for negotiations since, by definition, it would reduce the number of parties involved. There are also practical considerations and countries may feel that economic integration would provide security of markets among the participants. However, no matter what the motives for economic integration may be, it is still necessary to analyse the economic implications of such geographically discriminatory associations; that is one of the reasons why I have included political unification as one of the possible schemes.

At the customs union (CU) and free trade area (FTA) levels, the possible sources of economic gain from economic integration can be attributed to:

1. enhanced efficiency in production made possible by increased specialization in accordance with the law of comparative advantage, due to the liberalized market of the participating nations;

2. increased production levels due to better exploitation of economies of scale made possible by the increased size of the market;

3. an improved international bargaining position, made possible by the larger size, leading to better terms of trade (cheaper imports from the outside world and higher prices for exports to them);

4. enforced changes in efficiency brought about by intensified competition between firms;

5. changes affecting both the amount and quality of the factors of production due to technological advances, themselves encouraged by (4).

If the level of economic integration is to go beyond the free trade area and customs union levels, then further sources of economic gain also become possible:

6. factor mobility across the borders of the member nations will materialize only if there is a net economic incentive for them, thus leading to higher national incomes;

7. the co-ordination of monetary and fiscal policies may result in cost reductions since the pooling of efforts may enable the achievement of economies of scale;

8. the unification of efforts to achieve better employment levels, lower inflation rates, balanced trade, higher rates of economic growth and better income distribution may make it cheaper to attain these targets.

It should be apparent that some of these possible gains relate to static resource reallocation effects while the rest relate to long-term or dynamic effects. It should also be emphasized that these are *possible* economic gains, i.e. there is no guarantee that they can ever be achieved; everything would depend on the nature of the particular scheme and the type of competitive behaviour prevailing prior to integration. Indeed, it is quite feasible that in the absence of 'appropriate' competitive behaviour, economic integration may worsen the situation. Thus the possible attainment of these benefits must be considered with great caution:

Membership of an economic grouping cannot of itself guarantee to a member state or the group a satisfactory economic performance, or even a better performance than in the past. The static gains from integration, although significant, can be – and often are – swamped by the influence of factors of domestic or international origin that have nothing to do with integration. The more fundamental factors influencing a country's economic performance (the dynamic factors) are unlikely to be affected by integration except in the long run. It is clearly not a necessary condition for economic success that a country should be a member of an economic community as the experience of several small countries confirms, although such countries might have done better as members of a suitable group. Equally, a large integrated market is in itself no guarantee of performance, as the experience of India suggests. However, although integration is clearly no panacea for all economic ills, nor indispensable to success, there are many convincing reasons for supposing that significant economic benefits may be derived from properly conceived arrangements for economic integration. (Robson, 1985)

However, in the case of the EU, one should always keep in mind that the 'founding fathers' had the formation of a United States of Western (hopefully all) Europe as the ultimate goal and that economic integration became the immediate objective so as to facilitate the attainment of political unity via the back door (see Chapter 2). Those who fail to appreciate this will always undermine the EU's serious attempts at the achievement of economic and monetary union via the Maastricht Treaty as the ongoing discussion clearly demonstrates – see Chapter 6.

1.6 Areas of enquiry

The necessary areas of enquiry, emphasizing the economic aspects, are quite apparent now that we have established the nature of the EU. It is necessary to analyse the effects and consequences of the removal of trade impediments between the participating nations and to make an equivalent study of the establishment of the common external relations. These aspects are tackled in Chapters 5 and 7. It is also extremely important to discuss the role of competition and industrial policies and the presence of multinational firms. These aspects are covered in Chapters 9 and 10. Moreover, it is vital to analyse the implications and consequences of a special provision for agriculture (Chapter 11), fisheries (Chapter 12), transport (Chapter 13), EMU (Chapter 6), EMS (Chapter 17), fiscal aspects (Chapters 15 and 16), regional disparity (Chapter 18), energy (Chapter 14), social dimensions (Chapter 19), factor mobility (Chapter 21), environmental considerations (Chapter 20) and external trade and aid policies (Chapters 22 and 23). The book also contains chapters on the development and future of the EU (Chapters 23 and 25) as well as chapters on the 'economics of the single market' (Chapter 8) and the legal dimension (Chapter 3).

1.7 About this book

This book offers, more or less, a comprehensive but brief coverage of the theoretical issues: trade creation, trade diversion and the Cooper–Massell criticism; the domestic distortions argument; the terms of trade effects; the economies of scale argument. It also offers a fresh look at the different attempts at the economic justification of customs union formation. A full chapter deals with the methodology and results of the measurements of the effects of the EU formation on the member states and the outside world. These are discussed briefly since a comprehensive book on them is available – see El-Agraa (1989a and 1999). There is also a full treatment of all major policy considerations – see previous section.

Although chapters on EU political co-operation, distributional problems and political and legal considerations may seem to be absent, these aspects have not been omitted: some elements of political co-operation are discussed in Chapters 2 and 24, while some of the most significant elements of the distribution problem are tackled in the chapters on the role of the EU budget, fiscal harmonization, social policies and regional policies. This does not imply that these aspects are not worthy of separate chapters, as one could in fact argue that these are the most important issues facing the EU. The treatment given to them in this book is such that the significant aspects of these policies are tackled where they are particularly relevant. Moreover, with regard to some of these policies, the EU is not yet certain in which direction it is heading, and this in spite of the adoption and endorsement of the Maastricht Treaty, which specifies certain details. The wider political considerations lie outside our scope.

Appendix | WTO's Article XXIV

Territorial application – frontier traffic – customs unions and free trade areas

1. The provisions of this Agreement shall apply to the metropolitan customs territories of the contracting parties and to any other customs territories in respect of which this Agreement has been accepted under Article XXVI or is being applied under Article XXXIII or pursuant to the Protocol of Provisional Application. Each such customs territory shall, exclusively for the purposes of the territorial application of this Agreement, be treated as though it were a contracting party; *Provided* that the provisions of this paragraph shall not be construed to create any rights or obligations as between two or more customs territories in respect of which this Agreement has been accepted under Article XXVI or is being applied under Article XXXIII or pursuant to the Protocol of Provisional Application by a single contracting party.

2. For the purposes of this Agreement a customs territory shall be understood to mean any territory with respect to which separate tariffs or other regulations of commerce are maintained for a substantial part of the trade of such territory with other territories.

3. The provisions of this Agreement shall not be construed to prevent:
   (a) Advantages accorded by any contracting party to adjacent countries in order to facilitate frontier traffic;
   (b) Advantages accorded to the trade with the Free Territory of Trieste by countries contiguous to that territory, provided that such advantages are not in conflict with the Treaties of Peace arising out of the Second World War.

4. The contracting parties recognize the desirability of increasing freedom of trade by the development, through voluntary agreements, of closer integration between the economies of the countries parties to such agreements. They also recognize that the purpose of a customs union or of a free-trade area should be to facilitate trade between the constituent territories and not to raise barriers to the trade of other contracting parties with such territories.

5. Accordingly, the provisions of this Agreement shall not prevent, as between the territories of contracting parties, the formation of a customs union or of a free-trade area of the adoption of an interim agreement necessary for the formation of a customs union or of a free-trade area; *Provided* that:
   (a) with respect to a customs union, or an interim agreement leading to the formation of a customs union, the duties and other regulations of commerce imposed at the institution of any such union or interim agreement in respect of trade with contracting parties not parties to such union or agreement shall not on the whole be higher or more restrictive than the general incidence of the duties and regulations of commerce applicable in the constituent territories prior to the formation of such union or the adoption of such interim agreement, as the case may be;
   (b) with respect to a free-trade area, or an interim agreement leading to the formation of a free-trade area, the duties and other regulations of commerce maintained in each of the constituent territories and applicable at the formation of such free-trade area or the adoption of such interim agreement to the trade of contracting parties not

included in such area or not parties to such agreement shall not be higher or more restrictive than the corresponding duties and other regulations of commerce existing in the same constituent territories prior to the formation of the free-trade area, or interim agreement, as the case may be; and

(c) any interim agreement referred to in sub-paragraphs (a) and (b) shall include a plan and schedule for the formation of such a customs union or of such a free-trade area within a reasonable length of time.

6. If, in fulfilling the requirements of sub-paragraph 5(a), a contracting party proposes to increase any rate of duty inconsistently with the provisions of Article II, the procedure set forth in Article XXVIII shall apply. In providing for compensatory adjustment, due account shall be taken of the compensation already afforded by the reductions brought about in the corresponding duty of the other constituents of the union.

7. (a) Any contracting party deciding to enter into a customs union or free-trade area, or an interim agreement leading to the formation of such a union or area, shall promptly notify the CONTRACTING PARTIES and shall make available to them such information regarding the proposed union or area as will enable them to make such reports and recommendations to contracting parties as they may deem appropriate.

(b) If, after having studied the plan and schedule included in an interim agreement referred to in paragraph 5 in consultation with the parties to that agreement and taking due account of the information made available in accordance with the provisions of sub-paragraph (a), the CONTRACTING PARTIES find that such agreement is not likely to result in the formation of a customs union or of a free-trade area within the period contemplated by the parties to the agreement or that such period is not a reasonable one, the CONTRACTING PARTIES shall make recommendations to the parties to the agreement. The parties shall not maintain or put into force, as the case may be, such agreement if they are not prepared to modify it in accordance with these recommendations.

(c) Any substantial change in the plan or schedule referred to in paragraph 5(c) shall be communicated to the CONTRACTING PARTIES, which may request the contracting parties concerned to consult with them if the change seems likely to jeopardize or delay unduly the formation of the customs union or of the free-trade area.

8. For the purposes of this Agreement:

(a) A customs union shall be understood to mean the substitution of a single customs territory for two or more customs territories, so that

(i) duties and other restrictive regulations of commerce (except, where necessary, those permitted under Articles XI, XII, XIII, XIV, XV and XX) are eliminated with respect to substantially all the trade between the constituent territories of the union or at least with respect to substantially all the trade in products originating in such territories, and,

(ii) subject to the provisions of paragraph 9, substantially the same duties and other regulations of commerce are applied by each of the members of the union to the trade territories not included in the union;

(b) A free-trade area shall be understood to mean a group of two or more customs territories in which the duties and other restrictive regulations of commerce (except, where necessary, those permitted under Articles XI, XII, XIII, XIV, XV and XX) are eliminated on substantially all the trade between the constituent territories in products originating in such territories.

9. The preferences referred to in paragraph 2 of Article I shall not be affected by the formation of a customs union or of a free-trade area but may be eliminated or adjusted by means of negotiations with contracting parties affected. This procedure of negotiations with affected contracting parties shall, in particular, apply to the elimination of preferences required to conform with the provisions of paragraph 8(a)(i) and paragraph 8(b).

10. The CONTRACTING PARTIES may by a two-thirds majority approve proposals which do

not fully comply with the requirements of paragraphs 5 to 9 inclusive, provided that such proposals lead to the formation of a customs union or a free-trade area in the sense of this Article.

11. Taking into account the exceptional circumstances arising out of the establishment of India and Pakistan as independent States and recognizing the fact that they have long constituted an economic unit, the contracting parties agree that the provisions of this Agreement shall not prevent the two countries from entering into special arrangements with respect to the trade between them, pending the establishment of their mutual trade relations on a definitive basis.

12. Each contracting party shall take such reasonable measures as may be available to it to ensure observance of the provisions of this Agreement by the regional and local governments and authorities within its territory.

PART ONE

History, institutions and basic statistics

CHAPTERS

2   History and institutions
3   The legal dimension in EU integration
4   The basic statistics

The aim of this part of the book is to provide the reader with a general background to the EU. Chapter 2 gives a short account of the historical development of the EU and describes its institutions and their functioning. Chapter 3 explores the legal dimension in EU integration. Chapter 4 is a general statistical survey of the major economic indicators for members of the EU, but it also provides relevant information concerning the potential members of the EU and compares the state of the 15 nations plus the potential members with that of Canada, Japan, the United States and the Russian Federation.

2 History and institutions

C. D. E. COLLINS

2.1 Organizing Western Europe

The European Union (EU) is a unique political institution and this makes it diffi-cult to analyse and understand. The usual political models relate either to nation states, whether unitary or federal, or to traditional international organizations and the Union has elements drawn from all these strands. Furthermore, it is constantly evolving, often in very controversial ways. It is helpful to bear in mind the broader political environment within which the EU operates for this helps to explain many of the disagreements about its internal structure and future development. In the last analysis, the objectives of the Union are political rather than economic and, in the words of the preamble of the Treaty of Rome, are to 'lay the foundations of an ever closer union among the peoples of Europe' and by 'pooling their resources to preserve and strengthen peace and liberty'.

Historically, the aim of political union in Western Europe is an old one and although, in the past, it has failed to match the strength of nationalist feelings, beliefs in a common history, culture and destiny have helped to keep alive the view that a common political framework may one day be found. As the Second World War came to an end, the task appeared more urgent for Europe was physically dev-astated, too weak to restore itself without aid from the USA, and was shortly to be divided as the cold war began. Such circumstances made it possible to breach the psychological barriers preventing moves towards greater integration. There have remained, however, divergent views about how to proceed. A major divide soon appeared between those who wished to develop on the basis of very close inter-state co-operation and those who wished to take the plunge of moving towards a political entity of a federal nature and the fierce debates of the time, and more recently over the Maastricht Treaty and beyond, reflect the fact that there is still no agreement on a suitable future political shape for Western Europe. The Amsterdam Treaty of 1997 shows a willingness to accept variable structures in the future which may lead to a more differentiated Union than that so far developed.

It was in 1947 that General Marshall launched the plan of aid from the United States to revitalize the European economy, provided assistance programmes were organized on a continental and not a state basis. The following years saw the cre-ation of the Organization for European Economic Cooperation (OEEC) to control a joint recovery programme and to work for the establishment of freer trade, although this was limited to Western Europe only. Its later expansion into the Organization for Economic Cooperation and Development (OECD) brought world-wide membership and this gave expression to the world liberal trading area which forms part of the environment in which the EC (now the EU) took root. It continues to be an organization whose views on the activities of member states and the way they handle their economies have considerable influence.

Defence problems demanded special arrangements. The Brussels Treaty of 1948 was a pact of mutual assistance between the United Kingdom, France and the Benelux countries and was neatly balanced in aim between the perpetuation of the wartime alliance against Germany and the realization of a newer threat from the USSR. Recognition of the interdependence of the defence of Western Europe and wider defence needs was marked by the signature of the North Atlantic Treaty in 1949 by the Brussels Treaty powers in association with the United States and Canada, Denmark, Iceland, Italy, Norway and Portugal. This move brought a new dimension into European integration by recognizing that Western Europe was part of a larger military grouping but kept defence arrangements away from subsequent political and economic developments.

The same period saw yet another attempt to express the unity of Europe with the creation of the Council of Europe in 1949. This body has very broad political and cultural objectives, including the notable contribution of protecting the individual through the Convention for the Protection of Human Rights and Fundamental Freedoms. Its statute expresses a belief in a common political heritage based on accepted spiritual and moral values, political liberty, the rule of law and the maintenance of democratic forms of government. The Council of Europe was able to obtain wide support in Western Europe but it contained no real drive towards unification. It was impatience with this omission that led activists to try a new approach which was to result in the setting up of three European Communities and it was not long before an opportunity arose.

The establishment of a working relationship between the western alliance and West Germany was becoming urgent. The old Germany was now, in practice, divided but the western half was not accepted as a fully independent state. However, West Germany's economic recovery had begun and with the onset of the cold war she was needed as a contributor to the defence and prosperity of the West. A way had therefore to be found to re-establish West Germany without arousing the fears of her recent enemies and, in particular, of France.

The beauty of the proposal for the European Coal and Steel Community (ECSC) was its ability to appeal to many interests. It seemed rational to treat the coal and steel industries of the area as a single whole; greater efficiency and control of war-making capacity would thus be gained and it would be physically impossible for France and Germany to go to war with each other again. It was to be the first stone in the sound and practical foundation of a united Europe creating a base for economic unity under the guidance of a strong executive. Integration was here founded on a sectoral approach allowing for functional integration based on the belief that common solutions could be found for common problems. This approach, so different from classical diplomacy, formed the basis of what was to become known as the Community method. The ECSC was rapidly launched and appeared to work well, so it was not long before a new project was launched based upon the same approach.

The outbreak of the Korean war in 1950 resulted in American pressure on the west Europeans to do more to defend themselves against possible Soviet attack. This raised the issue of a military contribution from West Germany. Since the situation bore some resemblance to that which had made the launching of the ECSC possible, a similar attempt was made. The proposal was for a European Defence

Community (EDC) and the six members of the ECSC initialled a treaty in 1952. As before, the EDC was intended to kill several birds with one stone. It would be a further move to attach West Germany and the Germans to the West, in both a political and a psychological sense; it would produce the needed military contribution and it would introduce institutional controls. The novel feature was to be a European army, in which small national units would be merged into an integrated force which, in turn, would be subordinated to the NATO command. The whole structure bore a striking similarity to the ECSC arrangements.

However, it required a further element. A unified army made no sense if member states went their own ways in foreign policy or controlled their own defence efforts and a method of democratic control over the army would need to be found. Almost inevitably, therefore, the project had to be enlarged with a proposal for a parallel European political authority whose institutions would ultimately absorb those of the ECSC and EDC and which would push forward towards more general economic integration.

The project was larger and more sensitive than the ECSC and it failed to be accepted, with the result that the next move in European integration, the European Economic Community (EEC), steered very clear of foreign and defence policy whose development is, even now, in a much earlier stage than that reached in economic integration (see section 2.5 below). Meanwhile alternative solutions to immediate problems had to be found. The Brussels Treaty Organization was merged into a new body, the Western European Union (WEU); West Germany and Italy became members of WEU and it was agreed that West Germany should become a member of NATO (Italy had already joined). Other measures were agreed to clear up the aftermath of the Second World War and so, although formally the cause of European unity had received a setback, a line had been drawn under the past, means found whereby West Germany could become a full member of the Western community and the states of the area could concentrate upon the future.

A new attempt at integration was soon made and in June 1955 the foreign ministers of the six ECSC countries met at Messina. They discussed the possibility of pursuing general integration but also the idea of creating further functional organizations for transport and for the peaceful exploitation of atomic energy. Although general integration was seen as the way towards political unity this goal was not unduly stressed for fear of running into further antagonism, so it became an aspiration, relegated to a distant future. The meeting set up an intergovernmental committee under the chairmanship of Paul-Henri Spaak, then Foreign Minister of Belgium, and this committee produced the blueprint which was to form the Treaty of Rome creating the EEC. A second Treaty of Rome set up Euratom but the proposed transport community was not adopted.

Underlying the detail of the report is a vision of a revitalized western Europe, able to deal on equal terms with the superpowers and to influence world events. It looked for ways of liberating the abilities of the European people and of improving the foundations of European society. The chosen method was to be the setting up of a common market to provide the necessary productive base. This would require some collective measures, broadly common economic expansion and higher living standards and measures to utilize, and develop, European resources, including labour reserves. The resulting treaty contained the necessary detail, with a heavy emphasis upon the measures immediately required to create the common market but leaving a great deal to be decided in the future as the project unfolded. It was thus necessary for the new organization to have a general capacity to act. The treaty also set up the necessary institutions but these were politically cautious in their powers and it was generally held that the new organization was less supranational than the ECSC. Partly this reflected a change of mood, partly an unwillingness to run into more political controversy and partly a realization that the task of integrating whole economies was larger, more difficult and uncertain than handling a single sector. The price paid for the new venture was therefore caution in the political sphere and the institutions of the EEC left a great deal of power to the member states. It provided, however, a unique co-operative framework in which the clash of national interests could occur without being pushed to the point of mutual destruction. Unless they wished to break the edifice, member states were forced to find agreement.

2.2   The development of the EC

The EEC (which later adopted the title European Community to embrace the work of the three Communities) created a special set of institutions to handle its affairs. These centred on a Council of Ministers and a Commission, backed by a Parliament and a Court of Justice (see section 2.4). By the 1970s, however, it was clear that the EC needed institutional strengthening. The early tasks laid down in the Treaty of Rome had been completed, further internal objectives had to be formulated and a way found to ensure that the EC could act more effectively on the international stage. The result was to bring national political leaders more closely into EC affairs by the introduction of summit meetings. These were formalized under the name of the European Council in 1974 but the first major summit meeting was in 1969 when member states agreed that they were now so interdependent that they had no choice but to continue with the EC. This decision provided the necessary political will to reach agreement on the development of the common agricultural policy (CAP), on budgetary changes and, most importantly, on the need to work for enlargement. At the time, this meant settling the question of relations with the United Kingdom which had vexed the EC from the beginning.

Additionally, it was recognized that the EC needed institutional development to match its growing international stature. Its existing international responsibilities neither reflected its economic weight nor allowed effective consideration of the political aspects of external economic relations. Individual members still conducted most of their external affairs themselves and could easily cut across EC interests and this was apart from the issue of whether the EC should begin to move into the field of wider foreign affairs. Since member states had very different interests, and often different views on relations with the USA, with the USSR and on defence, it was clear that the EC was not ready to take over full competences. However, the foreign ministers were asked to study the means of achieving further political integration, on the assumption of enlargement, and to present a report. As a result, the EC began, in a gingerly fashion, to move into political co-operation with an emphasis on foreign affairs. This did not lead to a common foreign policy but it did mean efforts to identify common aims and it led to further institutional innovation alongside the institutions of the EC rather than as part of them although old and new gradually came closer together.

A second landmark summit meeting was held in 1972 and attended by three new members, Denmark, Ireland and the UK. It devoted considerable attention to internal affairs and notably to the need to strengthen the social and regional aims of the EC as part of an ambitious programme designed to lead to a full European Union. It also saw a continuing need to act externally to maintain a constructive dialogue with the USA, Canada and Japan and for member states to make a concerted contribution to the Conference on Security and Cooperation in Europe. Foreign ministers were to meet more frequently to discuss this last issue. This meeting marked the realization that heads of governments would have to meet more frequently than in the past. At first sight this seemed to strengthen the intergovernmental structure of the EC at the expense of the supranational element but this was not really so. Rather it showed that the future was a joint one, that the international climate was changing and often bleak and that, if members dealt with their internal economic difficulties alone, then this could undermine the efforts of the EC to strengthen the economies. Informal discussion of general issues, whether economic or political, domestic or worldwide, was a necessary preliminary to action which often seemed stronger if it were to be EC based. Through the summit meetings and the political co-operation procedure (EPC) the subject matter coming to the EC steadily enlarged.

By the 1980s it was clear that the political and economic environment in which the EC operated was changing fast. Tumultuous events in the former Soviet Union and the countries of the Warsaw Pact threw the institutional arrangements of western Europe into disarray and brought the need to reassess defence requirements, the role of NATO and the continuance of the American defence presence. The unsolved issue of whether the EC needed a foreign and defence policy, or at least some half-way house towards one, was bound to be raised once more. Meanwhile, the economic base upon which the EC had been able to develop had become much more uncertain. Recession, slow growth, industrial change, higher unemployment and worries about European competitiveness undermined previous confidence.

The twin issues of constitutional development and institutional reform continued to exercise EC circles but little progress was possible and the EC seemed to be running out of steam. The deepening of the integrative process required action which governments found controversial and the new members, now including Greece, Spain and Portugal, inevitably made for a less cohesive group while the recession hardened national attitudes towards the necessary give and take required for co-operative solutions. EC finances were constrained, with the result that new policies could not be developed and this, in turn, led to bitter arguments about the resources devoted to the CAP. Internal divisions were compounded by fears of a lack of dynamism in the EC economy threatening a relative decline in world terms. Such worries suggested that a significant leap forward was required to ensure a real common market, to encourage new growth and at the same time to modernize the institutions of the EC.

As the debate progressed, a major division emerged between those who were primarily interested in the ideal of political union and who wished to develop the EC institutions accordingly and those, more pragmatic in approach, who stressed the need for new policies. It was not until December 1985 that the lines of agreement could be settled. These were brought together in the Single European Act (SEA) which became operative on 1 July 1987. The key policy goal was to establish a true single market by the end of 1992 with free movement of capital, labour, services and goods. This was supported by other policies including responsibilities towards the environment, more encouragement of health and safety at work, technological research and development and co-operation in economic and monetary policy. The SEA also accepted that a policy of economic and social cohesion would be required to help the weaker states to develop so that they could participate fully in the single market. Foreign policy co-operation was brought more closely into the mainstream and given a stronger support structure. The other side of the bargain was a political strengthening of the institutions. It was agreed that the Council of Ministers should take decisions by qualified majority vote in relation to the internal market, research, cohesion and improved working conditions and that, in such cases, Parliament should share in decision making.

The single market provided a goal for the next few years and the EC busied itself with the necessary preparation, giving evidence of its ability to work as a unit. But it brought new complications. It raised the question of how much power should be held by the EC institutions, presented member states with heavy internal programmes to complete the changes necessary for the single market and exposed the very different economic conditions in member states which were bound to affect their fortunes in the single market. Meanwhile the unification of Germany fundamentally changed her position within the EC by giving her more political and economic weight but at the same time it required her to expend considerable effort eastwards.

A further challenge of the time came from new bids for membership. (So far there has been one withdrawal. The position of Greenland was renegotiated in 1984 but she remains associated and has a special agreement to regulate mutual fishing interests.) The single market policy finally convinced the doubters in Western Europe that they should try to join. This was both a triumph and an embarrassment for the EC in that it was preoccupied with its own internal changes and a belief that it had not yet fully come to terms with the southern enlargement which had brought in Greece, Spain and Portugal. An uncertain reaction was shown in that some member states wished to press on with enlargement as a priority while others wished to complete the single market and to tighten internal policies before opening the doors. A closer economic relationship was negotiated between the EC and the EFTA countries other than Switzerland (i.e. Austria, Sweden, Finland, Norway, Iceland, Liechtenstein) to form a European Economic Area (EEA) and this was assumed to be a preliminary step towards membership, a step taken in 1995 by Austria, Sweden and Finland. Switzerland has never formally withdrawn the application she made some years ago but still hesitates to take the final plunge. Subsequently, most states in Central and Eastern Europe expressed the desire to join and formal negotiations were opened with those thought most likely to succeed. However, the instability in the Balkans and the war in Kosovo showed the need to hasten the process and, at Helsinki in December 1999, it was agreed to open accession talks with a group originally thought of as being in the second round (see Chapter 24). There is now an active list of 13 candidates of which Cyprus, the Czech Republic, Estonia, Hungary, Poland and Slovenia are in the van but which includes Bulgaria, Latvia, Lithuania, Malta, Romania and Slovakia. After many years of trying, Turkey has been accepted as a candidate as well. Formal entry of the 13 is likely to be staggered over several years but a new sense of urgency surrounds the process. Finally, a recent change of regime in Croatia has brought her nearer to joining the group in the foreseeable future.

It is not easy to generalize about the issues involved in admitting such a variety of states to membership. The EU has a series of agreements with applicants through which it provides aid and advice on development and reform. In particular, it is looking for economic reform, the development of democratic political institutions and the protection of minority and human rights as necessary preconditions for closer relationships with the EU and, finally, full membership. Partnership and co-operation agreements with Russia and the newly independent states exist also but have no membership goal.

Clearly, an organization with such a large and varied membership would be very different from the original EEC of six and the applications challenge received wisdom as to its nature. They necessarily demand institutional change as it is accepted that the major institutions will become unworkable with such large numbers and this is one reason why pursuing the question of enlargement was made consequent upon the finalizing of the Maastricht Treaty and agreement upon new financial and budgetary arrangements for the existing members. Continuing issues about defence and the appropriate reaction to conditions in Central and Eastern Europe, the war with Iraq and the collapse of Yugoslavia all suggested that further consideration of foreign and defence capabilities was important.

It was, therefore, against a troubled background that the EC set up two inter-governmental conferences to prepare the way for a meeting of the European Council at Maastricht in December 1991 which produced a blueprint for the future. It aimed to integrate the EC further through setting out a timetable for full economic and monetary union, introduced institutional changes and developed political competences, the whole being brought together in a Treaty on European Union (TEU) of which the Economic Community formed a part of a wider European Union. It is not surprising that the ratification process, for which not a great deal of time was allowed, produced furious argument across Western Europe. Although each nation had its own particular worries, a general characteristic which the treaty made obvious was the width of the gap between political élites and the voters in modern society. Although political leaders rapidly expressed contrition that they had failed to provide adequate explanation for their moves they seemed less able to accept that there were strong doubts about many of the proposed new arrangements as being the best way forward and that a period of calm thinking, with less frenetic development, might in the end serve the EC and its people better.

Maastricht, therefore, left contentious problems which the Amsterdam conference was meant to solve. Although the hard core, consisting of changes to the voting system in the Council and the size of the European Commission, was still not tackled, the Treaty of Amsterdam in 1997 was useful in bringing objectives and policies up to date, in clarifying the position on foreign and defence policy and in justice and home affairs and in strengthening the Union's social side. The Treaty itself modified the existing treaties, notably the Treaty establishing the European Community (Treaty of Rome) and the Treaty of European Union (Maastricht Treaty) and these two treaties, together with the *acquis communitaire* (legislation deriving from the treaties) can be considered as a form of constitution for the EU. Supplementary treaties must be used when developments go beyond the existing ones. Past examples include changes in budget procedures, agreements to admit new members and the single market policy. In addition a unique arrangement attached to the Maastricht Treaty in 1991: an agreement and protocol were annexed because the UK could not accept changes in the social field agreed by other members and, although these no longer hold, the consequences have still not been fully worked through (see Chapter 19). The EC (i.e. the EEC, the ECSC and

EURATOM) forms the most developed section of the Union and its legislation takes precedence over national decisions in the appropriate field. A moment's reflection will show that this is a necessary precondition for the EC to work at all; it would otherwise be impossible to create a single economic unit, to establish the confidence necessary between members or to handle external relations.

2.3 The European Union

The Treaty of Amsterdam set out to give the Union a more coherent structure, a modern statement of goals and policies and to bring some necessary improvements in the working of the institutions. Naturally enough, it highlights those aspects which are new but this does not mean that they are necessarily more important than more long-standing policies. Events have determined that, for example, publicity has been given to the provisions on foreign and defence policy but they remain far less developed than arrangements in the economic sphere. Despite being thought of as a tidying up of Maastricht loose ends, the Treaty of Amsterdam is a substantial document. The treaty itself has three parts dealing respectively with substantive amendments to previous treaties, their simplification and modernization and, finally, their renumbering, ratification procedures and official language versions. In addition, however, there are an annexe, 13 protocols, often dealing with very difficult issues, 51 declarations and eight declarations by individual member states.

The EU has broad objectives. The classic aim, set out long ago, is to lay the foundations of, and subsequently develop, the 'ever closer union'. It promotes economic and social progress, an aim which includes the abolition of internal frontiers, better economic and social cohesion, an economic and monetary union and a single currency. It wishes to assert an international identity through a common foreign and defence policy and new provisions are designed to enhance this and to draw closer to the Western European Union (WEU). It has not only introduced a formal Union citizenship but taken steps to strengthen the commitment to democracy, to individual rights, to promote equality and to combat discrimination. It has a procedure to be followed should a member state appear to breach human rights. The treaty has also established the EU as an area of free movement, security and justice which is attempting to establish clearer and more uniform rules in these fields. These goals are supplemented by those of the Treaty of Rome (Articles 2, 3 EC). Internally, the EC has general economic objectives relating to the internal market, agriculture and transport, the goal of economic and social cohesion and a new emphasis on policy making in employment, social and environmental matters. The need for greater competitiveness for Community industry, the promotion of research and development (R&D), the construction of trans-European infrastructure, the attainment of a high level of health protection, better education, training and cultural development all find their place. Recognition is given to development policies, consumer protection and measures in energy policy and tourism. There are, of course, a host of subsidiary and supporting objectives.

After many arguments, the concept of flexible integration has now been brought out into the open. Articles 40, 43 and 44 (EU) allow some member states to establish closer co-operation between themselves with the aim of developing Union policies which not all members wish to pursue, but subject to a veto by a dissenting member. Such a move must be supported by a majority of members, not harm the interests of others and allow the non-participating members to be involved in the discussion of developments although not to vote on them. There are some important examples of policies which are less than fully inclusive. They include membership of the single currency, the Danish opt-outs from the free movement provisions although accepting the Schengen principle and from decisions with defence implications, and the British and Irish non-acceptance of the abolition of border controls.

The Maastricht conference touched fears of the creation of a super-state which it attempted to counter by introducing the doctrine of subsidiarity and the Treaty of Amsterdam tried to clarify this further. Article 5 (EC) explains that, where the EC does not have exclusive competence, it may only proceed if the member states cannot pursue the action themselves and it is an objective better achieved by Community action. A protocol attached to the Amsterdam Treaty has tried to clarify how this concept should be applied and, in particular, insists that the reasons for action must be stated, Community action must be simple and limited and a report given to Community institutions on what has been done. These provisions are meant as a check on an insidious growth of Community power, allowing it to slip in a direction which has never been consciously agreed. This brake is supported by the right of member states to bring a case in the European Court of Justice (ECJ) arguing that the EC is extending its powers unjustifiably (see Chapter 3).

An element in the debate about subsidiarity is doubt concerning the remoteness of decision taking in Brussels. There is a need to make the Community more responsive to the wishes of the general public and more sensitive to the effects of the intrusiveness that EC legislation appears to bring. The 'democratic deficit' is an issue that has long been discussed and there are several ways of addressing it, of which giving greater powers to the European Parliament (EP) is one. Individuals have long had the right to petition the EP and this has been supported by the appointment of an ombudsman, appointed by the EP but independent of it.

A particular issue is the undermining of national parliaments, especially those which have an important legislative function and which have found it hard to devise ways of exercising control over the EC. In practice, they have been limited to scrutiny of proposals which, once they are in an advanced stage, are very difficult to change. Some efforts have been made, through scrutiny committees, to discuss general issues as well, thus helping to suggest policy positions for the future, while Denmark, in particular, has tried to define the parameters within which ministers may negotiate. A protocol of the Treaty of Amsterdam tries to increase the influence of national parliaments. It requires that all Commission consultation papers be forwarded promptly, that proposed legislation should be made available in time for parliaments to consider it and that there should be a six-week gap between a legislative proposal being submitted to the European Parliament and the date it is sent to the Council of Ministers. A great deal is, of course, up to national parliaments to keep abreast of events and to improve contacts with the European Parliament. Associated with this was general acceptance of the need to keep the public better informed and to provide access to Community documentation. A declaration attached to the 1997 treaty stresses the importance of transparency, access to documents and the fight against fraud, Article 255 (EC) giving citizens a right of access to official documents. A further declaration accepts the importance of improving the quality of drafting in legislation. Over the years, efforts have been made, too, to help individuals question the EC. The right to petition the EP was buttressed by the establishment of an ombudsman, appointed by the EP but independent in investigations. A further change, directly affecting individuals, was to confer the citizenship of the Union on the nationals of member states (see Chapter 19). Although such changes are intended to encourage a greater openness in decision making, it will take time for them to be implemented. Actual decision taking in the Council of Ministers remains private.

Flexible policies and subsidiarity have been referred to together, although they deal with very different circumstances, because they both suggest that the EU is still uneasily balanced between the two opposing views on how to organize western Europe which have been so eloquently expressed since the end of the Second World War. The treaty, to some observers, represents one more step towards a federal Europe but to others, it is a means of keeping a check upon this drive and retaining a degree of national governmental control. The final outcome is still uncertain.

An over-arching institutional framework is clearly required to bring some consistency into such wide-ranging functions, to take appropriate decisions and to try to balance those forces that lie behind the EU so that unity is preserved. The next section turns to consider these arrangements.

2.4 The European institutions

The institutions of the Union have their functions under the respective sections of the treaties but their most comprehensive use is for the work of the European Community and the institutions are therefore explained within this context. However, in the Maastricht Treaty, the *European Council* (see section 2.2 above) was given a formal status and directed to provide the impetus for development and political guidance for the Union as a whole. It meets at least twice a year. The working institutions operate on a *modus vivendi*, developed over the years, which enables business to be carried on. In practice, tensions exist which can develop into a power struggle between them as happens between national governments and the Union itself. A critical example was the conflict between the Council and the Commission in 1965–6 which curbed the development of the Commission's powers and another period of difficulty appeared in the late 1970s when the Parliament tried to obtain greater power, especially over the budget. Both episodes contributed to periods of political stagnation and led to uneasy compromises.

Formally, a Community decision results in a regulation, a directive, a decision, a recommendation or an opinion. A *regulation* is generally and directly applicable as it stands, a *directive* is binding in objective on the member states but not in method of achievement, a *decision* is binding on those to whom it is addressed while *recommendations* and *opinions* have no binding force (Article 249 EC). These formal acts, notably the regulations and directives, are constantly adding to EC law. In 1997, a preference was expressed for the use of directives, and of a framework nature only, over regulations as part of a move to simplify Community actions. Decisions normally emanate from the Council of Ministers which decides the issue on procedures as laid down for the particular subject matter. Before this stage is reached, however, a complex process has been undertaken. The *Council of Ministers* consists of representatives of member governments. Its decisions are taken by unanimous, simple or qualified majority voting (QMV) and, when the last method is used, the votes are weighted so that at least some of the smaller members must assent. It is thereby hoped to arrive at a decision supported by a wide spectrum of opinion. The original intention was for the Council to move towards the use of majority voting and, although this has happened, it has been a slow and bumpy ride. The SEA extended the use of QMV to a wide range of decisions relating to the completion of the single market, R&D and the improvement of working conditions, and the EU Treaty goes even further along this road. Nevertheless, some matters remain subject to the unanimity rule. These include some treaty amendments, the accession of new members, some decisions relating to police and judicial co-operation (Article 34 EU), the principles of foreign policy and the possibility of permitting derogations. Unanimity also comes into play, along with absolute majority, in some procedural mechanisms for reaching final conclusions on proposals as they pass between Council, Parliament and Commission. However, the broad flow of policy now comes under QMV.

The Commission also attends Council meetings and plays an active part in helping to reach a decision, although it has no voting rights. It is here, however, that it can perform an important mediatory function between national viewpoints and its own, which is intended to represent the general Community interest.

The presidency of the Council is held by each member state in turn for a six-month period and the chairmanship of the many committees alters correspondingly. It has become the practice for each member state to try to establish a particular style of working and to single out certain matters to which it wishes to give priority. Since any chairman can influence business significantly, the president may occupy an important, albeit temporary, role. The president also fulfils some representational functions both towards other EC institutions, notably the European Parliament, and in external negotiations where the presidents of the Council and Commission may act in association.

Membership of the Council varies according to the subject matter under review and this growth has brought its own problems at home. As Community issues are handled by various ministers, briefed by their own civil servants, so it becomes harder for any government to see its European policy as a coherent whole. In turn, co-ordination within the government machine becomes important. For the Community, too, the greater specialization of business creates difficulties for it has become far harder to negotiate a package deal whereby a set of decisions can be agreed, and each member has gains to set off against its losses although, in the long run, governments need to show the benefits they have won.

The Council has its own secretariat and is also supported by a most important body, the *Committee of Permanent Representatives* (COREPER). Members of this committee, drawn from national administrations, are of ambassadorial rank and are the pinnacle of a structure of specialist and subordinate committees, often including members of home departments who travel to Brussels as required. COREPER prepares Council meetings and handles a great deal of work on behalf of the Council. It serves as an essential link between national bureaucracies, is in touch with the Commission during the process of formulating an intended proposal and is, in practice, involved in all major stages of policy making, ranging from early discussion to final Council decision taking. Many policy matters are, in reality, agreed by COREPER and reach the Council of Ministers only in a formal sense.

While this is one way of keeping business down to manageable proportions, it has meant that the Council itself has become concerned only with the most important matters or those which may not be of great substance but which are nevertheless politically sensitive. This has encouraged domestic media to present Council meetings as national battles in which there has to be victory or defeat and politicians, too, have become extremely adept at using publicity to rally support to their point of view. As a result, the effect has become the opposite of that originally intended when it was thought that the experience of working together would make it progressively easier to find an answer expressive of the general good and for which majority voting would be a suitable tool. Instead, conflict of national interests is often a better description. The Council also encounters practical problems. The great press of business, the fact that ministers can only attend to Council business part time, the highly sensitive nature of their activities and the larger number of members all contribute to a grave time-lag in reaching policy decisions and the move towards QMV was one measure designed to overcome this difficulty.

The Council is charged with the co-ordination of general economic policies of the members and, as power is transferred to the Community from the states so its powers must grow. The EU Treaty has also given it power to fine member states or to impose other sanctions with regard to government deficits (Article 104 EC). These measures suggest it is gaining in power *vis-à-vis* member states but, on the other hand, it is more circumscribed in other directions by the growing powers of the European Parliament (see below).

The second essential element in the making of EC policy is the *Commission*. This consists of 20 members, all nationals of the 15 member states and chosen on the grounds of competence and capacity to act independently in the interest of the EC itself. They are thus charged not to take instructions from governments. They do, however, need to be people familiar with the political scene, able to meet senior politicians on equal terms, for without this stature and ability to understand political pressures they would lose the senses of touch and timing which are essential for effective functioning. A few women have achieved commissioner rank but it remains largely a male preserve as do the top levels of the Commission's staff, although efforts are being made to change this imbalance.

France, Germany, Italy, Spain and the UK have two members each; the remaining states have one each. It has been known for some time that the Commission is too large a body for its tasks, a problem which enlargement will exacerbate, and a number of ideas exist for getting round this difficulty but so far national pride has prevented action. There is, however, general agreement that some reform is essential. An intergovernmental conference is at the time of writing (2000) discussing a solution which will be based on two ideas. There will be a limit on the size of the Commission, perhaps through the loss of the second commissioner post held by the major powers and, at the same time, a stronger voice for them in the Council of Ministers in order to represent population strengths rather better. This could be through a change in the weighting of votes and/or a dual majority voting system. A wholesale reorganization of the Commission is to occur at least a year before membership exceeds 20.

A new-style Commission took office in January 1995. Tenure now extends to five years and the period coincides with the life of the EP. Governments nominate the president of the Commission by common accord but the EP must approve. Governments then, in consultation with the presidential nominee, nominate the other members of the Commission and the whole team must be approved by the EP before being formally confirmed in office.

Following the exposure of the ineptness and laxity of some parts of the Commission, the EP has taken the question of approval even more seriously and has subjected nominees to detailed scrutiny including their suitability for their intended posts. It has also been made clear that the commissioners must work under the political guidance of the president (Article 219 EC) while the present commissioners have had to agree to resign if asked to do so by the President. The procedures have enhanced Parliament's powers considerably since it can satisfy itself about the Commission's programme and intended initiatives before giving its approval.

While the moves are intended to ensure a more efficient Commission, the episode has brought a latent contradiction to the surface. The Commission was designed as the powerhouse of political momentum for the EC, although this function is to some extent now shared with the European Council and the EP, and it has been less effective in administrative and managerial functions where its weakness has been exposed. This has led some critics to argue that reform should include a shift of responsibility away from policy towards execution so that the Commission becomes more like a national civil service.

Each commissioner has responsibility for one, or more, major areas of EC policy and, although in form the Commission is a collegiate body accepting responsibility as a group, in practice policy rests mainly with the responsible commissioner, perhaps in association with two or more colleagues. Adoption by the full Commission is often a formality but, unlike the Council, it has always used majority voting and no other method would enable it to get through the volume of work. At all stages of its work, it consults closely with the Council and is further developing its working relationships with the EP.

The commissioners are supported in two ways. Each commissioner has a private office, under a *chef de cabinet*, and these officers take many decisions on behalf of their chiefs. Second, there is the Commission staff itself. This is organized into *general directorates* (DGs) corresponding to the main areas of EC policy. In total there are about 15 000 civil servants of whom about 15% are necessary because of the heavy linguistic burden resulting from the use of 11 official EC languages. Often the work of the Commission seems rather slow but integrating the detail of national economies and undertaking the necessary consultations and translations are time consuming. Although the directorates are staffed by various nationalities, it is important to try to ensure that no one national viewpoint predominates, especially amongst the more senior staff. Over time, some directorates have acquired greater prestige than others; not surprisingly, those that deal with core Community policies count for most and, as the EC has developed, so the possibility of conflict between directorates over policy matters can arise. Competition and regional policy, Third World imports and agricultural policy are obvious examples. A new development brought with the 1999 Commission is to have a senior commissioner responsible for an oversight of external affairs whether of an economic or political nature. The reform of the Commission has begun. The personal Cabinets of the commissioners are being opened to wider recruitment so that they are less obviously national enclaves attached to a particular commissioner, reform of financial controls and stronger management systems are being put into place and merit is to account for more and nationality less for promotion to senior posts.

Personnel are to receive more training and be subject to tighter controls. These reforms are being undertaken by Mr Neil Kinnock, an energetic vice president, who is trying to bring the Commission up to modern standards of public administration but he is expected to meet strong resistance as union control of internal staff matters has traditionally been very tight.

The directorates are responsible for the initiation of proposals leading to a formal Commission proposal and they also administer agreed policy. The significance of this varies since a great deal of EC policy is administered nationally with the Commission employed more in monitoring and evaluation, tasks in which it is considered weak. Competition policy, however, requires direct contact with individual firms as do some functions relating to the coal and steel industries.

In recent years, the Commission has become more involved with the operation of the structural funds. It has considerable discretion in the allocation of monies, within broad guidelines, and has a series of advisory committees to assist it. Grants go through national administrations and there is close contact with them, and with lesser authorities over planning programmes and deciding which schemes will fit in best with the overall framework.

The implementation of the single market inevitably meant an active role for the Commission, which began a heavy programme of harmonizing directives and other legislation. This has led to considerable unease, not just on the part of national governments which are constantly being asked to change established rules and see power slipping away. The EP and politically concerned groups also worry about the Commission's lack of accountability and the difficulty of keeping abreast of its activities. The new arrangements brought by the EU Treaty for the EC to work on the principle of subsidiarity and for the EP to share in the appointment of commissioners were one response to these fears.

An important function of the Commission is to ensure that the members abide by their obligations or, as it is normally described, to act as the guardian of the treaties. It is essential that the rules are actively, and correctly, applied in member states or mutual confidence in the edifice will begin to slip. In many cases, keeping states and firms up to the mark results simply from day-to-day business and normal liaison but there are occasions when more formal steps are necessary. The Commission can investigate a suspected breach of obligation and issue a *reasoned opinion*. If matters are not set right, the Commission may refer the matter to the Court of Justice and this may, ultimately, lead to a fine (Article 228). Although the Commission has few direct sanctions, it has the power to fine firms which breach certain operational rules while member states have, so far, generally accepted their obligation to abide by EC rules. Recent evidence has suggested that states are beginning to resist implementation, and there has been considerable slippage on matters relating to the single market, a circumstance which has increased the argument that it would be better if the EC did less.

Considerable interest attaches to the functions of the Commission as initiator of policy and exponent of the EC interest. These responsibilities explain why it is the Commission which must initiate the policy proposals that go to the Council for decision (but see below for Parliament's role). Thus the working of the EC largely depends on the activity of the Commission and the quality of its work. With the need to develop a range of policies the Commission's role is crucial. However, in working out its proposals, the Commission is subject to a number of influences. It has to take Parliament's views into account, while the regular meetings of the

European Council provide broad guidelines for policy. In preparing a proposal, the appropriate directorate undertakes extensive discussions with COREPER, government departments and representatives of interested firms and other groups. It carries out, or more frequently commissions, initial studies and all this knowledge will contribute to a Commission proposal which will be further discussed by the European Parliament, the Economic and Social Committee and the Committee on the Regions after which it will probably be amended. These extensive and lengthy discussions, taken both before and after a proposal is formalized, are part of a process designed to obtain the highest level of agreement and acceptability to member states and, at the same time, to enhance the process of European integration.

To sum up, the Commission has a number of responsibilities. Some are executive in nature but its functions extend to the initiation of policy, the protection of EC interests, the mediation between national interests and the protection of the treaty structure. It also has the power to raise loans for agreed purposes. Thus the Commission cannot be equated with any equivalent national body. At one time it was thought that the Commission might simply become an organization for implementing decisions of the Council but its powers and its links with the EP prevent this happening. While the EU Treaty, by increasing the powers of Parliament, seems to curtail those of the Commission, the latter has a new position in the pillars for a common foreign and security policy (CFSP) and judicial and home affairs (JHA). Whether it will continue in its pre-eminent position as the driving force for change and development is less certain. Its future role is dependent on the evolution of the Union – and many believe that the impetus for this will have to come from governments, whether they act as a unit or as an inter-governmental group. Developments in foreign and defence policy and in justice and home affairs have shown elements of this mixed approach, while monetary union has required new institutional arrangements outside the Commission. If member states take advantage of the possibility of flexible development this would again inhibit an old style of initiative based on the Commission. Over the years, it may become primarily concerned to operate existing arrangements, notably the single market, while newer interests have their own achievements.

The *Court of Justice* is an integral part of the institutional structure (see Chapter 3). The Community is a highly complex body, created by treaties which lay down the operating rules for the various institutions and the basic rules for economic integration but which can also introduce general ideas for later clarification by the Court. Thus it is necessary for several reasons. It must ensure that the institutions act constitutionally, fulfilling their treaty obligations, but it must also help to ensure the observance of an ever-growing volume of EC rules by member states, firms and individuals. This is not just a matter of pronouncing upon any possible infringements of the EC legal system, although these may range from neglecting to implement a rule to slow and lax administration. It includes the need to guide national courts in their interpretation of EC law. A uniform application of the law is a slow business and difficult to achieve since it has to be incorporated into 15 legal systems, each with its own norms and methods of work. The difficulty is compounded since EC rules often operate alongside national ones where responsibilities are shared. It is not surprising that a great many court cases arise from policies for agriculture, competition and social security for migrants, where states have their own pre-existing policies and national and EC interests overlap.

The Court consists of 15 judges and nine advocates-general, the latter being responsible for preliminary investigation and for submitting a reasoned opinion to the Court to help it to come to a decision. In its method of working, the Court is heavily influenced by the legal systems of the members and particularly of the original six. It will hear cases brought by a Community institution, member state or directly concerned individual against the decisions of a Community institution or a national government which are thought incompatible with Community law, including a failure to act. It may impose penalties for infringements. States agreed they would abide by the decisions and the fact that, in practice, they mainly do so is an important factor in maintaining the validity of the system.

As the EC developed, the Court became worried about its ability to keep up and a backlog of cases developed. It is important that there should be no serious delay in making judgments since large business and commercial decisions may be at stake and the single market could be prejudiced if firms do not know where they stand. Similarly, if the Court delays, national courts will become chary of seeking rulings and will go their own way in interpreting the rules. The SEA, therefore, allowed for the setting up of a Court of First Instance to handle cases on the business side, including competition policy, together with staff cases and subject to a right of appeal. The EU Treaty also introduced the notion of a chamber of judges to deal with particular categories of cases and allows the Council to increase the number of judges if the Court so wishes (Article 221 EC).

The powers of the ECJ have not been greatly changed by recent treaties but they have been enlarged with greater emphasis upon fundamental rights and the development of police and judicial co-operation in recent treaties. It has power to fine a member state in some circumstances and Parliament's right to bring actions against the Council and Commission has been extended.

A relatively young institution is the *Court of Auditors* which the EU Treaty established as a major Community institution. It resulted from growing demands, notably from Parliament, for better external auditing of the budget and its clarification. Its work includes investigating the operations carried out in member states, pronouncing upon their effectiveness and publishing a report on its work in the *Official Journal*. Its influence grows along with EC business. A major concern has been about the misuse of Community funds and member states are expected to tighten up their control measures. The Court of Auditors is an important institution in exposing these events.

It is now time to turn to the place of the *European Parliament* (EP), the powers of which have steadily, but slowly, grown over the years. It has also become more adroit at exploiting its powers to gain a stronger position. A prime function is, of course, as a debating chamber and the other major institutions submit annual reports to it for this purpose. Much detailed work on matters of interest, and on legislative proposals, is carried out through a committee system and the EP formulates its views through debates on the committee reports. An important function is exercised in relation to the Commission and the appointments of its members. It has always had a formal control mechanism in the right to dismiss the whole Commission but this has been considered as rather impractical as it would bring the Community process to a halt, but votes of censure have been used occasionally to express strong disapproval of a policy line. It is possible to imagine that this mechanism may be used more readily now that the EP can influence the composition of any reappointed Commission. Parliament has also become better in the use of its power to ask questions, both verbally and in writing, as a means of keeping the Council and Commission up to the mark. The Political Committee holds policy discussions with the foreign ministers and this work is also subject to question time.

It has the right to set up committees of inquiry and to appoint an ombudsman and may be petitioned by any EU citizen or other resident. It must also draw up proposals for a uniform procedure for the electoral process which the Council is to recommend to members for adoption. Finding a solution to this problem has exercised the EC for many years and the anomalies extend to include severe imbalances of size and population between constituencies. The Amsterdam Treaty has limited the size of the EP to 700 seats, which allows for the enlargement process, but there is a case for examining the allocation of seats within this number.

A vexed question has been that of the site of Parliament. Nowadays, it normally meets in Strasbourg, most committee work is carried out in Brussels and a large part of the secretariat is based in Luxembourg. This arrangement has been confirmed although a more rational arrangement would ease many practical difficulties and help Parliament to become a more coherent and effective organization.

The European Parliament is remarkable for having achieved the first international election in June 1979 and members (MEPs) are elected every five years. Once elected, MEPs are organized in political, rather than national, groups and the EU Treaty gave formal recognition to parties and their importance to the integrative process (Article 191 EC). However, the groups still often consist of a collection of loosely co-operating national parties rather than forming a single coherent unit. It is important, however, for Parliamentarians to be members of a group since the business of Parliament is conducted through them. There are 626 members in all: 99 for Germany, 87 each for France, Italy and the UK, 64 for Spain, 31 for the Netherlands, 25 each for Belgium, Greece and Portugal, 22 for Sweden, 21 for Austria, 16 each for Denmark and Finland, 15 for Ireland and 6 for Luxembourg.

Following the 1999 election, the European People's Party/European Democrats (centre right) were returned with the largest number of seats (233) and the Party of European Socialists came second with 180. The other groupings are considerably smaller. The European Liberal, Democrat and Reformist Group has 50 members, the Greens and home rule parties together have 48, the confederal Group of Left/Green/Communist MEPs 42, the Union for Europe of Nations 31, the TGI (a group which brings together a number of disparate elements and whose existence is being considered by the Legal Affairs committee) has 18, the Europe of Democracies and Diversities Group (a miscellany of defence of rural traditions, UK independence and some anti-EU members) 16 and the Independent Group 8 members. There has always been considerable fluidity within and between the parties but it is unusual to have so many members who are seriously hostile to the EU.

The key question for the EP has always been its role in the legislative process. The original treaties laid down occasions upon which the EP must be consulted and, in practice, its opinion has been sought on all important issues. It could, nevertheless, be legally disregarded. However, consultation meant that the committees were able to build up close relations with the Commission while working on their reports. An important change came with the SEA which gave the EP a limited, but real, place in the legislative process under the 'co-operation procedure' (Article 252 EC), a method now reserved for some decisions relating to economic and monetary union. This requires two readings each by the Council and Parliament with a unanimous Council decision being able to overrule Parliament in the last resort. More important, today, is the *co-decision procedure* (Article 251 EC), which requires agreement from both institutions, with a conciliation procedure to reconcile their views where necessary. If this is impossible, the proposal is lost. It should be noted that, in the complex passages between institutions, timetables for action apply.

Two other ways in which the EP has a part to play in the decision-making process are assent and information. The Council may only go forward with assent in determining whether a member is in breach of fundamental rights of citizens (Article 7 EU), on the tasks of the structural funds (Article 161 EC), on recommending to states a uniform electoral procedure (Article 190 EC), on some international agreements (Article 300 EC) and on admitting new members (Article 49 EU). There are some measures for which the Council must inform Parliament of action taken.

Finally, passing the budget has its own special procedures. Once it had been agreed that the EC should be responsible for its own monies, some degree of parliamentary control was required. A treaty to start the process was signed in 1970, and amended subsequently.

A draft budget is made up by the Commission by September for expenditure the following year. This is then adopted by the Council on QMV and sent to Parliament for discussion. The key to understanding Parliament's budgetary control lies in the distinction between 'compulsory' and 'non-compulsory' expenditure. The former derives from treaty obligations and the bulk has always consisted of CAP expenditure. Compulsory expenditure may be modified in the first instance by a majority of votes cast, but these changes must subsequently be agreed, or rejected, by the Council. Non-compulsory expenditure may be modified by a majority of all members of Parliament but there is a given limit beyond which Parliament may not go. Although the Council may subsequently amend Parliament's decision, the total draft budget must return for a second parliamentary reading and, at this point, Parliament may reject the Council's changes in non-compulsory expenditure. Finally, Parliament is entitled to reject the draft budget entirely and to demand a new one or, alternatively, it must formally approve the final form. Parliament has made full use of the procedural powers thus given to it to try to force changes in budget expenditure.

Once both Council and Parliament had been given budgetary powers, it was necessary to strengthen procedures for consultation between them. The aim is to resolve disagreements through mutual discussion and compromise and to allow for early discussion of proposals likely to give rise to future expenditure.

An innovation in the EU Treaty was to give Parliament the right to ask the Commission to submit a proposal leading to a Community act. This was the first amendment made to the Commission's sole right of initiative and may well produce significant changes in the subject matter of decisions. The voice Parliament now has in approving the Commission and in sharing legislative decisions means that the original tandem of Council and Commission as the powerhouse for action has been seriously modified towards a triangle.

Parliament is still in an evolutionary stage and cannot be expected to follow the path of national parliaments which, in any case, differ among themselves. It operates in a different environment and its power struggles, so far, have been with the Council and Commission rather than national parliaments.

A considerable problem for the EC has always been that of keeping in touch with citizens and ensuring they are adequately consulted and informed. Parliament, of course, is one way of making public opinion more aware of EC activity and it is an important channel through which information and knowledge are fed back to member states. Additionally, there is a vast battery of machinery which acts as another link in the communications chain and which plays its part in shaping EC decisions. One of the formal mechanisms is the *Economic and Social Committee*, which has advisory status, and is designed to represent the various categories of economic and social activity such as employers, unions, farmers and the self-employed together with representatives from community and social organizations. It has 222 members, appointed by the Council on the basis of national lists, each member appointed for four years and acting in a personal capacity. In practice, members are considered as coming from three main groups, namely employers, unions and representatives of the general interest, and national delegations reflect this tripartite composition. It is usual to seek the opinion of the committee on all major policy proposals and the committee will also formulate its own opinion on subjects it considers important. Like many advisory bodies, the committee has found it hard to establish an effective voice but it is, nevertheless, helpful to the Council and Commission to have group views available before policy has hardened, and discussions in the committee provide this information. Meetings also enable like-minded people throughout the EC to meet and discuss, so that it helps to build up a core of people in the EC who are knowledgeable about EC affairs.

In addition, the Commission is supported by a set of advisory committees for its funding operations and by a range of working parties and committees for particular industries and problems. It freely uses outside experts and organizations to provide services, while Brussels is well known for the amount of pressure group lobbying that occurs. An *Employment Committee*, representing states and the Commission, is a reflection of concern with the economy, the effect of inflation and structural change on employment levels and the difficulties experienced by workers in declining industries. The meetings of employers and unions in the *social dialogue* are another way in which the Commission pursues consultation.

The EU Treaty also created a further advisory committee, the *Committee of the Regions,* representing regional and local bodies and also with 222 members. The committee has to be consulted by both Council and Commission on certain matters and can submit its own opinions. Its creation reflects the growing interest of authorities, such as the German *Länder*, and of national groups, including the Scots, Flemings and Catalans, in the work of the EC and their wish to influence its decisions directly. Whether the committee will be able to develop a significant role, as many hope, remains a matter for the future. Some members have a powerful regional structure, others none at all, and the committee has not yet become an effective political player on the European stage.

In some ways, both for interest groups and for the man or woman in the street who wishes to make the effort, the Commission is more accessible than national administrations. This is in part because the consultation processes, although clumsy, do bring a wide range of people into touch with EC affairs. The danger of this web of machinery and consultation is indecision and slowness of action. At the same time it puts a premium on the views of those who are effectively organized. Additionally, there is a well-established Commission policy of informing and educating the public in order to mobilize public opinion behind the integration process. Unfortunately, this policy often fails to reach its target, so that considerable unease remains and its relative success in establishing relations with bankers, organizational representatives, industrialists and other power groups has contributed to a widespread belief that the EU is an élitist institution far away from the ordinary citizen. Hence a new drive towards better information, and public access to it, was promised in the Maastricht Treaty and is continuing.

Standing apart from these institutions is the *European Investment Bank* (EIB) which was given the task of contributing to the balanced and steady development of the common market in the interests of the EC. It has three main fields of operation: to aid regional development; to help with projects made necessary by the establishment of the common market – for which normal financial means are lacking; and to assist projects of common interest. It is not a grant-aiding fund but a bank operating normal banking criteria whose capital is contributed by member states and by the money it can raise on normal markets. In addition to its lending operations, it is used as a channel for loans guaranteed by the EC budget and this is especially important for loans to the Third World and Mediterranean countries.

Finally, the EU Treaty set out the arrangements of the institutions necessary for economic and monetary union. These are the European System of Central Banks and the European Central Bank.

2.5 Foreign and security policy

The overwhelming concern of the EU has been to develop internal economic relationships and it is only relatively recently that it has begun to consider the need for a formal political presence on the international stage. It has a long way to go before it can be considered an international power in a traditional sense and, indeed, may never become one but its sheer size and wealth, its web of trading relationships and the traditional worldwide interests of some of its members have driven it to create machinery which will enable it to be a more effective international actor. It has, of course, always had external trading interests and is a major player in international trade negotiations. More recently, members have begun to share diplomatic and consular services, to co-ordinate political positions in other international bodies, such as the UN, and to react as a unit to calls for humanitarian assistance. However, it must be remembered that, in addition to having some common interests, its members also disagree on issues or have special interests which not all share. It is unrealistic to expect the Union to have an overall common foreign policy with the power to support it; it has, however, recognized that on some issues it can formulate a position and, although a defence policy is not around the corner, the existence of the EU has encouraged the discussion of issues of defence and procurement, allowed the EU to act jointly in peacekeeping and humanitarian missions and now recommends co-operation on armaments, building on the work already started under the WEU. It has recently formally recognized that some members wish to develop closer defence co-operation, as France and Britain did at St Malo in 1998. Shortly afterwards, France did not join Britain in supporting the USA in bombing Iraq, amply demonstrating some of the difficulties of the project in which the EU is now engaged.

The Treaty on European Union sets out the objectives of the foreign and security policy. They are to safeguard the common values, fundamental interests and integrity of the Union, to strengthen the Union, to preserve peace and international security, to promote international co-operation and to develop democracy and the rule of law. Member states have agreed not only to work together but to refrain from action which might cut across Union interests. It is for the European Council to define the principles and general guidelines as well as the common strategies needed to protect members' common interests on a unanimous vote but details are in the hands of the Council. A new idea is to allow a member to abstain in Council and not implement a decision although it must not obstruct the EU in its actions. It is also for the Council to take the necessary implementing decisions either in the form of 'joint actions' or by adopting 'common positions', both of which can be formulated on QMV subject to the right of a member to veto the decision (Article 23.2 EU). An important development is the creation of a permanent planning and early warning unit to advise the Council. In 1997 it was finally agreed that the Union should have a High Representative to handle CFSP matters and, to start with, this is the Secretary-General of the Council. It is intended, that, at long last, the Union will have a focal point for dealing with foreign policy matters. Although the EP has no formal power, it must be consulted and its views, which are actively expressed, taken into account and since operational expenditure falls normally on the budget this will also give an opportunity for Parliament to consider decisions taken. The Commission is brought fully into the structure and is involved at all stages. It has a right of initiative but shares this with member states, which may also bring matters to Council attention. The challenges faced by the EU in formulating foreign policy were amply demonstrated by events in Yugoslavia, Albania, Bosnia and Kosovo and it is to be hoped that the steps taken in 1997 to strengthen the arrangements prove more adequate. In particular, it is hoped that the EU will be able to react to sudden crises more effectively and to appoint a special representative when occasion demands.

At present, security policy simply envisages the possibility of an eventual framing of a common defence policy and that, in time, a common defence may emerge, a form of words which glosses over differences of view and the neutral status held by some members (Article 17 EU). However, the WEU has become an integral part of the Union in order to handle defence matters and a special Declaration of the TEU is concerned with its position. Since the Council of the WEU now brings together all members of the EU, European members of NATO and the states of central and eastern Europe who wish to enter both the EU and NATO, it has become a genuine framework for discussion on European security and defence issues as well as becoming more closely associated with implementing EU decisions. In particular, it now handles the humanitarian, peacekeeping and crisis management tasks and planning for such operations. However, the TEU has to recognize that members range from neutral countries to active members of the Atlantic Alliance and that there are serious disagreements amongst the latter over whether the EU requires an independent defence capability. The situation is further complicated by the concurrent discussions of the role and membership of NATO for which the WEU is the European pillar. Not all members of the EU belong to the WEU although they have observer status and there are many awkwardnesses to be worked out consequent upon the dual position held by the WEU in NATO and the EU and the reluctance of neutral members of the EU to find themselves committed to future action. The war in Kosovo undoubtedly stimulated thought on the EU's role in situations of instability or conflict on its doorstep. It brought home its dependency upon America for effective military operation, the inadequacy of its weaponry, the difficulty experienced by military forces in handling co-operative action and raised big questions about more uniformity and co-operation in armament production. One result was that, in December 1999, member states agreed to set up a rapid intervention force for conflict prevention and crisis management which should be ready by 2003. One of the big, unresolved issues is the degree of independence from, and integration with, the NATO arrangements and thus relations with the USA and the extent to which defence discussions should involve other European NATO allies. There seems little doubt that political and defence issues played their part in the welcome now given to Turkey's membership application.

2.6 Judicial and home affairs

Co-operation between members of the EU in matters such as the apprehension of terrorists and drug pedlars, questions of civil and criminal law, and to absorb the implications of the abolition of internal frontiers on the movement of goods and people, has grown steadily with the passing years. Steps have been taken to bring these arrangements into the Community framework, but they remain in a patchy and complicated half-way house. The main matters dealt with are those that arise from the common interest in asylum and immigration rules, police co-operation and arrangements to ensure the smooth working of civil and criminal law.

Visa, immigration and asylum matters have, since the Treaty of Amsterdam, been brought into the framework of the EC Treaty (Title IV). The Council, acting unanimously, must establish, within a five-year period, effective measures to set up external border controls, asylum and immigration rules, including the abolition of internal border checks. By protocols, the Schengen agreement on the abolition of checks at common borders has been brought into the EU but Britain and Ireland have opted out subject to their right to request to take part in some or all of it. Denmark also has special arrangements (while Norway and Iceland are bound by the Schengen principles in order to preserve the Nordic Passport Union). Judicial and customs co-operation is specifically covered, as is police co-operation to combat terrorism, drug trafficking and other international crimes. Forms of police co-operation and the use of Europol have all been strengthened by the TEU as has judicial co-operation with the aim of including measures to facilitate extradition, improve the compatibility and content of rules and generally improve co-operation between appropriate authorities. A co-ordinating committee of senior officials supervises the daily work and prepares the ground for Council meetings. The Council, in turn, may adopt a common position on a matter and also on framework positions to align the laws of members although only on a unanimous vote and after consulting Parliament. The ECJ now has competence to decide certain matters. Finally, it is possible for matters to be passed over to the full procedures of the European Community provided there is widespread agreement on the move. Overall, a good deal of the obscurity and ambiguity of the past has been cleared away without giving the EU significantly greater powers since so much depends upon co-operation based on unanimous voting in the Council.

The main task at present seems to be to flesh out the arrangements. Judicial and home affairs co-operation is not deemed to be a matter of creating a single European juridical code but of mutual recognition of each other's court rulings where necessary and agreed procedures to make extradition a more reliable instrument. Europol is currently being strengthened to permit better gathering and sharing of intelligence and the prevention of money laundering. On the civil side, consumer protection and the rights of small businesses and the civil and legal rights of long-resident third country nationals are some of the issues likely to benefit from consideration across the EU although, sometimes, wider international consideration is necessary. From time to time, the EU rules are found to be sufficiently uniform to translate into a regulation or directive but this is not always so. The need for common rules and policies is particularly felt at present for immigration and asylum matters. It is, for example, widely recognized that the definition of a refugee needs reconsideration to cover those fleeing from war-lords and tribal conflicts and not just from persecution by a state. State action can be difficult alone, for what it does has implications for others and particularly so as travel within the EU becomes progressively easier. It is clear that years of work lie ahead to create arrangements more suitable for a more integrated and mobile continent and world. The area of judicial and home affairs seems destined to remain a complex mixture of agreed principles, harmonized rules, inter-state co-operation and joint action.

2.7 Conclusion

It is always difficult to assess an organization which is under constant, and quite rapid, change. The TEU, together with the Amsterdam amendments, marks an important stage in European integration in that the balance shifted away from member states towards the Community. Whether the treaty proves just one more step towards further union or has provided a viable blueprint for a longer time cannot be predicted. Simply absorbing the applicant countries satisfactorily would seem, however, to be a sufficient task for the next few years, especially as it carries with it another institutional reform. The TEU does not solve the theoretical question of whether the EU should build on international co-operation or integration for it appears that the EU has opted for both ideas at this stage of its evolution. On one hand, the competence of the EU, the use in the Council of QMV and the powers of the EP are all extended within the concept of a Union. On the other, the idea of flexible integration has been accepted. Groups of members can act together to pursue closer links provided they respect the needs of others and the importance of keeping all together. This has already begun to happen over the single currency, ease of movement and common foreign and security policy decisions. The treaty further recognized that there should be limits on Community power in the grey areas that now exist between European and national government through the doctrine of subsidiarity and that international co-operation should be used as the only realistic method in common foreign and security policy and judicial and home affairs, at least for the present. Older ideas, such as that likening the Community to a bicycle which must move forward or fall over, do not seem to be applicable any longer. It has not fallen over, neither does it appear to be marching inexorably towards a European state. In reality, the Community has always known that it must work on consensus, sometimes difficult to achieve but in the end acceptable to all on the grounds of the overall benefits of membership. It is too simple to suggest that reluctant states will just be forced into line, and it presents a challenge to statesmanship to find a way through the difficulties so that the EU can continue to express the belief in common interests and likemindedness on which it was founded and which persists.

There are obvious questions for the immediate future relating to the institutions. Finding a satisfactory voting system for the Council of Ministers which allows for decisions but which effectively represents the forces at work in the Community is one of the hardest, but reforming the Commission to become an efficient machine and clarifying its role runs it close. The interrelationship of the European institutions with national systems of government receives less publicity but also requires attention. With the growth in importance of the EU and the loss of national power, the question must arise whether national parliaments can still perform a democratic role satisfactorily. It is clear that the EU has not been able to exert adequate control over the application of its policies within member states. The Community writ does not always run to achieve a uniform application of a regulation, an effective interpretation of a directive or even the proper use of Community funds. National parliaments have not shown much interest in controlling these matters on behalf of the Community, and it remains primarily up to the Commission to ensure the smooth running of policies on the ground. 'To do less but do it better' remains a valid goal.

Substantive policy issues are looming. Political events in the world change quickly, so that the foreign policy role of the EU and its corresponding security and defence policy, including the complications in the NATO relationship, are sure to be tested. Many practical difficulties must arise consequent upon the greater mobility of people both internally and would-be migrants from the rest of the world, so it is indeed essential that the institutional structure is adequate. But however good reform may be in itself, the changes will not endure if they are not supported by public opinion – and this has shown itself to be somewhat uncertain about the developments of recent years. The Maastricht Treaty was greeted with widespread hostility and was nearly lost in referendums in Denmark and France. The Commission has recently made efforts (of variable quality and accessibility) to counter public ignorance, and less has been done to improve awareness of the EP and the Council of Ministers. A major criticism of the latter remains its lack of openness and the failure of existing democratic institutions to control decisions taken. No obvious remedy exists. National Parliaments have perhaps too often allowed decisions and developments to pass them by, displaying little, or only a desultory, interest in the work of the European institutions. At the same time the institutions themselves have been too absorbed in the excitements of creating a political first to remember that time is needed for the general public to come to terms with these changes. All in all, there is indeed a democratic deficit in the EU, but this is not to be solved simply by increasing the powers of the EP – which is often put forward as the solution.

Understanding and support of the EU is not a question of reform of the institutions alone but of long years of hard grind and painstaking effort on everyone's part to ensure that the EU commands an unquestioned support.

Note on references

References to treaty articles followed by (EC) or (EU) refer to the consolidated versions of the Treaty establishing the European Community and the Treaty on European Union respectively. ISBN 92–828–1640–0. The Treaty of Amsterdam is required for the Protocols.

Many authors have dealt with the post-war organization of western Europe. These include Haas (1958) and Palmer and Lambert (1968). Wallace (1990) discusses more modern issues.

EC developments may be traced through *Bulletin* of the *European Communities/Union* and its supplements.

3 The legal dimension in EU integration

D. CHALMERS

In one sense, it should not be difficult to pinpoint the legal dimension to EU integration. As a political system, the EU has been traditionally centred around regulatory rather than redistributive or allocative activities. Its predominant concern has therefore been the adoption of binding acts (Majone, 1994; Wessels, 1997a). The acquisition of important stabilization functions, with the onset of economic and monetary union (EMU), has not diminished its capacity in this regard, but has endowed it with further law-making facilities. The extent of EC legislation alone can be gauged by estimates which suggested that 53% of legislation adopted in France in 1991 emanated from the EC and that 30% of all legislation in the Netherlands comprises provisions implementing EC Directives (on this see Mancini, 1998, p. 40).[1] Yet to stop there is to beg the question regarding the impact of legislation beyond simply being the end-process of the Brussels legislative procedures. How does it act upon and reconfigure the behaviour of the actors that invoke it and are subject to it? Instead of attempting the impossible task of trying to recount the contents of all this legislation, this chapter attempts to ask this latter question, considering in particular how the use of law as a plane of action steers the integration process.

'Integration through law' pulls this process in three broad directions. The first direction is an actor-interest based one. This considers the opportunity structures provided through the creation of specifically legal institutions (see Chapter 2), in the form of the European Court of Justice (ECJ) and the Court of First Instance (CFI), and of specifically 'legal relations' between these and national courts, most notably in the form of the Article 234 EC reference procedure, but more generally in the authority conferred on the formers' judgments by the latter. This leads not merely, in crude policy terms, to both national and EC courts becoming significant players and agenda-setters, with the Article 234 EC reference procedure having to be considered as influential a relationship in its own way as that of the Commission and Council (for a particularly important early analysis of this see Volcansek, 1986). It also leads to fresh opportunities for new types of actor, in the shape of litigants and lawyers, and for new forms of knowledge, in the form of EC law, at the expense of other actors and forms of knowledge.

Such approaches have been traditionally used in the field of judicial politics. Second, many EU legal scholars, by contrast, look not so much at the opportunities provided by EU law, but at its mapping functions, namely how it shapes expectations and understandings of the integration process, which in turn influences how parties act within that process. They thus note how debates about the values and directions of the EU, its legitimacy and the patterns of inclusion and exclusion established by it invariably involve, first and foremost, debates about the contours of EU law.

The third direction in which EU law pulls the integration process is in its communicative functions. The establishment of a series of networks by EU legal instruments creates a series of interrelationships between parties across a variety of fields within which parties have to adapt to and communicate with each other. The endurance of these relationships leads not only to the modification of identities, practices and understandings, but in so far as these relationships are generated in a 'transnational' manner, contributes to the emergence of a transnational society. It is in this that EU law is perhaps broadest in its embrace and most sweeping in its ambition.

3.1 Actor-interest based approaches

The capacity to determine the content of a legal provision is a cherished prize within any communal arrangement, be it an international, national or subnational one. For a legal provision will do a number of things. It will stabilize expectations as to what is required of parties and provide a benchmark by which each party judges the behaviour of the other. In addition, in so far as any legal provision must allow for the possibility that it will be obeyed out of a sense of duty, legal provisions can induce more wide-ranging assumptions over what constitutes appropriate behaviour. The ability to influence the content of norms occurs at a variety of points in their life cycle, be it in their formulation, enactment, application or enforcement. Within classic international treaty regimes, national governments, as both authors and addressees of the international treaty in question, preserve a monopoly over this capability through the device of autointerpretation, namely their ability to interpret the substantive content of the norms to which they are subject (Gross, 1984). This has been only marginally disturbed through the increasing resort, since the Second World War, to judicial or quasi-judicial decision-making bodies in both regional human rights and regional and global trade treaties (Merrills, 1998). Access to such bodies is limited and they do not disturb the national governments' monopoly of violence over their territories as no sanctions are provided for in the event of non-compliance with these bodies' rulings. The central actors brought into play by these instruments, therefore, continue to be bureaucrats, be they national civil servants or the international organizations or secretariats set up by the treaties.

The legal arrangements of the Treaty on EU, particularly those of the EC pillar, stand in marked contrast to this. The public spheres surrounding most EC legislative and quasi-legislative procedures involve a wide variety of actors beside national governments. Most explicitly, these procedures provide for the participation of a whole series of supranational institutions, depending upon the field in question. These can take the form of a wide array of bureaucratic interests, be they the Commission with its 26 Directorates-General or the European Central Bank (ECB, see Chapter 6); representative institutions in the form of the Economic and Social Committee and the Committee of the Regions; and, finally, directly elected interests in the shape of the European Parliament (EP). As a corollary to this, the opportunity structures provided by these procedures have, in turn, over the years attracted representatives of a wide variety of private interests, so that by 1995 it was possible to identify 1678 interest groups in Brussels (Wessels, 1997b). Even in those areas, such as Common Foreign and Security Policy (CFSP), which are characterized by limited supranational institutional influence and national government vetoes, the requirement to carry out measures through the Union institutional procedures generates structures and dialectics which constrain and shift preferences and curb unilateralism (Hill, 1997).

An even more potent feature of the EU than the pluralism surrounding its law making is that national governments have lost their monopoly over the application and enforcement of law in the EC pillar and, since the Treaty of Amsterdam, over certain areas of EU law in the Justice and Home Affairs (JHA) pillar. This has had particularly disempowering consequences for national governments as the legislative dynamics of the EU render unexpected interpretations or applications particularly difficult to remedy. Interpretations of the Treaties themselves can only be rectified through the unanimous agreement of the national governments (Article 48 TEU). Pressures militate against even amendment of secondary legislation. Most EC legislative procedures require a national government to negotiate amendments with a number of actors, notably the Commission and the Parliament, both of which, depending upon the legislative procedure deployed, may be able to veto any proposed amendments. In addition, the voting thresholds within the Council of Ministers will, depending upon the area in question, require the national government to co-opt either all or a qualified majority of its fellow governments into agreeing to its amendments. Within even highly rationalist accounts, which place national governments at the centre of the EU integration, these features grant those actors responsible for the application and enforcement of EC law a considerable degree of autonomy and power (Alter, 1998b; Garrett and Tsebelis, 1999). This autonomy has allowed these actors to develop autonomous dynamics and agenda-setting powers of their own (Armstrong, 1998; Armstrong and Bulmer, 1998, pp. 263–9).

3.1.1 The European Court of Justice

(a) The organization of the work of the European Court of Justice

The most salient of these actors is the European Court of Justice (ECJ). At the centre of the Court sit 15 judges, one from each member state (Article 221 EC). Judges do not need to have held prior national judicial office, but are to be chosen 'from persons whose independence is beyond doubt and who possess the qualifications required for appointment to the highest judicial offices in their respective countries or who are jurisconsults of recognised competence' (Article 223 EC). They are appointed for a renewable term of six years by the common accord of the national governments. To ensure continuity, half the Court is appointed or reappointed every three years (Article 223(3) EC). The Court works on the principle of collegiality. Drafted in the first place by a single judge, a *juge rapporteur*, and then negotiated between the different judges and their offices, a single judgment is given with no possibility for dissenting opinions. This, together with the relatively remote location of the Court in a rather drab Luxembourg suburb and the similar social backgrounds of the judges, is credited with giving it a certain *esprit de corps* which contributes to its collective autonomy (Edward, 1995; Kenny, 1998).[2]

The Court is assisted in its work by eight advocates-general. The conditions for office and length of term for these is the same as for judges of the Court. There is a convention that one is taken from each of the five larger member states and the other three are rotated among the smaller member states. The duty of the advocate-general is to present in open court 'with complete impartiality and independence . . . reasoned submissions on cases before the court' (Article 222 EC). The opinions of the advocate-general are in no way binding upon the Court.

The workload of the Court is considerable. Up until the end of 1998 it had given 4761 judgments (ECJ, 1999a, Table 3). Despite this, since the late 1970s, backlog has been a recurring feature of the caseload. This combination of workload and backlog has given rise to a number of problems. The most practical of these is obviously delay to individual litigants, which, in turn, provides incentives for national courts not to refer matters to the Court, irrespective of the wider importance of the legal questions raised. The workload has also affected the quality of judgments, partly, by placing the Court under considerable time constraints. The large number of judgments also gives national legal communities little time to digest EC law. This both contributes to the unfamiliarity of many national lawyers with important areas of EC law and prevents quick feedback on judgments, with unforeseen or unfortunate results (Jacqué and Weiler, 1990).

The ECJ made attempts to address this, first, by expanding the Chamber System. Unless a member state or EC institution is one of the parties, the case need not be heard by the full Court, but by a Chamber of three or seven judges. The full Court will also hear cases that involve difficult or important points of EU law. Yet the influence of the Chamber system is illustrated by its enabling the Court to decide 254 cases in 1998 as compared with an average of 133 cases per annum in the period 1979–81, with 190 of those decisions being made in Chambers (ECJ, 1999a, Table 16).

The second innovation was the establishment of a Court of First Instance (CFI) in 1988.[3] The CFI is essentially an 'administrative court' (Dehousse, 1998, p. 28) which has jurisdiction for all direct actions brought by individuals reviewing the action or inaction of the EC institutions. Like the ECJ, it has 15 judges whose terms of office are of the same length as those of the ECJ judges, and, as with the ECJ, it operates a Chamber system. Since many of the cases involve adjudication, particularly in competition cases, on highly involved and contested factual scenarios, its rate of decision is slower than that of the ECJ. In 1998 it gave 129 judgments (CFI, 1999, Table 7).

Third, the ECJ has developed a system of docket-control (Strasser, 1995; Barnard and Sharpston, 1997). It has refused to accept references where a dispute is not pending before a national court[4] or where it considers there is no genuine dispute at hand and the questions referred are merely hypothetical in nature. It will also refuse to answer references where it considers insufficient information is provided about the factual and national legal context to the dispute (ECJ, 1996). Yet such docket-control has proved to be controversial on the grounds both that it might lead to a 'denial of justice' in individual cases and that, through its second-guessing of national courts, the ECJ is introducing unwarranted hierarchies between it and national courts (O'Keeffe, 1998). In any case, it has led to the ECJ refusing to rule in less than 30 cases in the 1990s.

These largely internal developments have had little long-term impact on the problem of backlog. In 1998 the length of proceedings before the ECJ averaged, depending upon the procedure, between 20.3 and 21.4 months, and, at the end of 1998, 664 cases were still pending (ECJ, 1999a, Table 14). Matters were even worse for the CFI, which had 425 cases pending at the end of 1998 (CFI, 1999, Table 12).

This has prompted more wide-ranging calls for reform, with commentators arguing for specialized courts and regional courts to be set up, which could relieve the ECJ of some of its jurisdiction (Jacqué and Weiler, 1990). In their submissions to the intergovernmental conference prior to the Treaty of Amsterdam both the ECJ and CFI expressed opposition to any idea of super-regional courts on the grounds that they would threaten the position of the ECJ and the unity of EC law. The CFI also expressed hostility to the emergence of new specialized Euro-courts on the grounds that it would lead to problems of co-ordination and unnecessary fragmentation. With the increasing volume of EC law and imminent enlargement of the Union threatening to exacerbate the problem, the ECJ began to soften its stance. In 1999 it issued a communication which suggested, *inter alia*, that consideration be given to the creation or designation of judicial bodies in each member state which would receive rulings from other courts in that jurisdiction. These would act as intermediaries and would decide some matters by themselves and could, in turn, refer others to the ECJ (ECJ, 1999b, 28–9).

(b) The jurisdiction of the European Court of Justice

The feature that has led to the build-up of such an overwhelming workload for the ECJ and which simultaneously underpins its influence is its broad jurisdiction. In material terms this is very wide. The only parts of the TEU that the ECJ is now fully excluded from ruling upon are the opening Common Provisions and the Title on Common Foreign and Security Policy (Article 46 TEU). Since the Treaty of Amsterdam it is now possible for it to rule on the third pillar of the TEU – on police and judicial co-operation. This possibility is substantially reduced by its having no jurisdiction to review the validity of police or law enforcement agency operations or the exercise of member state responsibilities with regard to the maintenance of law and order and the safeguarding of internal security (Article 35(5) TEU).

The ECJ has contributed to this wide remit by bestowing upon itself a unique authority to comment upon the quality of EC law. In its judgments of *Van Gend en Loos* and *Costa* in 1963 and 1964, it began its 'constitutionalizing' jurisprudence which bestowed attributes upon EC law that are not possessed by any other international legal order.[5] In these judgments, the ECJ distinguished the EC Treaty from other international treaties, which it characterized as compacts between sovereign states. By contrast, in the EC Treaty the member states had transferred sovereignty to a new legal order which acted for the benefit not just of national governments and individuals. The immediate practical effects of this were that the ECJ considered in *Van Gend en Loos* that EC law contained provisions which could be invoked directly in national law and that, in *Costa*, in the instance of conflicts between EC law and national law the national courts should give precedence to EC law.

These judgments and the subsequent line of case law also had important institutional implications for the ECJ. It gave it a capacity to adjudicate upon conflicts between national law and EC law and upon the effects of provisions of EC law in national courts. This capacity has not really been questioned by national courts. The ECJ has also interpreted this as granting it the exclusive capacity both to adjudicate upon the boundaries between EC and national competencies[6] and to declare EC acts illegal.[7] This has been challenged by national courts. Most famously, both the German and Danish Constitutional Courts, in their respective judgments on the legality of the Maastricht Treaty, reserved the right for themselves to declare whether EU law violated their national constitutions.[8] A similar position has been taken by the Belgian Cour d'Arbitrage (Bribosia, 1998). Such decisions, however, suggest that national judicial decisions will be a matter of last resort, invoked only when EC law violates some national constitutional shibboleth. They therefore allow a considerable *de facto* hegemony for the ECJ to delimit the boundaries of national and EC jurisdiction. So much so in fact, that, although the *Kompetenz-Kompetenz* debate attracted considerable academic attention (Arnull, 1990; Schilling, 1996; Weiler and Haltern, 1998; Eleftheriadis, 1998; Kumm, 1999), there is no example of a judgment of the ECJ being actively challenged in these jurisdictions in recent years. The position has recently become different in England and Wales. In *ex parte First City Trading* the English High Court stated that the ECJ had no inherent jurisdiction, but only the powers conferred upon it by the TEU.[9] The High Court then inferred that the ECJ would have no powers to develop its doctrine of general principles of law and fundamental rights in such a way that these bound national measures generally, irrespective of what the ECJ might do. In similar mode the High Court stated in *ex parte IATA*, despite ECJ dicta to the opposite effect,[10] that the ECJ had no jurisdiction to interpret international agreements to which member states had acceded prior to EEC accession, which now fell within EC competence.[11] These suggest a far more active patrolling of the limits of ECJ judgments. Review is not centred around ring-fencing national constitutional sanctuaries but a more proactive engagement in determining the limits of the appropriate role of the ECJ in particular fields.

The sweeping material jurisdiction of the ECJ is limited by the circumstances in which actions can be brought before it. There are four routes. The first is an appeal from the CFI. Appeals accounted for 20 judgments in 1998 (ECJ, 1999a, Table 3). Second, a variety of enforcement actions can be brought before the ECJ. These accounted for 76 of its judgments in 1998. There are enforcement actions against individual EC institutions. Within the EC pillar a distinction is made between acts which breach EC law and failures to act. With regard to the latter, actions can be brought by the member states or any other institution (Article 232 EC). With regard to the former they can be brought by any member state, the Commission and the Council (Article 230(1) EC). They can also be brought by the ECB, the Court of Auditors and the European Parliament where the measure touches on their institutional prerogatives (Article 230(2) EC). In the case of policing and judicial co-operation, enforcement actions can only be brought against the Council and only by member states or the Commission. More common than enforcement actions against the EC institutions are enforcement actions against the member states. In theory, these can be brought by other member states or the Commission. Only once in the history of the ECJ has an action, however, been brought against one member state by another. It is more usual for them to co-opt the Commission into action. That said, the central dynamic of enforcement actions brought by the Commission against member states is negotiation in the shadow of litigation. In 1998 it commenced 1101 proceedings but referred only 123 to the ECJ (CEU, 1999c, Annex 2.1). Since the Maastricht Treaty the possibility has existed for the Commission to bring member states back to the ECJ to be fined if they failed to comply with ECJ judgments. The Commission did not instigate the proceedings until January 1997 when it brought a series of actions against Italy and Germany. These were settled and it was not until mid-1999 that the first hearings before the ECJ were heard. These involved an action against Greece (Case C–387/97

Commission v *Greece*). Third, member states, the Commission and the Council can ask the ECJ to rule on the EC's competence to sign an international agreement (Article 300(6) EC). In the 1980s and 1990s perhaps one ruling every two years was given on average under this heading. Fourth, the Treaty of Amsterdam provides that the ECJ shall rule on disputes between member states about the interpretation and application of any measures adopted under police and judicial co-operation where the matter has not been resolved by the Council within six months of its being referred to the Council by one of its members (Article 35(7) TEU). The same provision also allows for disputes between the Commission and any member state about the interpretation or application of any of the conventions adopted under the pillar to be brought before the ECJ. No case has yet been brought under this heading.

Finally, questions of EC law can be referred by national courts to the ECJ. Prior to the Treaty of Amsterdam the position was relatively simple. National courts against whose decisions there is no judicial remedy were required to refer those matters of EC law that were necessary to enable them to decide the dispute before them (Article 234(3) EC). Other courts had a discretion whether to refer (Article 234(2) EC). The matter was blurred both formally and in practice. In formal terms, all national courts were obliged to refer a matter if they considered a piece of EC secondary legislation might be invalid.[12] Conversely, higher courts were not obliged to refer where a materially identical question of EC law had already been resolved by the ECJ or where the interpretation of the provision is so clear as to 'leave no scope for any reasonable doubt'.[13] The matter is obscured in practice by there being no effective remedy against national courts of last resort that do not refer.

Undoubtedly facilitated by the ECJ's case law stating that some provisions of EC law generate rights that individuals may invoke in national courts, the preliminary reference procedure has been the ECJ's principal source of work. In 1998 it accounted for 157 out of the 254 cases decided by the ECJ. The matter was complicated by the Treaty of Amsterdam in two respects. Only national courts against whose decisions there is no judicial remedy in national matters may refer questions on the interpretation and application of the new Title in the EC Treaty on Visas, Asylum, Immigration and Other Provisions Relating to the Free Movement of Persons (Article 68(1) EC). In addition, non-judicial bodies, namely the Council, the Commission or a member state, may refer question on interpretation of this Title or acts adopted under it to the ECJ. The reason for barring lower courts from referring was, allegedly, that it would lead to the ECJ being swamped with references over asylum and other immigration related matters. The Treaty of Amsterdam also allowed member states to make a declaration stating whether they would allow national courts to refer questions to the ECJ about EC secondary legislation adopted under policing and judicial co-operation (Article 35(2) TEU). Those adopting this path had two options (Article 35(3) TEU). They could choose to allow any national court to refer, with courts of last resort being obliged to refer. This path has been adopted by Austria, Belgium, Germany and Luxembourg. They could alternatively allow courts of last resort a discretion as to referral – a route chosen by Greece.[14] The Netherlands has stated that it will make provision for the possibility of national judicial referral but has not decided which option to adopt. It is not clear whether those member states who have not given their courts the possibility to refer will be bound by judgments of the ECJ given in response to referrals from other jurisdictions.

(c) Explaining the powers of the European Court of Justice

The institutional design and jurisdiction of the ECJ raises interesting questions about its role in the integration process and the motivations behind its establishment. The most complete research on the historical background to the development of the ECJ (Alter, 1998a) suggests that the member states intended three roles for it. The first of these was to prevent the other EC institutions from exceeding their powers. Second, the ECJ was to solve the 'incomplete contract problem' by being a forum for dispute resolution where EC laws were vague. Third, while responsibility for monitoring compliance lay with the Commission, the enforcement action mechanisms allowed the ECJ to 'mediate Commission charges and Member state defences regarding alleged treaty breaches' (*ibid.*, p. 125). A similar pattern emerges with regard to the jurisdiction of the ECJ over policing and judicial co-operation except that the Commission is deprived of its monitoring role: national governments take that responsibility upon themselves. Central to this paradigm was a perception amongst participants that the preliminary reference was not to be used as a mechanism for reviewing national laws but more as a vessel for advice over EU law. This was certainly the view of the EEC Treaty negotiators in 1957, and a not dissimilar view is apparent in the Treaty of Amsterdam negotiations, where the possibility of references from national courts is left to the national government's discretion.

Notwithstanding this, a variety of writers have argued that a number of mechanisms exist at the disposal of the national governments which severely curtail the autonomy of the ECJ (Garrett, 1992, 1995; Garrett and Weingast, 1993; Garrett, Keleman and Schulz, 1998). These mechanisms include non-compliance with ECJ judgments; replacement of judges at the end of their term; and amendment of legislation to circumvent unfavourable judgments. Non-compliance with any unfavourable judgment would lead to a breakdown in the credibility of the rules underpinning the single market, which the authors argue is in the social and economic interests of the national governments to promote. As a strategic actor, however (so the argument goes), the ECJ is aware that it cannot diverge over a long period from the preferences of the central member states and a *de facto* principal-agent relationship emerges between it and the national governments.

If this was so, it was a foolish hope. As Bzdera has observed, central judicial institutions almost invariably have centralizing rather than particularist tendencies, and are therefore rarely sensitive to locally specific concerns of constituent states (Bzdera, 1992, pp. 133–4). There is little evidence, moreover, that the ECJ systematically behaves in a strategic manner, free from the arguments and legal reasoning presented to it in each individual case. It has taken decisions, for example, that were clearly against the interests of virtually all the national governments, such as declaring the European Economic Area agreement void[15] and holding national governments to be liable to individuals for loss suffered as a result of their failure to comply with EC law.[16]

Such principal-agent accounts suffer from two further structural weaknesses. The first is why, as principals, the national governments should, in these terms, allow such an inefficient agent to endure. The ECJ's inefficiencies lie not just in its backlog. The wide array of matters upon which it is called to adjudicate ranges from constitutional theory through to environmental science, questions of economics, fiscal arrangements and accounting. The ECJ being a collection of generalists, its expertise is obviously found wanting in some of these specializations, the most commented upon being competition (e.g. Bishop, 1981, pp. 294–5; Korah, 1997b, pp. 301–15). As an agent it is also inefficient in its inability to generate feelings of wider identification with and support for its behaviour. Studies have shown that while there is reasonable voter satisfaction with the behaviour of the ECJ, it was the least salient of the institutions and enjoyed low diffuse support (Gibson and Caldeira, 1995, 1998). This lack of any reservoir of goodwill renders it particularly vulnerable to attacks, where it makes decisions deviating from short-term public opinion.

The second weakness of this account is that it gives an impression which differs so radically from that of the lawyers who work in the field. There is considerable consensus that the judgments of the ECJ follow highly idiosyncratic paths, which appear simultaneously bereft of any long-term strategic vision and highly individualistic. Differences among legal scholars congregate rather around the normative characterization of this. To some, it is positive evidence of the upholding of judicial autonomy and the rule of law (Arnull, 1996; Tridimas, 1996) or the upholding of important liberal ideals (Cappelletti, 1987). To others, it smacks of a lack of judicial objectivity (Hartley, 1996, 1999) or unattractive centralising activism (European Research Group, 1997; Neill, 1996; Rasmussen, 1985, 1998). Yet the bedrock of all this debate is a shared agreement that the ECJ has behaved in such a highly autonomous manner that it is difficult to either explain or predict its case law on the basis of a relationship or series of relationships that it has with a group of other institutional actors.

3.1.2 The national courts

The constitutional case law of the ECJ has resulted in the emergence of three discrete doctrines which allow EC law to be invoked before national courts, and thereby bring them into play in the integration process.

The oldest is that of *direct effect*. This allows a provision, which is sufficiently clear and precise, to be invoked before a national court. It does not prescribe the remedy that must be applied if the provision is breached other than to stipulate the remedy should be effective and should not be less favourable than those remedies applying to similar domestic claims.[17] Typically, there are two forms of direct effect. Vertical direct effect is where a provision may be invoked against state or public bodies. It is particularly important in fields of market liberalization where a trader is normally arguing that a law, regulation or administrative measure be disapplied. Horizontal direct effect, by contrast, allows individuals to invoke an EC provision against other private individuals. It is central to fields that rely upon associative obligations such as labour law, consumer law and environmental law where, in the vast majority of cases, it will be a private party that is being sued. Depending upon the wording of the provision, EC Treaty provisions, provisions of regulations and provisions of certain international agreements entered into by the EC can be vertically and horizontally directly effective (for more on this see Weatherill and Beaumont, 1999, pp. 392–413). Directives, by contrast, are only vertically directly effective. They cannot generate a cause of action against private parties[18] although this has been tempered by their being allowed to be used as a shield against actions brought in national law by private parties.[19] As Directives are the central instruments used in the fields of the single market, the environment, social policy and consumer protection, this diminished judicial protection in these fields. It also gave rise to inequalities where the capacity of parties performing identical functions to sue depended on the wholly extraneous circumstance of the status of the defendant, namely whether it was a private or public body.[20]

A second doctrine emerged, that of *indirect effect*. This requires national courts to interpret all national law so as to conform with EC law in so far as it is given discretion to do so under national law. A strong interpretive duty is thereby placed on national courts which applies whether or not the national legislation was intended to implement EC law and whether or not the national precedes the EC provision in question.[21] The effect of this was to allow all binding EC law, including Directives, to be invoked, albeit indirectly, in disputes between private parties. Nevertheless, the results were unsatisfactory. Apart from the uncertainty and instability this doctrine brings to national law (De Búrca, 1992), there are circumstances where it will not guarantee the judicial application of EC law. The doctrine is of little effect where either the national provision explicitly or implicitly contradicts the EC provision or there is no national provision to interpret. There is a further exception which prevents this doctrine being applied to Directives where the effect would be to aggravate criminal liability.[22]

The third doctrine that seeks to compensate for this is that of *state liability*. Individuals can sue the state for compensation where an EC provision grants them individual rights and they have suffered loss as a consequence of the state's illegal conduct. While the doctrine provided strong incentives for national governments to implement and apply EC law, it met strong opposition from national administrations which, in the light of the inherent uncertainties in EC law, saw it as imposing open-ended, financially onerous duties upon them (United Kingdom Government, 1996, paras. 8–10). The doctrine was thus mitigated so that a breach of EC law by a member state, *simpliciter*, was insufficient to ground liability. It was necessary that the breach be serious. While the full doctrinal implications of this are still being probed, it appears there are three scenarios which justify liability. These are a failure to transpose a directive;[23] a failure to follow settled case law;[24] and a failure to follow EC law where there is no reasonable doubt about the application of the provision.[25]

While these doctrines still leave gaps where individuals will be unable to invoke EC provisions before national courts, their sweep is still considerable. The Registrar of the ECJ estimated therefore that it has, on its records, 30 000 instances of EC law being considered by national courts (conversation with author, 9 July 1999). In this, the importance of national courts is threefold.

First, they act as gatekeepers to the preliminary reference procedure. Enabling EC law to be invoked in national courts transformed the preliminary reference procedure into the central source of jurisdiction for the ECJ. In the UK, for example, it is estimated that about one in six of the recorded judgments in which EC law is considered in any depth by the national court results in a reference to the ECJ (Chalmers, 1999a). This is not simply a quantitative process, whereby approximately 65% of the ECJ's workload comes via this avenue. In qualitative terms, in all areas other than the institutional prerogatives of the EU institutions the most difficult and path-breaking questions upon which the ECJ has had to adjudicate have come via this procedure. This is, in itself, hardly surprising given the heterogeneity of courts and litigants who contribute to this procedure and the legal training and resources that these collectively can put into the formulation of questions of EC law.

Second, national courts have become important interlocutors of EC law. The disciplines of EC law have been generally accepted by national courts (Slaughter, Stone Sweet and Weiler, 1998). This entails a transformation of the national legal system, so that, in Weiler's words, national courts 'render Community law not as a counter-system to national law, but as part of the national legal order to which attaches "the habit of obedience" and the general respect, at least of public authority, to the "law"' (Weiler, 1994, p. 519). At its narrowest, the assertion that an EC provision can be invoked before a national court will involve the tailoring of surrounding national procedures and remedies. More far-reaching, however, it often involves substantial administrative reorganization. This can take the form of the creation of new powers of judicial review not previously available to the courts or the widening of those courts which are to have powers of judicial review. It can also mean that areas such as competition policy and environmental law, which traditionally were not dealt with in a substantial way previously in the judicial arena, have increasingly to be decided by judges. Matters previously dealt with through the language of collective goods now have to be considered in terms of individual rights.

There is, however, another aspect to national courts' roles as interlocutors of EC law. They act, in many ways, as laboratories for the understanding of and experimentation in EC law. National courts provide arenas for the testing, debating and refining of EC norms. Furthermore, the preliminary reference procedure allows the experiences of one national court and the responses of it and the ECJ to be communicated across the Union (de la Mare, 1999). This results in national courts acting, in many areas of EC law, as important dynamos for the transformation not just of national law but also of EC law.

National courts have a final role as enforcers of EC law. The application of EC law by national courts necessarily involves its enforcement against those against whom it is invoked. In this, their involvement significantly enhanced the formal effectiveness of EC law in a number of ways. The institutional position of national courts within national constitutional settlements resolves the compliance problems that have traditionally bedevilled judgments of international judicial bodies. For failure to comply with a judgment of a national court is seen as a breakdown in the rule of law in all EU jurisdictions. Application of EC law by national courts also allows for a wider interpretation of EC norms than would be likely to be the case if they were merely subject to the auto-interpretation of national ministries. Enforcement of EC law through national courts brings other benefits. It decentralizes the system of enforcement, thereby reducing costs and barriers to enforcement. By enabling private parties, through litigation, to become involved in the process of enforcement, it also provides incentives for more effective enforcement by attaching the power of initiative, in the form of the grant of individual rights to those whose property or interests are impaired.

That said, this system of decentralized judicial enforcement is not without its limits. By only allowing those who can show infringement of their individual rights to bring a matter before a national court, the constitutionalizing case law of the ECJ privileges private interests over collective goods, such as the protection of the environment, public health, social cohesion and prevention of regional disparities (Harlow, 1996). For a feature of the latter is that their 'public' nature prevents any one individual being able to appropriate and thereby assert an individual interest in them. The result is that legislation protecting the latter has generally been less fully applied and subject to more individual complaints about non-compliance by national governments than EC law asserting market or other private rights (CEU, 1996a).

In their capacity as gatekeepers, interlocutors and enforcers, national courts act as the fulcrum of the ECJ's power. It is certainly more highly dependent upon them than they upon it. This has prompted debate as to why they have been generally ready to accept EC law. Undoubtedly, such acceptance has been facilitated by the ECJ being sensitive to the arguments of higher national courts. Thus, it has responded to prompts from national courts that it develop a fundamental rights doctrine; not accord the EC unlimited powers; nor allow Directives to impose duties on individuals by tailoring EC law accordingly (Chalmers, 1997a). Yet these, by their nature are high profile and occasional. They cannot explain the structural conditions that might induce national courts more generally to apply EC law.

A variety of theories has emerged in this regard. There are, on the one hand, theories that cast national courts as strategic actors who apply EC law because it allows them to maximize their interests or preferences. It has been argued that acceptance of EC law was prompted by courts wishing to acquire or exercise powers of judicial review at the expense of other arms of government (Weiler, 1993; Burley and Mattli, 1993; Mattli and Slaughter, 1998b); lower courts wishing not merely to acquire new powers of review, but also to escape existing judicial hierarchies (Alter, 1996, 1998b; Mattli and Slaughter, 1998b); and courts wishing to exercise their own policy preferences at the expense of national legislatures (Golub, 1996a). While such analyses may have some force in some cases, they make highly contestable assumptions about the motivation for judicial decisions and disregard any impact that the surrounding legal context or legal reasoning will exert upon the decision. They are unable to explain why national courts should behave in this manner when, traditionally, there has been resistance to the application of international legal norms (Benvenisti, 1993). Empirical studies therefore suggest little general support for any of these theses (Stone Sweet and Brunell, 1997). Other arguments rely more upon courts acting as socialized institutions. It is therefore argued that they are induced to accept EC law by the formal pull of legal language (Weiler, 1993) or because it fits with their perception of this being the appropriate judicial thing to do either because this was being done by their peers or because EC law asserted rights-based discourses and notions of judicial autonomy (Chalmers, 1997a; Plötner, 1998). Others have observed that its incorporation into national legal orders results in a transmutation of EC law, with its becoming tailored to the culture and context of these legal orders, with a corollary limiting of its ability to bring about substantial change (Maher, 1998). These theories are more case sensitive and bring questions of identity and context more to the fore. Yet, by relying on existing identities, they suffer from being unable to explain transformation other than to rationalize it, unconvincingly, as being some form of extension of existing processes.

The limitations of these respective accounts has led some authors to amalgamate them in a manner that weight is given to all of the above factors (Slaughter, Stone Sweet and Weiler, 1998). Such amalgamations probably give a more complete list of the motives that are likely to lead national courts to accept EC law. Yet, in their inability to explain how competing variables should be weighed against each other, the last paradigms hint at the difficulties in this area of providing a single explanation across such a wide field where individual courts will be subject to varying institutional, cultural and sectoral contexts.

3.1.3 Litigants and other players

Most actor-based theories of EC law acknowledge that national courts, while important, act only as intermediaries. The opportunity structures they provide lead to their being surrounded by networks of actors and interests. They serve not merely to inform these interests of EC law and resolve disputes between them. As reactive bodies which must respond to the arguments and interests that appear before them, they enjoy a dialectical relationship with the former. These articulate, refract and test their judgments as well as provide the legal disputes and legal arguments that constitute the raw material of litigation. Attention has focused on a variety of groups.

Materialist analyses argue that the growth of transnational exchange within the EU has generated a demand for a supranational organization in order to reduce transaction costs. Part of any such organization must include a system of legal rules and a system of dispute resolution. Such analyses therefore draw a causal link between the degree of intra-EC trade and the quantity of litigation of EC law (Stone Sweet and Caporaso, 1998; Stone Sweet and Brunell, 1998). They infer this from two features. On the one hand, the increase in preliminary references over the long term mirrors the increase in intra-EC trade. In addition, fewer references have come from those jurisdictions where intra-EC trade constitutes a lower proportion of national GDP. Such analyses see the transnational merchant as someone who not only is the central motor behind the development of EC litigation, but has used the opportunities created by the EC court structure to develop a governance regime outwith the nation-state. Yet such actors have traditionally developed private legal regimes, such as the *lex mercatoria*, outside the court system altogether (Teubner, 1997). This transnationalization of exchange, combined with the restructuring and internationalization of the European legal profession, has led increasingly to large law firms and arbitrators acting as important additional generators of rules of the game for the single market (Dezalay, 1992; Trubek *et al.*, 1994).

As a paradigm, materialist analyses treat as unproblematic the processes which lead parties to go to court and which they use in going to court. There has been criticism of analyses which focus predominantly on transnational exchange. It has been argued that the time it takes for new transnational alliances to emerge is so great that they arrive on the 'scene too late to play the game' (Conant, 2000). Instead, on the basis of a comparative analysis of references from France, Germany and the UK, she argues that the extent to which EC law is invoked will depend far more upon pre-existing domestic institutions. They will be affected, on the one hand, by the extent to which they are able to adjust to and 'fit' with substantive EC law. Conant argues that equally important are pre-existing patterns of civil litigation and the presence of resources or public institutions that facilitate access to the courts. The high number of referrals in the UK, by contrast to the other two, in areas such as social security, labour law (and one could add VAT) is thus influenced by a system of accessible, low-cost tribunals and public support in the form of Citizens' Advice Bureaux.

Other commentators have noticed a division within domestic structures between 'one-shotters' and 'repeat players' (Mattli and Slaughter, 1998, pp. 186–92). The former are litigants merely interested in winning the particular case in hand. Repeat players, by contrast, treat litigation as part of a two-level game (on this more generally within the EU see Anderson and Liefferink, 1997). EC law and courts are used as a counterweight by parties where they have been unable to attain their objectives through local law or in national administrative and legislative arenas. They take a more prospective view of law in which the gains they seek are modifications of the rules of the game. As a consequence, they are less inclined to settle out of court and more likely to engage in repeated litigation, 'forum-shopping' before a number of tribunals. In a limited number of instances, such actors come directly before the ECJ (Harding, 1992). This institution's restrictive standing requirements and the proximity of the national courts have meant that, more frequently, they come before the latter. Such actors can be commercial groups of actors, as was the case in the Sunday trading saga, where a series of DIY stores engaged in repeated litigation under EC law to bring about a change in the legislation in Britain on trading hours (Rawlings, 1993). They can also be non-governmental organizations which seek to further certain post-material values and may seek to do this either by litigating directly or by providing support for litigants in areas of strategic interest – the latter tactic was pursued by the Equal Opportunities Commission in the UK (Barnard, 1995; Alter and Vargas, 2000). Repeat actors not only influence some areas of EC law – notably free movement of goods, gender discrimination and some areas of environmental law – disproportionately more than others, although their effects ripple out across the Union; their incidence is unevenly distributed across the different member states. Alter and Vargas have noted that a number of conditions normally have to inure for such groups to take action (Alter and Vargas, 2000). As litigation is an avenue of last resort, there have to be strong patterns of institutional exclusion from other arenas for such groups. It would appear to be an advantage that such groups have a narrow mandate and constituency. More dispersed groups may not have the concentration of expertise, and internal conflicts of interest might arise that will prevent litigation and provide incentives to spend resources elsewhere. Furthermore, such groups will seek narrowly focused policy gains, the costs for which may be widely distributed and therefore not strongly opposed.

All interest-group theories acknowledge that interest groups can not, alone, engineer EC legal change. They point, in particular, to the importance of sympathetic judiciaries (Mattli and Slaughter, 1998; Alter and Vargas, 2000). Yet there is another group of actors who are important to the development of EC law and that is the EC legal community. It was widely acknowledged that, certainly in the first 30 years, the capacity of the ECJ to establish EC law doctrine was dependent upon a community of lawyers and academics, specialists in EC law, who could provide new arguments for the fleshing out and development of EC law, analogize it to national legal systems and doctrines, and disseminate and advocate it amongst both lay and legal communities (Stein, 1981). This community was, certainly in each member state, relatively small and many of the high-profile writers had strong institutional links with either the Commission or the ECJ. It is also not unfair to suggest that most of the early writing was sympathetic both to the general idea of EC integration and to the process of integration being done through legal instruments and judicial interpretation (Schepel and Wesseling, 1997). The unfolding of EC law over time and its expansion into new areas have destroyed this cohesion. New academics, with axes to grind and totems to smash, have emerged on the one hand (for a discussion of this see Shaw, 1999), and academics and professionals from other fields, reticent about the destabilizing effects of EC law on those fields, have begun to discuss EC law (e.g. Teubner, 1998). This is not leading to legal communities ceasing to have influence over the integration process. It is probably more accurate to suggest a recasting of this influence within which specialized legal communities, increasingly brought together by the function of the law in which they specialize rather than its designation, have a heightened influence over narrow areas of expertise (on trade marks see Chalmers, 1997b).

3.2 The structuring of EU integration through EU law

All actor-interest theories of EU law conceive of EU law in relatively passive terms. It is something used by particular actors to prosecute particular advantages. Its enabling qualities are confined to the creation of particular legal institutions, notably courts, which provide opportunity structures for additional actors. Yet law is not infinitely malleable. Even as an agent of national preferences the ECJ can only express national preferences in terms of individual rights and win-lose (as opposed to mediated) scenarios and act on the basis of the limited information that parties, constrained by processes of standing and intervention, can put before it. The relationship is therefore a dialectic one, in which the very features of EU law that make it attractive to actors to be involved in its formulation and application also configure those and other actors' actions.

3.2.1 The symbolic effects of EU law

Giving legal value to certain arrangements carries with it certain symbolic effects (Dehousse and Weiler, 1990, p. 244). The formality of legal texts confers greater weight to commitments. Even instruments such as Recommendations, which do not formally oblige parties to do anything, nevertheless indicate a description of good practice agreed by all the parties who adopted the instrument. Yet, it is nevertheless true that the degree of commitment, in symbolic terms at least, is often reflected in the prescriptive terms of the instrument used. The increasing commitment to integrate environmental concerns into other EC policies was therefore reflected in the manner in which it started as an undertaking in the Third Action Plan on the Environment in 1983; was made a Treaty commitment (Article 130r(4) EC in 1986 by the SEA); was placed at the Head of the Title on the Environment by the Maastricht Treaty in 1991 (Article 130r(2) EC); and was then placed as one of the Principles of the Treaty by the Treaty of Amsterdam in 1996 (Article 6 EC). While the commitment was not actively pursued in a general manner until the mid-1990s (Wilkinson, 1997), this intensification made it increasingly difficult for the principle to be contested at the policy-making level, with debate focusing far more on the modalities of operation.

Translating a matter into law also confers a recognition upon it, which gives it both a greater importance and greater priority. Dehousse and Weiler therefore mention how it was the legal nature of the Elysée Treaty between France and Germany in 1963 on military co-operation that caused controversy. For it suggested a prioritization of defence links between these states over commitments to other states, despite the agreement being relatively empty of substantial commitments (Dehousse and Weiler, 1990, pp. 244–5). More recently, the European citizenship provisions introduced into the EC Treaty by the TEU conferred few new rights upon individuals. The provisions provoked such backlash, however, that the member states felt, at the Edinburgh European Council in 1992, that, to enable the second Danish referendum on Maastricht to be successful, the provision had to be revised to indicate explicitly that it did not encroach upon national citizenship. In symbolic terms, the adoption of laws at a EU level has a tri-dimensional quality.

As EU law signifies law beyond the nation-state, it relativizes national law, irrespective of the form it takes. EU law, whether intended to supplant or supplement national measures, exposes the functional limits of nation-state legal structures. A further feature of EU law is its authoritative nature. That is to say, it confers the power upon itself to regulate its own operations. In particular, it determines its own legal effects. This relativizes the authority of national legislation by pluralizing legal authority within the territory of any state. The nature of legal authority is constructed from a variety of sources rather than simply the national constitution (MacCormick, 1993, 1999). The opposition between EU law and national law leads to further dichotomies. At its crassest, the justifications for EU law residing in the limitations of national law create a characterization within which the EU acts as a form of enlightened, cosmopolitan counterweight to the atavistic qualities of the nation-state (Fitzpatrick, 1997); some even urge this (e.g. Weiler, 1997a). More astute commentators have noted an oppositionality within which EU law may justify itself by reason of arguments of rationalization, efficiency and integration, but the pluralization of its implementation creates new schisms and dislocations within the national legal system (Wilhelmsson, 1995; Schepel, 1997; Teubner, 1998).

Second, the 'Euro-centrism' of EU law lies also in its signifying an intensification of co-operation and integration between certain polities and societies to the exclusion of others. Numerous commentators have therefore pointed to its creating new insider/outsider pathologies (Geddes, 1995; Hervey, 1995; Ward, 1996, pp. 147–52). This dichotomy does not simply run along crude EU/non-EU lines. All legal instruments, in so far as they generate their own processes of bounding, will contain elements of integration/inclusion and elements of exclusion/disintegration. For any legislation will empower or disempower, impose duties or rights selectively (Shaw, 1996). As a text, it will, furthermore, translate roles, identities, etc. in a manner where only facets are recognized, to the exclusion of other aspects.

The third symbolic quality of EU law derives from the interaction between it and the policy domain it governs. EU law enlarges understanding of a policy domain, not through creating that policy domain for the first time – be it environment, health and safety, etc. – but by giving it a European dimension. The policy domain can no longer be understood without taking account of this dimension. A new horizon is added which might include new networks, technologies, instruments or values (Barry, 1993). In this manner, EU law is a practical manifestation of the manner in which 'Europe' transforms understandings and expectations of a particular field, irrespective of questions of fact, interests and preferences (Christiansen, 1997).

3.2.2 The stabilization of expectations about EU government

A feature of EU law is its normativity. This normativity provides that EU law cannot be falsified by subsequent conduct. That is to say, where conduct deviates from the norm, it will be the conduct rather than the norm that will be considered deviant (i.e. illegal). This results in EU law being the central instrument through which expectations are stabilized about the distribution, reach and modalities of power within the EU system of government. It is the legal instruments which detail what powers the EU enjoys and how it empowers and restricts those within its embrace.

At the very least, therefore, EU law sets out the rules of the game, which there is an expectation will be habitually obeyed. Rational choice institutionalists qualify this by claiming that while such rules may not affect parties' deep-seated preferences, they do, by forestalling certain options, determine the strategies adopted by the parties (e.g. Pollack, 1997; Tsebelis and Kreppel, 1998). Classically, therefore, legal constraints on national governments' ability to curb the Commission's exercise of its powers may lead to their trying to secure influence within the Commission. Even within the parameters of this analysis, the influence of EU law is considerable.

It prevents certain outcomes being achieved, irrespective of the preferences of the parties. The decision of the ECJ in 1975 that the Community enjoyed exclusive competence in the field of external trade did not bring about a uniform commercial policy.[26] Yet it forestalled national government unilateralism, by requiring any autonomous measure required to be first approved by either the Council or the Commission, with the consequence that any unilateral measure had to illustrate that it did not impinge excessively on other national or Community interests.

EU law also challenges existing asymmetries of power. In the case of the legislative influence of the European Parliament, not only do legal provisions 'constitute' the Parliament through providing for its existence, but it is the legal peculiarities of the co-operation and co-decision procedures which enable the Parliament to act, in many circumstances, as a 'conditional agenda-setter' (Tsebelis, 1994; Scully, 1997; Tsebelis and Garrett, 1997). For they make it easier for the Council to accept Parliamentary amendments (which with Commission agreement can be approved by qualified majority voting (QMV) in the Council) than to introduce its own (which require unanimity). The consequence of this is an increased propensity on the part of member states to accept Parliament's amendments. For the test is no longer whether this is an 'ideal' amendment, but, *faute de mieux*, becomes whether this is an improvement on the original proposal. In such circumstances, the legal procedures have resulted in the preferences of a player other than the national governments becoming important, and inevitably require that national governments realign their behaviour, and, to some degree, thereby adjust their preferences, if legislation contrary to their interests is not to be passed.

Legal structures determine outcomes in another way. As outcomes have to be translated into legal structures, actors are able to use prior legal structures to pattern outcomes and negotiations. Most famously, the Commission exploited the *Cassis de Dijon* judgment to provide the basis for its New Approach to Harmonisation which lay at the heart of the 1992 programme (Alter and Meunier-Aitsahalia, 1994). This judgment, it will be remembered, stated that Article 28 EC required member states, in the absence of a compelling public interest, to grant market access to products lawfully marketed or manufactured in another member state.[27] Undoubtedly, it shifted Article 28 EC away from being an instrument that exclusively tackled discriminatory, protectionist measures to one that was essentially deregulatory in nature, which was concerned with sweeping away measures that had unnecessarily restrictive effects upon inter-state trade. Beyond that, the parameters of the judgment were inconclusive (Barents, 1982; Chalmers, 1993). The Commission argued, however, that the judgment entrenched the principle of mutual recognition, whereby a member state should accept that the regulatory requirements of the member state where the good (or service) was produced were, in principle, equivalent to its own ([1980] OJ C256/2). This alleviated the need for total harmonization of regulatory requirements by the Community. Instead, an approach based on mutual recognition transformed the role of the EC legislature into that of providing minimum guarantees. It would harmonize only those essential health and safety standards that were necessary to prevent member states claiming that trade infringed some essential public interest ([1985] OJ C136/1). This governance structure was conceived as placing limits on EC legislative output, preserving national regulatory traditions and increasing consumer choice. To be sure, it allowed different interests to be reconciled in a manner which had not previously been possible. It also structured future relations and provided the source of future tensions. These included doubts about the standardization bodies' capacity to develop standards quickly enough or in a sufficiently pluralist manner (Vos, 1998, pp. 281–308); and breakdowns in the mutual trust and national internal administrative organization required to bring about mutual recognition (CEU, 1999d, pp. 4–5).

While the autonomy given to actors by EU legal structures affords them the possibility to use these strategically, a feature of legal autonomy is that it always gives actors the possibility of complying with the law for no ground other than simple legal obedience. Others have observed that in so far as EU law allows there exists the possibility of inculcating certain patterns of obedience and behaviour. In this manner, it is argued, EU law not only stabilizes patterns of behaviour, but also produces socializing effects which transform and adapt expectations and preferences (Armstrong and Bulmer, 1998; Armstrong, 1998; Shaw and Wiener, 1999). The general force of this argument is not undermined by such effects being difficult to prove or disprove in any one instance. It is also not necessarily incompatible with the argument that actors also use law strategically. In both instances, the law in question 'frames' the action in question. It influences the modalities of behaviour of the actor by simultaneously enabling and foreclosing certain courses of action (Fligstein, 1997). Thus, the legal structure of subsidiarity came to frame and emasculate debates about the intensity and breadth of EC law making in the post-Maastricht era, so that protagonists of all sides couched their arguments in terms of that structure (Maher, 1995). The question of whether an actor responds strategically to this frame is both largely a matter of degree and one of *ex post facto* rationalization. The degree to which legal or other structures condition actions will vary according to the dynamics of the relations entered into at the time (Granovetter, 1985). No actor is ever completely conditioned by any one structure, but analysis of the level of conditioning will be assessed by reference to the extent of determined calculation on the part of that actor; that is to say to what extent the actor uses other recognizable structures in interactions with legal instruments (Callon, 1998). In the *Cassis de Dijon* example, therefore, the Commission was taken to be acting strategically because it used the judgment as the basis for a series of political structures which distributed governmental power. Nevertheless, a degree of framing was present as it perceived these in terms of an overarching principle, namely free movement of goods. It will be obvious from this that not only may EU law appear to socialize some actors more heavily than others, but a condition of law is that it allows for the possibility of strategic and socialized interaction with all actors. The degree to which particular actors act strategically will therefore vary across context.

3.3   Law as the cipher for the legitimacy of the EU

One corollary to the normativity of law is that law always has the ability to acquire different meanings. A bald legal statement that 'theft is wrong' would transmutate, to prevent falsification, when confronted with the situation of the person who steals to survive, either by providing a justification or by modifying the definition of theft. This means that an invocation of law involves not merely its application to a particular situation but also an 'idealising moment of unconditionality that takes it beyond its immediate context' (Rehg, 1996, p. xiii). A legal interpretation is thus never just a description of the political settlement or social interaction it regulates, but also a prescriptive assertion of what it ought to be. Law is distinguished from morality or ethics in that it only governs social interaction and does not purport to regulate or judge behaviour that falls outside this interaction. Yet it is their shared features of normativity – namely that both prescribe norms which enjoy a priority to any subsequent conduct and which are never fully directly observable in that their meaning can never be derived from any single context – that allow government framed by law or enacted through legislation to describe itself as value oriented (Chalmers, 2000). It also leads to EU law being seen as the central cipher through which the values of the EU are to be understood. Most notably, therefore, debates about legitimacy and reform of the EU revolve around legal reform, as law is premised, perhaps falsely, as the enabling medium through which these questions can be gauged and re-established.

In this context legal integration, within the EC pillar of the TEU at least, has been seen as being characterized by a series of liberal attributes (Slaughter, 1995, pp. 510–14). These include the assurance of peaceful relations between member states; the assurance of some degree of civil and political rights, now brought together under the umbrella of 'European citizenship'; and the protection of transnational transactions and cross-boundary property rights. It also includes the emergence of transgovernmental communications, which not only involve ties between national administrations but collapse traditional foreign/domestic distinctions through the 'recognition of multiple actors exercising different types and modes of governmental authority' (*ibid.*, p. 513) in increasingly pluralistic and heterarchical patterns (MacCormick, 1993, 1997, 1999).

The liberal paradigm draws a nexus between legal integration and achievement of these values (Reich, 1997). Within this understanding, the broader the reach of EC legal integration and the more intensely it is pursued, the greater the likelihood that these values will be achieved. These attributes provide the source for much of the criticism of EU law. Thus, EC law is castigated for not going far enough to afford judicial protection to rights granted under EC law (Szyszczak, 1996); not extending market freedoms sufficiently widely (Arnull, 1991; Gormley, 1994); failing to extend its fundamental rights competence sufficiently broadly (Alston and Weiler, 1999); and not affecting third country nationals the same market rights as EU citizens (Hedemann-Robinson, 1996). Within the liberal paradigm, individual autonomy, protected through the grant of certain liberal rights, is to be complemented by the notion of public autonomy within which each individual agrees to limit his or her freedoms so as to ensure the freedom of others. The right to an equal distribution of liberties and constraints can only be given concrete shape, however, through the exercise of legislation in which all have the right to participate (Habermas, 1996, p. 125). It is possible, therefore, to argue that a similar line of liberal reasoning underpins those 'republican' theories which push for a broadening of participatory and dialogic opportunities for private parties in EC law making and administration (Craig, 1997; Weiler, 1997b; Scott, 1998; Bellamy and Warleigh, 1998). All the above suggest that all that is needed to remedy the 'legitimacy deficit' of the Union is for the reforms they suggest to be adopted. This legal vision of integration posits this deficit as simply residing in the Union not being sufficiently ideological.

This view has been criticized on the ground that there is an inevitable 'integration/disintegration' nexus to any liberal paradigm of law. Within this it is argued that, within the EU, any system of law inevitably generates new patterns not merely of inclusion but also of exclusion and alienation (Shaw, 1996). This is likely to be particularly the case with the liberal paradigm. By seeking to enhance the autonomy of the Imaginary Subject this rewards the attributes of the competitive and the efficient and those with the resources to translate their autonomy into substantive rewards at the expense of those without these capacities.

Others have also observed that it is too simplistic to attribute a single set of values to an organization such as the EU, and that within any legal instrument a plurality of values is present (Joerges, 1996). Thus, it has been argued that central structures within much of EC regulation are knowledge based, with EC regulation acting to secure the primacy of certain forms of knowledge over other forms (Sand, 1998). It has been noted in the field of policing that the principal values are those of 'securitization', the central pathologies of which are surveillance and re-establishing or consolidating certain territorial patterns of control (Chalmers, 1998). Within this mêlée, EU law acts more as an arena for bringing to the fore and institutionalizing conflicts between values. In so far as particular values are recognized, conflicts become patterned, recurrent and routinized (e.g. trade versus the environment, freedom versus security, etc.). Within such an environment it becomes increasingly difficult to argue for the priority of particular values. Instead, legitimization becomes centred around the perfection of dispute-resolution processes that seek to rationalize or mediate between these interests or values. This might be through seeking to optimalize a set of outcomes having regard to a set of pre-given preferences (Majone, 1998) or through exclusively processual means, such as requiring all decision makers either to recognize (Shaw, 1999) or to enter into dialogue with and be accountable to certain interests or identities (Joerges, 1997; Shapiro, 1996).

3.4 Actor network theories

Like the two sides of a coin, structural accounts of EU law encounter the reverse objections to those made against actor-interest accounts. By failing to consider the contexts in which EU law is invoked, which actors invoke EU law and which frames are adopted by actors when considering EU law, they are criticized for treating EU law in too isolated a manner. Nuances are, thus, drawn over and contingencies dismissed. Centrally, as they have no theory of agency, they struggle to explain how EU law is transformed over time or even adopted in the first place.

While both actor-interest and structural accounts present valuable insights into how EU law contributes to the integration process, it is the dichotomy that they draw which leads to the failings of each. More generally, they tend to centre upon law's contribution to EU government and administration. A feature of law, however, is that it transcends the political system. On the one hand, it is through law that claims are made against or to the political system. For law 'keep[s] one foot in the medium of ordinary language, through which everyday communication achieves social integration ..., it ... accepts messages that originate there and puts these into a form that is comprehensible to the steering codes of the power-steered administration' (Habermas, 1996, p. 81). Conversely, a feature of law is that it communicates a vision of governance to social, economic and cultural arenas outside the political system. This structures opportunities for actors outside the arena of government (within the EU context see Chalmers, 1999b; Zürn and Wolf, 1999; Shaw and Wiener, 1999). EC environmental, labour and health and safety legislation all structure how the workplace is organized, and can be used as instruments in negotiations, for example, between management and labour. EU law also serves to restructure expectations in these arenas. Thus, in its first significant review of the Single European Market in 1996 the Commission observed that a perennial complaint of traders was patchy transposition of EC Directives and uneven enforcement of EC law (CEU, 1996i, p. 20). Nevertheless, after the enactment of the programme, while there were mixed views on whether restrictions on trade had been removed, 29% of small and medium-sized enterprises (SMEs) and 7% of large firms felt that the process, necessarily a legal one, had encouraged them to export (*ibid.*, pp. 12–13).

A paradigm that seeks to capture these features, as well as the mutually transformative qualities of agency and structure, is actor network theory. This conceives of EU law as being both implicated in and generating a series of networks (Ladeur, 1997). These are:

> the process of co-operation itself which furnishes solutions to complex problems via joint problem definition and the drafting of a possible decision, which is then subject to ongoing evaluation on the basis of 'new' knowledge (that is new technology, new management forms, the definition of new social risks and so forth).... Networks do not merely consist in the identification of stable and pre-existing interests; rather they themselves generate new operating knowledge. (*ibid.*, p. 46)

Such networks straddle any form of political/economic or public/private delimitation. As the network defines the mode of participation of actors and the attributes through which others recognize them, it is the network that serves to reconfigure actors' identities. It will also be clear that at any one time any single actor will be participating in multiple networks. The model is not without its disadvantages. It is elusive on how networks emerge or terminate. In addition, while it emphasizes the interplay of relationships, as high levels of interdependence can stretch on indefinitely, it is obtuse about how networks bound themselves, so as to enable one network to start and another to stop. Yet it points to EU law contributing in a central manner to a transnational society through the putting in place of a series of interlocking, interdependent relationships which serve to reforge functions and identities around new axes.

In this, legal networks are differentiated from other networks by their relatively high levels of formalization and textual dependencies. A feature of any legislation is that it sets in place in a relatively immutable manner who may and who may not participate in a network and the forms of relationship participants may enjoy with others. While such relationships are not so rigid that transformation cannot take place, this feature contributes to legal networks having a high propensity for path dependency. The tracks down which the initial relationships are channelled cannot be changed. As time passes these routines become central to the constitution of the network, with the result that legal networks tend to be more stabilized and patterned than other forms. Through patterning and stabilization of transnational society, EU law performs another function, in that it allows this society to generate securities and routines which act as artifices for participants to look to, in an otherwise stable and fast-moving world.

The second feature of legal networks is that they revolve around interpretation of a legal text. They are thus distinct from epistemic communities, which are centred around some form of prized, shared knowledge, and economic networks, which are centred around some form of material exchange. As actors configure their actions around interpretation of this text, the text has the power to bring actors into mutually transformative relations not just with other actors but also with non-human objects (Callon, 1986; Latour, 1993). As others adapt their behaviour to the articulated qualities of these objects, EU law allows these to acquire a status and a power within the integration process.

For example, the qualities ascribed to Special Areas of Conservation (SAC) by the Habitats Directive, namely their high conservation status, and the need for their status to be restored or for them to maintain that status has shaped a number of policies.[28] The establishment of both the specific guidelines on TRENS and proposals for individual networks must take account of the needs of these areas.[29] They are eligible for specific funding under the funds earmarked for the environment[30] and grants under the Cohesion Fund will be influenced by whether a project contributes to a SAC.[31] The need for a development project to undergo an environment impact assessment will also depend upon whether it impairs a SAC.[32]

3.5   Conclusion

From all this, it will be clear that it is better to conceive of EU law as bringing a variety of new dimensions to the integration process. How central does all this render EU law to the integration process? The quantity of EU law and its territorial and material scope have already been alluded to. As a rider to this, however, all the above perspectives agree upon the quintessentially formal nature of EU law. This formality establishes very clear limits for its contribution to governance. The only opportunities, values, behaviour and relationships that can be influenced by EU law are ones that respond to formal structures, typically those centred around economic transactions or political opportunities. There are plenty of forms of interaction or (dis)integration that operate outside of and that are largely unresponsive to these structures (Snyder, 1999) – be they economic networks, the dissemination of cultural images or various forms of inter-subjective communication. It is also dangerous to view those that do respond purely through the prism of the legal instruments to which they respond (Chalmers, 1999b). Such confining analysis can obscure the variety of other structures and tensions that act upon these actors. Notwithstanding this, the sheer intensity and breadth of the EU render it the most important point of organization of interactions within Europe. For no other organization can match the combination of its authority, competencies, scale and level of interaction. The formality of EU law contributes to this power by emphasizing the saliencies and certainties of EU law. In the sum of the texts, one finds a vision both for integration within Europe – set out clearly in the primary texts – and for management of various policy sectors – explored in the secondary legislation. Even if actors choose not to respond to this vision – either positively or negatively – it inevitably forms a backdrop which casts a shadow over almost any form of participation in or resistance to transnational interaction.

Notes

1. The EC pillar is distinguished at various points throughout this chapter, as it involves a more intense form of 'legalization' in terms of the laws made and the actors implicated than the other two pillars.
2. No woman or member of an ethnic minority has ever served as a judge of the ECJ.
3. Decision 88/591/EEC, OJ 1988, L319/1.
4. Case 338/85 *Pardini* v *Ministero del commercio con l'estero* [1988] ECR 2041.
5. Case 26/62 *Van Gend en Loos* v *Nederlandse Administratie der Belastingen* [1963] ECR 1; Case 6/64 *Costa* v *ENEL* [1964] ECR 585.
6. *Opinion 1/91 on the Draft Agreement on a European Economic Area* [1991] ECR I-6079.
7. Case 314/85 *Firma Fotofrost* v *HZA Lubeck Ost* [1987] ECR 4199.
8. *Brunner* v *Treaty on EU* [1994] 1 CMLR 57; *Carlsen* v *Rasmussen*, Judgment of 6 April 1998.
9. *R* v *MAFF ex parte First City Trading* [1997] 1 CMLR 250, affirmed in *Marks and Spencer* v *CCE* [1999] 1 CMLR 1152.
10. Joined Cases 267–9/81 *SPI* [1983] ECR 801.
11. *R* v *Secretary of State for the Environment, Transport and the Regions ex parte IATA* [1999] 1 CMLR 1287.
12. Case 314/85 *Firma Fotofrost* v *HZA Lubeck Ost* [1987] ECR 4199.
13. Case 283/81 *CILFIT* [1982] ECR 3415.
14. [1997] OJ, C340/308.
15. *Opinion 1/91 on the Draft Agreement on a European Economic Area* [1991] ECR I-6079.
16. Joined Cases C 6 and 9/90 and C-9/90 *Francovich and Others* v *Italy* [1991] ECR I-5357.
17. Case 45/76 *Comet* v *Produktschap* [1976] ECR 2043.
18. Case 125/84 *Marshall* v *Southampton and South-West AHA* [1986] ECR 723.
19. Case 194/94 *CIA Security International* v *Signalson* [1996] ECR I-2201.
20. See the Opinion of Advocate-General Jacobs in Case C–316/93 *Vaneetveld* v *Le Foyer* [1994] ECR I-763.
21. Case C–106/89 *Marleasing* v *La Comercial* [1990] ECR I-4135.
22. Joined cases C 58, 75, 112, 119, 123, 135, 140–1, 154 and 157/95 *Gallotti* [1996] ECR I-4345.
23. Joined Cases C 178, 179, 188–190/94 *Dillenkofer* v *Germany* [1996] ECR I-4845.
24. Case C–46/93 *Brasserie du Pêcheur* v *Germany* [1996] ECR I-1029.
25. Case C–5/94 *R* v *MAFF ex parte Lomas* [1996] ECR I-2553.
26. Opinion 1/75 *Local Cost Standard Opinion* [1975] ECR 1355.
27. Case 120/78 *Rewe* v *Bundesmonopolverwaltung für Branntwein* [1979] ECR 649.
28. Directive 92/43/EC, [1992] OJ, L206/7, Articles 3 and 4(4).
29. Decision 1692/96/EC, [1996] OJ, L228/1, Article 6. See also the proposal for a high-speed train network, [1994] OJ, C 134/6.
30. Regulation 1404/96/EC, [1996] OJ, L181/1, Article 2(1)(a) (LIFE).
31. e.g. Decision 93/707/EC on the grant of aid to the Closa rising bog in Ireland, [1993] OJ, L331/20; Decision 93/714/EC on the restoration of natural resources in natural parks in Spain, [1993] OJ, L331/83.
32. Directive 97/11/EC, [1997] OJ, L73/5, Annex III, 2(e).

4 The basic statistics

A. M. EL-AGRAA

This chapter provides the reader with a brief summary of the basic statistics of the EU which are used in the analytical chapters. For comparative purposes and in order to preserve a general sense of perspective, similar information is given for Canada, Japan, the United States, the Russian Federation and for the immediate potential EU member countries: the member nations of EFTA, which, except for Switzerland, are members of the European Economic Area (EEA), which is considered as a stepping-stone to full EU membership (see Chapters 1 and 2); Bulgaria, Cyprus, the Czech Republic, Estonia, Hungary, Latvia, Lithuania, Malta, Poland, Romania, the Slovak Republic, Slovenia and Turkey because they have applied for EU membership (but for some of which most data are not available).

The main purpose of this chapter is to provide information; the analysis of most of these statistics and the economic forces that determine them is one of the main tasks of the rest of this book. For example, the analysis of the composition and pattern of trade prior to the inception of the EU and subsequent to its formation is the basic aim of the theoretical and measurement section of the book. Moreover, the policy chapters are concerned with the analysis of particular areas of interest: the Common Agricultural Policy (CAP), the role of the EU general budget, competition and industrial policies, the EU regional policy, etc., and these specialist chapters contain further relevant information.

4.1 The basic statistics

4.1.1 Area, population, life expectancy and health

Table 4.1 (the tables may be found in the appendix at the end of the chapter) gives information about area, population and life expectancy at birth, and the later Table 4.17 provides supporting data on health. The data are more or less self-explanatory but a few points warrant particular attention.

The EU of 15 has a larger population (about 375 million) than any country in the advanced Western world. This population exceeds that of the Russian Federation (about 147 million) and of the United States (about 270 million) and is only just short of being three times that of Japan. It exceeds the combined population of the United States and Canada (member nations of the North American Free Trade Agreement, NAFTA) by about 74 million, is about 22 million short of the combined population of all three NAFTA nations (Mexico has a population of about 96 million), and is only about 21 million less than the combined population of the United States and Japan, the world's two largest economies.

A quick comparison of the first two columns of Table 4.1 reveals that the EU member nations have higher population densities than Canada and the United States. However, the population densities within the EU exhibit great diversity with the Netherlands and Belgium at the top of the league and Spain, Greece and Ireland at the bottom. It should be stressed that population density has important implications for the potential economic growth and the future of the social and environmental policies of the EU.

The average rate of increase of population between 1965 and 1980 was quite variable for the member nations of the EU. It was low in West Germany (0.2%), the United Kingdom (0.2%), Austria (0.3%), Belgium (0.3%), Finland (0.3%) and Portugal (0.4%), but high in the Netherlands (0.9%), Spain (1.0%) and Ireland (1.2%). The remaining EU nations occupied the middle ground. For the same period, among the three EFTA countries, Norway and Switzerland had roughly the same rates as Denmark, Italy and Sweden, which are near the average for the EU as a whole. All the other countries shown in the table had high rates, with Turkey being completely out of line with a rate of 2.4%. For the period 1980–90, the rates declined for virtually all the countries except for Finland, Switzerland and Latvia, where it increased by about one-tenth of a percentage point, and the United Kingdom where it remained at the previous rate. For the period 1990–97, the change is dramatic in both directions, but, since this is a shorter period, no serious comparison can be made. However, Turkey continued to be the only country out of line within this group of nations.

Note that for the countries listed in the table, life expectancy at birth is between 61 and 79 years for males and between 72 and 83 for females. For the EU nations, the range is between 71 and 77 for males and 79 and 82 for females. For the other potential EU members, the range is 64–79. The general pattern that can be detected from the entire list is that there is a positive relationship between the level of economic development and life expectancy but there is no clear relationship between public expenditure on health and life expectancy. Although these figures do not seem far apart, a difference in life expectancy of about five years is in reality quite substantial in terms of the required provision for old age, a question that is becoming a real headache for countries such as Japan, but some EU nations are almost on a par with Japan.

However, one should be careful not to read too much into such comparisons – there is always the danger that they may distract the reader from some obvious and basic realities of life: the cultural diversity of the member nations of the EU relative to the almost common historical evolution and economic development of the United States, the contrasting political systems of the countries compared, the frequency of natural disasters, etc.

4.1.2 GNP and inflation

Table 4.2 gives per capita GNP (the structure and total GDP are provided in Tables 4.5 and 4.6) and its average annual rate of growth between 1985 and 1998. The table also provides the GDP implicit deflator, i.e. the annual inflation rates, for the period 1980–98. One of the salient features of this table is the disparity between the member nations of the EU in terms of per capita GNP: Portugal, Greece, Spain and Ireland lag, in that order, far behind the rest, with Portugal on $10 690. All three member countries of EFTA have per capita incomes exceeding the average for the

EU, while all the EU potential partners, with the exception of Cyprus, Malta and Slovenia, have per capita GNPs in the range of 11–47% that of Portugal. Note that in this respect Luxembourg and Denmark are ahead of the United States.

For the period 1958–64, the United Kingdom showed the slowest rate of growth of GDP in comparison with the original six member nations of the EC (this information is not provided in the table). Indeed, if a longer period is considered (1953–64), the average exponential growth rate of the United Kingdom was only 2.7%, with the United States next with 3.1% (Kaldor, 1966, p. 5). On the other hand, Japan had exceptionally high growth rates – for the period 1953–64 the average exponential growth rate was 9.6%. Although during 1965–80 (Table 4.6) these rates declined for all the countries concerned, relative performance did not change much, but during 1990–98 dramatic changes were beginning to happen, with Ireland, the United States and Denmark being the stars and the United Kingdom not so far behind its EU partners and exceeding the performance of nine of them.

With regard to the rate of growth of GNP per capita for the period 1965–90 (not given in the table), except for the fact that the rates declined overall and that the United Kingdom's position was taken over by Switzerland, the Netherlands, the United States and Sweden (in that order), the United Kingdom occupied the fourth lowest position. However, during 1985–95, although the United Kingdom did a little better than the United States and was on a par with Italy, its overall performance within the EU ranked tenth (equal), and its performance in 1997–98 was even worse, coming second to last.

Table 4.2 also provides information on the annual inflation rates for 1980–98. During 1980–90 Portugal, Greece and Italy had exceptionally high rates; they were the only three EU member nations with double-digit rates (18%, 18% and 10% respectively). Taking the rate for the United States as the standard, only two EU nations did better. Note that, with the exception of the Netherlands, Japan continued to occupy the bottom of this league with a low rate of 1.7%. During 1990–98 there have been some dramatic changes, but the overall picture remains intact. Thus the data clearly demonstrate the disparity of performance by the member nations of the EU in this respect.

4.1.3 Work

Table 4.3 provides data on the percentage of civilian working population, the unemployment rates and the sectoral distribution of the labour force in terms of the broad categories of agriculture, industry and services. Of course, from this information and the total population figures given in Table 4.1, one can easily arrive at the absolute total for the labour force.

With regard to the percentage of civilian working population, there was no striking difference between the member nations of the EU in 1965 except for the fact that Ireland (with 57%) stood below the 62–66% range that covered the rest. For the same year, of all the relevant nations in the table, Turkey stood out with a figure of 53%. In 1994, this rate declined for all the countries in the table, and, except for Denmark, the rate was 50% or below for the EU nations. Note that although Ireland still occupied the bottom position within the EU with 40%, this time it was joined by France, Greece and Spain, with Belgium close by, and Turkey was still far below the rest, being the only country with less than 40%. However, one should again be careful with regard to this information since it does not include those employed in the military field, and the decline in rates may reflect an increase in the number of those going for higher education as well as lengthening of the duration of such education; the reader is advised to glance at Table 4.15 on education which may prove helpful in this respect.

The unemployment rates were high for all the member countries of the EU except for Luxembourg and Austria, if one were again to adopt the rate for the United States as the norm. Since by present standards any rate below 3% can be regarded as exceptionally good, Luxembourg would stand out. However, Luxembourg is so small and so dominated by EU bureaucrats and parliamentarians that it should be discounted in any serious comparison. Although Denmark, Finland, Greece, Ireland and Portugal had double-digit rates and hence can be classified as EU countries with extremely worrying unemployment rates, the same can be said about the other eight EU nations since they had rates in excess of 7%. Given this arbitrary classification, only Austria can claim to have performed extremely well. All three member nations of EFTA registered good rates, especially Iceland with 3%. Of the 'other countries', Japan passes as exceptionally good.

Of particular interest is the relative size of the services sector. This is mainly the tertiary sector (it comprises such divergent items as banking, distribution, insurance, transport, catering and hotels, laundries and hairdressers, professional services of a more varied kind, publicly and privately provided, etc.) and was, for all the EU, EFTA and Other countries, the largest in 1995, exceeding 60% in the majority of them. This is a significant point, particularly since it has frequently been alleged in the past that the size of this sector was the cause of the slow rate of growth of the UK economy; there is nothing in the data to suggest that the UK is unique in this respect. Moreover, the increasing size of this sector over time has led to the doctrine of 'deindustrialization': as this sector grows in percentage terms, it automatically follows that the other sectors, especially industry, must decline in relative terms.

As one would expect (since it is a natural characteristic of development), all the countries considered show a decline in the percentage of the labour force engaged in agriculture, even for the United Kingdom whose percentage has remained consistently near the 2–3% level: when the percentage is so low it is difficult for it to fall further, especially when most countries deem some agriculture to be necessary for food security (see Chapter 11). However, Greece, Ireland, Portugal and Spain were the only EU countries with double-digit percentages. Again, note that Turkey, with 53%, is in a league of its own.

4.1.4 Employment and unemployment

Although some aspects of EU employment and unemployment are tackled in various chapters of the book, especially those on the social and competition and industrial policies, this may be the appropriate point to consider briefly certain aspects of this topic which are not tackled in those chapters. Employment is a political and socioeconomic issue which needs to be tackled in all its manifestations, and that is why, at the particular insistence of France, the Amsterdam Treaty incorporates it as a new policy area. It is quite obvious that the solution to the unemployment problem necessitates a close integration of economic policies as well as social and manpower policies. The unemployment problem has two basic features. First, there is the transitional problem: given existing levels of unemployment and possible rates of growth of population, the achievement of acceptable levels of manpower utilization will inevitably be slow and in some countries may take many years. In addition, there is the longer-term problem: the effect of evolving structures of the labour force, attitudes to work and changing social objectives which may affect employment in a fundamental sense.

Table 4.4 gives a longer-term perspective for manpower utilization and unemployment rates. It should be noted that between 1973 and 1975 unemployment grew steadily in all the countries included in the table, except for Italy, and that the rates of growth were much higher than during the boom years of the 1960s. In terms of employment, the maximum declines in the 1973–5 recession were much greater than any that had occurred in the 1960s. However, the reader should note that the absolute levels of unemployment for these countries are not strictly comparable owing to differences in measurement techniques. For example, some of those considered as fully employed in Japan will not pass as such elsewhere (see El-Agraa 1988a).

In spite of the above observation, a great deal of the slack in manpower utilization which developed during the period 1973–5 was absorbed by various measures which diverted the growth of overt unemployment. Working hours fell in a number of countries and jobs were preserved by subsidies to employers, by restrictions on dismissals or by deterrents such as redundancy payments which made employers reluctant to dismiss labour. As a result, output per employee fell in many cases.

The table also gives some indication of the change in working hours in the major countries. Many of the figures refer only to manufacturing and may therefore be more sensitive to a recession than those for the economy as a whole, but they do indicate that working hours dropped more than the 1960–70 trend would have suggested. The biggest fall was in Japan. This explains some of the fall in output per employee, but the reduction in working hours does not by any means explain the whole of this decline.

The bottom half of the table gives recorded unemployment for the EU countries for various years.

4.1.5 Demand

Table 4.7 gives information on the structure of demand in 1998, i.e. on the distribution of GDP between private consumption, collective consumption of the general government, investment expenditure, savings, the export of goods and non-factor services and resource balance. With regard to private consumption, the lowest percentage within the EU belonged to Denmark, Finland, Ireland and Sweden (52–54%) and the highest was that of Greece (75%). As to gross domestic investment, the lowest percentage belonged to Sweden (15%) and the highest was that of Austria and Portugal (24%). The percentages for savings showed a larger divergence between the lowest (11% for Greece) and the highest (33% for Ireland). Note that of the EU nations only Spain had an equality between the percentages devoted to savings and domestic investment, but Austria, Germany and the United Kingdom were close to that. Exports of goods and non-factor services loomed large in the case of Ireland (76%), Belgium (73%) and the Netherlands (56%) but varied between 15% and 44% for the rest. Norway and Switzerland fitted into the general picture for the EU, but the divergence was somewhat wider for the remaining nations, with the United States being almost in a league of its own in terms of savings and exports as well as Japan with its very high savings and domestic investment rates and low exports rate. Note that all these comparisons relate to 1998 data; longer-term data can be guessed from the growth rates for 1965–80 and 1990–98 given in Table 4.6. Here, it suffices to state that the excess of domestic savings over investment in Japan is far in excess of the 2% given in 1998, and the same qualification applies to the opposite relationship between investment and savings in the United States.

4.1.6 Government sector

Tables 4.7, 4.8, 4.9 and 4.11 and parts of 4.10 and 4.12 provide data on what can loosely be referred to as the 'government sector'. They give information about current government revenue and expenditure as percentages of GDP, net official development assistance to developing countries and multilateral agents, total official reserves, money and interest rates, etc.

There was a dissimilarity between the member nations of the EU with respect to both their current government expenditure and revenue as percentages of their GDPs in 1997. In terms of total current expenditure, the range was between 28.5% for Greece and 46.0% for the Netherlands. This was in stark contrast to those for Japan (14.8%), Canada (20.8%), the United States (21.0%) and Switzerland (25.3%). A similar range (24.7–39.3%) existed between the potential EU nations. With regard to total capital expenditure, the ranges are also wide, but the percentages are smaller. There were also wide ranges in terms of total expenditure on defence and social services. Of particular interest in the case of the EU is the variation in the size of the overall budget deficit since it is one of the criteria set for the introduction of the single currency (see Chapters 5 and 17).

A particularly interesting feature is the percentage of GDP spent on net official assistance extended to developing countries and multilateral agents, given in Table 4.12. Denmark (1.03%), Norway (1.01%) and Sweden (0.98%) came at the top of the league while the United States (0.15%) and Japan (0.26%) came at the bottom if one rightly excluded Greece (0.10%) and Ireland (0.20%) from this comparison since their level of development in 1993 does not match that of this group of countries. One does not want to dwell too much on this matter, but the information suggests that the advanced world, in resisting the demands made by the developing world, is more concerned about absolute figures than about percentages. The latter clearly indicate the significant implications for official development assistance of the developing countries' plea (through UNCTAD) that this figure should be raised to 0.5% (originally 1.0%) of the major donor countries' GDP: Germany, Japan, the United Kingdom and the United States. Therefore, as far as developing countries are concerned, only Denmark, Norway, Sweden, the Netherlands and France will be applauded. One should add however that a movement for the writing off of the debt of the poorest nations is now under serious discussion.

For a proper and detailed discussion of the role played by the governments' budgets, the reader is advised to turn to the chapters on the role of the EU general budget (16) and on fiscal harmonization (15).

4.1.7 Exports, imports and balance of payments

Tables 4.10, 4.13 and 4.14 give information on exports and imports, foreign direct investment, current account balance, imports from and exports to the EU nations and gross international reserves.

All these tables are more or less self-explanatory, but Tables 4.13 and 4.14 warrant particular attention. They should be considered together since they give the percentages for the share of imports of the importing country coming from the EU and the share of exports of the exporting country going to the EU. The reader should be warned that these percentages are not strictly comparable, because for the year 1957 the EU refers to the original six, while for 1974 it refers to the nine, for 1981 to the 10, for 1986 and 1990 to the 12, and for 1995 to the 15. For an analysis of the proper trends, the reader should consult Chapter 7, and for a full analysis consult El-Agraa (1989b and 1999).

The tables show that, in 1995, EU member nations' imports from each other varied from about 55% for the United Kingdom to about 75% for Austria. The percentages for exports varied likewise, with the lowest being over 57% for Germany and the highest over 80% for Portugal. Thus, on average, Portugal comes at the top. Of the potential EU partners, all three member nations of EFTA conducted more than half of their total trade (both exports and imports) with the EU, with Norway and Switzerland closer to 75%.

4.1.8 Education

Table 4.15 gives public expenditure on education as a percentage of GNP, the enrolment rates at the primary, secondary and tertiary levels of education, the percentage of cohort reaching grade 5 and the adult illiteracy rate. The table shows that for 1996 there were on the whole no drastic differences between the countries compared with regard to the primary levels, but that major deviations are noticeable at the secondary and tertiary levels. However, the table also reveals that five EU nations did not provide primary education to every child, and that public expenditure on education varied greatly, with Greece (3%) and Belgium (3.2%) at the bottom and Sweden (8.3%) and Denmark (8.2%) at the top.

At the tertiary level, Canada (103%), the United States (81%) and Finland (63%) stand out while Portugal (23%) recorded the lowest percentage within the EU, but much lower rates can be seen in many of the countries that are EU potential members. These rates may suggest that a general positive relationship exists between economic development and high rates of enrolment at the tertiary level, but there is no such relationship if one concentrates on the most advanced of the nations in the table; for example, Japan and Switzerland are the two countries with the highest per capita GNP in the world in 1996 yet their enrolment rate at the tertiary level is only higher than that of Portugal. Moreover, the data are not strictly comparable since what is deemed to be university education in one country may not pass as such in others.

4.1.9 Income–consumption distribution

Table 4.16 gives some information on the distribution of income and consumption. The table shows that, within the EU and EFTA nations, Canada, Japan and the United States, the highest 10% received between 19.3% and 28.5% of income while the lowest 10% received between 1.5% and 4.4%. At the same time, the highest 20% received a share of between 33.3% and 45.2% of income while the lowest 20%

received only between 4.8% and 10.4%. It is interesting to note that the disparity is widest for both the United States and Russia.

4.1.10 Tariffs

Table 4.18 provides information on the average tariff levels in the original six as well as in Denmark, the United Kingdom, Canada and the United States. To see how these compare with the tariff levels that are at present in existence, one should turn to Chapter 22 on EU external trade policy.

4.2 Conclusion

As stated at the beginning of this chapter, there are no conclusions to be drawn from this general statistical survey; the information is provided only for the purpose of giving a general sense of perspective. The reader who is seeking conclusions should turn to the relevant specialist chapter or chapters.

Appendix The statistical tables

In all tables, na means not available. Unless otherwise stated, the sources for all the tables are the World Bank's *World Development Report*, Eurostat's *Basic Statistics of the EU* and *Statistical Review*, and OECD publications for various years. The data are subject to technical explanations as well as to some critical qualifications; hence the reader is strongly advised to turn to the original sources for these.

Table 4.1 Area and population

	Area (000 km²)	Population (mill.) 1998	Average annual growth of population (%)			Life expectancy at birth (years) 1997	
			1965–80	1980–90	1990–98	Males	Females
EU countries							
Austria	84	8.1	0.3	0.7	0.7	74	81
Belgium	31	10.2	0.3	0.4	0.3	73	80
Denmark	43	5.3	0.5	0.1	−0.1	73	78
Finland	338	5.1	0.3	0.8	0.5	73	81
France	552	58.8	0.7	0.9	0.5	74	82
Germany	357	82.1	0.2	0.5	0.5	74	80
Greece	132	10.6	0.7	0.9	0.5	75	81
Ireland	70	3.7	1.2	0.8	0.7	73	79
Italy	301	57.6	0.5	0.2	0.2	75	82
Luxembourg	3	0.4	na	0.4	0.3	74	81
Netherlands	42	15.7	0.9	1.0	0.7	75	81
Portugal	92	9.9	0.4	0.2	0.1	71	79
Spain	506	39.4	1.0	0.5	0.2	75	82
Sweden	450	8.9	0.5	0.6	0.5	77	82
United Kingdom	244	59.2	0.2	0.5	0.4	75	80
EU (15)	3 245	375.0					
EFTA countries							
Iceland	103	0.27	na	na	na	79[b]	79[b]
Norway	324	4.4	0.6	0.8	0.6	76	81
Switzerland	41	7.0	0.5	1.2	0.8	76	82
EU potential members							
Bulgaria	111	8.4	0.4[a]	−0.7	−0.8	67	74
Cyprus	9	0.73	na	na	na	78[b]	78[b]
Czech Republic	79	10.3	0.5[a]	0.1	−0.1	71	78
Estonia	45	1.5	0.8[a]	−0.3	−1.2	64	76
Hungary	93	10.2	0.4[a]	−0.6	−0.3	66	75
Latvia	64	2.5	0.4	−0.4	−1.3	64	75
Lithuania	65	3.7	na	0.8	−0.1	70	75
Malta	0.3	0.38	na	na	na	77[b]	77[b]
Poland	313	38.7	0.8	0.8	0.2	69	77
Romania	238	22.5	na	0.1	−0.5	65	73
Slovak Republic	49	5.4	0.9[a]	0.8	0.3	69	77
Slovenia	20	2.0	0.9[a]	0.4	−0.1	71	79
Turkey	775	63.0	2.4	3.6	1.8	67	72
Other countries							
Canada	9 971	31.0	1.3	2.2	1.4	76	82
Japan	378	126.0	1.2	0.8	0.3	77	83
Russian Federation	17 075	147.0	0.6[a]	0.6	−0.1	61	73
United States	9 364	270.0	1.0	1.7	1.1	73	79

[a]The rate is for 1970–80.
[b]The average life expectancy rate.

Table 4.2 GNP per capita and inflation rates

| | GNP per capita | | | | |
| | US$ | Average annual growth rate (%) | | GDP implicit deflator | |
	1998	1985–95	1997–98	1980–90	1990–98
EU countries					
Austria	26 850	1.9	3.2	3.3	2.5
Belgium	25 380	2.2	2.7	4.4	2.3
Denmark	33 260	1.5	2.6	5.6	1.7
Finland	24 110	−0.2	4.8	6.8	1.8
France	24 940	1.5	2.9	6.0	1.7
Germany	25 850	na	−0.4	na	2.2
Greece	11 650	1.3	3.4	18.0	10.6
Ireland	18 340	5.2	8.5	6.6	1.9
Italy	20 250	1.4	2.2	10.0	4.4
Luxembourg	43 570	0.9	4.2	na	na
Netherlands	24 760	1.9	3.3	1.6	2.1
Portugal	10 690	3.6	3.9	18.0	5.8
Spain	14 080	2.6	3.7	9.3	4.2
Sweden	25 650	−0.1	3.5	7.4	2.3
United Kingdom	21 400	1.4	2.0	5.7	3.0
EFTA countries					
Iceland	28 010	1.0	5.1	na	na
Norway	34 330	1.7	2.4	5.6	1.8
Switzerland	40 080	0.2	2.1	3.4	1.7
EU potential members					
Bulgaria	1 230	−2.6	na	1.8	109.5
Cyprus	na[a]	na	na	na	na
Czech Republic	5 040	−1.8	na	1.5	17.1
Estonia	3 390	−4.3	na	2.3	75.5
Hungary	4 510	−1.0	na	8.9	22.8
Latvia	2,430	−6.6	na	0.0	87.7
Lithuania	2 440	−11.7	5.6	na	111.5
Malta	9 440	na	4.1	na	na
Poland	3 900	1.2	5.4	53.8	27.0
Romania	1 390	−3.8	−5.6	2.5	113.3
Slovak Republic	3 700	−2.8	na	1.8	12.6
Slovenia	9 760	na	na	na	32.3
Turkey	3 160	1.2	na	45.2	79.3
Other countries					
Canada	20 020	0.4	6.1	4.5	1.6
Japan	32 380	2.9	−2.6	1.7	0.4
Russian Federation	2 300	−5.1	−6.6	na	235.3
United States	29 340	1.3	3.7	4.2	2.2

[a]Estimated to be high income ($9361 or more).

Table 4.3 Labour force and unemployment rates

| | Civilian working population (% of total population) | | % of labour force in | | | | | | Unemployment rates (annual averages in %) |
| | 1965 | 1994 | Agriculture | | Industry | | Services | | |
			1965	1994	1965	1995	1965	1995	1995
EU countries									
Austria	63	48	19	7	45	37	36	55	3.8
Belgium	63	41	6	3	46	28	48	69	9.9
Denmark	64	54	14	5	37	28	49	66	8.2
Finland	65	49	24	8	35	31	41	61	17.2
France	62	40	18	5	39	29	43	66	11.5
Germany	65	49	11	3	48	38	41	59	8.2
Greece	65	40	47	21	24	28	41	58	9.1
Ireland	57	40	31	13	28	29	41	58	12.4
Italy	66	43	25	8	42	32	34	59	11.9
Luxembourg	na	43	na	3	na	26	na	70	2.9
Netherlands	62	48	9	7	41	26	51	69	7.3
Portugal	62	49	38	12	30	34	32	48	7.3
Spain	64	40	34	10	35	33	32	55	22.9
Sweden	66	49	11	4	43	25	46	71	9.2
United Kingdom	65	50	3	2	47	29	50	69	8.8
EU (15)				5		30		64	10.7
EFTA countries									
Iceland	na	55	na	9	na	26	na	63	5.0
Norway	63	49	16	5	37	25	48	69	4.9
Switzerland	65	56	9	4	49	35	41	59	4.4[a]
EU potential members									
Bulgaria	na	na	na	14[a]	na	50	na	36	na
Cyprus	na	na	na	na	na	na	na	na	na
Czech Republic	na	na	na	11[a]	na	45	na	44	na
Estonia	na	na	na	14[a]	na	41	na	45	na
Hungary	na	na	na	15[a]	na	38	na	47	na
Latvia	na	na	na	16[a]	na	42	na	42	na
Lithuania	na	na	na	18[a]	na	41	na	41	na
Malta	na	na	na	na	na	na	na	na	na
Poland	na	na	na	27[a]	na	36	na	37	na
Romania	na	na	na	24[a]	na	47	na	29	na
Slovak Republic	na	na	na	12[a]	na	32	na	56	na
Slovenia	na	na	na	5[a]	na	44	na	51	na
Turkey	53	34	75	53[a]	35	18	14	29	6.8[a]
Other countries									
Canada	59	51	10	4	33	25	57	72	11.6[a]
Japan	67	54	26	6	32	34	42	59	3.1
Russian Federation	57[b]	57	34	15	33	42	33	44	1.0[a]
United States	60	50	5	3	35	28	60	69	5.6

[a]The rate is for 1993.
[b]Working age population.

Table 4.4 Manpower utilization, unemployment rates and recorded unemployment

| | Changes (%) | | | | | | | |
| | Employment | | Hours worked per person | | Output per man-hour | | Unemployment % of labour | |
	1960–73	1973–75	1960–73	1973–75	1960–73	1973–75	1960–73	1974
EC countries								
Belgium[a]	0.7	na	−1.2	na	5.4	na	2.2	2.6
Denmark	1.3	na	−1.5	na	5.0	na	1.1	2.1
France	0.7	−0.5	−0.5	−2.1	5.5	3.6	1.6	2.3
Germany	0.1	−2.8	−0.9	−2.7	5.5	4.0	0.8	2.2
Ireland	na	na	na	na	na	na	na	na
Italy	−0.7	1.2	1.9	na	7.8	na	3.3	2.9
Netherlands	0.9	na	na	na	na	na	1.3	3.0
United Kingdom	0.1	0.0	−0.5	−0.8	3.4	0.1	1.9	2.1
Other countries								
Canada	2.9	3.1	−0.3	−1.4	−2.8	−0.8	5.3	5.4
Japan	1.2	−0.8	−1.0	−5.3	10.1	6.2	1.3	1.4
United States	1.9	0.1	0.1	−0.2	2.3	−2.4	4.8	5.4

| | Unemployment (annual average % of labour force) | | | | | Estimated number (annual averages in 1 000) |
	1973	1979	1985	1991	1995	1995
Austria	na	na	na	3.5	3.8	147
Belgium[a]	3	8	14	8.3	9.9	416
Denmark	1	5	12	8.6	8.2	198
Finland	na	na	na	7.6	17.2	430
France	2	6	12	9.7	11.5	2 850
Germany	1	3	7	4.3	8.2	3 209
Greece	na	na	8	7.0	9.1	380
Ireland	6	8	15	16.1	12.4	178
Italy	5	7	12	10.3	11.9	2 683
Netherlands	2	4	12	7.0	7.3	535
Portugal	na	na	na	4.0	7.3	347
Spain	na	na	na	16.4	22.9	3 574
Sweden	na	na	na	2.7	9.2	404
United Kingdom	2	5	16	9.4	8.8	2 501
EU 15						17 856

[a]Includes Luxembourg.

Table 4.5 Structure of production, 1998

	GDP (million US$)	Distribution of gross domestic product (%)			
		Agriculture	Industry	(of which manufacturing)	Services etc.
EU countries					
Austria	212 069	3	26	14	71
Belgium	247 076	1	27	18	72
Denmark	174 272	4	29[c]	21[c]	67[c]
Finland	125 673	4	34	25	62
France	1 432 902	2	26	19	72
Germany	2 142 018	1	55	24	44
Greece	120 304	21	36[c]	218[c]	43[c]
Ireland	80 880	8[b]	9[b]	3[b]	83[b]
Italy	1 171 044	3	31	20	66
Luxembourg	18 587	2[a]	36[a]	na	62[a]
Netherlands	382 487	3	2[c]	18[c]	70[c]
Portugal	106 650	6[a]	39[a]	na	55[a]
Spain	551 923	4[a]	34[a]	na	62[a]
Sweden	224 953	2	32[c]	23[c]	66[c]
United Kingdom	357 429	2	31	21	71
EU (15)	8 348 267				
EFTA countries					
Iceland	7 675	na	na	na	na
Norway	145 896	2	32	11	66
Switzerland	264 352	4[a]	40[a]	na	56[a]
EU potential members					
Bulgaria	10 085	23	26	18	50
Cyprus	na	na	na	na	na
Czech Republic	52 035	6	39[c]	na	55[c]
Estonia	5 462	8	28[c]	17[c]	64[c]
Hungary	45 725	6	34	25	60
Latvia	5 527	7	31	21	62
Lithuania	10 517	11	36[c]	30[c]	53[c]
Malta	3 564	na	na	na	na
Poland	148 863	4	26	17	70
Romania	34 843	21	40	na	39
Slovak Republic	19 461	5	33	na	62
Slovenia	18 201	5	39	29	57
Turkey	189 878	15	28	18	57
Other countries					
Canada	598 847	3[a]	40[a]	na	57[a]
Japan	3 783 140	2	38[c]	24[c]	60[c]
Russian Federation	446 982	9	42	na	49
United States	8 210 600	2	27	18	71

[a]The rate is for 1992.
[b]The rate is for 1994.
[c]The rate is for 1995.

Table 4.6 Growth of production

	GDP		Average annual growth rate (%)					
			Agriculture		Industry		Services	
	1965–1980	1990–1998	1980–1990	1990–1998	1980–1990	1990–1998	1980–1990	1990–1998
EU countries								
Austria	4.1	2.0	1.1	−0.7	1.9	1.3	2.3	2.2
Belgium[f]	3.8	1.6	1.8	1.6	2.2	0.7	1.8	1.3
Denmark	2.7	2.8	3.1	1.7	2.9	1.9	2.1	1.4
Finland	4.0	2.0	−0.2	0.2	3.3	2.1	3.7	−0.1
France	4.0	1.5	2.0	0.4	1.1	0.1	3.0	1.6
Germany	3.3[a]	1.6	1.7	0.8	1.2	1.1[b]	2.9	3.0[b]
Greece	5.6	2.0	−0.1	2.0	1.3	−0.5	2.3	1.8
Ireland	5.0	7.5	na	−6.2[c]	na	na	na	3.8[c]
Italy	4.3	1.2	0.6	1.3	2.2	0.8	2.7	1.1
Netherlands	3.8	2.6	4.1[d]	3.7	0.8[d]	1.2	1.6[d]	2.3
Portugal	5.3	2.3	−0.9[d]	−0.4	1.0[d]	0.5	1.3[d]	2.3
Spain	4.6	1.9	0.9[d]	−2.5	0.4[d]	−0.4	2.1[d]	−13.1
Sweden	2.9	1.2	1.5	−1.9	2.8	−0.7	2.1	−0.1
United Kingdom	2.4	2.2	3.1[d]	na	1.3[d]	na	3.0[d]	na
EFTA countries								
Iceland	na	na	na	na	na	na	na	na
Norway	4.4	3.9	0.9	4.5	3.5	5.6	2.6	3.1
Switzerland	2.0	0.4	na	na	na	na	na	na
EU potential members								
Bulgaria	na	−3.3	−2.1	−3.1	5.2	−5.5	4.8	−0.6
Cyprus	na	na	na	na	na	na	na	na
Czech Republic	na	−0.2	−0.4[e]	na	0.3[e]	na	1.2[e]	na
Estonia	na	−2.1	−1.9	−4.3	1.6	−5.9	−0.5	0.5
Hungary	5.6	−0.2	0.6	−3.8	−2.6	1.1	4.8	0.3
Latvia	na	−8.5	2.3	−10.8	4.3	−15.9	3.1	−0.2
Lithuania	na	−5.2	na	−1.4	na	−10.1	na	−0.4
Malta	na	na	na	na	na	na	na	na
Poland	na	4.5	0.7	−1.6	0.1	4.7	2.2	3.0
Romania	na	−0.6	na	−0.2	na	−0.8	na	−0.2
Slovak Republic	na	0.6	0.6	−0.4	2.2	−6.5	1.7	8.1
Slovenia	na	1.4	na	0.2	na	0.8	na	3.8
Turkey	6.2	4.1	4.4	1.1	6.4	5.0	5.5	4.1
Other countries								
Canada	4.8	2.2	1.5	1.2	2.9	1.8	3.6	1.8
Japan	6.4	1.3	1.1	−2.0	4.9	0.2	3.7	2.0
Russian Federation	na	−7.0	na	−6.9	na	−8.1	na	−4.7
United States	2.6	2.9	4.0	2.0	2.8	4.3	3.1	1.9

[a]The figure is for West Germany.
[b]The percentage is for 1980–92.
[c]The percentage is for 1980–90.
[d]The percentage is for 1980–88.
[e]The percentage is for Czechoslovakia for 1980–91.
[f]Includes Luxembourg.

Table 4.7 Structure of demand, 1998

	Distribution of gross domestic product (%)					Resource balance
	General government consumption	Private consumption etc.	Growth domestic investment	Growth domestic savings	Exports of goods and services	
EU countries						
Austria	20	57	24	23	42	−1
Belgium[a]	15	63	18	22	73	5
Denmark[b]	25	54	16	21	35	6
Finland	22	53	17	25	33	9
France	19	61	17	20	24	3
Germany	20	58	21	22	27	2
Greece	14	75	19	11	15	−9
Ireland	14	53	18	33	76	15
Italy	16	61	17	22	27	4
Netherlands	14	60	20	26	56	7
Portugal	18	65	24	17	31	−9
Spain	16	62	21	21	26	1
Sweden	26	52	15	21	44	7
United Kingdom	21	64	16	15	29	0
EFTA countries						
Iceland	na	na	na	na	na	na
Norway	20	48	23	32	41	7
Switzerland	14	61	20	24	40	4
EU potential members						
Bulgaria	12	70	12	17	61	6
Cyprus	na	na	na	na	na	na
Czech Republic	20	51	34	28	58	−5
Estonia	21	62	26	17	76	−9
Hungary	10	63	27	27	45	0
Latvia	23	67	20	10	50	−10
Lithuania	20	67	28	14	50	−14
Malta	na	na	na	na	na	na
Poland	16	65	24	20	25	−4
Romania	10	77	20	13	24	−7
Slovak Republic	22	49	35	28	56	−7
Slovenia	20	57	24	23	57	−1
Turkey	12	68	25	19	25	−6
Other countries						
Canada	21	58	18	21	41	2
Japan[b]	10	60	29	31	9	2
Russian Federation	10	67	20	24	27	3
United States	16	68	18	16	12	−1

[a]Includes Luxembourg.
[b]The percentages are for 1995.

Table 4.8 Central government expenditure, 1997

	Total expenditure (%) of GDP		% of total expenditure on		Overall deficit/surplus[a] (% of GNP)
	Current	Capital	Defence[e]	Social services[b]	
EU countries					
Austria	38.6	3.1	3.7	65.7	−4.1
Belgium	45.9	2.4	7.0	60.2[d]	−3.2
Denmark	40.0	1.5	4.0	54.5	−1.9
Finland	38.5	1.6	3.9	53.6	−6.3
France	44.6	2.0	5.6[c]	72.5[e]	−3.5
Germany	32.1	1.3	na	68.8[d]	−1.4
Greece	28.5	4.3	8.9	36.8	−8.5
Ireland	34.4	3.7	3.0	60.3	−1.4
Italy	45.4	2.5	na	48.8[d]	−3.1
Luxembourg	na	na	na	na	na
Netherlands	46.0	1.7	3.9	63.9	−1.7
Portugal	36.2	5.3	na	46.0[d]	−2.3
Spain	34.9	1.9	6.8	49.2	−6.0
Sweden	43.2	1.1	5.6	58.1	−1.3
United Kingdom	39.6	2.1	10.4[c]	51.7	−5.3
EFTA countries					
Iceland	na	na	na	na	na
Norway	35.1	1.7	6.5[c]	50.2	5.1
Switzerland	25.3	1.0	15.2	70.6	−1.2
EU potential members					
Bulgaria	30.9	2.6	6.3	42.0	2.1
Cyprus	na	na	na	na	na
Czech Republic	32.6	3.3	5.7	71.3	−1.1
Estonia	28.7	2.9	3.1	57.5	2.4
Hungary	38.5	4.1	4.3	8.7	−4.9
Latvia	30.6	1.5	2.6	58.3	0.9
Lithuania	25.0	2.4	1.9	50.2	−1.9
Malta	na	na	na	na	na
Poland	39.3	1.9	na	71.4	−1.4
Romania	29.1	2.9	6.2	49.0	−3.9
Slovak Republic	na	na	na	na	na
Slovenia	na	na	na	na	na
Turkey	24.7	2.2	15.8	19.0	−8.4
Other countries					
Canada	20.8[d]	0.2[d]	10.8	51.4[c]	−4.5[c]
Japan	14.8[d]	3.6[d]	4.1	59.2[c]	0.0
Russian Federation	25.8[e]	1.3[e]	16.4	31.1	−4.5
United States	21.0	0.7	18.1	53.5	−0.3

[a]Includes grants.
[b]Refers to education, health, social security, welfare, housing and community amenities.
[c]The figure is for 1994.
[d]The figure(s) is (are) for 1980.
[e]The figure is for 1995.

Table 4.9 Central government revenue, 1980 and 1997

	Percentage of GDP			
	Current tax revenue		Current non-tax revenue	
	1980	1997	1980	1997
EU countries				
Austria	31.2	34.4	2.6	2.8
Belgium	41.2	43.0	1.8	1.1
Denmark	30.7	33.7	4.0	5.1
Finland	25.1	28.4	2.1	5.1
France	36.7	39.2	2.9	2.6
Germany	na	26.7	na	5.0
Greece	22.6	20.6	2.7	2.4
Ireland	30.9	32.4	3.9	1.6
Italy	29.3	42.2	2.5	2.5
Luxembourg	na	na	na	na
Netherlands	44.1	42.7	5.3	3.0
Portugal	24.1	31.1	1.9	3.1
Spain	22.1	28.3	1.9	2.0
Sweden	30.1	36.9	4.9	5.1
United Kingdom	30.6	33.4	4.6	2.8
EFTA countries				
Iceland	na	na	na	na
Norway	33.7	32.5	3.5	9.2
Switzerland	17.2	21.1	1.4	1.6
EU potential members				
Bulgaria	na	25.2	na	6.8
Cyprus	na	na	na	na
Czech Republic	na	32.7	na	1.2
Estonia	na	30.1	na	3.4
Hungary	44.8	32.5	8.6	4.7
Latvia	na	29.2	na	3.3
Lithuania	na	25.4	na	1.0
Malta	na	na	na	na
Poland	na	35.2	na	3.4
Romania	10.1	24.4	35.2	2.1
Slovak Republic	na	na	na	na
Slovenia	na	na	na	na
Turkey	14.3	15.2	3.7	3.1
Other countries				
Canada	16.0	19.5[a]	2.5	2.5[a]
Japan[b]	11.0	17.6	14.8	15.4
Russian Federation	na	17.9	na	1.1
United States	18.5	19.8	1.7	1.5

[a]The figure is for 1994.
[b]The figures are for 1995.

Table 4.10 Exports and imports of goods and services, current account balance and international reserves

	Exports		Imports		Current account balance		Gross international reserves	
	1980	1997	1980	1997	1980	1997	1980	1997
EU countries								
Austria	26 650	88 266	29 921	91 446	−3 865	−4 996	17 725	25 208
Belgium[a]	70 498	185 415	74 259	173 865	−4 931	13 939	27 974	21 013
Denmark	21 989	63 680	21 727	57 971	−1 875	833	4 347	15 881
Finland	16 802	48 228	17 307	37 976	−1 403	6 664	2 451	10 271
France	153 179	365 342	155 915	319 781	−4 208	39 474	75 592	73 773
Germany[b]	224 224	590 984	225 599	558 835	−13 319	−2 774	104 702	108 265
Greece	8 122	14 863	11 145	25 601	−2 209	−4 860	3 607	18 501
Ireland	9 610	61 447	12 044	51 711	−2 132	1 984	3 071	9 527
Italy	97 298	310 550	110 265	261 884	−10 587	33 424	62 428	53 880
Netherlands	90 380	216 530	91 622	193 107	−855	21 985	37 549	31 155
Portugal	6 674	32 339	10 136	40 684	−1 064	−1 877	13 863	21 606
Spain	32 140	148 357	38 004	142 478	−5 580	2 486	20 473	60 881
Sweden	38 151	100 989	39 878	84 779	−4 331	7 301	6 996	15 457
United Kingdom	146 072	375 033	134 200	375 128	6 864	10 304	31 755	38 830
EFTA countries								
Iceland	na	na	na	na	na	na	na	na
Norway	27 264	63 213	23 749	52 286	1 079	8 112	6 746	18 947
Switzerland	48 595	120 696	51 843	107 187	−201	23 714	64 748	65 158
EU potential members								
Bulgaria	9 302	6 277	7 994	5 730	954	427	na	3 127
Cyprus	na	na	na	na	na	na	na	na
Czech Republic	na	29 868	na	32 713	na	−3 271	na	12 625
Estonia	na	3 609	na	4 142	na	−562	na	813
Hungary	9 671	24 514	9 152	25 067	−531	−982	na	9 348
Latvia	na	2 871	na	3 348	na	−345	na	117
Lithuania	na	5 224	na	6 237	na	−981	na	1 463
Malta	na	na	na	na	na	na	na	na
Poland	16 061	39 717	17 842	46 367	−3 417	−5 744	574	27 383
Romania	12 087	9 853	13 730	12 448	−2 420	−2 338	2 511	3 793
Slovak Republic	na	10 959	na	12 367	na	−1 359	na	3 240
Slovenia	na	10 450	na	10 631	na	37	na	3 639
Turkey	3 621	52 004	8 082	56 536	−3 408	−2 679	3 298	20 568
Other countries								
Canada	74 977	247 438	70 259	236 225	−6 088	−9 261	15 462	24 023
Japan	146 980	478 542	156 970	431 094	−10 750	94 354	38 919	222 443
Russian Federation[c]	na	102 196	na	90 065	na	2 569	na	12 043
United States	271 800	937 434	290 730	1 043 473	2 150	−155 375	171 413	146 006

[a]Includes Luxembourg.
[b]Data prior to 1990 refer to West Germany before unification.
[c]Excludes trade with other members of the Commonwealth of Independent States.

Table 4.11 Money and interest rates

	Average annual nominal growth of money and quasi money (%) 1985–95	Nominal bank interest rates (average annual %)		Interest rate spread (lending minus deposit rate) Percentage points	
		Deposit rate 1995	Lending rate 1995	1990	1998
EU countries					
Austria	7.0	2.2	na	na	3.8
Belgium	13.0	4.0	8.4	6.9	na
Denmark	4.4	3.9	10.3	6.2	4.8
Finland	6.6	3.2	7.7	4.1	3.3
France	3.7	4.5	8.1	6.0	3.3
Germany	8.1	3.9	10.9	4.5	6.1
Greece	15.1[a]	15.8	23.1	8.1	7.9
Ireland	11.4	0.4	6.6	5.0	5.8
Italy	7.9[a]	6.4	12.5	7.3	4.7
Luxembourg	na	na	na	na	na
Netherlands	5.6	4.4	7.2	8.4	3.4
Portugal	15.5	8.4	13.8	7.8	3.9
Spain	11.2	7.7	10.0	5.4	2.1
Sweden	na	6.2	11.1	6.8	4.0
United Kingdom	16.3[a]	4.1	6.7	2.2	2.7
EFTA countries					
Iceland	na	na	na	na	na
Norway	5.9	5.0	7.8	4.6	0.7
Switzerland	4.6	1.3	5.5	−0.9	3.4
EU potential members					
Bulgaria	44.7[a]	na	na	8.9	10.3
Cyprus	na	na	na	na	na
Czech Republic	na	7.0	12.8	na	4.7
Estonia	na	8.7	16.0	na	8.6
Hungary	18.2[a]	26.1	32.6	4.1	3.2
Latvia	na	102.0	319.5	na	9.0
Lithuania	na	8.4	27.1	na	6.2
Malta	na	na	na	na	na
Poland	87.2	26.8	33.5	462.5	6.3
Romania	51.3	na	na	na	na
Slovak Republic	na	9.0	15.6	na	4.9
Slovenia	na	15.3	24.8	142.0	5.5
Turkey	73.9	76.1	na	na	na
Other countries					
Canada	8.9	7.1	8.6	1.3	1.6
Japan	5.9	0.7	3.4	3.4	2.1
Russian Federation	na	na	na	na	24.7
United States	3.9	5.9[b]	8.8	na	na

[a]The figure is for 1985–94.
[b]Certificate of deposit rate.

Table 4.12 Official development assistance and foreign direct investment

	Official development assistance						Foreign direct investment in US$m	
	Amount in US$m[a]			% of donor country GNP				
	1975	1985	1993	1975	1985	1993	1990	1997
EU countries								
Austria	79	248	544	0.21	0.38	0.33	653	2 354
Belgium	378	440	808	0.59	0.55	0.39	na	na
Denmark	205	440	1 340	0.58	0.80	1.03	1 132	2 792
Finland	48	211	355	0.18	0.40	0.46	812	2 128
France	2 093	3 995	7 915	0.62	0.78	0.63	13 183	23 045
Germany	1 689[a]	2 942[a]	6 954[a]	0.40[a]	0.47[a]	0.37[a]	2 532	−334
Greece	na	−11	na	na	0.10	0.10	1 005	984
Ireland	8	39	81	0.09	0.24	0.20	627	2 727
Italy	182	1 098	3 043	0.11	0.26	0.31	6 411	3 700
Netherlands	608	1 136	2 525	0.75	0.91	0.82	12 352	9 012
Portugal	na	−101	na	na	0.50	na	2 610	1 713
Spain	na	0	na	na	0.00	na	13 984	5 556
Sweden	566	840	1 769	0.82	0.86	0.98	1 982	9 867
United Kingdom	904	1 530	2 908	0.39	0.33	0.31	32 518	37 007
EFTA countries								
Iceland	na	na	na	na	na	na	na	na
Norway	184	574	1 014	0.66	1.01	1.01	1 003	3 545
Switzerland	104	302	793	0.19	0.31	0.33	4 961	5 506
EU potential members								
Bulgaria	na	na	na	na	na	na	4	498
Cyprus	na	na	na	na	na	na	na	na
Czech Republic	na	na	na	na	na	na	207	1 286
Estonia	na	na	na	na	na	na	82	266
Hungary	na	na	na	na	na	na	0	2 079
Latvia	na	na	na	na	na	na	29	521
Lithuania	na	na	na	na	na	na	0	355
Malta	na	na	na	na	na	na	na	na
Poland	na	na	na	na	na	na	89	4 908
Romania	na	na	na	na	na	na	0	1 215
Slovak Republic	na	na	na	na	na	na	0	165
Slovenia	na	na	na	na	na	na	na	321
Turkey	na	−175	na	na	0.60	0.10	684	805
Other countries								
Canada	880	1 631	2 373	0.54	0.49	0.45	7 581	7 132
Japan	1 148	3 797	11 259	0.23	0.49	0.26	1 777	3 200
Russian Federation	na	na	na	na	na	na	0	6 241
United States	4 161	9 403	9 721	0.27	0.24	0.15	47 918	93 448

[a] Data refer to West Germany before unification.

Table 4.13 Exports to EU (12) countries

Exporting country	% share of total exports of exporting country					
	1957	1974	1981	1986	1990	1995
EU countries						
Austria	na	na	na	60.1	65.2	65.5
Belgium[a]	46.1	69.9	70.0	72.9	75.1	76.5
Denmark	31.2	43.1	46.7[b]	46.8	52.1	66.7
Finland	na	na	na	38.3	46.9	57.5
France	25.1	53.2	48.2	57.8	62.7	63.0
Germany	29.2	53.2	46.9	50.8	53.6	57.1
Greece	52.5	50.1	43.3	63.5	64.0	59.1
Ireland	na	74.1	69.9	71.9	74.8	73.4
Italy	24.9	45.4	43.2	53.5	58.2	56.8
Netherlands	41.6	70.8	71.2	75.7	76.5	79.9
Portugal	22.2	48.2	53.7	68.0	73.5	80.1
Spain	29.8	47.4	43.0	60.9	64.9	67.2
Sweden	na	na	na	50.0	54.3	59.3
United Kingdom	14.6	33.4	41.3	47.9	52.6	59.8
EFTA countries						
Iceland	na	na	52.2[b]	na	na	62.7
Norway	na	na	83.5	65.1	64.9	77.9
Switzerland	na	na	60.9	54.9	58.1	62.1
EU potential members						
Bulgaria	na	na	28.5[b]	na	na	50.4
Cyprus	na	na	32.0[b]	na	na	34.8
Czech Republic	na	na	na	na	na	45.7
Estonia	na	na	na	na	na	na
Hungary	na	na	26.6[b]	na	na	62.8
Latvia	na	na	na	na	na	na
Lithuania	na	na	na	na	na	na
Malta	na	na	76.7[b]	na	na	71.1
Poland	na	na	27.4[b]	na	na	70.1
Romania	na	na	27.7[b]	na	na	53.6
Slovak Republic	na	na	na	na	na	45.7
Slovenia	na	na	na	na	na	na
Turkey	na	na	47.3[b]	44.0	53.3	51.3
Other countries						
Canada	9.3	12.6	10.7	6.8	8.1	5.9
Japan	na	10.7	12.4	14.8	18.8	15.9
Russian Federation	na	na	na	na	na	33.7
United States	15.3	21.9	22.4	24.5	25.0	21.2

[a] includes Luxembourg.
[b] The figure is for 1980.

Table 4.14 Imports from EU (12) countries

Importing country	% share of total imports of importing country					
	1957	1974	1981	1986	1990	1995
EU countries						
Austria	na	na	na	66.9	68.6	75.9
Belgium[a]	43.5	66.1	59.3	69.9	70.7	72.2
Denmark	31.2	45.5	47.9[b]	53.2	53.7	71.0
Finland	na	na	na	43.1	46.3	65.0
France	21.4	47.6	48.2	64.4	64.8	68.5
Germany	23.5	48.1	48.2	54.2	54.1	58.6
Greece	40.8	43.3	50.0	58.3	64.1	68.8
Ireland	na	68.3	74.7	73.0	70.8	63.9
Italy	21.4	42.4	40.7	55.4	57.4	60.5
Netherlands	41.1	57.4	52.4	61.0	59.9	63.2
Portugal	37.1	43.5	38.0	58.8	69.1	73.9
Spain	21.3	35.8	29.0	51.3	59.1	67.5
Sweden	na	na	na	57.2	55.3	68.6
United Kingdom	12.1	30.0	39.4	50.4	51.0	55.3
EFTA countries						
Iceland	na	na	51.7[b]	na	na	58.3
Norway	na	na	70.8[b]	50.1	45.8	71.7
Switzerland	na	na	74.5[b]	73.0	71.7	79.7
EU potential members						
Bulgaria	na	na	4.6[b]	na	na	54.0
Cyprus	na	na	55.8[b]	na	na	51.7
Czech Republic	na	na	na	na	na	64.1
Estonia	na	na	na	na	na	na
Hungary	na	na	30.7[b]	na	na	61.5
Latvia	na	na	na	na	na	na
Lithuania	na	na	na	na	na	na
Malta	na	na	77.7[b]	na	na	72.9
Poland	na	na	na	na	na	64.7
Romania	na	na	20.5[b]	na	na	50.4
Slovak Republic	na	na	na	na	na	38.9[c]
Slovenia	na	na	na	na	na	na
Turkey	na	na	33.8[b]	41.0	41.9	47.9
Other countries						
Canada	4.2	6.9	8.0	11.3	11.5	11.0
Japan	na	6.4	6.0	11.1	15.0	14.7
Russian Federation	na	na	na	na	na	38.8
United States	11.7	9.0	16.0	20.5	18.6	17.8

[a]Includes Luxembourg.
[b]The figure is for 1980.
[c]The figure is for 1994.

Table 4.15 Education, 1996

	Public expenditure on education % of GNP	Net enrolment ratio % of relevant age group			% of cohort reaching grade 5		Adult illiteracy (%)	
		Primary	Secondary	Tertiary[a]	Female	Male	Female	Male
EU countries								
Austria	5.6	100	88	43	99[b]	97[b]	c	c
Belgium[d]	3.2	98	99	na	na	na	c	c
Denmark	8.2	91	87	41	99	100	c	c
Finland	7.6	99	93	63	100	100	c	c
France	6.1	100	94	50	95[b]	100[b]	c	c
Germany	4.8	100	87	36	99[b]	97[b]	c	c
Greece	3.0	90	87	na	99[b]	98[b]	na	na
Ireland	5.8	100	86	34	99[b]	98[b]	c	c
Italy	4.7	100	na	37	100	100	c	c
Netherlands	5.2	99	91	45	na	na		
Portugal	5.5	104	78	23	na	na	na	na
Spain	4.9	105	na	41	95[b]	94[b]	na	na
Sweden	8.3	102	98	38	97	98	c	c
United Kingdom	5.4	100	92	37	na	na	c	c
EFTA countries								
Iceland	na	na	na	na	na	na	na	na
Norway	7.5	99	96	54	100	100	c	c
Switzerland	5.3	na	na	31	na	na	c	c
EU potential members								
Bulgaria	3.3	92	74	23	91[b]	93[b]	na	na
Cyprus	na	na	na	na	na	na	na	na
Czech Republic	5.4	91	87	16	na	na	na	na
Estonia	7.3	87	83	38	96	97	na	na
Hungary	4.7	97	87	17	97	97	na	na
Latvia	6.5	90	97	39	na	na	na	na
Lithuania	5.6	na	80	39	na	na	na	na
Malta	na	na	na	na	na	na	na	na
Poland	5.2	95	85	26	97	98	na	na
Romania	3.6	95	73	12	94	93	na	na
Slovak Republic	4.9	na	na	17	na	na	na	na
Slovenia	5.8	95	na	28	na	na	na	na
Turkey	2.2	96	50	16	98	98	28	8
Other countries								
Canada	7.0	95	93	103	98[b]	95[b]	c	c
Japan	3.6	103	98	30	100	100	c	c
Russian Federation	4.1	93	na	45	na	na	na	na
United States	5.4	95	90	81	na	na	c	c

[a]The figures are for 1993.
[b]The figure is for 1990.
[c]According to UNESCO, illiteracy is less than 5%.
[d]Includes Luxembourg.

Table 4.16 Distribution of income or consumption[a]

| | Survey year[a] | Gini index | % share of income or consumption | | | | | | |
			Lowest 10%	Lowest 20%	Second quantile	Third quantile	Fourth quantile	Highest 20%	Highest 10%
EU countries									
Austria	1987	23.1	4.4	10.4	14.8	18.5	22.9	33.3	19.3
Belgium[b]	1992	25.0	3.7	9.5	14.6	18.4	23.0	34.5	20.2
Denmark	1992	24.7	3.6	9.6	14.9	18.3	22.7	34.5	20.5
Finland	1991	25.6	4.2	10.0	14.2	17.6	22.3	35.8	21.6
France	1989	32.7	2.5	7.2	12.7	17.1	22.8	40.1	24.9
Germany	1989	28.1	3.7	9.0	13.5	17.5	22.9	37.1	22.6
Greece	na	na	na	na	na	na	na	na	na
Ireland	1987	35.9	2.5	6.7	11.6	16.4	22.4	42.9	27.4
Italy	1991	31.2	2.9	7.6	12.9	17.3	23.2	38.9	23.7
Netherlands	1991	31.5	2.9	8.0	13.0	16.7	22.5	39.9	24.7
Portugal	na	na	na	na	na	na	na	na	na
Spain	1990	32.5	2.8	7.5	12.6	17.0	22.6	40.3	25.2
Sweden	1992	25.0	3.7	9.6	14.5	18.1	23.2	34.5	20.1
United Kingdom	1986	32.6	2.4	7.1	12.8	17.2	23.1	39.8	24.1
EFTA countries									
Iceland	na	na	na	na	na	na	na	na	na
Norway	1991	25.2	4.1	10.0	14.3	17.9	22.4	35.4	21.2
Switzerland	1982	36.1	2.9	7.4	11.6	15.6	21.9	43.5	28.6
EU potential members									
Bulgaria	1992	30.8	3.3	8.3	13.0	17.0	22.3	39.3	24.7
Cyprus	na	na	na	na	na	na	na	na	na
Czech Republic	1993	26.6	4.6	10.5	13.9	16.9	21.3	37.4	23.5
Estonia	1995	35.4	2.2	6.2	12.0	17.0	23.1	41.8	26.2
Hungary	1993	27.9	4.1	9.7	13.9	16.0	21.4	38.1	24.0
Latvia	1995	28.5	3.3	8.3	13.8	18.0	22.9	37.0	22.4
Lithuania	1993	33.6	3.4	8.1	12.3	16.2	21.3	42.1	28.0
Malta	na	na	na	na	na	na	na	na	na
Poland	1992	27.2	4.0	9.3	13.8	17.7	22.6	36.6	22.1
Romania	1994	28.2	3.7	8.9	13.6	17.6	22.6	37.3	22.7
Slovak Republic	1992	19.5	5.1	11.9	15.8	18.8	22.2	31.4	18.2
Slovenia	1993	29.2	4.0	9.3	13.3	16.9	21.9	38.6	24.5
Turkey	na	na	na	na	na	na	na	na	na
Other countries									
Canada	1994	31.5	2.8	7.5	12.9	17.2	23.0	39.3	23.8
Japan	1979	na	na	8.7	13.2	17.5	23.1	37.5	22.4
Russian Federation	1996	48.0	1.4	4.2	8.8	13.6	20.7	52.8	24.2
United States	1994	40.1	1.5	4.8	10.5	16.0	23.5	45.2	28.5

[a]The data refer to income shares by percentiles of population and are ranked by per capita income.
[b]Includes Luxembourg.

Table 4.17 Health

	Public expenditure on health % of GDP 1990–97	% of total population with access to		Infant mortality rate (per 1000 live births)		Total fertility rate Births per woman		Maternal mortality rate (per 100 000 live births)
		Safe water 1995	Sanit-ation 1995	1980	1997	1980	1997	1990–97
EU countries								
Austria	5.7	100[a]	100[a]	14	5	1.6	1.4	10[b]
Belgium[c]	6.7	100[a]	100[a]	12	6	1.7	1.6	10[b]
Denmark	5.1	100[a]	100	8	6	1.5	1.8	9[b]
Finland	5.7	98	100	8	4	1.6	1.9	11[b]
France	7.7	100[a]	96[a]	10	5	1.9	1.7	15[b]
Germany	8.1	100[a]	100[a]	12	5	1.4	1.4	22[b]
Greece	5.3	100[a]	96[a]	18	7	2.2	1.3	10[b]
Ireland	5.1	100[a]	100[a]	11	5	3.2	1.9	10[b]
Italy	5.3	100[a]	100[a]	15	5	1.6	1.2	12[b]
Netherlands	6.2	99	100	9	5	1.6	1.5	12[b]
Portugal	4.9	82	100[a]	24	6	2.2	1.4	15[b]
Spain	5.8	99[a]	97	12	5	2.2	1.4	7[b]
Sweden	7.2	100[a]	100[a]	7	4	1.7	1.7	7[b]
United Kingdom	5.7	100	96	12	6	1.9	1.7	9[b]
EFTA countries								
Iceland	na	na	na	na	na	na	na	na
Norway	6.2	100	100	8	4	1.7	1.9	6[d]
Switzerland	7.1	100	100[a]	9	5	1.5	1.5	6[d]
EU potential members								
Bulgaria	3.5	100[a]	99[a]	20	18	2.0	1.1	20[d]
Cyprus	na	na	na	na	na	na	na	na
Czech Republic	6.4	na	na	16	6	2.1	1.2	2[d]
Estonia	5.8	na	na	17	10	2.0	1.2	52[d]
Hungary	4.5	100[a]	94[a]	23	10	1.9	1.4	14[d]
Latvia	3.5	na	na	20	15	2.0	1.1	15[d]
Lithuania	5.0	na	na	20	10	2.0	1.4	13[d]
Malta	na	na	na	na	na	na	na	na
Poland	4.8	100[a]	100[a]	26	10	2.3	1.5	5[d]
Romania	2.9	62	44	29	22	2.4	1.3	41[d]
Slovak Republic	6.1	77[a]	51	21	9	2.3	1.4	8[d]
Slovenia	7.1	98	98	15	5	2.1	1.3	5[d]
Turkey	2.7	92[a]	94[a]	109	40	4.3	2.5	180[d]
Other countries								
Canada	6.3	99	95	10	6	1.7	1.6	6[b]
Japan	5.7	96	100	8	4	1.8	1.4	18[b]
Russian Federation	4.1	na	na	22	17	1.9	1.3	53[b]
United States	6.6	73	85[a]	13	7	1.8	2.0	12[b]

[a]The figure is for 1993.
[b]Official estimation.
[c]Includes Luxembourg.
[d]UNICEF–WHO estimate based on statistical modelling.

Table 4.18 Average tariffs (%), 1958[a]

	Benelux	France	West Germany	Italy	EC(Six)	Denmark	United Kingdom	Canada	United States
Instruments (86)	13	22	8	17	16	3	27	19	29
Footwear (851)	20	21	10	21	19	19	25	24	19
Clothing (84)	20	26	13	25	21	19	26	25	32½
Furniture (821)	13	23	8	21	17	11	20	25	24
Building parts and fittings (81)	15	19	8	25	17	8	15	16	20
Transport equipment (73)	17	29	12	34	22	8	25	17	13
Electric machinery, etc. (72)	11	19	6	21	15	8	23	18	20
Machinery other than electric (71)	8	18	5	20	13	6	17	9	12
Manufactures of metals (699)	11	20	10	23	16	6	21	18	23
Ordnance (691)	9	14	7	17	11	1	22	13	26
Iron and steel (681)	5	13	7	17	10	1	14	12	13
Silver, platinum, gems, jewellery (67)	5	13	3	7	6	5	11	13	29
Non-metallic mineral manufactures (66)	12	16	6	21	13	5	17	21	13
Textiles, etc. except clothing (65)	14	19	11	20	16	9	23	21	26
Paper, paperboard, etc. (64)	14	16	8	18	15	6	13	17	10½
Wood manufactures, etc. except furniture (63)	11	19	7	22	16	4	15	12	18
Rubber manufactures (62)	17	17	10	19	18	8	21	18	18
Leather, etc. (61)	11	11	12	18	12	11	16	17	17
Chemicals (59)	7	16	8	17	12	4	15	11	24

[a] The figures are subject to the reservations stated in the source. The figures in parentheses refer to SITC classification.
Source: PEP (1962).

PART TWO

Theory and measurement

Part Two of the book is devoted to the discussion of the theoretical aspects of the EU and to the measurement of the impact of the formation of the EU on trade, production and factor mobility (the policy aspects of this are discussed in Chapter 21).

The whole part is basically concerned with three concepts: 'trade creation', 'trade diversion' and 'unilateral tariff reduction'. These can be illustrated rather simplistically as follows. In Table II.1 the cost of beef per kg is given in pence for the United Kingdom, France and New Zealand. With a 50% non-discriminatory tariff rate the cheapest source of supply of beef for the United Kingdom consumer is the home producer. When the United Kingdom and France form a customs union, the cheapest source of supply becomes France. Hence the United Kingdom saves 10p per kg of beef, making a total saving of £1 million for ten million kg (obviously an arbitrarily chosen quantity). This is *'trade creation'*: *the replacement of expensive domestic production by cheaper imports from the partner.*

In Table II.2 the situation is different for butter as a result of a lower initial non-discriminatory tariff rate (25%) by the United Kingdom. Before the customs union, New Zealand is the cheapest source of supply for the UK consumer. After the customs union, France becomes the cheapest source. There is a total loss to the United Kingdom of £1 million, since the tariff revenue is claimed by the government. This is *'trade diversion'*: *the replacement of cheaper initial imports from the outside world by expensive imports from the partner.*

Table II.1 Beef

	United Kingdom	France	New Zealand
The cost per unit (p)	90	80	70
UK domestic price with a 50% tariff rate (p)	90	120	105
UK domestic price when the UK and France form a customs union (p)	90	80	105

Total cost before the customs union = 90p × 10 million kg = £9 million
Total cost after the customs union = 80p × 10 million kg = £8 million
Total savings for the UK consumer = £1 million

Table II.2 Butter

	United Kingdom	France	New Zealand
The cost per unit (p)	90	80	70
UK domestic price with a 25% tariff rate (p)	90	100	87½
UK domestic price when the UK and France form a customs union (p)	90	80	87½

Total cost to the UK government before the customs union =
  70p × 10 million kg = £7 million
Total cost to the UK after the customs union = 80p × 10 million kg = £8 million
Total loss to the UK government = £1 million

In Tables II.3 and II.4 there are two commodities: beef and butter. The cost of beef per kg is the same as in the previous examples and so is the cost of butter per kg. Note that Table II.3 starts from the same position as Table II.1 and Table II.4 from the same position as Table II.2. Here the United Kingdom does not form a customs union with France; rather, it reduces its tariff rate by 80% on a non-discriminatory basis, i.e. it adopts a policy of unilateral tariff reduction.

Now consider Tables II.3 and II.4 in comparison with Tables II.1 and II.2. The total cost for Tables II.1 and II.2 before the customs union = £9 million + £7 million = £16 million.

The total cost for Tables II.1 and II.2 after the customs union = £8 million + £8 million = £16 million.

Table II.3 Beef

	United Kingdom	France	New Zealand
The cost per unit (p)	90	80	70
UK domestic price with a 50% tariff rate (p)	90	120	105
UK domestic price with a non-discriminatory tariff reduction of 80% (i.e. tariff rate becomes 10%) (p)	90	88	77

Total cost to the UK before the tariff reduction = 90p × 10 million kg = £9 million
Total cost to the UK after tariff reduction = 70p × 10 million kg = £7 million
Total savings for the UK = £2 million

Table II.4 Butter

	United Kingdom	France	New Zealand
The cost per unit (p)	90	80	70
UK domestic price with a 25% tariff rate (p)	90	100	87½
UK domestic price with a non-discriminatory tariff reduction of 80% (i.e. tariff rate becomes 5%) (p)	90	84	73½

Total cost to the UK before the tariff reduction = 70p × 10 million kg = £7 million
Total cost to the UK after the tariff reduction = 70p × 10 million kg = £7 million
Total savings for the UK = nil

The total cost for Tables II.3 and II.4 after the customs union = £7 million + £7 million = £14 million.

This gives a saving of £2 million in comparison with the customs union situation. Hence, a non-discriminatory tariff reduction is more economical for the United Kingdom than the formation of a customs union with France. Therefore, *unilateral tariff reduction is superior to customs union formation.*

This dangerously simple analysis (since a number of simplistic assumptions are implicit in the analysis and all the data are chosen to prove the point) has been the inspiration of a massive literature on customs union theory. Admittedly, some of the contributions are misguided in that they concentrate on a non-problem, as explained in the following chapter.

Chapter 5 tackles the basic concepts of trade creation, trade diversion and unilateral tariff reduction, considers the implications of domestic distortions and scale economies for the basic analysis and discusses the terms of trade effects. Chapter 6 contains an analysis of the vital issue of monetary integration. Chapter 7 discusses the measurement of the theoretical concepts discussed in Chapter 5. Finally, Chapter 8 concentrates on the specific issues of the EU's 'internal market'.

5 The theory of economic integration

A. M. EL-AGRAA

In reality, almost all existing cases of economic integration were either proposed or formed for political reasons even though the arguments popularly put forward in their favour were expressed in terms of possible economic gains. However, no matter what the motives for economic integration are, it is still necessary to analyse the economic implications of such geographically discriminatory groupings.

As mentioned in Chapter 1, at the customs union (CU) and free trade area (FTA) level, the *possible* sources of economic gain can be attributed to the following:

1. Enhanced efficiency in production made possible by increased specialization in accordance with the law of comparative advantage.
2. Increased production level due to better exploitation of economies of scale made possible by the increased size of the market.
3. An improved international bargaining position, made possible by the larger size, leading to better terms of trade.
4. Enforced changes in economic efficiency brought about by enhanced competition.
5. Changes affecting both the amount and quality of the factors of production arising from technological advances.

If the level of economic integration is to proceed beyond the CU level, to the economic union level, then further sources of gain become *possible* as a result of:

6. Factor mobility across the borders of member nations.
7. The co-ordination of monetary and fiscal policies.
8. The goals of near-full employment, higher rates of economic growth and better income distribution becoming unified targets.

I shall now discuss these considerations in some detail.

5.1 The customs union aspects

5.1.1 The basic concepts

Before the theory of second best was introduced, it used to be the accepted tradition that CU formation should be encouraged. The rationale for this was that since free trade maximized world welfare and since CU formation was a move towards free trade, CUs increased welfare even though they did not maximize it. This rationale certainly lies behind the guidelines of the GATT–WTO Article XXIV (see Appendix to Chapter 1) which permits the formation of CUs and FTAs as the special exceptions to the rules against international discrimination.

Viner (1950) and Byé (1950) challenged this proposition by stressing the point that CU formation is by no means equivalent to a move to free trade since it amounts to free trade *between* the members and *protection vis-à-vis* the outside world. This combination of free trade and protectionism could result in trade creation and/or trade diversion. Trade creation (TC) is the replacement of expensive domestic production by cheaper imports from a partner and trade diversion (TD) is the replacement of cheaper initial imports from the outside world by more expensive imports from a partner. Viner and Byé stressed the point that trade creation is beneficial since it does not affect the rest of the world, while trade diversion is harmful; it is the relative strength of these two effects that determines whether or not CU formation should be advocated. It is therefore important to understand the implications of these concepts.

Assuming perfect competition in both the commodity and factor markets, automatic full employment of all resources, costless adjustment procedures, perfect factor mobility nationally but perfect immobility across national boundaries, prices determined by cost, three countries H (the home country), P (the potential EU partner) and W (the outside world), plus all the traditional assumptions employed in tariff theory, we can use a simple diagram to illustrate these two concepts.

In Figure 5.1 I use partial-equilibrium diagrams because it has been demonstrated that partial- and general-equilibrium analyses are, under certain circumstances, equivalent – see El-Agraa and Jones (1981). S_W is W's perfectly elastic tariff-free supply curve for this commodity; S_H is H's supply curve while S_{H+P} is the joint H and P tariff-free supply curve. With a non-discriminatory tariff (t) imposition by H of AD ($= t_H$), the effective supply curve facing H is $BREFQT$, i.e. its own supply curve up to E and W's, subject to the tariff [$S_W(1 + t_H)$] after that. The domestic price is therefore OD, which gives domestic production of Oq_2, domestic consumption of Oq_3 and imports of q_2q_3. H pays q_2LMq_3 ($= a$) for the imports while the domestic consumer pays q_2EFq_3 ($a + b + c$) with the difference ($LEFM = b + c$) being the tariff revenue which accrues to the H government. This government revenue can be viewed as a transfer from the consumers to the government with the implication that, when the government spends it, the marginal valuation of that expenditure should be exactly equal to its valuation by the private consumers so that no distortions should occur.

If H and W form a CU, the free trade position will be restored so that Oq_5 will be consumed in H and this amount will be imported from W. Hence free trade is obviously the ideal situation. But if H and P form a CU, the tariff imposition will still apply to W while it is removed from P. The effective supply curve in this case is $BRGQT$. The union price falls to OC resulting in a fall in domestic production to Oq_1, an increase in consumption to Oq_4 and an increase in imports to q_1q_4. These imports now come from P.

The welfare implications of these changes can be examined by employing the concepts of consumers' and producers' surpluses. As a result of increased consumption, consumers' surplus rises by $CDFG$ ($= d + e + c + f$). Part of this (d) is a fall in producers' surplus due to the decline in domestic production and another part (c) is a portion of the tariff revenue now transferred back to the consumer subject to the same condition of equal marginal valuation. This leaves e and f as gains

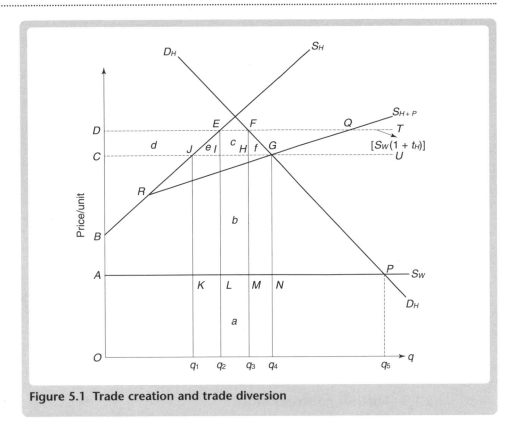

Figure 5.1 Trade creation and trade diversion

from CU formation. However, before we conclude whether or not these triangles represent net gains we need to consider the overall effects more carefully.

The fall in domestic production from Oq_2 to Oq_1 leads to increased imports of q_1q_2. These cost q_1JIq_2 to import from P while they originally cost q_1JEq_2 to produce domestically. (Note that these resources are assumed to be employed elsewhere in the economy without any adjustment costs or redundancies.) There is therefore a saving of e. The increase in consumption from Oq_3 to Oq_4 leads to new imports of q_3q_4 which cost q_3HGq_4 to import from P. These give a welfare satisfaction to the consumer equal to q_3FGq_4. There is therefore an increase in satisfaction of f. However, the *initial* imports of q_2q_3 cost the country a, but these imports now come from P costing $a+b$. Therefore these imports lead to a loss in government revenue of b (c being a retransfer). It follows that the triangle gains ($e+f$) have to be compared with the loss of tariff revenue (b) before a definite conclusion can be made regarding whether or not the net effect of CU formation has been one of gain or loss.

It should be apparent that q_2q_3 represents, in terms of our definition, trade diversion, and $q_1q_2+q_3q_4$ represents trade creation, or alternatively that areas $e+f$ are trade creation (benefits) while area b is trade diversion (loss). (The reader should note that I am using Johnson's 1974 definition so as to avoid the unnecessary literature relating to a trade-diverting welfare-improving CU promoted by Gehrels (1956–7), Lipsey (1960) and Bhagwati (1971).) It is, then, obvious that trade creation is economically desirable while trade diversion is undesirable: hence Viner and Byé's conclusion that it is the relative strength of these two effects which should determine whether or not CU formation is beneficial or harmful.

The reader should note that if the initial price is that given by the intersection of D_H and S_H (due to a higher tariff rate), the CU would result in pure trade creation since the tariff rate is prohibitive. If the price is initially OC (due to a lower tariff rate), then CU formation would result in pure trade diversion. It should also be apparent that the size of the gains and losses depends on the price elasticities of S_H, and S_{H+P} and D_H and on the divergence between S_W and S_{H+P}, i.e. cost differences.

5.1.2 The Cooper–Massell criticism

Viner and Byé's conclusion was challenged by Cooper and Massell (1965a). They suggested that the reduction in price from OD to OC should be considered in two stages: first, reduce the tariff level indiscriminately (i.e. for both W and P) to AC which gives the same union price and production, consumption and import changes; second, introduce the CU starting from the new price OC. The effect of these two steps is that the gains from the trade creation ($e+f$) still accrue while the losses from trade diversion (b) no longer apply since the new effective supply curve facing H is BJGU which ensures that imports continue to come from W at the cost of a. In addition, the new imports due to trade creation ($q_1q_2+q_3q_4$) now cost less, leading to a further gain of KJIL plus MHGN. Cooper and Massell then conclude that *a policy of unilateral tariff reduction (UTR) is superior to customs union formation.*

5.1.3 Further contributions

Following the Cooper–Massell criticism have come two independent but somewhat similar contributions to the theory of CUs. The first development is by Cooper and Massell (1965b) themselves, the essence of which is that two countries acting together can do better than each acting in isolation. The second is by Johnson (1965b) which is a private plus social costs and benefits analysis expressed in political economy terms. Both contributions utilize a 'public good' argument, with Cooper and Massell's expressed in practical terms and Johnson's in theoretical terms. However, since the Johnson approach is expressed in familiar terms this section is devoted to it – space limitations do not permit a consideration of both.

Johnson's method is based on four major assumptions:

1. Governments use tariffs to achieve certain non-economic (political, etc.) objectives.

2. Actions taken by governments are aimed at offsetting differences between private and social costs. They are, therefore, rational efforts.

3. Government policy is a rational response to the demands of the electorate.

4. Countries have a preference for industrial production.

In addition to these assumptions, Johnson makes a distinction between private and public consumption goods, real income (utility enjoyed from both private and public consumption, where consumption is the sum of planned consumption expenditure and planned investment expenditure) and real product (defined as total production of privately appropriable goods and services).

These assumptions have important implications. First, competition among political parties will make the government adopt policies that will tend to maximize consumer satisfaction from both 'private' and 'collective' consumption goods. Satisfaction is obviously maximized when the *rate of satisfaction per unit of resources is the same in both types of consumption goods*. Second, 'collective preference' for industrial production implies that consumers are willing to expand industrial production (and industrial employment) beyond what it would be under free international trade.

Tariffs are the main source of financing this policy simply because GATT–WTO regulations rule out the use of export subsidies, and domestic political considerations make tariffs, rather than the more efficient production subsidies, the usual instruments of protection.

Protection will be carried to the point where *the value of the marginal utility derived from collective consumption of domestic and industrial activity is just equal to the marginal excess private cost of protected industrial production.*

The marginal excess cost of protected industrial production consists of two parts: the marginal production cost and the marginal private consumption cost. The marginal production cost is equal to the proportion by which domestic cost exceeds world market costs. In a very simple model this is equal to the tariff rate. The marginal private consumption cost is equal to the loss of consumer surplus due to the fall in consumption brought about by the tariff rate which is necessary to induce the marginal unit of domestic production. This depends on the tariff rate and the price elasticities of supply and demand.

In equilibrium, the proportional marginal excess private cost of protected production measures the marginal 'degree of preference' for industrial production. This is illustrated in Figure 5.2 where S_W is the world supply curve at world market prices; D_H is the constant-utility demand curve (at free trade private utility level); S_H is the domestic supply curve; S_{H+u} is the marginal private cost curve of protected industrial production, including the excess private consumption cost (*FE* is the first component of marginal excess cost – determined by the excess marginal cost of domestic production in relation to the free trade situation due to the tariff imposition (*AB*) – and the area *GED* (=*IHJ*) is the second component which is the dead loss in consumer surplus due to the tariff imposition); the height of *vv* above S_W represents the marginal value of industrial production in collective consumption and *vv* represents the preference for industrial production which is assumed to yield a diminishing marginal rate of satisfaction.

The maximization of *real* income is achieved at the intersection of *vv* with S_{H+u} requiring the use of tariff rate *AB/OA* to increase industrial production from Oq_1 to Oq_2 and involving the marginal degree of preference for industrial production v. Note that the higher the value of v, the higher the tariff rate, and that the degree of protection will tend to vary inversely with the ability to compete with foreign industrial producers. It is also important to note that, in equilibrium, the government is maximizing real income, not real product: maximization of real income makes it necessary to sacrifice real product in order to gratify the preference for collective consumption of industrial production. It is also important to note that this analysis is not confined to net importing countries. It is equally applicable to net exporters, but lack of space prevents such elaboration – see El-Agraa (1984a) for a detailed explanation.

The above model helps to explain the significance of Johnson's assumptions. It does not, however, throw any light on the CU issue. To make the model useful for

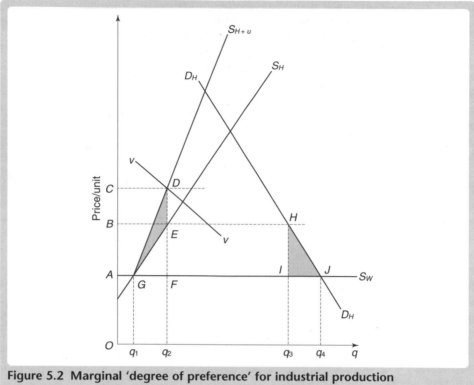

Figure 5.2 Marginal 'degree of preference' for industrial production

this purpose it is necessary to alter some of the assumptions. Let us assume that industrial production is not one aggregate but a variety of products in which countries have varying degrees of comparative advantage, that countries differ in their overall comparative advantage in industry as compared with non-industrial production, that no country has monopoly–monopsony power (conditions for optimum tariffs do not exist) and that no export subsidies are allowed (GATT–WTO).

The variety of industrial production allows countries to be both importers and exporters of industrial products. This, in combination with the 'preference for industrial production', will motivate each country to practise some degree of protection.

Given the third assumption, a country can gratify its preference for industrial production only by protecting the domestic producers of the commodities it imports (import-competing industries). Hence the condition for equilibrium remains the same: $vv=S_{H+u}$. The condition must now be reckoned differently, however: S_{H+u} is slightly different because, first, the protection of import-competing industries will reduce exports of both industrial and non-industrial products (for balance of payments purposes). Hence, in order to increase total industrial production by one unit it will be necessary to increase protected industrial production by more than one unit so as to compensate for the induced loss of industrial exports. Second, the protection of import-competing industries reduces industrial exports by raising their production costs (because of perfect factor mobility). The stronger this effect, *ceteris paribus*, the higher the marginal excess cost of industrial production. This will be greater the larger the industrial sector compared with the non-industrial sector and the larger the protected industrial sector relative to the exporting industrial sector.

If the world consists of two countries, one must be a net exporter and the other necessarily a net importer of industrial products and the balance of payments is settled in terms of the non-industrial sector. Therefore for each country the prospective gain from reciprocal tariff reduction must lie in the expansion of exports of industrial products. The reduction of a country's own tariff rate is therefore a source of loss which can be compensated for only by a reduction of the other country's tariff rate (for an alternative, orthodox, explanation see El-Agraa, 1979b).

What if there are more than two countries? If reciprocal tariff reductions are arrived at on a 'most-favoured nation' basis, then the reduction of a country's tariff rate will increase imports from *all* the other countries. If the tariff rate reduction is, however, discriminatory (starting from a position of non-discrimination), then there are two advantages: first, a country can offer its partner an increase in exports of industrial products without any loss of its own industrial production by diverting imports from third countries (trade diversion); second, when trade diversion is exhausted, any increase in partner industrial exports to this country is exactly equal to the reduction in industrial production in the same country (trade creation), hence eliminating the gain to third countries.

Therefore, discriminatory reciprocal tariff reduction costs each partner country less, in terms of the reduction in domestic industrial production (if any) incurred per unit increase in partner industrial production, than does non-discriminatory reciprocal tariff reduction. On the other hand, preferential tariff reduction imposes an additional cost on the tariff-reducing country: the excess of the costs of imports from the partner country over their cost in the world market.

The implications of this analysis are as follows:

1. Both trade creation and trade diversion yield a gain to the CU partners.
2. Trade diversion is preferable to trade creation for the preference-granting country since a sacrifice of domestic industrial production is not required.
3. Both trade creation and trade diversion may lead to increased efficiency due to economies of scale.

Johnson's contribution has not been popular because of the nature of his assumptions. For example, an:

> economic rationale for customs unions on public goods grounds can only be established if for political or some such reasons governments are denied the use of direct production subsidies – and while this may be the case in certain countries at certain periods in their economic evolution, there would appear to be no acceptable reason why this should generally be true. Johnson's analysis demonstrates that customs union and other acts of commercial policy may make economic sense under certain restricted conditions, but in no way does it establish or seek to establish a general argument for these acts. (Krauss, 1972)

5.1.4 General equilibrium analysis

The conclusions of the partial equilibrium analysis can easily be illustrated in general equilibrium terms. To simplify the analysis we shall assume that H is a 'small' country while P and W are 'large' countries, i.e. H faces constant t/t (t_p and t_w) throughout the analysis. Also, in order to avoid repetition, the analysis proceeds immediately to the Cooper–Massell proposition.

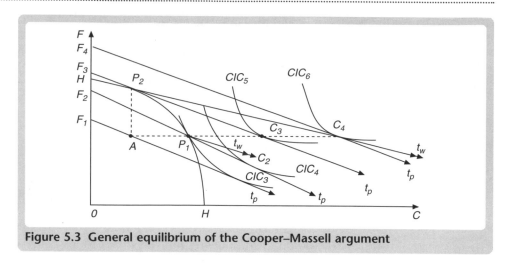

Figure 5.3 General equilibrium of the Cooper–Massell argument

In Figure 5.3, HH is the production possibility frontier for H. Initially, H is imposing a prohibitive non-discriminatory tariff which results in P_1 as both the production and consumption point, given that t_w is the most favourable t/t, i.e. W is the most efficient country in the production of clothing (C). The formation of the CU leads to free trade with the partner, P, hence production moves to P_2 where t_p is at a tangent to HH, and consumption to C_3 where CIC_5 is at a tangent to t_p. A unilateral tariff reduction (UTR) which results in P_2 as the production point results in consumption at C_4 on CIC_6 (if the tariff revenue is returned to the consumers as a lump sum) or at C_3 (if the tariff is retained by the government). Note that at C_4 trade is with W only.

Given standard analysis, it should be apparent that the situation of UTR and trade with W results in exports of AP_2 which are exchanged for imports of AC_4 of which C_3C_4 is the tariff revenue. In terms of Johnson's distinction between consumption and production gains and his method of calculating them (see El-Agraa, 1983b, Chapters 4 and 10), these effects can be expressed in relation to food (F) only. Given a Hicksian income compensation variation, it should be clear that: (i) F_1F_2 is the positive consumption effect; (ii) F_2F_3 is the production effect (positive due to curtailing production of the protected commodity); and (iii) F_3F_4 is the tariff revenue effect. Hence the difference between CU formation and a UTR (with the tariff revenue returned to the consumer) is the loss of tariff revenue F_3F_4 (C_4 compared with C_3). In other words, the consumption gain F_1F_2 is positive and applies in both cases but in the Cooper–Massell analysis the production effect comprises two parts: (i) a *pure* TC effect equal to F_2F_4; and (ii) a *pure* TD effect equal to F_3F_4. Hence F_2F_3 is the difference between these two effects and is, therefore, rightly termed the *net* TC effect.

Of course, the above analysis falls short of a general equilibrium one since the model does not endogenously determine the t/t (ibid., Chapter 5). However, as suggested above, such analysis would require the use of offer curves for all three countries both with and without tariffs. Unfortunately such an analysis is still awaited – the attempt by Vanek (1965) to derive an 'excess offer curve' for the potential union partners leads to no more than a specification of various possibilities; and the contention of Wonnacott and Wonnacott (1981) to have provided an analysis incorporating a tariff by W is unsatisfactory since they assume that W's offer curve is perfectly elastic – see Chapter 4 of El-Agraa (1999).

5.1.5 Dynamic effects

The so-called dynamic effects (Balassa, 1961) relate to the numerous means by which economic integration may influence the rate of growth of GNP of the participating nations. These ways include the following:

1. Scale economies made possible by the increased size of the market for both firms and industries operating below optimum capacity before integration occurs.

2. Economies external to the firm and industry which may have a downward influence on both specific and general cost structures.

3. The polarization effect, by which is meant the cumulative decline either in relative or absolute terms of the economic situation of a particular participating nation or of a specific region within it due either to the benefits of trade creation becoming concentrated in one region or to the fact that an area may develop a tendency to attract factors of production.

4. The influence on the location and volume of real investment.

5. The effect on economic efficiency and the smoothness with which trade transactions are carried out due to enhanced competition and changes in uncertainty.

Hence these dynamic effects include various and completely different phenomena. Apart from economies of scale, the possible gains are extremely long term and cannot be tackled in orthodox economic terms: for example, intensified competition leading to the adoption of best business practices and to an American type of attitude, etc. (Scitovsky, 1958), seems like a naïve sociopsychological abstraction that has no solid foundation with regard to either the aspirations of those countries contemplating economic integration or to its actually materializing.

Economies of scale can, however, be analysed in orthodox economic terms. In a highly simplistic model, like that depicted in Figure 5.4 where scale economies are internal to the industry, their effects can easily be demonstrated – a mathematical discussion can be found in, *inter alia*, Choi and Yu (1984), but the reader must be warned that the assumptions made about the nature of the economies concerned are extremely limited, e.g. H and P are 'similar'. $D_{H,P}$ is the identical demand curve for this commodity in both H and P and D_{H+P} is their joint demand curve; S_W is the world supply curve; AC_P and AC_H are the average cost curves for this commodity in P and H respectively. Note that the diagram is drawn in such a manner that W has constant average costs and is the most efficient supplier of this commodity. Hence free trade is the best policy resulting in price OA with consumption that is satisfied entirely by imports of Oq_4 in each of H and P giving a total of Oq_6.

If H and P impose tariffs, the only justification for this is that uncorrected distortions exist between the privately and socially valued costs in these countries – see Jones (1979) and El-Agraa and Jones (1981). The best tariff rates to impose are Corden's (1972a) made-to-measure tariffs which can be defined as those that encourage domestic production to a level that just satisfies domestic consumption without giving rise to monopoly profits. These tariffs are equal to AD and AC for H and P respectively, resulting in Oq_1 and Oq_2 production in H and P respectively.

When H and P enter into a CU, P, being the cheaper producer, will produce the entire

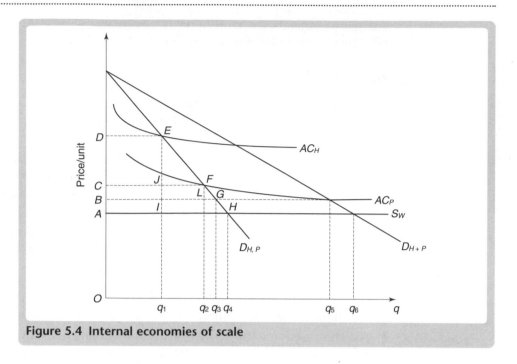

Figure 5.4 Internal economies of scale

union output – Oq_5 – at a price OB. This gives rise to consumption in each of H and P of Oq_3 with gains of $BDEG$ and $BCFG$ for H and P respectively. Parts of these gains, $BDEI$ for H and $BCFL$ for P, are 'cost-reduction' effects. There also results a production gain for P and a production loss in H due to abandoning production altogether.

Whether or not CU formation can be justified in terms of the existence of economies of scale will depend on whether or not the net effect is a gain or a loss, since in this example P gains and H loses, as the loss from abandoning production in H must outweigh the consumption gain in order for the tariff to have been imposed in the first place. If the overall result is net gain, then the distribution of these gains becomes an important consideration. Alternatively, if economies of scale accrue to an integrated industry, then the locational distribution of the production units becomes an essential issue.

5.1.6 Domestic distortions

A substantial literature has tried to tackle the important question of whether or not the formation of a CU may be economically desirable when there are domestic distortions. Such distortions could be attributed to the presence of trade unions which negotiate wage rates in excess of the equilibrium rates or to governments introducing minimum wage legislation – both of which are widespread activities in most countries. It is usually assumed that the domestic distortion results in a *social* average cost curve which lies below the private one. Hence, in Figure 5.5, which is adapted from Figure 5.4, I have incorporated AC^s_H and AC^s_P as the *social* curves in the context of economies of scale and a separate representation of countries H and P.

Note that AC^s_H is drawn to be consistently above AP_W, while AC^s_P is below it for higher levels of output. Before the formation of a CU, H may have been adopting

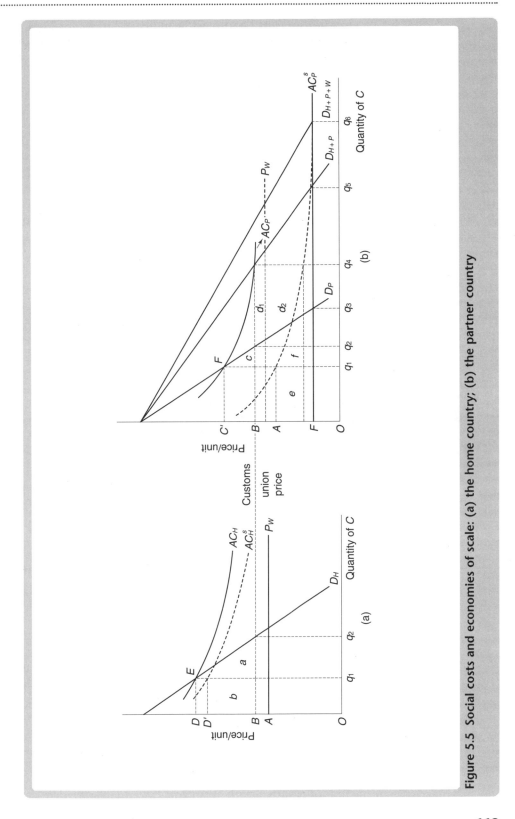

Figure 5.5 Social costs and economies of scale: (a) the home country; (b) the partner country

a made-to-measure tariff to protect its industry, but the first best policy would have been one of free trade, as argued in the previous section. The formation of the CU will therefore lead to the same effects as in the previous section, with the exception that the cost-reduction effect (Figure 5.5(a)) will be less by DD' times Oq_1. For P, the effects will be as follows:

1. As before, a consumption gain of area c.
2. A cost-reduction effect of area e due to calculations relating to social rather than private costs.
3. Gains from sales to H of areas d_1 and d_2, with d_1 being an income transfer from H to P, and d_2 the difference between domestic social costs in P and P_W – the world price.
4. The social benefits accruing from extra production made possible by the CU – area f – which is measured by the extra consumption multiplied by the difference between P_W and the domestic social costs.

However, this analysis does not lead to an economic rationale for the formation of CUs, since P could have used first best policy instruments to eliminate the divergence between private and social cost. This would have made AC^s_P the operative cost curve, and, assuming that D_{H+P+W} is the world demand curve, this would have led to a world price of OF and exports of q_3q_5 and q_5q_6 to H and W respectively, with obviously greater benefits than those offered by the CU. Hence the economic rationale for the CU will have to depend on factors that can explain why first best instruments could not have been employed in the first instance (Jones, 1980). In short, this is not an absolute argument for CU formation.

5.1.7 Terms of trade effects

So far the analysis has been conducted on the assumption that CU formation has no effect on the terms of trade (t/t). This implies that the countries concerned are too insignificant to have any appreciable influence on the international economy. Particularly in the context of the EU and groupings of a similar size, this is a very unrealistic assumption.

The analysis of the effects of CU formation on the t/t is not only extremely complicated but is also unsatisfactory since a convincing model incorporating tariffs by all three areas of the world is still awaited – see Mundell (1964), Arndt (1968, 1969) and Wonnacott and Wonnacott (1981). To demonstrate this, let us consider Arndt's analysis, which is directly concerned with this issue, and the Wonnacotts' analysis, whose main concern is the Cooper–Massell criticism but which has some bearing on this matter.

In Figure 5.6, O_H, O_P and O_W are the respective offer curves of H, P and W. In section (a) of the figure, H is assumed to be the most efficient producer of commodity Y, while in section (b), H and P are assumed to be equally efficient. Assuming that the free trade t/t are given by OT_O, H will export q_6h_1 of Y to W in exchange for Oq_6 imports of commodity X, while P will export q_1p_1 of Y in exchange for Oq_1 of commodity X, with the sum of H and P's exports being exactly equal to OX_3.

When H imposes an *ad valorem* tariff (percentage tariff), its tariff revenue-distributed curve is assumed to be displaced to $O'H$ altering the t/t to OT_1. This leads to a contraction of H's trade with W and, at the same time, increases P's trade with W.

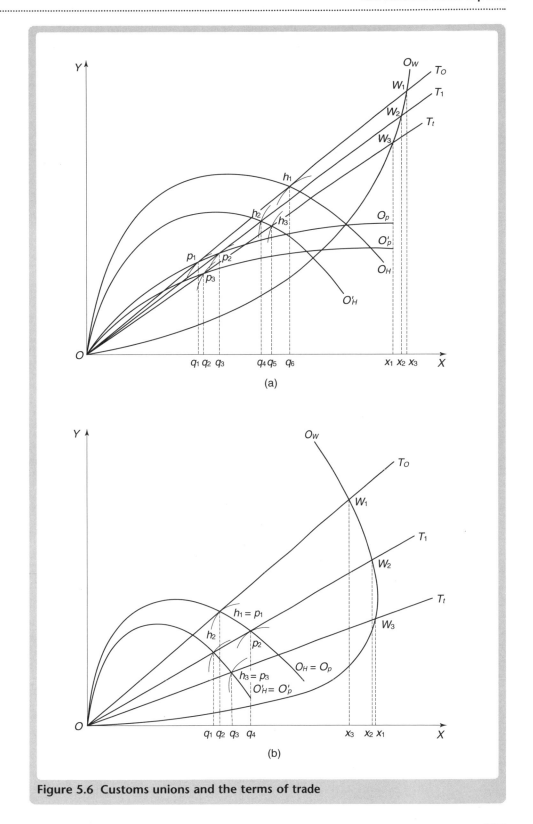

Figure 5.6 Customs unions and the terms of trade

In section (a) of the figure, it is assumed that the net effect of H and P's trade changes (contraction in H's exports and expansion in P's) will result in a contraction in world trade. It should be apparent that, from H's point of view, the competition of P in its exports market has reduced the appropriateness of the Cooper–Massell alternative of a (non-discriminatory) UTR.

Note, however, that H's welfare may still be increased in these unfavourable circumstances, provided that the move from h_1 to h_2 is accompanied by two conditions. It should be apparent that the larger the size of P relative to H and the more elastic the two countries' offer curves over the relevant ranges, the more likely it is that H will lose as a result of the tariff imposition. Moreover, given the various offer curves and H's tariff, H is more likely to sustain a loss in welfare, the lower her own marginal propensity to spend on her export commodity, X. If, in terms of consumption, commodity Y is a 'Giffen' good in country H, h_2 will be inferior to h_1.

In this illustration, country H experiences a loss of welfare in case (a) but an increase in case (b), while country P experiences a welfare improvement in both cases. Hence, it is to H's advantage to persuade P to adopt restrictive trade practices. For example, let P impose an *ad valorem* tariff and, in order to simplify the analysis, assume that in section (b) H and P are identical in all respects such that their revenue-redistributed offer curves completely coincide. In both sections of the figure, the t/t will shift to OT_t, with h_3, P_3 and w_2 being the equilibrium trading points. In both cases, P's tariff improves H's welfare but P gains only in case (b), and is better off with unrestricted trade in case (a) in the presence of tariff imposition by H.

The situation depicted in Figure 5.6 illustrates the fundamental problem that the interests, and hence the policies, of H and P may be incompatible:

> Country [H] stands to gain from restrictive trade practices in [P], but the latter is better off without restrictions – provided that [H] maintains its tariff. The dilemma in which [H] finds itself in trying to improve its terms of trade is brought about by its inadequate control of the market for its export commodity. Its optimum trade policies and their effects are functions not only of the demand elasticity in [W] but also of supply conditions in [P] and of the latter's reaction to a given policy in [H].
>
> Country [H] will attempt to influence policy making in [P]. In view of the fact that the latter may have considerable inducement to pursue independent policies, country [H] may encounter formidable difficulties in this respect. It could attempt to handle this problem in a relatively loose arrangement along the lines of international commodity agreements, or in a tightly controlled and more restrictive set-up involving an international cartel. The difficulty is that neither alternative may provide effective control over the maverick who stands to gain from independent policies. In that case a [CU] with common tariff and sufficient incentives may work where other arrangements do not. (Arndt, 1968, p. 978)

Of course, the above analysis relates to potential partners who have similar economies and who trade with W, with no trading relationships between them. Hence, it could be argued that such countries are ruled out, by definition, from forming a CU. Such an argument would be misleading since this analysis is not concerned with the static concepts of TC and TD; the concern is entirely with t/t effects, and a joint trade policy aimed at achieving an advantage in this regard is perfectly within the realm of international economic integration.

One could ask about the nature of this conclusion in a model which depicts the potential CU partners in a different light. Here, Wonnacott and Wonnacott's (1981) analysis may be useful, even though the aim of their paper was to question the general validity of the Cooper–Massell criticism, when the t/t remain unaltered as a result of CU formation. However, this is precisely why it is useful to explain the Wonnacotts' analysis at this juncture: it has some bearing on the t/t effects and it questions the Cooper–Massell criticism.

The main point of the Wonnacotts' paper was to contest the proposition that UTR is superior to the formation of a CU; hence the t/t argument was a side issue. They argued that this proposition does not hold generally if the following assumptions are rejected:

1. That the tariff imposed by a partner (*P*) can be ignored.
2. That *W* has no tariffs.
3. That there are no transport costs between members of the CU (*P* and *H*) and *W*.

Their approach was not based on t/t effects or economies of scale and, except for their rejection of these three assumptions, their argument is also set entirely in the context of the standard two-commodity, three-country framework of CU theory.

The basic framework of their analysis is set out in Figure 5.7. O_H and O_P are the free trade offer curves of the potential partners while O_H^t and O_P^t are their initial tariff-inclusive offer curves. O_W^1 and O_W^2 are *W*'s offer curves depending on whether the prospective partners wish to import commodity X (O_W^1) or to export it (O_W^2). The inclusion of both O_H^t and O_P^t meets the Wonnacott's desire to reject assumption (1) while the gap between O_W^1 and O_W^2 may be interpreted as the rejection of (2) and/or (3) – see Wonnacott and Wonnacott (1981, pp. 708–9).

In addition to these offer curves, I have inserted in Figure 5.7 various trade indif-

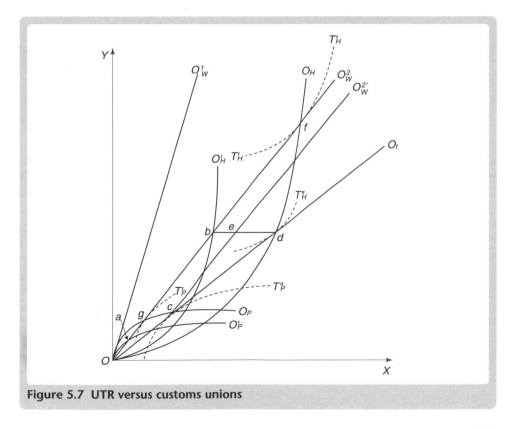

Figure 5.7 UTR versus customs unions

ference curves for countries H and P ($T_{H}\cdots$ and $T_{P}\cdots$ respectively) and the pre-CU domestic t/t in H (O_t). $O_W^{2'}$ is drawn parallel to O_W^2 from the point c where O_p intersects O_t.

The diagram is drawn to illustrate the case where a CU is formed between H and P with the CET set at the same rate as H's initial tariff on imports of X and where the domestic t/t in H remain unaltered so that trade with W continues after the formation of the CU. With its initial non-discriminatory tariff, H will trade along O_W^2 with both P (Oa) and with W (ab). The formation of the CU means that H and P's trade is determined by where O_p intersects O_t (i.e. at c) and that H will trade with W along $cO_W^{2'}$ (drawn parallel to OO_W^2). The final outcome for H will depend on the choice of assumptions about what happens to the tariff revenue generated by the remaining external trade. If there is no redistribution of tariff revenue in H, then traders in that country will remain at point d. The tariff revenue generated by the external trade of the CU with W is then shown to be equal to ed (measured in units of commodity X) which represents a reduction of be compared with the pre-CU tariff revenue in H. Further, if procedures similar to those of the European Union were adopted, the revenue ed would be used as an 'own resource' (see Chapter 16) to be spent or distributed for the benefit of both members of the CU whereas the pre-union tariff (bd) would be kept by country H.

It can be seen that country P will benefit from the formation of the CU even if it receives none of this revenue, but that H will undoubtedly lose even if it keeps all the post-union tariff revenue. This is the case of pure TD (trade diversion) and, in the absence of additional income transfers from P, H clearly cannot be expected to join the CU even if it considers that this is the only alternative to its initial tariff policy. There is no rationale, however, for so restricting the choice of policy alternatives. UTR is unambiguously superior to the initial tariff policy for both H and P and, compared with the non-discriminatory free trade policies available to both countries (which take country H to T_H' at f and country P to T_P' at g), there is no possible system of income transfers from P to H which can make the formation of a CU Pareto-superior to free trade for both countries. It remains true, of course, that country P would gain more from membership of a CU with H than it could achieve by UTR but, provided that H pursues its optimal strategy, which is UTR, country P itself can do no better than follow suit so that the optimal outcome for both countries is multilateral free trade (MFT).

Of course, there is no *a priori* reason why the CU, if created, should set its CET at the level of country H's initial tariff. Indeed, it is instructive to consider the consequences of forming a CU with a lower CET. The implications of this can be seen by considering the effect of rotating O_t anticlockwise towards O_W^t. In this context, the moving O_t line will show the post-union t/t in countries H and P. Clearly, the lowering of the CET will improve the domestic t/t for H compared with the original form of the CU and it will have a trade-creating effect as the external trade of the CU will increase more rapidly than the decline in intra-union trade. Compared with the original CU, H would gain and P would lose. Indeed, the lower the level of the CET, the more likely is H to gain from the formation of the CU *compared with the initial non-discriminatory tariff*. As long as the CET remains positive, however, H would be unambiguously worse off from membership of the CU than from UTR and, although P would gain from such a CU compared with any initial tariff policy it may adopt, it remains true that there is no conceivable set of income transfers associated with the formation of the CU which would make both H and P simultaneously better off than they would be if, after *H*'s UTR, *P* also pursued the optimal unilateral action available – the move to free trade.

It is of course true that, if the CET is set to zero, so that the rotated O_t coincides with $O_W^{2'}$ then the outcome is identical with that for the unilateral adoption of free trade for both countries. This, however, merely illustrates how misleading it would be to describe such a policy as 'the formation of a CU'; a CU with a zero CET is indistinguishable from a free-trade policy by both countries and should surely be described solely in the latter terms.

One can extend and generalize this approach beyond what has been done here – see El-Agraa (1989) and Berglas (1983). The important point, however, is what the analysis clearly demonstrates: the assumption that the t/t should remain constant for members of a CU, even if both countries are 'small', leaves a lot to be desired. But it should also be stressed that the Wonnacotts' analysis does not take into consideration the tariffs of *H* and *P* on trade with *W* nor does it deal with a genuine three-country model since *W* is assumed to be very large: *W* has constant t/t.

5.2 Customs unions versus free trade areas

The analysis so far has been conducted on the premise that differences between CUs and FTAs can be ignored. However, the ability of the member nations of FTAs to decide their own commercial policies *vis-à-vis* the outside world raises certain issues. Balassa (1961) pointed out that free trade areas may result in deflection of trade, production and investment. Deflection of trade occurs when imports from *W* (the cheapest source of supply) come via the member country with the lower tariff rate, assuming that transport and administrative costs do not outweigh the tariff differential. Deflection of production and investment occur in commodities whose production requires a substantial quantity of raw materials imported from *W* – the tariff differential regarding these materials might distort the true comparative advantage in domestic materials, therefore resulting in resource allocations according to overall comparative disadvantage.

If deflection of trade does occur, then the free trade area effectively becomes a CU with a CET equal to the lowest tariff rate which is obviously beneficial for the world – see Curzon Price (1974). However, most free trade areas seem to adopt 'rules of origin' so that only those commodities which originate in a member state are exempt from tariff imposition. If deflection of production and investment does take place, we have the case of the so-called tariff factories; but the necessary conditions for this to occur are extremely limited – see El-Agraa in El-Agraa and Jones (1981, Chapter 3) and El-Agraa (1984b, 1989a).

5.3 Economic unions

The analysis of CUs needs drastic extension when applied to economic unions. First, the introduction of free factor mobility may enhance efficiency through a more rational reallocation of resources but it may also result in depressed areas, therefore creating or aggravating regional problems and imbalances – see Mayes (1983a) and Robson (1985). Second, fiscal harmonization may also improve efficiency by eliminating non-tariff barriers (NTBs) and distortions and by equalizing their effective protective rates – see Chapter 15. Third, the co-ordination of monetary and fiscal policies which is implied by monetary integration may ease unnecessarily severe imbalances, hence resulting in the promotion of the right atmosphere for stability in the economies of the member nations.

These economic union elements must be tackled *simultaneously* with trade creation and diversion as well as economies of scale and market distortions. However, such interactions are too complicated to consider here: the interested reader should consult El-Agraa (1983a, 1983b, 1984a, 1989a). This section will be devoted to a brief discussion of factor mobility. Since monetary integration is probably the most crucial of commitments for a regional grouping and because it is one of the immediate aspirations of the EU, the following chapter is devoted to it.

With regard to *factor mobility*, it should be apparent that the removal (or harmonization) of all barriers to labour (L) and capital (K) will encourage both L and K to move. L will move to those areas where it can fetch the highest possible reward, i.e. 'net advantage'. This encouragement need not necessarily lead to an increase in actual mobility since there are sociopolitical factors which normally result in people remaining near their birthplace – social proximity is a dominant consideration, which is why the average person does not move. If the reward to K is not equalized, i.e. differences in marginal productivities (MPs) exist before the formation of an economic union, K will move until the MPs are equalized. This will result in benefits which can be clearly described in terms of Figure 5.8, which depicts the production characteristics in H and P. M_H and M_P are the schedules which relate the K stocks to their MPs in H and P respectively, given the quantity of L in each country (assuming two factors of production only).

Prior to formation of an economic union, the K stock (which is assumed to remain constant throughout the analysis) is Oq_2 in H and Oq^*_1 in P. Assuming that K is immobile internationally, all K stocks must be nationally owned and, ignoring taxation, profit per unit of K will be equal to its MP, given conditions of perfect competition. Hence the total profit in H is equal to $b+e$ and $i+k$ in P. Total output is, of course, the whole area below the M_p curve but within Oq_2 in H and Oq^*_1 in P, i.e. areas $a+b+c+d+e$ in H and $j+i+k$ in P. Therefore, L's share is $a+c+d$ in H and j in P.

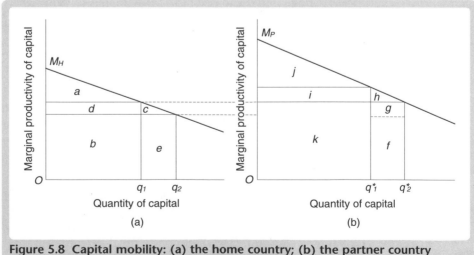

Figure 5.8 Capital mobility: (a) the home country; (b) the partner country

Since the MP in *P* exceeds that in *H*, the removal of barriers to *K* mobility or the harmonization of such barriers will induce *K* to move away from *H* and into *P*. This is because nothing has happened to affect *K* in *W*. Such movement will continue until the MP of *K* is the same in both *H* and *P*. This results in q_1q_2 $(=q^*_1q^*_2)$ of *K* moving from *H* to *P*. Hence the output of *H* falls to *a+b+d* while its *national* product including the return of the profit earned on *K* in *P* (=*g+f*) increases by (*g − c*). In *P*, *domestic* product rises by (*f+g+h*) while *national* product (excluding the remittance of profits to *H*) increases by area *h* only. Both *H* and *P* experience a change in the relative share of *L* and *K* in national product, with *K* owners being favourably disposed in *H* and unfavourably disposed in *P*.

Of course, the analysis is too simplistic since, apart from the fact that *K* and *L* are never perfectly immobile at the international level and multinational corporations have their own ways of transferring *K* (see McManus, 1972; Buckley and Casson, 1976; Dunning, 1977), the analysis does not take into account the fact that *K* may actually move to areas with low wages after the formation of an economic union. Moreover, if *K* moves predominantly in only one direction, one country may become a depressed area; hence the 'social' costs and benefits of such an occurrence need to be taken into consideration, particularly if the economic union deems it important that the economies of both *H* and *P* should be balanced. Therefore, the above gains have to be discounted or supplemented by such costs and benefits.

5.4 Macroeconomics of integration

We have seen that trade creation and trade diversion are the two concepts most widely used in international economic integration. We have also seen that their economic implications for resource reallocation are usually tackled in terms of particular commodities under conditions of global full employment. However, the economic consequences for the outside world and their repercussions on the integrated area are usually left to intuition. Moreover, their implications for employment are usually ruled out by assumption.

In an effort to rectify these serious shortcomings, I have used a macroeconomic model (see Chapters 6–8 of El-Agraa and Jones, 1981, and El-Agraa, 1989a) with the purpose of investigating these aspects; the model has been refined (see A. J. Jones, 1983). However, even the crude model indicates that the advantages of using a macro model are that it clearly demonstrates the once and for all nature of trade creation and trade diversion. It also shows the insignificance of their overall impact given realistic values of the relevant coefficients: marginal propensities to import, marginal propensities to consume, tariff rates, etc. The model also demonstrates that trade creation is beneficial for the partner gaining the new output and exports but is detrimental to the other partner and the outside world and that trade diversion is beneficial for the partner now exporting the commodity but is detrimental for the other partner and the outside world.

5.5 Economic integration in developing countries

It has been claimed that the body of economic integration theory as so far developed has no relevance for the Third World. This is because the theory suggests that there would be more scope for trade creation if the countries concerned were initially very competitive in production but potentially very complementary and that a CU would be more likely to be trade creating if the partners conducted most of their foreign trade among themselves – see Lipsey (1960) and Meade (1980). These conditions are unlikely to be satisfied in the majority of the developing nations. Moreover, most of the effects of integration are initially bound to be trade diverting, particularly since most of the Third World seeks to industrialize.

On the other hand, it was also realized that an important obstacle to the development of industry in these countries is the inadequate size of their individual markets – see Brown (1961), Hazlewood (1967, 1975) and Robson (1980, 1983, 1985). It is therefore necessary to increase the market size so as to encourage optimum plant installations: hence the need for economic integration. This would, however, result in industries clustering together in the relatively more advanced of these nations – those that have already commenced the process of industrialization.

I have demonstrated elsewhere (El-Agraa, 1979a) that there is essentially *no theoretical difference* between economic integration in the advanced world and the Third World but that there is a major difference in terms of the *type* of economic integration that suits the particular *circumstances* of developing countries and that is politically feasible: the need for an equitable distribution of the gains from industrialization and the location of industries is an important issue (see above). This suggests that any type of economic integration that is being contemplated must incorporate as an essential element a common fiscal authority and some coordination of economic policies. But then one could equally well argue that *some degree* of these elements is necessary in *any* type of integration – see the Raisman Committee recommendations for the EAC (1961).

5.6 Economic integration among communist countries

The only example of economic integration among communist countries was the CMEA. However, there the economic system perpetuated a fundamental lack of interest of domestic producers in becoming integrated with both consumers and producers in other member countries. As Marer and Montias (1988) emphasize, the integration policies of member nations must focus on the mechanism of state-to-state relations rather than on domestic economic policies which would make CMEA integration more attractive to producers and consumers alike. That is, integration must be planned by the state at the highest possible level and imposed on ministries, trusts and enterprises. It should also be stated that the CMEA operated different pricing mechanisms for intra- and extra-area trade. Moreover, the attitude of the former USSR was extremely important since the policies of the East European members of the CMEA were somewhat constrained by the policies adopted by the organization's most powerful member, for economic as well as political reasons. CMEA integration, therefore, had to be approached within an entirely different framework but this is not the appropriate place for discussing it, especially since the CMEA met its demise soon after the collapse of socialism in the former USSR and Eastern Europe.

5.7 Conclusions

The conclusions reached here are consistent with my 1979 and 1989a conclusions and with those of Jones in El-Agraa and Jones (1981). They are as follows.

First, the rationale for regional economic integration rests upon the existence of constraints on the use of first best policy instruments. Economic analysis has had little to say about the nature of these constraints, and presumably the evaluation of any regional scheme of economic integration should incorporate a consideration of the validity of the view that such constraints do exist to justify the pursuit of second rather than first best solutions.

Second, even when the existence of constraints on superior policy instruments is acknowledged, it is misleading to identify the results of regional economic integration by comparing an arbitrarily chosen common policy with an arbitrarily chosen national policy. Of course, ignorance and inertia provide sufficient reasons why existing policies may be non-optimal; but it is clearly wrong to attribute gains which would have been achieved by appropriate unilateral action to a policy of regional integration. Equally, although it is appropriate to use the optimal common policy as a point of reference, it must be recognized that this may overstate the gains to be achieved if, as seems highly likely, constraints and inefficiencies in the political processes by which policies are agreed prove to be greater among a group of countries than within any individual country.

Although the first two conclusions raise doubts about the case for regional economic integration, in principle at least, a strong general case for economic integration does exist. In unions where economies of scale may be in part external to national industries, the rationale for unions rests essentially upon the recognition of the externalities and market imperfections which extend beyond the boundaries of national states. In such circumstances, unilateral national action will not be optimal while integrated action offers the scope for potential gain.

As with the solution to most problems of externalities and market imperfections, however, customs union theory frequently illustrates the proposition that a major stumbling block to obtaining the gains from joint optimal action lies in agreeing an acceptable distribution of such gains. Thus the fourth conclusion is that the achievement of the potential gains from economic integration will be limited to countries able and willing to co-operate to distribute the gains from integration so that all partners may benefit compared with the results achieved by independent action. It is easy to argue from this that regional economic integration may be more readily achieved than global solutions but, as the debate about monetary integration in the EU illustrates (see Chapter 6), the chances of obtaining potential mutual gain may well founder in the presence of disparate views about the distribution of such gains and weak arrangements for redistribution.

6 European monetary integration

A. M. EL-AGRAA

The previous chapter was devoted to a discussion of the economic consequences of tariff removal and the establishment of the common external tariff (CET), i.e. the chapter was concerned mainly with the customs union (CU) and some of the economic union aspects of the EU. However, it is now well recognized that monetary integration, more precisely economic and monetary union (EMU), is by far the most challenging feature of the EU, or any scheme of economic integration that may decide to embrace it. The aim of this chapter is to explain the reasons for the challenge as well as to trace the EU endeavours in this respect. Before doing so, however, one needs to explain what monetary integration means.

6.1 What is monetary integration?

Monetary integration has two essential components: an exchange-rate union and capital (K) market integration. An exchange-rate union is established when member countries have what is in effect one currency. The actual existence of one currency is not necessary, however, because, if member countries have *permanently* and *irrevocably* fixed exchange rates among themselves, the result is effectively the same. Of course, one could argue that the adoption of a single currency would guarantee the irreversibility of undertaking membership of a monetary union, which would have vast repercussions for the discussion in terms of actual unions; but one could equally well argue that if a member nation decided to opt out of a monetary union, it would do so irrespective of whether or not the union entailed the use of a single currency.

Convertibility refers to the *permanent* absence of all exchange controls for both current and K transactions, including interest and dividend payments (and the harmonization of relevant taxes and measures affecting the K market) within the union. It is, of course, absolutely necessary to have complete convertibility for trade transactions, otherwise an important requirement of CU formation is threatened, namely the promotion of free trade among members of the CU, which is an integral part of an economic union – see Chapter 1. That is why this aspect of monetary integration does not need any discussion; it applies even in the case of a free trade area (FTA). Convertibility for K transactions is related to free factor mobility and is therefore an important aspect of K market integration which is necessary in common markets (CMs), not in CUs or FTAs.

In practice, this definition of monetary integration should specifically include the following:

1. An explicit harmonization of monetary policies.
2. A common pool of foreign exchange reserves.
3. A single central bank.

There are important reasons for including these elements. Suppose union members decide either that one of their currencies will be a reference currency or that a new unit of account will be established. Also assume that each member country has its own foreign exchange reserves and conducts its own monetary and fiscal policies. If a member finds itself running out of reserves, it will have to engage in a monetary and fiscal contraction sufficient to restore the reserve position. This will necessitate the fairly frequent meeting of the finance ministers or central bank governors, to consider whether or not to change the parity of the reference currency. If they do decide to change it, then all the member currencies will have to move with it. Such a situation could create the sorts of difficulty which plagued the Bretton Woods System:

1. Each finance minister might fight for the rate of exchange that was most suitable for his/her country. This might make bargaining hard; agreement might become difficult to reach and the whole system might be subject to continuous strain.
2. Each meeting might be accompanied by speculation about its outcome. This might result in undesirable speculative private K movements into or out of the union.
3. The difficulties that might be created by (1) and (2) might result in the reference currency being permanently fixed relative to outside currencies, e.g. the US dollar.
4. However, the system does allow for the possibility of the reference currency floating relative to non-member currencies or floating within a band. If the reference currency does float, it might do so in response to conditions in its own market. This would be the case, however, only if the union required the monetary authorities in the partner countries to vary their exchange rates so as to maintain constant parities relative to the reference currency. They would then have to buy and sell the reserve currency so as to maintain or bring about the necessary exchange-rate alteration. Therefore, the monetary authorities of the reference currency would, in fact, be able to determine the exchange rate for the whole union.
5. Such a system does not guarantee the permanence of the parities between the union currencies that is required by the appropriate specification of monetary integration. There is the possibility that the delegates will not reach agreement, or that one of the partners might finally choose not to deflate to the extent necessary to maintain its rate at the required parity or that a partner in surplus might choose neither to build up its reserves nor to inflate as required and so might allow its rate to rise above the agreed level.

In order to avoid such difficulties, it is necessary to include in monetary integration the three elements specified. The central bank would operate in the market so that the exchange parties were permanently maintained among the union currencies and, at the same time, it would allow the rate of the reference currency to fluctuate, or to alter intermittently, relative to the outside reserve currency. For instance, if the foreign exchange reserves in the common pool were running down, the common central bank would allow the reference currency, and with it all the partner currencies, to depreciate. This would have the advantage of economizing in the use of foreign exchange reserves, since all partners would not tend to be in deficit or surplus at the same time. Also surplus countries would automatically be helping deficit countries.

However, without explicit policy co-ordination, a monetary union would not be effective. If each country conducted its own monetary policy, and hence could engage in as much domestic credit as it wished, surplus countries would be financing deficit nations without any incentives for the deficit countries to restore equilibrium. If one country ran a large deficit, the union exchange rate would depreciate, but this might put some partner countries into surplus. If wage rates were rising in the member countries at different rates, while productivity growth did not differ in such a way as to offset the effects on relative prices, those partners with the lower inflation rates would be permanently financing the other partners.

In short,

> Monetary integration, in the sense defined, requires the unification and joint management both of monetary policy and of the external exchange-rate policy of the union. This in turn entails further consequences. First, in the monetary field the rate of increase of the money supply must be decided jointly. Beyond an agreed amount of credit expansion, which is allocated to each member state's central bank, a member state would have to finance any budget deficit in the union's capital market at the ruling rate of interest. A unified monetary policy would remove one of the main reasons for disparate movements in members' price levels, and thus one of the main reasons for the existence of intra-union payment imbalances prior to monetary union. Second, the balance of payments of the entire union with the rest of the world must be regulated at union level. For this purpose the monetary authority must dispose of a common pool of exchange reserves, and the union exchange rates with other currencies must be regulated at the union level. (Robson, 1980)

Monetary integration which explicitly includes the three requirements specified will therefore enable the partners to do away with all these problems right from the start. Incidentally, this also suggests the advantages of having a single currency.

6.2 The gains and losses

The gains due to membership of a monetary union could be both economic and non-economic, e.g. political. The non-economic benefits are too obvious to warrant space; for example, it is difficult to imagine that a complete political union could become a reality without the establishment of a monetary union. The discussion will therefore be confined to the economic benefits, which can be briefly summarized as follows:

1. The common pool of foreign exchange reserves already discussed has the incidental advantage of economizing in the use of foreign exchange reserves in terms of the facts both that member nations are not likely to go into deficit *simultaneously* and that intra-union trade transactions will no longer be financed by foreign exchange. In the context of the EU this will reduce the role of the US dollar or reduce the EU's dependence on the dollar.

2. In the case of forms of economic integration like the EU, the adoption of the

common currency (the Euro) would transform that currency into a major world medium able to compete with the US dollar or Japanese yen on equal terms. The advantages of such a currency are too well established to discuss here. However, the use of an integrated area's currency as a major reserve currency doubtless imposes certain burdens on the area; but, in the particular case of the EU, it would create an oligopolistic market situation which could either lead to collusion, resulting in a stable international monetary system, or intensify the reserve currency crisis and lead to a complete collapse of the international monetary order. The latter possibility is, of course, extremely likely to result in the former outcome; it is difficult to imagine that the leading nations in the world economy would allow monetary chaos to be the order of the day; indeed, the group of seven (G7) was created in 1986 to establish a system of international co-ordination between the most advanced nations in the world for precisely such a reason.

3. Another source of gain could be a reduction in the cost of financial management. Monetary integration should enable the spreading of overhead costs of financial transactions more widely. Also, some of the activities of the institutions dealing in foreign exchanges might be discontinued, leading to a saving in the use of resources.

4. There also exist the classical advantages of having permanently fixed exchange rates (or one currency) among members of a monetary union for free trade and factor movements. Stability of exchange rates enhances trade, encourages K to move to where it is most productively rewarded and ensures that labour (L) will move to where the highest rewards prevail. It seems unnecessary to emphasize that this does not mean that *all L* and *all K* should be mobile, but simply enough of each to generate the necessary adjustment to any situation. Nor is it necessary to stress that hedging can tackle the problem of exchange-rate fluctuations only at a cost, no matter how low that cost may be.

5. The integration of the K market has a further advantage. If a member country of a monetary union is in deficit (assuming that countries can be recognized within such a union), it can borrow directly on the union market or raise its rate of interest to attract K inflow and therefore ease the situation. However, the integration of economic policies within the union ensures that this help will occur automatically under the auspices of the common central bank. Since no single area is likely to be in deficit permanently, such help can be envisaged for all the members. Hence, there is no basis for the assertion that one country can borrow indefinitely to sustain real wages and consumption levels that are out of line with that nation's productivity and the demand for its products.

6. When a monetary union establishes a central fiscal authority with its own budget, then the larger the size of this budget, the higher the degree of fiscal harmonization (the *McDougall Report*, CEC, 1977). This has some advantages: regional deviations from internal balance can be financed from the centre and the centralization of social security payments financed by contributions or taxes on a progressive basis would have some stabilizing and compensating effects, modifying the harmful effects of monetary integration.

7. There are negative advantages in the case of the EU in the sense that monetary integration is necessary for maintaining the EU as it exists; for example, realizing the 'single market' would become more difficult to achieve and the common

agricultural prices enshrined in the *Common Agricultural Policy* (CAP – see Chapter 11) would be undermined if exchange rates were to be flexible.

These benefits of monetary integration are clear and there are few economists who would question them. However, there is no consensus of opinion with regard to its costs.

The losses from membership of a monetary union are emphasized by Fleming (1971) and Corden (1972a). Assume that the world consists of three countries: the home country (H), the potential partner country (P) and the rest of the world (W). Also assume that, in order to maintain both internal and external equilibrium, one country (H) needs to devalue its currency relative to W, while P needs to revalue *vis-à-vis* W. Moreover, assume that H and P use fiscal and monetary policies for achieving internal equilibrium. If H and P were partners in an exchange-rate union, they would devalue together – which is consistent with H's policy requirements in isolation – or revalue together – which is consistent with P's requirements in isolation – but they would not be able to alter the rate of exchange in a way that was consistent with both. Under such circumstances, the alteration in the exchange rate could leave H with an external deficit, forcing it to deflate its economy and to increase–create unemployment, or it could leave it with a surplus, forcing it into accumulating foreign reserves or allowing its prices and wages to rise. If countries deprive themselves of rates of exchange (or trade impediments) as policy instruments, they impose on themselves losses that are essentially the losses emanating from *enforced departure from internal balance* (Cordon, 1972a).

In short, the rationale for retaining flexibility in the rates of exchange rests on the assumption that governments aim to achieve both internal and external balance, and, as Tinbergen (1952) has shown, to achieve these *simultaneously* at least an equal number of instruments is needed. This can be explained in the following manner. Orthodoxy has it that there are two macroeconomic policy targets and two policy instruments. Internal equilibrium is tackled via financial instruments, which have their greatest impact on the level of aggregate demand, and the exchange rate is used to achieve equilibrium. Of course, financial instruments can be activated via both monetary and fiscal policies and may have a varied impact on both internal and external equilibria. Given this understanding, the case for maintaining flexibility in exchange rates depends entirely on the presumption that the loss of one of the two policy instruments will conflict with the achievement of both internal and external equilibria.

With this background in mind, it is vital to follow the Corden–Fleming explanation of the enforced departure from internal equilibrium. Suppose a country is initially in internal equilibrium but has a deficit in its external account. If the country were free to vary its rate of exchange, the appropriate policy for it to adopt to achieve overall balance would be a combination of devaluation and expenditure reduction. When the rate of exchange is not available as a policy instrument, it is necessary to reduce expenditure by more than is required in the optimal situation, with the result of extra unemployment. The *excess* unemployment, which can be valued in terms of output or whatever, is the cost to that country of depriving itself of the exchange rate as a policy instrument. The extent of this loss is determined, *ceteris paribus*, by the marginal propensity to import and to consume exportables, or, more generally, by the marginal propensity to consume tradables relative to non-tradables.

The expenditure reduction which is required for eliminating the initial external account deficit will be smaller the higher the marginal propensity to import. Moreover, the higher the marginal propensity to import, the less the effect of that reduction in expenditure on demand for domestically produced commodities. For both reasons, therefore, the higher the marginal propensity to import, the less domestic unemployment will result from abandoning the devaluation of the rate of exchange as a policy instrument. If the logic of this explanation is correct, it follows that as long as the marginal propensity to consume domestic goods is greater than zero, there will be some cost due to fixing the rate of exchange. A similar argument applies to a country which cannot use the exchange-rate instrument when it has a surplus in its external account and internal equilibrium: the required excess expenditure will have little effect on demand for domestically produced goods and will therefore exert little inflationary pressure if the country's marginal propensity to import is high.

This analysis is based on the assumption that there exists a trade-off between rates of change in costs and levels of unemployment – the Phillips curve. Assuming that there is a Phillips (1958) curve relationship (a negative response of rates of change in money wages – $\dot{W}$ – and the level of unemployment – U), Fleming's (1971) and Corden's (1972a) analysis can be explained by using a simple diagram devised by de Grauwe (1978). Hence, in Figure 6.1, the top half depicts the position of H while the lower half depicts that of P. The top right and the lower right corners represent the two countries' Phillips curves, while the remaining quadrants show their inflation rates corresponding to the rates of change in wages – $\dot{P}$. WI_H (which stands for *wage-rate change* and corresponding *inflation*) and WI_P are, of course, determined by the share of L in total GNP, the rate of change in the productivity of L and the degree of competition in both the factor and the commod-

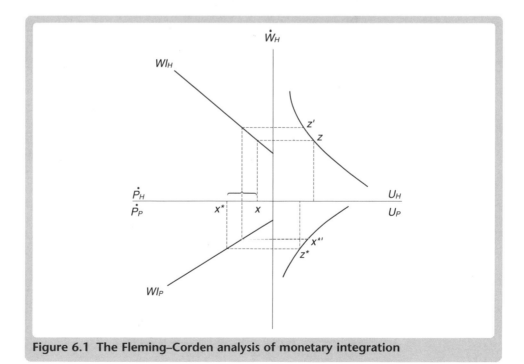

Figure 6.1 The Fleming–Corden analysis of monetary integration

ity markets, with perfect competition resulting in the *WI*s being straight lines. Note that the intersection of the *WI*s with the vertical axes will be determined by rates of change of *L*'s share in GNP and its rate of productivity change. The diagram has been drawn on the presumption that the *L* productivity changes are positive.

The diagram is drawn in such a way that countries *H* and *P* differ in all respects: the positions of their Phillips curves, their preferred trade-offs between $\dot{W}$ and $\dot{P}$, and their rates of productivity growth. *H* has a lower rate of inflation, *x*, than *P*, $x^\star$ (equilibria being at *z* and $z^\star$); hence, without monetary integration, *P*'s currency should depreciate relative to *H*'s; note that it is only a chance in a million that the two countries' inflation rates would coincide. Altering the exchange rates would then enable each country to maintain its preferred internal equilibrium: *z* and $z^\star$ for countries *H* and *P*, respectively.

When *H* and *P* enter into an exchange-rate union, i.e. have irrevocably fixed exchange rates *vis-à-vis* each other, their inflation rates cannot differ from each other, given a model without traded goods. Each country will therefore have to settle for a combination of *U* and $\dot{P}$ which is different from what it would have liked. The Fleming–Corden conclusion is thus vindicated.

However, this analysis rests entirely on the acceptance of the Phillips curve. The controversy between Keynesians and monetarists, although still far from being resolved, has at least led to the consensus that the form of the Phillips curve just presented is too crude. This is because many economists no longer believe that there is a trade-off between unemployment and inflation; if there is any relationship at all, it must be a short-term one such that the rate of unemployment is in the long term independent of the rate of inflation: there is a 'natural rate' (now referred to as NAIRU, which stands for non-accelerating inflation rate of unemployment) of unemployment which is determined by rigidities in the market for *L*. The crude version of the Phillips curve has been replaced by an expectations-

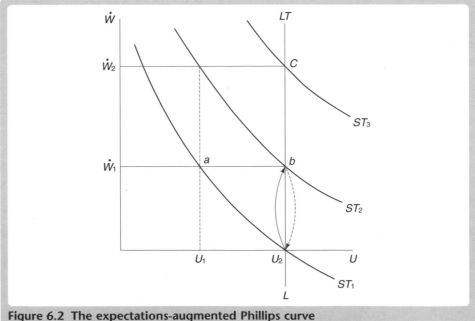

Figure 6.2 The expectations-augmented Phillips curve

adjusted one along the lines suggested by Phelps (1968) and Friedman (1975), i.e. the Phillips curves become vertical in the long run. This position can be explained with reference to Figure 6.2 which depicts three Phillips curves for one of the two countries. Assume that unemployment is initially at point U_2, i.e. the rate of inflation is equal to zero, given the short-term Phillips curve indicated by ST_1. The expectations-augmented Phillips curve suggests that, if the government tries to lower unemployment by the use of monetary policy, the short-term effect would be to move to point a, with positive inflation and lower unemployment. However, in the long term, people would adjust their expectations, causing an upward shift of the Phillips curve to ST_2 which leads to equilibrium at point b. The initial level of unemployment is thus restored but with a positive rate of inflation. A repetition of this process gives the vertical long-term curve labelled LT.

If both partners H and P have vertical LT curves, Figure 6.1 will have to be adjusted to give Figure 6.3. The implications of this are that:

1. Monetary integration will have no long-term effect on either partner's rate of unemployment since this will be fixed at the appropriate NAIRU for each country – U_H, U_P.
2. If monetary integration is adopted to bring about balanced growth as well as equal NAIRU, this can be achieved only if other policy instruments are introduced to bring about uniformity in the two L markets.

Therefore, this alternative interpretation of the Phillips curve renders the Fleming–Corden conclusion invalid.

Be that as it may, it should be noted that Allen and Kenen (1980) and P. R. Allen (1983) have demonstrated, using a sophisticated and elaborate model with financial assets, that, although monetary policy has severe drawbacks as an instrument for adjusting cyclical imbalances within a monetary union, it may be able to

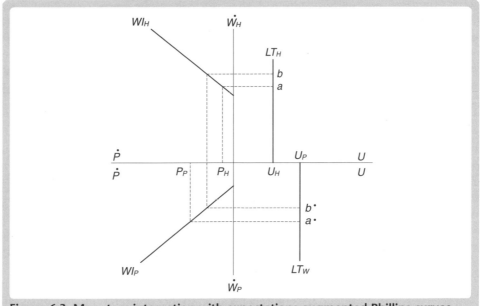

Figure 6.3 Monetary integration with expectations-augmented Phillips curves

influence the demand for the goods produced by member countries in a differential manner within the short term, provided that the markets of the member nations are not too closely integrated. Their model indicates that economic integration, in this sense, can come about as a consequence of the substitutability between nations' commodities, especially their financial assets, and of country biases in the purchase of commodities and financial assets. The moral of this is that the central bank of a monetary union can operate disparate monetary policies in the different partner countries without compromising their internal and external equilibria – a severe blow to those who stress the costs from monetary integration.

Moreover, once non-traded goods are incorporated into the model and/or K and L mobility is allowed for, it follows that the losses due to deviating from internal equilibrium vanish into oblivion, a point which Corden (1972a, 1977) readily accedes to. Finally, this model does not allow for the fact that monetary integration involves at least three countries; hence W has to be explicitly included in the model. Allen and Kenen (1980) tried to develop a model along these lines, but their model is not a straightforward extension of that depicted in Figure 6.1.

In concluding this section, it may be appropriate to highlight the limitations in the argument put forward by Fleming and Corden:

1. It is clearly stated in the definition of monetary integration that the fixity of exchange-rate parities within a monetary union (or the adoption of one currency) does not mean that the different member currencies cannot vary in unison relative to extra-union currencies. Hence the monetary union is not forgoing the availability of exchange rate variations relative to the outside world.

2. In a proper monetary union, an extra deficit for one region can come about only as a result of a revaluation of the union currency – the union as a whole has an external surplus *vis-à-vis* the outside world. Such an act would increase the foreign exchange earnings of the surplus region, and therefore of the union as a whole, provided that the conditions for a successful revaluation exist. The common central bank and the integration of monetary policies will ensure that the extra burden on the first region is alleviated: the overall extra earnings will be used to help the region with the extra deficit. Needless to say, such a situation does not lead to surplus regions financing deficit regions indefinitely because no single region is likely to be in deficit or surplus permanently and because the policy co-ordination will not allow one region to behave in such a manner unless there are reasons of a different nature which permit a situation to be sustained.

3. Even if one accepts the Fleming–Corden argument at its face value, the assumptions are extremely controversial. For instance, devaluation can work effectively only when there is 'monetary illusion'; otherwise it would be pointless since it would not work. Is it really permissible to assume that trade unionists, wherever they may be, suffer from money illusion? Many authors have disputed this assumption, but Corden's response has been to suggest that exchange-rate alterations may work if money wages are forced up because the catching-up process is never complete. Such an argument is far from convincing simply because the catching-up process has no validity as a true adjustment; it cannot be maintained indefinitely because, sooner or later, trade unionists will allow for it when negotiating money wage increases.

4. One must remember that in practice there would never be a separation between the exchange-rate union and K market integration. Once one allows for the role of convertibility for K transactions, K will always come to the rescue. Corden has reservations about this too since he argues that K integration can help in the short run, but, in the long term, while it has its own advantages, it cannot solve the problem. The rationale for this is that no region can borrow indefinitely on a private market, no matter how efficient and open the market is, to sustain levels of real wages, and hence real consumption levels, which are too high, given the productivity level in the region. Clearly, this is a switching of grounds: devaluation is nothing but a temporary adjustment device as the discussion of the monetary approach to the balance of payments has shown. Why then should devaluation be more desirable than short-term K adjustment? Moreover, for a region that is permanently in deficit, all economists would agree that devaluation is no panacea.

5. We have seen that monetary integration can be contemplated only when the countries concerned have an economic union in mind. In such conditions, the mobility of L will also help in the adjustment process. This point is conceded by Corden, but he believes that L mobility may help only marginally since it would take prolonged unemployment to induce people to emigrate, and, if monetary integration proceeded far in advance of 'psychological integration' (defined as the suppression of existing nationalisms and a sense of attachment to place in favour of an integrated community nationalism and an American-style geographic rootedness), nationalistic reactions to any nation's depopulation may become very intense. This reasoning is similar to that in the previous case since it presupposes that the problem region is a *permanently* depressed area. Since no region in the union is ever likely to experience chronic maladjustments, L mobility needs only to be marginal and national depopulation is far from the truth.

6. Finally, and more fundamentally, a very crucial element is missing from the Fleming–Corden argument. Their analysis relates to a country in internal equilibrium and external deficit. If such a country were outside a monetary union, it could devalue its currency. Assuming that the necessary conditions for effective devaluation prevailed, then devaluation would increase the national income of the country, increase its price level or result in some combination of the two. Hence a deflationary policy would be required to restore the internal balance. However, if the country were to lose its freedom to alter its exchange rate, it would have to deflate in order to depress its imports and restore external balance. According to the Fleming–Corden analysis, this alternative would entail unemployment in excess of that prevailing in the initial situation. The missing element in this argument can be found by specifying how devaluation actually works. Devaluation of a country's currency results in changes in relative price levels and is price inflationary for, at least, both exportables and importables. These relative price changes, given the necessary stability conditions, will depress imports and (perhaps) increase exports. The deflationary policy which is required (to accompany devaluation) in order to restore internal balance should therefore eliminate the *newly injected* inflation as well as the *extra* national income. By disregarding the 'inflationary' implications of devaluation, Fleming and Corden reach the unjustifiable *a priori* conclusion that membership of a

monetary union would necessitate extra sacrifice of employment in order to achieve the same target. Any serious comparison of the two situations would indicate that no such *a priori* conclusion can be reached – one must compare like with like.

In addition to the above limitations, one should point out a fundamental contradiction in the analysis of those who exaggerate the costs. If a nation decides to become a member of a monetary union, this implies that it accedes to the notion that the benefits of such a union must outweigh any possible losses and/or that it feels that a monetary union is essential for maintaining a rational economic union. It will want to do so because its economy is more interdependent with its partners than with *W*. Why then would such a country prize the availability of the exchange rate as a policy instrument for its own domestic purposes? The answer is that there is no conceivable rational reason for its doing so: it will want to have an inflation rate, monetary growth target and unemployment rate which are consistent with those of its partners. Also, the use of an economic union's rate of exchange *vis-à-vis* *W*, plus the rational operations of the common central bank and its general activities, should ensure that any worries on the part of the home country are alleviated. For such a country to feel that there is something intrinsically good about having such a policy instrument at its own disposal is tantamount to its not having any faith in or a true commitment to the economic union to which it has voluntarily decided to belong.

Expressed in terms of Tinbergen's criterion of an equal number of policy instruments and objectives, it should be remembered that the formation of a *complete* economic union is effectively just a step short of complete political union. However, given that the necessary conditions for an effective economic union require a great deal of political unification, economic union and complete political integration are hardly distinguishable in a realistic situation. In forming an economic union, the countries concerned will actually be acquiring a free policy instrument: they will have two instruments for internal policy adjustments and one for external (joint) adjustment when all they effectively need is only one of the former instruments. Therefore, an analysis which does not explicitly incorporate this dimension can hardly claim to have any relevance to the situation under consideration.

6.2.1 A 'popular' cost approach

As we have seen, the purely economic costs of EMU are very technical; too technical for even the average economist! In this section, I shall introduce a simpler version of their presentation, made popular in the context of the discussions concerning the Euro as the single currency for the EU. Note that I use the term 'purely economic' since the literature under consideration deals with only the economic conditions necessary for countries to adopt permanently fixed exchange rates; the terminology used by the profession being 'optimum currency areas' (Mundell, 1961; Fleming, 1971), some implications of which are known within the EU as the 'impossible trilogy' or 'inconsistent trinity' principle.

The principle states that only two out of the following three are mutually compatible:

(a) completely free capital mobility;

(b) an independent monetary policy; and

(c) a fixed exchange rate.

This is because with full capital mobility a nation's own interest rate is tied to the world interest rate, at least for a country too small to influence global financial markets. More precisely, any difference between the domestic and world interest rates must be matched by an expected rate of depreciation of the exchange rate. For example, if the interest rate is 6% in the domestic market, but 4% in the world market, the global market must expect the currency to depreciate by 2% this year. This is technically known as the 'interest parity condition', which implies that integrated financial markets equalize expected asset returns; hence assets denominated into a currency expected to depreciate must offer an exactly compensating higher yield.

Under such circumstances, a country that wants to conduct an independent monetary policy, raising or lowering its interest rate to control its level of employment or unemployment, must allow its exchange rate to fluctuate in the market. Conversely, a country confronted with full capital mobility, which wants to fix its exchange rate, must set its domestic interest rate to be exactly equal to the rate in the country to which it pegs its currency. Since monetary policy is then determined abroad, the country has effectively lost its monetary independence.

The loss from EMU membership can be calculated in terms of the employment sacrificed, or increased unemployment due to fixing the exchange rate between EMU members – see the previous section. The extent of this loss is evaluated relative to the three criteria, known as the Mundell–McKinnon–Kenen criteria, under which two or more countries can adopt a common currency without subjecting themselves to serious adverse economic consequences. These criteria relate to elements which render price adjustments through exchange rate changes less effect or less compelling. They are:

(a) openness to mutual trade;

(b) diverse economies; and

(c) mobility of factors of production, especially of labour.

Greater openness to mutual trade implies that most prices would be determined at the union level, which means that relative prices would be less susceptible to being influenced by changes in the exchange rate. An economy more diverse in terms of production would be less likely to suffer from country-specific shocks, reducing the need for the exchange rate as a policy tool. Greater factor mobility enables the economy to tackle *asymmetric shocks* via migration; hence reducing the need for adjustment through the exchange rate.

The EU nations score well on the first criterion since the ratio of their exports to their GDP is 20–70% while that for the USA and Japan is, respectively, 11% and 7%, the USA being the preferred reference nation on the assumption that it is an optimum currency area! They also score well in terms of the second criterion, even though they are not all as well endowed with oil and gas resources as Denmark and Britain. As to the third criterion, they score badly in comparison with the USA since EU labour mobility is rather low due to the Europeans' tendency to stick to place of birth, not only nationally but also regionally. Indeed, while in the USA and employee who moves to San Francisco after being made redundant in Nashville enters the national statistics as a happy example of internal mobility, an Italian who moves to Munich after losing a job in Milan is seen in a different light. To the Italian government, emigration would have overtones of domestic policy failure, and to the German government the inflow of Italian workers might be seen as exacerbating Germany's unemployment problem. In the EU there is also the language factor, but Europeans are increasingly becoming bilingual, with English being the dominant tongue. Moreover, in the EU, casual observation will reveal that it is the unskilled from the south who tend to be relatively less immobile in terms of moving north in search of jobs, i.e. they move because they have no other choice.

Although there is no definitive estimate of the costs due to the relative lack of labour mobility, most economics specialists suggest that it is very high, and assert that even if it is not, it must be far in excess of the benefits of the EU's version of EMU; hence they cannot comprehend why the EU nations want to have the Euro. However, as we have seen in Chapter 2, if one takes a historical perspective one can argue that the purely economic approach is misguided: it ignores the wider dimension of unity via the back door, a process in which the adoption of the Euro is a tactical manoeuvre. Although some EU nations insist that EMU is for purely economic reasons, those in the driving seat know very well that is not the case. None the less, even on purely economic grounds alone, the longer-term perspective will not lend support to the economists' pessimistic assessment. Consider, for example, Krugman's (1990) model, which utilizes such a perspective when examining the costs and benefits of EMU. In Figure 6.4, the costs are represented by *CC* and the benefits by *BB*, and both costs and benefits are expressed in relation to GDP. The benefits from the single currency are shown to rise with integration, since, for example, intra-EU trade, which is expected to increase, and has been doing so for a long time (El-Agraa, 1988a and Tables 2.9a and 2.9b therein), with integration over time, will be conducted with lesser costs, while the losses from giving up the exchange rate as a policy variable decline with time. To put it in modern economic jargon, as we have seen, changes in the exchange rate are needed to absorb asymmetric shocks but these will decline with time owing to the shocks becoming less asymmetric as integration proceeds and becomes more intensive. In short, the essence of Krugman's analysis is that as the member economies become more inte-

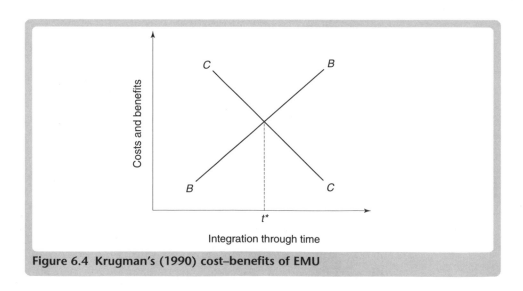

Figure 6.4 Krugman's (1990) cost–benefits of EMU

grated, the use of the exchange rate instrument for variations against member nations' currencies would become less and less desirable. Thus, for countries seriously and permanently involved in an EMU, sooner or later a time will come when the benefits will exceed the costs: the two lines are bound to intersect at some future point in time, indicating 'bliss' thereafter.

One should add that those who ignore the political dimension, and who also insist on the net outcome being a negative sum, are not only relying on pure gut feeling but also ignoring the fact that the EU has 'structural funds' aimed at assisting the poorer regions and member nations. Admittedly, these funds are presently small relative to EU GDP, but they are set to rise with further integration. Moreover, when the European Central Bank (ECB) becomes well established and the EU general budget is increased due to fiscal harmonization and further integration (see above), deviations from the desired levels of economic activity can be catered for from EU central coffers.

6.3 The road to EMU

The aim of achieving EMU, although enshrined in the Maastricht Treaty, is not a new phenomena for the EU – see Chapters 2 and 24. This section provides a historical perspective by travelling, albeit in the fast lane, on the route taken by the EU in this direction.

6.3.1 The Werner Report

In 1969, during The Hague summit (see Chapters 2 and 25), the Six decided that the EC should progressively transform itself into an EMU, and set up a committee, led by Pierre Werner, then Prime Minister of Luxembourg, to consider the issues involved. The Werner Committee presented an interim report in June 1970 and a final report in October of the same year. The latter became generally known as the 'Werner Report', and was endorsed by the Council in February 1971.

According to the Council resolution, the EC would:

1. Constitute a zone where persons, goods, services and capital would move freely – but without distorting competition, or creating structural and regional imbalances – and where economic undertakings could develop their activities on a Community scale;
2. Form a single monetary entity within the international monetary system, characterised by the total and irreversible convertibility of currencies; the elimination of fluctuation margins of exchange rates between the [members]; the irrevocable fixing of their parity relationships. These steps would be essential for the creation of a single currency, and they would involve a Community-level organisation of central banks;
3. Hold the powers and responsibilities in the economic and monetary field that would enable its institutions to ensure the administration of the economic union. To this end, the necessary economic policy decisions would be taken at Community level and the necessary powers would be attributed to community institutions.

The Community organisation of central banks would assist, in the framework of its own responsibilities, in achieving the objectives of stability and growth in the Community.

These three principles would apply to:

(a) The internal monetary and credit policies of the union;
(b) Monetary policy *vis-à-vis* the rest of the world;

(c) Policy on a unified capital market and capital movements to and from non-member countries;

(d) Budgetary and taxation policies, as related to the policy for stability and growth . . .;

(e) Structural and regional action needed to contribute to the balanced development of the Community.

As progress was made in moving closer to the final objectives, Community instruments would be created whenever they seemed necessary to replace or complement the action of national instruments. All actions would be interdependent; in particular, the development of monetary unification would be backed by parallel progress in the convergence, and then the unification of economic policies.

The Council decided that EMU could be attained during that decade, if the plan had the permanent political support of the member governments. Implementation was envisaged to be in three stages, with the first beginning in 1971 and the final completed by 1980. The Council made quite clear how it envisaged the process leading to full EMU (emphasis added):

(a) The first phase should begin on January 1, 1971, and could technically be completed within three years. This phase would be used to make the Community instruments more operational and to mark the beginnings of the Community's individuality within the international monetary system;

(b) The first phase should not be considered as an objective in itself; it should be associated with the complete process of economic and monetary integration. *It should therefore be launched with the determination to arrive at the final goal*;

(c) In the first phase consultation procedures should be strengthened; the budgetary policies of the member states should accord with Community objectives; some taxes should be harmonised; monetary and credit policies should be coordinated; and integration of financial markets should be intensified.

Thus, it should be clear that the EMU launched by the EC in 1971 was consistent with and satisfied all the above requirements for a proper EMU. What is of significance for our purposes, however, is that EMU is not a new venture for the EC since it goes back to more than two decades. Yet, the 1971 venture did fail after an earlier than expected successful negotiation of the first phase and some progress during the second, but the failure was not due to lack of commitment, determination or both: the Nixon shock, the first oil shock and the enlargement shock (the admission of three new members, each bringing with it its own unique problems) were the real culprits.

6.3.2 The EMS

In some quarters, the European Monetary System (EMS) has been considered as the next EC attempt at EMU, but in reality the EMS was no more than a mechanism devised to check the monetary upheavals of the 1970 by creating a 'zone of monetary stability'. Although Chapter 17 is devoted to a full coverage of the EMS, here a few words on the EMS are in order.

The route to EMS was a fairly short one: the Bremen Declaration on 6 and 7 July 1978 was followed by its affirmation in Bonn on 16 and 17 July and then by its adoption by the Council, in the form of a resolution 'on the establishment of the European Monetary System (EMS) and related matters', on 5 December of the same year.

The EMS was introduced with the immediate support of six of the EC nations at the time. Ireland, Italy and the United Kingdom adopted a wait-and-see attitude; 'time for reflection' was needed by Ireland and Italy and a definite reservation was expressed by the United Kingdom. Later, Ireland and Italy joined the system, while the United Kingdom expressed a 'spirit of sympathetic cooperation'. The EMS was to start operating on 1 January 1979, but France, which wanted assurances regarding the MCA system (see Chapter 11), delayed that start to 13 March 1979.

The main features of the EMS are given in the annex to the conclusions of the EC presidency (*Bulletin of the European Communities*, no. 6, 1978, pp. 20–1):

1. In terms of exchange rate management, the ... (EMS) will be at least as strict as the 'snake'. In the initial stages of its operation and for a limited period of time, member countries currently not participating in the 'snake' may opt for somewhat wider margins around central rates. In principle, intervention will be in the currencies of participating countries. Changes in central rates will be subject to mutual consent. Non-member countries with particularly strong economic and financial ties with the Community may become associate members of the system. The European Currency Unit (ECU) will be at the centre of the system; in particular, it will be used as a means of settlement between EEC monetary authorities.

2. An initial supply of ECUs (for use among Community central banks) will be created against deposit of US dollars and gold on the one hand (e.g. 20% of the stock currently held by member central banks) and member currencies on the other hand in an amount of a comparable order of magnitude.

    The use of ECUs created against member currencies will be subject to conditions varying with the amount and the maturity; due account will be given to the need for substantial short-term facilities (up to 1 year).

3. Participating countries will coordinate their exchange rates policies *vis-à-vis* third countries. To this end, they will intensify the consultations in the appropriate bodies and between central banks participating in the scheme. Ways to coordinate dollar interventions should be sought which avoid simultaneous reserve interventions. Central banks buying dollars will deposit a fraction (say 20%) and receive ECUs in return; likewise, central banks selling dollars will receive a fraction (say 20%) against ECUs.

4. Not later than two years after the start of the scheme, the existing arrangements and institutions will be consolidated in a European Monetary Fund.

5. A system of closer monetary cooperation will only be successful if participating countries pursue policies conducive to greater stability at home and abroad; this applies to deficit and surplus countries alike.

Thus, in essence, the EMS is concerned with the creation of an EC currency zone within which there is discipline for managing exchange rates. This discipline is known as the 'exchange rate mechanism' (ERM), which asks a member nation to intervene to reverse a trend when 75% of the allowed exchange rate variation of ±2.25% is reached; this is similar to that which was practised within the 'snake' arrangements that preceded the EMS. The ERM, however, did not apply to all the member nations of the EMS, since wider margins of fluctuation for those not participating in the snake were allowed for (±6%). The ECU, which is similar to the European Unit of Account in that it is a basket of *all* EC currencies, lies at the heart of the system; it is the means of settlement between the EC central banks. The EMS is supported by a European Monetary Fund (EMF) which (supposedly within two years) was to absorb the short-term financing arrangement operating within the snake, the short-term monetary support agreement which was managed by the European Monetary Cooperation Fund (EMCF) and the medium-term loan facilities for balance of payments assistance (*Bulletin of the European Communities*, no. 12,

1978). The EMF is backed by approximately 20% of national gold and US dollar reserves and by a similar percentage in national currencies. The EMF issues ECUs which are used as new reserve assets. An exchange-stabilization fund able to issue about 50 billion US dollars was to be created (*Bulletin of the European Communities* no. 12, 1978).

It is clear from the above that the EMS asks neither for permanently and irrevocably fixed exchange rates between the member nations nor for complete capital convertibility. Moreover, it does not mention the creation of a common central bank to be put in charge of the member nations' foreign exchange reserves and to be vested with the appropriate powers. Hence, the EMS is not EMU, and although it could be seen as paving the way for one, the 1992 crisis, which resulted in the complete withdrawal of the United Kingdom from the ERM and the widening of the margin of exchange rate fluctuations to ±15%, completely erases such a vision.

6.3.3 The Delors Report and the Maastricht Treaty

The EC summit which was held in Hanover on 27 and 28 June 1988 decided that, in adopting the Single Act, the EC member states had confirmed the objective of 'progressive realisation of economic and monetary union'. The heads of state agreed to discuss the means of achieving this in their meeting in Madrid in June of the following year, and to help them in their deliberations then they entrusted to a committee of central bankers and others, chaired by Mr Jacques Delors, then President of the EC Commission, the 'task of studying and proposing concrete stages leading towards this union'. The committee reported just before the Madrid summit and its report is referred to as the Delors Report on EMU.

The committee was of the opinion that the creation of the EMU must be seen as a single process, but that this process should be in stages which progressively led to the ultimate goal; thus the decision to enter upon the first stage should commit a member state to the entire process. Emphasizing that the creation of the EMU would necessitate a common monetary policy and require a high degree of compatibility of economic policies and consistency in a number of other policy areas, particularly in the fiscal field, the Report pointed out that the realization of the EMU would require new arrangements which could be established only on the basis of a change in the relevant Treaty of Rome and consequent changes in national legislation.

The first stage should be concerned with the initiation of the process of creating the EMU. During this stage there would be a greater convergence of economic performance through the strengthening of economic and monetary policy co-ordination within the existing institutional framework. The economic measures would be concerned with the completion of the internal market and the reduction of existing disparities through programmes of budgetary consolidation in the member states involved and more effective structural and regional policies. In the monetary field the emphasis would be on the removal of all obstacles to financial integration and on the intensification of co-operation and co-ordination of monetary policies. Realignment of exchange rates was seen to be possible, but efforts would be made by every member state to make the functioning of other adjustment mechanisms more effective. The committee was of the opinion that it would be important to include all EC currencies in the exchange-rate mechanism of the EMS during this stage. The 1974 Council decision defining the mandate of central bank governors would be replaced by a new decision indicating that the committee itself should formulate opinions on the overall orientation of monetary and exchange-rate policy.

In the second stage, which would commence only when the Treaty had been amended, the basic organs and structure of the EMU would be set up. The committee stressed that this stage should be seen as a transition period leading to the final stage; thus it should constitute a 'training process leading to collective decision-making', but the ultimate responsibility for policy decisions would remain with national authorities during this stage. The procedure established during the first stage would be further strengthened and extended on the basis of the amended Treaty, and policy guidelines would be adopted on a majority basis. Given this understanding, the EC would achieve the following:

1. Establish 'a medium-term framework for key economic objectives aimed at achieving stable growth, with a follow-up procedure for monitoring performances and intervening when significant deviations occurred'.

2. 'Set precise, although not yet binding, rules relating to the size of annual budget deficits and their financing.'

3. 'Assume a more active role as a single entity in the discussions of questions arising in the economic and exchange rate field.'

In the monetary field, the most significant feature of this stage would be the establishment of the European System of Central Banks (ESCB) to absorb the previous institutional monetary arrangements. The ESCB would start the transition with a first stage in which the co-ordination of independent monetary policies would be carried out by the Committee of Central Bank Governors. It was envisaged that the formulation and implementation of a common monetary policy would take place in the final stage; during this stage exchange-rate realignments would not be allowed except in exceptional circumstances.

The Report stresses that the nature of the second stage would require a number of actions, e.g.:

1. National monetary policy would be executed in accordance with the general monetary orientations set up for the EC as a whole.

2. A certain amount of foreign exchange reserves would be pooled and used to conduct interventions in accordance with the guidelines established by the ESCB.

3. The ESCB would have to regulate the monetary and banking system to achieve a minimum harmonization of provisions (such as reserve requirements or payment arrangements) necessary for the future conduct of a common monetary policy.

The final stage would begin with the irrevocable fixing of member states' exchange rates and the attribution to the EC institutions of the full monetary and economic consequences. It is envisaged that during this stage the national currencies would eventually be replaced by a single EC currency. In the economic field, the transition to this stage is seen to be marked by three developments:

1. EC structural and regional policies may have to be further strengthened.

2. EC macroeconomic and budgetary rules and procedures would have to become binding.

3. The EC role in the process of international policy co-operation would have to become fuller and more positive.

In the monetary field, the irrevocable fixing of exchange rates would come into effect and the transition to a single monetary policy and a single currency would be made. The ESCB would assume full responsibilities, especially in four specific areas:

1. The formulation and implementation of monetary policy.

2. Exchange-market intervention in third currencies.

3. The pooling and management of all foreign exchange reserves.

4. Technical and regulatory preparations necessary for the transition to a single EC currency.

As agreed, the Report was the main item for discussion in the EC summit which opened in Madrid on 24 June 1989. In that meeting member nations agreed to call a conference which would decide the route to be taken to EMU. This agreement was facilitated by a surprisingly conciliatory Mrs Thatcher, the British Prime Minister then, on the opening day of the summit. Instead of insisting (as was expected) that the United Kingdom would join the exchange-rate mechanism of the EC 'when the time is ripe', she set out five conditions for joining:

1. A lower inflation rate in the United Kingdom, and in the EC as a whole.

2. Abolition of all exchange controls (at the time and for two years after, Italy, France and Spain had them).

3. Progress towards the single EC market.

4. Liberalization of financial services.

5. Agreement on competition policy.

Since these were minor conditions relative to the demands for creating the EMU, all member nations endorsed the Report and agreed on 1 July 1990 as the deadline for the commencement of the first stage. Indeed, the economic and finance ministers of the EC at a meeting on 10 July 1989 agreed to complete the preparatory work for the first stage by December, thus giving themselves six months to accommodate the adjustments that would be needed before the beginning of the first stage.

The three-stage timetable for EMU did start on 1 July 1990 with the launching of the first phase of intensified economic co-operation during which all the member states were to submit their currencies to the EMS's *exchange-rate mechanism* (ERM) (see above and below). The main target of this activity was the United Kingdom whose currency was not subject to the ERM discipline; the United Kingdom joined in 1991 while Mrs Thatcher was still in office, but withdrew from it in 1992, and so did Italy – see Chapter 17.

The second stage is clarified in the Maastricht Treaty. It was to start in 1994. During this stage the EU was to create the *European Monetary Institute* (EMI) to prepare the way for a European Central Bank which would start operating on 1 January 1997. Although this was upset by the 1992 turmoil in the EMS, the compromises reached in the Edinburgh summit of December 1992 (deemed necessary for creating the conditions which resulted in a successful second referendum on the Treaty in Denmark and hence in ratification by the United Kingdom – see Chapter 2) did not water down the Treaty too much. Be that as it may, the Treaty already allowed

Denmark and the United Kingdom to opt out of the final stage when the EU currency rates will be permanently and irrevocably fixed and a single currency floated. However, in a separate protocol, all the then 12 EC nations declared that the drive to a single currency in the 1990s was 'irreversible'. Denmark, which supported the decision, was an exception because its constitution demands the holding of a referendum on this issue; the United Kingdom, apart from its cultural and institutional differences from the rest of the EC, has always been the black sheep of Europe – see Chapters 1, 2, 25 and 26.

A single currency (the Euro), to be managed by an independent European Central Bank, was to be introduced as early as 1997 if seven of the then 12 EC nations passed the strict economic criteria required for its successful operation, and in 1999 at the very latest. These conditions are as follows:

1. *Price stability*. Membership required 'a price performance that is sustainable and an average rate of inflation, observed over a period of one year before the examination, that does not exceed by more than [1.5] percentage points that of, at most, the three best performing' EC member countries. Inflation 'shall be measured by means of the consumer price index on a comparable basis, taking into account differences in national definitions'.

2. *Interest rates*. Membership required that,

   observed over a period of one year before the examination, a Member State has had an average nominal long-term interest rate that does not exceed by more than two percentage points that of, at most, the three best performing Member States in terms of price stability. Interest rates shall be measured on the basis of long-term government bonds or comparable securities, taking into account differences in national definitions.

3. *Budget deficits*. Membership required that a member country 'has achieved a government budgetary position without a deficit that is excessive' (Article 109j). However, what is to be considered excessive is determined in Article 104c(6) which simply states the Council shall decide after an overall assessment 'whether an excessive deficit exists'. Given the general trend at present, one could argue that the deficit should be less than 3% of GDP.

4. *Public debt*. The Protocol does not state anything on this, but by present standards this is interpreted to mean that membership required a ratio not exceeding 60% of GDP.

5. *Currency stability*. Membership required that a member country

   has respected the normal fluctuation margin provided for by the exchange-rate mechanism of the [EMS] without severe tensions for at least two years before the examination. In particular, [it] shall not have devalued its currency's bilateral central rate against any other Member State's currency on its own initiative for the same period.

One is of course perfectly justified in asking about the theoretical rationale for these convergence criteria. The answer is simply that there is not one; for example, the inflation criterion is not even based on NAIRUs (i.e. inflation bears no relationship to that consistent with a natural rate of unemployment) and there is no way to evaluate whether or not a 60% of GDP public debt is better or worse than, say, a 65% of GDP rate. The only rationale is that 3% of GDP happened to be the average level of public investment at that time, and the member nations deemed this percentage acceptable. Given this, it has to be financed by a budget deficit of that amount and calculating this at the steady state of equilibrium and a compound rate of interest of 5% per annum results in a public borrowing of 60% of GDP (see Buiter, Corsetti and Roubini, 1993). Also, these criteria are consistent with Germany's, hence adopting them implies that the ECB will be as solid as the Bundesbank in controlling inflation, which is the sole role attributed to the ECB, i.e. it cannot offer credit or make bailouts; the exchange rate will be the responsibility of Ministers.[1] The important point is that the performance of the member countries must not diverge so much as to make it difficult for the EMU to operate, and for the Euro to be stable, and the members, in their wisdom, decided that the convergence criteria agreed upon are the ones that will ensure against such an outcome.

It is interesting to note that if one had conducted this test in 1992, only France and Luxembourg would have scored full marks, i.e. five points. The others would have scored as follows: Denmark and the United Kingdom four points each; Belgium, Germany and Ireland three points each; the Netherlands two points; Italy and Spain one point each; Greece and Portugal zero points each. Hence, the EMU could not have been introduced since seven countries would have needed to score full marks for this purpose. The position at the end of 1996 was even worse since only Luxembourg qualified – see Figure 6.5. However, in the previous edition I stressed that one should hasten to add three provisos regarding this test. The first is that it is an extremely severe one since it is based on the most demanding scenario stated in the protocol. The second is that not only has the text been written in a vague manner, but the vagueness has been enforced by Article 6 of the Protocol which states that the

> Council shall, acting unanimously on a proposal from the Commission and after consulting the European Parliament, the EMI or the ECB as the case may be, and the Committee referred to in Article 109c, adopt appropriate provisions to lay down the details of the convergence criteria referred to in Article 109j of the Treaty, which shall then replace this Protocol.

The third is that the day of reckoning is yet to arrive.

I added that these criteria are no more than general guidelines; hence they can be eased or made more difficult, depending on the order of the day in 1997 (delayed to 1998). Indeed, it was later decided that 1 January 1999 should be the earliest day for introducing the Euro.

The data on which the decision on 2 May 1998 was based indicated that, in the opinion of the EU Commission, 11 nations had passed the test – see Table 6.1. Of the remaining four, three (Denmark, the UK and Sweden) had already decided not to join in the first wave, and Greece has never tried. Note that the Commission's interpretation of the government's performance is consistent with my 'flexible' interpretation:

> Fourteen Member States had government deficits of three per cent of GDP or less in 1997: Belgium, Denmark, Germany, Spain, France, Ireland, Italy, Luxembourg, the Netherlands, Austria, Portugal, Finland, Sweden and the United Kingdom. Member States have achieved significant reductions in the level of government borrowing, in particular in 1997. This remarkable outcome is the result of national governments' determined efforts to tackle excessive deficits combined with the effects of lower interest rates and stronger growth in the European Economy. The Commission's report critically examines one-off measures which have contributed to some Member States' 1997 figures. In particular it analyses Budget measures for 1998 and other factors to assess whether the budgetary situation is sustainable. *The report concluded that the major part of the deficit reductions are structural.*

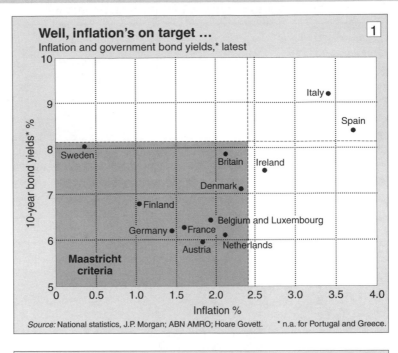

Well, inflation's on target ...
Inflation and government bond yields,* latest

Source: National statistics, J.P. Morgan; ABN AMRO; Hoare Govett.   * n.a. for Portugal and Greece.

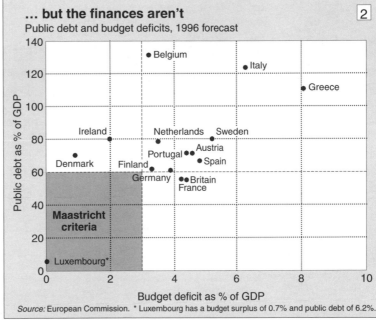

... but the finances aren't
Public debt and budget deficits, 1996 forecast

Source: European Commission.   * Luxembourg has a budget surplus of 0.7% and public debt of 6.2%.

Figure 6.5 Performing to the convergence criteria, 1996

Table 6.1 EU member states' performance to convergence criteria

	Inflation		Government budgetary position					Exchange rates	Long-term interest rates[d]
	HICP[a]	Existence of an excessive deficit[b]	Deficit (per cent of GDP)[c]	Debt (per cent of GDP)				ERM participation	
	January 1998		1997	1997	Change from previous year			March 1998	January 1998
					1997	1996	1995		
Reference value	2.7[e]		3	60					7.8[f]
Austria	1.1	yes[g]	2.5	66.1	−3.4	0.3	3.8	yes	5.6
Belgium	1.4	yes[g]	2.1	122.2	−4.7	−4.3	−2.2	yes	5.7
Denmark	1.9	no	−0.7	65.1	−5.5	−2.7	−4.9	yes	6.2
Finland	1.3	no	0.9	55.8	−1.8	−0.4	−1.5	yes[k]	5.9
France	1.2	yes[g]	3.0	58.0	2.4	2.9	4.2	yes	5.5
Germany	1.4	yes[g]	2.7	61.3	0.8	2.4	7.8	yes	5.6
Greece	5.2	yes	4.0	108.7	−2.9	1.5	0.7	yes[h]	9.8[i]
Ireland	1.2	no	−0.9	66.3	−6.4	−9.6	−6.8	yes	6.2
Italy	1.8	yes[g]	2.7	121.6	−2.4	−0.2	−0.7	yes[j]	6.7
Luxembourg	1.4	no	−1.7	6.7	0.1	0.7	0.2	yes	5.6
Netherlands	1.8	no	1.4	72.1	−5.0	−1.9	1.2	yes	5.5
Portugal	1.8	yes[g]	2.5	62.0	−3.0	−0.9	2.1	yes	6.2
Spain	1.8	yes[g]	2.6	68.8	−1.3	4.6	2.9	yes	6.3
Sweden	1.9	yes[g]	0.8	76.6	−0.1	−0.9	−1.4	no	6.5
United Kingdom	1.8	yes[g]	1.9	53.4	−1.3	0.8	3.5	no	7.0
EU (15)	1.6		2.4	72.1	−0.9	2.0	3.0		6.1

[a] Percentage change in arithmetic average of the latest 12 monthly harmonized indices of consumer prices (HICP) relative to the arithmetic average of the 12 HICP of the previous period.

[b] Council decisions of 26.09.94, 10.07.95, 27.06.96 and 30.06.97.

[c] A negative sign for the government deficit indicates a surplus.

[d] Average maturity 10 years; average of the last 12 months.

[e] Definition adopted in this report: simple arithmetic average of the inflation rates of the three best performing Member States in terms of price stability plus 1.5 percentage points.

[f] Definition adopted in this report: simple arithmetic average of the 12-month average of interest rates of the three best performing Member States in terms of price stability plus two percentage points.

[g] Commission is recommending abrogation.

[h] Since March 1998.

[i] Average of the available data during the past 12 months.

[j] Since November 1996.

[k] Since October 1996.

Source: EU Commission Services.

In 1997 government debt was below the Treaty reference value of 60 per cent of GDP in four Member States – France, Luxembourg, Finland and the United Kingdom. According to the Treaty, countries may exceed this value as long as the debt ratio is 'sufficiently diminishing and approaching the reference value at a satisfactory pace'. This was the case in almost all Member States with debt ratios above 60 per cent in 1997. Only in Germany, where the ratio is just above 60 per cent of GDP and the exceptional costs of unification continue to bear heavily, was there a small rise in 1997. In 1998, all countries above 60 per cent are expected to see reductions in their debt levels. *The Commission concludes that the conditions are in place for the continuation of a sustained decline in debt ratio in future years.* (EU Commission Services, 1998, italics added)

Thus, it should be clear that the EMU envisaged in the Delors Report and detailed and endorsed in the Maastricht Treaty is consistent with and satisfies all the requirements of a full economic and monetary union. However, I did caution in the fourth edition of this book (p. 124) that it was needless to add, 'sceptics will insist that this does not mean that the EMU will actually materialize since there is always the possibility of a loss of momentum (Delors has been both vigorous and successful), more British stalling and German vacillation, and that the process itself may take more than two decades to complete'; the continuing debate vindicates this.

6.4 The transition to EMU

It was pointed out earlier that the most pessimistic conclusion an economist can reach is that the gains from EMU must exceed any possible losses from its adoption. That being the case, why is it that the Corden–Fleming argument is still so dominant in this field, as clearly reflected by the position taken especially by the United Kingdom and Denmark?

The answer is twofold. First, it is because economists had failed to point out the fallacy in their argument. Second, it is due to Corden's distinction between a *complete* and a *pseudo* exchange rate union and to his equating the latter with the EMU envisaged in the Werner Report, and, by extension, with the EMU enshrined in the Maastricht Treaty, since the two are more or less equivalent (see above).

The *pseudo* EMU, unlike the *complete* EMU, does not allow for economic policy co-ordination, a pool of foreign exchange reserves and a common central bank. It is therefore subject to the problems discussed in the definitional section. However, as we have seen, both the EMU of the Werner Report and that of the Maastricht Treaty are *complete* EMUs.

6.5 Conclusions

In the previous edition, I stated that one need stress only two conclusions. The first is that the alleged net disadvantages of EMU apply mainly to the so-called pseudo exchange rate unions. Such unions are consistent neither with the first stage of the EMU envisaged in both the Werner Report and the Maastricht Treaty nor with their nature as processes leading to complete EMUs. All economists would concede the difficulties associated with the transitional phase, but none of them, in their strict area of competence, should interpret this to mean that the losses exceed the benefits of the Community's EMUs.

The second is that the EU, but not the entirety of its present membership, is set to achieve full EMU more or less on target. The reason for the optimism is that the convergence criteria have been specified in such a way that they can always be modified to ensure that all those EU member countries that wish to join can do so on the relevant day. Moreover, although the recent trend has been to emphasize the economic dimension, in reality the driving force behind EMU has always been political (see Chapter 25), and as long as Germany and France are committed and Italy and Spain think of EMU as panacea to their ills, nothing can happen to deter the present momentum; the decision by the EU Finance Ministers on 6 April 1997 to impose fines of up to 0.5% of GDP on any member nation that undermines the Euro with slack finance and to use the proceeds to reward 'virtuous members' signifies the members' determination.

One should add that the first conclusion remains valid and the second has been vindicated, since the 11 EU member nations mentioned on p. 144 have adopted the Euro. Moreover, Greece has practised its option of applying to adopt the Euro when it has passed the necessary criteria and it set to do so by the beginning of 2001. Furthermore, Sweden is expected to conduct a referendum on adoption at the beginning of 2002, but the Danish rejection on 27 September 2000 may have a negative effect on this, although Germany and France have reacted immediately by reviving the issue of a two-speed Europe.

Note

1. The ECB has a Board of Governors, which comprises an Executive Board (consisting of the President, Vice-President and four others, all appointed for eight years), 15 national bank governors, and, as non-voting members, the Presidents of the Commission and Council of Ministers. The ECB must issue quarterly reports, and make annual submissions to the European Parliament, and can be called to testify before its Committees. Within this context, Feldstein's assertion that those appointed to set policy at the ECB will continue to act in their national interest because they 'would be political appointees of their national governments' (Feldstein, 1997, p. 38) is a gross misrepresentation of EU political and constitutional reality: members of the EU Commission are so appointed, yet once in office, they are mandated to act in the interest of the EU as a whole, and can be taken to the Court of Justice if they act otherwise, and on the whole they have always acted as mandated – see Chapter 3. If Feldstein has made an inappropriate use of the word 'appointees', meaning the national central bank governors, then his assertion is tantamount to stating that all Council of Ministers' deliberations have been to no avail in terms of EU-wide interests, which would obviously be far off the mark.

7 Measuring the impact of economic integration

A. M. EL-AGRAA

A growing area of research in the field of economic integration is concerned with the measurement of the impact of the formation of the EU, EFTA, NAFTA and similar associations on the economies of member states and on the outside world. The purpose of this chapter is to explain the nature of the problem and to evaluate briefly the attempts at measurement that have so far been made. The reader who is interested in a comprehensive survey and assessment of the actual estimates that have been carried out is advised to read El-Agraa (1989a and 1999).

7.1 The nature of the problem

It is extremely important to comprehend the nature of the methodology of measuring the impact of economic integration in order to appreciate the difficulties associated with such measurements.

Assume that the world is constituted of three mutually exclusive and collectively exhaustive areas: the EU, EFTA and the rest of the world (*W*). The object of the exercise is to contrast the world trade matrix[1] *Y* as it appears in year *t* (indicated by a subscript), with the situation that would have materialized in year *t* if the EU and EFTA had not been formed. The latter is referred to as the '*anti-monde*' – an alternative world in which all events except one are identical – or non-integration position. The differences between this hypothetical position and the actual position can then be attributed to the following:

1. *Trade creation:* the substitution of cheaper imports from the partner country for expensive domestic production.
2. *Trade diversion:* the replacement of cheap *initial* imports from non-partners by expensive imports from a partner country.
3. *External trade creation:* the replacement of expensive domestic production by cheaper imports from a non-partner country due to a reduction in the common external tariff rate which is necessary in a customs union but not in a free trade area.
4. 'Supply-side diversion'; i.e. the replacement of exports to non-partners by exports to partners.[2]
5. Balance of payments induced adjustments due to the preceding points (1)–(4), which are made necessary for equilibrating purposes.

   Let us adopt the notation used by Williamson and Bottrill (1971) where:

   c_{ii} = intra-*i*th area trade creation

d_{ij} = diversion of the ith area's imports from area j

d_{ii} = $\sum_{j \neq 1} d_{ij}$ = diversion of ith's imports (to area i)

e_{ij} = increase in i's imports from j caused by external trade creation

e_i = $\sum_j e_{ij}$ = total external trade creation of area i

r_{ij} = increase in i's imports from j caused by balance of payments reactions

s_{ij} = reduction in j's exports to i caused by supply-side constraints

x_{ij} = (hypothetical) imports of area i from area j in the non-integration position

x_i = $\sum_j x_{ij}$ = (hypothetical) imports of area i in the non-integration position

y_i = $\sum_j y_{ij}$ = actual imports of area i

The world trade matrix Y is:

		Exports by			
		EU	EFTA	*W*	Total
Imports of	EU	y_{11}	y_{12}	y_{13}	y_1
	EFTA	y_{21}	y_{22}	y_{23}	y_2
	W	y_{31}	y_{32}	y_{33}	y_3

The world trade matrix can be disaggregated to show the various effects that followed the formation of the EU and EFTA. Both these areas could have led to internal trade creation and/or could have diverted imports from *W*. Also, the EU may have been responsible for external trade creation (in the partner countries that levelled down their external tariff rates) and external trade destruction (in the low tariff partner countries which raised their external tariff rates to the level of the common external tariff rates):

> The attractions of partners' markets may have directed some [EU] and EFTA exports away from non-partners' markets, but this effect may have been partially, wholly, or more than fully offset by the greater competitiveness of exports from those blocs resulting from the advantages of a larger 'home' market. (Williamson and Bottrill, 1971, pp. 324–5)

Moreover, every trade flow in the matrix may have been affected by reactions made necessary in order to re-equilibrate payments positions.

The Y matrix can be disaggregated to show all these changes:

$$\begin{bmatrix} y_{11} & y_{12} & y_{13} \\ y_{21} & y_{22} & y_{23} \\ y_{31} & y_{32} & y_{33} \end{bmatrix} =$$

$$\begin{bmatrix} x_{11}+c_{11}+d_{11}+r_{11} & x_{12}-d_{12}+e_{12}-s_{12}+r_{12} & x_{13}-d_{13}+e_{13}+r_{13} \\ x_{21}-d_{21}-s_{21}+r_{21} & x_{22}+c_{22}+d_{22}+r_{22} & x_{23}-d_{23}+r_{23} \\ x_{31}-s_{31}+r_{31} & x_{32}-s_{32}+r_{32} & x_{33}+r_{33} \end{bmatrix} \quad (7.1)$$

Most of the studies in this field have disregarded some of these effects, particularly the supply-side constraints and the balance of payments re-equilibrating reactions. This amounts to assuming that s_{ij} and v_{ij} are equal to zero and leads to the much simpler framework:

$$\begin{bmatrix} y_{11}\ y_{12}\ y_{13} \\ y_{21}\ y_{22}\ y_{23} \\ y_{31}\ y_{32}\ y_{33} \end{bmatrix} = \begin{bmatrix} x_{11}+c_{11}+d_{11} & x_{12}-d_{12}+e_{12} & x_{13}-d_{13}+e_{13} \\ x_{21}-d_{21} & x_{22}+c_{22}+d_{22} & x_{23}-d_{23} \\ x_{31} & x_{32} & x_{33} \end{bmatrix} \tag{7.2}$$

This implies that:

$$y_i = x_i + c_{ii} + e_i \tag{7.3}$$

Even though this methodology is very useful for analysing the *overall* effects of the formation of the EU and EFTA, it is inadequate for analysing the effects on particular countries. For example, the method cannot provide information about the consequences for the United Kingdom of membership of the EU. In order to deal with this problem, it is necessary to alter the matrix so as to allow for at least two areas for each of the EU and EFTA. This would provide the freedom to investigate the impact of the formation of EFTA and the EU on one member of the EU (United Kingdom), on that country's relationship with EFTA, with a particular member of EFTA (Norway) and with the rest of the world. Hence, the matrix should look like this:

			Exports by				
			EU		**EFTA**		**W**	**Total**
			(1) UK	**(2)** Rest of EU	**(3)** Norway	**(4)** Rest of EFTA		
	EU	**(1)**	y_{11}	y_{12}	y_{13}	y_{14}	y_{15}	y_1
		(2)	y_{21}	y_{22}	y_{23}	y_{24}	y_{25}	y_2
Imports of	**EFTA**	**(3)**	y_{31}	y_{32}	y_{33}	y_{34}	y_{35}	y_3
		(4)	y_{41}	y_{42}	y_{43}	y_{44}	y_{45}	y_4
	W	**(5)**	y_{51}	y_{52}	y_{53}	y_{54}	y_{55}	y_5

Disaggregating in terms of trade creation, trade diversion and external trade creation (assuming $s_{ij}=0$ and $r_{ij}=0$) gives:

$$\begin{bmatrix} y_{11}\ y_{12}\ y_{13}\ y_{14}\ y_{15} \\ y_{21}\ y_{22}\ y_{23}\ y_{24}\ y_{25} \\ y_{31}\ y_{32}\ y_{33}\ y_{34}\ y_{35} \\ y_{41}\ y_{42}\ y_{43}\ y_{44}\ y_{45} \\ y_{51}\ y_{52}\ y_{53}\ y_{54}\ y_{55} \end{bmatrix} =$$

$$\begin{bmatrix} \underline{\quad\quad} & x_{12}+c_{12}+d_{12} & x_{13}-d_{13}+e_{13} & x_{14}-d_{14}+e_{14} & x_{15}-d_{15}+e_{15} \\ x_{21}+c_{21}+d_{21} & \underline{\quad\quad} & x_{23}-d_{23}+e_{23} & x_{24}-d_{24}+e_{24} & x_{25}-d_{25}+e_{25} \\ x_{31}-d_{31} & x_{32}-d_{22} & \underline{\quad\quad} & x_{34}+c_{34}+d_{34} & x_{35}-d_{35} \\ x_{41}-d_{41} & x_{42}-d_{42} & x_{43}+c_{43}+d_{43} & \underline{\quad\quad} & x_{45}-d_{45} \\ x_{51} & x_{52} & x_{53} & x_{54} & x_{55} \end{bmatrix} \tag{7.4}$$

The matrix could, of course, be made more suitable for studying the impact of the formation of the EU and EFTA on particular areas of the rest of the world, e.g. the impact of UK membership of the EU on imports from New Zealand. This can easily be done by an appropriate breakdown of *W*. The most significant consideration that remains is the effect of the formation of the EU and EFTA on their economies and on the outside world.

Thus the problem of measuring the impact of economic integration relates to the empirical calculation of the indicated changes in the world trade matrix. However, it seems evident that any sensible approach to the analysis of these changes should have the following characteristics:

1. It should be capable of being carried out at the appropriate level of disaggregation.

2. It should be able to distinguish between trade creation, trade diversion and external trade creation.

3. It should be capable of discerning the effects of economic growth on trade that would have taken place in the absence of economic integration.

4. It should be 'analytic': it should be capable of providing an economic explanation of the actual post-integration situation.

5. It should be a general-equilibrium approach capable of allowing for the effects of economic integration on an interdependent world.

The above approach relates to the measurement of changes in only the trade flows, but economic integration is not confined to customs unions and free trade areas. In the case of common markets, the impact of factor mobility needs to be taken into account and in economic unions so too must the effects of common policies, considerations which are especially pertinent in the case of the EU (see Chapters 1 and 21). Since most of these issues are considered in, respectively, Chapter 21 and the following chapter, a brief statement on factor mobility only may be in order.

Factor mobility complicates the estimation of the impact of economic integration on goods and services since they can be both complements to and substitutes for them. A new foreign investment may require an inflow of skilled labour and imports for some of its inputs and may export part of its output. Alternatively, a firm may decide to invest in a new plant using local labour to supply the local market, both substituting for goods and services it previously supplied from its home market. These interactions are very difficult to separate, especially since the theoretical literature on factor movements is relatively undeveloped and factors may not respond to any changes that are meant to enhance their movement.

7.2 The effects on trade

The general trend of the empirical work on economic integration has been to examine various specific aspects of integration (mainly the effects on trading patterns) and to analyse them separately. The most important practical distinction made is between 'price' and 'income' effects. This is largely because the main initial instruments in economic integration are tariffs and quotas and other trade impediments which act mainly on relative prices in the first instance. However, all sources of possible economic gain (see Chapter 5) incorporate income as well as price effects.

The removal of quotas and other trade impediments is usually subsumed within the tariff changes for estimation purposes. These tariff changes are thought to result in a series of relative price changes: the price of imports from the partner countries falls, for commodities where the tariff is removed, relative to the price of the same commodity produced in the domestic country. In third countries which are excluded from the union, relative prices may change for more than one reason. They will change differently if the tariff with respect to third countries is shifted from its pre-integration level or they may change if producers in third countries have different pricing reactions to the change in price competition. Some third country producers may decide to absorb rather more of the potential change by reducing profits rather than by increasing prices relative to domestic producers. Relative prices are also likely to change with respect to different commodities and hence there is a complex set of interrelated income and substitution effects to be explained.

The immediate difficulty is thus the translation of tariff changes and other agreed measures in the customs union treaty into changes in prices and other variables which are known to have an impact on economic behaviour. Such evidence as there is suggests that there are wide discrepancies among the reactions of importers benefiting from tariff cuts and also among competitors adversely affected by them (EFTA Secretariat, 1968) and that reactions of trade to tariff changes are different from those to price changes (Kreinin, 1961). Two routes would appear to be open: one is to estimate the effect of tariff changes on prices and then to estimate the effects of these derived price changes on trade patterns; the other is to operate directly with observed relative price movements. This latter course exemplifies a problem which runs right through the estimation of the effects of economic integration and makes the obtaining of generally satisfactory results almost impossible. It is that to measure the effect of integration one must decide what would have happened if integration had not occurred (see previous section). Thus, if in the present instance any observed change in relative prices was assumed to be the result of the adjustment to tariff changes, all other sources of variation in prices would be ignored, which is clearly an exaggeration and could be subject to important biases if other factors were affecting trade at the same time.

7.3 The dynamic effects

While in the discussion of the exploitation of comparative advantage, the gains from a favourable movement in the terms of trade and often those from economies of scale are expressed in terms of comparative statics, it is difficult to disentangle them from feedback on to incomes and activity. The essence of the gains from increased efficiency and technological change is that the economy should reap dynamic gains. In other words, integration should enhance the rate of growth of GDP rather than just giving a step-up in welfare. Again it is necessary to explain how this might come about explicitly.

There are two generalized ways in which this can take place, first through increased productivity growth at a given investment ratio or second through increased investment itself. This is true whether the increased sales are generated internally or through the pressures of demand for exports from abroad through integration. Growth gains can, of course, occur temporarily in so far as there are slack resources in the economy. Again it is possible to observe whether the rate of growth has changed; but it is much more difficult to decide whether that is attributable to economic integration.

Krause (1968) attempted to apply a version of Denison's (1967) method of identifying the causes of economic growth but suggested that *all* changes in the rate of business investment were due to the formation of the EC (or EFTA in the case of those countries). Mayes (1978) showed that if the same contrast between business investment before and after the formation of the EC (EFTA) were applied to Japan a bigger effect would be observed than in any of the integrating countries. Clearly changes in the rate of business investment can occur for reasons other than integration.

7.4 Previous studies

As stated in the introduction to this chapter, a comprehensive survey of the studies covering up to the late 1980s is available in El-Agraa (1989a) and is updated in El-Agraa (1999). There is therefore no need to go through these studies here. However, a few general comments and a short summary may be in order.

Most of the measurements can be broadly classified as *ex ante* or *ex post*. The *ex ante* estimates are based on *a priori* knowledge of the pre-integration period (i.e. structural models), while the *ex post* studies are based on assumptions about the actual experience of economic integration (i.e. residual-imputation models). However, recall that either type can be analytic or otherwise.

There are two types of *ex ante* studies: those undertaken before the EC and EFTA were actually operative and those undertaken after they became operative.[3] The most influential studies to use this approach are those of Krause (1968), who predicted the trade diversion that would be brought about by the EC and EFTA on the basis of assumptions about demand elasticities, and Han and Leisner (1970), who predicted the effect on the United Kingdom by identifying those industries that had a comparative cost advantage/disadvantage *vis-à-vis* the EC and finding out how they were likely to be affected by membership, on the assumption that the pattern of trade prior to UK membership provided an indication of the underlying cost conditions and that this would be one of the determinants of the pattern of trade and domestic production after membership. This approach is of very limited value, however, for the simple reason that 'it does not provide a method of enabling one to improve previous estimates on the basis of new historical experience' (Williamson and Bottrill, 1971, p. 326).

The most significant studies to use the *ex post* approach are those of Lamfalussy (1963) and Verdoorn and Meyer zu Schlochtern (1964), who all use a relative shares method, Balassa (1967 and 1975), who uses an income elasticity of import demand method,[4] the EFTA Secretariat, which uses a share of imports in apparent consumption method,[5] Williamson and Bottrill, who use a more sophisticated share analysis,[6] Prewo, who uses an input–output method,[7] and Barten *et al.*, who use a medium-term macroeconomic method.[8] The advantage of the *ex post* method is that it can be constructed in such a way as to benefit from historical experience and hence to provide a basis for continuous research. However, the major obstacle in this approach concerns the difficulty regarding the construction of an adequate hypothetical post-integration picture of the economies concerned.

This section now provides an integrated summary of the studies of the impact of economic integration up to the early 1970s; later contributions are either refinements on these or too complex to go through here – the interested reader is advised to consult El-Agraa (1989b and 1999) – or relate to the internal market, in which case they are considered in the following chapter. In reading this summary, it is vital to bear in mind the distinction between short-term static effects, whereby changes in the impediments to trade lead to once and for all changes in the composition and pattern of trade, and longer-run dynamic effects, whereby economic integration over time leads to permanent changes in the rate of change of economic parameters. With this distinction in mind, one can classify the studies into *static* and *dynamic* along the lines suggested above.

The static studies can be put together into two major groups under the headings of *residual* and *analytic* models.

7.4.1 Residual models

Residual models depend largely on their ability to quantify the situation in the absence of economic integration, i.e. on the construction of the *anti-monde*. It should be clear from the contributions discussed that the construction of a satisfactory *anti-monde* will depend on a thorough accounting for the omissions mentioned above. These models are set out here in order of increasing complexity.

(a) Import models

The general tendency in import models is to emphasize variables drawn from only the importing country. This has the advantage of easy data collection, but one must ask the question of whether or not this adequately compensates for the inaccuracy of the estimates. To answer this question meaningfully, we need to follow Mayes' (1978) classification of this category of studies.

(i) The demand for imports

Studies of the demand for imports are based on the assumption that in the absence of economic integration imports would have grown over time as they did in the past. These studies have the obvious limitation that the extrapolation of trends has cryptic drawbacks for a cyclical activity such as international trade. Hence, many of the contributors assumed that imports would continue to be subject to the same linear relation to total expenditure, GDP and GNP respectively, in the *anti-monde* as they had been prior to the integration era – see, for example, Wemelsfelder (1960), Walter (1967) and Clavaux (1969). These contributions were built on the untenable premise that the marginal propensity to import remained constant throughout; evidence suggests that this parameter rises as income grows. Moreover, the estimation of the actual marginal propensity to import over the pre-integration periods would always be obscured by other changes in the international trading arrangements which had occurred then, and would not represent an *anti-monde* where no change had taken place.

The relative significance of changes in assumptions in terms of their quantitative impact is depicted in Figure 7.1 where the results of various estimates for the economic impact of the formation of the EC on trade are portrayed. Clearly, ideal comparison would require one to use each of the models with the *same* set of data, and where the quantity of recomputation was minimal, Mayes (1978) carried it out and included it in the figure. However, the data used in the various models were very different, so Mayes opted for the original results; these are also included in the figure with a time axis denoting the year for which they are estimates. The conclu-

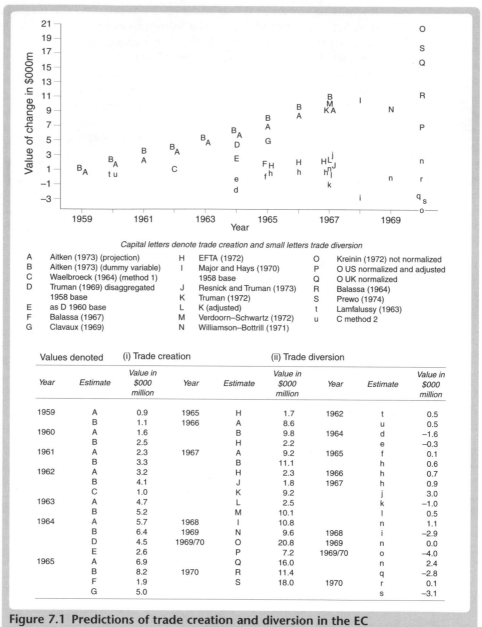

Capital letters denote trade creation and small letters trade diversion

A	Aitken (1973) (projection)	H	EFTA (1972)	O	Kreinin (1972) not normalized
B	Aitken (1973) (dummy variable)	I	Major and Hays (1970) 1958 base	P	O US normalized and adjusted
C	Waelbroeck (1964) (method 1)	J	Resnick and Truman (1973)	Q	O UK normalized
D	Truman (1969) disaggregated 1958 base	K	Truman (1972)	R	Balassa (1964)
E	as D 1960 base	L	K (adjusted)	S	Prewo (1974)
F	Balassa (1967)	M	Verdoorn–Schwartz (1972)	t	Lamfalussy (1963)
G	Clavaux (1969)	N	Williamson–Bottrill (1971)	u	C method 2

Values denoted		(i) Trade creation				(ii) Trade diversion		
Year	Estimate	Value in $000 million	Year	Estimate	Value in $000 million	Year	Estimate	Value in $000 million
1959	A	0.9	1965	H	1.7	1962	t	0.5
	B	1.1	1966	A	8.6		u	0.5
1960	A	1.6		B	9.8	1964	d	−1.6
	B	2.5		H	2.2		e	−0.3
1961	A	2.3	1967	A	9.2	1965	f	0.1
	B	3.3		B	11.1		h	0.6
1962	A	3.2		H	2.3	1966	h	0.7
	B	4.1		J	1.8	1967	h	0.9
	C	1.0		K	9.2		j	3.0
1963	A	4.7		L	2.5		k	−1.0
	B	5.2		M	10.1		l	0.5
1964	A	5.7	1968	I	10.8		n	1.1
	B	6.4	1969	N	9.6	1968	i	−2.9
	D	4.5	1969/70	O	20.8	1969	n	0.0
	E	2.6		P	7.2	1969/70	o	−4.0
1965	A	6.9		Q	16.0		n	2.4
	B	8.2	1970	R	11.4		q	−2.8
	F	1.9		S	18.0	1970	r	0.1
	G	5.0					s	−3.1

Figure 7.1 Predictions of trade creation and diversion in the EC

Source: Mayes (1978), p. 6.

sion one reaches from a portrayal of the estimates is that the use of more observations tends to improve the results.

(ii) Shares in apparent consumption

Estimation can also be carried out by examining the relative share performance in total consumption, as against the absolute value of imports, of different suppliers. Truman (1969) adopted the simplest solution by assuming that the relative share of each supplier would remain constant over time, but, as already indicated, it would be desirable to allow changes in these ratios over time on the basis of historical experience. The studies by the EFTA Secretariat (1969, 1972) tackle this by assuming that the linear trend in relative shares during the period 1954–9 would have been maintained by the participating nations in the absence of economic integration. There are two objections to this premise: first, 1954 and 1959 may not lie on the actual trend and, second, the form of the trend itself is too simple. Estimation by, for example, regression analysis to improve on the results is not really worth while, given the naïvety of the original assumption.

Table 7.1 gives two alternative estimates of the impact on the aggregate trade flows for EFTA depending on whether or not one assumed a linear trend or no change in the *anti-monde*. Not only the differing results but also the almost random distribution of the negative and positive signs should be noted.

(iii) Changes in the income elasticity of demand for imports

This method tries to tackle the problem of changes in the relative shares from the opposite direction by discerning what the actual changes imply for the elasticity of demand for different types of imports with respect to income. Balassa (1967) estimates the income elasticities of demand for imports from member countries separately from those from non-participating nations. He advanced the proposition that an increase in the elasticity of demand for imports from all sources indicated trade creation and that a decline in the elasticity of demand for imports from non-participants, given an increase in the elasticity for imports from the partners, indicated trade diversion. The results are given in Figure 7.1. Note that the *anti-monde* here was that these elasticities would not have changed in the absence of economic integration. To reiterate the criticism advanced in El-Agraa (1989a), Mayes (1978, pp. 8–9) argues that since the estimated elasticities are not unitary and not equal for imports from member and non-member countries, this means that changes in the shares of total imports in apparent consumption and imports from non-member countries (and hence member countries) in total imports can and do take place in the *anti-monde*. Although Balassa made allowances for changes in prices, his esti-

Table 7.1 Alternative estimates of aggregate effects of EFTA, 1965 ($ million)

Country	Trade creation hypothesis		Trade diversion hypothesis	
	(1)	(2)	(1)	(2)
Austria	−121.5	163	178.3	79
Denmark	−180.6	−122	322.1	−166
Finland	−204.9	−59	149.0	−136
Norway	−32.7	63	261.6	−73
Portugal	63.8	62	−15.1	43
Sweden	364.4	276	96.5	−110
Switzerland	−357.8	218	288.3	117
United Kingdom	831	−343	−619.1	−594
Total	361.7	258	661.6	−840

Source: Mayes (1978), p. 8.

mates were similar to those of the general trend in Figure 7.1, but both positive and negative results were observed.

Both the Balassa (1967) and the EFTA Secretariat (1969) methods leave unanswered the question as to why the substantial liberalization in world trade prior to economic integration left unaffected the estimation of trade relationships during that period. Indeed, Clavaux (1969) showed that if this factor were taken into consideration, i.e. trade liberalization were excluded from the *anti-monde*, Balassa's calculations for trade creation by 1966 would have more than doubled. However, as Mayes (1978, p. 9) clearly argues, the most important aspect of this criticism is that price elasticities imply a level of sophistication not reflected in the methods employed: without equations depicting supply conditions, there would arise identification problems which would bias estimates of price elasticities towards zero; the neglect of supply conditions implied that the price elasticities of supply would be infinite. Note that Balassa's (1974) calculation of *ex post* income elasticities incorporated supply constraints, but for the pre-integration situation as well. Moreover, Sellekaerts (1973) demonstrated that income elasticities varied widely over both the pre- and post-integration eras. Hence, the selection of appropriate periods for comparison purposes is of the utmost importance.

(b) Inclusion of supply parameters

The explicit incorporation of supply conditions would improve the specification of models since trade between any two countries is determined by parameters within both of them. The simplest method dealing with this was built on the premise that, under *normal* circumstances, trade between any two countries would be purely a function of the total trade of each of the two countries. Most particularly, the trade between any two countries would vary proportionately with the total exports of the exporting country and the total imports of the importing country in the *anti-monde*. The *RAS* advanced by Stone and Brown (1963) was the earliest input–output model to be adapted by Kouevi (1965) and Waelbroeck (1964) for this purpose. The major deficiency of this model is that total imports and exports were constrained to their actual values; hence, it was not possible to estimate trade creation.

An advance on this simple approach was the 'gravitational' method pioneered by Tinbergen and developed by Pulliainen (1963), Polyhonen (1963a, 1963b) and Linnemann (1966). The model presumed that the trade flow between any two countries would be a function of their respective national incomes and populations and the distance between them. The model was estimated by cross-section data and the economic impact of any integration scheme was calculated by the unexplained residual in the regression, or by the inclusion of dummy variables (DVs) for trade between participating nations as was the case in the estimates by Aitken (1973). These two methods gave very different results because of the substantial variability over time in the parameters. The estimates by Aitken (1973) gave a figure of $1264 million for trade creation by EFTA in 1967, employing the 1958 variables (this is labelled 'projection' in Figure 7.1), while the use of the 1967 values themselves together with the DVs made the results increase by 92%. Note that Aitken's results were the only ones to be estimated over a sequence of years; hence their great influence on the overall pattern of Figure 7.1. Even though these estimates are fairly consistent with the others, they tend to form an upper bound in some instances: for example, in 1965 they were three to four times as large as the lower bound. But one should hasten to add that the absolute magnitude of all the estimates was small. The main reason for these differences was the variability in the estimated parameters from year to year indicating that, to project with fixed parameters, one needed to take great care; this was confirmed in a disaggregated study by Bluet and Systermanns (1968). Mayes (1978, pp. 11–12) argued that much of the

> variability in the estimators occurs because a cross-section cannot represent a relationship which responds to cycles in economic activity and the very process of trade liberalisation in general. Pooling data helps to some extent but the model's main disadvantage is the omission of relative prices.

Verdoorn and Schwartz (1972) tried to tackle this drawback in their second model where they combined the advantages of the gravitational method with the effects of prices both on the overall demand for imports and the substitution between imports from different sources. While the results were mainly calculated on a residual basis, two DVs were used to explain some of the residual, but the explanation was statistical, not economic. The results are given in Table 7.2, and, as can be observed from Figure 7.1, they generally conform with the broad results, thus indicating that more sophisticated models do not leave us much the wiser.

(c) Incorporating information from third countries

Estimation using the share approach, without incorporating supply factors, could include third country behaviour. Lamfalussy (1963) showed that if one took into consideration the change in the shares of trade of non-participating countries and member nations of the EC in other markets, where neither was affected by economic integration, as the basis of one's expectations of how shares in the participating nations' markets would have changed in the absence of integration, one

Table 7.2 Resnick and Truman's (1974) estimates (R&T) of trade creation and trade diversion in the EC and EFTA compared with those of Verdoorn and Schwartz (1972) (V&S) ($ million)

	Trade creation		Trade diversion	
	R&T	V&S	R&T	V&S
Country	1968	1969	1968	1969
EC				
Belgium and Luxembourg	152	913	281	183
Netherlands	93	868	190	216
West Germany	−659	3 874	1 732	267
Italy	1 022	1 336	62	154
France	582	3 073	737	248
Total	1 190	10 064	3 002	1 068
EFTA				
UK	81	204	394	249
Other EFTA	131	161	231	547
Total	212	365	625	796
EC + EFTA	1 402	10 429	3 627	1 864

Source: Mayes (1978), p. 12.

Table 7.3 A comparison of the effects of different *anti-mondes* on the imports of the EC and EFTA in 1969 ($ million)

Anti-monde	Exporter	Importer	
		EC	EFTA
(1)		5091	−1042
(2)	EC	1018	−3610
(1)/(2)		5.00	0.29
(1)		−2258	2542
(2)	EFTA	−1594	2644
(1)/(2)		1.42	0.96
(1)	W	−2833	−1500
(2)		576	966

(1) Share of exporter *i* in the market of importer *j* would change between 1959 and 1969 at the same linear rate as the share of *i*'s exports in the imports of rest of world (*W*) changed during the same period (shares constrained to sum to unity).
(2) Share of exporter *i* in the market of importer *j* would change between 1959 and 1969 at the same linear rate as it did between 1954 and 1959.
Source: Mayes (1978), p. 13.

would get a different set of answers relative to those from trend extrapolation in the markets of the member countries alone. This is shown in Table 7.3, where the differences depict a fairly clear pattern: the share of EC exports in both EC and EFTA imports is much greater under the first hypothesis and the share of *W* in both markets falls under the first hypothesis but rises under the second. EFTA shares in both markets are greater under the second hypothesis but only very marginally so for intra-EFTA trade. As we observed earlier, it is also apparent that Lamfalussy's pessimistic conclusions were largely due to a limited period of observation – the first three years in the life of the EC. This was demonstrated by Williamson and Bottrill (1971) by using more observations and sophisticated extrapolation methods of the *anti-monde* shares. Recall, however, that their approach does not allow one to estimate trade creation and trade diversion without introducing further assumptions concerning their relative sizes.

Third countries can be used as a 'control' group or a 'normalizer' for estimating what the *anti-monde* would have been by incorporating them explicitly in the model. Kreinin (1972) does so by adapting the technique of projecting the *anti-monde* on the basis of predicted import/consumption ratios. The advantage of this method is that it allows one to observe more clearly how the normalization procedure works, and, therefore, should enable one to evaluate the tenability or otherwise of the assumptions on which it is built. However, it is an illusion to believe that a control group can be found, particularly for such schemes of integration as the EU and EFTA, since the control variables themselves are affected by the very experiment one is seeking to isolate.

(d) Estimation of the *anti-monde*

We have observed that the number and range of estimates of the impact of economic integration by imputation of the unaccounted-for residual are large, and it should be apparent that, the more relevant parameters are incorporated into the estimation of the *anti-monde*, the more acceptable are the results. Also, the incorporation of such refinements as disaggregation and intermediate products should lead to even more satisfactory results. However, the results of the study by Prewo (1974) depicted in Figure 7.1 give a very different pattern of estimates relative to other models, but this may be attributable to the simplicity of some of his other assumptions. Yet, as Mayes has argued, the problem of establishing a hypothetical *anti-monde* is in itself not an attractive proposition: 'While it is possible to point out the existence of biases it is not possible to know whether an unbiased estimate has been achieved, one can merely judge on the grounds of plausibility' (Mayes, 1978, p. 15). Plausibility is determined by the incorporated parameters not just in the importing and exporting countries, but also in the way they influence the trade cycle and changes in world prices. Hence, it is necessary to develop *analytic* models which are capable of explaining actual trade flows and their changes, as opposed to the estimation of *anti-mondes* and the imputation of residual differences to determine the impact of economic integration.

7.4.2 Analytic models

By *analytic* models one means methods which provide an economic rationale for the actual situation after economic integration has taken place. Such approaches are vital for all *ex ante* methods since the future values of trade flows are not known. Owing to the inherent complexity of prediction, such models are usually very simple and rely mainly on economic behaviour in the importing country. As we have seen, they assume that imports are determined by a measure of income or economic activity and the level of prices of imported and domestic products. Therefore, on the premise of a relationship between tariffs and prices, trade creation can be predicted from the change in the level of tariffs. Also, if one has knowledge about the elasticity of substitution with regard to changes in prices between member countries and the non-participants, one can estimate trade diversion.

This simple method will not provide acceptable estimates even if more sophisticated import demand functions are incorporated unless the effect of price changes on the level of prices can be explained. The EFTA Secretariat (1968) expected prices to fall by the amount of tariff changes, but it turned out that only part of the tariff changes seemed to be passed on. There is also a fair amount of evidence, at the microeconomic level, to suggest that the pricing of imports of many commodities depends mainly on the prices of existing competing domestic products. It is even suggested that the situation is far worse since importers tend to anticipate tariff changes, indicating that the growth of trade will anticipate the 'determining' tariff changes – see Walter (1967). Moreover, the attempts by Krause (1962) and Kreinin (1961) to calculate the tariff elasticities directly have not been successful; Mayes (1974) demonstrates that the estimates from this method do not correspond closely to those from the residual models.

Since different goods and/or nations are unlikely to behave in an identical fashion, one should expect that the greater the extent of disaggregation the more reasonable the estimates will be. Mayes (1971) uses a 97-commodity breakdown of manufactures and allows for a complete system of demand equations with the volume and price of imports from each country being distinguished to give a whole matrix of direct substitution elasticities (with those of Barten, 1970) to reach estimates for a projected *Atlantic Free Trade Area* comprising Canada, EFTA, Japan and the United States. These results are given in Table 7.4. They display an expected pattern of signs for overall trade creation and trade diversion, and are also robust to quite significant changes in the variables. Other estimates utilize more global values based on either simple assumptions or crude extrapolation from calculations for the United States; the different sets of assumptions employed by Balassa (1967), Kreinin (1967) and Krause (1968) lead to estimates given respectively in columns (2), (3) and (4) of the table, as recalculated by Mayes (1978). The results are somewhat similar, but this is attributable to offsetting changes: greater trade creation being matched by greater trade diversion. However, the striking feature of these results is that they are small relative to those given by residual models; for example, Kreinin (1969) found the effect of the formation of the EC for the period 1962–5 to be less than $100 million.

More elaborate models (Armington, 1970; Resnick and Truman, 1975) allow for the determination of imports by a series of allocative decisions while the studies by

Table 7.4 A comparison of *ex ante* predictions of the effects of economic integration on trade for an Atlantic free trade area[a] (effects on total exports) ($ million), 1972 (estimated)

Country	(1)[b]	(2)[c]	(3)[d]	(4)[e]
United States	2454	2318	2509	2645
Canada	2141	2610	2547	2650
Belgium–Luxembourg	−88	−124	−93	−117
France	−127	−146	−159	−199
Germany	−444	−538	−538	−673
Italy	−131	−144	−163	−204
Netherlands	−48	−56	−64	−80
Total EC	−838	−1008	−1017	−1273
Denmark	22	30	24	24
Norway	15	23	18	18
Sweden	128	156	144	148
United Kingdom	607	821	726	756
Rest of EFTA	241	263	255	269
Total EFTA	1013	1293	1167	1215
Japan	1879	2380	2301	2448
Rest of the world	−646	−806	−719	−898
Total	6002	6786	6786	6786

[a] Defined here as an area comprising the USA, Canada, EFTA and Japan – this corresponds closely to the definitions used by Balassa (1967).
[b] Mayes (1971).
[c] Using elasticities used by Balassa (1967).[f]
[d] Using same import elasticity as Balassa but assuming elasticity of substitution is −2.5, as assumed by Kreinin (1967).
[e] As d but assuming elasticity of substitution is −2, as assumed by Krause (1968).
[f] Commodity categories are different so these results do not represent an exact updating of the original results.
Source: Mayes (1978), p. 18.

Balassa (1967) and Kreinin (1967) use simple assumptions for supply constraints, but, as can be seen from Figure 7.1 and Table 7.2, the estimates of these models do not fit happily with those from the residual models. For example, the estimates of trade diversion from the Resnick and Truman model are only one-eighth of those from the Verdoorn and Schwartz (1972) model. Also, because the establishment of the CETs meant that West Germany had to raise its tariff levels, trade creation is negative in the analytic case but is the largest positive estimate in the residual model. This indicates that factors other than tariff changes had a very substantial and positive effect on West Germany's post-EC trade. There is, therefore, 'much more to be explained which *is not* covered by the analytic models and *cannot* be covered by the residual ones' (Mayes, 1978, p. 18).

However, the main attraction of the analytic models is that they can be tested after the event and can be used for forecasting as well as for ex post estimation. In this respect, the models used by Grinols (1984) and Winters (1984a), which cannot be discussed here owing to space limitations, represent a way forward – see El-Agraa (1989a and 1999).

7.4.3 Dynamic studies

The static models are predominantly concerned with the impact of price changes alone on the level, composition and pattern of trade. However, it could be argued that the static models leave out the most dominant effects of economic integration. This is due to the fact that the feedback into incomes and the rate of economic growth or the necessity for the use of expenditure-switching policies for balance of payments equilibrating purposes may be considerable and either positive or negative. For example, Kaldor (1971) argues not only that membership of the EC will inflict costs on the United Kingdom, but that the costs will be reinforced by adverse dynamic effects. However, there are very few estimates of the dynamic effects, with Krause (1968) being the exception. Krause tries to explain changes in the rate of real economic growth in the EC and EFTA by increasing business investment and efficiency. The expectation is that an increase in the ratio of investment to GDP will increase capital accumulation, and if the marginal capital/output ratios are constant, both output and the rate of growth must increase. But the fixity of the capital/output ratios automatically excludes economies of scale which lie at the very heart of the dynamic effects. The increase in efficiency is due to a decrease in input costs from imports: hence the increase in the ratio of imports to output is estimated and multiplied by the average tariff rate to calculate the income effect of the cost reduction, and this can be expressed as an annual rate.

Clearly, this method suffers from the same limitations as the static models: equating tariff changes and consequent price changes, and attributing all changes to economic integration.

7.5 A critique of previous studies

There are some general and some specific points of criticism to be made against these studies:

1. All the studies, excepting the Brada and Méndez (1985), Truman (1975) and Williamson and Bottrill (1971) studies, and to a certain extent the Aitken (1973)

and Mayes (1978) estimates, assume that the formation of the EC (or EFTA) has been the sole factor to influence the pattern of trade. Since the EC and EFTA were established more or less simultaneously (there is a year's difference between them), it is not justifiable to attribute changes in the pattern of trade to either alone. After all, EFTA was established in order to counteract the possible damaging effects of the EC. Moreover, a few years after the establishment of these two blocs, a number of schemes were formed all over the world – see El-Agraa (1982c, 1988b, 1997, 1999) and Chapter 1 of this book for a detailed specification and discussion of these. The impact of these latter groupings should not have been ignored by studies conducted in the late 1960s and thereafter.

2. Most of the recent studies ignore the fact that Britain used to be a member of EFTA before joining the EC. Since the United Kingdom is a substantial force as a member of either scheme, it seems misleading to attempt estimates which do not take into consideration this switch by the United Kingdom. A similar argument applies to Denmark. This point of course lends force to the previous one.

3. In the period prior to the formation of the EC and EFTA, certain significant changes were happening on the international scene. The most important of these was that the discrimination against the United States was greatly reduced. Is it at all possible that such developments had no effect whatsoever on the trade pattern of the EC and EFTA? It seems unrealistic to assume that this should have been the case.

4. All the studies, except for Truman's (1975) and to some extent Winters' (1984a), dealt with trade data in spite of the fact that a proper evaluation of the effects of economic integration requires analysis of *both* trade *and* production data. Trade creation indicates a reduction in domestic production combined with new imports of the same quantity from the partner, while trade diversion indicates new imports from the partner combined with less imports from the rest of the world (W) and a reduction in production in W.

5. Tariffs are universally recognized as only one of the many trade impediments, yet all the studies, except Krause's (1968), Prewo's (1974) and the EU study discussed in the following chapter, were based on the assumption that the only effect of integration in Western Europe was on discriminatory tariff removal. This is a very unsatisfactory premise, particularly if one recalls that the EC had to resort to explicit legislation against cheaper imports of textiles from India, Japan and Pakistan in the 1960s and early 1970s. The EC later forced Japan to adopt voluntary export restraints (VERs) with regard to cars, and some unusual practices were adopted, such as France's diverting of Japanese video recorders to Poitiers (poorly manned for customs inspection) to slow down their penetration of the French market – see El-Agraa (1988a) for a detailed specification of these issues. Moreover, the level of tariffs and their effective protection is very difficult to measure:

> Tariff schedules are public, but their interpretation is often made difficult by peculiar institutional clauses. Furthermore, it is difficult to obtain a good measure of the restrictive impact of tariffs. Average tariff rates will not do, for, if the rate is zero on one good and prohibitive on another, the average tariff is zero. It is necessary to use *a priori* weights, which inevitably is arbitrary ... [Others] raised a more subtle issue by proposing to use input–output analysis to measure the effective *rates of protection* achieved by tariffs on value added. This approach raises a host of problems. The assumptions of fixed

technical coefficients and of perfectly competitive price adjustments are both debatable. It is clear that the concept of effective protection ... relies on oversimplified assumptions. (Waelbroeck, 1977, p. 89)

6. The Dillon and Kennedy Rounds of tariff negotiations resulted in global tariff reductions which coincided with the first stage of the removal of tariffs by the EC. Does this not mean that any evidence of external trade creation should be devalued, and any evidence of trade diversion is an underestimate?

More specifically, however:

In all these studies, the integration effect, whether trade creation or trade diversion, is estimated by the difference between actual and extrapolated imports for a post-integration year. The extrapolation of imports is done by a time trend of imports or by relating imports with income or consumption in the importing country. The difference between the actual and estimated imports would be due to (i) autonomous changes in prices in the supplying and importing countries, (ii) changes in income, consumption or some other variable representing macroeconomic activity, (iii) changes in variables other than income/consumption and autonomous price movements, (iv) revisions of tariffs and/or other barriers as a result of integration, (v) residual errors due to the random error term in the estimating equation, misspecification of the form of the equation, errors in the data, omission or misrepresentation of certain variables, etc. The studies ... try to segregate the effect of (ii) only. The remaining difference between the actual and estimated imports would be due to (i), (iii), (iv) and (v), but it is ascribed only to (iv), i.e. the effect of revision of tariff and/or other barriers to trade as a result of integration. Clearly, it is a totally unreliable way of estimating the integration effect on trade creation or trade diversion. Even if prices are included as an additional variable in the estimating equation, it would amount to segregating the effect of (i) and (ii), so that the difference between the actual and estimated imports would be due to (iii), (iv) and (v). It would still be wrong to ascribe it to (iv) only. The error term at (v) is often responsible for a divergence of ±10% between the actual and estimated imports, which might often overshadow the effect of integration. For this reason, the 'residual method' used by Balassa, the EFTA Secretariat and many others, is highly unreliable for estimating the trade creation and trade diversion effects of integration. (Dayal and Dayal, 1977, pp. 136–7)

Moreover, the effects of economic integration, be they trade creation or trade diversion, occur in two stages: the effects of changes in tariffs on prices and the effect of price changes on trade. These two effects have to be separately calculated before the trade creation and trade diversion effects of economic integration can be estimated. This procedure is not followed.

In addition, the accuracy of the *ex ante* forecasts of the impact of economic integration on the level and direction of trade rests on the reliability of the price elasticities utilized. Furthermore, apart from this general problem, a critical issue is whether the effect of a tariff is the same as that of an equivalent price change; tariff elasticities substantially exceed the usual import demand elasticities, and the elimination of a tariff is perceived by the business world as irreversible.

It therefore seems inevitable to conclude that

All estimates of trade creation and diversion by the [EC] which have been presented in the empirical literature are so much affected by *ceteris paribus* assumptions, by the choice of the length of the pre- and post-integration periods, by the choice of benchmark year (or years), by the methods to compute income elasticities, changes in trade matrices and in relative shares and by structural changes not attributable to the [EC] but which occurred during the pre- and post-integration periods (such as the trade liberalisation amongst industrial countries and autonomous changes in relative prices) that the magnitude of no ... estimate should be taken too seriously. (Sellekaerts, 1973, p. 548)

Moreover, given the validity of those criticisms, one should not take seriously such statements as:

> There are a number of studies that have reported attempts to construct ... estimates. Individually the various methods must be judged unreliable. ... But collectively the available evidence is capable of indicating conclusions of about the same degree of reliability as is customary in applied economics. That is to say, there is a wide margin of uncertainty about the correct figure, but the order of magnitude can be established with reasonable confidence. (Williamson and Bottrill, 1971, p. 323)

Since no single study can be justified in its own right and the fact that the degree of reliability in applied economics leaves a lot to be desired, it is difficult to see the collective virtue in individual misgivings.

7.6 The alternative

It seems evident that there is nothing wrong with the methodology for the empirical testing of integration effects, but that the problems of actual measurement are insurmountable. However, these difficulties are due to some basic misconceptions regarding the welfare implications of trade creation and trade diversion: trade creation is good while trade diversion is bad – using the Johnson (1974) definition.

In an interdependent macroeconomic world, trade creation is inferior to trade diversion for the country concerned – see Chapter 6 of El-Agraa (1989a) – and both are certainly detrimental to the outside world. This conclusion is also substantiated by Johnson's work which incorporates the collective consumption of a public good – see Chapter 5 of this book and Johnson (1965a). It therefore seems rather futile, for estimation purposes, to attach too much significance to the welfare implications of trade creation versus trade diversion in this respect. Lest it be misunderstood, I should hasten to add that this is not a criticism of the trade creation–trade diversion theoretical dichotomy, rather the futility or impossibility of its empirical estimation. Moreover:

> trade creation and trade diversion ... are static concepts. Their effects are once-for-all changes in the allocation of resources. At any date in the future their effects must be measured against what *would otherwise have been*, not by what is happening to trade at that time. In the economic theorist's model without adjustment lags, the introduction of a scheme for regional integration causes a once-for-all shift to more intra-integrated area trade and less trade with the outside world, and the forces that *subsequently* influence the allocation of resources become once again cost changes due to technological advance, and demand changes due to differing income elasticities of demand as real income rises as a result of growth [,] ... call the first set of forces affecting the allocation of resources *integration induced* and the second set *growth induced* ... The two sets of forces ... are intermixed (the problem becomes even more complex conceptually if integration itself affects the growth rate). The more sudden the integration, the more likely it is that integration induced effects will dominate, at least for the first few years; but the longer the time lapse the more would normal growth-induced effects dominate. The morals are: (1) the longer the time since a relatively sudden move towards integration, the harder it is to discern the effects by studying changes in the pattern of trade; and (2) the more gradually the integration measures are introduced, the more will the effects be mixed up, even in the short term, with growth-induced effects. (Lipsey, 1977, pp. 37–8)

For all these reasons I have suggested (see the first edition of this book) that the measurement of the impact of economic integration should be confined to ɾɾ mating its effect on intra-union trade and, if at all possible, to finding out wheth or not any changes have been at the expense of the outside world. Although th, macroeconomic framework is subject to some serious limitations, it provides, at the very least, a genuine alternative against which one can judge the quality of the estimates obtained from the previous models.

This suggestion has now been taken up by a number of leading international organizations, but has been narrowed down to a single calculation of the changes in the volume of trade between the member countries. I would go along with this for advanced nations since increased trade *may* reflect enhanced integration, but I very much doubt the usefulness of this for very poor nations where investments generated by the scheme of integration would be more important.

Notes

1. An equivalent world production matrix is also necessary, see points (1)–(3) below.
2. It is possible that the fast growth of EEC and EFTA intra-trade in the years immediately following their formulation (and also of EC intra-trade in 1969) was particularly at the expense of slower growth in exports to [W]. There is no conclusive evidence as to whether this was an important factor. In the long run, however, one would expect supply bottlenecks to be overcome, and one might also expect their effect to be counteracted by the greater competitive strength resulting from a larger 'home market'. We therefore follow a well-established precedent in assuming $s_{ij}=0$ (no supply-side diversion exists). (Williamson and Bottrill, 1971, p. 325)
3. See, for instance, Verdoorn (1954), Janssen (1961), Krause and Salant (1973a) and the Eᴄ study discussed in the following chapter.
4. *Ex post* income elasticities of import demand were defined as the ratio of the average annual rate of change of imports to that of GNP, both expressed in constant prices. Under the assumption that income elasticities of import demand would have remained unchanged in the absence of integration, a rise in the income elasticity of demand for intra-area imports would indicate gross trade creation – increases in intra-area trade – irrespective of whether this resulted from substitution for domestic or for foreign sources of supply. In turn, a rise in the income elasticity of demand for imports from all sources taken together would give expression of trade creation proper, i.e. a shift from domestic to partner-country sources. Finally, trade diversion, a shift from foreign to partner country producers, would be indicated by a decline in the income elasticity of demand for extra-area imports. (Balassa, 1975, p. 80)
5. The EFTA Secretariat's study is based on the assumption that had EFTA not been established, the import shares in the apparent consumption of a particular commodity in any of the EFTA countries would have developed in the post-integration period in precisely the same fashion as they had during the pre-integration period 1954–9. (See EFTA Secretariat 1969 and 1972.)
6. We believe that the most promising hypothesis is that originally introduced by Lamfalussy. According to this, the share performance of the *j*th supplier in markets where he neither gains nor loses preferential advantages gives a good indication of his hypothetical performance in markets which were in fact being affected by integration. In terms of the present analysis, the rest of the world provides a control which indicates what share performance would have been in EEC and EFTA markets if these two organizations had not been formed. (Williamson and Bottrill, 1971, p. 333)

The methods selected are:

(1) Using an *a priori* formula which ensures that the predicted gain in market shares will be small if the previous market share was either very small or very large.

(2) Extrapolating from a regression of data on relative export shares.

(3) Assuming that market shares would have remained constant in the absence of economic integration.

7. Prewo (1974) uses a gravitational model which links the national input–output tables of the EC countries by a system of trade equations. In this model, trade between members of the EC is assumed to be proportional to demand in the importing, and supply in the exporting, country and inversely proportional to trade impediments, whereas extra-area imports are assumed to be related to demand in the EC countries. In this model, changes in final demand have a direct effect on imports of final goods, as well as an indirect effect through their impact on the imports of inputs for domestic production.

The basis of the analysis is that the 'difference between the actual trade flows of the customs union and the hypothetical trade flows of the customs union's antimonde is taken to be indicative of the integration effects.' (Prewo, 1974, p. 380)

8. 'It basically consists of eight similarly specified country models which are linked by *bilateral trade equations* and equations specifying the formation on import and export prices.' (Barten *et al.*, 1976, p. 63)

8 The economics of the Single Market

A. M. EL-AGRAA

In this book, the Single European Act (SEA), incorporating the package proposed by the Commission in its White Paper (CEC, 1985a) for the creation of an internal market by 31 December 1992, is tackled as a natural but significant extension and development of the EU. Therefore, the reader who is interested in the details of the SEA and the internal market, and their implications for both the EU and the rest of the world, will have to go through virtually every chapter of the book for information; the implications of the Single Market are too wide and far reaching to be tackled in a vacuum. This approach may offend those who believe that the future should be highlighted and the past forgotten; but the emphasis in this book is on the evolution and dynamism of the EU. To follow the bandwagon by concentrating entirely on the economics of the Single Market or economic and monetary union (EMU) would be to negate the very foundations of our approach. However, it is appropriate to devote a chapter to the internal market, emphasizing its theoretical and measurement aspects – the general heading of this section of the book – especially since the assessment of the gains expected from it have led to a novel approach, and vast resources have been devoted to the exercise.

8.1 The aspirations of the White Paper

According to Lord Cockfield, then Commission Vice-President with a portfolio including the internal market, the completion of the Single Market was the first priority of the Commission to which he belonged. He went so far as to state that its accomplishment would be the greatest achievement of the Commission during its term of office. This was put more succinctly in the *Bulletin of the European Communities* (no. 6, 1985, p. 18):

> From the words of the Treaties themselves through successive declarations by the European Council since 1982, the need to complete the internal market has been confirmed at the highest level. What has been missing has been an agreed target date and a detailed programme for meeting it. The Commission has welcomed the challenge of providing the missing piece. It has interpreted the challenge in the most comprehensive way possible: the creation by 1992 of a genuine common market without internal frontiers.

According to the White Paper the completion of the internal market will become a reality when the EU has eliminated any physical, technical and fiscal barriers among its member nations. Before elaborating on these, it should be stressed that the Commission felt that the single market programme contained three main features:

(i) there are to be no more attempts to harmonize or standardize at any price – a method originating in too rigid an interpretation of the Treaty; in most cases, an 'approximation' of the parameters is sufficient to reduce differences in rates or technical specifications to an acceptable level [see Chapter 15];

(ii) the programme will propose no measures which, while supposedly facilitating trade or travel, in fact maintain checks at internal frontiers and therefore the frontiers themselves, the symbol of the Community's fragmentation; their disappearance will have immense psychological and practical importance; [and]

(iii) a major factor for the success of the programme is its two-stage, binding timetable, with relatively short deadlines, relying as far as possible on built-on mechanisms; the programme is a comprehensive one, which means that it has the balance needed if general agreement is to be forthcoming. (*Bulletin of the European Communities*, no. 6, 1985, p. 18)

With regard to physical frontiers, the aim is to eliminate them altogether, not just to reduce them. The Commission argued that it is not sufficient simply to reduce the number of controls carried out at the borders because, as long as persons and goods have to stop to be checked, the main aim will not be achieved: 'goods and citizens will not have been relieved of the costly delays and irritations of being held up at frontiers, and there will still be no real Community'.

In the White Paper the Commission provided a specification of all the functions carried out at border-crossing points. It drew attention to those functions that could or should be unnecessary in a true common market. Moreover, where the function carried out at the frontier checkpoint was still deemed to be necessary, the Commission recommended alternative ways of achieving it without border crossing-points. For example, with regard to health protection, the Commission suggested that checks on veterinary and plant health should be limited to destination points, the implication being that 'national standards be as far as possible aligned on common standards'. With regard to transport, quotas had to be progressively relaxed and eliminated, and common safety standards introduced for vehicles so that systematic controls could be dispensed with.

The Commission was quick to stress that it was quite aware of the implications of the elimination of border crossing-points for such sensitive issues as tax policy and the fight against drugs and terrorism. It admitted that it 'recognises frankly that these are difficult areas, which pose real problems', but maintained its belief that the objectives justify the effort that would be needed to solve them. Thus, it promised to put forward directives regarding the harmonization of laws concerning arms and drugs.

As to the question of technical barriers, the Commission argued that the elimination of border crossing-points would be to no avail if both firms and persons inside the EU continued to be subjected to such hidden barriers. Therefore, the Commission carefully considered these technical barriers and suggested ways of eliminating them to a detailed timetable. The Commission proposals covered goods and services, freedom of movement for workers and professional persons, public procurement, capital movements and the creation of conditions for industrial co-operation.

In the case of goods, the Commission emphasized that, provided that certain health and safety-related constraints and safeguards are met, goods which are 'lawfully' made and sold in one EU member nation should be able to move freely and go on sale *anywhere* within the EU. For this purpose, the EU's new approach to technical harmonization and standards (see *Official Journal of the European Committees*, no. 136, 4 April 1985) was applied and extended.

With regard to the freedom to provide services, the Commission recognized that there had been much slower progress here than with the situation regarding goods. It claimed that the distinction between goods and services had never been a valid one and that the EU had undermined its own economic potential by retaining it. This was because the service sector not only was growing fast as a 'value-adding provider of employment in its own right', but also gave vital support and back-up for the manufacturing sector. It stressed that this was already the case not just in such traditional services as banking, insurance and transport, but also in the new areas of information, marketing and audiovisual services. Thus the White Paper put forward proposals and a timetable for action covering all these services until 1992. The Commission concluded that, with the creation of a true common market for the services sector in mind, it should be possible to enable the exchange of 'financial products' such as 'insurance policies, home-ownership savings contracts and consumer credit, using a minimum coordination of rules as the basis of mutual recognition'. With regard to transport, proposals were to be sent to the Council for the 'phasing out of all quantitative restrictions (quotas) on road haulage and for the further liberalisation of road passenger services by 1989, of sea transport services by the end of 1986 and of competition in air transport services by 1987' (see Chapter 13).

In the case of audiovisual services, the aim should be to endeavour to create a single EU-wide broadcasting area. For this purpose, the Commission was to make specific proposals in 1985 based on its Green Paper of May 1984 on the establishment of a common market for broadcasting.

As to capital movements, the Commission stated that from 1992 onwards any residual currency control measures should be applied by means other than border controls (see Chapter 17). The Commission stated that, in the case of employees, freedom of movement was already almost entirely complete. Moreover, the rulings of the Court of Justice restricted the right of public authorities in the EU member nations to reserve jobs for their own nationals. However, the Commission was to bring forward the necessary proposals to dismantle any obstacles that still prevailed. It was also to take measures to eliminate the cumbersome administrative procedures relating to residence permits (see Chapter 19). With regard to the right of establishment for the self-employed, the Commission conceded that little progress had been made. This was because of the complexities involved in trying to harmonize professional qualifications: in professions such as accounting and auditing practitioners perform completely different jobs and receive completely different training in the EU member nations and hence harmonization implies a drastic change in both education and training before the profession can hope to be seen as performing the same task (see Chapter 16 of the first edition of this book on the accounting profession). However, such efforts had led to a substantial degree of freedom of movement for those in the health sector and in 1985 the Council adopted measures which extended such freedom to architects after '18 years of protectionist pressure and exaggerated defensive arguments' (*Bulletin of the European Communities*, no. 6, 1985, p. 20). The Commission concluded by stating that, in an effort to remove obstacles to the right of establishment, it would lay before the Council (in 1985) a framework directive on a general system of recognition of degrees and diplomas (see Chapter 19), the main features of which would be:

> the principle of mutual trust between the [member nations]; the principle of comparability of university studies between the [member nations]; the mutual recognition of degrees and diplomas without prior harmonization of the conditions for access to and the exercise of professions.

Any difference between the member nations, especially with regard to training, would be compensated by professional experience.

In the field of fiscal frontiers, the Commission was of the opinion that taxation would be one of the principal areas in which the challenge of the Single Market had to be faced. It argued that the rates of indirect taxation in the EU member nations were in some cases so divergent (see Chapter 15) that they would no doubt create trade distortions, leading to loss of revenue to the exchequers of the member states. It was convinced that frontier controls could not be eliminated if substantial differences in VAT and excise duties prevailed between the member nations. Its conclusion was that, if frontiers and associated controls were to be eliminated, 'it will be necessary not only to set up a Community clearing system for VAT and a linkage system of bonded warehouses for excised products, but also to introduce a considerable measure of approximation of indirect taxes'. The first question that this raised was how close the approximation should be. As stated in Chapter 15, the 'Commission argued that the experience of countries like the United States indicated that controls could be eliminated without a complete equalisation of rates'. Variations would have to be narrowed, but 'differences of up to 5% may coexist without undue adverse effects. This would suggest a margin of 2.5% either side of whatever target rate or norm is chosen' (*Bulletin of the European Communities*, no. 6, p. 20). The Commission stated that a great deal of statistical and econometric work would have to be carried out before it could make specific proposals. However, it felt that it would be of great assistance if the Council agreed to exert extra effort to finalize work on the proposals it had already presented to it. At the same time, the Commission would propose a 'standstill clause' to guarantee that prevailing variations in the number and levels of VAT rates would not be widened, hoping that in 1986 it would propose target rates or norms and allowed ranges of variation. However, it stressed that the approximation of indirect taxation would result in a number of problems for some of the EU member nations, and hence it might be necessary to provide for derogations. Needless to add, the discussion in Chapter 15 clearly shows that the Commission has delivered these proposals as promised.

Finally, the Commission concluded by making it clear that the proposed measures to accomplish a single EU domestic market would not become a reality without some institutional changes. It argued that in many areas the possibility of reaching decisions by majority voting must be entertained and left this issue for a separate document.

8.2 Actions promised by the Commission

The details of the actual proposals put forward by the Commission to enable the creation of the Single Market are by now not only common knowledge (see *The Economist* of 9 July 1988 and 8 July 1989), but can be found in a number of academic books (see, *inter alia*, Emerson *et al.*, 1988; Pelkmans and Winters, 1988) as well as in the majority of the chapters in this book. They therefore need not detain us here. However, in the Commission's view, the achievement of the internal market meant the enactment of 300 directives, 21 of which were quietly dropped by 1988 but a similar number of which proved necessary, thus restoring the 300 figure. By the end of December 1992, the EU was forced to concede that only 95% of the 300 directives had been launched, but all internal EU border checks were abolished by then. Indeed, Mr Jaques Delors, then President of the EU Commission, stated that as a gradual process the Single Market project was never supposed to end with a 'big bang' on 1 January 1993. However, if the discussion in Chapter 2 is recalled, it will be remembered that directives have to be incorporated into national law before they are put into practice, and some of the early directives had been in the pipeline long before the White Paper was published in 1985. Moreover, Butt Philip (1988) argues that although the *average* time taken for legislative proposals to pass through the Council is three years, many proposals have been in gestation in the Council for longer than this. He shows that, in February 1987, 126 proposals from the Commission had been part of this 'logjam for over five years. Some thirty-eight proposals had been "under consideration" for over a decade.' His main explanation (p. 2) for such legislative delays at the EU level is that the negotiators for some of the member nations, 'in anticipation of implementation problems ahead, adopt a tough stance in order to ensure that the resulting decisions can be implemented by their own national administrations', and adds that other member nations such as Italy are 'less diligent in briefing their negotiators, and more frequently encounter administrative and other difficulties' when they come to apply the rules they have already endorsed. Furthermore, many of the directives have a contingent or voluntary outcome, especially those pertaining to the harmonization of technical standards and the mutual recognition of rules. Although I added in the fourth edition of this book that, be that as it may, one can still confidently assert that the internal market will be fully realized after a few months' delay, in its 1995 *General Report* the Commission stated that the 'overall rate of transposal for the 15 [members] was 93.2% at the end of the year. However, the level remained below that figure in a number of areas, such as public procurement, intellectual property rights and insurance' (p. 51). Although the legal process is now complete, the Commission introduced a regular publication, the *Single Market Scoreboard*, which reports on the progress made and difficulties encountered in the various sectors of the internal market. Also, on 24 November 1999, it set out its strategic objectives for the internal market for 2000–2004, which include improving quality of life, enhancing the efficiency of product and capital markets and improving the business environment.

8.3 The expected benefits

8.3.1 The Cecchini estimates

According to the Cecchini Report, which summarizes in 16 volumes the findings of a study carried out on behalf of the EC Commission (see CEC, 1988i; a popular version is to be found in Cecchini, 1988), the completion of the internal market will regenerate both the goods and services sectors of the EU. The study estimates (see below for the methodology employed and section 8.4 for theoretical analysis) the total potential gain for the EC (the 12) as a whole to be in the region of 200 billion ECU, at constant 1988 prices. This would increase EC gross domestic product (GDP) by 5% or more. The gains would come not only from the elimination of the costs of barriers to intra-EC trade, but also from the exploitation of economies of scale which were expected to lower costs by about 2% of EC GDP. The medium-term impact of this on employment will be to increase it by about two million jobs.

These estimates are considered to be minimal since the study points out that, if the governments of the member nations of the EU pursue macroeconomic policies that recognize this potential for faster economic growth, the total gains could reach 7% of EC GDP and increase employment by about five million jobs. If these predictions become a reality, the EU will gain a very substantial competitive edge over non-participating nations.

The summary of the Cecchini Report given in Cecchini (1988) is written for the general public. The definitive technical work is that by Emerson *et al.* (1988); Emerson is a leading economist who then worked for the Directorate-General for Economic and Financial Affairs, and in this capacity his (and his collaborators') work presents the official Commission analysis; hence the interested reader is advised to consult this work. Here it should be asked why the elimination of the various barriers mentioned above should lead to economic benefits for the EU. To answer this question meaningfully, one needs to specify the barriers, which are all of the non-tariff type, slightly differently, and in a more general context:

1. Differences in the technical regulations adopted in the various member nations which tend to increase the cost of intra-EU trade transactions.

2. Delays in the customs procedures at border crossing-points and related extra administrative tasks on both private firms and public organizations which further increase the costs of intra-EU trade transactions.

3. Public procurement procedures which effectively limit if not completely eliminate competition for public purchases to own member nation suppliers, a procedure often claimed to raise the price of such purchases.

4. Curtailment of one's ability either to transact freely in certain services, especially finance and transport, where barriers to entry are supposedly great, or to get established in them in another EU member nation.

No claim has been made to suggest that the cost of eliminating each of these barrier categories is substantial, but Emerson *et al.* (1988) have argued that the combination of these barriers, in an EU dominated by oligopolistic market structures, amounts to 'a considerable degree of non-competitive segmentation of the market', with the implication that the cost of eliminating all the barrier categories then becomes considerable. Since the emphasis is on costs (the Cecchini Report stresses them as the 'cost of non-Europe' – see Chapter 7), it follows that the elimination of these barriers will reduce the costs, i.e. increase the benefits; these are two sides of the same coin.

Here, it may be appropriate to provide a brief explanation of this methodology. Recall that the majority of the 300 or so areas of barrier identified with the cost of Europe related to differences in technical requirements, whether product standards, required qualifications for workers, location for financial services or domestic ownership for public procurement. The remainder were labelled as fiscal barriers, through the differential operation of tax systems (see Chapter 15), or physical, such as border controls. Identifying these areas was a major challenge, and trying to quantify their importance was even more so. Instead of carrying out a microeconomic exercise assessing the degree to which each measure could be translated into a value equivalent (see Chapter 7), an almost impossible task, Cecchini (or the EU Commission in disguise) opted for this novel approach to examining the impact of economic integration by measuring departures from it. This inverted the procedure of trying to explain what the counterfactual might have been had economic integration not taken place. Instead the comparison became one with a specified view of what the integrated economy might have looked like. In such an economy there would be little price dispersion (see section 8.4) and firms would have operated on an EU-wide level. Thus, in setting out the potential impact, the Cecchini study looked at the extent of departures from the lowest prices and the extent to which economies of scale had not been exploited. Thus, this approach did not estimate the likely impact of economic integration; rather, it provided an estimate of the scope for gains (Mayes, 1997d).

These benefits can also be expressed forthrightly. The elimination of the costs of non-Europe is tantamount to the removal of constraints which 'today prevent enterprises from being as efficient as they could be and from employing their resources to the full' (Emerson *et al.*, 1988, p. 2). They go on to argue that since these are constraints, their removal will 'establish a more competitive environment which will incite [the enterprises] to exploit new opportunities' (p. 2). They then claim that the combination of the elimination of the constraints and the creation of a more competitive situation will have four major types of effect:

1. A significant reduction in costs due to a better exploitation of several kinds of economies of scale associated with the size of production units and enterprises.

2. An improved efficiency in enterprises, a rationalization of industrial structures and a setting of prices closer to costs of production, all resulting from more competitive markets.

3. Adjustments between industries on the basis of a fuller play of comparative advantages in an integrated market.

4. A flow of innovations, new processes and new products, stimulated by the dynamics of the internal market.

They were quick to add that these processes free resources for alternative productive uses, and, when they are so utilized, the total sustainable level of consumption and investment in the EU economy will be increased. They stressed that this was their fundamental criterion of economic gain.

Given the definitive nature of the Emerson *et al.* (1988) book, it may be useful, at the risk of duplication, to quote the estimates of the gains as presented by them. To make sense of their calculations and, of course, of the overall results given above, it has to be recalled that all the calculations relate to 1985 when the total EC GDP was 3300 billion ECU for the 12 member nations. However, the actual calculations were made for the seven largest EC member countries (accounting for 88% of EC GDP for the 12) with a total GDP of 2900 billion ECU.

They claim that the overall estimates range from 70 billion ECU (2.5% of EC GDP) for 'a rather narrow conception of the benefits' of eliminating the remaining barriers to the single market, to about 125–190 billion ECUs (4.5–6.5% of EC GDP) in the case of a more competitive and integrated market. Applying the same percentages to the 1988 GDP data, the gains were estimated to be between 175 and 255 billion ECUs. These gains were expected to increase the EC's annual growth rate by about one percentage point for the years until 1992. Also, 'there would be good prospects that longer-run dynamic effects could sustain a buoyant growth rate further into the 1990s' (p. 5).

These gains were obtained on the understanding that it might take five or more years for the upper limits to be achieved and that policies at both the microeconomic and the macroeconomic level would ensure that the resources (basically labour) released by the savings in costs would be fully and effectively utilized elsewhere in the EC. These assumptions were made to simplify the analysis. However, in order to make the calculations look more professional, they used the estimates to generate macroeconomic simulations from macrodynamic models (see Chapter 7). For this purpose, the effects of the single market were classified into four groups according to their type of macroeconomic impact:

1. The elimination of customs delays and costs.
2. The exposing of public markets to competition.
3. The liberalization and integration of financial markets.
4. Broader supply-side effects, 'reflecting changes in the strategic behaviour of enterprises in a new competitive environment' (p. 5).

The results of the simulations are then presented according to whether or not passive macroeconomic policies are pursued.

At this juncture, one needs to present the calculations and the methodologies employed in a suitable manner. Table 8.1 provides the assessment on an industry-by-industry and barrier-by-barrier basis in ECU billions. Taking the sector-by-sector analyses and a view on possible feedback, gives an estimate of the scope for gain in percentage terms; these are given in Table 8.2. These percentages then provide an input for the use of macroeconomic models, such as the EU Commission's own HERMES and the OECD's INTERLINK, to trace through the economy-wide feedback on the realization of these microeconomic effects; these are provided in Table 8.3.

Table 8.1 Estimated costs of barriers, EC 12, 1985 (billion ECU)

Barriers	
Specific barriers	
Customs formalities	8–9
Public procurement	21
In specific industries	
Food	0.5–1
Pharmaceuticals	0.3–0.6
Automobiles	2.6
Textiles and clothing	0.7–1.3
Building materials	2.8
Telecommunications	3–4.8
In specific services	
Financial services	22
Business services	3.3
Road transport	5
Air transport	3
Telecommunication services	6

Source: Adapted from various pages in Emerson *et al.* (1988)

Table 8.2 Partial equilibrium calculations of the costs of non-Europe (percentage of real GDP, EC 7, 1985)

	A	*B*
Costs of barriers affecting trade only	0.2	0.3
Costs of barriers affecting all production	2.0	2.4
Economies of scale from restructuring and increased production	2.0	2.1
Competition effects of X-inefficiency and monopoly rents	1.6	1.6
Total	5.8	6.4

Note: Variants *A* and *B* relate to the use of different primary source material.
Source: As Table 8.1.

Table 8.3 Macroeconomic consequences of completing the internal market (percentage change from base, EC 12)

	1 year	2 years	Medium term Simulation	Range
Real GDP	1.1	2.3	45.5	3.2 to 5.7
Consumer prices	−1.5	−2.4	−6.1	−4.5 to −7.7
Employment (000s)	−525.0	−35.0	1804.0	1350.0 to 2300.0

Source: As Table 8.1.

In the case of passive macroeconomic policies, the overall impact of the measures is felt most sharply in the earlier years in reduced prices and costs; but after a modest time lag output begins to increase. It is reported that the major impact is felt in the medium term (five to six years) when a cumulative impact of 4.5% increase in GDP and a 6% reduction in the price level may be expected. The effect on employment is slightly negative at the beginning, but increases by two million jobs (almost 2% of the initial level of employment) by the medium term. Moreover, there is a marked improvement in the budget balance and a significant improvement in the current account.

In the case of more active macroeconomic policies, it is argued that since the main indicators of monetary and financial equilibrium would then be improved, it would be perfectly in order to 'consider adjusting medium-term macroeconomic strategy onto a somewhat more expansionary trajectory' (p. 6). Obviously, the extent of adjustment rests upon which constraint (inflation, budget or balance of payments deficit) is considered crucial. In the text, a number of variants is illustrated. For example, in the middle of the range there is a case in which the level of GDP is 2.5% higher after the medium term. Since this is additional to the 4.5% boost obtained with passive macroeconomic policies, the total effect is therefore 7%. It is pointed out that, in this instance, inflation would still be below its projected value in the absence of the Single Market, the budget balance would also be improved and the balance of payments might be worsened by a 'moderate but sustainable amount'.

Before going further, it is important to be explicit about certain assumptions behind these estimates:

It is implicit, in order to attain the highest sustainable level of consumption and investment, that productivity and employment be also of a high order. In particular, where rationalisation efforts cause labour to be made redundant, this resource has to be successfully re-employed. Also implicit is a high rate of growth in the economy. The sustainability condition, moreover, requires that the major macroeconomic equilibrium constraints are respected, notably as regards price stability, balance of payments and budget balances. It further implies a positive performance in terms of world-wide competitivity. (Emerson *et al.*, 1988, p. 2)

Although these estimates depend largely on a number of crucial qualifications, Emerson *et al.* state that, irrespective of these qualifications, the upper limits to the gains are unlikely to be overestimates of the potential benefits of a fully integrated EC market. This is because

the figures exclude some important categories of dynamic impact on economic performance. Three examples may be mentioned. Firstly, there is increasing evidence that the trend rate of technological innovation in the economy depends upon the presence of competition; only an integrated market can offer the benefits both of scale of operation and competition. Secondly, there is evidence in fast-growing high technology industries of dynamic or learning economies of scale, whereby costs decline as the total accumulated production of certain goods and services increase[s]; market segmentation greatly limits the scope of these benefits and damages performance in key high-growth industries of the future. Thirdly, the business strategies of European enterprises are likely to be greatly affected in the event of a rapid and extensive implementation of the internal market programme; a full integration of the internal market will foster the emergence of truly European companies, with structures and strategies that are better suited to securing a strong place in world market competition. (Emerson *et al.*, 1988, pp. 6–7)

8.3.2 The Baldwin estimates

Although these expected gains have generated tremendous enthusiasm for the internal market, they are not really substantial enough to cause countries such as Japan and the United States to react in a panic so as to avoid missed opportunities. However, later estimates by Baldwin (1989) may have sown the seeds for such a response. Baldwin argues that the gains may be about five times those given in Cecchini.

Baldwin's approach differs from that of Cecchini in one significant respect. He questions Cecchini for not making an allowance for an increase in the long-term rate of growth. He contends that the methodological background to the estimates in Cecchini is based on traditional growth theory which assumes that countries become wealthier because of technological change, and that the dismantling of barriers to trade and increasing the size of markets will not permanently raise the rate of technological progress. Thus, both Cecchini and the traditional methodology are built on the premise that the liberalization of markets cannot permanently raise the rates of growth of the participating countries.

Cecchini addressed the question of how the internal market will alter the *level*, not the *rate of growth*, of output. Thus, he reached the conclusion that the creation of the internal market will squeeze more output from the same resources, for reasons such as the lower costs due to economies of scale and enhanced competition, giving the predicted benefits reported by Cecchini. Note, however, that, although these expected gains will take some time to realize, the underlying methodology envisages them as a step increase; this is depicted as line 1 in Figure 8.1.

Baldwin's claim that this approach underestimates the gains rests on two distinct arguments. The first endorses the traditional approach, but asks about what the expected rise in output will do to savings and investment. He argues that, if savings and investments stay as constant percentages of national income, they will both rise in absolute terms. Consequently, the stock of physical capital will also increase, leading to a further rise in output which will raise savings and investment again; thus a virtuous cycle will set in.

The traditionalists will challenge the assertion that this burst of faster growth will continue indefinitely. They will argue that, as the capital stock rises, a larger percentage of each year's investment will simply replace existing capital owing to depreciation. Thus the capital stock will grow at a diminishing rate and, sooner or later, investment will match depreciation, bringing to a halt any further increase in the capital stock. The economy then reaches a new equilibrium with a larger capital stock and a higher level of output than initially, but with the economy once more growing at the earlier long-term rate. Therefore, it follows that, even if there is no permanent rise in the growth rate, Cecchini must have missed this vital element: the expected rise in GDP of about 6.5–7% will raise the levels of savings and investment and increase the capital stock, making the EC grow faster while this process continues. Baldwin thinks that half of this adjustment might take about ten years. He labels this a 'medium-term growth bonus'; this is depicted by line 2 in Figure 8.1. Converting this into an equivalent change in the level of output, and relying on conservative assumptions, Baldwin concludes that the gains from the internal market will be in the region of 3.5–9%, as against the 2.5–7% predicted by Cecchini.

However, Baldwin is not content with this. He declares that the medium-term

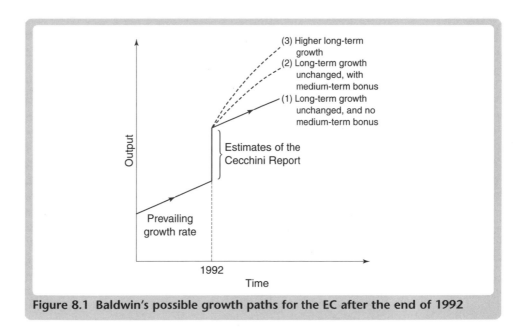

Figure 8.1 Baldwin's possible growth paths for the EC after the end of 1992

bonus may be augmented by a permanent rise in growth, giving a 'long-term growth bonus'. This is because, unlike orthodox theory (which argues that there is a 'steady state' in which the capital stock grows at the same rate as the labour force, thus with the constant labour force assumed by Cecchini there will be a constant capital stock), he follows the model proposed by Romer (Chicago University) which is built on the premise that the capital stock can rise indefinitely. This leads him to believe that the increase in EC investment after 1992 will raise the growth rate for the EC permanently by something in the range of a quarter to three-quarters of a percentage point; this is depicted by line 3 in Figure 8.1. Expressed as an equivalent increase in the level of output, the total bonus (the combined bonuses from the medium and long terms) would be about 9–29% of GDP. Adding this estimate to that by Cecchini, one gets an overall figure of 11–35% increase in GDP.

The Baldwin estimates, taken at face value, should have made any non-EC country think hard about its strategy for such an expanded and more competitive EC market. Japan, which was being, and continues to be, increasingly asked by the United States to open its markets more, was even more concerned; hence it decided to enhance its investments there and in Eastern Europe (see Chapter 21).

8.4   Theoretical illustration

Before stating explicit reservations, it may be useful to provide some theoretical framework for some of the stated gains. Let us consider two cases. The first is one in which comparative advantage can be exploited by trade. The second concerns the case of enhanced competition where there is no comparative advantage between countries. The basic model behind the diagrams used below is fully set out in Chapter 5 and in standard trade theory books – see El-Agraa (1989b). No explanation will therefore be provided here.

The first case is illustrated by Figure 8.2. Because of the removal of certain market

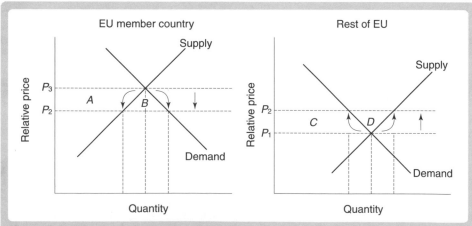

Figure 8.2 Effects of eliminating market barriers and the distortions for a given commodity (the case in which comparative advantage can be exploited by trade)

Source: Emerson *et al.* (1988), adapted.

barriers and distortions, the relative price of a particular commodity is equalized throughout the entire EU market at the lower P_2 in the EU member country under consideration. As we have seen, this is because it is assumed that the presence of these barriers is costly, leading to the higher price level P_3 in that country. Since this country is a net importer from the rest of the EU, comparative advantage lies with the EU or, alternatively, this country has a comparative disadvantage.

In this member country, the removal of the barrier increases consumer surplus by areas A and B and reduces producer surplus by area A, giving a net benefit of area B. In the rest of the EU, there is an increase in producer surplus of areas C and D and a reduction in consumer surplus of area C, resulting in a net benefit of area D. Therefore, the total benefit to the EU as a whole is the sum of the two net benefits, i.e. areas B plus D. In short, the analysis in the case of the member country is the reverse of the one for tariffs considered in Chapter 11, while the analysis for the rest of the EU is exactly the same as that in the same chapter applied to agricultural surpluses.

The second case is illustrated by Figure 8.3. As barriers are removed, importers are able to reduce their prices from P_2 by the amount of direct costs saved. Domestic producers respond by reducing their own prices through reductions in their excess profits and wages or by eliminating inefficiencies of various types (overhead costs, excess manning and inventories, etc.). As prices fall, demand increases beyond Q_1

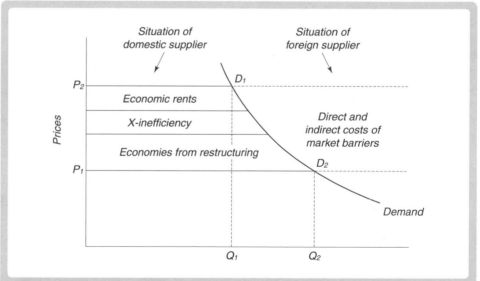

Figure 8.3 Effects of eliminating cost-increasing trade barriers (the case of enhanced competition where are no comparative advantages between countries)

Note: Economic rents consist of the margins of excess profit or wage rates that result from market protection. X-inefficiency consists of, for example, the costs of overmanning, excess overhead costs and excess inventories (i.e. inefficiencies not related to the production technology of the firm's investments). Economies of restructuring include, for example, the greater economies of scale or scope obtained when inefficient production capacity is eliminated and new investments are made. Direct costs are those, such as delays at frontiers and the cost of differing technical regulations, that would immediately fall if the market barriers were eliminated. Indirect costs are those that would fall as foreign suppliers adjust to the more competitive situation with more efficient production and marketing.

Source: Emerson *et al.* (1988), adapted.

and this induces investment in productive capacity in this industry which results in economies of scale and further price reductions. However, this is not the end of the story since this more competitive market environment is supposed to make industries reconsider their business strategies in a fundamental way, leading to restructuring (mergers and acquisitions, liquidations and investment) over a number of years until output increases to Q_2.

As can be seen from Figure 8.3, there is an increase in consumer surplus equal to area $P_2D_1D_2P_1$, but what happens to producer surplus is not so clear. On the one hand, producers may be able to compensate for price cuts in terms of cost reductions; but they will lose some economic rent. On the other hand, since they have become more competitive, they may be able to sell outside the EU and so increase their output and profits. For the EU economy as a whole, it can be said that there is a net benefit since the gains to the EU consumer are in excess of the losses incurred by the EU producers. However, in the light of the discussion in Chapter 5, it must be emphasized that this analysis is extremely simple.

8.5   Reservations

There are two reservations to consider. The first is advanced by Pelkmans and Robson (1987). It is that the categorization by the EU of these three types of barrier is somewhat arbitrary. Physical barriers are concerned with frontier controls on the movement of goods and persons. Fiscal barriers consist of all impediments and substantial distortions among member states that emanate from differences in the commodity base as well as in the rates of VAT and the duties on excises (see Chapter 15). All remaining impediments fall into the category of technical barriers. Therefore, this category includes not only barriers arising from absence of technical harmonization and public procurement procedures, but also institutional impediments on the free movement of people, capital and financial services, including transport and data transmission. It also includes a miscellaneous collection of obstacles to the business environment which take the form of inadequately harmonized company law and the lack of an EU patent and of an EU trade mark, together with issues of corporate taxation and several diverse problems concerned with the national application of EU law. However, even though this categorization may make analysis more cumbersome, the approach adopted in this book shows that this is not a serious reservation.

The second reservation is more serious. It is that the estimates given in the Cecchini Report should not be taken at face value. First, in spite of the endorsement of the SEA by all the member nations, there does not seem to be a philosophy common to all of them to underpin the internal market. Second, these estimates do not take into consideration the costs to be incurred by firms, regions and governments in achieving them. Third, the internal market aims at the elimination of internal barriers to promote the efficient restructuring of supply, but it remains silent on the question of demand; thus the internal market seems to be directed mainly at the production side. Fourth, putting too much emphasis on economies of scale, when their very existence has to be proved, will encourage concentration rather than competition, and there is no evidence to support the proposition that there is a positive correlation between increased firm size and competitive success. Finally, the estimates are for the EU as a whole; thus it is likely that each member nation will strive to get the maximum gain for itself with detrimental consequences for all, i.e. this is like the classical oligopoly problem where the best solution for profit-maximization purposes is for oligopolists to behave as joint monopolists, but if each oligopolist firm tries to maximize its own share of the joint profit, the outcome may be losses all round.

Since Baldwin's estimates start from Cecchini's, these reservations apply equally to them. Moreover, not many development economists, or, for that matter, any economist, will endorse the concept of an indefinitely rising capital stock, especially when the doctrine of steady growth is built on an elegant mathematical structure, but the new theory leaves a lot to be desired in this respect. Of course, this is not meant to suggest that mathematical elegance is all that is needed in economics, rather either that some theoretical justification should be provided or that a solid and indisputable empirical foundation should be advanced.

A rigorous specification of these reservations is fully set out in Chapters 5 and 6 of this book and in El-Agraa (1989a). In the fourth edition of this book, I added that here

> it is sufficient to state that such potential benefits may prove rather elusive since the creation of the appropriate environment does not guarantee the expected outcomes. However, this does not mean that the EC should not be congratulated for its genuine attempts to create the necessary competitive atmosphere, only that one should not put too much emphasis on estimates which can easily be frustrated by the realities of everyday EC economic life. However, some of the quotations given above clearly show that the experts are aware of these problems.

The part of that statement relating to the benefits expected from the internal market remains true at the time of writing.

8.6 Conclusion

The conclusion is evident: the EU has been successful not only in achieving *negative integration* (see Chapter 1), but also in adopting elements of *positive integration*. Because in the latter progress has been slow, the EU has set itself an extensive programme, with deadlines, for accomplishing a true internal market and an EMU. Only history can tell whether or not the EU has been unduly optimistic, but in terms of the philosophy of the founding fathers it could be argued that the EU is at last on target. As to the future, only politics can help, which is why it is left to the final chapter.

PART THREE

Major EU policies

Part Two of this book was devoted to the theoretical and empirical aspects of the common market elements of the EU and to an analysis of European monetary integration. Part Three provides an extensive discussion of virtually all the major policies of the EU.

9 Competition policy

W. SAUTER

9.1 Introduction

The main purpose of competition policy is generally seen as protecting the market mechanism from breaking down by promoting competitive market structures and policing anti-competitive behaviour, thereby enhancing both the efficiency of the economy as a whole and consumer welfare. In the EU this objective is pursued by means of enforcing prohibitions against anti-competitive agreements between different companies, as well as against anti-competitive behaviour by companies that are large enough – either individually or jointly – to harm competition, and by vetting mergers between companies to verify whether these are likely to result in non-competitive market structures. These are features that the EU shares with numerous countries, including all EU member states that have implemented national competition policies.

However, EU competition policy has three important characteristics that are not commonly found elsewhere. First, it aims to promote and protect market integration between the member states of the EU. Second, apart from addressing private distortions of competition, it also curbs distortions of the market process by these member states. Both result from the third distinguishing feature of EU competition policy: it is implemented in a multi-level political system, that of the European Union and its member states. In this context, it is worth noting that although until recently the application of the EU competition rules was highly centralized in the hands of the European Commission, this is about to change. All these aspects are examined further below.

This chapter first discusses in greater detail the rationale for competition policy generally, and of EU competition policy in particular. Next, it sets out the basic instruments of the EU competition policy, its rules and procedures, and the manner in which they are implemented. Finally, three important shifts in EU competition policy are addressed: the focus on public intervention; its shift to a more economic approach; and, most recently, toward decentralisation.

9.2 The rationale for EU competition policy

The reasons for introducing competition rules have varied, both between different jurisdictions, and over time. Although it is possible to draw up a long pedigree for competition law by pointing to Roman law, the Magna Carta, common law or the statutes of medieval city states, the first set of competition rules that are clearly related to the EU rules is contained in the US Sherman Act (1890). They were adopted as the result of political concern over the railroad, oil and financial 'trusts' emerging in the United States at the end of the nineteenth century, an economic concentration of power that threatened to upset the popular consensus underpinning its economic as well as its political system. In various European countries from the early twentieth century onward, national competition rules typically sought to balance the perceived benefits of economic collaboration between undertakings – cartels – against their acknowledged political and economic dangers (Gerber, 1998). Such competition policies often sought to provide protection against the socially and therefore politically undesirable results of 'unfair' competition, and aimed to ensure the survival of established undertakings by foreclosing markets from unregulated entry. In some cases, the legislation concerned enabled public authorities to impose the terms of existing private cartel agreements on entire economic sectors, as an alternative for state-designed market regulation, e.g. in the interest of price control. Both in Germany and Japan after the Second World War, the allied occupation forces imposed new anti-monopoly legislation to curb the power of the financial-industrial combines that were widely seen as having powered the war effort of these two countries. For similar reasons antitrust provisions were introduced into the 1954 Paris Treaty on Coal and Steel (ECSC), that consequently, unlike the EC Treaty, included control of concentrations from the outset.

For the European Community beyond coal and steel, competition rules were introduced in the 1957 EEC Treaty, albeit for a different reason. In this case, the competition rules served mainly to ensure that restrictions on trade between member states – tariff and non-tariff barriers – that the member states' governments agreed to remove under this Treaty, would not be replaced by cartels between undertakings following national lines (Goyder, 1999). Hence, remarkably, competition rules addressed to undertakings were introduced into what at the time of its conclusion was otherwise still widely seen as an international Treaty between, and addressed to, independent states.

Initially, therefore, the EU competition rules essentially served to complement an inter-state trade policy of reducing trade barriers and market integration. From this starting-point, promoting market integration has developed into the overriding rationale of EU competition policy, alongside that of maintaining 'effective competition' (Bishop and Walker, 1999). This integration rationale has had a profound impact on the orientation of EU competition policy that has at times led it into conflict with the developing economic consensus. For example, the integration rationale has long militated against vertical agreements with territorial effects.

In spite of these varied origins, and while it is difficult to find a case where pure economic reasoning motivated the introduction of competition rules, the rationale of competition policy is increasingly defined in economic terms. Evidently, the relevant economic theory has evolved over time as well.

The economic reasoning concerning the goals and limits of competition policy has been developed in particular in the United States, where an early willingness of courts to entertain economic arguments was subsequently stimulated by the appointment of law and economics scholars to the bench and to influential regulatory positions alike (including, for example, justices Easterbrook and Posner). Over the past century, the resulting debate has had a profound impact on the way competition policy is applied both in the USA and beyond. Originally, competition policy focused on the results of market structure and the behaviour of market participants associated with the earlier 'Harvard School'. Increasingly, the so-called Chicago School of antitrust economics, focusing on efficiency, price effects, and the self-policing nature of the market (Posner, 1976), has become the new mainstream of industrial organization, and hence of much analysis underlying competition policy (Scherer and Ross, 1990). In addition, game theoretic approaches are increasingly used to deal with, for example, problems of collusion and joint dominance in oligopolistic markets (Philips, 1995). EU competition policy has followed these trends to varying degree, modified in particular by the intervening variable of its overriding integration objective (Mehta and Peeperkorn, 1999).

Today, the market is generally seen as the most efficient instrument to allocate resources and set prices. To a large extent, however, the success of markets in doing this is determined by the degree of competition in the market involved. Economists have traditionally illustrated this argument by analysing 'ideal types' of the two theoretical extremes: contrasting, on the one hand, the maximum imaginable number of competitors in a given market, and, on the other hand, the least possible number. 'Perfect competition' in fully contestable markets can be demonstrated to lead to Pareto-optimal, or maximal allocative efficiency: a situation in which the welfare of any single participant cannot be increased without another participant being disproportionately worse off. Conversely, monopoly markets can be demonstrated to lead to monopoly rents and net welfare losses, further aggravated by technical developments and efficiencies forgone, and further losses caused by attempts to lock in monopoly advantage by political 'rent seeking'. However, 'perfect competition', which presupposes homogeneous products, and full transparency of prices and costs, as well as the absence of market barriers, economies of scale and scope, and learning effects, is not a real-world phenomenon. Instead, market imperfections, or market failures, are likely to lead to restrictions of competition that produce sub-optimal results. Consequently, the role of competition policy is to substitute for competitive pressure by ensuring that restrictions on competition between undertakings that are harmful to the competitive process (rather than to individual competitors) are prevented or removed.

Because market outcomes are likely to be theoretically sub-optimal in many cases, this leaves ample room for different views on what amounts to a restriction of competition that merits policy intervention. For example, views vary on whether vertical restraints, pricing below cost, or even the effects of mergers on market structure and degree of concentration as such – the number of firms present, and their relative size – form appropriate targets of competition policy.

In the context of EU competition policy, the key concept in this regard is that of maintaining 'effective competition' or 'workable competition': here again there is debate about whether that concerns the process of competition as such, or the outcome that markets produce in terms of improving consumer welfare – generally equated with efficiency. In any event, it is by now well established that effective competition is seen in terms of preventing harm to competition as such, not to particular competitors (Bishop and Walker, 1999). The determination of whether there is effective competition has to be made in a specific 'relevant market', defined both in terms of the product concerned, and geographically. Factors taken into account such as the existence of market power, the number of competitors, relative market share and degree of concentration, demand and supply substitution, the existence of barriers to market entry and exit, and potential competition, affect both the evaluation of the degree of effective competition in the relevant market and market definition itself (CEU, 1997j).

The result is an approach that considers both market structure and the efficiency of market outcomes, although the emphasis assigned between these two may be shifting, as is emphasized in particular by the new policy on vertical restraints that emerged in recent years (CEU, 1996v; 1997b).

9.3 Legal framework

Although EU competition policy is increasingly driven by economic considerations, its origins are found in law, and it must evidently operate within the constraints of its legal framework. This legal framework consists of the substantive, procedural and institutional rules that govern EU competition policy (see Chapter 3).

The legal basis of EU competition policy is found, first of all, in the EU Treaty itself (Articles 3, 10, 81–6 and 87–9). Second, it is found in implementing legislation adopted by the Council and Commission in the form of Regulations and Directives, which develop in particular the wide-ranging powers of the European Commission in this field (notably, Council Regulations 17 of 1962, and 19 of 1965). The much more recent Council Regulation 4064 of 1989 provides the framework for merger control by the Commission (European Council, 1989, 1997). In addition, an increasing number of notices and guidelines that are not formally binding provide essential information on the manner in which the Commission intends to apply EU competition policy. An example is the Commission notice on the definition of the relevant market referred to above (CEU, 1997j). By issuing such guidance both on how it interprets the binding rules of EU law, and on how it intends to use the margin of discretion inherent in its policy powers, the Commission increases the predictability of its policy – and thereby facilitates the enforcement of EU competition law between private parties and at national level.

The ultimate arbiter of the various rules, and on whether Commission policy remains within the bound of its powers, is the European Court of Justice (ECJ). The ECJ is seized either directly on a 'pre-judicial' reference by a national court, or in judicial review proceedings following a first appeal against Commission Decisions to the EU's Court of First Instance (CFI). In principle, the standards applied are those of administrative review of policy: i.e., they focus on formal competence to act and enforcing minimum standards of reasoned rationality. Remarkably for a judicial institution, the ECJ has, nevertheless, on a number of occasions led the way in demanding higher standards of economic argument, rather than more formal reasoning, from the Commission (Korah, 1997b).

The institution that is responsible at EU level for the implementation of EU competition law and policy is the European Commission, which takes most formal decisions by simple majority, as a collegiate body. These decisions are prepared by the Directorate General for Competition, DG COMP (formerly known as DG IV), which reports to the commissioner responsible for competition policy, since September 1999 Mr Mario Monti. Competition commissioners have usually lasted more than a single four-year term and carried considerable clout within their respective Commissions, adding to the stature of the office. The Commission can be seized of a competition problem by notification, following a complaint by an undertaking or member state, and act on its own initiative ('ex officio') to investigate either specific cases, or entire economic sectors ('sector inquiries'). It has considerable powers to require undertakings to collaborate in its investigations, backed up by fines, including the right to obtain evidence by unannounced inspections of company offices ('dawn raids'). In addition, the Commission can penalize all infringements of the competition rules, including the cartel prohibition, with significant financial penalties, including fines of up to 10% of the (global) group turnover of the companies involved, without any absolute upper limit. Fines of well over a hundred million Euros have already been imposed in a number of cases.

Apart from the Commission, most national competition authorities in the member states now have powers to apply the EU rules, although the equivalent national rules may give them broader policy-making powers, do not require an effect on trade between the member states and are therefore often likely to remain their instruments of choice, where such a choice exists. Under the recent proposals for decentralization however, the importance of the national competition authorities' role in enforcing the EU competition rules is scheduled to increase significantly.

Finally, because the Treaty prohibitions on restrictions of competition are directly effective, parties may choose to invoke these rules in procedures before national courts of all levels in the EU member states. This in turn gives rise to requests by such national courts for the pre-judicial rulings on points of law by the ECJ that are an important mechanism to ensure the coherent application of EU competition law and policy.

There are three core substantive norms of EU competition law that are addressed to undertakings: the prohibition of agreements and concerted practices between firms restricting competition; the prohibition of abuse of (single firm or joint) dominance; and the obligation to submit mergers and acquisitions for prior clearance under the merger control rules. In addition there are specific competition rules that apply to aid by the member states, and to companies privileged in their relation to public authority.

The prohibition of collusion restricting competition (cartels) is found in Article 81(1) EC. Prohibited cartel agreements cover, e.g., market sharing, price fixing, tying, and discrimination. By force of Article 81(2), infringement of the prohibition of Article 81(1) triggers the nullity of the restrictive clauses of the agreements involved, which can lead to civil law liability and hence claims for damages under national law. As mentioned, the Commission can in addition penalize infringements by means of fines. Article 81(3), however, provides for the possibility of exemptions from the Article 81(1) prohibition. Exemptions are given for a limited period of time and may be subject to conditions and reporting requirements. Under the present system of Council Regulation 17/62, such exemptions can only be awarded by the Commission, and only following mandatory notification of the agreements involved to the Commission. The reform of this highly centralized system is the focus of the Commission's pending modernization proposals (CEU, 1999j).

The prohibition of abuses of dominant position (monopolies and oligopolies) in Article 82 EC focuses on the abusive anti-competitive behaviour associated with market power rather than on the acquisition of high market shares as such. Although therefore it is not illegal to be dominant, provided dominance is achieved based on legitimate commercial advantage won in the market, there are evidently no exemptions for abuse of such dominance. Like the restrictions of competition covered by the cartel prohibition, possible abuses of dominance include unfair (e.g. excessive or predatory) pricing, discrimination and tying. However, unlike the cartel prohibition, which in principle applies to all undertakings, the prohibition of abuse of dominance is asymmetrical in nature: it only applies to those firms that can afford to behave – and price – independently of their competitors, suppliers and customers. The prohibition on abuse of dominance is intended to force such firms to behave as if they were subject to effective competition by abstaining from anti-competitive behaviour. In order to establish an Article 82 infringement, first the relevant (product and geographic) market must be established, second, the existence of dominance in that relevant market, and finally, the existence of an abuse must be shown, as well as an effect on trade between member states. It would be possible to examine mergers under Article 82, as they may affect the market structure in a manner constituting abuse. However, it is generally not attractive to do so, as remedies following the consumption of a merger, such as the forced divestiture of assets, are likely to be highly burdensome on the undertakings involved. Moreover, merger control by means of Article 82 is not systematic, is therefore unpredictable, and is at odds with legal certainty. These drawbacks have stimulated the introduction of a separate system of prior merger control.

Unlike the prohibitions on cartels and abuse of dominance, which are normally enforced after the alleged infringement occurs (or *ex post*), EU merger control is based on a system of pre-notification (or *ex ante* control) that is elaborated in the Merger Control Regulation. This system is intended to provide legal certainty to firms before they consume their transaction, and to allow the Commission to vet all such transactions of a certain size (or Community dimension), based on a complex system of turnover thresholds. Merger control aims at preserving 'effective' or workable competition, based on an assessment of the structural characteristics of the relevant product and geographical markets. The relevant test is whether a merger is likely to create or strengthen a dominant position as a result of which effective competition in the internal market would be significantly impeded. As elsewhere in EU competition policy, market definitions are essential here: if wide product and geographical market definitions are used, mergers are evidently less likely to be considered problematic than if narrower markets are concerned: size, and the effects of size, are relative to a specific factual context. In principle, mergers are considered useful to allow undertakings to realize potential efficiencies of scale and scope in contestable markets. Mergers cannot normally be executed until they have been formally approved. Such approval may be given subject to structural remedies (e.g. divestiture), and frequently is. In addition, behavioural remedies are sometimes considered (Jones and Gonzalez-Diaz, 1992).

The EU was long denied merger policy powers, as its member states preferred to vet themselves (or indeed promote) the creation of national 'industrial champions', in particular in a wide and often ill-defined set of industries considered to be of strategic or political importance. The failure of such mutually exclusive national strategies, the increasing desire of businesses to merge across national borders without engaging in multiple notifications subject to different rules, and the merger boom triggered by the 1985 internal market initiative, were all instrumental in finally convincing the member states to adopt the Merger Control Regulation in 1989 (Neven, Nutall and Seabright, 1993). Since then, merger control has become widely acclaimed as a model for EU competition policy generally. The main reasons for this success are strict rules and deadlines that force the Commission to produce binding decisions within a limited time-frame, and undertakings to collaborate fully in the process of reaching these decisions. The scope of Community competence in this area – determined by the thresholds in the Regulation – remains politically sensitive: the member states are reluctant to agree to extending it further. In 1997, the Merger Control Regulation was nevertheless amended to lower the turnover thresholds above which it applies, bringing a larger number of mergers within its scope, and to apply to co-operative joint ventures (European Council, 1997). In the case of co-operative joint ventures, the Article 81(3) test is applied to decide whether they are likely to give rise to unacceptable anti-competitive economic effects, in particular in adjacent upstream or downstream markets where both parents remain present.

In addition to the rules that apply to undertakings in general, the EU Treaty includes specific provisions governing the application of competition rules for undertakings that are controlled, favoured or charged with executing key economic tasks by public authorities.

Article 86 EC provides rules concerning state-owned undertakings, undertakings that benefit from certain legal advantages assigned in an arbitrary manner or from legal monopoly rights and undertakings charged with tasks in the general economic interest, such as utilities (e.g. in the energy, transport and communications sectors). Article 86 states that, in principle, the competition rules apply to such companies without limitation, unless this makes it impossible for undertakings charged with services in the general economic interest to carry out their tasks. The Commission can address secondary rules based on Article 86 to undertakings as well as member states. Exceptionally, it does not require permission from the European Parliament or the Council to adopt such rules. The importance of Article 86, long a dormant provision of the Treaty, has increased markedly since 1988, when it was applied to the telecommunications sector. This is because 'natural monopoly' arguments long held to apply to public utilities have become contested, and public ownership is increasingly unpopular. Consequently, the application of the competition rules has worked in favour of the spread of independent private enterprise in sectors traditionally controlled by the state. The Treaty itself, however, remains formally neutral concerning public and private ownership, by force of its Article 222.

Finally, in its Articles 87–9, the Treaty contains rules on restrictions of effective competition that result from member states' authorities at any level favouring some companies over others by means of subsidies: state aid (Hancher, Ottervanger and Slot, 1999; see also Chapter 10). Illegal state aid covers subsidies in any form, including outright financial subsidies as well as tax advantages or exceptions, favourable loan terms, credit guarantees, the sale or lease of goods and real estate below market prices, and many other forms of discrimination that may occur between undertakings by public authorities. Some types of state aid are, however, acceptable. Hence, state aid is governed by a rule in Article 87(1) prohibiting aid that distorts competition, and two possible exceptions to this rule: first, aid that is by definition considered compatible with the internal market, as listed in Article 87(2) (e.g. social aid to consumers and disaster relief); and, second, aid that the Commission may clear by decision, following mandatory notification, as listed in Article 87(3) (e.g. certain regional and sectoral aid). Commission findings of illegal aid can in theory be overruled by the Council, although in practice this rarely occurs (Ehlermann, 1995). Although they are also applied by DG COMP, the state aid rules constitute a separate system under which the Commission is attributed powers that are considerably less significant than those it enjoys in relation to private undertakings, in particular because the Council was long unable to agree on any secondary implementing legislation for state aid. As will be discussed below, this has changed over recent years.

Whether directed at private undertakings or member states, the EU competition norms are triggered only if constraints on competition both are appreciable, and have the effect of restraining trade between the member states (CEU, 1997k). This is consistent with the integration rationale of EU competition policy: unless they obstruct trade flows, restrictions of competition do not hamper integration, and consequently do not concern the EU. However, the integration rationale also means that certain types of territorial protection are prohibited that might not otherwise be objectionable from an economic perspective, if they have the effect of reinforcing trade barriers along national lines. This still leaves EU competition policy a broad scope, which has often made it difficult to enforce effectively.

9.4   Enforcement

The Commission's relatively limited human resources have long been dedicated largely to the enforcement of the cartel prohibition contained in Article 81 (although, more recently, the relative weight of state aid policy has increased). This is the result of interrelated systemic, political and practical constraints.

Article 82 decisions are relatively rare, in large part due to the high burden of proof the European Courts have imposed on the Commission, given the inherently intrusive nature of this prohibition, which bars individual behaviour by companies based on their size, that would otherwise be acceptable business practice. A clear indication of the difficulties involved is that over the period of almost 40 years that the Commission has actively applied the competition rules, it has adopted only 39 such decisions: evidently, it is likely that in reality over this period significantly higher numbers of grave abuses of dominance occurred. Due to political resistance, cases involving public authorities (including state aid) and public undertakings have also traditionally been difficult to pursue. The manner in which the system of Article 81 is implemented, on the other hand, is clearly biased in favour of attracting cases to the Commission.

Article 81(1) EC prohibits agreements and parallel behaviour that restrict or distort competition within the common market. However, it is not always clear whether restrictions capable of affecting trade are involved, and in any event the benefits of such restrictions may be more significant than their negative effects. In practice, there are therefore many agreements, which are on their face restrictive, that ought not to be prohibited, and are not. Because under Article 81(2) EC agreements that infringe the prohibition of Article 81(1) EC are automatically void, undertakings require assurances that their prospective agreements are not caught by this prohibition. However, because under the key implementing Regulation 17/62 only the Commission can provide exemptions of the prohibition on policy grounds and, because notification to the Commission of the agreements involved is a precondition for obtaining an exemption, this has resulted in a flood of thousands of notifications from the first day this system entered into force. Due to the capacity constraints imposed on DG COMP (even today, a total of only about 150 'A-grade' Commission officials is responsible for dealing with the enforcement of the rules on merger control, cartel infringements and dominance abuse), a timely handling of all of these notifications has eluded the Commission from the outset. Moreover, the purpose of this system is by no means self-evident in terms of measurable results: harmful cartels are rarely caught in this manner, as clearly illegal cartels are more likely to be carefully kept secret, than notified. In over 35 years, the Commission has adopted only nine decisions prohibiting cartel infringements based on notified agreements, without in addition a complaint having been lodged against them (CEU, 1999j).

Over time, the Commission has developed a number of different ways of dealing with this problem. These solutions share the common feature of increasing reliance on instruments that allow the Commission to provide collective, rather than individual, clearances and exemptions, and to employ informal administrative solutions, rather than fully reasoned formal decisions that are subject to judicial appeal. Both the instruments defined by the Treaty and those developed under secondary legislation or in administrative practice are categorized as based either on clearances, or on exemptions.

Clearances concern cases in which the Commission considers that an agreement does not restrict competition or does not affect trade between the member states, and is therefore not caught by the prohibition of Article 81(1). They are rarely awarded on a formal basis: when addressed to individual undertakings, clearances are usually based on informal administrative letters instead (in fact, over 90% of all notifications are closed informally, including informal clearances and informal exemptions). The most important instrument providing a collective negative clearance is the *de minimis* notice, concerning agreements of minor importance: i.e., with negligible effects on trade between the member states or on competition (CEU, 1997k). This concerns primarily agreements between small and medium-sized enterprises (SMEs) with an aggregate turnover below 300 million Euro, that do not affect goods and services representing more than 5% of the relevant market, where the agreement is made between undertakings operating at the same level of production or of marketing (i.e. a 'horizontal' agreement); or 10% of the relevant market, where the agreement is made between undertakings operating at different economic levels (a 'vertical' agreement). In such cases restrictions of competition between the undertakings involved are assumed sufficiently unlikely to result in uncompetitive markets to merit a contestable presumption of legality.

Aside from agreements covered by the *de minimis* notice, few agreements benefit from a negative clearance, largely because the Commission has traditionally preferred to perform its antitrust analysis under Article 81(3) EC. This approach has been consistently criticized by advocates of a 'rule of reason' approach under Article 81(1). Under Article 81(3), an agreement that is in principle prohibited under Article 81(1) may, if its effects are on balance considered beneficial to competition, obtain a waiver, or 'exemption' from this prohibition. Such waivers or exemptions can be subject to structural and behavioural conditions, and are limited in time. They include the following categories :

- formal individual exemption decisions under Article 81(3) EC;
- informal individual exemptions by means of administrative 'comfort letters';
- general block exemptions covering certain types of agreements found across

different sectors (concerning exclusive distribution, exclusive purchasing, franchising, specialization, technology transfer and R&D agreements);

● sector-specific block exemptions for agreements prevalent in particular sectors (e.g. air and sea transport, insurance, motor vehicle and beer distribution).

In order to be eligible for an exemption, agreements must make a contribution to production, distribution or technical or economic progress, and allow consumers to share the resulting benefits (generally seen in terms of price and availability of new products). Moreover, the particular restraints of competition involved must be indispensable for achieving these benefits, and may not eliminate competition completely, for example by foreclosing market entry. In determining whether any competition remains, 'potential competitors', and hence barriers to entry, are taken into account.

Formal individual exemptions are relatively rare because the Commission is not required to respond to a notification within a specific deadline, and because due to its limited resources in any event it could not in this way address the numerous agreements that might qualify. Instead, alongside the issuing of administrative 'comfort letters', reliance on the block exemptions has become the main solution to the problem of obtaining legal certainty for businesses, and to the problem of overwhelming numbers of notifications for the Commission. The system of block exemptions allows large numbers of agreements to be cleared, based on 'white' lists of admissible restrictions and 'black' lists of strictly prohibited restrictions: if agreements contain only white-listed restrictions and no black-listed ones, they need not be notified. This has the disadvantage that businesses must design their agreements to fit the template of an individual block exemption (as the benefits of several block exemptions cannot be applied to a single agreement), leading to a 'strait-jacket effect' that is unlikely always to coincide with the optimal business case. Similarly, undertakings will often seek to structure transactions so as to fall within the merger control regime, which provides the certainty of obtaining decisions within strict deadlines. This in turn has added to the rapidly growing merger caseload, in effect shifting rather than resolving at least part of the notification problem.

Its monopoly on exemptions from the cartel prohibition gives the Commission sole control of key levers of competition policy. Although the direct effect of the EU competition prohibitions means that undertakings and individuals can invoke these norms in legal proceedings before national courts, the possibility that the Commission may still act to exempt the agreements involved ties the hands of the national authorities involved. The resulting centralization of EU competition law enforcement in the hands of the Commission has considerable benefits in terms of consistency and credibility, and was probably indispensable in order to allow a full-fledged EU competition policy to develop. With few exceptions (notably Germany), in the EU a true competition policy was long pursued only at Community level, and even there it was constructed step by step.

Over recent years, however, this situation has changed fundamentally. All member states now accept, at least in principle, that state intervention and tolerance or promotion of private cartel arrangements cannot efficiently substitute for the market allocation of resources. Hence, in a process of 'spontaneous harmonization' most member states have adopted national competition rules based on the EU model, and work toward their increasingly effective enforcement. At the same time, it is clear that in order to advance the development of competition policy further, the Commission would have to focus on new problems such as those which arise in recently liberalized markets, in oligopolistic markets and in markets that extend beyond the EU. Likewise, to ensure proactive enforcement, it would have to focus more on complaints, and on (time-consuming) own-initiative action to pursue the gravest cartels and dominance abuses. This means that many of the initial arguments to concentrate policy competence at EU level in the hands of the Commission no longer hold, or at least no longer outweigh the negative effects of centralization, given the capacity constraints as sketched above.

Hence, at the time of writing, the centralization resulting from the Article 81(3) EC notification and exemption system is subject to fundamental review. In addition, the Commission is in the process of rationalizing its existing Article 85(3) practice by streamlining and consolidating its block exemptions, and by moving toward an approach that relies more on economic insights, in particular in the area of vertical restraints. Already at an earlier stage, following the momentum generated by the internal market programme, the Commission had started focusing its competition policy more on public undertakings and state intervention. These three developments are each in turn discussed below, in rough chronological order.

9.5   The public turn

During the first three decades of its competition policy, the Commission focused on the basic task of enforcing the Article 81 EC and Article 82 EC prohibitions against private undertakings. This required it to elaborate implementing rules (the procedural Regulations and group exemption Regulations discussed above) and to develop its practice concerning a range of standard competition policy problems in this area. After consolidating this part of its competencies, the Commission started expanding the scope of its enforcement efforts to cover the politically more delicate areas of the public sector and state aid over the course of the 1980s and 1990s. This trend has been defined as the 'public turn' of EU competition law (Gerber, 1998).

In the first place, the Commission has begun more active enforcement of the competition rules against public undertakings, and undertakings that enjoy special and exclusive rights, such as legal monopolies, and licences or concessions limited in number and awarded on discretionary grounds. In doing so, it had begun to address not only the undertakings benefiting from such privileges, but also the member states responsible for awarding them. In some previously sheltered sectors, notably that of telecommunications, the Commission actually abolished such exclusive and special rights by means of competition law Directives. In a number of other sectors concerned, such as posts, energy and transport, it relied more heavily on Treaty infringement actions and sector-specific harmonization legislation adopted by the Council and European Parliament, albeit inspired by the drive to create competitive conditions, and fuelled by (potential) competitors' complaints under the competition rules. Once statutory prerogatives are removed, the competition rules come to play a key role in ensuring the markets involved are contestable. This means that, although significant differences in the degree to which they are subject to effective competition are likely to persist for some time, there are no longer any economic sectors that are immune from the competition rules.

The Commission's policy on state aid has matured, in particular following the completion of the internal market programme (Ehlermann, 1995). This policy has included: targeting aid to public enterprises; the elaboration of the 'market investor test', which means aid is not acceptable unless private investors might have taken similar investment decisions; and enforcing the repayment of illegal aid. At the same time, the conviction that state control over the economy is inversely related to its performance is now widely shared by policy makers at national level. This realization has been reinforced by the move to Economic and Monetary Union (EMU), which imposes budgetary constraints that make member states reluctant to expose themselves to the significant potential liabilities represented by public investment that is not guided by efficiency considerations, and indeed by public ownership as such (Devroe, 1997).

An indication of the fundamental change in the attitude of the member states is that the Council has at last, and for the first time, introduced secondary legislation implementing the state aid provisions of the Treaty. In the past few years it adopted both a Regulation concerning the conditions under which horizontal state aid may be acceptable (European Council, 1998), and a Regulation concerning procedural rules for state aid (European Council, 1999a) that also delegates new rule-making powers to the Commission. These implementation measures not only provide the Commission with improved enforcement instruments, but also increase the transparency of state aid policy, and therefore offer greater legal certainty to undertakings and national authorities.

Although the developments that constitute the 'public turn' of EU competition policy can certainly also be seen as a form of modernization and rationalization, they still remain distinct from the changes to its traditional core, antitrust enforcement (discussed below). In the utilities sectors, where traditional monopoly markets must be opened up to competitive entry, sector specific competition rules enforced by independent sector-regulators will continue to play an important role at least in the medium term, when application of the general (or horizontal) competition rules may suffice. Meanwhile, the existence of such sector-specific national regulators helps to relieve the burden on the competition services of the Commission, and to spread an understanding of how the process of competition may be protected in technically often highly complex fields, such as telecommunications. A similar phasing out of the rules on state aid is of course not contemplated, as the need to distinguish legitimate public measures from illegal aid will persist as long as public authorities are tempted to interfere in markets. Moreover, because, unlike the antitrust provisions, the state aid rules are by definition not suited to decentralized application, and no such rules exist at national level, they must be enforced in a centralized manner.

Hence, there is a clear case for the Commission services to focus on state aid, mergers and other cases with a significant Community interest due to the size, trans-national nature and precedent value of the problems involved, while leaving the large majority of competition cases to national competition authorities and, at least until effective competition in previously monopolized utility sectors takes off, to sector-specific regulators. As a significant Community interest or dimension is arguably not involved in the bulk of competition cases currently examined under Article 81, this would require the empowering of national authorities to deal with such cases. In addition, rolling back the scope of the prohibitions where their economically useful effects are limited would help to allow a clearer focus on more serious competition problems both at national and at EU level. Recent developments in the area of vertical restraints, and toward modernization, clearly indicate a policy trend this direction.

9.6   Rationalization

Many commentators have criticized EU competition policy for its lack of economic analysis, in particular in relation to restraints on competition under Article 81 (Korah, 1998). In part, the Commission's approach was a logical consequence of the integration objective, with its focus on formal and territorial restraints. The system of parallel block exemption regulations for similar types of agreements led to inconsistencies, and the practice of identifying exempted restrictions rather than just those restrictions held illegal led to the 'straitjacket' effects mentioned above. Moves toward consolidation and reform started in 1996, when the Commission adopted a single block exemption for technology transfer agreements, replacing previously separate Regulations concerning patent and know-how licences. Recent developments indicate more far-reaching changes as part of a shift of EU competition policy away from an approach based on legal form, toward an approach based on economic effects.

The most important example so far concerns the Commission's approach to vertical restraints: recently, it adopted a single block exemption Regulation for vertical restraints, replacing the formerly separate legal instruments concerning exclusive distribution, exclusive purchasing and franchising agreements. In addition, the new block exemption covers selective distribution agreements, which were previously dealt with under individual decisions (CEU, 1999i). Vertical agreements are entered into between undertakings operating at different levels of the production or distribution chain that relate to the purchasing, sale or resale of certain goods and services. The restraints involved in such agreements typically cover various forms of exclusivity, non-competition clauses, branding and pricing constraints that may foreclose market entry, reduce in particular intra-brand competition and create obstacles to market integration. Especially for the latter reason, they have generally been frowned upon and a systematic policy based on the potential benefits of vertical agreements has been slow to develop. However, as the various specific block exemptions recognized, these potential benefits can be significant: vertical agreements can improve economic efficiency by reducing the transaction and distribution costs of the parties involved, and lead to an optimization of their respective sales and investment levels, in particular where there is effective competition between brands. Moreover, and most important from an integration perspective, vertical agreements offer particularly effective ways of opening up or entering new markets. The objective of the new block exemption is to secure these positive effects in a turning away from EU competition law's earlier focus on integration through protecting inter-brand competition (Peeperkorn, 1998).

In a first important move going beyond past practice, the block exemption for vertical restraints is no longer based on exemptions for specifically listed agreements: instead, there is a general exemption, subject only to a prohibition of a limited number of blacklisted clauses (such as resale price maintenance, and most territorial constraints), leaving broader freedom for commercial contracts. As the efficiency-enhancing effects of vertical agreements are likely to outweigh the anti-competitive effects of restrictions they may contain, unless the undertakings involved enjoy market power, the block exemption creates a presumption of legality for vertical agreements concerning the sale of goods and services which are concluded by companies with less than 30% market share. Only cases involving undertakings that fall above this threshold have to be notified to the Commission for exemption. However, if cumulative effects occur in markets that are in large part covered by similar vertical restraints, the Commission can decide the block exemption no longer applies, requiring individual notifications. In a move toward decentralization, national authorities are authorized to withdraw the benefits of the block exemption if vertical agreements have effects incompatible with Article 81(3) EC on a geographically distinct market within their jurisdiction. Guidelines will serve to inform undertakings of the way the block exemption is applied.

Over the next few years, this approach, based on more economic analysis, focus on market power and guidance to undertakings, will be extended to horizontal cooperation agreements, leading to a new generation of a limited number of block exemptions.

9.7 Modernization

For more than 35 years, following the Council's adoption of the key procedural Regulation 17 in 1962, the Commission has been responsible for the administration of a highly centralized authorization system for exemptions to the cartel prohibition of Article 81(1). This system rests on the notification requirement and exemption monopoly introduced by Regulation 17. Over time, it has served the uniform application of EU competition law, which in turn fostered a 'culture of competition' now shared with national competition authorities in all 15 member states, a majority of which have authority to apply both Community and national competition law (Temple Lang, 1998). However, as described earlier in this chapter, this success has come at significant cost to effective enforcement: mass notifications overburden the Commission services, leading to administrative solutions that do not provide adequate legal certainty for undertakings, and which can be used strategically to trump national courts and competition authorities in their own enforcement of the directly effective cartel prohibition (Wils, 1999).

Many elements of the widespread criticism of this system (Forrester and Norall, 1984; Bright, 1995; Neven, Papandropoulos and Seabright, 1998) have come to be shared by the Commission itself. In addition, it has identified the impending further enlargement of the EU, the effects of economic restructuring following EMU, and the need to reallocate resources to respond adequately to the broadening geographic scope of various anti-competitive practices as the result of economic globalization, as reasons to adopt a programme of far-reaching modernization and reform of the manner in which Article 81 is applied. In its modernization White Paper of 1999 (CEU, 1999j), the Commission sets the following three objectives for this exercise, that is to lead to proposals for legislative changes over 2000 and 2001: ensuring effective supervision, simplifying administration and easing the constraints on undertakings while providing them with a sufficient degree of legal certainty (Rodger, 1999; Wesseling, 2000).

The key element of the modernization proposals would be replacing the mandatory notification and authorization system by a directly applicable legal exception system. In effect, this would constitute a shift from a system of *ex ante* control to a system of *ex post* supervision that relies more on direct effect, and hence on the national authorities and the undertakings concerned. Undertakings would be required to assess themselves whether their contemplated agreements are likely to infringe the prohibition of Article 81(1), and, if they do, whether they remain within the scope of the legal exception of Article 81(3), because the restrictions involved are the minimum necessary to realize legitimate economic benefits shared with consumers, consistent with established EU competition policy practice. This assessment would remain subject to challenge before national courts and by the competition authorities both at national and at Community level. Enforcement at national level would be facilitated by Commission guidance. In its own handling of such cases, the Commission has announced that it will limit the scope of its review to undertakings with market power. Hence, as with to the approach adopted to vertical restraints, market shares will come to play a key role.

This fundamental reform still requires a large number of legal changes that remain to be worked out. Procedures to facilitate co-ordination between national authorities require new structures and additional practical and legal measures at both Community and national level. For example, seven national authorities still have to be authorized by their national governments to apply the EU rules at all. Likewise, new mechanisms to ensure consistent application of the competition rules by national courts will have to be elaborated. Perhaps most important, if decentralization of EU competition policy is to be implemented with minimal inconsistencies, a more concentrated focus on a limited number of – predominantly economic – objectives appears to be required.

Consultation on the modernization proposals has produced criticism not only on a large number of technical points, but also on the assumptions that uniformity of competition law can be maintained in a decentralized system, and that among national courts and competition authorities sufficient unused capacity is available to ensure that overload problems are not moved around, but resolved. To what extent such criticism will affect the forthcoming legislative changes remains to be seen. Locating capacity problems at national level will presumably give the individual member states a stronger incentive to address them. However, it is true that because giving up formal centralization will give rise to an increased need for co-ordination, it is by no means certain that the Commission's ambitions to refocus its own enforcement activities on intensified *ex post* control – including that against the gravest cartels – can be realized without additional resources. Whether sharing responsibility for competition law enforcement more broadly will create momentum in favour of providing the necessary means, remains an open question. At a minimum, it will provide the Commission with increased flexibility in reordering its priorities.

9.8 Conclusion

Following its initial system-building efforts, EU competition policy became increasingly hampered by a mismatch between the scope of the European Commission's powers and its capacity for effective enforcement. To some extent the Commission has been the victim of its own success at centralizing its competence in order to secure its key mission of promoting market integration. Nevertheless, its efforts have spawned the spontaneous harmonization of competition policy and an increasingly effective enforcement culture at national level that are now considered the key to reform.

EU competition policy is in a process of rationalization and modernization that involves imposing increasingly stringent curbs on public intervention, and moving away from its former primary focus on the integration objective, toward increasing reliance on economic logic and on enforcement at national level.

Although significant advances have already been made concerning previously privileged economic sectors, state aid, revising the block exemptions, the ongoing review of the EU's competition policy instruments is not complete: a review of policy on market power and dominance, including approaches to dominance and collusion in oligopolistic markets, remains to be worked out. The Commission will have to strengthen the proactive enforcement of its anti-cartel policy. The process of decentralizing the enforcement of the principles established so far forms a pre-condition for such further modernization that has only recently begun. Nevertheless, the contours of a full-fledged 'second generation' system of EU competition law are emerging.

10 Industrial policy

V. CURZON PRICE

This chapter is divided into four sections. Section 10.1 briefly defines industrial policy and discusses its intellectual foundations. Sections 10.2 and 10.3 describe and analyse the two main areas where the EU has an active industrial policy: the control of state aid and support for research and development. The final section (10.4) attempts an evaluation.

10.1 What is industrial policy?

It is important to define what we mean by industrial policy before proceeding to discuss the EU's approach to the issue. Industrial policy has several dimensions of interest to us. If we adopt the broadest possible definition, '[industrial policy] embraces all acts and policies of the state in relation to industry' (Bayliss and El-Agraa, 1990), it is clear that *no industrial policy at all* could be an industrial policy by default. This policy option, while not central to our story, should be kept in mind.

Second, while it is conventional to speak of 'industrial' policy, it is clear that we do not intend to limit our domain to policies directed only at manufacturing. The term 'industrial' is retained only because it has entered into common usage. It goes without saying that a policy to support a service activity, like a bank or an airline, qualifies as an 'industrial' policy. For the same reason, one should include agricultural policy (although we shall not do so in this chapter), for the simple reason that it also affects the allocation of resources, not only within the agricultural sector itself, but also between agriculture and other activities. Indeed, a broad *economic* definition of industrial policy might be 'all acts and policies of the state to alter the allocation of resources between sectors'.

The *level of generality* of the 'acts and policies' is an issue in deciding what to include in a definition of industrial policy. Thus, while it is true that the rate of interest affects investment, hence industry, few people would hold that monetary policy is part of industrial policy. In fact, broad general policies which do not discriminate between economic activities, and therefore do not affect the inter-sectoral allocation of resources, are usually defined as lying outside the boundary of industrial policy. The EU refers to these as 'horizontal' policies (fiscal, competition, regional, social, labour, environmental policies, etc.). However, some general policies can fit a broad definition of industrial policy (see above). Thus, 'completing the internal market' was for many years considered to be an EU industrial policy in its own right. Geroski and Jacquemin (1989) also adopt a broad definition: 'in our view, [industrial policy] should be designed not to specify and enforce particular *outcomes* but to alter market *processes* by attacking the rigidities which impede ...

the force of market selection' (p. 298). They specify their preference for an industrial policy which provides 'a framework in which private sector flexibility is encouraged and adjustment to shocks is facilitated' (p. 305). They express disapproval of industrial policy which 'might try to lead the private sector through a more or less explicit planning procedure' because it would take the form of ' "picking winners", predicting the emergence of "sunrise" sectors, and charting the rationalization of "sunset" sectors' (p. 305).

Geroski and Jacquemin's (normative) definition of industrial policy thus includes horizontal policies at a high level of generality, designed to improve the natural forces of the market. It is clear, however, that any practical definition of industrial policy must *also* allow for policies which target a sector of economic activity, or a type of product (even if one does not, like Geroski and Jacquemin, approve of them), and which therefore affect the inter-sectoral allocation of resources. In its most specific form, industrial policy supports a firm in particular (and discriminates against other firms in the same sector). To affect the inter-firm allocation of resources, however, flies in the face of market processes.

There has been an evolution in the philosophy underlying government intervention in economic affairs in the last forty years or so. Thus, in the 1960s and 1970s people approached microeconomic intervention (and hence specific industrial policies) with enthusiasm, convinced that government should and could correct market failures of various kinds. For instance, according to Geroski and Jacquemin, European industrial policies 'aimed to create European super-firms to compete with the US giants' (p. 299). By the 1990s, however, the tide had turned. We had become less convinced that government action was effective, even in the presence of market failures, and respect for market forces had increased. For instance, Martin Bangemann (1994), Commissioner for Industry from 1989 to 1999, endorsed the by-then fashionable general definition of industrial policy and proclaimed that 'it should promote adaptation to industrial change in an open and competitive market'. This gives us a benchmark for the Commission's views at the time. It is clear that these two definitions of industrial policy are not easy to reconcile. I propose to resolve this difficulty by retaining the distinctions between 'firm-specific industrial policy', 'sector-specific industrial policy' and 'general industrial policy'. Another semantic way of distinguishing between these concepts might be to refer respectively to 'micro-microeconomic', 'microeconomic' and 'macroeconomic' industrial policy, and I shall sometimes do so in what follows.

Competition policy is a special case, and in another context would have had to be included in our discussion of industrial policy. It is general in intent, but is often specific in application. Thus the EU Commission's Directorate General for Competition (DG COMP, formerly known as DG IV) affects the internal structure of industries by controlling mergers, joint ventures and minority acquisitions, and by attempting to prevent cartels. It can support or discourage certain types of agreements between firms (for instance, collaborative R&D arrangements). It possesses considerable administrative discretion, and can even allow a 'restructuring cartel' to ease the burden of adjustment in a declining sector (see below). However, since these aspects are covered in Chapter 9, they will only be touched upon here.

Fourth, it is a matter of empirical observation that microeconomic industrial policy is often dualistic and contradictory. Governments tend to simultaneously support 'sunrise' and 'sunset' industries, an apparently irrational approach, which encourages economists, when they come across the phenomenon, to use the theory of public choice to explain it (see below).

It is worth noting that in the examples just given, the policy is assumed to be proactive: its aim is to *help* a targeted activity, whatever one might think about the wisdom of such an approach. In fact, there are very few examples of state interventions which explicitly penalize or run down an industry (this is understandable from a political point of view). However, one should bear in mind that a decision to *remove* a life-support machine, or to cut off a past stream of subsidies (as the UK has done with its coal mines and France with its shipyards), is indeed part of industrial policy as well (see the very first point, above, that having no industrial policy is an industrial policy by default).

The opportunity cost of specific industrial policy should also not be forgotten. Thus sums which are devoted to support A, B and C must come from somewhere, and will penalize all non-supported activites from D to Z. No government, as far as I know, has ever attempted to evaluate this hidden cost of industrial policy, and the public are certainly not aware of it.

A brief word is needed on the *instruments* of specific industrial policy. The favoured instruments of microeconomic or micro-microeconomic intervention, whether forward or backward looking, are subsidies and protection from (foreign) competition. Both instruments are easy to aim at the desired target – the sector or firm selected for preferential treatment. There is much overlap between the two, and it is not even very clear whether the distinction can be maintained at all. For instance, a public procurement policy to 'buy national' at twice the price and half the quality of a foreign competitor is both a form of hidden subsidy and a clear non-tariff barrier against foreign competition. Any protective barrier, whether tariff or non-tariff in nature, against foreign competition permits local firms to raise their prices, which means that they enjoy a hidden subsidy which does not transit through government coffers, but is transferred directly from consumers to producers. Regulations can also be implicit or explicit instruments of industrial policy, since they can shape a sector and determine to a very great extent whether it is 'successful' or not (see, for instance, the furore over the regulatory environment for High Definition TV (HDTV) in the mid-1990s). The EU has exclusive competence over external trade policy, shared (but growing) competence over regulatory policy, a duty to supervise member states' subsidies to industry, and small (but growing) subsidy policy of its own – not to speak of competition policy, just mentioned. Space and time constraints compel us to restrict this chapter to the third and fourth aspects of industrial policy listed above, namely the supervision of member states' aid to industry on the one hand (traditional microeconomic industrial policy) and the encouragement of pre-competitive scientific and technological R&D (new 'macroeconomic' or general industrial policy). We shall argue that it is sometimes difficult, in practice, to maintain the generality of support for R&D, and that as it moves closer and closer to the market place, it is bound to become sector and even firm-specific.

10.2   Industrial policy: for and against

International trade theorists have long asked why, as a matter of empirical observation, discriminatory protection (favouring some industries and penalizing others) is so prevalent. Most of the work on why governments practise *specific* industrial policy has therefore already been done by trade theorists. It just needs transposing to the slightly broader framework of industrial policy. Since the arguments are familiar, I shall simply mention them, without going into great detail. The case for *general* industrial policy, however, is based simply on improving the competitive functioning of markets.

10.2.1 Market failure in general

An economic case for government action can be made whenever an instance of general market failure can be spotted. For example, firms are naturally inclined to form cartels to reduce competition if the cost of forming the arrangement is lower than the expected benefit (often the case when a small number of firms is involved). For this reason antitrust policies are devised to improve the competitive functioning of markets. The failure of the market to account properly for damage to the environment is another well-known and widely acknowledged reason for government action. Finally, it is often claimed that the market will under-supply useful scientific and industrial knowledge because of the public-goods aspect of information. It is on this that public funding of R&D is based. We shall return to this question below.

In the area of specific industrial policy, however, the case for market failure is much harder to make, because the underlying assumption is that the government is better at allocating resources than the market, or at any rate can improve substantially upon it. This is increasingly questioned and has led to growing scepticism regarding selective industrial policy.

Several different types of market failure arise under this head which are discussed below.

10.2.2 Infant industries

This is the oldest and most popular of the (economic) arguments for subsidization and/or protection. Even in its traditional formulation, it appeals to the notion of economies of scale. It asserts that an 'infant' industry operating below optimum size will never achieve the low costs associated with large-scale production of established firms, because the latter possess a 'first mover advantage' that the newcomer simply cannot overcome. For this reason, it needs a start-up subsidy. Once it is up and running it will become competitive, in theory at least. In practice, many infants never grow up. The art is in selecting the right sector – in 'picking the winners'. This is not easy, even for entrepreneurs investing their own money. It is much harder for public officials, investing other people's money. The process tends to become politicized, of which more below.

10.2.3 Strategic industrial policy

In the 1980s, under the leadership of Paul Krugman (1979), trade theory turned to models of imperfect competition to explain phenomena such as intra-industry trade between developed countries. From this exercise there emerged not only an explanation for certain empirical observations in terms of oligopolistic rivalry, but also some policy prescriptions (see, in particular, Brander and Spencer, 1983).

For many observers, however, the policy prescriptions looked remarkably like the old infant-industry argument, dressed up in modern clothes. What is perhaps new is the idea that comparative advantage is no longer a matter of traditional factor endowments, but can be *consciously shaped* by judicious industrial policy. This at any rate is the claim of the new trade theory.

In a world where *technology* determines the competitiveness of firms and where location is no longer a question of hard geographic facts, but rather proximity to other firms in the same sector, economic activity can become (fairly) 'footloose'. Attracting specific sectors to particular locations therefore becomes a feasible, and potentially profitable, object of public policy. The market-failure reasons why markets need a helping hand are the same as before: first-mover advantages, barriers to entry due to economies of scale and perhaps lack of appropriate general infrastructure (high-speed communication networks, universities, publicly funded research laboratories, etc.). The problem, as always, lies in whether the response to the observed market failure is to be selective or general.

10.2.4 Industrial agglomerations

The idea that economies of scale are paramount, that geographic location is no longer an issue and that comparative advantage can be 'shaped', has led to some spectacular failures when, combining industrial with regional policy, governments erected 'cathedrals in the desert' (such as huge steel and chemical complexes in Italy's Mezzogiorno). Clearly, something was missing from the recipe. Geography matters – but what kind? The failure of old-style regional policy to create viable industries in blighted areas, as well as the astonishing success of Silicon Valley, has led to a renewed interest in the economics of agglomeration (Fujita and Thisse, 1996). The notion that people following the same skilled trade derive advantages from proximity to each other goes back to Alfred Marshall, who noted that they gained from lower factor prices and economies of scale (Marshall, 1920).

The 'pull' factors which reduce costs for members of an agglomeration include: positive externalities based on mass production of specialized inputs (i.e. access to lower costs from efficient suppliers), access to specialized labour, specialized services, shared consumers, shared infrastructure (especially universities), flow of information (especially tacit information and informal gossip) and the sheer efficiency of markets as co-ordinating agents (as compared with the corresponding inefficiency of hierarchical management as a method of co-ordination beyond a certain degree of complexity). An agglomeration reduces costs by allowing firms to contract out all but their very core activities, but this is only efficient if the specialized suppliers can themselves operate on a large enough scale, thus offsetting market transaction costs.

For instance, some hospitals no longer employ nurses directly, but contract out this seemingly core activity to a nursing-services agency.[1] However, such a practice will only get good results if there are many hospitals and many service providers, offering similar (but often subtly differentiated) specialized nursing services. The truly spectacular benefits will come when specialization and economies of scale, in turn, hit the nursing services supply industry as well, spreading pecuniary externalities (Scitovsky, 1954) throughout the agglomeration and creation of a Silicon Valley for health care. At one point, the hospital might become just a Coasian locus for a multitude of contracts (Coase, 1937).

One important implication for industrial policy is that while the agglomeration may be very large, most of the firms which compose it will be very small, at least relative to the traditional multinational corporation or national champion. In fact, the economies of agglomeration can be interpreted as being both substitutes for and complements of technical economies of scale. Thus an agglomeration of small specialized firms might compete head-on with a large, vertically integrated corporation, each being equally efficient. On the other hand, a complementary structure would involve large firms capturing the available technical economies of scale, surrounded by a dense network of suppliers and sub-contractors, all working to keep costs and prices down, and variety and innovation up.

This means that industrial policy can no longer simply target large firms and hope for the best. Support for SMEs is (perhaps) needed too. But we are far from understanding industrial agglomerations and even further from knowing how to create them. This is not an argument for an industrial policy based on market failure, but rather one based on mysterious market success, which we would dearly like to duplicate.

10.2.5 Domestic distortions

In a world of political and social constraints, with numerous public policies affecting every aspect of business life, it might be efficient to adopt an industrial policy to offset some of the unintended consequences of other types of policies. For instance, if is often claimed that Europe's expensive social welfare system, the cost of which appears to fall mostly on firms, discourages them from hiring extra employees, creating new enterprises or investing in R&D. Rather than dismantle the entire welfare system (which would anyway be politically impossible) it might be preferable to adopt an industrial policy to offset some of the negative side-effects. Here the argument for industrial policy is based on policy, rather than market failures.

10.2.6 Support for research and development

The importance of technological change in explaining economic growth has long been recognized (Solow, 1957; Denison, 1974). Furthermore, it has long been acknowledged that firms will only invest in research and development if they can appropriate for themselves the new knowledge they have created. However, since much scientific knowledge, once discovered, is freely available for anyone to use, firms have little incentive to produce it (the free-rider problem). This market failure (due to the public-goods nature of knowledge) gives rise to two broad policy responses: the patent system on the one hand, giving inventors a temporary and exclusive right to exploit the new knowledge they have created; and public funding of basic research at universities and technical laboratories on the other. The question is whether firms need *more* than the patent system to encourage them to create new knowledge. For instance, should the government offer to defray part of the cost of R&D? Irrespective of the answer to this question (which indeed remains open) most developed countries do actually devote substantial public funds to financing R&D in private industry. The argument in favour of doing so must rest on something more than the free-rider problem, since this could be remedied by strengthening and, above all, lengthening the time of protection under the patent system.

Public funding of R&D, however, allows governments to be selective up to a point, in other words, to adopt a microeconomic industrial policy under the banner of a well-recognized general market failure in the area of knowledge creation. Governments can promote *indirectly* those industries which they wish to support (see the infant industry and strategic arguments outlined above) by sponsoring R&D in selected areas. However, this is less risky than 'picking the winners' directly (by supporting investment in new production facilities, for instance) since the new knowledge thus created might 'spill over' into other areas and be generally useful. For instance, the Apollo space programme is often credited with having developed the transistor, the grandfather of the silicon chip.

These technological loops, linkages, feedbacks and spill-overs (all terms frequently used by true believers) are in fact at the heart of the argument. They help to translate scientific knowledge into commercially useful innovations, and vice versa. Industrial research by one firm takes known science, applies it to solving a particular problem and, in the course of this work, adds to general scientific knowledge which can be exploited by other firms and perhaps find its way back to the universities. Thus the creation of new knowledge by one firm is assumed to generate positive externalities for other firms, both in the form of better and cheaper products, and in the form of new scientific (non-patented) information, as well as ensuring the firm's own longer-term survival through the development of patented information (Grossman and Helpman, 1991).

A further point made by Grossman and Helpman is that the ability to assimilate existing technologies and generate new ones is by no means universal, but has to be cultivated. Countries in which technological research is carried out acquire a *comparative advantage in the form of human capital resource endowments that may persist for some time* (Ruttan, 1998).

Efforts to include technology in standard economic theory (known as 'endogenizing technological change') are beginning to be made, despite the daunting task of modelling the unknown. When successful, the implications are staggering. Thus Romer (1994) argues that if, when tariffs come down, firms do not choose simply between known goods X and Y, but include in their choice set the as-yet-undiscovered sector Z, the cost of protection is very high – namely, a lack of dynamism and innovation. Standard neoclassical economics cannot capture these effects because it assumes perfect knowledge (Hayek, 1945). In fact it is a tribute to the 'Austrian' school that mainstream economists are now beginning to go beyond the world of perfect knowledge, where people chose among known means to achieve known ends, and are entering a world where sheer ignorance is prevalent. In such a world, everyone is an entrepreneur, since we must constantly add novelties to our stock of known options.

The main question for policy makers is not so much whether R&D needs public support (there seems little doubt, even in the minds of sceptical academics) but how and at what stage. The process of transforming general scientific knowledge into useful commercial applications can be viewed as a kind of pipeline, running from academic institutions as far from the business world as is possible to imagine, with links to general industrial research laboratories, where much scientific knowledge is created, but few innovations emerge, to the more focused development of prototype products or processes in an engineering laboratory, on to the testing of innovations on a small scale and finally, after much trial and error, if successful, to their full-scale development and marketing on a broad scale. New knowledge is created at each stage in the process. But which stage is the most deserving of public support? Generally speaking, the further away from 'the market place' and the more general the type of research, the more appropriate it is for public funding. In this way, one can avoid targeting public funds to particular firms which, as we have already seen, is a politically dangerous and degenerate form of industrial policy. For this reason, as we shall see, the EU promotes 'pre-competitive' R&D, i.e. it in principle does not fund the development of prototypes or anything 'too close' to the market.

Agglomerations, discussed above, are also conducive to technological change. Information and ideas circulate informally within an agglomeration, speeding up the process of product development (Lucas, 1988). Thus, support for agglomerations, if such could be devised, might be an indirect way of promoting innovation.

10.2.7 Problems with industrial policy

The principal problem with industrial policy is the fact that it often implies selectivity *in practice*. As we saw in section 10.1, if a policy is general and 'horizontal', it does not distinguish between sectors and it avoids all the problems of 'picking the winners'. But support for R&D, for instance, often ends up targeting particular sectors. *Someone* must do the selecting. If not the market, then who? Are public officials so wise and far-seeing that they can really do better?

Second, if all governments enter the industrial policy game, each supporting the sectors they think are promising or in need of help, there is a fair chance that we shall collectively spend too much on industrial policy, that our efforts will cancel out and that much useless duplication of effort will occur.

Third, the process of allocating industrial policy funds is bound to become ever more politicized with time. Once 'hooked' on industrial policy funds, sectors grow beyond their market-determined size and hence enjoy more political support than is really their due. Industrial policies become 'path dependent' (i.e. one can predict with fair accuracy where next year's budget will be spent simply by looking at last year's budget). Industrial policies become self-perpetuating.

If industrial policy is hijacked by rent-seekers, as is likely (see Tullock, 1967; Kreuger, 1974 for seminal articles on 'public choice'), it will end up reducing rather than improving welfare. Its ostensible purpose is to improve on markets by offsetting market failures, but in reality it will have been captured by special interest groups. The latter have a direct interest in the creation of public support programmes and in their expansion over time. Lobbying public authorities for privileges of one kind or another diverts resources from producing real goods and services of marketable value. The loss to society is thus twofold: not only do lobbies extract rents from the less well organized members of society, generating the usual opportunity costs, but they also waste real resources to obtain them. Furthermore, the whole process can become dynamic (Olson, 1982) as more and more firms try to join the gravy-train. According to Olson, there is no end to this process (except long-term decline in growth as firms invest more and more in rent-seeking and less and less in innovation). The principal victims (consumers and taxpayers) remain 'rationally ignorant', allowing themselves to be regularly fleeced by rationally knowledgeable and politically active interest groups. And the public choice school does not even discuss the problem of outright corruption, favouritism and nepotism, which surfaced in the EU Commission in the later 1990s.

Finally, one does not need the apparatus of public choice theory to spot the occasions when industrial policy degenerates into pure political opportunism, as when subsidies are given to loss-making firms to 'save jobs' (especially politicians' jobs).

10.2.8 Conclusion

If any general conclusion is to be drawn from this brief summary of the intellectual case for state intervention at a microeconomic level in the economy it is this: it is not enough to demonstrate the existence of a market failure to justify government intervention. Government action is costly in its own right. In fact, the direct and indirect costs of government action might be far greater than the original market imperfection. This is not to say that no industrial policy is the best policy, but to make a plea for very close scrutiny of what is advanced under this banner.

10.3 Industrial policy in the EC: the control of state aid

The Treaty of Rome does not provide for a 'Common Industrial Policy' in the same way as it provides, for instance, for a Common Agricultural Policy, a Common Transport Policy and a Common Social Policy. It did not even provide for a Common Regional Policy until 1987. This is no accident. Common policies were necessary in areas where government intervention at member-state level was so extensive that freeing markets could only produce a distorted outcome and policy competition. Where these loomed, and the political will was present, the problem was elevated to Community level and a 'common' policy was born. Sometimes (as in the case of road transport) the problem was never dealt with and remains a source of tension to this day.

In the case of industrial policies, the founding fathers deemed it sufficient to grant the Commission powers of supervision to ensure that state aid did not distort conditions of competition in the common market. Articles 87–9 (formerly Articles 92–4) set forth the general rules.

Article 87(1) states that:

> Save as otherwise provided in this Treaty, any aid granted by a Member State or through State resources in any form whatsoever which distorts or threatens to distort competition by favouring certain undertakings or the production of certain goods shall, in so far as it affects trade between Member States, be incompatible with the common market.

Apart from the introductory caveat (see next paragraph), this is an extremely sweeping prohibition. It covers aid in 'any form whatsoever', targeted either at the level of individual firms ('favouring certain undertakings'), or at the level of an entire sector ('the production of certain goods'). Its purpose is to prevent member states' industrial policies from undermining the common market by distorting competition.

However, some industrial policies may be deemed compatible with the common market. Article 87(3) lists in this regard aid to promote development of depressed or backward areas, aid for 'important projects of common European interest', aid for 'certain economic activities' or 'certain economic areas' (aid granted to shipyards is expressly mentioned) and 'such other categories of aid as may be specified by decisions of the Council'. In 1992 the Maastricht Treaty introduced a specific derogation for State aid to culture and heritage conservation (Article 87(3)(d)). In fact, Article 87(3) allows the Commission considerable leeway in developing a policy with regard to state aid.

Article 88 empowers the Commission to 'keep under constant review all systems of aid' in member states and Article 89 allows the Commission to propose appropriate regulations to ensure the proper application of Articles 87 and 88.

It was some time before the Commission developed these powers into a 'policy', since the role of *gendarme* was not an easy one to assume when the miscreants were member states. On the whole, however, the 1960s and early 1970s were good years and there was little excuse, or perceived need, for state intervention in industry. According to the Commission's *First Report on Competition Policy* (published in 1972) the only sectors in trouble were shipbuilding, textiles and film production, and the Commission limited itself to exhortations to keep national aid within rather vague 'guidelines'. General aid schemes to promote investment were approved, and even dowries for industrial weddings in the French electronics industry (Machines Bull and CII) were passed without difficulty.

In fact, during this period, the term 'industrial policy' was either not in use at all, or subsumed under the generic term 'completion of the internal market' (see, for instance, the Commission's 'Colonna Report', CEC, 1970d). It covered the elimination of non-tariff barriers, the regulation of public procurement to avoid hidden subsidies, and the creation of a single regulatory environment for European industry. In a word, industrial policy at that time took the form of a *withdrawal* of the state from the market place, in order to create the 'common' market.

The 1970s and early 1980s, on the other hand, were much more turbulent. Two successive oil price increases plunged Europe into a prolonged recession, characterized by high rates of inflation and unemployment. Traditional macroeconomic policies were powerless to cope with this hitherto unprecedented combination. Firms continued to fail, unemployment continued to rise, exchange rates gyrated. Many EC members resorted to the direct subsidization of loss-making firms.

To begin with, the Commission did not appreciate the danger. It found that 'Member States, in an attempt to protect employment, were justified in boosting investment by granting firms financial benefits . . . it agreed to financial aid being granted to ensure the survival of firms which have run into difficulties, thereby avoiding redundancies' (CEC, 1976a, para. 133). The list of sectors 'in difficulty' expanded to include automobiles, paper, machine tools, steel, synthetic fibres, clocks and watches and chemicals. The number of subsidy schemes notified to the Commission rose from a mere handful in the early 1970s to well over 100 by the end of the decade. The race for subsidization was in full swing.

Finally waking up to the danger, the Commission decided to take a less lenient view of subsidies to preserve employment (CEC, 1979e, paras 173, 174), putting more emphasis on the 'need to restore competitiveness' and to 'face up to worldwide competition'. The change in policy and circumstance emerges quite clearly from Table 10.1, which shows that while the total number of cases trebled from 1977 to 1978, the ratio of 'objections' to 'total decisions' halved to only 12–14%. This period of excessive leniency was succeeded by one (1979–86) where the rate of 'objections' rose again to between 30% and 55% – evidence of a battle royal between the Commission and the member states. From 1987 onwards, not only did the economy pick up somewhat, but one may also assume that member states had learned to avoid, as much as possible, the inconvenience and embarrassment

Table 10.1 Accumulated data on state subsidies, 1970–97.

(1) Year	(2) Total decisions	(3) No objection	(4) Objection	(5) Of which final negative decision	(6) Objections/ total (col. 4/col. 2)
1970	21	15	6	1	0.29
1971	18	11	7	3	9.39
1972	35	24	11	3	0.31
1973	22	15	7	4	0.32
1974	35	20	15	0	0.43
1975	45	29	16	2	0.36
1976	47	33	14	2	0.30
1977	112	99	13	1	0.12
1978	137	118	19	0	0.14
1979	133	79	54	3	0.41
1980	105	72	33	2	0.31
1981	141	79	62	14	0.44
1982	233	104	129	13	0.55
1983	195	101	94	21	0.48
1984	314	201	113	21	0.36
1985	178	102	76	7	0.43
1986	181	98	83	10	0.46
1987	274	205	69	10	0.25
1988	410	303	107	14	0.26
1989	343	259	84	16	0.24
1990	492	415	77	14	0.16
1991	597	493	104	7	0.17
1992	552	473	79	8	0.14
1993	467	399	68	6	0.15
1994	527	440	87	3	0.17
1995	619	504	115	9	0.19
1996	474	373	101	23	0.21
1997	502	385	117	9	0.23

Source: EU Commission, Annual Competition Reports.

of going through the Commission's 'objection' process. The rate of 'objections' thus fell back to below 25%.

Another problem which emerged during those dark years was an open conflict between DG III (Industrial Affairs) and DG IV (Competition). Etienne Davignon, Commissioner for Industrial Affairs, sponsored 'temporary crisis cartels' in two stricken industries – steel and synthetic fibres. They were plagued by over-capacity, chaotic price cutting and huge losses. Viscount Davignon offered an 'orderly' way out, which involved all producers bearing equal shares of the agony of cutting back capacity. However, while the steel cartel was in accordance with the Treaty of Paris, the synthetic fibre cartel was not compatible with the Treaty of Rome, and DG IV duly condemned it (CEC, 1979e, para. 42).

What was the industry to do? One Commission Directorate told them to set up a cartel, the other told them to dismantle it! In fact, DG IV did not pursue the matter, and the synthetic fibre agreement continued in a kind of legal twilight until 1982, when the Commission published its 'policy' on the matter.

The statement on the application of competition rules to agreements aimed at reducing 'structural over-capacity' reads as follows:

> The Commission may be able to condone agreements in restraint of competition which relate to a sector as a whole, provided they are aimed solely at achieving a coordinated reduction of overcapacity and do not otherwise restrict free decision-making by the firms involved. The necessary structural reorganization must not be achieved by unsuitable means such as price-fixing or quota agreements, nor should it be hampered by State aids which lead to artificial preservation of surplus capacity. (CEC, 1983, para. 39)

The synthetic fibre producers duly amended their agreement and obtained an exemption in 1984 (CEC, 1985c, paras. 81–2).

The Commission justified its policy towards crisis cartels on the grounds that 'production can be considered to be improved if the reductions in capacity are likely in the long run to increase profitability and restore competitiveness'. This represented a total capitulation to the chemical lobby, for there is a world of difference between the 'reductions in capacity' that market competition would have produced (the weakest firms would have collapsed) and the 'coordinated reduction of overcapacity' by agreement between firms (each firm, irrespective of its efficiency, reduced capacity by an agreed amount). The latter process guaranteed the survival of the un-fittest. Quite *why* the Commission believed that the latter process would 'restore competitiveness' was not revealed. In the meantime, the Commission did not prosecute, but permitted, under close supervision, the continuing subsidization by member states of 'sectors in difficulty' (coal-mines, shipyards, textiles, etc.). For this it was much criticized as having a purely negative industrial policy, supporting only 'sunset' sectors.

The latter 1980s were marked by a spectacular renewal of the European Community: the adoption in 1985 of the Commission's White Paper on completing the internal market, the entry into force in 1987 of the Single European Act (SEA), and the launching of Economic and Monetary Union (EMU) were huge steps undertaken, in part, as a response to the terrible decline into which the oil-price induced recession had thrown all European countries. The creation of a genuine single market made it more important than ever that member states should not thwart the competitive process by extensive use of state aid. It was therefore agreed in 1985 that the Commission should issue a general report on the subject every three years. At the time of writing (2000) there have been six of these reports, which give a good idea of the evolution of state aid over time (see Tables 10.2–10.6)

State aid to R&D received special attention in 1986, when the Commission adopted its first 'Framework on State Aid for Research and Development'. The Commission emphasized its favourable attitude to this type of aid, warned of the dangers of fruitless duplication of effort and hence pointed to the need for proper co-ordination by the Commission (see below). It called for the notification of all R&D subsidies in excess of 20 million ECU. A good part of the increase in the number of subsidies investigated by the Commission from 1987 onwards (see Table 10.1) was due to the adoption of this new framework. Other reasons include the increase in membership from 1970 to 1997, and the growing efficiency with which the Commission tracks such aid (CEC, 1987d, para 174), but not an increase in the total volume of state aid (see Tables 10.2 and 10.4).

Table 10.2 State aid as a percentage of GDP

	1981–6	1986–8	1988–90	1990–2	1992–4	1994–6
Austria						0.6
Belgium	4.1	3.2	2.8	2.3	1.7	1.3
Denmark	1.3	1	1.1	1	1.1	1
Finland						0.5
France	2.7	2	2.1	1.8	1.4	1.1
Germany	2.5	2.5	2.5	2.4	2.5	1.9
Greece	2.5	4.5	3.1	2.2	1.3	1.2
Ireland	5.3	2.7	1.9	1.5	1	0.8
Italy	5.7	3.1	2.8	2.8	2.1	2
Luxembourg	6	4	3.9	3.9	2.4	1
Netherlands	1.5	1.3	1.1	0.9	0.7	0.7
Portugal		1.5	2	1.4	1	0.9
Spain		2.7	1.8	1.3	1.1	1.2
Sweden						0.8
UK	1.8	1.1	1.2	0.6	0.4	0.5
EU average	**3**	**2.2**	**2.1**	**1.9**	**1.6**	**1.3**

Source: EU Commission, *Surveys of State Aid in the European Union* (1st to 6th surveys).

The adoption of the framework on state aid for R&D in 1986 was no accident. In 1985 President Mitterrand had launched his Eureka initiative (see section 10.4.3) to counter President Reagan's 'Star Wars' programme, and since this was supposed to involve large sums of money being channelled towards large firms, the French government wanted some kind of recognition at Community level that their programme would not be thwarted by Brussels.

Because of the growing caseload, the Commission proposed a regulation to grant group exemptions for certain categories of state aid, which was adopted by the Council in 1998.[2] The types of state aid which are deemed to be compatible with the Treaties are: horizontal aid (in particular, aid to SMEs, R&D, environmental protection employment and training), regional aid and *de minimis* aid. This list is indicative of the Commission's own policy towards industrial policy, already suggested in the way the statistical surveys of state aid are structured. We can see that it follows current thinking in allowing general aid and, in particular, aid to SMEs and R&D. In future years we can therefore expect the number of cases to drop substantially.

Tables 10.2 and 10.4 show that state aid has fallen steadily from 1981 to 1996 as a proportion of GDP (from 3% to 1.3% on average). All countries have participated in this trend, the most spectacular declines being registered by Italy (from 5.7 to 2%), Ireland (5.3 to 0.8%), and Belgium (4.1 to 1.3%), with most of the reductions taking place in the 1990s. This trend is doubtless due partly to the need for these countries to meet the Maastricht criteria for EMU membership, and partly to the realization that public handouts often miss their mark. In any event, by 1994–6 only Germany and Italy were still financing domestic industrial policy to the tune of 2% of GDP, while most other member states were well below 1%. This is a dramatic turnaround by comparison with 1981–6.

Table 10.3 State aid to manufacturing by objectives (%)

	1981–6	1986–8	1988–90	1990–2	1992–4	1994–6
Horizontal objectives	22	40	42	38	30	30
of which R&D	*4*	*9*	*10*	*10*	*7*	*9*
Regional objectives	14	34	38	50	53	57
Sectoral objectives	63	26	20	12	17	13

Source: EU Commission, *Surveys of State Aid in the European Union* (1st to 6th surveys).

Another trend is to be found in the breakdown of state aid to manufacturing by objective (see Table 10.3). In its statistical surveys of state aid, the Commission distinguishes between 'horizontal' aid programmes, regional aid and 'sectoral' aid programmes (mainly aimed at traditional sectors in difficulty, such as steel, coal, shipyards, automobiles, etc.). Regional objectives have taken an ever larger share in total state aid, rising from 28 to 57% of the total (see Chapter 18). Regional aid, as we have seen, is permitted under Article 87(c), and the Treaty of Rome as amended by the SEA in 1987 and the Amsterdam Treaty in 1999, provides explicitly in Title XVII, Articles 158–62, for regional policies to promote social and economic cohesion throughout the Union. It is therefore logical that state spending should reflect this emphasis. Since the EU's regional policy and its competition policy with regard to member states' regional aid is being run by two different directorates, there is room for improved co-ordination and harmonization of definitions, but otherwise no major conflicts arise.

This trend leaves an ever smaller share of an ever smaller total for sectoral aid programmes (falling from 28% in 1981–6 to 13% in 1994–6). In other words, although help is still available for 'sunset' industries, it is gradually on its way out. 'Horizontal' aid has also fallen from 44 to 30%, while state aid to R&D has remained steady in relative terms (but has obviously fallen in absolute terms).

Table 10.4 charts the trend of state aid on an annual basis from 1981 to 1996, for

Table 10.4 State aid to the manufacturing sector (million ECU)

	EUR 10	EUR 12	EUR 15
1981–6 annual average	42 161		
1986		35 580	
1987		32 620	
1988		37 690	
1989		30 253	
1990		42 059	
1991		35 734	
1992		39 062	
1993		44 057	
1994		41 198	
1995		37 386	38 591
1996		34 106	35 163

Source: EU Commission, *Surveys of State Aid in the European Union* (1st to 6th surveys).

the EU as a whole. Although a direct comparison over time is to be avoided (for reasons such as inflation, changing EU membership, etc.), it is clear that the 35 billion ECU spent on aid to manufacturing by 15 member states in 1996 represented much less than the annual average of 42 billion ECU spent by 10 member states in the period 1981–6. This is amply borne out by the trend of subsidies as a percentage of GDP, already noted in Table 10.2.

The sixth report on state aid, however, strikes a note of concern. There is a rising tendency for member states to grant *ad hoc* aid outside any structured programme or authorized scheme (see Table 10.5). As the official publication *European Economy* puts it: 'Because such aids are concentrated on a small number of firms, often operating in oligopolistic markets, they present a danger of significant distortions of competition through rent shifting' (Vanhalewyn, 1999). A significant proportion of this *ad hoc* aid relates to the restructuring of East German industry ('Treuhand aid') but this proportion is gradually falling. However, *ad hoc* aid *excluding* 'Treuhand aid' has risen from 6% in 1992 to 16% of total aid in 1996. This aid, given to individual firms to help them restructure, mainly in the air transport and banking sectors, is in principle incompatible with the competition rules of the EU and falls into the aforementioned category of micro-microeconomic industrial policy. These troubled service sectors are, in some countries, replacing steel, textiles and shipyards as new 'lame ducks'.

The principal culprits are France, Italy, Spain and Germany (see Table 10.6), while for their size, Portugal, Austria, Ireland and Greece are by no means blameless. Denmark, Finland, Luxembourg, the Netherlands, Sweden and the UK do not offer *ad hoc* aid at all (at least not during the years surveyed).

Table 10.7 looks at the number of state subsidy *cases*, by country, for 1997. These data are published annually in the Commission's *Reports on Competition Policy*. The same countries crop up as being the sources of most of the cases examined by the Commission (Germany, Spain, Italy, France – and now Austria). Column 6 looks at the rate of 'objections', to see which countries get into the most trouble with the Commission. This throws up one or two anomalies (Luxembourg, with a 100% 'objection rate' (since its one case was objected to), and Sweden with a 50% 'objection rate' (since five out of ten cases were objected to). But for the rest, Greece, Italy, France, Spain and Germany once again appear with above-average 'objection rates', so there is some overlap between statistical data on *ad hoc* subsidies and the negative decisions issued by the Commission's Competition Directorate.

Table 10.5 *Ad hoc* aid to individual enterprises

	Ad hoc aid	Treuhand aid	Total *ad hoc* aid	Total aid	Total *ad hoc* aid as % of total	*Ad hoc* aid excluding Treuhand (% of total)
1992	2 422	5 161	7 583	39 062	19	6
1993	5 742	8 854	14 596	44 800	33	13
1994	6 922	11 013	17 935	43 466	41	16
1995	5 776	6 682	12 458	41 732	30	14
1996	5 888	4 839	10 727	37 877	28	16

Source: EU Commission, *Sixth Survey of State Aid, 1998.*

Table 10.6 *Ad hoc* aid to individual enterprises: country breakdown (million ECU)

	1992–4		1994–6	
	Value	%	Value	%
Austria	–*		65	1.0
Belgium	31	1.0	29	0.5
Denmark	0	0.0	0	0.0
Germany	686	14.0	584	10.0
Greece	75	1.0	44	0.5
Finland	–*		0	0.0
France	1663	33.0	2532	41.0
Ireland	53	1.0	58	1.0
Italy	1864	37.0	1453	23.0
Luxembourg	0		0	0.0
Netherlands	0		0	0.0
Portugal	184	4.0	365	6.0
Spain	473	10.0	1088	18.0
Sweden	–*		0	0.0
UK	0		0	0.0
EU	5029	100	6218	100

Source: EU Commission, *Sixth Survey of State Aid, 1998*.
*Not then members.

Table 10.7 State subsidy decisions by member state, 1997

(1)	(2)	(3)	(4)	(5)	(6)	(7)
	Total decisions	No objection	Objections	Of which final negative	Objections/ total (col. 4/col. 2)	Breakdown by country (col. 1, %)
Austria	32	28	4	1	0.13	6.4
Belgium	11	11	0	0	0.00	2.2
Denmark	16	14	2	1	0.13	3.2
Finland	8	8	0	0	0.00	1.6
France	38	24	14	1	0.37	7.6
Germany	194	142	52	4	0.27	38.6
Greece	5	3	2	0	0.40	1.0
Ireland	2	2	0	0	0.00	0.4
Italy	63	46	17	1	0.27	12.5
Luxembourg	1	0	1	0	1.00	0.2
Netherlands	33	30	3	0	0.09	6.6
Portugal	15	12	3	0	0.20	3.0
Spain	53	39	14	1	0.26	10.6
Sweden	10	5	5	0	0.50	2.0
UK	21	21	0	0	0.00	4.2
Total/average	502	385	117	9	0.23	100.0

Source: EU Commission, *27th Report on Competition Policy*.

Finally, Table 10.8 looks at reimbursments of illegal state aid (requested, effectively reimbursed and outstanding) from 1982 to 1993. This is the final test of the effectiveness of the Commission in disciplining subsidies, and the willingness of member states to submit to its authority. We note that Italy is the main culprit: it not only heads the list of reimbursments demanded, but had (at the time of the survey) not enforced the reimbursment of any of the illegal aid given. The Netherlands and Spain were also noteworthy for not clawing back any of the aid which the Commission had determined was illegal. Belgium had given plenty of illegal aid, but had reimbursed 72% of it by the end of the period under consideration. Denmark, Greece, Ireland, Luxembourg and Portugal were all 'clean', having given no illegal aid at all. The UK had reimbursed 97%.

In conclusion, it may be said that state aid is gradually being brought under control, but most governments find it difficult to relinquish this instrument of policy. That France, Italy and Spain should appear at the head of the list is of no surprise, given their tradition of state intervention and 'indicative' planning, but they too have radically reduced the absolute level of public aid. That Germany should frequently appear heading the same group is more surprising. Much of this is due to the reunification process, which has turned Germany into a more interventionist state. Thus, while France, Italy and Spain radically reduced their levels of intervention from a high initial starting point in 1981 (see Table 10.2), Germany started from a comparatively low point and maintained it through 1992–4. The end result is that Germany now stands out as an interventionist member state. The Commission still has problems enforcing discipline on member states, but the overall level of state aid is declining. Time will tell whether this is because economic conditions have improved, or whether state aid at member state level has been replaced by public aid at Community level. To this question we now turn.

Table 10.8 Reimbursements demanded by the Commission, 1982–93 (million ECU)

	Amount	Reimbursed	Outstanding	% reimbursed
Italy	566.46	0.00	566.46	0.00
Belgium	403.16	292.00	111.16	72.43
France	180.24	98.74	81.50	54.78
Netherlands	136.84	0.00	136.84	0.00
Spain	113.90	0.00	113.90	0.00
Germany	108.06	17.70	90.36	16.38
UK	59.39	57.89	1.50	97.47
Denmark	–	–	–	–
Greece	–	–	–	–
Ireland	–	–	–	–
Luxembourg	–	–	–	–
Portugal	–	–	–	–
EU	1568.05	466.33	1101.72	29.74

Source: EU Commission, *23rd Report on Competition Policy, 1993*.

10.4 Industrial policy in the EU: research and technological development

EU policy towards Research and Technological Development (R&TD) is inspired by the idea that Europe fails to realize its full scientific and technological potential because its research efforts are dispersed, expensive and given to wasteful duplication. Much is made of the 'technology gap' which separates Europe from the United States and Japan, and the EU Commission regularly publishes depressing statistics on all aspects of this problem (CEC, 1994a, 1997b). The answer, in the view of the Commission, is to create a 'European technological community' by fostering long-term collaborative ventures between Community firms; between European firms and publicly funded research institutions; and between universities themselves, at a European level.

To this end, the EU uses two broad policy instruments: a dispensation from Article 81 (formerly Article 85) for R&TD collaborative agreements between large firms, and direct subsidies to encourage such agreements.

10.4.1 Competition aspects of policy on research and technological development

The Treaty of Rome makes express provision for co-operative R&TD within the private sector which 'contributes to improving the production or distribution of goods or to promoting technical or economic progress' (Article 81(3)). This is one of the principal exceptions to the blanket prohibition of agreements between undertakings laid down in Article 81(1). As early as 1968 the Commission established guidelines for the application of Article 81, which permitted agreements between firms (even large ones) for the exclusive purpose of developing joint R&D, provided the co-operation remained 'pre-competitive' (i.e. did not extend to actual production), and on condition that the results of the R&D were freely available to the members of the consortium, and preferably also to outsiders on a licensing basis (CEC, 1972b, paras 31–2).

In December 1984 the Commission adopted a 'block exemption' for R&D agreements between firms which established a new, more favourable policy. Co-operative R&D schemes no longer had to be individually notified and could extend downstream to the joint exploitation of the results. This represented a considerable shift in policy for which European industry had been asking for some time, on the grounds that it made little sense to pool R&D efforts if, once they were successful, competition between the members of the pool wiped out all the potential monopolistic rents: under such circumstances, firms would prefer not to pool R&D resources at all, but take the risk of going it alone.

We saw earlier (in sections 10.1 and 10.2) that the level of generality of industrial policy is an issue. We come across the problem again here. Thus, giving all firms, large and small, special dispensation from normal antitrust rules to permit long-term collaborative research agreements does not pre-judge the sectors which will avail themselves of the opportunity. It is therefore a truly *general* or macroeconomic industrial policy. Because it is so general, the EU, as we have just seen, after some arm-twisting, now allows the antitrust dispensation to cover not only pre-competitive research, but also *technological development and marketing* of actual products. The general industrial policy thus becomes *specific* in its effect. However, the process of selection is market based and the Commission is not in the business of 'picking the winners'.

In terms of the policy pipeline described earlier, the competition policy arm of the EU's R&TD policy goes all the way to the market place, and it can do so without attracting criticism because it is so general.

However, the subsidy arm of the R&TD policy only goes as far as the 'pre-competitive' (i.e. pre-market) stage because, by its very nature, it is selective to start with. It cannot go all the way to supporting the market-based stage of developing prototypes without laying itself open to accusations that it is 'picking the winners'. These two branches of Community policy (antitrust dispensation and direct subsidies) enable a third, non-Community instrument of joint industrial policy – the 'Eureka' initiative – to flourish under the benign dispensation from the European antitrust authorities, *and with financial support from member states*, which is the level at which 'picking the winners' takes place (see Table 10.3, section 10.3 above and the discussion of 'horizontal' subsidies). Thus selective support for R&TD at national level is permitted by the Commission as long as it involves agreements between firms from two or more member countries. As such, it promotes the 'ever-closer union among the peoples of Europe' which is the over-riding political objective of the EU.

10.4.2 European subsidies to research and technological development

Despite the obvious advantages of pooling R&D efforts at a European level (as compared with strictly national support for R&D), the Treaty of Rome does not mention joint European technology policy and it has taken many years to develop one.

Member states have long been hesitant to relinquish their prerogatives. Industrial policy based on subsidizing 'sunrise' sectors, after all, was the last remaining area in which they might still exercise some national policy of their own. However, their experience at pooling research efforts in the nuclear field had not been a happy one (Guzzetti, 1995). France under President de Gaulle was not inclined to share the results of French nuclear research, while Germany, Italy and the Netherlands followed American technology when developing their nuclear reactors. The Joint Research Centres, set up in these early days, were for a long time the only manifestation of joint R&D at European level. By 2000 what remained was a recognized European presence in nuclear fission research and a distant (and very expensive) experimental technology aimed at producing pollution-free energy from smashing atoms in huge cyclotrons.

However, this had very little to do with what, over the years, has become a major worry: Europe's declining 'competitiveness' in commercially useful high technology.

The origins of EU technology policy lie in the disastrous state of the European economy after the two oil price increases of the 1970s, to which it proved slow in adapting. By contrast, both the United States and Japan shook off the negative effects quickly. At the same time that Viscount Davignon was organizing 'crisis cartels' in declining industries (see section 10.3), he also, to his credit, was trying to drum up support for a programme to help 'sunrise' industries. His idea was aimed as much at 'building Europe' as at improving the competitiveness of European firms. He believed that there was a case for European high-technology firms to pool their R&D efforts, to avoid useless duplication and to benefit from trans-European synergies. Following the wake-up call by Servan-Schreiber (1967), he and others were upset by the distressing tendency of European firms to form technological alliances, if at all, with American or Japanese partners.

During 1979–80 Davignon invited the heads of Europe's biggest electronics and information technology companies[3] to participate in a set of 'round table' discussions to see if there was any appetite for joint R&D projects among them. The response was not overwhelming, but gradually a strategy emerged which involved linking universitites, research institutes, the major European companies and some SMEs in an effort to narrow the 'technology gap' which had opened up between Europe and the United States in the area of electronics and information technology. The pilot proposal was prepared in 1980, approved by the Council in 1981 and given funding of 11.5 million ECU in 1982 (Peterson and Sharp, 1998, pp. 70–1). Davignon's strategy of involving from the very start 12 major European firms, which then lobbied their respective governments to support the scheme, had paid off. The rest, as the saying goes, is history. The pilot project was heavily oversubscribed and formed the basis for the next phase.

The ESPRIT programme (acronym for European Programme for Research in Information Technology), proposed by the Commission in May 1983 and adopted unanimously by the Council in February 1984, proved hugely popular with industry. It provided 750 million ECU of Community funding over the period 1984–8, matched ECU for ECU by private funding from the participating companies. Calls for research proposals produced over 900 projects, only 240 of which were finally approved, after consultation with the round table representatives.

Other sectoral support programmes soon followed. Davignon and his advisers had noticed that the European telecommunications industry was in danger of slipping well behind that of the USA and Japan. Not only did both these countries offer a far larger domestic market to their telecoms hardware producers, but the United States was in the process of deregulating AT&T, introducing competition and new electronic technologies into an industry which, in Europe, was dominated by entrenched public monopolies, the famous PTTs (combined postal, telegraph and telephone services). Each country's market was in fact a bilateral monopoly: a single public-sector buyer (not accountable to shareholders in a competitive capital market), and a single (highly protected) private-sector supplier. Breaking this system up and forging a 'single market' in telecommunications, with firms accountable in the normal way to market-based shareholders, is one of the Commission's major achievements.

The pilot phase of Research in Advanced Communications for Europe (RACE) was launched in 1985 with a small budget of 21 million ECU, and a much larger programme followed in 1989: RACE I ran from 1990 to 1994 with a budget of 460 million ECU; RACE II ran from 1992 to 1994 with a budget of 489 million ECU. In the meantime, the Commission sponsored research in developing European standards in the area of telecommunications (establishing the European Telecommunications Standards Institute – ETSI) and broke open the old PTT monopolies with the 'open network provision' as part of the Single Market programme. The PTTs and their local suppliers viewed all this activism with little enthusiasm and the Commission, in desperation at the foot-dragging it encountered, in 1988 declared that PTTs were subject to Article 86 (formerly Article 90). This Article states:

> In the case of public undertakings and undertakings to which Member States grant special or exclusive rights, Member States shall neither enact nor maintain in force any measure contrary to the rules contained in this Treaty.

After a protracted battle, the European Court of Justice agreed that Article 86 was directly applicable and endorsed the Commission's directive on opening up members' markets for telecommunication terminal equipment.[4]

Another important sector was targeted in the same way. Thus the programme Basic Research in Technologies/Advanced Materials for Europe (BRITE/EURAM) was launched at the same time with a 100 million ECU pilot phase in the period 1985–8. This developed into two major programmes with budgets of 450 million ECU and 660 million ECU running from 1986 to 1992.

Smaller programmes can only be mentioned by their acronyms (see Table 10.9).

In short, by the late 1980s European technology policy had been well and truly launched. In this it was helped by the Single European Act (1987) which for the first time gave the Community a legal basis for all these schemes. A new title VI entitled 'Research and technological development' (R&TD) was added (Articles 163–173 – formerly 130(F) – 130(Q)) gives the Community a new aim: 'to strengthen the scientific and technological bases of Community industry and to encourage it to become more competitive at international level'. To achieve this end, the Community decided to 'adopt a multiannual framework programme setting out all its activities' (Article 166). While decisions relating to establishing the budget of the multiannual framework programme (MFP) were to be taken unanimously by the Council on a proposal from the Commission and after consulting the European Parliament (EP), decisions on its implementation through specific programmes and detailed arrangements were to be taken by the Council by qualified majority voting in co-operation with the EP. The provisions requiring both unanimity in the Council *and* consultation of the EP in the first phase of the MFP, as well as the need, in the second stage, to obtain Council *and* EP approval for individual research projects, proved to be politically fraught, contentious and time consuming (Peterson and Sharp, 1998, pp. 172–3).

The Maastricht Treaty downgraded the EP's role to consultation in 1992, which made it easier for the Commission to construct qualified majorities for its detailed proposals to the Council (*idem.*, p. 175).

Another Maastricht Treaty innovation was to add a qualifying phrase to Article 163 to the effect that Community R&TD policies, besides strengthening the scientific and technological bases of Community industry and encouraging it to become more competitive at international level, should also promote 'all the research activities deemed necessary by virtue of other Chapters of this Treaty'. This allows for R&TD which is not directly concerned with competitiveness of European indus-

Table 10.9 Various R&TD programmes soon to be integrated into the multiannual framework programmes

	Budget (million ECU)	Years
BAP	75	1985–89
BRIDGE	100	1989–93
ECLAIR	80	1989–94
FLAIR	25	1989–94
COMETT	230	1987–94

Source: Peterson and Sharp (1998), pp. 74–5.

try, such as basic science, or research connected with social objectives. This modification, though modest in appearance, in fact represents a very great shift in Community R&TD policy. Whereas before it was focused entirely on making European industry more competitive, it is now diffused across the entire range of Community objectives, such as regional and social cohesion, quality of life, the environment, etc. This is clear from the evolution of the Fourth and Fifth framework programmes by comparison with previous ones (see Tables 10.10 and 10.11).

Table 10.10 Aims of EU R&TD multiannual framework programmes: trends from 1984 to 1998 (%)

	MFP I 1984–7	MFP II 1987–91	MFP III 1990–4	MFP IV 1994–8	Actual[a] MFP IV up to 1998
Information and communications	25	42	38	28	41
Industrial technologies	11	16	15	16	14
Environment	7	6	9	9	5
Life sciences	5	7	10	13	16
Energy	50	22	16	18	13
Other	2	7	12	16	11
Total (million ECU/Euro)	3750	5396	6600	13 100	5777[b]

[a]As at the end of 1998. [b] Provisional.

Sources: EU Commission, *The European Report on Science and Technology Indicators 1994* (DGXII, Luxembourg, 1994); EU Commission, *Annual Report on Research and Technological Development Activities of the European Union 1999* COM (99) 284 final.

Table 10.11 Aims of EU and R&TD: multiannual framework programmes IV and V (1994–2002, million ECU)

	MFP IV 1994–8		MFP V 1999–2002	
	Value	%	Value	%
Quality of life and management of living resources	1 835	14.0	2 413	16.1
User-friendly information society	3 604	27.5	3 600	24.1
Competitive and sustainable growth	1 722	13.1	2 705	18.1
Energy and Environment and sustainable growth	1 597	12.2	2 125	14.2
Nuclear fission and fusion	1 017	7.8	1 260	8.4
Joint Research Centre	1 095	8.4	739	4.9
International co-operation	575	4.4	475	3.2
SMEs	312	2.4	363	2.4
Training, mobility, human capital	792	6.0	1 280	8.6
Other	551	4.2		
Total	13 100	100	14 960	100

Source: Commission, *Annual Report on Research and Technological Development Activities of the European Union 1999*, COM (99) 284 final.

The Maastricht Treaty also added a new Title called 'Industry' (Article 157, formerly 130), in which the Community was given a broad mandate to promote the competitiveness of European industry by improving its ability to adjust to structural change, to encourage SMEs, to favour co-operation between enterprises and to increase the effectiveness of the Community's R&TD policies by promoting their dissemination. Decisions, if any, were to be taken unanimously. This new Article was the result of a compromise between those countries which wanted the EU to possess a clear mandate to develop a fully-fledged industrial policy, and those which did not. It remains a legal hook upon which to hang such an industrial policy, but for the time being the Commission finds it more convenient to pursue these aims under the R&TD Title because of the QMV rights it has obtained for the Council in this area.

Thus the Amsterdam Treaty lifted the unanimity requirement with regard to establishing the MFPs for R&TD, but did nothing to alter the 'Industry' Title, despite strong representations from the Commission and the then Industry Commissioner, Madame Edith Cresson.

In the meantime, as the Council approved successive MFPs, it refined its objectives. Thus in 1990, the Third MFP specified two new aims, namely to 'increase economic and social cohesion while ensuring the scientific and technical excellence of research projects' and to 'take account of safeguarding the environment

Table 10.12 Annual R&TD expenditures at Community level, 1984–2002, million ECU and million €, current prices

Year	Annual expenditure					
1984	593.0	MFP I				
1985	735.0	MFP I				
1986	874.0	MFP I				
1987	939.3	MFP I	MFP II			
1988	1128.0	MFP I	MFP II			
1989	1412.2		MFP II			
1990	1784.4		MFP II	MFP III		
1991	1887.4		MFP II	MFP III		
1992	2863.2			MFP III		
1993	2691.2			MFP III		
1994	2753.5			MFP III	MFP IV	
1995	2985.8				MFP IV	
1996	3153.5				MFP IV	
1997	3485.6				MFP IV	
1998	3499.3				MFP IV	MFP V
1999	3450.0					MFP V
2000	3600.0					MFP V
2001	3900.0					MFP V
2002	4010.0					MFP V
Grand total 1984–2002	45745.4					
% of Community budget		2.42	3.18	4.05	4.00	3.73

Source: Commission, *Annual Report on R&TD Activities of the European Union 1999*, Brussels, COM (99) 284 final, Table 10.

225

and the quality of life' and in 1992, as has already been mentioned, the broadening of the aims of the MFPs received official sanction in the Maastricht Treaty.

Tables 10.10–10.12 chart the evolution of the MFPs from their inception. Over the years since the first MFP in 1984–7, total funding of R&TD has risen from 2.5% of the Community budget, to 3.73% for the Fifth MFP which runs from 1999 to 2002. The annual sums involved, currently some 3500 million ECU a year, are about 10% of national state aid to industry (see Table 10.4). However, most of the latter – 57% – is currently devoted to regional, rather than industrial policy (see Table 10.3). In fact, comparing like with like, we note that about 10% of *national* state aid to industry currently supports R&D (see Table 10.3), roughly the same amount which is now being channelled through the EU budget, giving a total R&TD effort (national plus Community) of about 8000 million ECU annually (by 2000). This is obviously a big change from the first MFP, when Community expenditure on R&TD represented only a quarter of national R&D budgets (CEC, 1989i, para. 21), which themselves represented only about 4% of total state support to industry (see Table 10.3 again). The trend is something of a political triumph for the Commission, given the great opposition on the part of many member states to transferring an industrial policy mandate to Brussels in the 1960s and 1970s.

This expenditure growth has also gone hand in hand with a massive decline in national aid to 'sectoral objectives' (the notorious steel shipyards and coal subsidies – see Table 10.3), from which we can conclude that there has been a noticeable shift of emphasis away from supporting 'sunset' industries and firms, to supporting 'sunrise' sectors. Where the balance actually lies, however, is impossible to determine without much greater statistical detail than is provided by official EU data.

Comparing the structure of the first four MFPs allows us to note a few trends on the Community's side of total R&TD expenditure. Table 10.9 charts the allocation of resources for each MFP up to MFP IV. The data must be interpreted with care, for the overlap between programmes covers sometimes one, sometimes two years (see Table 10.12), and the level of disbursements in any one year for any one sector may vary due to one-off circumstances. This being said, there has been a clear shift away from energy, IT and telecommunications. These sectors used to absorb 75% of all EU R&TD, but by MFP IV they had dropped to only 36% of the total, the gains for other sectors being in life sciences, industrial technologies and 'other' sectors.

A direct comparison with MFP V does not appear to be possible, as the Commission, in response to various criticisms concerning the old system (seen as unfocused and too heavily dependent on the major 'Round Table' participants), and as a consequence of the much broader list of objectives which EU R&TD now has to meet (see above) has entirely revamped its classification system. Comparing Table 10.10 with Table 10.11 shows just how extensive the change is. Important new items are now highlighted, such as SMEs, training, mobility, human capital, international co-operation, sustainable growth, a 'user-friendly' information society and a wonderful new category called 'quality of life and management of living resources'. Who ever accused international civil servants of lacking poetic inspiration? The latter three categories account for 58% of the total EU R&D budget. However, it would be nice if the Commission could supply a Rosetta stone to enable us to translate the one into the other, for unkind souls might suggest, for instance, that the IT and telecoms barons have recovered pride of place at the R&TD table.

10.4.3 Non-EU technological co-operation

No account of European industrial policy would be complete without a brief description of the Eureka (European Research Co-ordinating Agency) programme. Variable geometry applies in the field of industrial policy. In 1985 President Mitterrand of France launched the Eureka programme. He was clearly frustrated with the lack of anything resembling EU industrial policy, and alarmed at the implications of President Reagan's 'Star Wars' or Strategic Defence Initiative (SDI). This was scheduled to spend $26 billion on advanced electronic, nuclear and space technology, and threatened to siphon off the best European intellectual talent in these areas. President Mitterrand gathered together the then 12 members of the European Community, plus Spain, Portugal, Turkey, the EFTA countries and the European Commission, and founded an intergovernmental organization with a tiny secretariat in Paris.

Its purpose is to promote, through public subsidies, any 'near market' R&D project involving firms in more than one member country. It possesses no central allocative function. Projects are generated in member states and circulated among members to see if other firms or governments might like to join. The Eureka secretariat simply keeps track of what is going on. It has no 'policy' as such and therefore fits the definition of a truly general or macroeconomic industrial policy (although individual projects are obviously the outcome of individual governments' different industrial policies). Any attempt to define an overall objective would have foundered anyway, given Eureka's intergovernmental structure and the fact that member states are free to give the Eureka 'label' to whatever project they consider fits the bill (Peterson and Sharp, 1998, p. 92). The only organizing principle is that projects must involve more than one country and in principle should promote the *development* phase of R&D (so as to comply with EU competition rules – see p. 221 above).

Eureka has thrived over the years and, according to Peterson and Sharp, represents 'a total research effort only marginally smaller than the Framework programme' (p. 90). Unlike the EU itself, Eureka opened its arms to Central and Eastern Europe and beyond to Russia, in the 1990s. It has welcomed non-member observers, from the US government to the Vatican City. It may perhaps have become too successful in some respects.

After starting off with two *grands projets* which absorbed large amounts of public money (the ill-fated HDTV project and the more successful Joint European Submicron Silicon Initiative – JESSI), Eureka has settled down to sponsoring an ever-larger number of smaller research projects.[5] By so doing, it substantially increases the chances of 'stumbling on winners' and decreases the incidence of R&D disasters.

Its birth coincided with the launching of the Commission's own proposal for an expanded role in R&D (see above) and was viewed with deep suspicion in Brussels. Meanwhile, Germany under Chancellor Kohl was torn between accepting participation in the American SDI programme and teaming up with France and President Mitterrand. In the end, the Franco-German axis withstood the strain and Eureka survived.

Calming the Commission's fears that R&D had somehow escaped from its fold was another matter. The ostensible division of labour between the two was that the EU should devote its energies to 'pre-competitive' R&TD (essentially research and technology), while Eureka should sponsor 'near-market' development. In practice, Eureka offers EU member states a welcome alternative to the EU's cumbersome MFPs. The Commission of course retains its overarching supervisory function. As we have already seen, it has long taken a favourable view of state aid to R&D, but in 1986 insisted on the 'notification' of any aid in excess of a paltry 20 million ECU (see section 10.2 above), the timing of which suggests an insitutional reaction to the Eureka programme. In 1996 the Commission issued a new set of guidelines for state aid to R&D[6] to bring Community practice into line with new WTO obligations. In particular, the Commission highlighted the distinction between WTO-compatible support for R&D (squarely in the pre-competitive box) and illegal R&D support (aid to the commercial introduction of industrial innovations or the marketing of new products). This left very little space between the Commission's own 'pre-competitive' MFPs, and the 'near-market' Eureka projects. The battle for turf continues. The only concession to Eureka projects made by the Commission in the 1996 guidelines was to increase the notification threshold to 40 million ECU (but it has never challenged a Eureka project in practice).

The Commission, overwhelmed by the caseload all this had generated, made a strategic withdrawal towards the end of the 1990s. It decided to sponsor a new Council regulation to grant group exemptions, *inter alia* for R&D state aid[7] which meets its criteria for acceptibility. It nevertheless retains its overarching supervisory function.

While there is clearly some overlap between Eureka and the EU's MFPs, there is also plenty of complementarity. At least theoretically, a project sponsored by the EU at the top end of the R&TD pipeline could be taken up by a Eureka project at the lower end of the process. However, the much wider membership of Eureka might have got in the way of such a neat division of labour. Is it then a pure coincidence that the Fifth MFP puts a new emphasis on international co-operation (see Table 10.11)?

In short, Mitterrand's Eureka failed to become the spearhead for massive government-sponsored R&D projects in clear opposition to the EU's attempts to co-ordinate R&D at a European level. Instead it gradually evolved into a useful complement, offering public support for a multitude of international R&D ventures spreading far beyond the EU's borders.

10.5   Conclusion

The EU's industrial policy has come a long way since it first sponsored 'crisis cartels' in the 1970s. It has shifted, slowly but surely, away from supporting 'sunset' sectors to sponsoring 'sunrise' industries. It is critical of member states' *ad hoc* subsidies to individual firms and is managing to claw back a growing proportion of illegal aid. It has launched its own R&TD programme in the teeth of member state opposition. It has tried hard to avoid the trap of 'picking the winners' by supporting only 'pre-competitive' R&TD. The Commission has even come to live with the rival Eureka programme initiated by its two main supporters, France and Germany.

There are by now countless evaluations of all these efforts to support innovation in Europe, all of which are globally positive while pointing out some of the obvious deficiencies. Academic sources are naturally more critical, and emphasize problems such as the eternal *juste retour*, the inevitable politicization of the R&TD

funding process,[8] holding private beneficiaries to account,[9] and so on. Looking back over the last 15 years, with an accumulated R&TD expenditure of 46 billion Euro at EU level, and roughly the same again at member state level, who can tell where European industry would have been today without it? The HDTV experiment was a fiasco,[10] but clearly support for telecommunications research has paid off handsomely, since the European global mobile telephone system (GSM) has proved to be a huge commercial success, and some of this success is surely attributable to the ESPRIT and BRITE programmes (and their successors). The fact is that no one will ever know what the *anti-monde* would look like.

Is enough public money being spent on R&TD? Is enough being done to develop an innovation-friendly environment? Is enough thought being devoted to creating the right pro-innovation institutions at a European level? The answers to these questions must remain political. R&TD competes with many other EU policies for political attention. Agriculture, structural and regional issues, enlargement and external relations all receive substantial funds from the EU budget. The share allotted to each reflects complex political choices which, if we accept as legitimate the process through which they are reached, must be 'right', at least in these terms. These are big 'ifs', however. The economic approach is tempted to reflect on the fact that the EU spends eleven times more on agriculture than on R&TD, and nine times more on structural problems. The opportunity cost of supporting farming or trying to deal with structural inequalities could thus be evaluated in terms of fewer resources being devoted to innovation and economic growth.

Looking to the future, it is clear that support for R&TD at European level (and perhaps also at member state level) will become more and more involved with aims which have nothing to do with the competitiveness of European firms. Since the Maastricht Treaty, R&TD is supposed to serve any and all the EU's many objectives. Is this to be welcomed or deplored? The advancement of knowledge on as broad a front as possible is probably to be welcomed. However, care must be exercised to ensure that knowledge is indeed advanced, otherwise the lack of focus will open the doors to plenty of nonsense.

Two new departures are needed in the years to come. First, the EU lacks a common 'European Institute of Technology', like MIT or Imperial College. It needs a post-graduate European institute of higher scientific learning, in order to promote basic research, to attract the best of its young graduates and provide an extra tier to the European academic career ladder. At present, far too many young Europeans go to the United States for their doctoral and post-doctoral research, never to return. Money spent at the top end of the R&TD pipeline is by far the most effective in the long run.

Second, the multiannual framework programmes must encourage links with firms from non-EU countries, not only current applicants and future candidates as is already the case, but also with American, Japanese or *any* firms, from any country at all. There should be an end to the idea that R&D should carry the burden of 'building Europe'. Europe is pretty well built by now, and can well afford to set its technological community free to seek partnerships wherever they happen to be the most fruitful. Discriminating between European and non-European firms cannot possibly promote efficiency and might be positively harmful in the long run.

Notes

1. An astonishing example along the same lines was provided by the *Financial Times* in a story entitled 'Police to hire investigators for company fraud cases' (1 March 2000, p. 7). After contracting out the task of running prisons, the British police are now extending the concept to detective work. What next? Presumably the taxpayer benefits from unbundling policework and using markets instead of hierarchies to deliver this complex set of services.
2. Council Regulation (EC) 994/98 on the application of Articles 87 and 88 of the EC Treaty to certain categories of horizontal state aid.
3. The Round Table of industrialists (also known as the 'Big 12') brought together by Viscount Davignon in 1982 was composed of the chief executives of the following companies: for Germany: AEG, Nixdorf and Siemens; for France: Bull, CGE-Alcatel and Thomson; for the UK: GEC, ICL and Plessey; for Italy: Olivetti and STET; and for the Netherlands: Philips. This influential group is credited not only with supporting the EU's R&TD policy, but with backing Eureka (see pp. 227–8) and with shaping much official policy in this area. In turn the group is suspected of being the principal beneficiaries.
4. *France* v. *Commission*, Case C–202/88, ECJ decision of 19 March 1991.
5. See *Eureka News* and consult the Eureka web site for information.
6. 'Community framework for state aid for research and development', OJ C 405 17/2/96, pp. 0005–0014.
7. Council Regulation 994/98 on the application of Articles 87 and 88 of the EC Treaty to certain categories of horizontal state aid [1998] OJ L142, 14/5/1998.
8. Peterson and Sharp, 1998, provide an excellent and balanced account.
9. The Court of Auditors (Annual Report, 1995) C 340 12/11/96, Chapter 9, complains that the Commission audited only 60 contracts out of 13 500 in 1995 (recovering 9 million ECU in the process), while its own audit of eight projects revealed 'grave anomalies' in each and every one!
10. See Court of Auditors, *op. cit.*, paras. 9.12–9.49.

11 The Common Agricultural Policy

A. M. EL-AGRAA

Unlike EFTA, the EU extends its free trade arrangements between member states to agriculture and agricultural products. The term 'agricultural products' is defined as 'the products of the soil, of stockfarming and of fisheries and products of first-state processing directly related to the foregoing' (Article 32.1, Amsterdam Treaty, to which all the articles in this chapter refer), although fisheries has developed into a policy of its own – see Chapter 12. Moreover, in 1957, the EEC Treaty dictated that the operation and development of the common market for agricultural products should be accompanied by the establishment of a 'common agricultural policy' among member states (Article 32.4).

One could ask: why were the common market arrangements extended to agriculture? or why was agriculture (together with transport) singled out for special treatment? Such questions are to some extent irrelevant. According to the General Agreement on Tariffs and Trade (GATT, now WTO, the World Trade Organization – see Appendix to Chapter 1):

> a customs union shall be understood to mean the substitution of a single customs union territory for two or more territories, so that ... duties and other restrictive regulations of commerce are eliminated with respect to substantially all the trade between the constituent territories of the union. (Dam, 1970)

Since agricultural trade constituted a substantial part of the total trade of the founding members, especially so in the case of France, it is quite obvious that excluding agriculture from the EEC arrangements would have been in direct contradiction of this requirement (see next section). Moreover, free agricultural trade would have been to no avail if each member nation continued to protect agriculture in its own way (see section 11.4) since that would have amounted to replacing tariffs with non-tariff trade barriers (NTBs) and might also have conflicted with EC competition rules (see Chapter 9). In any case:

> a programme of economic integration which excluded agriculture stood no chance of success. It is important to appreciate that the Rome Treaty was a delicate balance of national interests of the contracting parties. Let us consider West Germany and France in terms of trade outlets. In the case of West Germany the prospect of free trade in industrial goods, and free access to the French market in particular, was extremely inviting. In the case of France the relative efficiency of her agriculture ... as compared with West Germany held out the prospect that in a free Community agricultural market she would make substantial inroads into the West German market ... Agriculture had therefore to be included. (Swann, 1973, p. 82)

The purpose of this chapter is to discuss the need for singling out agriculture as one of the earliest targets for a common policy; to specify the objectives of the

Common Agricultural Policy (CAP); to explain the mechanisms of the CAP and their development to date; to make an economic evaluation of its implications and to assess the performance of the policy in terms of its practical achievements (or lack of achievements) and in terms of its theoretical viability.

Before tackling these points, it is necessary to give some general background information about agriculture in the EU at the time of the formation of the EC and at a more recent date.

11.1 General background

The economic significance of agriculture in the economies of member states can be demonstrated in terms of its share in the total labour force and in GNP. Table 11.1 gives this information. The most significant observations that can be made regarding this information are as follows:

1. At the time of the signing of the treaty many people in the original six were dependent on farming as their main source of income; indeed, 25% of the total labour force was employed in agriculture – the equivalent percentage for the United Kingdom was less than 5 and for Denmark was about 9.

2. The agricultural labour force was worse off than most people in the rest of the EC: for example, in France about 26% of the labour force was engaged in agriculture, but for the same year the contribution of this sector to French GDP was about 12%.[1]

3. A rapid fall in both the agricultural labour force and in the share of agriculture in GNP occurred between 1955 and 1995,[2] and this trend is being maintained, albeit at a slower pace.

It is also important to have some information about the area and size distribution of agricultural holdings. This is given in Table 11.2. The most significant factor to note is that in the original six, at the time of the formation of the EC, approximately two-thirds of farm holdings were between 1 and 10 hectares in size. At about the same time, the equivalent figure for the United Kingdom was about two-fifths. Since then there has been a steady increase in the percentage of larger size holdings.

A final piece of important background information that one needs to bear in mind is that, except for Italy and the United Kingdom, the EU farming system is an owner-occupier system rather than one of tenant farming.

11.2 The problems of agriculture

The agricultural sector has been declining in relative importance and those who have remained on the land have continued to receive incomes well below the national average. Governments of most developed countries have, therefore, always found it necessary to practise some sort of control over the market for agricultural commodities through price supports, subsidies to farmers, import levies, import quotas, etc. In this section I shall analyse the background to such practices.

It should be plain to all that the production of many agricultural commodities is

Table 11.1 Share of agriculture in total labour force and GDP (%)

		Belgium	France	Germany	Italy	Luxembourg	Netherlands	Denmark	Ireland	UK	Greece	Portugal	Spain	Austria	Finland	Sweden
Labour force	1955	9.3	25.9	18.9	39.5	25.0	13.7	25.4	38.8	4.8	–	–	–	–	–	–
	1970	4.5	13.5	8.6	20.2	9.7	5.8	11.5	27.1	2.7	40.8	–	29.5	18.7	24.4	8.1
	1975	3.4	10.9	7.1	15.5	6.1	6.5	9.3	23.8	2.7	33.2	–	–	–	–	–
	1980	2.9	8.5	5.3	14.3	5.5	4.5	8.1	18.3	2.4	30.3	28.6	19.3	10.6	13.5	5.1
	1985	3.2	7.3	5.3	10.9	4.0	4.8	6.2	15.8	2.6	28.5	21.9	16.1	–	–	–
	1990	2.7	5.6	3.7	8.8	3.3	4.6	4.4	15.0	2.2	23.9	18.0	11.8	2.9	8.4	3.4
	1995	2.7	4.9	3.2	7.5	3.7	3.7	5.7	12.0	2.1	20.4	11.5	9.3	7.3	7.7	3.7
National output	1955	8.1	12.3	8.5	21.6	9.0	12.0	19.2	29.6	5.0	–	–	–	–	–	–
	1970	4.2	6.6	3.0	8.0	3.3	6.0	7.0	17.0	3.0	–	–	8.9	7.0	12.0	–
	1975	3.2	5.6	2.9	8.7	3.5	4.7	7.4	18.1	1.9	19.0	7.3	–	–	–	–
	1980	2.0	4.0	1.9	6.0	2.8	3.0	5.0	11.3	2.0	14.0	–	–	4.0	10.0	4.0
	1985	2.0	4.0	2.0	5.0	–	4.0	6.0	14.0	2.0	17.0	10.0	6.0	–	–	–
	1990	2.0	4.0	1.7	4.0	2.4	4.0	5.0	10.5	1.5	17.0	5.5	4.7	3.0	6.0	3.0
	1995	1.6	2.0	0.8	2.6	0.9	3.2	2.5	5.4	0.9	7.5	2.0	2.7	2.2	1.8	1.0

Source: Various issues of The Agricultural Situation in The Community, European Union (EU Brussels) and World Bank's World Development Report.

Table 11.2 Size distribution of agricultural holdings (% of total)

Hectares	Belgium	Denmark	France	Germany	Greece	Ireland	Italy	Luxembourg	Netherlands	Portugal	Spain	UK	Austria	Finland	Sweden
1960															
1–<5	48.5	18	26	45	na	20	68	32	38	na	na	29.5	na	na	na
5–<10	26.5	28	21	25	na	24	19	18	27	na	na	13	na	na	na
10–<20	18	28	27	21	na	30	8.5	26	23	na	na	16	na	na	na
20–<50	6	23	21	8	na	21	3	22	11	na	na	22.5	na	na	na
50+	1	3	5	1	na	5	1.5	2	1	na	na	19	na	na	na
1973															
1–<5	31	12	22	36	72	15	68	21	25	78	56	16	na	na	na
5–<10	23	20	16	20	20.5	16.5	17.5	13	22	12.5	18	13	na	na	na
10–<20	27	29	24	24	6	31	8.5	20	31	5	12	16	na	na	na
20–<50	16	32	28	18	1.5	29	4	41	20	2.5	8.5	26	na	na	na
50+	1	7	10	2	0.0	8.5	2	7	2	2	5.5	29	na	na	na
1980															
1–<5	28.4	11.1	20.4	34.5	72	15.2	68.1	19.1	24.0	77.9	55.8	11.8	na	na	na
5–<10	19.8	17.6	14.6	18.6	19.9	11.9	16.7	10.6	20.2	12.6	18.0	12.5	na	na	na
10–<20	26.6	26.5	21.1	22.7	6.2	30.3	8.7	14.9	28.9	5.2	12.0	16.0	na	na	na
20–<50	20.9	34.7	30.4	20.3	1.6	29.8	4.5	38.3	23.9	2.5	8.7	27.1	na	na	na
50+	4.2	10.1	13.3	3.9	0.2	8.8	2.0	17.0	2.9	1.8	5.5	32.6	na	na	na
1987															
1–<5	27.7	1.7	18.2	29.4	69.4	16.1	67.9	18.9	24.9	72.5	53.3	13.5	na	na	na
5–<10	18.1	16.3	11.7	17.6	20.0	15.2	16.9	9.9	18.4	15.0	19.0	12.4	na	na	na
10–<20	24.5	25.3	19.1	22.1	7.6	29.2	8.7	12.4	25.0	7.2	12.3	15.3	na	na	na
20–<50	23.9	39.4	32.8	24.8	2.5	30.5	4.6	32.5	27.3	3.4	9.4	25.4	na	na	na
50+	5.8	17.2	18.1	6.1	0.5	9.0	1.9	26.2	4.4	1.9	6.0	33.3	na	na	na
1995															
1–<5	31.1	2.7	26.7	31.2	74.8	9.3	77.9	24.5	31.3	76.4	54.3	13.0	28.1	10.0	11.9
5–<10	14.4	16.5	9.5	14.8	14.9	13.4	10.4	8.8	16.0	11.5	16.6	12.6	18.8	17.8	17.5
10–<20	17.9	21.7	12.1	17.6	6.7	26.5	5.6	7.9	18.3	6.3	11.5	15.4	22.1	30.1	21.4
20–<50	25.8	33.8	24.1	23.3	2.7	37.3	4.2	20.8	26.3	3.3	9.0	24.1	16.1	34.9	27.8
50+	8.4	24.9	27.0	12.6	0.4	13.2	1.6	37.4	6.3	2.2	7.6	34.2	3.6	6.8	21.0

na = not available

Source: Calculated from various issues of *The Agricultural Situation in The Community, European Union, Eurostat Review 1977–86* and *Eurostat Yearbook 1998/9*, all published by EU Commission, Brussels.

subject to forces that lie beyond the direct control of the farmers concerned. Drought, floods, earthquakes and to some extent invasions of pests, for instance, would lead to an actual level of agricultural production far short of that *planned* by the farmers. On the other hand, exceptionally favourable conditions could result in *actual* production being far in excess of that *planned* by farmers. It is therefore necessary to have some theoretical notions about the effects of such deviations between planned and actual agricultural produce on farmers' prices and received incomes.

The predictions of economic theory can be illustrated by reference to a simple diagram. In Figure 11.1, SS represents the range of quantities that farmers plan to supply to the market at various prices in a particular period of time given a certain set of 'market circumstances', for example agricultural input prices, farmers' objectives for production, agricultural technology, etc. DD represents the various quantities that consumers of agricultural products plan to purchase at alternative prices in a specific period of time given a certain set of 'market circumstances', for example consumers' tastes for agricultural products, their incomes, population size and composition, etc. D_1D_1 and D_2D_2 represent two such demand curves, with D_2D_2 being less elastic than D_1D_1.

If consumers' plans and producers' plans actually materialize, P_3 will be the equilibrium price which will clear the equilibrium output Oq_2 off the market. As long as this situation is maintained, agricultural prices (represented by P_3) will remain stable and agricultural incomes (represented by the area OP_3Eq_2) will also remain stable. However, actual agricultural production may fall short of, or exceed, the equilibrium planned production Oq_2 for any of the above-mentioned reasons. If a shortage occurs such that actual output is Oq_1, the price will rise above the equilibrium level to P_5 (for D_2D_2) or P_4 (for D_1D_1). In the case of an actual supply of Oq_3, the price will fall to P_1 or P_2 respectively. Therefore, when actual agricultural production deviates from the planned output, fluctuations in agricultural prices will

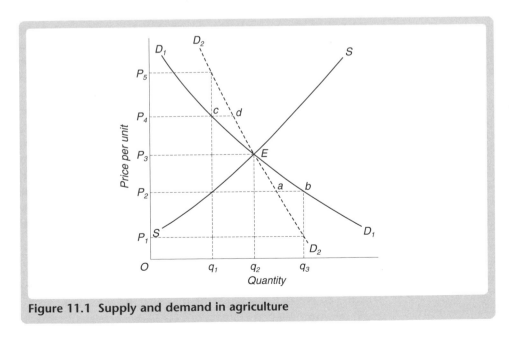

Figure 11.1 Supply and demand in agriculture

result, such that an excess actual output reduces prices and a shortage in output increases prices. The extent of these price fluctuations is determined by the price elasticity of demand: the more (less) price inelastic the demand curve, the wider (narrower) the margin of price fluctuations.

Moreover, as long as the demand curve does not have a price elasticity of unity, agricultural incomes will fluctuate from the planned level OP_3Eq_2: with a price elastic (inelastic) demand curve, an actual shortage will result in a lower (higher) income for the farmers and an actual excess supply will lead to higher (lower) incomes.

At this point it is appropriate to mention two further characteristics of agriculture in advanced economies. First, as people's incomes rise they tend to spend a smaller proportion of it on agricultural products: the income elasticity of demand is low. (People spend relatively less on food as their incomes rise, therefore they spend even less on agricultural products because a higher proportion of the expenditure on food goes on processing, packaging and presentation.) Hence poor (rich) nations tend to spend a large (small) proportion of their income on agricultural products.

Second, because of advances in technology and growth of factors of production, average incomes have been rising in developed economies. Agricultural economists would argue that, for the same reason, agricultural outputs tend to rise at least at the same rate as those of the non-agricultural sector. Once it is realized that consumers would want to spend relatively more on non-agricultural products as their living standards rise (the income elasticity of demand is high for these products), it is inevitable to conclude that there would be a relative tendency for a fall in the demand for farm products. Hence farm incomes would tend to lag behind the incomes of those engaged in the non-farm sector.

Furthermore, once one appreciates that the demand for most agricultural (non-agricultural) products has a low (high) price and income elasticity and that agriculture as an industry is becoming at least as efficient as the national average (because of technological progress in the agricultural sector, the supply curve is moving to the right all the time), then it is easy to understand that agricultural (non-agricultural) price levels and incomes have a tendency to relative decline (rise) with economic growth. This adds a new dimension to the problem, in that, if an 'agricultural stabilization policy' is to be introduced, its aim must not simply be one of stabilizing agricultural prices and incomes, but also of raising agricultural incomes to the national average – if only because policy dictates so.

However, the assumption that agricultural outputs tend to rise at at least the same rate as those of the non-agricultural sector does not stand up to close scrutiny. In the United Kingdom, according to the Cambridge Department of Applied Economics Programme for Growth 12, agricultural productivity grew at a rate of 1.6% per annum compound during the period 1948–68, as against 1.8% for manufacturing. In the United Kingdom, manufacturing productivity growth had been low and agricultural productivity growth, because of the form of policy, high. In the rest of Europe the disparity would have been much greater. Since agriculture started as a low-productivity industry, the disparity has indeed worsened – the impact of science and technology on farming is less than on manufacturing for two reasons: first, agriculture is characterized by decreasing returns to scale while manufacturing is characterized at least by constant returns to scale; second, there are severe institutional constraints on increasing the size of farms, and therefore technology can make its impact only from specialization within the existing farm structure. Economies of specialization are limited within this constraint and furthermore there are offsetting losses of economies of joint production (from rotations, etc.) which are more pronounced in agriculture than elsewhere and are virtually lost from specialization. Hence the problem of agricultural incomes stems from declining agricultural productivity (in comparison with manufacturing productivity) rather than from inelastic demand for agricultural products. In any case, the elasticity has not been so low once population growth is taken into account. (For a forceful and detailed explanation of these points, see Bowers, 1972.)

This is a more convincing argument in that it suggests that the setting of reasonable agricultural prices, given the declining relative efficiency of agriculture, ensures declining agricultural incomes. Hence, the way to increasing agricultural productivity is to encourage the marginal agricultural labour to seek alternative employment. This view is consistent with the structural problem of the EU, where declining farm incomes are attributed to the fact that labour does not flow out of agriculture quickly enough (trapped resources with low salvage values).

The above suggests why most advanced mixed economies have been adopting some kind of agricultural support policies. Other arguably more important considerations include historical factors, strategic considerations and the strengths of the agricultural lobby; indeed, it is commonly accepted that the latter is the main determining factor of these apparently uneconomic policies.

11.3 Agricultural support policies

With the foregoing analysis and observations, we are in a position to attempt a specification of the necessary elements in an agricultural policy and to point out the difficulties associated with such a policy.

In most advanced mixed economies where living standards have been rising, agricultural policies were introduced with the aim of achieving the following:

1. As a minimum requirement, avoid impeding the *natural* process of transferring resources from the agricultural sector to the non-agricultural sector of the economy, and if necessary promote this process.

2. Aim at protecting the incomes of those who are occupied in the agricultural sector. The definition of the farm sector raises a number of problems, for instance:

   should one's policy be devised to guarantee prosperity to any who might wish at some future date to enter agriculture – and moreover to assure a reasonable rate of return for any amount of capital that they may wish to invest in farming? Or should one's policy be geared to those already in the industry who have made resource allocation decisions based on expectations of the future which governments then feel under an obligation to realise? (Josling, 1969, p. 176)

3. Aim at some kind of price stability, since agriculture forms the basis of living costs and wages and is therefore the basis of industrial costs.

4. Make provision for an adequate agricultural sector since security of food supplies is essential for a nation.[3]

5. Ensure the maintenance of agriculture as a family business, and the maintenance of some population in rural villages.

Unfortunately these objectives are, to a large extent, mutually contradictory. Any policy which aims at providing adequate environmental conditions, secure food supplies and agricultural incomes equal to the national average interferes with the economy's natural development. Moreover, the provision of stable farm incomes, let alone rising farm incomes, is not compatible with the provision of stable agricultural prices. This point can be illustrated by reference to Figure 11.1.

Suppose that D_1D_1 is a demand curve which has unit price elasticity along its entire range. In order to keep farmers' incomes constant it would be necessary to operate along this curve, keeping farmers' incomes equal to OP_3Eq_2. If agricultural production deviates from Oq_2, the following will ensue:

1. When an output is equal to Oq_3, the authority in charge of the policy must purchase ab in order to make certain that the price level falls only to P_2 rather than P_1, therefore ensuring that farmers' incomes remain at the predetermined level.

2. When output is equal to Oq_1 the authority must sell cd in order to achieve the price level P_4 rather than P_5.

Hence a policy of income stability can be achieved only if the price level is allowed to fluctuate, even though the required level of fluctuation in this case is less than that dictated by the operation of the free market forces.

On the other hand, a policy of maintaining constant price levels (constant P_3) will give farmers higher incomes when output is Oq_3 (by $q_2q_3 \times OP_3$) since the authority will have to purchase the excess supply at the guaranteed price, and lower incomes when output is Oq_1 (by $q_1q_2 \times OP_3$). Therefore, a policy of price stability will guarantee income fluctuations in such a manner that higher (lower) agricultural outputs will result in higher (lower) farmers' incomes.

This throws light on another aspect of agricultural polices: if average farm prices are set at too high a level this will encourage farmers to increase production, since at the guaranteed price they can sell as much as they can produce. This, in effect, results in a perfectly elastic supply curve at price level P_3. Under such circumstances, an excess supply of these commodities could result. This is a point that has to be borne in mind when assessing the CAP.

11.4 EC member policies

Prior to the formation of the EC, member countries (except for the Netherlands) had adopted different practices in their agricultural stabilization policies. This is an appropriate point to turn to a discussion of these policies.

Agricultural policies in Western Europe as a whole since the Second World War have been rather complicated, but a substantial element of these policies had been the support of prices received by farmers for their produce. In this respect, a variety of methods have been practised:

1. *Deficiency payments schemes* (supplements to market-determined prices): these refer to policies of guaranteed farm prices which the government ensures by means of deficiency payments. These prices become the farmers' planning prices. This system was used in the United Kingdom before it joined the EC; however, the United Kingdom was moving away from this system for budgetary reasons, not as a preparation for joining the EC.

2. *Variable levies* or *import quota systems*: these systems are concerned with policies which effectively impose threshold prices and charge levies on imports equal to the difference between world prices and the threshold prices.

3. *Market control systems*: these aim at limiting the quantities of agricultural produce that actually reach the market. This can be achieved by ensuring that the produce is marketed by single private authorities (agencies) or by certain government departments. The quantity that is not allowed to reach the market can

> either be destroyed, stored (to be released when prices rise), exported, donated to low income countries or needy groups within the home economy, or converted into another product which does not compete directly with the original one. Examples of this last course of action are 'breaking' of eggs for use as egg powder and rendering some cereals and vegetables unfit for human consumption (usually by adding a dye or fish oil) but suitable for animal feed. (Ritson, 1973, p. 99)

This system was widely used in the original Six.

4. *Direct income payments*: this term describes schemes whereby incomes are transferred to the farmers without these bearing any relationship to the level of output. The nearest to this system was the Swedish system.

5. *Non-price policies*: a miscellaneous set of policies such as import subsidies on both current and capital inputs, output increasing measures (R&D), export subsidies and production quotas. Of course, input subsidies do add to the effective protection afforded to agriculture.

Let us now turn to an analytical consideration of these schemes. The analysis of (1), (2) and (4) is slightly different from that illustrated by Figure 11.1 in that one needs to deal with products which compete with imports. This is because most Western European countries, specially the original Six, were net importers of most agricultural products at the time of the inception of the EC; the nearest they came to self-sufficiency was in livestock.

Assume (unrealistically in the context of the EU, since Western Europe is a large consumer) that the level of imports does not influence the world prices of agricultural commodities and that, allowing for transport costs and quality differentials, the import price level is equal to the domestic price. Then consider the different support systems with reference to Figure 11.2.

In Figure 11.2, P_w is the world price, Oq_1 is the domestic production level and q_1q_4 is the level of imports given free trade conditions. When a deficiency payment scheme is in operation, P_d becomes the guaranteed farmer price. This leads to an increase in domestic production (from Oq_1 to Oq_2) which guarantees the farmer a deficiency payment of P_wP_dbc (equal to $(P_d - P_w) \times Oq_2$) and which results in foreign exchange savings of q_1acq_2. On the assumption that the supply curve is a reflection of the marginal social opportunity cost of resources used in production (for a detailed discussion of this see El-Agraa and Jones, 1981) it is possible to make some significant remarks regarding this new farm revenue.

The area q_1abq_2, in an extremely simple analysis, approximates the value of the extra inputs attracted into agriculture by the deficiency payment policy. The area P_wP_dba represents the additional producer's surplus, or economic rent.[4] This can be thought of as an income transfer in favour of the farming sector.[5] Area abc represents the net loss to the society for adopting this policy; this is because the price for the consumer remains at P_w and therefore the level of imports is equal to cf.

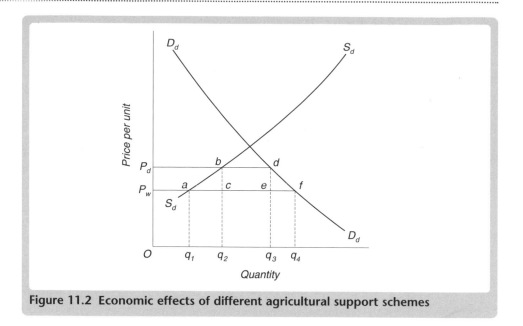

Figure 11.2 Economic effects of different agricultural support schemes

When a variable levy scheme is in operation, the relevant farmer price equals the threshold price so that P_d becomes the price facing both farmers and consumers. Hence, the effects on the agricultural producing sector are exactly the same as in the previous case. However, the foreign exchange savings would now be equal to q_1acq_2 plus q_3efq_4 due to the fall in consumption by q_3q_4 (from Oq_4 to Oq_3) – imports fall to bd. The loss of the policy is therefore equal to the areas abc and def. Area $bced$ (the revenue accruing from the levy) represents a transfer from the consumers to the government.

Under extremely restrictive assumptions, it can be demonstrated that the operation of an import quota system equal to q_2q_3 produces the same result as a variable levy of the same equivalence.[6] There is another problem here relating to who gains the area $bced$, which in the variable levy system represents government revenue: if the government assumes responsibility or if the importers are well organized there is no problem, but if the foreign exporters are well organized they can absorb this area in the form of economic rent or excess profit – see El-Agraa (1989b).

In a purely static theoretical analysis, direct income subsidies have no economic costs (see Johnson, 1965a), particularly since they do not harm the consumer or the foreign supplier. However, for these subsidies to be strictly neutral in their economic impact, they should be paid in such a manner as to 'allow the recipients to leave farming without prejudice to their income from the payment scheme'.[7] Moreover, in the real world costs will be incurred in the process of dispersing the income, and there is also the question of where the money to finance the subsidies should come from.

From the foregoing analysis it is evident that the income transfer system, given the stated provisos, is the most efficient mechanism for farm support and that the variable levy or import quota system is the least efficient in this respect.[8] This is because the income subsidies and deficiency payment schemes allow the consumer to decide according to the cheapest international prices available, while the variable levy and import quota systems interfere with both producers and consumers. This comparison should be borne in mind when reading the conclusions of this chapter.

11.5 Objectives of the CAP

Owing to the variety of agricultural support policies that existed in Western Europe at the time of the formation of the EC, it was necessary, for the reasons given at the beginning, especially French insistence, to subject agriculture to equal treatment in all member states. Equal treatment of coal and steel (both necessary inputs for industry and therefore of the same significance as agriculture) was already under way through the ECSC and the importance of agriculture meant that equal treatment here was vital.

The objectives of the CAP are clearly defined in Article 33. They are as follows:

1. To increase agricultural productivity by promoting technical progress and by ensuring the rational development of agricultural production and the optimum utilization of all factors of production, in particular labour.

2. To ensure thereby 'a fair standard of living for the agricultural community, in particular by increasing the individual earnings of persons engaged in agriculture'.

3. To stabilize markets.

4. To provide certainty of supplies.

5. To ensure supplies to consumers at reasonable prices.

The Treaty also specifies that in

working out the Common Agricultural Policy, and any special methods which this may involve, account shall be taken of:
(i) the particular nature of agricultural activity, which results from agriculture's social structure and from structural and natural disparities between the various agricultural regions;
(ii) the need to effect the appropriate adjustments by degrees;
(iii) the fact that, in the member states, agriculture constitutes a sector closely linked with the economy as a whole.

The Treaty further specifies that in order to attain the objectives set out above a common organization of agricultural markets shall be formed:

This organisation shall take one of the following forms depending on the product concerned:
(a) common rules as regards competition;
(b) compulsory co-ordination of the various national marketing organisations; or
(c) a European organisation of the market.

Moreover, the common organization so established:

may include all measures required to achieve the objectives set out . . . in particular price controls, subsidies for the production and distribution of the various products, stock-piling and carry-over systems and common arrangements for stabilisation of imports and exports.

The common organisation shall confine itself to pursuing the objectives set out . . . and shall exclude any discrimination between producers and consumers within the Community.

Any common policy shall be based on common criteria and uniform methods of calculation.

Finally, in order to enable the common organization to achieve its objectives, 'one or more agricultural orientation and guarantee funds may be set up'.

The remaining articles (34–38) deal with some detailed considerations relating to the objectives and the common organization.

The true objectives of the CAP were established after the Stresa conference in 1958 which was convened in accordance with the Treaty. The objectives were in the spirit of the Treaty:

(i) to increase farm incomes not only by a system of transfers from the non-farm population through a price support policy, but also by the encouragement of rural industrialisation to give alternative opportunities to farm labour;

(ii) to contribute to overall economic growth by allowing specialisation within the Community and eliminating artificial market distortions;

(iii) preserving the family farm and . . . ensuring that structural and price policies go hand in hand.

It can be seen, therefore, that the CAP was not preoccupied simply with the implementation of common prices and market supports; it also included a commitment to encourage the structural improvement of farming, particularly when the former measures did not show much success (see the later section on assessment). Regarding the latter point, the main driving force has been the Mansholt Plan of 1968.[9] Dr Sicco Mansholt, who was the Agricultural Commissioner at the time, emphasized that market supports by themselves would not solve the agricultural problem. The plan, which basically relates to the guidance aspects of the CAP, proposed the following principal measures:

(a) A first set of measures concerns the structure of agricultural production, and contains two main elements:

(i) One group of measures, varying widely in character, must be taken to bring about an appropriate reduction in the number of persons employed in agriculture. Older people will have to be offered a supplementary annual income allowance if they agree to retire and thereby release land; younger farmers should be enabled to change over to non-farming activities; the children of farmers, finally, should be given an education which enables them to choose an occupation other than farming, if they so desire. For the two latter categories, new jobs will have to be created in many regions. These efforts at reducing manpower should be brought to bear with particular force on one group of persons within agriculture, namely, those who own their farm businesses, inasmuch as the structural reform of farms themselves . . . largely depends upon the withdrawal of a large number of these people from agriculture.

(ii) Secondly, far-reaching and co-ordinated measures should be taken with a view to the creation of agricultural (farming) enterprises of adequate economic dimensions.[10] If such enterprises are to be set up and kept running, the land they need will have to be made available to them on acceptable terms; this will require an active and appropriate agrarian policy.

(b) A second group of measures concerns markets, with the double purpose of improving the way they work and of adjusting supply more closely to demand:

(i) Here a major factor will be a cautious price policy, and this will be all the more effective as the enterprises react more sensitively to the points offered by the market.

(ii) A considerable reduction of the area of cultivated land will work in the same direction.

(iii) Better information will have to be made available to all market parties (products, manufacturers and dealers), producers will have to accept stricter discipline and there will have to be some concentration of supply. Product councils and groupings of product councils will have to be set up at European level to take over certain responsibilities in this field.

(c) In the case of farmers who are unable to benefit from the measures described, it may prove necessary to provide personal assistance not tied either to the volume of output or to the employment of factors of production. This assistance should be payable within specified limits defined in the light of regional factors and the age of the persons concerned.

After a lengthy discussion the Council issued three directives (72/159–72/161) in April 1972: Directive 72/159 allowed member nations to support their farmers' modernization through grants or subsidized interest rates on the condition that these farms were capable of generating income levels comparable with those of other local occupations; Directive 72/160 permitted member nations to extend lump-sum payments or annuities to farm workers aged between 55 and 65 years to lure them into leaving the industry; Directive 72/161 aimed at encouraging member countries to establish 'socio-economic guidance services' to entice farm workers to retrain and relocate. However, although the precise method of implementation, itself not mandatory, of these directives was left to the discretion of national governments, about a quarter of the necessary outlay (65% for Ireland and Italy) would be borne by the CAP guidance section. Thus, these directives were in the spirit of the Mansholt Plan.

Yet the EC expenditure on the structural aspects of the CAP remained very small. Indeed, the annual grants under all of the three directives over the decade 1975–84 averaged no more than about 100 million ECUs (at 1986 prices) for about four million farms of less than 10 hectares in area in 1975. However, these directives were replaced by a new ten-year structural plan in 1985. The rationale for this was the realization by then that the surpluses generated at the time did not justify a policy of trying to solve the plight of small farms through increased output, and that the slower rates of economic growth being experienced then made it more difficult for farmers to find alternative employment. Thus the new plan shied away from fundamental changes in the farm structure and put emphasis on cost reductions and quality improvement, and at the same time the aim of achieving incomes for the sector comparable with those in non-agricultural occupations was abandoned altogether. In other words, the aim was no longer to transform small farms into larger ones to enable them to obtain higher incomes, but rather to make it possible for small farmers to survive with a reasonable quality of living. In support of the plan, an average of 420 million ECUs per annum was to be provided over the period 1985–94 and a further annual sum of 270 million ECUs was to be made available for schemes aimed at improving agricultural marketing and processing. Despite these aspirations, total budgetary expenditure on guidance was 3.7 billion ECUs in 1996, or about 4.5% of the total budget and under 10% of total expenditure on the CAP. However, since the adoption of new proposals first made in *Agenda 2000* (CEU, 1997a), which are discussed in section 11.9, this aspect of the CAP has been subsumed within the structural funds of the EU general budget (see Chapter 16), and given enhanced support funding.

11.6 The CAP price support mechanism

The original CAP machinery did not apply to every product and, in the cases where it did, it varied from one product to another – see Table 11.3. Although major changes have since been introduced (see section 11.9), the mechanism still applies to some products and sheds light on some of the disastrous consequences of the policy earlier on; hence it is instructive to give it some consideration.

Where the original system still applies, the farmers' income support is guaranteed by regulating the market so as to reach a price high enough to achieve this objective. The domestic price is partly maintained by various protective devices. These prevent cheaper world imports from influencing the EU domestic price level. But, in addition, certain steps are taken for official support buying within the EU, so as to eliminate from the market any actual excess supply that might be stimulated by the guaranteed price level. These surpluses may be disposed of in the manner described in the section on the policies of the EC member nations.

More specifically, the basic features of the system can be represented by that originally devised for cereals, the first agricultural product for which a common policy was established.

A 'target' price is set on an annual basis and is maintained at a level which the product is expected to achieve on the market in the area where cereal is in shortest supply – Duisburg in the Ruhr Valley. The target price is not a producer price since it includes the costs of transport to dealers and storers. The target price is variable, in that it is allowed to increase on a monthly basis from August to July in order to allow for storage costs throughout the year.

The 'threshold price' is calculated in such a way that when transport costs incurred within the EU are added, cereals collected at Rotterdam (Europe's major port) should sell at Duisburg at a price equal to or slightly higher than the target price, the consequence being that adding the levy and transport costs to Duisburg would make it unprofitable to sell cereals anywhere in the EU at less than the target price. An import levy is calculated on a daily basis and is equal to the margin between the lowest priced consignment entering the EU on the day – allowing for transport costs to the major port (Rotterdam) – and the threshold price. This levy is then charged on all imports allowed into the EU on that day. All this information is illustrated in Figure 11.3.

It is quite obvious that, as long as the EU is experiencing excess demand for this product, the market price is held above the target price by the imposition of import levies. Moreover, import levies would be unnecessary if world prices happened to be above the threshold price since in this case the market price might exceed the target price.

If target prices result in an excess supply of the product in the EC (see Figure 11.3), the threshold price becomes ineffective in terms of the objective of a constant annual target price and support buying becomes necessary. A 'basic intervention price' is then introduced for this purpose. This is fixed for Duisburg at about 7% or 8% below the target price. Similar prices are then calculated for several locations within the EU on the basis of costs of transport to Duisburg. National intervention agencies are then compelled to buy whatever is offered to them (provided that it conforms to standard) of the 'proper' product at the relevant intervention price. The intervention price is therefore a minimum guaranteed price.

Moreover, an export subsidy or *restitution* is paid to EU exporters. This is determined by the officials and is influenced by several factors (world prices, amount of

Table 11.3 Price and market regimes for agricultural products

Product	Target price	Guide price	Norm price	Basic price	Intervention price	Withdrawal price	Minimum price	Production aid	Deficiency payment	Threshold price	Sluice-gate price	Reference price	Variable levy	Supplementary levy	Customs duty	Export refund
Common wheat	x				x					x			x			x
Durum wheat	x				x			x[a]		x			x			x
Barley	x				x					x			x			x
Rye	x				x					x			x			x
Maize	x				x					x			x			x
Rice	x				x					x			x			x
Sugar: white	x				x					x			x			x
beet							x									
Oilseeds: colza	x				x				x							
rape	x				x				x							
sunflower	x				x				x							
soya beans		x							x							
linseed		x							x							
castor		x					x		x							
cotton								x								
Peas and field																
beans	x[b]						x		x							
Dried fodder								x	x							
Fibre flax and																
hemp								x								
Milk products:																
butter					x					x			x			x
smp					x					x			x			x
cheese[c]					x					x			x			x
Beef: live		x														
meat					x								x		x	x
Pigmeat				x	x						x			x		x
Eggs											x			x		x
Poultry											x			x		x
Fish		x			x[d]	x						x			x	x
Silkworms								x								
Fresh fruit and																
vegetables					x	x						x			x	x
Live plants															x	
Olive oil	x				x			x	x[e]	x					x	x
Wine		x			x[f]							x			x	x
Hops								x							x	
Seeds for sowing								x				x[g]				
Tobacco			x		x				x						x	x

[a] Certain regions only. [b] Activating price. [c] Italy only. [d] Sardines and anchovies only.
[e] Olive oil consumer subsidy. [f] Wine storage contracts and distillation. [g] Hybrid maize only.
Source: Adapted from R. Fennell (1979), p. 106.

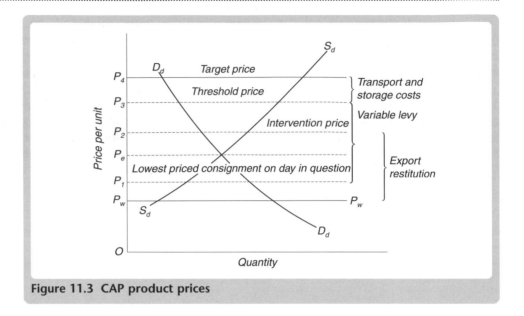

Figure 11.3 CAP product prices

excess supply, expected trends) and is generally calculated as the difference between the EU intervention price (P_2) and the world price (Pw).

For the latest position on this mechanism and the new methods that the EU has introduced to tackle the problems of excess supply, see section 11.9 on development and assessment.

11.7 The green money

The various agricultural support prices were fixed by the Council in units of account. For each member country there was a 'green rate' at which the support prices were translated into national prices. Green rates are needed for administrative convenience since otherwise it would have been cumbersome to alter prices every time there was a change in exchange rates, but when the Euro becomes the single currency for all member countries, green rates will no longer be needed. The unit of account originally had a gold content equal to a US dollar, but in 1973 was linked to the 'joint float'; with the introduction of the European Monetary System (EMS) in March 1979 it was given a value equal to the European currency unit (ECU), called a 'green ECU' and since January 1999, with the adoption of the Euro, all prices are expressed in the single currency. This implies that if a member country devalued (revalued) its currency, its farm prices expressed in terms of the national currency would rise (fall). It should also be noted that the scope for changing green currency rates (allowed because of the desire of member states to stabilize farm prices in the face of exchange rate fluctuations at the time) gave the member countries scope for altering internal farm prices *independently* of price changes determined at the annual review for the EC as a whole. In August 1969 the French franc was devalued by 11.11%, which obviously disturbed the common farm price arrangements in favour of the French farmers, and the rise in their price level would obviously have stimulated their farm production and aggravated the excess supply problem (see next section). Moreover, the devaluation of the unit of account would not have improved matters in such a situation, since it would have depressed the price level for the farmer in the rest of the EC, even though it would have nullified the effects of the devaluation of the French franc. Therefore, a more complicated policy was adopted: the French intervention price was reduced by the full amount of the devaluation so as to eliminate the unfair benefit to the French farmer; French imports from and exports to the rest of the EC were to be restored by asking France to give import subsidies and levy duties on its exports to compensate for the effects of the devaluation. The term 'monetary compensatory amounts' (MCAs) was coined to describe this system of border taxes and subsidies. Since then, the MCA system became general in application and more complicated, with the changes in the rates of exchange of the currencies of other EC members and new members.

Even though the EC persisted in announcing its intention to discontinue the MCA system, it has not completely succeeded in doing so. It did make an attempt through the introduction of the 'switchover mechanism' in 1984, which was meant, *inter alia*, to neutralize exchange rate changes by tying the common support price levels to the strongest EC currency, the German mark, starting from 1984, but this was to no avail. Also, although it did suspend the MCA system altogether in 1993 with the introduction of the single market, the widening of fluctuations within the Exchange Rate Mechanism to ±15 (see Chapters 6 and 17) has not helped. However, if everything goes according to plan, the *full* introduction of the Euro (i.e. when all member nations have adopted it), would ensure its demise. The system therefore warrants some further explanation. It should be remembered that one of the basic aims of the CAP was to establish a uniform set of agricultural prices for all the participating nations. Since these prices were expressed in units of account, when a member country decided to devalue its currency (i.e. its official rate), the prices of agricultural products would rise in terms of the domestic currency by the full percentage of devaluation (given a simple analysis). This increase in the domestic prices would distort trade between the member nations and its effect on intra-EC trade could have been fully eliminated (again in a simple analysis) by imposing equivalent taxes on the export of these products and by granting equivalent subsidies to the imports of the products. This in effect amounted to operating a system of multiple exchange rates. On the other hand, when a member of the EC decided to revalue its currency, it would have had to tax intra-EC imports and subsidize intra-EC exports to eliminate a fall in agricultural prices. Since the green rates of exchange – known as 'representative rates' – were officially used for converting prices expressed in units of account into national currencies – official rates – it followed that, when the green rate deviated from the official rate, these taxes on, and subsidies to, intra-EC traded agricultural products were used to maintain uniform agricultural prices. This was the MCA system which, once adopted by a member of the EC, would have remained until that country was able to restore its green rate to that on the foreign exchange market.

The MCA system is therefore basically simple; it became complicated because of several factors. First, the French devaluation of 1969 was followed almost immediately by the German revaluation and the French and the Germans asked for the adoption of MCAs which were to be eliminated within periods of two and three years respectively. Second, the EC agreed to these arrangements and met part of the cost, hence increasing the financial burden of the CAP. Third, the later weakness of the US dollar was used as a reason by the EC to introduce MCAs in order to protect its farmers from worldwide unfair competition – the EC claimed this was because the United States, being a net exporter of agricultural products, was able to determine the world price level for agricultural products and this was in spite of the fact that the unit of account was fixed in terms of dollars. Fourth, the enlargement of the EC added new currencies. Finally, the floating of the pound sterling in 1972 and the Italian lira in 1973, which led to the depreciation of both, encouraged the use of MCAs to protect the stronger EC currencies from agricultural price increases.

The reader who is particularly interested in this area of the CAP is advised to read Irving and Fearne (1975), Josling and Harris (1976), Mackel (1978), Hu (1979), Fennell (1979) and Marsh and Swanney (1980, 1985).

11.8   Financing the CAP

Intervention, export restitution and the MCA system need to be financed. The finance is supplied by the EU central fund called FEOGA (Fonds Européen d'Orientation et de Garantie Agricole) due to the dominance of French during the EC of six. In English it is referred to as the European Agricultural Guidance and Guarantee Fund (EAGGF), so named to incorporate the two basic elements of the CAP: support and guidance. At the time of inception of the CAP it was expected that the revenues collected from the imposition of extra area import levies would be sufficient to finance EAGGF. Since then, the rapid rise in agricultural output has led to a reduction in EC imports and therefore to a reduction in receipts from levies.

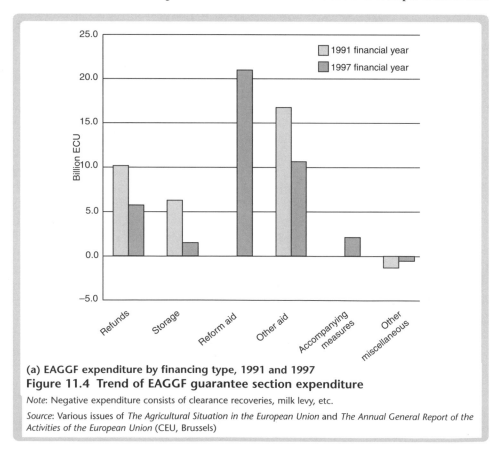

(a) EAGGF expenditure by financing type, 1991 and 1997

Figure 11.4 Trend of EAGGF guarantee section expenditure

Note: Negative expenditure consists of clearance recoveries, milk levy, etc.

Source: Various issues of *The Agricultural Situation in the European Union* and *The Annual General Report of the Activities of the European Union* (CEU, Brussels)

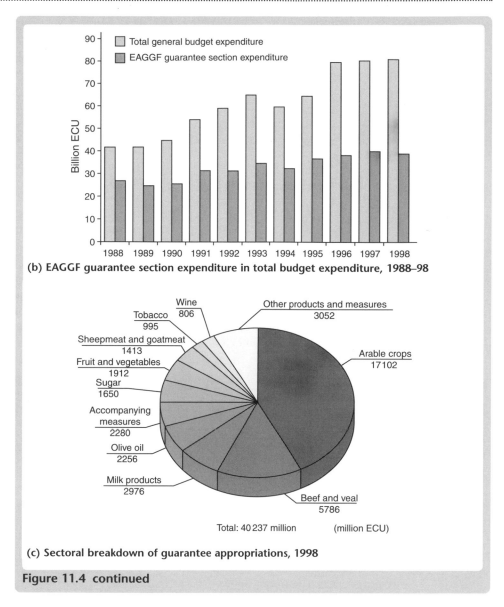

(b) EAGGF guarantee section expenditure in total budget expenditure, 1988–98

(c) Sectoral breakdown of guarantee appropriations, 1998

Figure 11.4 continued

Also, the cost of the support system has increased beyond expectation (see the McDougall Report (CEC, 1977c) and Chapter 16). Thus the EC deemed it necessary to make provision for direct budgetary contributions from national governments on the basis of a formula which is discussed in some detail in the McDougall Report. However, in 1970 the EC switched to a system of own resources, which became fully operative in 1980 – see Chapter 16.

In order to put the expenditures in their proper perspective, it should be noted that the general budget of the EU makes provision for the administrative expenses of the European Parliament, the Council of Ministers, the ECJ, the ECSC, and the European Development Fund (EDF), and for the administrative costs and the other operational expenditures of the Commission, which include the EAGGF, the Social Fund, the Regional Development Fund and the structural funds. For the financial year 1998 the budget amounted to some 90 billion ECU or, roughly, $72 billion, of which guaranteed agricultural expenditure accounted for about 48%. The revenue from agricultural levies was about 2 billion ECU, approximately 2.4% of the total budget – see Figure 11.4 for trends of EAGGF guidance expenditures, their relation to the general budget, their allocation by type and the 1998 commodity breakdown of its allocation.

11.9 Change in the support system

Due to both internal EC pressures and external demands, some parts of the CAP support system have undergone substantial change. The internal pressures arose mainly from the need to save on costs and to protect the environment. The external demands, especially by the United States during the Uruguay round of the GATT (now WTO) negotiations, were directed mainly against the export restitution payments, which were regarded as serious obstacles to the promotion of fairer international trade since they enabled the selling of EC products in third markets. A chronological description of all the changes would prove both boring and unhelpful, hence it is sufficient to concentrate on only the salient changes.

One of the internal pressures for change arose from some consequences of the original support mechanism, the main purpose of which was to eradicate post-Second World War memories of food shortages and rural poverty. As is clear from the above, this was to be achieved through the provision of a secure domestic market. However, the system of helping farmers through increased prices and agricultural levies resulted in the highly publicized embarrassing surpluses: the butter and beef mountains; the wine lakes; earlier on, the grain and sugar surpluses; and later on, the milk lakes. The first, although not the immediate, response to these was the introduction of a 'co-responsibility levy' in 1977 and 'budget stabilizers' soon after, the purpose of which was to hold the farmers partly responsible for the cost of disposing of the surpluses they created. The minor changes before that amounted to *ad hoc* devices brought in after the event of surpluses which included the introduction of 'buying-in prices' set below the intervention prices.

The next major change became effective on 31 March 1984 when the member nations agreed on a package which reduced the EC's common farm prices by 0.5% and relied on a system of quotas to restrict milk production from 103 million tonnes in 1983 to 99.2 million tonnes in 1984 and 1985; thereafter it was to be pegged for a further three years. Moreover, the quotas which had already been applied to sugar beet were extended to other surplus products such as cereals, oilseeds and processed tomatoes. In order to reduce wine production, new vine plantings were banned until 1990. Finally, various production and consumption subsidies to livestock, butter, fruit and vegetables were reduced, and the MCAs were to be phased out over four years. It should be added that the EC Council decided in February 1988 that the annual growth rate of EAGGF guarantee expenditure should not exceed 70–80% (later specified as 74%) of the annual growth rate of EC GDP. New agricultural stabilizers were to be introduced. For example, the threshold for cereals was set at 155–160 million tonnes per year for the period 1988–91, and an additional co-responsibility levy of 3% was charged at the beginning of each marketing year to ensure that agricultural expenditure stayed within the specified limits. Similar quotas were set for oilseeds and protein products, then existing stabilizers were continued for olive oil and cotton, the quota system for milk was extended for another three years, etc. What was significant, however, was that the Council not only cut some prices, but also agreed to adopt provisions to limit the supply by withdrawing land from production. This so-called 'set-aside' programme was devised to complement policy measures, and was compulsory for member countries but optional for producers. The EC therefore took reasonable, if not serious, measures for tackling the problems of surpluses. (The reader should note that these developments and their financial implications for the EC general budget are fully discussed in Chapter 16).

Digressing from surpluses, one should mention that a significant element of the 1988 reform package just mentioned was the introduction of a system enabling direct income subsidies to farmers. It was agreed that farmers earning well below the national average farm income could receive up to 1500 ECU per annum, 70% of the cost of which was to be borne by member nations. This was significant because, for the first time, direct subsidies became part of the system.

However, in spite of the seriousness of these measures, agricultural surpluses persisted. The EC had no alternative, given the above-mentioned pressure by the United States, but to reinforce and forcefully pursue this approach. Thus a digression regarding this element is in order.

For much of the GATT's Uruguay round, the EC resisted changes to its CAP support instruments when the negotiations demanded their abandonment. This was because: the variable agricultural levies were to be converted into fixed tariffs, 'tariffication' being the in-word; export subsidies, i.e. restitution payments, were to be discontinued; and all domestic support was to be phased out, except for research and extension, domestic and international food aid and some other supports with negligible impacts on trade. Moreover, protection levels were to be reduced by up to 75% over a decade. The EC's response was to agree conditionally to change its levy system and to reduce the overall level of support by 30% (measured by the so-called 'support measurement unit') over five years, thus making little change to the CAP. In the meantime, the EC support was already falling relative to its 1986 level, when the round started, and this led the EC to question the need for further CAP reform.

These opposing attitudes came to a head during the summer of 1990, when, despite several attempts by President Bush at 'arm twisting' and Mats Hellström, the Swedish Minister of Agriculture, at compromising, the talks collapsed. However, within hours of the collapse, the EC Commissioner in charge of Agriculture, Ray MacSharry of Ireland, was circulating a document containing new proposals to his colleagues in the EC Commission. These were agreed and later adopted, after some modification, by the Council.

What this amounted to was that in June 1992, a further package of reforms was adopted and came to be known as the MacSharry reform package. The support prices for cereals, oilseeds and pulses were to be cut, but the cuts were to be offset by compensation payments to farmers. Also, dairy and beef prices were to be cut and their producers compensated. These price cuts in combination with the set-aside system would hopefully lower production, stimulate demand and, hence, would enable the EC to reduce its restitution payments and meet the requirements of the GATT negotiators. The package must therefore be stated in more precise terms:

1. Target prices for cereals were to be cut, relative to their 1991–92 buying-in levels, by 29% over three years starting in 1993–94. The reduction was expected to

bring EC prices down to then current world prices. However, a minimum import price was set to maintain a margin of about 40% of EC preference. In addition, an agreed amount of arable land was to be taken out of cereals production each year in line with forecast market needs. This amount was 15% in the first year, but this reduction did not apply to farmers with holdings of 20 hectares below the EC average. Farmers were to receive full and direct compensation for loss of earnings resulting from price cuts, but the 15% reduction in land under cereals, oilseeds and protein crops was to be a precondition for the receipt of compensation. The payments were to be in the form of direct income support and were to be calculated on the basis of the average yields in each farming region. Compensation was also to be paid on the same basis for land taken out of production. Small farmers, producing less than 92 tonnes, qualified for full compensation without setting aside any land. Naturally, the co-responsibility levy was to be abolished, starting in 1992–93.

2. Oilseeds and pulses were to receive no support from 1993–94. However, area payments per hectare were to continue, but at levels below those in 1992–93, with linseed added to the list of eligible products. Also, the production controls were to be the same as those for the cereals set-aside programme.

3. Beef intervention prices were to be cut by 15% over the three years starting in 1993–94, and a limit of 350 000 tonnes was to be set on intervention buying by 1997. Farmers raising beef cattle on open grazing land were to receive extra per capita premiums; the idea was to discourage intensive factory farming since premiums would not be available to farmers raising cattle in stalls, but they were to be able to offset the drop in beef prices through the use of cheaper cereals as animal feed. Also, then existing premiums paid for bulls, steers and suckling cows were to be increased.

4. Payment for ewe premiums were to be restricted by producer quotas based on premiums paid in 1991. In return, the quotas were to have a market value and special extensification premiums were to be available for reduced stock levels; there would also be the benefit of reduced cereal prices. However, if the quota is sold without land, 15% of it would be taxed to national reserves. Also, quotas could not be transferred outside then prevailing 'less favoured areas'.

5. Butter intervention prices were to be cut by 5% in 1994–95 and the milk quota and its associated value were to continue until at least the year 2000. The co-responsibility levy was to be abolished from 1992–93 and future cuts in the quota may be possible.

6. These measures were to be accompanied by others aimed at developing more environmentally friendly types of agriculture (using fewer pesticides and fertilizers), financing afforestation programmes and ensuring the management of land taken out of production.

7. The EC was also to finance an improved early retirement scheme for farmers aged 55 years or over who make way for younger people.

Since these reforms were for a number of years, the prices for 1993–96 simply reinforced these aims. For example, for 1996–97 prices were frozen across the board at the 1995 level except for rice (fixed in December 1995) and fibre flax (pending restructuring for the common organization of its market).

The EU has claimed that these measures marked a watershed in the reform of the

CAP not only because they applied the previous sensible reforms to the most significant agricultural products but also because they came under the category of 'compulsory expenditures', i.e. payment for them out of the EU general budget is a priority spending (see Chapters 2 and 16). One should stress, however, that these reforms did not come entirely from within; indeed, as just mentioned, it was the persistent pressure applied by the United States during the Uruguay round of the GATT negotiations that was the driving force.

The latest changes were adopted by the Council in May 1999. The EU has claimed that these measures, although not as far-reaching as had originally been proposed, are the most radical and wide-ranging reform of the CAP in its history. This is not because the guaranteed prices are to be cut, gradually, by 20% in the case of beef and 15% in arable crops and dairy products, and direct payments to farmers are to be increased since these are along the lines of the MacSharry reforms. It is because these are to be accompanied by the following measures:

1. A new policy for rural development where each member nation sets its own programmes, but in correspondence with EU guidelines, and receives financial support from the EU. Within this context, agriculture and forestry are recognized as complementary to each other and the environment must be an integral element of rural development.

2. The involvement of local people in finding local solutions.

3. The integration of environmental goals into the CAP through 'agri-environmental measures' to support the sustainable development of rural areas by encouraging farmers to adopt practices consistent with environmental protection and natural resource conservation.

4. The creation of Sapard as a fund with 529 million Euro per year to assist the farm sectors and rural economies of the potential Central and Eastern European countries to prepare for membership.

These new initiatives are along the lines first spelled out in *Agenda 2000*, the document published in July 1997 and adopted, with modifications, by the EU at the summit meeting held in Berlin in March 1999. (The modifications include reducing the amount of the cut in the guaranteed prices for cereals from 20% to 15%, to be implemented later, with the possibility of further price cuts 'in the light of market developments'; a reduction of the figure for beef, from 30% to 15%; and the delay, until 2005, of the 15% cut in guaranteed prices for butter and skim milk powder.) The document sets out the new directions for the EU. Hence it deals with such issues as the EMU, the CAP and enlargement.

11.10   Analysing surpluses and set-asides

The analysis of surpluses and these changes is straightforward since it requires no more than a simple adaptation of Figure 11.3. As can be seen from Figure 11.5, a target or buying-in price of P_3 would result in a surplus of *ad* which the EU authorities have the obligation to buy from the farmers. Assuming that the world price is P_1, a subsidy, i.e. a restitution payment, equal to area *adnj* would be needed to dispose of the surplus in world markets. At an intervention or buying-in price of P_2, the surplus would be *fg* and the cost to the EU would be area *fgmk*. In either case,

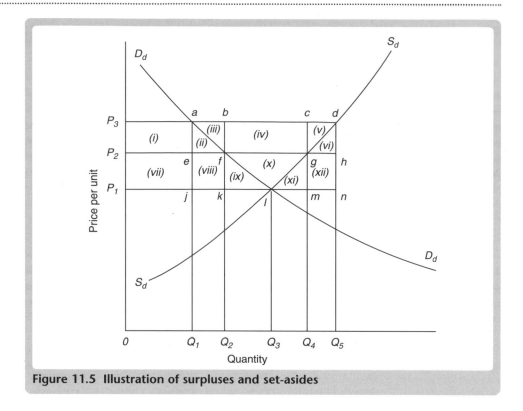

Figure 11.5 Illustration of surpluses and set-asides

however, the actual cost would be in excess of these amounts since there would also be storage and/or disposal expenses (such as the cost of destroying or changing the product in the manner discussed above); the product itself may deteriorate in quality while in store, thus it cannot fetch the intervention price; and the product may have to be sold in the international market at a price below P_1. The impact on consumers' and producers' surpluses can then be determined as before. For example, if P_1 were the world price and P_3 the intervention price, there would be self sufficiency under free trade, but with CAP support there would be the surplus of ad. Then, consumers' surplus would decrease by the sum of areas (i), (ii), (vii), (viii) and (ix); for ease of exposition, call this sum A. Producers' surplus would increase by the sum of areas (iii), (iv), (v) and (x), call this sum B, plus A. There would therefore be a net welfare gain of A. It is important not to equate these welfare changes with per product CAP costs since if, for example, the surplus is sold to Russia, area $adnj$ would be the needed restitution subsidy, and this, together with such costs as those paid for storage, would be the CAP cost of this product.

This analysis can then easily be extended to cater for marketing quotas. Assume that instead of having the right to sell into intervention all the surplus of ad at price P_3, farmers are restricted to selling only ac. Then the EU authorities would save costs equal to the sum of areas (v), (vi) and (xii) and consumers' surplus would remain intact while producers' surplus would fall by area (v). Note that if the marketing quota itself were allocated inefficiently between farmers, leading to a distortion in the supply curve itself, i.e., instead of the quota resulting in the supply curve simply becoming vertical from point g going through point c, it shifts up, say, from point l to connect directly with point c, then one has to take into consideration area lcg (not drawn, to avoid cluttering the figure). This should not detain us, however, since if one assumes that competitive forces are at work, the supply curve would be restored to the one just adjusted, i.e. that with the vertical section connecting g to c.

If instead of the marketing quota, the EU opts for a cut in price from P_3 to P_2, consumers' surplus would increase by areas (i) and (ii) while producers' surplus would decrease by the sum of areas (i), (ii), (iii), (iv) and (v), resulting in a net welfare loss equal to the sum of areas (iii), (iv) and (v). Note, however, that this loss is less than the saving in costs that the authorities would achieve if they had to buy the surplus at the original intervention price P_3, i.e. less than the sum of areas (ii), (iii), (iv), (v) and (vi). Recall, however, that one should not confuse costs and welfare changes.

The same figure can then be used to analyse the policy linking price cuts to set-asides. The farmers who opt for set-asides would, by definition, incorporate them into their plans in advance of actual production. It is correct to say 'opt', because each farmer would have to choose between setting aside and accepting a lower price. Assuming that the farmers go for set-asides and that all farmers are equally efficient, the supply curve would shift to the left by the full quota of the set-aside, i.e. there would be a new supply curve going through point c and running parallel and to the left of the original supply curve in Figure 11.3. It is then easy to see that, relative to the original price P_3, direct income compensations to the farmers equal to area (v) would induce a reduction in production matching the set-asides quota.

However, neither P_3 as the original intervention price nor P_1 as the assumed world price is likely to remain the same with the set-asides. This is because P_3 has to fall as a consequence of the trade-off with the set-asides, and the reduction in surplus would reduce the amount to be sold outside the EU, hence resulting in a higher world price. With the intervention price being lower than P_3 and the world price higher than P_1, it should be clear that all the areas involving changes in consumers' and producers' surpluses would be smaller in comparison with their original. It should also be apparent that if farmers were not equally efficient in production, the new supply curve would not run parallel and to the left of the original one since it would shift along the lines just discussed, with similar consequences.

11.11 Prospects for further change

In spite of claims by the EU that these changes are 'historic', agriculture and trade therein continue to be highly protected relative to their non-agricultural counterpart, and not just in the EU. For example, while tariffs on non-agricultural trade now average 5–10% (see Chapter 22), those on agricultural trade average about 40%, with tariff peaks, called 'megatariffs', of over 300% – see Table 11.4 and Josling (1998, p. 6). Moreover, the size of total transfers to agriculture from taxpayers and consumers consequent on the mix of OECD agricultural policies changed little between 1986–88 and 1996, from about $280 million to about $300 million per annum, with the EU accounting for about 40% in both cases – see Table 11.5 and OECD (1997b). Therefore, more needs to be done, but in the face of EU euphoria with its past achievements, one needs to ask about the possibility of further reform.

A consideration of such a possibility requires reflection on the circumstances leading to the major CAP changes. At the time of the excessive surpluses, it was the escalating disposal costs, given a severely constrained general budget, which forced the changes despite the political clout of the farming lobbies. Hence, truly internal

Table 11.4 Average unweighted *ad valorem* bound tariff rates, post-Uruguay Round, for 10 agricultural products in 20 countries[a]

Product	Tariff rate
Grains	46.7
Oilseeds	41.7
Fats and oils	41.6
Meats	39.3
Milk	40.7
Dairy products	47.1
Sugar	48.7
Fresh fruit and vegetables	35.5
Processed fruit and vegetables	35.3
Other agricultural goods	24.4

[a]The countries are: Australia, Brazil, Canada, Chile, Colombia, European Union, India, Indonesia, Hong Kong, Japan, South Korea, Malaysia, Mexico, New Zealand, Philippines, Singapore, Sri Lanka, Thailand, United States and Venezuela.
Note: The table shows the unweighted average *ad valorem* tariff of the numerous individual tariff lines relating to the product groups identified. Two cautions should be noted. First, the unweighted average tariff does not distinguish between the importance of the individual items either in the current trade basket or in any potential pattern of trade. Second, the average omits specific tariffs that cannot be averaged without assumptions about the level of world prices. An ambitious attempt to convert the specific tariffs often found in agricultural trade into *ad valorem* equivalents has been proceeding at the World Bank (Ingco and Hathaway, 1996). This indicates that specific tariffs are often higher than the *ad valorem* tariffs. More importantly, the Japanese and South Korean protection of rice imports is not yet in the form of a tariff and is not included in the table. Nor is the EU protection of grains, as this is limited to a level below the bound tariff. The bound tariffs can overstate the level of protection actually applied: several Latin American countries apply tariffs that are well below their bound levels.
Source: WTO Secretariat.

pressure was the driving force. Since then, however, the changes have been driven by what can loosely be described as external factors. The 1984 changes were introduced at a time when the negotiations concerning the Iberian enlargement were progressing well. Thus, with the imminent accession of Portugal and Spain, which happened in 1986, CAP costs and financing had to be addressed before matters got out of hand. The MacSharry reforms, as just mentioned, were no doubt influenced by the Uruguay round of the GATT negotiations. The *Agenda 2000* reforms were introduced under circumstances which included some that replicated those preceding the Iberian enlargement. In the face of expansion to include the countries of Central and Eastern Europe, which have large agricultural sectors requiring vast support expenditures, not only CAP finances but the entire general budget would have become unsustainable in the absence of reform. Having internalized two of the three external factors and adjusted the system to cater, 'historically', for the last major enlargement of the EU, further reform can come about only through WTO pressure.

To find out how forceful such pressure would be, one needs to examine the implications of the Uruguay Round Agreement on Agriculture (URAA). Since the conclusion of the round, well-defined quantitative WTO commitments regarding what countries can do with their agricultural policies have been introduced. The EU has so far had no major problems meeting its commitments, but with further reductions to be made, these constraints will soon begin to bite. Hence, more on this is in order.

Table 11.5 Agricultural policy transfers by country, 1986–96 (US$ billion)

	1986–88	1993–5	1994	1995	1996
Total transfers					
European Union	114.1	132.5	128.5	138.6	120.3
United States	68.2	74.1	76.4	62.4	68.7
Japan	62.5	89.9	87.2	100.5	77.4
Canada	7.3	6.1	5.8	5.7	4.8
OECD	278.9	332.1	328.2	332.9	297.1
Transfers per farmer (full-time farmer equivalent)					
European Union	12 785	18 657	18 336	19 478	17 474
United States	27 892	29 384	30 285	24 742	27 240
Japan	17 280	31 647	29 402	38 440	30 091
Canada	15 742	14 085	13 750	13 318	11 225
OECD	11 100	15 651	15 440	15 955	14 493
Transfers per hectare					
European Union	851	953	944	951	825
United States	159	174	179	146	161
Japan	11 705	17 553	17 013	19 618	15 107
Canada	99	84	80	78	66
OECD	236	284	280	284	254

Source: OECD (1997a).

WTO members now have commitments on what they can and cannot do in three areas relating to agriculture: (a) market access, (b) export competition and (c) domestic support. These commitments, for the EU, are as follows:

1. *Market access*. In this area, EU commitments have so far turned out to be rather generous. This is due to a combination of 'dirty' tariffication, the special safeguard provisions in the URAA, specific EU arrangements in tariffication, EU policy changes after the policy period and EU use of preferential trading arrangements with non-members to fulfil access commitments under the URAA (see Tangermann, 1999). For example, because the MacSharry cereal price cuts substantially lowered the rates of levies, WTO pressured the EU into not using its full tariff-binding levels, but instead to ensure that EU tariff-inclusive prices for cereals should not be higher than 155% of the intervention price. This means that the EU cannot use its full tariff-binding level unless world prices fall to much lower levels. Consequently, there was a lot of 'water' in the EU cereal tariff binding during the first few years after the GATT agreement. Since then, however, as a result of the combination of a built-in decline in tariff binding and lower world prices, the water has largely evaporated. This can be clearly seen from Figure 11.6 where the tariffs actually applied by the EU, using the 155% rule, are contrasted with their tariff-binding counterparts for wheat and barley. In the case of wheat, because the EU tariff applies to all qualities, the lower qualities are hit the hardest. It can be seen that low quality wheat reached its year 2000 tariff-binding level in 1998; hence it can no longer be protected by the EU

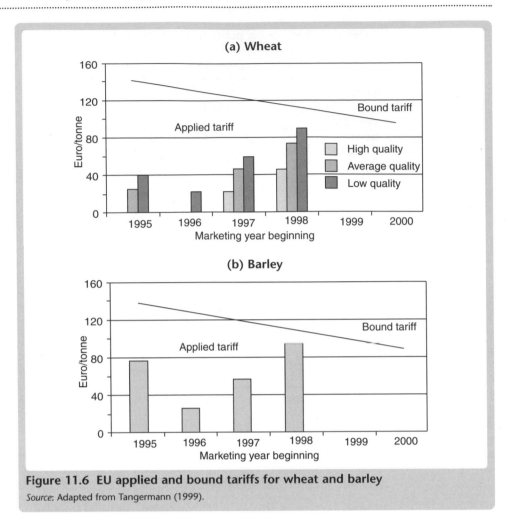

Figure 11.6 EU applied and bound tariffs for wheat and barley

Source: Adapted from Tangermann (1999).

at the planned level. In the case of barley, the 1998 level exceeded the tariff-binding level. Tangermann (1999) provides an excellent analysis of this issue for a number of products.

2. *Export subsidies*. In this area, the URAA commitments have either already begun to bite or are about to do so. This is evident from Figure 11.7 for 1996, the second year of implementation, and for 2000. In 1996 the subsidies exceeded the basic EU commitments in wine, beef, olive oil, rice and wine. For 2000, the majority of products did likewise. Note that the EU experienced no difficulties in the first year.

3. *Domestic support*. Tactical problems apart, WTO commitments have a direct bearing on what levels of support the EU can extend to its farming sector. Since tariffication is meant to make protection transparent so that further tariff reductions can be negotiated in new rounds, one needs to examine the implications of such reductions on EU domestic policy. For example, intervention prices, which the EU intends to retain especially for cereals and dairy products, cannot exceed world prices plus tariffs, otherwise world supplies would flood into EU intervention markets. As tariffs are reduced, intervention prices cannot be sustained unless they are reduced in tandem. This will have a direct bearing

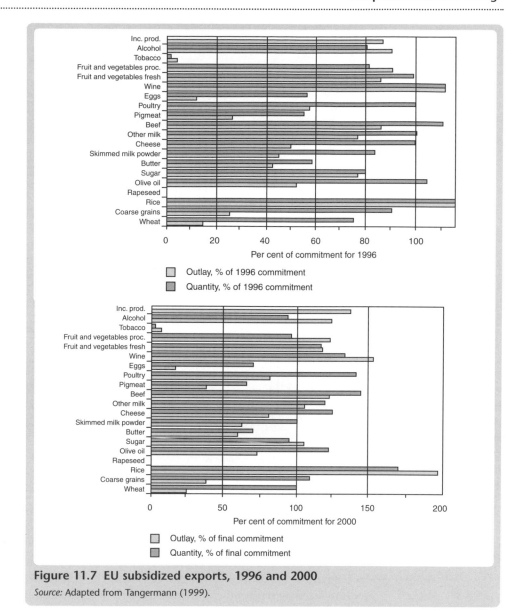

Figure 11.7 EU subsidized exports, 1996 and 2000

Source: Adapted from Tangermann (1999).

on the dairy and sugar sectors since they were not subject to the MacSharry price cuts. More importantly and immediately, even the URAA present commitments for export subsidies will force a change in EU support. This is not just because of what is mentioned in point (2) above. Comparing existing WTO commitments (constraints) with recent subsidized EU exports (which are rising because of growth in production and stagnant consumption, declining in the case of beef), as becomes clear from Figure 11.8 for wheat and coarse grains, but is of general applicability, we see that the EU will have to act soon. If the EU has to sustain its present price levels, it will have to increase the level of its quasi-mandatory set-aside from 17.5% to about 25% by 2005 (Tangermann, 1999, p. 1166). The situation becomes even tighter when one realizes that the present WTO commitments on export subsidies will be negotiated downwards in future rounds,

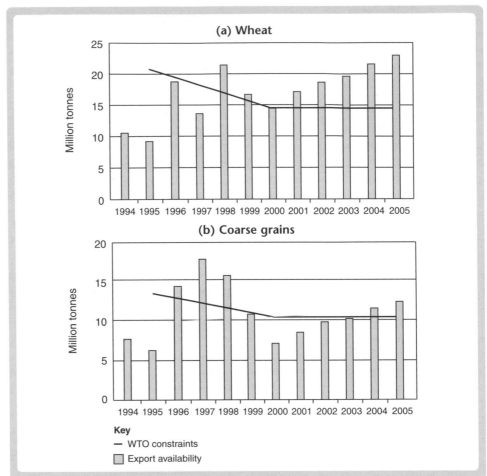

Figure 11.8 Export availability and WTO constraints on subsidized exports of wheat and coarse grains

Source: Adapted from Tangermann (1999).

with the EU being the primary target since it is the largest holder of such rights – see Figure 11.9. Indeed, both the USA and the Cairns Group (of small and medium-sized agricultural exporting countries which championed the causes of better access to the markets of advanced nations and less market disruption from their policies during the Uruguay round) have already committed themselves to negotiating substantial reductions, if not complete elimination, of export subsidies during the next round.

Before jumping to the conclusion that this implies plenty of room for further reform, one has to factor in the changes agreed in Bonn, based on *Agenda 2000*, mentioned above. For example, the agreed cuts in cereal prices, when accompanied by further reductions, in the light of market developments, would enable the EU to export without subsidies. On the other hand, sugar was not included in *Agenda 2000* (since powerful and active lobbies would have disrupted the whole package), so its price remains high, with tariffs in excess of the 150% extended to the dairy sector. In short, the agreed package, based on this document (see above), somewhat

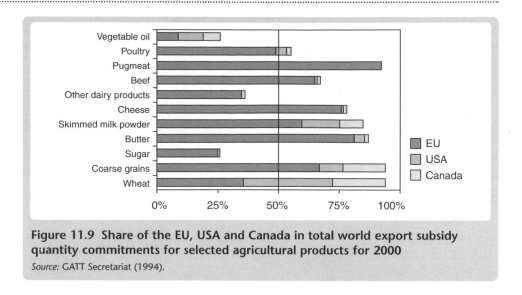

Figure 11.9 Share of the EU, USA and Canada in total world export subsidy quantity commitments for selected agricultural products for 2000
Source: GATT Secretariat (1994).

lessens, but does not eliminate, the need for the introduction of immediate further reforms. What is of particular significance, however, is that most indications suggest that future reform will have to rely heavily on cuts in EU agricultural prices. That must be welcomed by all concerned since free and fair trade is what should be promoted, and cuts in prices will take the EU in that direction.

This leaves the question of when the next round of WTO negotiations can be expected to start. One of the accomplishments of the URAA was the resolve to resume the process of agricultural policy reform in the future, with a 'built-in agenda' for another round of negotiations on agriculture to be initiated in 1999. However, the December 1999 Seattle meeting ended in failure, not just because the non-governmental organizations (NGOs) and interested parties disrupted the meeting, but also because, with WTO now having 135 members, the interests have become so diverse that even agreeing on the agenda would require major efforts. Moreover, as history has shown, rounds of negotiations are bound to be lengthy; the Uruguay round started in 1986 but finished in 1994. It would therefore seem that the reforms that have so far been achieved by the EU will remain in force for at least a decade.

11.12   Conclusion

Since the prospects for change have already been discussed, the conclusion should be in the nature of an assessment of the CAP as it developed over the four decades or so since its inception. Before doing so, however, one needs to remind the reader that the CAP support system has become rather complicated since it retains the original system for certain products while applying new methods for others and/or building them on top of the old.

With regard to assessment, judged in terms of its own objectives, the CAP would seem to have had several successes. First, the various agricultural support systems that existed prior to the formation of the EC have been liquidated and a common, although highly complicated, system has been achieved. Second, to a qualified extent, intra-EU free trade in agricultural products has been accomplished through the removal of most intra-EU trade impediments. Third, the EU as a whole has become more or less self-sufficient in farm products going to the final consumer (in 1993–94, the EC of 12 members had self-sufficiency rates between 101% and 211% for most agricultural products except for wine and sheepmeat and goatmeat, with respectively 97% and 87%; the latest situation is similar – see above). Fourth, Directive 75/268, which dealt with mountain and hill farming in certain disadvantaged areas, was adopted in 1975, signalling a recognition of the fact that special provision would have to be made for these areas. Fifth, agriculture has experienced high rates of technical progress, increased productivity and stability in agricultural markets, achievements which are, together with increasing self-sufficiency, consistent with the objectives set out in Article 39 of the EEC Treaty (Article 33 in the Amsterdam Treaty). Finally, much progress has been achieved in increasing the size of farm holdings and in reducing the number of farm businesses – see Table 11.2.

On the debit side, the CAP has failed to make progress on the structural aspect of encouraging farmers to seek alternative occupations (even though the drift from land to industry is a natural process – see above). That is why this objective was finally abandoned. Moreover, the CAP has been the cause of the aforementioned embarrassing surpluses, which, in spite of the measures undertaken earlier, continue to have excessively high book values for at least cereals, skimmed milk powder and beef – see Figure 11.10 for figures for 1995–7. Furthermore, the CAP has had the effect of making the prosperous farmers richer, but has not helped the poorer farmers as it has retained them in the industry through its high intervention price levels; the latest measures adopted to rectify the situation are a step in the right direction, but will not tackle the problem immediately or for a long time, given the amount of direct support extended. Finally, in spite of the latest cuts, the CAP has failed to provide reasonable and stable prices for the consumer. For more information on this, see section 16.6.

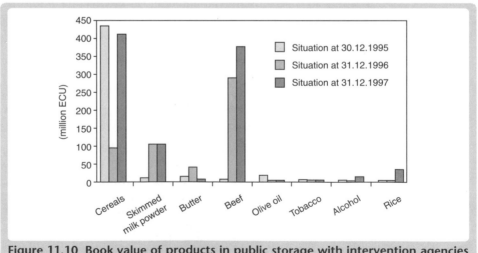

Figure 11.10 Book value of products in public storage with intervention agencies
Source: The Agricultural Situation in the European Union 1998 (CEU, 1999k).

These successes and failures have to be examined more carefully. First, most economists would agree that the embarrassing surpluses were, and continue to be, caused by the high levels of intervention prices; these were initially set at the high West German levels. This of course had serious consequences for the financing of the policy, and it was only after the costs had become unmanageable that efforts were introduced to alleviate the situation. However, even with the latest cuts, the problem is yet to be fully resolved – see section 11.10.

Second:

> Low earnings in agriculture are the consequence of low alternative earnings arising from disparities in education levels in rural areas. But [under] these circumstances any price policy based on some concept of giving to farm resources the ability to achieve parity incomes with the non-farm population is doomed to failure. Higher prices are largely translated into the purchase of more inputs from the non-farm sector (fertilizers and machinery) and into the values of assets the supply of which is fixed (mainly land). Input suppliers and landlords gain, but the new entrants get no benefit. This accounts for the seemingly insatiable appetite of farm programmes for public money and the desire to hide the appropriations in the form of higher food costs even if the same transfer could be made more efficiently by direct payments. Agriculture adjusts in size to the level of support it is given; price support policies have never influenced long-run resources returns appreciably. The implication of this is that the only way to raise farm incomes is to control the inflow of resources into agriculture, or to increase the level of education in rural areas. (Josling, 1969, pp. 268–9)

In spite of the fact that Josling wrote this about three decades ago, it remains relevant today.

Third, the MCA system, which most observers had thought was a temporary phenomenon, became well established in the CAP mechanism; as mentioned above, it was only a few years ago that it was discontinued. The MCA system, together with the 'green money', came to be used in a very sophisticated way to enable farmers to accommodate their national interests within the CAP (Ritson and Tangermann, 1979). The system came to be a positive deterrent to intra-EC trade since traders had great difficulty in predicting the MCAs and hence offset them by adding them to their margins. This created unequal prices and justifiably led to the term 'the uncommon market'.

In global terms, the CAP has been seen as undermining the interests of the United States and the Third World. This point has two elements to it: first, by disposing of surpluses at subsidized prices (restitution payments) to countries such as the former USSR and now Russia, the EU is depriving the poorer nations of export earnings and the United States of real income (since EU sales are achieved at the cost of American exports); second, and most importantly, the EU, in protecting its own agriculture, is competing unfairly against imports from these same countries. Indeed, some economists would argue that under free and fair trade conditions, Western Europe would have no comparative advantage in most agricultural products. However, this is not an entirely accurate assessment since the United States also subsidizes its farmers, but in spite of the recent changes, the EU still appears to be out of line in this respect – see the previous section.

A possible response to these claims is that 'it would be churlish to question such a goal of prosperous agriculture contributing to economic growth in the [EC]' (Josling, 1969, p. 268), particularly in a world where agriculture is a highly protected industry, as is the case in the EU's most eminent competitors, the United

States and Japan. Moreover, agriculture should be seen as an industry for which the EU has a sociopolitical preference (secure food supplies and pleasant environmental conditions) in terms of output and employment; this is the case of a preference for a collective good discussed in detail elsewhere (see, for example, El-Agraa and Jones, 1981) and in Chapter 4. Additionally, absolutely free trade in agriculture would have been detrimental to the interests of countries such as France and Italy, unless the argument for free trade applied simultaneously to *all* industries. Finally, the EU does not produce the same range of agricultural products as does the Third World.

However, such responses have no solid foundation. First, although a prosperous agriculture would no doubt contribute to growth, it is difficult to see why it is churlish to question this. This goal can be achieved, if at all, only at the expense of alternative goals; hence one needs to know relative rates of growth before reaching a conclusion – the question is one of priorities. Second, the EU *does* compete with such countries as Australia, Canada, New Zealand, the United States and several developing countries in terms of beef, cereals, sugar and vegetables; the figures on self sufficiency published by the EU Commission do not reflect this, simply because they are a manifestation of the protectionist nature of the CAP itself. Recall that most EU member nations were net importers of most agricultural products at the time of the inception of the EEC. Third, it is nonsensical to equate countries in a comparison by simply referring to the fact that protection exists in all of them; one needs their 'effective protective rates' before doing so. Fourth, the argument for a social preference for employment in agriculture is not very appealing in the context of the EU, particularly since world supplies are cheaper than those of the EU and the movement away from agricultural employment not only is natural but is an objective of the CAP itself. Finally, the argument for security of food supplies does not hold much water these days since absolute food shortages have become rare and fleeting and are usually caused by administrative mismanagement or political turmoil; hence a 'country's best guarantee of food security is a diversified export sector that provides the funds for needed imports, along with sound macroeconomic policy to keep those exports competitive' (Josling, 1998, p. 9).

The gist of this argument is that some economists seem preoccupied with the 'trade creation' elements of the CAP. Because the 'trade diversion' aspects have been almost completely ignored, the successes have been exaggerated while the failures have been underestimated. The reader who is interested in a full survey of the actual cost estimates of the CAP should consult Chapter 12 of El-Agraa (1999), Baldwin *et al.* (1988) and references given there.

Notes

1. A rough indication of the average levels of income for farmers, relative to the incomes of those in other occupations, can be obtained by comparing the share of agriculture in total labour force and national output. Such a comparison indicates that at the time of the inception of the EEC, average agricultural incomes in the three largest countries (France, Germany and Italy) were only about 50% of those of other occupations (Ritson, 1973, p. 96).
2. 'Agricultural incomes have risen, but in France, Germany and Italy there is little evidence that the gap in incomes between agriculture and other occupations has diminished' (*ibid.*).
3. It is argued by some that the provision of an adequate agricultural sector incidentally

helps to ensure a pleasant environment for the nation's inhabitants. However, there is considerable argument that intensive agriculture is detrimental to the environment, e.g. removal of hedges, odours from intensive livestock farming, etc. (Bowers, 1972).

4. 'This does not, however, accrue to farmers alone: in fact it represents increased return to fixed factors in both farming and the purchased input industries' (Josling, 1969, p. 296).

5. 'It is possible to derive expressions of the average cost (in terms of extra resources or budget payments) of achieving a unit of objective, in this case income transfer. Such calculations are meaningful if comparing the policy with a free market. More relevant in the case of a policy where the level of guaranteed price can be changed from year to year is the marginal cost of gaining an additional unit of objective.' (Josling, 1969, p. 272)

6. Bhagwati (1965) demonstrates that tariffs and quotas can be equivalent in their effects only if it is assumed that free competition exists in both the exporting and importing countries and in the industry under consideration – see El-Agraa (1983b, Chapters 8–10, and 1989b, Chapters 8–10).

7. Josling (1969, p. 277). For a more detailed discussion of distortions, the reader should consult Johnson (1965a) and Chapter 5.

8. For an estimate of the average and marginal costs of some of these policies, the reader should consult Josling (1969, pp. 278–80).

9. This refers to a series of documents, which were submitted to the Council in December 1968. The first of these was called 'Memorandum on the Reform of Agriculture in the European Community', in *Bulletin of the European Community*, 1969, Supplement. The series is available in one volume as *Le Plan Mansholt*, Brussels, July 1969 – see Fennell (1979, 1997) for details.

10. The average size of holding in the United Kingdom in 1970–1 was more than three times that in the Original Six – and if one were to include farms of less than one hectare, the difference would be more extreme.

12 The Common Fisheries Policy

A. M. EL-AGRAA

It was stated in the previous chapter that in the EEC Treaty of Rome fisheries were included in the definition of agricultural products; but in 1966 an effort was made by the EC Commission to establish a Common Fisheries Policy (CFP – in its *Report on the Situation of the Fisheries Sector in the Member States of the EEC and the Basic Principles for a Common Policy*, 1966); prior to that, many fish stocks in what are now EU waters were controlled by the North-East Atlantic Fisheries Commission (NEAFC). However, agreement on the CFP was not reached until 1983, after six years of negotiations and hard bargaining. The purpose of this chapter is to examine briefly the background to these developments and to explain the nature and implications of the CFP. The reader who is interested in a detailed account of the developments leading to the creation of this policy together with its geographical and political implications is advised to read Wise (1984).

However, before we tackle the main body of this chapter, a few points should be made. The first is about the inclusion, initially, of fisheries in agriculture. This is not altogether illogical since the two industries have a lot in common: both are subject to price instability (owing to the highly specialized human and physical capital in the fisheries industry, making its short-term supply highly inelastic, and to fish having a rather low price elasticity); both have low income elasticity for their products; both are prone to random shocks owing to natural causes over which they have no control; both have large numbers of small, self-employed producers. The second concerns the need for a common policy. Many analysts would argue that a common policy for fisheries makes more sense than one for agriculture since most fishing activity is conducted across and beyond national territorial waters, and fish take no notice of national frontiers (for example, about 90% of the North Sea cod-fish spend their first year in waters off the coasts of Denmark, Germany and Holland, but by the time they are three years old and ripe for catching, most of them will have migrated to British territorial waters). However, others would counter by stressing that even when activities ancillary to fishing are added (such as processing, transport and ship maintenance), the total industry involved no more than 1% of the entire EC of the early 1970s (1.2 million; dropping to 263 019 fishermen in 1995), but the response would be that the industry, like agriculture, had political clout due mainly to its concentrated nature, involving whole communities in remote areas with no prospects for alternative employment; and that, being a risky industry, it draws a lot of sympathy, especially when disaster strikes. The third is that during the 1960s there was agreement that any vessel can fish anywhere except in a 12-mile coastal zone reserved for vessels belonging to the country whose coast borders this zone, exception being granted to vessels from other nations that had traditionally fished there, i.e. those that had traditional rights.

However, prompted by a unilateral action by Iceland in 1970, claiming exclusive fishing rights within 50 miles of its coast, the United Nations decided two years later that any country could establish an Exclusive Economic Zone (EEZ) in waters up to 200 miles from its coastline, appropriate consideration being allowed for overlapping zones. Needless to add, this had drastic implications for most EC nations, given their traditional fishing areas. Finally, because of advances in vessel technology fish catches were beginning to outstrip existing stocks, and hence something had to be done to stop biological disaster.

12.1   Background

It could be argued that what prompted the emergence of a CFP was the situation in 1966. Then, production in the original Six began to stagnate, the attitude of non-member nations regarding their 12-mile limits became increasingly restrictive and there was a sharp decline in the Community's self-sufficiency rates for the major fish species. As a consequence of this, proposals were advanced in June 1968 which amounted to a set of basic ingredients for a CFP, and the basic foundations were agreed at the end of June 1970, on the day before membership negotiations were due to commence with the new applicants. These proposals were adopted by the Council in October 1970 (Regulation 2141/70 on conservation rules and Regulation 2142/70 on the establishment of a common marketing organization with an intervention price system to be run by recognized producer organizations in each member state; hence the mechanism resembles that for the CAP) and came into force in February 1971.

The striking feature of this policy was the recognition by all six member states of the principle of 'equal access' for all EC fishermen to the territorial waters of the EC together with a free EC market for fish. This was opportune, given the fact that the waters of the three prospective member countries of the EC (as well as those of Norway, which finally decided not to join the EC, arguably because of this very issue) were rich in fish: the total catch of the original Six was half that of the three soon to become members. Hence, the negotiation of 'access' was vital if the CFP were to become a reality.

It should be added that the agreements reached between the original Six and the three new member nations included arrangements for fisheries which entitled the fishermen of coast countries (those countries highly dependent on fishing for their livelihood) to a general and exclusive six-mile zone and to a 12-mile exclusive zone in some areas with the proviso that these zones would become EC waters after 1982 if no review of the CFP took place in the meantime. However, the three nations did not view this as a permanent solution since they felt that they were losing more than they expected to gain. Thus an atmosphere ripe for conflict was created.

However, during the period 1974–6, the United Nations Convention on the Law of the Sea (UNCLOS III) was in session and one of the points which occupied a large part of its deliberations was the issue regarding the extension of national fishing zones to 200 miles. The nine member nations of the EC were actually about to implement such an exclusive zone limit, but preferred to await the outcome of the conference. In the end, UNCLOS III failed to reach agreement on this issue, and when Canada, Norway and the United States announced their intention of adopting a 200-mile zone, the EC decided (in The Hague in October 1976) to follow suit and to implement what it had already intended, especially since the United Kingdom was threatening to do so unilaterally. At the meeting in The Hague, it was also decided to ask the EC Commission to proceed with negotiations with third countries. Obviously, without specific agreements, the 200-mile zone limit was bound to exclude countries which had in the past fished in what came to be known as the 'Community pond'. It should be clear that whether or not these countries should be allowed access to the EC pond would depend on the size of catch granted and the extent of reciprocity extended to the EC in terms of EC fishermen having access to the waters of such countries. Not surprisingly, the EC Commission, for this purpose, classified third countries into three categories:

1. Possible reciprocators such as Iceland and Norway.
2. Countries like Canada and the United States which have no interest in the EC pond but which might have surpluses in their waters to which the EC fishermen might want to gain access.
3. Countries which would like access to the EC pond but could not reciprocate, such as the nations of Eastern Europe.

By 1976 the same old questions began to surface again. Were the member nations to have completely free access to the EC pond or would they be granted exclusive zones on a permanent basis? Would the EC go for a maximum catch, partly determined with conservation in mind, which would be shared out between the member states on a percentage basis? Would the EC perhaps opt for both these possibilities? What compensation would Ireland and the United Kingdom receive, in terms of access to the EC pond, for losing some of their own waters to countries like Iceland because of the common 200-mile zone?

The position of the United Kingdom was that the 12-mile limit was unacceptable, and the British government started by demanding a 100-mile exclusive zone, but later dropped this limit by 50%. During the negotiations that followed, more emphasis was placed on a limit on the total catch to be divided into national quotas and less on exclusive zones. Late in 1977, the EC Commission proposed possible national quotas, giving about 30% to the United Kingdom; but this was only two-thirds of what the United Kingdom had hoped for.

The first detailed proposals of a CFP went to the Council in September 1976. These comprised measures for 'conserving fishery resources (through determining total allowable catches – TACs – and quotas), for safeguarding, as far as possible, employment and incomes in coastal regions, and for adjusting fleet size in the light of the catch available' (*Bulletin of the European Communities*, no. 1, 1983, p. 1). It should be emphasized that TACs are determined by biological, not economic, criteria; they are calculated in terms of the maximum number of fish to be caught without reducing the total fish population to a level at which it would not be capable of maintaining itself. Therefore, they would naturally vary from year to year in accordance with variations in the size of the fish stocks. In October 1976 the Six agreed to extend their fishing limits to 200 nautical miles as from 1 January 1977 (North Sea and North Atlantic). It should therefore not be surprising to learn that the negotiations were very tense and difficult since it was not just that the question of access had to be solved but also that TACs had to be fixed and then allocated to each member country of the EC on a quota basis at a time when there was evidence of over-fishing. Indeed, final resolution of the matter was not reached until 25 January 1983 when the ministers in charge of fisheries in the ten member nations of the EC agreed on the new CFP. This was based on the proposals that the EC Commission had itself initiated. The relief expressed by the EC Commission on reaching an agreement, after six years of hard bargaining, should not be underestimated.

12.2 The policy

The delight of the EC Commission with the new CFP can be clearly captured from their statement that a 'Blue Europe' had been born (CEC, 1983c, p. 193).

In that report, the EC Commission states that the following ground rules were laid down for EC fishery activities:

1. 'Equality of access to resources in Community waters except, by way of derogation and for a renewable period of 10 years, for the preferential arrangements for in-shore fishermen within the 12-mile limit.'

2. 'Compliance with a common policy for the conservation of resources, including both technical measures concerning the different fisheries and such stock management measures as the fixing of total allowable catches ... and annual quotas.'

3. 'The scope of agreements with non-Community countries to be reinforced and extended so as to safeguard fishing possibilities in their waters.'

4. 'Market support by implementation from 1 January 1983 of a common organisation of the market, with the changes decided upon on 29 December 1981.'

5. 'Modernization of development of the fishery and aquaculture sector, through measures financed by a Community budget of 250 million ECU over three years.'

The Report added that in 1983, the Blue Europe was experiencing some difficulties in settling down with the new ground rules. To cater for this, 'structural rules' were introduced on 4 October and TACs and catch quotas for 1983 were determined on 20 December of the same year, thus reinforcing the agreement.

In short, the new CFP covers four aspects. First, the policy has a 'system' for the conservation of sea resources within the EU. Second, the policy has a common organization of the market. Third, the policy includes 'structural' measures. These were originally financed by EAGGF, but following the reform of structural funds in 1993, a separate fund, the Financial Instrument for Fisheries Guidance (FIFG) was set up for this purpose – see Chapter 16. Finally, the policy asks for fisheries agreements with non-EU countries and for formal consultations between EU nations so that they can act in concert in the context of international agreements.

With regard to the conservation of resources, the Council has adopted a regulation which establishes an EU system which provides for measures to curtail fishing activities, sets rules for utilizing resources and makes special provisions for coastal fishing. More specifically, a conservation box has been established around the Orkney and Shetland Islands and the number of licences offered to EU fishermen over-fishing endangered species has been made more limited. Hence both 'access' and TACs are aspects of crucial importance here.

Table 12.1 provides information on the 1984 and 1985 TACs and the individual country quotas together with the TACs for 1982, 1986 and 1997. I have provided

Table 12.1 Allocations for 1984 and 1985 catch quotas in EC waters and in water managed in co-operation with non-member countries and TACs for 1982, 1983–6 and 1997 (tonnes)

	Cod	Haddock	Saithe	Whiting	Plaice	Redfish	Mackerel	Herring[a]
Belgium								
1984	8 230	1 670	80	3 680	12 030	0	100	0
1985	9 030	1 830	90	3 970	12 990	0	400	8 920
Denmark								
1984	234 350	18 615	7 550	34 190	46 110	4 890	7 400	43 770
1985	166 420	11 690	8 390	15 870	42 100	0	8 000	90 260
France								
1984	36 390	19 340	69 850	37 510	7 250	2 410	17 100	1 930
1985	39 540	20 270	95 020	41 400	7 500	4 410	14 930	35 430
West Germany								
1984	84 380	7 110	21 110	3 900	9 860	62 820	25 600	22 180
1985	87 840	7 530	25 260	4 330	10 780	62 535	22 190	65 760
Ireland								
1984	11 520	4 370	3 060	17 800	3 070	0	85 300	27 170
1985	11 520	3 820	3 730	22 700	3 730	0	72 640	31 900
Netherlands								
1984	23 230	1 120	190	8 630	66 890	0	37 300	7 850
1985	25 950	1 270	210	9 290	71 810	0	32 180	82 900
United Kingdom								
1984	117 910	140 840	20 860	79 480	53 710	380	234 700	38 800
1985	129 550	151 540	27 400	92 890	59 570	375	200 160	98 180
EC[b]								
1982	524 700	201 700	101 760	208 120	159 960	70 500	375 000	219 400
1984	516 010	193 065	122 700	185 190	198 920	70 500	407 500	141 700
1985	469 350	197 950	160 100	191 450	208 480	65 320	350 500	413 350
1986	377 470	245 630	157 000	176 200	212 690	0	349 000	514 415
1997[c]	321 662	155 000	139 000	146 340	109 240	0	343 855	801 770
EU share	310 592	146 900	79 200	122 960	106 130	0	295 885	727 330

[a] The herring quotas excluded provisional North Sea allocations to six of these countries – Belgium (1570), Denmark (6920), West Germany (4350), France (4520), Netherlands (9030) and the United Kingdom (7910).
[b] Greece and Italy are not involved in the TACs simply because they conduct all their fishing in the Mediterranean.
[c] There are now also TACs for the following (the first figure is the total TAC while the second is the EU share): anchovy (45 000; same), anglerfish (55 900; same), Atlantic salmon (1 204 750; same), blue whiting (522 500; 205 500), capelin (0; 0), deep water prawn (10 500; 5610), hake (69 130; same), horse mackerel (422 000; 430 000), megrim (35 840; same), Norway lobster (65 980; same), Norway pout (36 505; same), 'Panaeus' prawn (4108; 4000), pollock (22 100; same), sole (36 505; same) and sprat (401 540; 370 540).
Source: Calculated from the various issues of the *Bulletin of the European Communities*, vol. 17, no. 1, 1984, p. 37.

fuller data for 1984–5 simply for ease of exposition. This is because the Council decided that fishing during the first few months of 1983 should have been conducted on the basis of the 1982 TACs and quotas (due allowance being given to normal seasonal fluctuations), thus making the 1982 figures provisional in nature.

Moreover, the levels for 1984 can easily be compared with those of 1983: the 1984 figures were slightly lower for cod, haddock and whiting and slightly higher for mackerel, plaice and saithe, with the TAC for redfish remaining unchanged at 70 500 tonnes. For 1997, the TACs have declined for all categories except for herring, but new categories have been included. Thus there is enough information to compare the TACs in the three years, but such a comparison is too obvious to warrant specification. However, attention should be drawn to the fact that although the TAC for cod declined over the period 1983–5, Denmark absorbed more than the total decline since all the countries in the table increased their share, with Ireland maintaining its quota. A more drastic situation also applies to Denmark with regard to haddock, plaice and whiting since the TACs have increased relative to 1984. The reader who is interested in following the detailed yearly changes in the TACs and their allocation between the member nations of the EU is advised to consult the *Official Journal of the European Communities*; these yearly comparisons will not be pursued here nor updated on a yearly basis simply because the variations in them are not determined just by the bargaining position of the individual nations: as already indicated, changes in conservation criteria and in the natural catch environments are crucial.

The market organization covers fresh fish and frozen and preserved products and its main objective is to apply common marketing standards and to facilitate trading between the member nations of the EU. More precisely, however, it should be stated that the objectives of the marketing aspect are to guarantee an adequate income to the producers, to enhance rational marketing, to alter supply in accordance with market requirements, to ensure that consumer prices are reasonable and to promote common marketing standards – see Cunningham and Young (1983, p. 2).

The strutural measures can be described more precisely by stating their aims. The main objectives are to ensure that the resources of the sea are rationally utilized, to ensure that the fishermen of the different member nations of the EU are treated on an equal basis and to conserve resources or to reduce overcapitalization (Cunningham and Young, 1983, p. 3). With regard to these aspects, the Council agreed on 25 January 1983 to activate, within six months, special EC measures which were designed to 'adjust capacity and improve productivity of fishing and aquaculture'. These measures consisted largely of proposals put forward by the EC Commission between 1977 and 1980 and included 'aids for laying up, temporarily or permanently, certain fishing vessels so that capacity can be adjusted in the light of the conservation needs', 'aids for exploratory fishing and cooperation with certain non-member countries in the context of joint ventures in order to encourage the redeployment of the Community's fishing activity' and 'aids for the construction and modernisation of certain fishing vessels and aquaculture facilities and for the installation of artificial structures to facilitate restocking and develop the fishing industry generally' (*Bulletin of the European Communities*, no. 1, 1983, p. 2). As stated above, these measures were to apply for three years and were to qualify for EC financing to the total of 250 million ECU: 76 million ECU for capacity adjustment; 18 million ECU for exploratory fishing and joint ventures; 156 million ECU for restructuring, i.e. for encouraging investment in the fishing industry (see Table 12.2 for details). It should be added, however, that the EU's financial contribution to any approved project is generally limited to 50% of its total cost, and that these are EU monies for which EU citizens can apply irrespective of their nationality. With regard to the latter point, Wise (1984, p. 244) argues that since a large percentage of

Table 12.2 EC funds to assist the fisheries sector, 1983–6.

Proposed measures	Total expenditure (million ECU)
1. Directive on adjusting capacity	
(a) temporary withdrawal	44
(b) permanent withdrawal	32
2. Regulation on exploratory fishing and joint ventures	
(a) exploratory fishing	11
(b) joint ventures	7
3. Regulation on a common measure for restructuring, etc.	
(a) construction and modernisation of fishing vessels	118
(b) aquaculture	34
(c) artificial structures intended for restocking	4
Total expenditure over three years	250

Source: Official Journal of the European Communities, 26, C28, 3 February 1983, 1.

these funds was 'designed to help fleets adjust to nearer-water fishing following the loss of rights in far-off grounds, Britain could expect to continue as a major recipient of [EC] structural aid following a pattern established over the previous 10 years'. The United Kingdom received about 40.8 million ECU during 1973–82 for the construction and modernization of vessels from EAGGF; this amounted to 35.8% of total EAGGF expenditures on this item over the specified period – see below.

Finally, with regard to agreements with non-EU countries, framework fisheries agreements were signed with the Faeroe Islands, Guinea, Guinea-Bissau, Norway, Spain, Sweden and the United States. In 1991, new protocols were concluded with Senegal, Morocco, Mauritania and São Tomé and Príncipe. The Council also decided on the provisional application of the protocol with Morocco, Guinea-Bissau, the Comoros, Mozambique and Guinea and adopted two decisions on extension and amendment of agreements with the United States and the extension of the agreement with South Africa. The EU Commission was also authorized to negotiate fisheries agreements with the Caribbean countries of Antigua, Dominica, Saint Lucia and Suriname, all of which have been concluded. It was also authorized to negotiate agreements with Ecuador and Venezuela. Multilateral agreements were concluded with a view to the Community's participation in international agreements covering the north-east and north-west Atlantic, the Antarctic and salmon in the north Atlantic, and talks were in progress with regard to the EU's participation in international agreements on tuna and whaling and to its joining the organizations that control fishing in the Baltic, and in the central and south-east Atlantic.

One could continue along these lines by adding the annual changes that have been introduced, but such developments are easy to follow by reading the appropriate sections of various EU publications. Thus all that needs adding is to state that the major external events in this sector in 1996 were the signing on 26 February of a new four-year agreement on co-operation in the sea fisheries sector between the EU and Morocco, the work carried out in various international organizations, especially the signing of the agreement on the implementation of UNCLOS regarding the conservation and management of straddling stocks and highly migratory species, and the EU's accession, within the framework of FAO, to the agreement to promote compliance with international conservation and management measures by fishing vessels on the high seas. Within the EU, the Commission adopted a proposal for a decision on the objectives of and rules for restructuring the EU's fishing industry for 1997–2002, with a view to achieving a sustainable balance between resources and their exploitation.

12.3 Developments in the CFP

The progress of the CFP has been almost along the expected lines, especially when two years after the inauguration of the CFP, the EU began to take decisions on TACs and their country allocation in December so as to inform the EC fishermen of their expected catches well before they started fishing. Although later agreements on the TACs and individual country quotas took longer to reach than expected, the delays were mainly for technical reasons and took no longer than two or three months, which is natural, given the bargaining nature of the situation.

With regard to the promised assistance for the restructuring of the fishing industry, Table 12.3 gives some indication of the progress made in this regard. The table shows that for the period 1983–6 the EC intended to extend aid totalling about 219 million ECU, but for the first three years the total was only about 174 million ECU. Thus it would seem that the aid for the restructuring of the fisheries industry fell short of the promised of 250 million ECU for the first three years of the CFP. If, however, one were to include aid amounting to about 68 million ECU granted under Regulation 355/77, which was adopted on 15 February 1977 and which comes under the EAGGF structural fund (now general structural funds – see above and Chapter 16), then the latter sum is only about 8 million ECU short of the target.

Another way of looking at the finances provided by the EC to support the restructuring of the fisheries industry is simply to quote the figures from the EC General Budget which come under the heading of fisheries (chapters 40–47). These are given in Table 12.4. It does not matter which three years cover the appropriate sum mentioned in the CFP since it is evident that the total of 250 million ECU was exceeded between 1983 and 1986. The comparison is made even more difficult by the EC's decision to inject a further 850 million ECU for restructuring over the five-year period 1988–92: if one took the 1988 figure as the starting point, the EC would be on target, and the drastic fall since 1993 corroborates this.

It should be added that the projects covered by the 1983 regulation amounted to 4271 while those covered by the 1977 regulation added a further 299 to this total. Moreover, a large number of new projects are being added each year: for example,

Table 12.3 Aid granted under the common measures for the restructuring, modernizing and developing of the fisheries industry and for developing aquaculture under Regulation (EC) 2908/83 (million ECU)

Appropriations	1983	1984	1985	1986	1987	1988
Belgium	0.35	3.95	2.41	2.38	0.41	0.10
Denmark	2.71	4.60	4.09	7.69	1.21	3.29
France	6.07	12.80	5.86	13.78	12.42	4.74
West Germany	3.13	3.18	1.12	4.92	4.41	1.39
Greece	6.70	2.44	3.95	9.51	6.37	5.41
Ireland	5.91	3.07	1.45	3.50	1.84	4.99
Italy	10.68	22.11	11.22	18.99	16.12	11.40
Netherlands	1.87	2.06	0.46	2.68	0.66	0.57
Portugal	–	–	–	–	11.22	2.85
Spain	–	–	–	–	32.30	18.11
United Kingdom	7.39	9.90	5.04	11.07	7.23	7.50
Total	44.81	64.11	35.60	74.52	94.09	60.35

Source: Calculated from various issues of the *Bulletin of the European Communities*.

in 1991 alone, 591 projects were approved for the modernization of vessel capacity. Also, Wise's expectation that the United Kingdom would get about 36% of the total aid is way off target since the average received by the United Kingdom between 1983 and 1986 was about 15% – see above.

Table 12.4 Allocations from the EC General Budget for the restructuring of the fisheries industry

Year	Million ECU
1983	107.24
1984	112.35
1985	111.73
1986	189.62
1987	197.29
1988	325.89
1989	348.24
1990	431.57
1991	530.80
1992	594.90
1993	25.00
1994	25.64
1995	28.20
1996	35.50
1997[a]	49.95
1998	48.10
1999	49.93

Source: *EC General Budget*, various years.

These figures also point to the most significant development in the CFP: the accession of Portugal and Spain. These countries were expected to increase the number of EC fishermen by 90%, the fishing capacity by 80% and fish consumption by EC citizens by about 50%. The changes in these totals reflect this reality. It should be added that as a result of the Iberian enlargement the EU has become the third largest fishing area in the world, and this position is further consolidated with the addition of Finland and Sweden.

Finally, as already indicated, the EU continues to negotiate agreements with third countries.

Before bringing this section to an end, it should be mentioned that the EU Commission decided that the measures that have been introduced have not succeeded in halting the danger to fish stocks, owing to excessive mortality, particularly in the case of juveniles, and over-capacity of the fishing fleet. It therefore recommended that the CFP should be amended, with special attention given to the following:

1. Distribution of responsibility in accordance with the 'subsidiarity' principle, conferring responsibility on the parties concerned, especially fishing organizations.

2. More stringent regulation of access to resources by a system of licences to cut back excess capacity.

3. A new classification of fishing activities (multiannual, multispecies and analytical TACs, as appropriate).

4. More stringent control mechanisms, by improving in particular the monitoring of vessel movements.

5. Enforcement of rules which are in the common interest, through suitable economic incentives and, where appropriate, the use of deterrent sanctions.

6. Greater synergy between management of internal and external resources.

7. Maintenance of certain principles established, notably the principle of relative stability with regard to fishing activities, the derogation from the principle of freedom of access within the 12-mile limit and the present arrangement for the Shetland area (possibly extending this to other regions).

8. Stronger structural management, mainly by the inclusion of structural measures under the reform of the structural funds.

9. Introduction of appropriate social accompanying measures, in accordance with the principle of cohesion, with particular emphasis on the concentration of EU resources and instruments in support of those regions least developed and most dependent on fisheries.

That might sound like political rhetoric, but the Commission would be justified in claiming that it has largely succeeded in its efforts to entice the member nations to follow its directions, citing as proof the major developments in the CFP to date:

1. The adoption in 1997 by the Council of Decision 97/413/EC on the objectives and detailed rules for restructuring the sector for 1997–2002 with reference to the achievement of a balance on a sustainable basis between resources and their exploitation, which, *inter alia*, set new targets for the reduction of fishing effort in each section of the fleet.

2. The adoption in 1998 of a regulation banning the use of driftnets from 1 January 2002 by all vessels in EU waters, other than the waters of the Baltic, the Belts and the Sound, and, in other waters, by all EU fishing vessels, the implementation of which was to be accompanied by social measures and compensation for the fishermen involved.

3. The adoption in 1999 of, *inter alia*, the regulations on the FIFG and on a new common organization of the markets in fishery and aquaculture products, and the taking of steps to improve dialogue with all groups concerned with the CFP and to promote nature conservation in the marine environment.

4. The agreement by the ministers in early 2000 to the biggest cuts ever in the TACs by between 20% and 40%, with cod catches in the Irish Sea to fall by 62%.

Thus, at least in the Commission's opinion, the recent developments in the CFP should galvanize all concerned into undertaking more appropriate action.

12.4 Reservations

Although the agreement on the CFP has been much applauded, a great deal of caution should be exercised. First, the use of such words as 'rational' and 'fair' immediately reminds one of the problems of the CAP where similar terminology came to mean self-sufficiency and an income to farmers much closer to, if not in excess of, the national average. Indeed, one aspect of the CFP is that, when the price of fish falls, the fishermen can withdraw their excess stocks from the market in return for the receipt of financial assistance from the funds designated for the purpose. Second, there is the apparent conflict between the structural aspects and the market organization, since the structure seeks conservation, while the market organization encourages larger catches by giving price supports which are directly related to the size of the catch. Third, it is inevitable that TACs will be negotiated annually; hence a tense bargaining atmosphere is likely to be generated over quota allocations. This reminds one of the classical case where it is desirable for oligopolists to pursue a policy of joint profit maximization, but where the outcome is for each oligopolist to try to maximize his or her share of the profit. Fourth, as Cunningham and Young (1983, p. 3) rightly state, even if the structural measures could be achieved,

> almost complete reliance is placed on management methods which might be termed 'biological' in that, while they generally improve the condition of the fish stock itself, they will not result in any long-term improvement in the economic health of the [fishing industry]. Typical of such biological techniques are net mesh size restrictions, closed seasons, closed areas and limitations on the use of certain efficient methods of capture.

12.5 Conclusion

In earlier editions, I stated that

> Although the CFP is about a decade old and the accession of Portugal and Spain has gone smoothly and no problems are envisaged regarding the membership of Finland and Sweden (Austria has no concerns here), it is still too early to make firm predictions about the appropriateness or otherwise of this policy. This is because the points mentioned in the previous section do indicate that there are potential problems which the EU Commission must keep

constantly in mind if the situation is not to be potentially explosive. Moreover, as we have seen the Commission feels that the CFP has been facing severe problems; hence its proposals for further drastic action.

Since then, not only have the members joining the EU in 1995 been fully accommodated, but also much progress with realizing the aims of the CFP has been achieved. This has been facilitated by the multi-annual guidance programmes (MAGPs), which, since 1983, set conditions for fleet development and PESCA (the Community Initiative Concerning the Restructuring of the Fisheries Sector), which provided assistance for those in areas heavily dependent on the fishing sector to create and develop alternative activities, jobs and training programmes. That stated, one must conclude by sharing in the applause for the reaching of agreement in 1983 after negotiations which took six years of hard bargaining and mackerel wars with Denmark, and for the smooth incorporation of the Iberian countries into the agreement. This was finalized through the adoption of Regulation 2027/95, relating to the establishment of a system for the management of fishing activities in certain EU fishing areas and resources. This Regulation came into force on 1 January 1996. One must also add that since the CFP puts emphasis on restrictions on output and sets prices which bear some relationship to actual market prices, it would seem that the excesses and absurdities of the CAP will not be repeated here.

13 Transport policy

K. BUTTON

13.1 Introduction

Transport has always been important in shaping the human geography of Europe. The military conquests of the past were largely along well-defined transport corridors and the growth of cities has mainly been at important junctions in transport networks. Advances in technology and changes in political ambition, as well as new economic conditions and institutional developments, have altered the nature of this link but its fundamental importance remains. The role of transport as a lubricator of economic reconstruction was appreciated in the post-Second World War period. Institutions such as the European Conference of Ministers of Transport (ECMT) were set up under the Marshall Plan to assist in reconstructing transport infrastructure and the considerable energies of the European Coal and Steel Community (ECSC) were devoted to improving the efficiency of the European rail transport system (Meade *et al.*, 1962). It was even more transparent in the formation of the European Economic Community (EEC) whereby the explicit creation of a Common Transport Policy (CTP) was mandated under the EEC.

Transport is a major industry in its own right, directly employing about 7% of the European Union (EU – the term largely used throughout this chapter for simplicity although the title has changed over the years) workforce, accounting for 7% of total EU GDP and for about 30% of final energy consumption. But this, however, is not really the important point. The crucial thing about transport from an economic perspective is its role in facilitating trade and in allowing individuals, companies, regions and nation states to exploit their various comparative advantages. Early debates concerning the merits of free trade tended to assume away the friction associated with moving goods to markets and the analysis of migration patterns exhibited similar tendencies to assume transport costs to be negligible. Some economists, such as von Thünen (1826), did take account of transport costs when trying to explain local land use patterns but such explicit consideration of space and the problems of transversing it was exceptional. The situation changed with the advent of new transport technologies in the middle of the nineteenth century and as countries and regions appreciated that manipulation of the transport system could influence their economic conditions. Manipulation of transport rates and the strategic design of infrastructure networks were used to protect domestic industries in ways akin to those of tariff barriers and other trade barriers. Individual European states sought to develop transport policies that were to their short-term benefit irrespective of their consequences for overall trade.

Today the upsurge of interest in supply chain management, just-in-time production and the like has led to a wider appreciation of the general need to enhance the efficiency of European transport if the region as a whole is to compete successfully in the global economy. The concern is that the effectiveness of transport logistics in the EU area are at least comparable with those elsewhere to ensure that the labour, capital and natural resources of member states can be exploited in a fully efficient economic manner.

It was against this broad background that the EU initially sought to develop a transport policy, of which the CTP has been but one element, designed to reduce artificial friction. It has taken time for the CTP and other elements of transport policy to come together to represent anything like a coherent strategy. There have been shifts of emphasis since the signing of the EEC Treaty and frequent changes in the types of policy deemed appropriate to meet these moving objectives. This chapter provides more details of the underlying problems and issues that have been central to these efforts and charts out some of the paths that have been pursued to confront them. The process has not been smooth and has involved a number of almost completely discrete phases. To pre-empt the conclusions, it can be said that ultimately, and after many tribulations, the EU has emerged with a relatively coherent approach to transport that has largely removed many of the potential bottlenecks to economic integration that dogged the early development of the Union.

13.2 Issues surrounding the European transport system

Problems with the creation of a transport policy began early. The EEC Treaty contained an entire chapter on transport, although apparently limiting itself to movement of freight by road, rail and inland waterways. Strictly the treaty said, 'The Council may, acting unanimously, decide whether, to what extent and by what procedure appropriate provisions may be laid down for sea and air transport.' It is thus not clear whether these modes were excluded only from the transport clauses or from the treaty as a whole, including its competition provisions. The Netherlands, having considerable maritime interests, were particularly concerned about retaining autonomy in these areas, and this concern contributed to the ambiguity.

While the treaty gave indications of what national obligations should be, it was not until 1961 that a memorandum appeared setting out clear objectives (CEC, 1961) and not until the following year that an Action Programme was published. The emphasis of these initiatives was to seek means to remove obstacles to trade posed by the institutional structures governing transport and to foster competition once a level playing field of harmonized fiscal, social and technical conditions had been established. That it has subsequently taken over forty years to make significant progress towards a CTP is in part due to the nature of European geography and the underlying transport market, although continued insistence on nation states pursuing their individual agendas was also a causal factor.

A simple examination of a map of the EU provides information on some of the problems of devising a common transport policy. Even when the Community consisted of only six members, the economic space involved hardly represented a natural market. Ideally transport functions most effectively on a hub and spoke basis with large concentrations of population and economic activity located at corners and in the centre and with the various transport networks (roads, railways and the like) linking them. The central locations act as markets for transport services in their own rights but also as interchange and consolidation points for traffic between the corner nodes. In many ways the USA fits this model rather well but the EU never has. When there were six members the bulk of economic activity was at the core, with limited growth taking place at the periphery. The joining of such states as Ireland, Greece, Portugal, Finland and Sweden added to the problems of serving peripheral and often sparsely populated areas. The geographical separation of some states and the logical routeing of traffic through non-member countries, together with the island nature of others, posed further problems.

The CTP also was not initiated with a clean slate – member states had established transport networks and institutional structures that could not rapidly be changed even if a common set of principles could have been established. At the outset countries such as France and West Germany carried a significant amount of their freight traffic by rail (34% and 27% by tonne-kilometres respectively). Others, such as Italy and the Benelux nations, relied much more on road transport; the average length of domestic hauls being an important determining feature. The resultant differences were also not simply physical (including variations in railway gauges, vehicle weight limits and different electricity currents). They also reflected fundamental differences in the ways transport was viewed.

At a macro, political-economy level there were two broad views on the way transport should be treated. Following the Continental philosophy of transport policy, the objective was to meet wide social goals that require interventions in the market involving regulations, public ownership and direction. This approach particularly dominated much of twentieth-century transport policy thinking in Continental Europe and has its genesis in the Code Napoléon with its focus on centralism. Its place has been taken in recent years by a wider acceptance of the Anglo-Saxon approach to transport policy. This treats the transport sector as little different to other economic activities. Transport provision and use should be efficient in its own right. Efficiency is normally best attained by making the maximum use of market forces. Of course, the extremes of the Continental approach never existed and nowhere has the strict Anglo-Saxon philosophy been fully applied; it has been a matter of degree. Even in countries such as the UK that had in the past been seen as a bastion of the Anglo-Saxon ideology there existed extensive regimes of regulation and control and large parts of the transport system were in state or local government ownership.

The periodic enlargements of the EU, together with broader shifts in the way that transport is viewed that transcended the narrow European situation, have resulted in a move away from the Continental way of thinking to a more market-based approach to a CTP. The interventionist positions of Germany and France were initially set against the more liberal approach of the Netherlands. With the accession of the UK and Denmark in 1973 the more interventionist approach was now in the minority. Subsequent enlargements added to the impetus for less regulation of transport markets.

The situation can also be looked at from a more analytical, economic perspective over time. This is in terms of the ways that efficiency is viewed. The approach until the 1970s was to treat efficiency in transport largely in terms of maximizing scale efficiency while limiting any deadweight losses associated with monopoly power. Most transport infrastructure was seen as enjoying economies of scale that could only be completely exploited by co-ordinated and, *ipso facto*, regulated and often subsidized, development. State ownership, the extreme of regulation, was also often adopted. Many aspects of operations were also seen as potentially open to monopoly exploitation and hence in need of oversight. This situation has changed since the late 1970s. From a pragmatic perspective, the high levels of subsidies enjoyed by many elements of the transport sector became politically unsustainable. Economists began to question whether the regulations deployed were actually achieving their stated aims. They may, for example, have been captured by those that are intended to be the regulated or have been manipulated to the benefit of individuals responsible for administering the regime. Government failures, it was argued, were larger than the market failures they were trying to correct.

New elements also came into play in the 1970s, and especially concern about the wider environmental implications of transport. Attitudes towards the environmental intrusion associated with transport vary between member states as well as having changed more generally over time. To some extent this has been part of a wider effort within the Union to improve the overall environment and to fulfil larger, global commitments on such matters as reducing emissions of global warming gases (CEC, 1992g; CEC, 1995a) – see also Chapter 20. Transport impacts the environment at the local level (noise, lead, carbon monoxide, particulates and so on), at the regional level (e.g. nitrogen oxide emissions and maritime pollution) and at the global level (carbon dioxide). It is this diversity of implications and the trade-offs between them, as well as the absolute scale of some of the individual environmental intrusions, that make policy formulation difficult. Local effects, because they impinge on nationals, have largely been left to the individual countries but as the implications of regional and global environmental intrusions have become more widely appreciated so EU transport policy has become proactive in these areas. The main problem with these types of environmental issue is that their effects are often trans-boundary and thus give little incentive for individual action by governments.

13.3 The early phases of policy

As we have seen, the past thirty years have seen important changes in the ways in which transport is viewed. There have always been periodic swings in transport policy but the period since the late 1970s provides a classic watershed (Button and Gillingwater, 1986) that has permeated EU thinking. The change has been a dramatic one that transcends national boundaries and modes. The liberalization of transportation markets throughout the world and the extension of private sector ownership has also had the wider influence of providing important demonstration effects to other sectors that in turn have also been liberalized (Button and Keeler, 1993).

The early thinking regarding the CTP centred on the idea of harmonization so that a level playing field could ultimately be created on which competition would be equitable. The ECSC had initiated this approach in the early 1950s and it continued as EU interest moved away from primary products. The ECSC had removed many artificial tariff barriers relating to rail movements of primary products and the CTP initially attempted to expand this idea in the 1960s to cover the general carriage of goods and especially those moved on roads. Road transport was viewed rather differently to railways. In particular, it was perceived that the demand and supply features of road haulage markets could lead to excessive competition and supply uncertainties.

The early efforts involved such actions as seeking to initiate common operating practices (e.g. relating to driving hours and vehicle weights), common accounting procedures and standardizing methods of charging. A forked tariff regime for trucking, with rates only allowed between officially determined maxima and minima, was aimed at meeting the dual problems of possible monopoly exploitation in some circumstances and of possible inadequate capacity due to excess competition in others. A differential between the maximum and minimum rate on international movements within the EU was stipulated and statutory charges established on this basis. Practically, there were problems in setting the cost-based rates but beside that, questions must be raised concerning a policy that was aimed at simultaneously tackling monopoly and excess competition (Munby, 1962). Limitations on the number of international truck movements across borders were marginally reduced by the introduction of a small number of Community quota licences – authorizing the free movement of holders over the entire EU road network (Button, 1984).

The enlargement of the Union from the original six to nine members in 1973 stimulated a renewed interest in transport policy. At about the same time, the Commission also raised legal questions concerning the inertia of the Council of Ministers to move on creating a genuine CTP. The new members – the UK, Ireland and Denmark – tended to be more market oriented in terms of transport policy objectives. Also, there was inevitable horse-trading across policy areas and with the enlargement came the opportunity to review a whole range of policy areas. It also followed a period of rapid growth in trade within the Union, with a shift towards greater trade in manufactures. As a result infrastructure capacity issues were coming to the fore and the case for more flexible regulation of road freight transport was being strongly argued (Button, 1990).

The outcome, however, was not dramatic although new sectors entered the debates, most notably maritime transport, and wider objectives concerning environmental protection and energy policy played a role (see Table 13.1). Overall, the actions in this period were a gentle move to liberalization. Making of the quota licence system permanent and expanding the number of licences increased international intra-EU road freight capacity. The option of using reference tariffs rather than forked tariffs was a reflection of the inherent problems with the latter. A major element of the measures initiated involved transport infrastructure in terms of improving decision-making regarding its provision and with regard to consideration of the way that charges should be levied for its use. The importance of transport links outside of the EU borders, but part of a natural European network, also began to play a part in policy formulation with the Union beginning to develop mechanisms for financing investment in such infrastructure.

The enlargements of the Union as Greece, and then Spain and Portugal, joined had little impact on the CTP. It still essentially remained piecemeal. The only significant change prior to major developments in the early 1990s was the gradual widening of the modes covered. There were, for example, moves to bring maritime and air transport policy in line with Union competition policy.

Efforts to develop a common policy on maritime transport represent one of the spheres in which there was a broadening out of EU transport policy (Brooks and Button, 1992) from the mid-1980s. Since 35% of the international, non-intra EU trade of member states involves maritime transport (some 90% of the Union's aggregate imports and outputs) it may seem surprising that it took so long for this

> **Table 13.1 Summary of the policy of EC-9**
>
> *Emphasis on*
> - Links between transport and: regional; social; fiscal; industrial; environmental and energy affairs
> - Intervention with transport within a Community-led framework
> - The joint movement forward on consistency of regulations and liberalization
> - The increasing importance attached to co-ordination of infrastructure investment
>
> *Policy*
> - Infrastructure co-ordination
>   (Important in the Action Programme, 1974–1976)
>   - New consultation procedure with a Transport Infrastructure Committee (1978)
>   - Oort's study of infrastructure pricing (Dort and Maaskant, 1976)
>   (Contained in the 'Green Paper' of 1979)
>   - Creation of an Infrastructure Fund
>   - Extension of interest in the infrastructure of non-members (e.g. Austria and Yugoslavia) where it affects links between members
> - Liberalization
>   - Reference tariff system (1978)
>   - Permanent quota system (1976)
>   - Common method for determining bilateral quotas (1980)

mode to come within the CTP. The reason for this, as we have seen, was that the EEC Treaty required unanimous decisions regarding the extent to which sea transport was to be included in EU policy – although it was unclear whether this applied to EU policy as a whole or purely to the CTP. Inertia, initially at least, was largely a function of a lack of clarity in the Commission's remit.

The accession to membership in the 1970s and early 1980s of countries such as the UK and Greece with established shipping traditions brought maritime issues to the table and then the Single European Act (SEA) of 1987 provided a catalyst for initiating a maritime policy (Erdmenger and Stasinopoulos, 1988). A series of measures were introduced aimed at bringing shipping within the Union's competition policy framework (see Chapter 9). This came at a time when major changes were beginning to permeate the way in which maritime services were provided. Technical shifts, such as the widespread adoption of containerization, had begun to influence the established cartel arrangements that had characterized the provision of scheduled maritime services. (These arrangements were mainly conferences that co-ordinated fares and sailings but later were more integrated consortia.) The ability to discriminate in relation to price that these cartels enjoyed was beginning to be eroded as it became more difficult to isolate cargoes. Conferences had been permitted in most European countries since the late nineteenth century because they were thought to be the only way to offer scheduled services of less than a ship-load at relatively stable rates to shippers. Action by the United Nations to limit the power of these cartels in the 1970s was largely aimed at protecting developing countries but was in conflict with national policies of some EU members while others ratified it. A perceived need for a more co-ordinated maritime policy emerged (Brooks and Button, 1992).

This view was reinforced in the 1980s as the size of the EU shipping sector declined significantly. The relative size of the sector had been falling for many years but accelerated in the face of competition from Far East and Communist bloc fleets. Taxation and policies on such matters as wages and technical standards were adding to the problem by stimulating operators to 'flag out' and register in non-member states.

The 'First Package' in 1985 sought to improve the competitive structure of the European shipping industry and its ability to combat unfair competition from third countries (CEC, 1985h). It gave the Commission the power to react to predatory behaviour by third party ship owners which when initially applied (e.g. the *Hyundai* case) exerted a demonstration effect, especially on Eastern bloc ship owners. The measures also set out an interpretation of competition policy that allowed block exemptions for shipping cartels (shipping conferences) albeit with safeguards to ensure the exemption was not exploited.

In 1986 a 'Second Package' – the Positive Measures Package – was initiated by the European Commission with four main regulations aimed at addressing the decline in the competitiveness of the EU's fleets as well as covering such matters as safety and pollution. Greater co-ordination of fleets was seen as a cornerstone of policy and as part of this a common registry was proposed (CEC, 1991g). It has not, however, proved a success, and fleet sizes have continued to decline, bringing forth new ideas for capacity reduction from the EU Commission. Also as part of the general effort to liberalize the European market and enhance the efficiency of the industry, agreement on cabotage (the provision of a domestic service within a country by a carrier from another nation) was reached but with exceptions in some markets, e.g. the Greek Islands.

Air transport in general, since the initiatives of the USA in the late 1970s that had liberalized its domestic passenger and freight markets and fostered an Open Skies policy for international aviation, was moving away from a tradition of strict regulation that had pertained since the pioneering days (Button *et al.*, 1998). Until the early 1980s, however, it had also generally been thought that aviation policy was outside of the jurisdiction of the EU Commission and a matter for national governments. Following a number of legal decisions by the European Court of Justice (e.g. the *Nouvelles Frontières* – see below – and *Ahmed Saeed* cases, both regarding the applicability of various aspects of EU competition rules to air transport), however, this changed.

The European bilateral system of air transport agreements covering scheduled air services between member states was, like those in other parts of the world, tightly regulated. Typical features of a bilateral agreement involving EU members meant that: only one airline from each country was allowed to fly on a particular route with the capacity offered by each bilateral partner also often restricted; revenues were pooled; fares were approved by the regulatory bodies of the bilateral partners; and the designated airlines were substantially state owned and enjoyed state aid. Domestic air markets were also highly controlled. The charter market, largely catering for holiday traffic from northern Europe to southern destinations, represented about 50% of the revenue seat miles within the EU and was less strictly regulated but the regulations were such that services seldom met the needs of business travellers.

The changing policy climate began in 1979 when the Commission put forward general ideas for regulatory reform in its *Civil Aviation Memorandum No. 1*, with more specific ideas following in *Civil Aviation Memorandum No. 2* (CEC, 1984d). The practical push for reform came from the ECJ's verdict in the *Nouvelles Frontières* case concerning the cutting of air fares. This encouraged the Commission to adopt the view that its powers to attack fare-fixing activities were greater than the implementing regulation suggested. The Council subsequently decided that the best way to regain control was to agree to introduce deregulation but of a kind, and at a pace, of its own choosing. Hence the 1987 'First Package'.

The basic philosophy was that deregulation would take place in stages, with workable competition being the objective. A regulation was adopted that enabled the Commission to apply the antitrust rules directly to airline operations. Only interstate operations were covered; intrastate services and services to countries outside the EU were not at this stage affected. Certain technical agreements were also left untouched. The Council also adopted a Directive designed to provide airlines with greater pricing freedom. While airlines could collude, the hope was that they would increasingly act individually. The authorities of the states approved applications for air-fare changes. Also the new arrangements did not constitute free competition since an element of regulation remained. While conditions were laid down that reduced the national authorities' room for manoeuvre in rejecting changes in air fares, they could still reject them. However, if there was disagreement on a fare the disagreeing party lost the right of veto under arbitration.

The 1987 package also made a start on liberalizing access to the market. To this end the Council of Ministers adopted a decision in 1987 that provided for a deviation from the traditional air services agreement which set a 50/50 split. The capacity shares related to total traffic between the two countries. Member states were required to allow competition to change the shares up to 55/45 in the period to 30 September 1989 and thereafter to allow it to change to 60/40. Normally they could only take action if capacity shares threatened to move beyond such limits. Fifth freedom traffic[1] was not included in these ratios but was additional. There was also a provision in which serious financial damage to an air carrier could constitute grounds for the Commission to modify the shift to the 60/40 limit.

The decision also required member states to accept multiple designations on a country-pair basis by another member. A member state was not obliged to accept the designation of more than one air carrier on a route by the other state (that is, a city-pair basis) unless certain conditions were satisfied. These conditions have become progressively less restrictive over time. The decision also made a limited attempt to open up the market to fifth freedom competition.

In 1989 the Council returned to the issue of air transport deregulation. The 'Second Package' involved more deregulation. From the beginning of 1993 a system of double disapproval was accepted. Only if both civil aviation authorities refused to sanction a fare application could an airline be precluded from offering it to its passengers. From the same date the old system of setting limits to the division of traffic between the bilateral partners was to disappear totally in a phased manner. Member states also endorsed the vital principle that governments should not discriminate against airlines provided they meet safety criteria and address the problem of ownership rules. In the past, an airline had typically to be substantially owned by a European state before it could fly from that country, but the Council abolished this rule over a two-year period.

Air cargo services were liberalized so that a carrier operating from its home state to another member country could take cargo into a third member state or fly from one member state to another and then to its home state. Cabotage and operations between two free-standing states were not liberalized.

13.4   The CTP and other aspects of policy in the 1990s

The creation of the Single European Market in 1992, and subsequent moves towards greater political integration, brought important changes to the CTP and related transport policies (Button, 1992). Broadly, the 1987 SEA stimulated a concerted effort to remove institutional barriers to the free trade in transport services. At about the same time, efforts at further political integration led to major new initiatives to provide an integrated European transport infrastructure – e.g. the Trans-European Networks (TENs) (CEC, 1989j). These strategic networks were aimed at facilitating higher levels of social and political integration at the national and regional levels. They also had purely economic objectives.

While there were moves to liberalize industries such as air transport from the late 1980s, the broad basis of the current phase of EU transport policy was established in the Commission's White Paper on *The Future Development of the Common Transport Policy* (CEC, 1992o). This set out as a guiding principle the need to balance an effective transport system for the EU with a commitment to the protection of the environment. The environmental theme was expanded subsequently (CEC, 1992e). This was to be set in the context of defending the needs and interests of individual citizens as consumers, transport users and people living and working in areas of transport activity.

Even if these effects were not present, questions arose at the time regarding the ability of regulators to serve the public interest with the information that they had at hand. The development of economic theories involving such concepts as contestable markets (where potential competition could be as effective as actual competition in blunting the power of monopoly suppliers), although subsequently the centre of intellectual and empirical debate, provided new ways of thinking about transport markets and were central to several EU initiatives. There was also a switch away from concern about problems of optimal scale and monopoly power that had been the intellectual justification for state ownership and regulation of such industries as railways and air transport, to attempts at seeking to create conditions favourable to X-efficiency and dynamic efficiency. Technically, this was largely but not exclusively a concern with reducing costs replacing that of containing consumer exploitation. In particular, there was mounting concern about the costs of regulated transport that had macroeconomic implications for inflation and also often led to the need for high levels of public subsidy. These undertakings were neither producing at the lowest possible costs for the technology they were using at the time nor moving forward to adopt lower-cost technologies.

One can also look at the situation in the much wider context of the past thirty years being a period of important economic change as the information age has gradually taken over. Improved new forms of communication of all types have come to the fore that affect both production and consumption activities. Transport is part of the supply side in that it involves the facilitation of personal and commercial interactions but it is also part of the demand side, being a major user of information services. Modern aviation services, for example, could not operate without this technology and innovations in freight transport such as just-in-time management would hardly be possible on the scale on which they are now practised without it. As the structure of production has changed, not only in the EU but throughout the world, and as social changes have taken place it would have been almost impossible for the institutional structure of a key industry such as transport to have been unaltered. In this sense EU policy in the 1990s must be seen as partly flowing with much stronger international tides.

The nature of the policy changes, however interpreted, have not been uniform in either time or space. Countries and regional groupings have differed in their approach. The USA tended to lead the way as it deregulated its domestic transport markets between 1977 and 1982. Demonstration effects resulted in other countries following. The reforms in the USA were, however, only partly copied elsewhere. There were different starting points but also later reformers benefited from the experiences of the first-time movers. Transport systems differ across countries. In the USA, for instance, the average car is driven about 12 500 miles a year whereas in Europe the figure is less than 9000. Western Europe has only about 30% of the freeway mileage of the USA. Similarly, the demands placed on transport systems vary according to such things as the goods produced and the physical structure of the area. There are, however, common lessons to be learned, but these need to be taken in the context of the geography of the countries involved, the individual details of the reforms, their wider institutional context and their particular timing (Button, 1998). In some senses the EU benefited from the experiences of pre-1990s reforms when devising its current transport priorities and strategies.

Although terms such as multi-modalism abound in the official literature and, indeed, some initiatives have transcended the conventional bounds of modal-based actions, a useful and pragmatic way of treating these recent developments is by mode.

13.4.1 Road transport

Road transport is the dominant mode of both freight and passenger transport in the EU. The share of freight going by rail, for example, has fallen from 32% of the EU total in 1970 to about 14% today. Over the period, the total freight tonnage in Europe has increased 2.5 times and the share of this going by road has risen from 48% to 74%. The initial efforts to develop a common policy regarding road transport, however, as we have seen, proved problematic. Technical matters were more easily solved than those of creating a common economic framework of supply although even here issues concerning such matters as maximum weight limits for trucks have tended to be fudged. Economic controls lingered on as countries with less efficient road haulage industries sought to shelter them from the more competitive fleets of countries such as the UK and the Netherlands. There were also more legitimate efficiency concerns throughout the EU over the wider social costs of road transport, regarding both environmental matters and narrower questions of infrastructure utilization.

The Single Market initiative, also later influenced by the potential of new trade with the post-Communist states of Eastern and Central Europe (Button, 1993b), has resulted in significant reforms to economic regulation in recent years. From the industrial perspective, road freight transport offers the flexibility that is required by modern, just-in-time production management; but from the social perspective it can be environmentally intrusive and, in the absence of appropriate infrastructure pricing, can contribute to excessive congestion costs.

Earlier measures had helped expand the supply of international permits in Europe, the EU quota complementing bilateral arrangements, and reference tariffs had introduced a basis for more efficient rate determination. The 1990s were concerned with building on this rather fragile foundation. In particular, as part of the 1992 Single Market initiative, a phased liberalization was initiated that both gradually removed restrictions on trucking movements across national boundaries and phased in cabotage that had hitherto not been permitted by member states.

The long-standing bilateral arrangements for international licensing led to high levels of economic inefficiency. This was not only because the system imposed an absolute constraint on the number of movements but also because cabotage was not permitted, and combinations of bilateral licences permitting trucks to make complex international movements were difficult to obtain – trucks had to travel long distances without cargo. The system also added to delays at borders as documents were checked. Besides leading to the gradual phasing out of bilateral controls and the phasing in of cabotage rights, the 1992 initiative also led to considerable reductions in cross-border documentation.

Passenger road transport policy has largely been left to individual member states, although in the late 1990s the Commission began to advocate the development of a 'citizens' network' and more rational road-charging policies (notably systems of congestion pricing). Perhaps the greatest progress has been made regarding social regulations on such matters as the adoption of catalytic converters in efforts to limit the environmental intrusion of motor vehicles. It has taken time to develop a common policy regarding public transport despite efforts in the 1970s to facilitate easier cross-border coach and bus operations.

13.4.2 Railways

Rail transport, while largely filling a niche market in many countries, is an important freight mode in much of continental Europe and provides important passenger services along several major corridors. At the local level, it serves as a key mode for commuter traffic in larger cities. Much of the important economic reform of European railways was undertaken in the early phase of integration by the ECSC, with actions on such matters as the removal of discriminatory freight rates. The recent phase has been concerned less with issues of economic regulation and with operations and more with widening access to networks and with technological developments, especially regarding the development of a high-speed rail network as part of the TENs initiative.

The earlier phase had initially sought to remove deliberate distortions to the market that favoured national carriers but from the late 1960s and 1970s had shifted to the rationalization of the subsidized networks through more effective and transparent cost accountancy. However, the exact incidence of subsidies still often remained uncertain. The Union has also instigated measures aimed at allowing the trains of one member to use the track of another with charges based upon economic costs. The aim of EU Directive 91/440 (CEU, 1995c) was to develop truly European networks but at the time of writing the open access rules explicitly do not apply to the new high-speed rail lines such as the French and Belgian Lignes à Grande Vitesse and the German Neubaustrecken networks. The implementation of the open access strategy has been slow and has had limited impact (CEU, 1998d).

The EU has traditionally found it difficult to devise practical and economically sound common pricing principles to apply to transport infrastructure despite the proposals of the Oort Report (Oort and Maaskant, 1976). With regard to railways, the gist of the overall proposals are for short-run marginal costs (which are to include environmental and congestion costs as well as wear on the infrastructure) to be recovered. Long-run elements of cost are only to be recovered in narrowly defined circumstances and in relation only to passenger services. This clearly has implications, especially on the freight side, if genuine full cost-based competition is to be permitted with other transport modes.

Rail transport has also received considerable support from the Commission as an integral part of making greater use of integrated, multi-modal transport systems. Such systems would largely rely upon rail (including piggy-back systems and kangaroo trains) or waterborne modes for trunk haulage, with road transport used as the feeder mode. This is seen as environmentally desirable and as contributing to containing rising levels of road traffic congestion in Europe.

The success of some of the French TGV services, and especially that between Paris and Lyon, where full cost recovery has been attained, has led to a significant interest in this mode. In 1990 the Commission set up a high-level working group to help push forward a common approach to high-speed railway development. A master plan for 2010 was produced. The EU's efforts to harmonize the development of high-speed rail has not been entirely successful and there are significant technical differences, for example between the French and German systems. Indeed, both countries actively market their technologies as superior (Viegas and Blum, 1993).

The difficulties that still remain with rail transport reflect technical variations in the infrastructure and working practices of individual states that are only slowly being co-ordinated. Some countries, such as the Netherlands, Sweden and the UK, have pursued the broad liberalization philosophy of the EU and gone beyond the minimal requirements of the CTP, but in others rigidities remain and the rail network still largely lacks the integration required for full economies of scope, density and market presence to be reaped.

13.4.3 Inland waterway transport

Inland waterway transport was already an issue in the early days of the EU. This is mainly because it is a primary concern of two founder member countries, the Netherlands and Germany, which in 1992 accounted for 73.1% of EU traffic. France and Belgium also had some interest in this mode of transport. Progress in formulating a policy has tended to be slow, in part because of historical agreements covering navigation on the Rhine (e.g. the Mannheim Convention) but mainly because the major economic concern has been that of over-capacity. In 1998 over-capacity was estimated at between 20% and 40% at the prevailing freight rates. Retraction of supply is almost always inevitably difficult to manage, both because few countries are willing to pursue a contraction policy in isolation and because of the resistance of barge owners and labour.

As in other areas of transport, the EU began by seeking technical standardization, and principles for social harmonization were set out by the Commission in 1975 and 1979 (CEC 1975d; 1979f) but economic concerns have taken over in the 1990s. In 1990 the EC initiated the adoption of a system of subsidies designed to stimulate scrappage of vessels. Subsequent measures only permitted the introduction of new vessels into the inland fleet on a replacement basis. Labour subsidies operated in the Netherlands, Belgium and France (the rota system that provides minimum wages for bargemen) have also been cut back in stages. They will be removed entirely in 2000.

These measures were coupled with an initiative in 1995 to co-ordinate investment in inland waterway infrastructure (the Trans-European Waterway Network), designed to encourage, for environmental reasons, the greater use of waterborne transport.

13.4.4 Maritime transport

Much of the emphasis of the EU maritime policy in the late 1990s has been on the shipping market rather than on protecting the Union's fleet. In other words, it is user rather than supplier driven. In the 1990s the sector became increasingly concentrated as, first, consortia grew in importance, mergers took place (e.g P&O and Nedlloyd in 1997) and then the resultant large companies formed strategic alliances. (In 1999 all shipping companies, with the exception of two of the world's largest, were part of alliances.) An extension of the 1985 rules to cover consortia and other forms of market sharing was initiated in 1992 and subsequently extended as the nature of maritime alliances have become more complex (CEU, 1995c).

The Commission also initiated a number of actions supporting this position. In 1994 it took action to ban the Transatlantic Agreement that had been reached the preceding year by the major shipping companies to gain tighter control over the loss-making North Atlantic routes. It did so on the grounds of capacity manipulation and rate manipulation and because it contained agreements over pre- and on-carriage over land. In the same year it also fined 14 shipping companies that were members of the Far East Freight Conference for price fixing. The main point at issue was that these prices embodied multi-modal carriage and while shipping *per se* enjoyed a block exemption on price agreements multi-modal services did not.

Ports also attracted the attention of the EU in the 1990s. Ports are major transport interchange points and in 1994 handled about 24% of the world's ton equivalent units. Advances in technology have led to important changes in the ways in which ports operate, and there has been a significant concentration in activities as shipping companies have moved towards hub-and-spoke operations. The main EU ports have capacity utilization levels of well over 80% and some are at or near their design capacity. Whether this is a function of a genuine capacity deficiency or reflects inappropriate port pricing charges that do not contain congestion cost elements is debatable. The Commission has produced further proposals for co-ordinating investment in port facilities (CEU, 1997g).

13.4.5 Air transport policy

While liberalization of EU transport may be considered one of the successes of the CTP in the late 1980s, the market was still heavily regulated at the time of the Cockfield Report that heralded the Single Market. The final reform – the 'Third Package' – came in 1992 and was phased in from the following year. The programme aimed for a regulatory framework for the EU by 1997 similar to that for US domestic aviation (Button and Swann, 1992). The measures removed significant barriers to entry by setting common rules governing safety and financial requirements for new airlines. Since January 1993, EU airlines have been able to fly between member states without restriction and within member states (other than their own) subject to some controls on fares and capacity. National restrictions on ticket prices were removed; the only safeguards related to excessive falls or increases in fares.

Consecutive cabotage was introduced, allowing a carrier to add a 'domestic leg' to a flight which started from an airport other than its home base and flew to a destination in another member state, if the number of passengers on the second leg did not exceed 50% of the total on the main flight. From 1997, full cabotage has been permitted, and fares are generally unregulated. Additionally, foreign ownership among Union carriers is permitted, and these carriers have, for EU internal purposes, become European airlines. This change does not apply to extra-Union agreements where national bilateral arrangements still dominate the market. One result has been a considerable increase in cross-share holdings and a rapidly expanding number of alliances among airlines within the Union.

Early analysis of reforms by the UK Civil Aviation Authority (1993) and the Commission indicated that the reforms of the 1990s produced, in terms of multiple airlines serving various market areas, greater competition on both EU domestic routes and international routes within the EU. The changes varied but countries such as Greece and Portugal increased the number of competitive international services considerably. Many routes, however, either because multiple services are simply not technically sustainable or institutional impediments still limited market entry, remained monopolies in 1994.

More recently, the Commission, in examining the impact of the Third Package, reported important consumer benefits (CEU, 1996c). It found that the number of routes flown within the EU rose from 490 to 520 between 1993 and 1995, that 30% of Union routes are now served by two operators and 6% by three operators or more, that 80 new airlines have been created while only 60 have disappeared, that fares have fallen on routes where there are at least three operators and that overall, when allowance is made for charter operations, 90–95% of passengers on intra-EU routes are travelling at reduced fares. One caveat is that there have been quite significant variations in the patterns of fares charged across routes.

There has been little change in fares on routes that remain monopolies or duopolies. The number of fifth freedom routes doubled to 30 between 1993 and 1996 although this type of operation remains a relatively small feature of the market and seventh freedoms[2] have been little used. Indeed, much of the new competition has been on domestic routes where routes operated by two or more carriers rose from 65 in January 1963 to 114 in January 1996, with the largest expansions being in France, Spain and Germany. The charter market has also continued to grow and in some countries accounts for more than 80% of traffic.

13.5 Conclusions

Papers written only a decade or so ago were extremely pessimistic about the prospects for any viable transport policy being initiated within the EU. That transport was important was seldom questioned, but prior attempts to do anything other than tinker with the prevailing, largely national driven, transport policies had proved disappointing. Early efforts in the 1960s to draw up what essentially amounted to a master plan or blueprint policy had failed. The problems of continued enlargement of the Union, coupled with fresh, often radical thinking on how transport as a sector should be treated, seemed to pose almost insurmountable problems for policy makers in the 1970s and 1980s. These problems were not helped by mounting concerns over physical and institutional bottlenecks in the transport system of Europe that were manifestly an impediment to any radical shift towards a more rapid phase of economic integration.

At the time of writing the picture is entirely different. Certainly many issues remain to be resolved, such as the initiation of more rational pricing for most modes, but by and large transport is no longer seen as a major threat to further economic and political integration within the EU. There is broad agreement that transparency and market-based systems afford an efficient way to meet the EU's transport needs. While there has been much wasted time and effort, and significant economic, social and political costs are inevitably associated with this, the current phase of transport policy formulation can be seen as one of the important successes of the EU in the 1990s.

Notes

1. The right of an airline of one country to carry traffic between two countries outside its country of registry as long as the flight originates or terminates in its country of registry.
2. The right of an airline to operate stand-alone services entirely outside the territory of its home state, that is, to carry traffic between two foreign states.

14 Energy policy

A. M. EL-AGRAA and F. MCGOWAN*

A full discussion of the EU Common Energy Policy (CEP) should cover a number of topics. It should give a full account of the policies pursued by the individual member nations of the EU; assess the energy balances for various years, including the latest available; describe the EU institutions which are particularly concerned with energy matters; and document the history of EU energy efforts and proposals. Such a comprehensive coverage is not attempted here simply because the diversity of policies pursued by the individual nations precludes a discussion of these aspects, and also because all the relevant EU institutions are presented and discussed in Chapter 2. In any case, such a comprehensive coverage would in effect require a whole book, hence this chapter concentrates mainly on the objectives of and recent developments in the CEP.

This chapter considers the EU's role in energy policy, notes past attempts to create a CEP, assesses the factors behind their failure and examines why the Community has been able to influence national policies more successfully during the past few years. After discussing the current policy proposals and the context to them, the situation in the different EU energy industries is reviewed, noting their main characteristics and the balance of past and present EU policy towards them. Finally, some of the difficulties the Commission faces both in developing a credible CEP and in addressing the energy industries within such a framework are assessed. Before carrying out all these tasks, however, it is necessary to consider the rationale for an EU energy policy.

14.1 The need for an EU energy policy

It is important to ask: is there an economic rationale for a CEP? In order to provide a meaningful answer, it is vital to realize that the energy sector comprises several major industries (see Table 14.1) which contribute about 10% of Community GDP: coal; natural gas; nuclear energy; oil; and petroleum. Moreover, since the oil crises of the 1970s another, but overlapping, field has emerged: it comprises a miscellaneous set of measures aimed at reducing both industrial and domestic heating consumption (conserving resources) and at encouraging the discovery and utilization of alternative energy sources, including solar, tidal and wave energy. Each industry has its own general characteristics and problems. These industries interact with secondary ones: electricity generation and distribution; oil refining and distribution of its products; gas collection and distribution, etc. These various and diverse industries

---

* This chapter was originally contributed by Dr Yao-Su Hu while he was with Chatham House, London, working for the Federal Trust. It was then revised in collaboration with A. M. El-Agraa before being rewritten by Francis McGowan. The present version adapts and updates McGowan's text.

Table 14.1 The EU energy picture in 1997 (million tonnes of oil equivalent – Mtoe)

	Production						Net imports (exports–imports)				
	Hard coal	Crude oil and NGL	Petroleum products	Natural gas	Nuclear energy	Hydro energy	Coal	Oil	Electricity	Gas	Total energy
Austria	0.29	1.02	10.60	1.22	na	3.09	3.13	11.04	−0.07	5.13	19.26
Belgium	0.22	na	37.28	0.00	12.35	0.03	8.17	29.15	0.28	11.28	48.87
Denmark	0.01	11.59	9.05	6.96	na	0.00	7.88	−0.77	−0.62	−2.78	3.71
Finland	2.63	0.06	12.01	na	5.45	1.05	4.82	10.55	0.66	2.91	18.93
France	4.43	2.20	94.12	2.13	103.07	5.35	9.74	89.57	−5.62	29.34	123.10
Germany	70.22	3.46	115.01	16.07	44.41	1.49a	14.88	137.37	−0.20	58.14	210.19
Greece	7.71	0.48	21.06	0.04	na	0.33	0.76	18.39	0.20	0.13	19.48
Ireland	0.74	na	2.96	1.91	na	0.06	2.05	6.80	0.00	0.87	9.71
Italy	0.01	6.17	98.96	15.78	na	3.58	10.71	89.04	3.34	31.97	135.37
Luxembourg	na	na	na	na	na	0.01	0.31	1.96	0.45	0.63	3.34
Netherlands	na	3.04	82.65	60.57	0.63	0.01	10.54a	36.80	1.09	−25.24	23.18
Portugal	na	na	13.42	na	na	1.31	3.69	14.78	0.25	0.10	18.82
Spain	9.80	0.38	58.02	0.16	14.41	2.98	6.75	63.02	−0.26	11.54	81.04
Sweden	0.25	na	21.85	na	18.22	5.94	2.49	17.40	−0.23	0.72	20.37
United Kingdom	29.61	134.24	100.35	77.46	173.66	0.36	12.86	−49.14	1.43	−0.59	−35.44

a Estimate.

na = data not available.

Source: Various issues of Energy Balances of OECD Countries and Energy Statistics of OECD Countries, International Energy Agency, Paris. These are also the sources for the remaining tables in this chapter.

have different organizational structures ranging from the small private firm to nationalized enterprises and multinational corporations. They are also subject to numerous contradictory domestic pressures on governments from producers, consumers, environmentalist lobbies and trade unionists, some of whom have been successful in persuading their governments to deviate from their planned strategies. Of course, apart from this multiplicity and the contradictions, the Community energy sector was subjected to two very severe external shocks in the early and late 1970s.

Since energy is not only an input which affects industrial costs, but also an industrial sector in its own right, it follows that it is doubly vital that the EU should have a common approach to it since the EU is more than a common market and is in the process of transforming itself into a complete economic, monetary and political union (EMU; see Chapter 1). If effective free trade and a consistent industrial structure are to be promoted it is necessary that equal treatment should be applied to this sector across the membership of the Union, otherwise there would be a significant non-tariff barrier to free trade. Of course, it could be argued that the industrial organization aspect of the sector should be tackled under the competition and industrial policies of the EU (see Chapters 9 and 10) and the trade aspects under the general rules of free trade within the EU (see Chapter 8). That, however, would be a misconceived approach since a separate treatment of two interrelated aspects of the same industrial sector is bound to result in an incoherent philosophy. In any case, such an argument could equally well be applied to transport, a sector to which the Treaty of Rome has given special treatment (see the previous chapter). However, it would be a contradiction in terms to accept this argument in the case of transport and to reject it for energy.

On the other hand, if by a policy one means a combination of a clear vision of the future, a coherent set of principles, a range of policy instruments adequate to the objectives that are set, and the existence of sufficient legitimacy and authority to carry the measures through, many analysts would argue that the EU does not need a CEP. This is because even a full political and economic union like the United States, with its vast resources, does not have an energy policy in this sense.

Be that as it may, the idea of a CEP for the EU is almost as old as the Community itself. In the years since the EEC was founded in 1957, numerous policy proposals have been made by the Commission or its predecessor, although they have been marked by a shifting balance of priorities and a range of proposed mechanisms, depending on the conditions in the energy markets and the influence of the Commission. For the most part, however, these attempts came to nothing, with member states variously rejecting or ignoring them. Since the early 1980s the Commission has again been active in the energy sector, as the momentum of the Single Market debate has gathered pace and environmental concerns have intensified. Yet, although there has been an enhanced Community profile in this sector, a CEP remains elusive, as demonstrated by the failure to incorporate an energy chapter into either the Maastricht or Amsterdam treaties.

14.2 Past attempts and present successes

14.2.1 The treaties and energy

That the EC attached great importance to the energy sector is demonstrated by the fact that two of the three treaties on which the EC is based are specifically concerned with energy: the 1951 Treaty of Paris creating the European Coal and Steel Community (ECSC) and the 1957 Treaty of Rome establishing Euratom were devoted to the coal and nuclear sectors. The details of these treaties (and their rationale) are covered in Chapter 2, but their significance for energy policy is clear enough. The 1951 ECSC treaty reflected the dominance of coal in the energy balance of member states (as well as its role in the steel industry); by tackling coal, most EC energy supply and demand issues were addressed. The 1957 Euratom treaty sought to foster co-operation in the development of civil nuclear power, then perceived as the main source of future energy requirements (Lucas, 1977). Both treaties, moreover, were in principle geared towards the creation of free and integrated markets in these sectors: the ECSC sought to abolish all barriers to trade between member states while controlling subsidies and cartel-like behaviour amongst producers; Euratom also paid lip-service to the idea of a common market in nuclear products.

A common market for other energy sectors was addressed in the EEC Rome Treaty. While the EEC was orientated towards more or less competitively structured sectors, it was also intended to cover the more oligopolistic or monopolistic sectors such as oil, gas and electricity. Accordingly, in addition to being subject to the EEC Treaty's general provisions on opening up markets, these energy industries' special characteristics were covered by the Treaty's provisions on state enterprises and their conduct.

14.2.2 Policy efforts, 1951–1973

The gap between intentions expressed in the Treaties and the outcomes, however, has been a large one for energy, more so than for most other parts of the economy. The Commission's attempts to develop an energy policy of any sort, let alone one reflecting the ideals of the treaties, have proved to be of only limited success.

From the 1950s on, the Commission or its equivalents sought to develop a policy first for coal and then for energy more broadly (see El-Agraa and Hu, 1984). On coal, the High Authority was unable to impose the spirit of the Paris Treaty on national industries; it was mainly involved in tackling the crises which beset the European coal industry from the mid-1950s on (Lindberg and Scheingold, 1970). In the sphere of energy more generally, initial efforts were made as the negotiations for the EEC were progressing. The Messina conference recommended that the potential for co-ordinated energy policy be considered, but the Spaak Committee determined that this would not be necessary (von Geusau, 1975).

Following the establishment of the new Communities, there was a renewed attempt to develop a CEP. The formation of an interexecutive Committee on energy in 1959 sought to develop a policy focusing on the creation of a common energy market. The main concerns of the Committee were with the effect of energy prices on industrial competitiveness and, to a lesser extent, with the security of energy supply (PEP, 1963). However, governments largely rejected the Committee's attempts to gain access to energy policy; instead they exercised benign neglect towards the energy sector. This inertia on energy policy reflected the largely untroubled energy markets of the period. However, when there was concern over supply in the 1950s and 1960s (such as in the wake of the Suez crisis), governments were keen to retain their autonomy.

The merger of the Communities in 1968 saw the Commission renew its efforts to develop a CEP. In its document 'First Guidelines Towards a EC Energy Policy' (CEC,

1968), the Commission noted that barriers to trade in energy persisted and stressed the necessity of a common energy market. Such a market, based on the needs of consumers and competitive pressures, would help obtain security of energy supplies at the lowest cost. To this end the Commission suggested three broad objectives: a plan for the sector involving data collection and forecasting as a means of influencing members' investment strategies; measures to bring about a common energy market (tackling issues such as tax harmonization, technical barriers, state monopolies, etc.); measures to ensure security of supply at lowest cost.

The proposals proved difficult to put into practice partly because of the scale of objectives and the contradictions between the substance of different goals, but mainly because of the resistance of member states to the goals. Even though the Council approved the strategy, it ignored most of the Commission's subsequent attempts to enact the proposals. The principal measures adopted in the wake of the Commission's proposals concerned oil stocks (following OECD initiatives) and some requirements for energy investment notification. These actions owed more to growing concern about security of supply than to the creation of a common energy market, and presaged a wider shift in Commission and member state perceptions of the priorities of energy policy. The reaction to the 1973–4 oil crisis confirmed the change in orientation of energy policy proposals away from markets and towards security.

14.2.3 Energy crises, 1973–1986

The backdrop for the new emphasis on security of supply was the development of the Community's energy balances and the changes in global energy markets generally. Since the 1950s, the member states had become less reliant upon domestically produced coal and more reliant on imported resources, primarily oil. This shift in demand reflected the growth in energy demand overall, but also a gradual but absolute decline in energy resources among the then member states. By 1970 over 60% of the EC's needs were imported, leaving it highly vulnerable to the supply disruptions and price increases of 1973–4 (see Table 14.2).

In the midst of the first oil shock, the EC attempted a crisis management role but failed even to provide a united front *vis-à-vis* OAPEC over their oil embargo of the Netherlands (Daintith and Hancher, 1986). Member states pursued their own policies or worked through the International Energy Agency (IEA). Formed in 1974, the IEA overshadowed the EC both in breadth of membership (covering all the OECD countries except France) and in terms of its powers on oil sharing in a new crisis (van der Linde and Lefeber, 1988).

Even so, the shock of oil price increases reinforced the reassessment of energy policies in member states and the Commission. The Commission attempted to develop a more strategic approach to the management of energy supply and demand. The 'New Strategy' (*Bulletin of the European Communities, Supplement 4/1974*) which was only agreed to after much wrangling and dilution (a proposal for a European energy agency was abandoned after member state opposition – see Lucas, 1977) envisaged a number of targets to be met by 1985 (COM (74) 1960). These included the reduction of oil imports, the development of domestic energy capabilities (notably nuclear power) and the rational use of energy (see Table 14.3). The policy, while only indicative, mobilized resources for R&D and promotional programmes on energy, covering conventional and nuclear technologies but also

Table 14.2 EU energy balances (Mtoe)

	Energy production	Net imports	Supply[a]
1960	360.3	206.2	551.4
1970	408.1	650.2	1015.0
1980	584.3	687.6	1218.1
1990	711.1	649.7	1328.4
1995	749.0	658.2	1380.7
1996	773.4	685.9	1428.5
1997	767.0	699.9	1421.2

Figures for all years are for EU-15.

[a] Includes adjustments for stocks.

Sources: See Table 14.1.

(albeit to a limited extent) renewables and energy efficiency technologies. The new strategy also provided the basis for a handful of directives designed to restrict the use of oil and gas.

The policy clearly entailed a change in emphasis for energy policy and the goal of a common energy market was demoted, although it was alluded to in areas such as pricing policies and some measures directed at the oil sector (see below). Overall, policy was concerned with changing the structure of energy balances rather than the structure of energy markets. The condition of energy markets (notably after the second oil shock) and concern over energy prices and security in the early 1980s were such that the policy was sustained into the decade. Further rounds of energy policy objectives were agreed in 1979 (to be met by 1990) and 1986 (for 1995). The 1995 objectives included a number of 'horizontal' objectives, aimed at more general energy policy concerns, such as its relationship with other EC policies. Each round sought to build on the previous one, and although in general the goals appeared to be on target, in some cases they reflected a degree of failure either across the EC or in certain member states, and subsequent rounds would adopt a rather less ambitious agenda (COM (84) 88 and COM (88) 174). The objectives approach reappeared as part of more recent EU energy strategy (COM (96) 431).

By the mid-1980s, therefore, the Commission had succeeded in establishing a place in energy policy making, but it was far from being central to member states' energy policy agendas, let alone one being sufficiently influential to dictate the development of a common energy market. Instead, its role consisted of information gathering, target setting and enabling activities (the latter had a substantial budget for energy R&D and promotion). While these measures ensured that the Commission had an influence on policy, they were not without problems – some of the objectives were showing few signs of achievement while aspects of the Commission's funding strategies were also open to criticism (Cruickshank and

Table 14.3 The EU's energy objectives for 1985, 1990, 1995 and 2010

1985 objectives

To increase nuclear power capacity to 200 GW.

To increase Community production of oil and natural gas to 180 million tonnes oil equivalent.

To maintain production of coal in the Community at 180 million tonnes oil equivalent.

To keep imports to no more than 40% of consumption.

To reduce projected demand for 1985 by 15%.

To raise electricity contribution to final energy consumption to 35%.

1990 objectives

To reduce to 0.7 or less the average ratio between the rate of growth in gross primary energy demand and the rate of growth of gross domestic product.

To reduce oil consumption to a level of 40% of primary energy consumption.

To cover 70–75% of primary energy requirements for electricity production by means of solid fuels and nuclear energy.

To encourage the use of renewable energy sources so as to increase their contribution to the Community's energy supplies.

To pursue energy pricing policies geared to attaining the energy objectives.

1995 objectives

To improve the efficiency of final energy demand by 20%.

To maintain oil consumption at around 40% of energy consumption and to maintain net oil imports at less than one-third of total energy consumption.

To maintain the share of natural gas in the energy balance on the basis of a policy aimed at ensuring stable and diversified supplies.

To increase the share of solid fuels in energy consumption.

To pursue efforts to promote consumption of solid fuels and to improve the competitiveness of their production capacities in the Community.

To reduce the proportion of electricity generated by hydrocarbons to less than 15%.

To increase the share of renewables in energy balances.

To ensure more secure conditions of supply and to reduce risks of energy price fluctuations.

To apply Community price formation principles to all sectors.

To balance energy and environmental concerns through the use of best available technologies.

To implement measures to improve energy balance in less-developed regions of the Community.

To develop a single energy market.

To co-ordinate external relations in the energy sector.

2010 objectives

To meet Treaty objectives, notably market integration, sustainable development, environmental protection and supply security.

To integrate energy and environmental objectives and to incorporate the full cost of energy in the price.

To strengthen security of supply through improved diversification and flexibility of domestic and imported supplies on the one hand and by ensuring flexible responses to supply emergencies on the other.

To develop a co-ordinated approach to external energy relations to ensure free and open trade and to secure investment framework.

To promote renewable energy resources with the aim of achieving a significant share of primary energy production by 2010.

To improve energy efficiency by 2010 through better co-ordination of both national and Community measures.

Walker, 1981). Moreover, aside from a few legislative measures, the Commission's policy had few teeth. The locus of power remained with national governments, which generally chose to follow their own energy policies, resisting too strong a Commission role.

14.2.4 The new energy policy agenda: competition and the environment

In the course of the 1980s, however, the agenda for energy policy began to change. Developments in energy markets, the attitudes of governments towards the energy industries and the overall position of the Commission in policy making contributed to a turnaround in the concerns of EC energy policy. The new agenda rests on two broader objectives: the creation of a competition-oriented single energy market and the pursuit of environmental protection.

A key factor in the changed regime was the shift in energy markets. Prices stabilized and faltered in the early 1980s and continued to weaken until the 1986 oil price collapse. The reasons for this were more fundamental than the rows within OPEC which precipitated the fall in prices. The price increases of the early 1980s had had the effect of boosting output in OPEC countries, as well as fostering exploration and production in the rest of world. Furthermore, many countries had sought to improve energy efficiency and diversify sources of energy (if not to the levels sought by the Commission). The economic recession of the 1980s also dampened demand. The combined effect of these factors was a massive over-capacity in supply and minimal demand growth (see Table 14.2) which forced down prices. The effects were not only confined to oil: gas and coal were in equally plentiful supply, while the consequences of past over-investment in electricity capacity also boosted the energy surplus.

The combined effect of these developments was to weaken the scarcity culture which had prevailed among suppliers, consumers, governments and the Commission. As prices fell and markets appeared well supplied so the concerns of policy focused less on energy supply *per se* and more on the price of supply and existence of obstacles to the lowest price.

This change in market conditions made many energy policies, especially those fostering conservation or diversification from high-price fuels, hard to sustain or justify. In any case, in some countries, governments were abandoning traditional approaches to energy policy. The United Kingdom was the most notable example, making an explicit move to rely on market forces for determining supply and demand. A major plank of that policy was deregulation, with attempts to introduce competition to gas and power, and privatization, with the sale of oil interests and then the gas and electricity industries (Helm *et al.*, 1989). Shifts in policies were under review in other parts of the EC (Helm and McGowan, 1989), although these were often conceived at a less ambitious level or pursued for rather different reasons.

The deregulatory thrust was not confined to the energy sector – indeed it was probably more widely spread initially in other areas of the economy. It was, for example, to the fore in the Commission's plans for the Single European Market (SEM; see Chapters 2 and 8) as covered in the White Paper (CEC, 1985a). Partly as a reflection of past energy policy failures, the Commission did not include energy in the initial agenda for the SEM. However, areas where energy was affected indirectly by more general SEM measures (such as indirect taxation and procurement policies) meant that the sector was not untouched by the proposals.

Indeed, there were already some signs of a different policy towards energy. The issue of price transparency was extended across the energy industries with attempts to agree a directive on the issue. While the moves failed, they indicated a greater interest in the issue by the Commission. The Commission was also taking a greater interest in energy subsidies (as in the case of Dutch support to its horticultural industry through the provision of cheap gas). Other indications of change included moves to tackle state oil monopolies and the types of support given to the coal industry in a number of member states.

The potential for more radical action was indicated by a number of moves taken by the Competition Directorate of the Commission towards other 'utility' industries. It sought the introduction of more competitive arrangements in the civil aviation industry and was able to threaten use of legal powers to this end. In the field of telecommunications, it sought to open access for equipment and service sales, using powers under Article 90 to do so (see Chapter 10). These moves demonstrated not only a willingness to act but also a range of mechanisms which could be used in other sectors. The further the policy went in one industry the more likely that it would be applied to others.

This changing agenda meant that the idea of an internal energy market (IEM) was once again an issue for the EC. While the 1995 goals were largely flavoured by energy security concerns, one of the 'horizontal' objectives was the creation of an IEM. As the prospect of an SEM became realizable with the '1992' campaign the idea of extending it to energy took root, and in 1987 the Energy Commissioner Mr Nicolas Mosar announced a study of the barriers to an IEM.

The Commission's thinking was revealed in 'The Internal Energy Market' (COM (88) 238), a review which set out the potential benefits of an IEM and the obstacles that faced it. The IEM would cut costs to consumers (particularly to energy-intensive industries), thereby making European industry as a whole more competitive; it would increase security of supply by improving integration of the energy industries; it would rationalize the structure of the energy industries and allow for greater complementarity among the different supply and demand profiles of member states. The benefits would stem from a mixture of cost-reducing competition and the achievement of scale economies in a number of industries. Taken together these would more than recover the 0.5% of EC GDP which the Commission claimed was the 'cost of non-Europe' in the energy sector (although, as noted, energy was not part of the original SEM debate nor of the 'cost of non-Europe' exercise which assessed the benefits of the SEM – see Cecchini (1988) and Emerson et al. (1988)).

According to the Commission, the obstacles to the IEM were to be found in the structures and practices of the energy industries. These ranged from different taxation and financial regimes to restrictive measures which protected energy industries in particular countries and conditions which prevented full co-ordination of supplies at the most efficient level (the latter applying to the gas and electricity industries). However, as the Commission admitted, the effects of particular practices were difficult to assess given the special nature of the energy industries. Indeed, in certain cases, the Commission appeared hesitant over the extent of the IEM. Nonetheless, the document demonstrated that the Commission was committed to implement an IEM and would examine all barriers to its development. It has followed up that commitment with measures to implement the White Paper proposals (on taxation and procurement) and to apply EC law to the sector.

In the period since the IEM document was published, the Commission has completed the programme of measures liberalizing the energy industries' procurement practices, but has been unable to achieve an effective harmonization of indirect taxation (see Chapter 15). It has also made some progress on liberalizing the electricity and gas supply markets and the offshore exploration industry but very little has been achieved by way of coal industry reform. To the extent that the policy has been successful, it has been aided not only by changes in EC decision-making procedures, notably the majority voting conditions allowed under the Single European Act (SEA), but also by the prospect of the Commission using its powers to investigate the energy sector from a Treaty of Rome perspective. However, there remain many aspects of the policy to be implemented, where the Commission will have to overcome the opposition of member states.

Since 1988, the IEM has played a major role in Commission proposals on energy policy. It has, for all its problems, shifted the emphasis in Community policy towards the energy sector. Over the same period, however, another element has also gained a higher profile in deliberations on the sector: the environment.

The Commission's interest in environmental issues is not new. The formal commitment of the EC to environmental policy dates from early 1972 when, in the wake of the Stockholm conference, the Council agreed a programme of action, while some measures on environmental problems predated even this initiative (Haigh, 1987). While the Commission's concerns on environment are very wide ranging (see Chapter 20), covering issues such as chemical wastes, water quality and noise pollution, the consequences of energy choices are a major part of the policy.

The importance of EC environmental policy for the energy sector has paralleled the ascent of the issue up the political agenda in an increasing number of member states, particularly as the Greens have become a political force. In those cases where governments have been obliged to introduce new controls on pollution, they have sought to have them accepted across the EC so as not to lose competitiveness. The best example has been the acid rain debate where the German government, forced to introduce major controls on domestic emissions from industrial and electricity plants, has pressed for similar controls in all member states (Boehmer-Christiansen and Skea, 1990). These were agreed in 1988, setting targets for emission reduction into the next century.

The emergence of the environment has given the Commission a higher profile in energy matters and another, more robust, lever on energy policy (Owens and Hope, 1989). The importance of the issue to energy policy was demonstrated in the 1995 objectives where environmental concerns were identified as a major consideration in policy. The status of environmental issues overall was confirmed in the SEA where it was given its own provisions (allowing it to enforce decisions on a majority vote). The SEM proposals also identify the need for high standards of environmental protection in the EC and this has impacted on the IEM debate.

Integrating environment and energy has not been easy for the Commission; a document on the issue was apparently the focus for considerable dispute within the Commission because of the different perspectives of the Directorates for Energy and for the Environment (COM (89) 369). However, the issue which has both brought the environment to the centre of Community energy policy making and exposed the tensions between the two policies most starkly has been the greenhouse effect.

The Commission has sought to co-ordinate a common European response to the threat of global warming. In 1991 the member states, with the exception of the United Kingdom, agreed to stabilize emissions of CO_2 by the year 2000. In the following year it produced proposals for decreasing emissions of greenhouse gases, particularly CO_2 (COM (92) 246). These comprised four elements: programmes to encourage the development of renewable energy sources (which have zero or very low carbon dioxide emissions) and of energy efficiency, a monitoring system and a carbon-energy tax to discourage use of fossil fuels.

While much has been achieved by the Commission in incorporating conservation and renewables into a strategy for tackling global warming, the carbon tax has all but been abandoned. The proposed tax consists of two elements, one related to the energy used and the other to the carbon emitted by the fuel in question. The tax therefore penalizes coal use most strongly but not as much as if it were a pure carbon tax. Small renewable-based energy sources are not covered by the proposal. More importantly, large industrial consumers are also exempt from it and the proposal will not be put into effect unless equivalent steps are taken by other industrialized countries (Pearson and Smith, 1991). Despite these conditions, which were included after considerable lobbying of the Commission, the proposal has drawn a good deal of criticism from industries and governments, and, although modifications have been made, the chances of an agreement in the Council appear slim. Subsequent attempts to use taxation as an instrument of environmental policy in the energy sector have also been opposed (Finon and Surrey, 1996).

Although the Single Market and the environment dominate energy policy, the Commission continues to pursue a variety of other energy policy objectives. It continues with its support for energy efficiency and renewables through research budgets and other measures designed to encourage their use (such as recommendations for preferential terms for renewable sources of supply). It has developed policies for supporting energy infrastructures primarily in less-developed areas of the Community, although this goal has been broadened in the light of attempts to increase integration of gas and electricity supply, through the initiative on fostering 'trans-EC networks' (McGowan, 1993b).

The Commission has even sought to develop a role in the traditionally difficult area of security of supply. The policy it has proposed addresses two aspects of the problem: the development of indigenous energy resources and the management of Community activities in the event of supply disruption. The first element, which was developed in response to the British government's desire to protect the nuclear industry after privatization, allows authorities to subsidize up to 20% of their energy requirements on the grounds that, while subsidization may infringe the Treaty's free market provisions, it also supports the Community's own energy resources (Brittan, 1992). The second element of the policy comprises a variety of measures designed to establish a clearer role for the Commission in energy crisis management and diplomacy.

It is largely for securing supplies that an increasingly important part of the Community's energy policy activities is the links with the rest of the world. These are focused on immediate neighbours to the north, east and south of the EU. The principal element of these links has been its efforts to draw Eastern Europe into secure energy links through the European Energy Charter (COM (91) 36). This was the initiative of the Dutch Prime Minister, Mr Lubbers, who sought to use an agreement on energy, symbolically echoing the ECSC in ending the cold war, and, more importantly, acting as a framework for closer energy links between the Community and the East. An agreement on a basic charter was reached at the end of 1991 and an Energy Charter Treaty signed at the end of 1994. The Treaty sets out the basic conditions for investment in markets but important related questions such as energy transit and the application of competition rules have been incorporated in only the most limited manner.

The Energy Charter Treaty and the protocol on energy efficiency and related environmental aspects became effective on 16 April 1998, but was not fully ratified until 1999 when the remaining two EU nations, France and Ireland, did so. With the approval in December 1999 of the Altener (promotion of renewable energy sources) and SAVE (promotion of energy efficiency) programmes, the European Parliament and the Council put the finishing touches on a 1997 multiannual framework programme for action in the energy sector (1998–2000) and its six specific programmes. The framework programme itself and the four specific programmes designated as ETAP (studies, analyses, forecasts and related work), SYNERGY (international co-operation), CARNOT (clean and efficient use of solid fuels) and SURE (nuclear transport safety and international co-operation) were adopted in 1998. These developments have kept the Commission busy. For example, on 8 November 1999, after a lengthy screening of the energy sector in the new applicants, it adopted a communication on strengthening the northern dimension of the CEP, which the Council endorsed a month later; it signed a memorandum of understanding on industrial co-operation with Russia, which included energy; on 4 May 1999, it adopted its second report on the state of liberalization of the energy markets, which it found to be 'highly satisfactory'; etc.

In financial terms, the SAVE II programme adopted in December 1999 is allocated a budget of 66 million Euro. This is hardly a sum to be elated about, but it is an improvement on the 7.4 million Euro for the original SAVE programme, under which 52 projects benefited in 1999.

14.2.5 The prospects for a common energy policy

Such a variety of activities, along with the increased recourse to the Community institutions by member states and pressure groups on energy matters, would suggest that the Commission anticipated the Community finally taking responsibility for energy policy. However, attempts to formalize its role in the Maastricht Treaty were unsuccessful. While the Commission was able to insert a relatively weak commitment to a Community role, which was kept in the draft Treaty up to the very last negotiations, a number of member states indicated their objections to it and obtained its removal at the last stage in the negotiations. The Commission subsequently embarked on an extensive consultation exercise in order to clarify its role in energy policy making. A Green Paper was published at the end of 1994 with a White Paper following at the end of 1995. Both documents stressed the importance of energy matters by drawing attention to the prospect of increased energy dependence: Commission forecasts suggested that imported energy would account for as much as 70% of energy needs by 2020 (CEC, 1995c). The documents reiterated the need for a Community energy policy on the basis of reconciling the objectives of supply security, environmental protection and an internal market (see previous section); a Community dimension was justified on the basis of existing treaty powers (particularly in competition policy and the internal market), the international nature of energy markets and problems and existing policy and budgetary commitments (CEC, 1995c). The White Paper established an Energy Consultative Committee to ensure transparency and set out an extensive work programme for the Community in the energy sphere (although interestingly the Commission has also been willing to review, and where necessary to discard, existing policies). Since the White Paper the Commission has conducted two reviews of energy legislation and recommended the rescinding of some measures (including those affecting oil and gas use in such sectors as power generation).

Despite its ambitious scale, the White Paper did not seek to justify the inclusion of energy in the next round of Treaty negotiations. However, the Maastricht Treaty had included a condition that the status of energy – along with some other policies – be reviewed as part of those discussions. In its report the Commission, while being careful not to call explicitly for a chapter on energy, indicated that inclusion was desirable given the various goals of Community energy policy and the need to rationalize the coverage of the energy sectors across the Treaties. The Commission followed this up since the latter part of 1996 with documents designed to justify a Community role: although these documents spelled out a range of recommendations (including a new set of energy policy objectives) they were clearly designed to strengthen the case for a formal CEP (COM (96) 431). The 1997 Treaty makes no new mention of energy, let alone a new chapter (though it has been suggested that provisions could be added if the proposed rationalization of Treaty texts takes place).

14.3 The EU and the energy industries

14.3.1 Coal

The coal industry in the EU has undergone a major restructuring since the 1950s when it was the mainstay of the industrial European economy. Indigenous production of hard coal has been in more or less constant decline (lignite and peat have actually shown a slight increase but they are relatively unimportant owing to their low thermal value). In 1960, coal production accounted for almost 85% of energy production and 55% of energy supply in the countries which now make up the Community. By 1997 production accounted for only about 16% of energy produced and under 9% of energy supply. This decline reflected a restructuring of demand away from domestic and industrial markets towards power generation and away from local production towards imports: in 1960 net imports accounted for just over 5% of coal supply; by 1997 they constituted about 44% of coal supply (see Table 14.4).

Imports might account for an even greater amount of coal consumed were it not for the barriers to entry in a number of member states which maintain a domestic industry. The restructuring of the sector has seen some countries close down the industry, while some have maintained capacity, often on a large scale. The competitiveness of these industries varies considerably, depending on developments in world coal prices, although some are clearly only maintained by a mixture of direct subsidy and government-backed agreements with electricity utilities (IEA, 1988a, 1988b). In a number of countries these measures have come under increasing criticism – primarily from the consumers who have to bear the higher cost of electricity production – and the pressures for reform have intensified.

Considering the major restructuring under way in the industry and its position in the EU's treaties and institutions, the role of the Commission in coal policy has been limited. As noted, many of the attempts to develop policy from the 1950s on came to little as a result initially of a series of crises (which were largely dealt with at a national level) and subsequent concerns over the EC's vulnerability to imported sources of energy (concerns which worked to the advantage of indigenously produced coal).

Table 14.4 EU coal balances (Mtoe)

	Coal production	Net imports	Supply[a]
1960	304.6	18.4	331.7
1970	281.7	36.3	326.0
1980	250.9	63.8	304.7
1990	209.3	87.9	300.1
1995	139.9	94.5	239.8
1996	130.5	95.8	234.3
1997	125.9	98.8	222.9

Figures for all years are for EU-15.
[a] Includes adjustments for stocks.
Source: See Table 14.1.

The relative impotence of the Commission is demonstrated by its failure to control national subsidies. The Paris Treaty all but prohibited the provision of state aid to the industry, yet such support was endemic across the Community. The Commission sought to rectify this conflict by making its approval of aid subject to conditions and ultimate phasing out (Lucas, 1977). However, national support largely continued without much Commission interference for much of the first thirty years of the ECSC.

The Commission attempted to adopt a tougher policy towards the sector in the 1980s. In 1985, the Commission proposed a much more stringent set of controls of government policies including a major reduction in the level of subsidy to the industry. As the Commission noted, whereas the old rules were dominated by supply concerns, the new ones would emphasize 'the need to achieve viability ... and reduce the volume of aid even if this means substantial reductions in uneconomic capacity' (CEC, 1985a, p. 130). The proposals were opposed by most coal-producing countries and the Commission was obliged to accept a less ambitious policy. This policy set a framework for continuing aid until 1993 on the basis of three criteria: to improve the industry's competitiveness; to create new economically viable capacity; to solve the social and regional problems related to developments in the coal industry. In addition, the Commission developed a more detailed procedure for approving aid and for reviewing progress made on improving the industry's financial and economic position and for bringing into line the different forms of aid offered by member states.

The effect of the Commission's scrutiny policy has been difficult to assess since many countries were already pushing their own rationalization policies. In a recent review, the Commission noted that, after some years of decline, the level of aid had increased in 1994 although this was largely a function of the closure of relatively low-cost capacity in the United Kingdom (CEC, 1996e). The process of rationalization in the high-cost industries of Germany and Spain has been much less dramatic (largely because of the greater political sensitivities surrounding the issue in those countries). These two governments opposed a Commission initiative to reduce subsidies through a 'reference price' (*International Coal Report*, 1992). Under this proposal member states would have been able to subsidize their coal industries to the level of the average production costs within the Community (the two plus the United Kingdom). However, since both industries' cost structures exceed the proposed price level they would have been obliged to shut down capacity much more rapidly than was politically feasible. Instead it has been left to each state to determine the pace of rationalization (and ironically it has been the United Kingdom, which has the cheapest coal resources in the Community, which has cut capacity most dramatically (see McGowan *et al.*, 1993).

If anything, the Community's effect on the coal sector has been primarily felt on the demand side, where environmental policies have been to the fore. The area of Community policy which is most damaging to the coal industry's survival is, however, the environment. Attempts to combat the problems of acid rain and global warming have targeted coal as the main culprit. The principal initiative for controlling emissions causing acid rain has been the Large Combustion Plants Directive, which, by restricting national emission levels of the principal gases, effectively requires the installation of capital-intensive equipment in power stations, or the use of low-sulphur fuels or alternatives such as natural gas. In some countries, the effect of the directive has been to accelerate the reduction in the domestic coal industry (Boehmer-Christiansen and Skea, 1990).

However, whereas the control of acid rain can be reconciled with the use of coal (whether from the Community or elsewhere), such a bargain is much harder with regard to the control of emissions of carbon dioxide. Although all fossil fuels emit CO_2, coal emits the most. Consequently, most strategies for controlling or reducing emissions seek to restrict the use of coal: the Commission's plans for a carbon tax would penalize coal more than other fossil fuels. If the momentum behind the greenhouse effect debate continues, coal is likely to play an ever shrinking role in Community energy balances. The Commission has indicated that it is keen to encourage the clean use of coal (its research programme has subsidized various 'clean coal' technologies) and on 14 December 1998 it succeeded in this respect when the Council adopted a decision, under the Framework Programme for 1998–2002, on a multiannual programme of actions to promote the clean and efficient use of solid fuels.

14.3.2 Oil

As in the rest of the world, the importance of oil in EU energy balances has increased dramatically since the 1950s, even allowing for the levelling off which has occurred since the 1980s. By 1960 oil accounted for 25% of energy requirements in the original six countries which constituted the EC. By the early 1970s, it had risen to over 60% before gradually declining and stabilizing at just over 45% in the mid-1980s. The bulk of these requirements was met by imports since EC production was limited until the mid-1970s. It was then that North Sea oil began to come on stream: output increased from 14.5 million tonnes in 1970 to nearly 160 million tonnes in the mid-1990s, up from 8% to 28% of oil requirements. Output stayed at about 163 million tonnes during the period 1995–7 (see Table 14.5).

Table 14.5 EU crude oil balances (Mtoe)

	Oil production	Net imports	Supply[a]
1960	14.5	187.4	178.4
1970	17.7	611.8	578.5
1980	97.7	595.2	629.8
1990	122.0	466.9	555.2
1995	163.9	452.7	585.9
1996	163.6	471.5	598.2
1997	162.6	475.9	598.4

Figures for all years are for EU-15.
[a] Includes adjustments for stocks.
Source: See Table 14.1.

The major factors controlling demand have been the oil shocks of the 1970s which demonstrated the EC's vulnerability to supply disruptions and price increases. In response, member states shifted policies (at different intensities), with some attaining major reductions in oil dependence (for example, Denmark cut its reliance on oil from nearly 90% of energy requirements in 1973 to 57% in 1986). However, oil remains the largest single element of primary fuel requirement.

The structure of the industry is quite diverse, reflecting in part the existence or otherwise of indigenous reserves. Where a production capability emerged (either at home or in colonies or dependencies), there has been a strong domestic element – often publicly owned – involved in the industry. In others, the multinationals have dominated through their subsidiaries and have played a part in the development of almost every industry (although for many years state companies enjoyed near monopolies in imports, refining and distribution – see Osborne and Robinson, 1989).

Given this diversity, and particularly the influence of international companies and markets, the industry is apparently more competitive than other energy industries. There is not the same natural monopoly element in distribution and marketing found in other sectors, while production and refining is notionally competitive. However, the close-knit structure of the international industry has prompted fears of collusion, while the dominance of state firms in some countries also raised fears of unfair trade practices.

As noted, much of EU policy effort on energy has been focused on the oil sector, with policies aimed at reducing vulnerability and maintaining security of supply. The objectives set in the 1970s and 1980s have been supplemented with actions to restrict use of oil in power stations and encouraging stockpiling arrangements. Another aspect has been the encouragement of oil exploration in the EC and supervising the restructuring of the refinery industry which underwent severe over-capacity when demand turned down in the 1970s and 1980s (COM (88) 491). Finally, policy has sought to maintain a diversified source of supply and to continue a dialogue with major supply countries. More ambitious policies such as the attempts to develop a minimum support price have largely failed (Weyman Jones, 1986). The Commission has sought to increase the transparency of oil industry pricing. It also sought to tackle the practices of state oil monopolies in a number of member states (notably the new Mediterranean members).

In applying the IEM to oil, the Commission has sought to maintain these two aspects of past policy, but with the emphasis on market conduct. While accepting that the oil industry was structured more competitively than other energy industries, the Commission noted the persistence of a number of barriers, including exploration and production monopolies, exploration and production licensing procedures, oil field development conditions, taxation of oil production, landing obligations, restrictions on imports of oil and its byproducts, flag protection for shipments of oil, restrictions on refining and marketing rights, differences in technical norms and rules, pricing systems, and indirect taxation conditions.

The Commission's initial target was the implementation of the White Paper goals on taxation (harmonizing excise duties and VAT and abolishing other taxes – see Chapter 15), standards (uniform standards on product quality and equipment) and procurement (opening up markets for offshore exploration equipment). Its efforts have met with limited success: although the procurement rules are now in place, most national offshore industries have successfully obtained exemption from the procedures which the Commission wanted to apply. Nonetheless, the Commission has pushed ahead with further proposals to open up the market, primarily on the producer and exploration sides. The Commission's aim has been the harmonization of access conditions for these activities and it has managed to overcome the opposition of some member states.

More problematic have been efforts to tackle the demand side of the oil market. Aside from the limited progress on taxation issues, the Commission has also experienced considerable opposition to its attempts to address the environmental aspects of oil use, particularly in the transport sector. The 'Auto-Oil' programme is an initiative to improve environmental standards in both the quality of fuels and the efficiency and effectiveness of fuel use in new vehicles. So far the initiative has had little impact despite (or perhaps because of) the intervention of the petroleum and automobile industries (COM (96) 143).

The Commission has been keen not to ignore the traditional importance of supply security issues in the oil sector. However, national authorities also have maintained their reluctance to see the Community play the leading role in energy crisis management. The Commission attempted to revive this issue at the time of the Gulf War, with measures to co-ordinate member states' actions. Although the issue remains unresolved, it is unlikely that the Commission will be any more successful in this area than in the past. Nonetheless the Community dimension to dialogue with oil producers (notably in the co-operation programme with the Gulf Co-operation Council) continues to develop.

14.3.3 Natural gas

The EU gas industry has seen dramatic growth in the last twenty years, considering that the industry was rooted in town gas for most of its history and seemed in

Table 14.6 EU gas balances (Mtoe)

	Gas production	Net imports	Supply
1960	10.2	0	10.2
1970	61.3	1.5	62.8
1980	135.5	47.3	182.8
1990	132.7	89.9	222.6
1995	167.0	109.2	274.9
1996	188.8	118.3	305.3
1997	182.3	124.1	302.7

Figures for all years are for EU-15.
Source: See Table 14.1.

definite decline. The discovery of natural gas, first in Groningen after the Second World War and then in the North Sea, indicated its potential to supply Europe with energy. Production in the countries which constitute the EU today has risen from just over 10 million tonnes of oil equivalent in 1960 to just under 160 million tonnes of oil equivalent by the mid-1990s. Demand has outpaced supply and imports have met a steadily rising proportion of consumption (currently approximately 37%) (see Table 14.6). While natural gas accounted for 3% of energy requirements for the EC in 1960, it had risen to just under 20% by 1994.

The gas industry shares the characteristics of the exploratory production industries such as oil and the network utility industries such as electricity. On balance the industry is dominated not so much by production companies but by the transmission companies which import and carry gas. Production is widespread (with the Netherlands and United Kingdom predominant – see Table 14.1) and is carried out by oil exploration companies. Transmission and imports are normally carried out by national monopolies (Germany is the exception where the monopolies are organized regionally). Distribution is also a monopoly and is generally carried out by local companies. Ownership is largely public with the exception of Germany and the United Kingdom. The extent to which monopoly or oligopoly prevails is reinforced by the substantial degree of vertical integration in the industry, thanks to long-run contracts between the suppliers and transmission companies and between the transmission companies and the distributors. Some attempts have been made to introduce competition into the industry, with the United Kingdom the most advanced, but they are not widespread in the EU.

The EU's past policy towards the gas industry was mainly concerned with supply security (limiting gas use in power stations) and price discrimination (investigating prices charged to large consumers in the Netherlands). The first signs of a wider agenda for gas came with the publication of the Commission's review of the natural gas industry in the EC (COM (86) 518). This indicated not only that the prospects for supply and demand appeared healthy (and underscored the fuel's relatively benign environmental effects), but that the industry should move towards a European structure with as much competition as possible in the system. The IEM objectives for the gas market straddle the two components of the industry. To the extent that the gas is produced in the EU, then considerations related to oil production and barriers to that market would also apply to the gas industry (as discussed in the previous section). To the extent that the gas industry at the distribution level approximates the natural monopolies such as electricity, it is subject to similar proposals on extending grid integration, encouraging competition and determining regulation (see the next section).

One of the Commission's main objectives is to see the creation of an EU-wide gas network. While applauding the widespread integration of the system of continental Europe and the joint ventures created, the Commission has sought to integrate the whole of the Community into the gas market and to improve links with neighbouring states. Community funds have been used to bring gas to Greece and Portugal while the TransEuropean Networks initiative has sought to strengthen the network across the continent (in the latter case, however, financial support is limited to supporting feasibility studies and facilitating other sources of funding).

While there has been general support for extending the network, the issue of competition in the gas market is much more controversial. Although some member states already permit consumers to buy direct from gas suppliers using the network as a common carrier, the idea is not supported by the industry as a whole or by many governments. Attempts to introduce rules for the transit of gas between utilities were opposed by a number of member states and the Commission's proposals were eventually passed by majority vote. Measures to liberalize the market proved controversial. Opponents of reform argue that such a system (by introducing competition) would not provide the certainty required for the long-run investments needed in the sector and would jeopardize existing contractual arrangements. Progress in liberalizing the European electricity market (see below) rekindled the prospects for a similar arrangement in the gas sector but so far the Council has failed to resolve the differences between member states. However, a directive was adopted in 1998 for applying the internal market to gas, with implementation coming under the IEM.

Whatever the outcome of this debate, however, it is unlikely to stem the growing share of gas in Community energy balances. The Commission has accordingly placed great importance on ensuring stable supplies of gas, particularly from the former Soviet Union. The European Energy Charter covers all fuels but there is no doubt that ensuring gas supplies to the Community is the primary concern (Stern, 1992).

14.3.4 Electricity

Electricity has seen the most rapid growth in the post-war period. Electricity demand and production in the EC rose rapidly for many years (in the 1950s and 1960s by an average of 8% annually). Although the mix of production technologies has changed over the years, for many decades (with a decline in the role of coal and the rise of nuclear power) the industry has benefited from a virtuous circle of improving supply technologies reducing costs and prices on the one hand and

Table 14.7 EU electricity generation by fuel

	Electricity total production (TWh)	Coal (%)	Oil (%)	Gas (%)	Nuclear (%)	Hydro (%)	Net imports (Mtoe)
1960	511.9	55.6	8.5	1.5	0.4	33.2	na
1970	1104.3	45.3	24.1	4.9	3.9	20.7	0.43[a]
1980	1672.7	42.0	20.4	7.6	12.6	16.6	1.87[b]
1990	2140.7	37.4	9.1	6.9	33.6	12.1	2.33
1995	2308.6	31.6	8.8	10.3	35.1	12.6	1.50
1996	2390.7	30.5	8.3	11.7	35.5	12.2	−0.14
1997	2403.7	28.3	7.7	13.8	35.8	12.3	0.67

Figures for all years are for EU-15.
na = not available.
[a] The figure is for 1971.
[b] The figure is for 1982.
Source: See Table 14.1.

increasing demand on the other (see Table 14.7). In the last decade the electricity sector has seen slower growth rates for demand and greater investment in gas and renewables-based capacity at the expense of coal and nuclear fuel.

The electricity supply industry (ESI) retains a wide diversity of institutional forms, with differing levels of public and private participation and/or centralized or decentralized organization (Hughes, 1983; McGowan and Thomas, 1992). The diversity owes much to the origins of the industry in each country, whether in rural co-operatives, municipal companies or industrial firms selling surplus power. The determining factor in shaping the development of the ESI, however, has been the political-economic structure of the country; much of the way in which industries have evolved can be attributed to the balance of power between public authority and private enterprise in the economy and between central and local government in the political realm (Hughes, 1983).

The shared position of the utilities has extended to international contacts. Despite the different structures and practices of the industry, for the most part they share a common perception of their obligations and future options, and are organized within a common pressure group for international issues. Co-operation has also extended to operational aspects – most EU utilities are linked into common despatch systems for optimizing the use of peak and reserve capacity (Bruppacher, 1988).

In more recent years, the pattern of steady improvement and the status of the utility have faltered. Technological improvements turned out to be harder to obtain and (in scale economies) self-defeating, demand faltered, and costs and prices rose. The industry's record on environmental affairs also came under criticism in the 1970s and 1980s. However, the most important factor in change was in the relationship between the utilities and the consumers (particularly the largest industrial users).

In the 1980s, a number of large consumers sought to gain access to the national systems in various member states (to buy either from private producers or from exporters), but without success. In this environment, tensions between utilities also increased, and in the face of irreconcilable positions a number of consumers (primarily large German industrial users seeking to purchase cheap nuclear surplus power from France) threatened the use of the Rome Treaty to support their goals (Lippert, 1987).

As noted the idea of a European component to the ESI pre-dates the EEC, and figured in the debate on the development of the EC at some stages. However, an EC role was rejected in the 1950s and most moves on integrating systems have occurred outside the EC framework. Commission interest has intermittently focused on the EC (such as on investment notification and rules for equipment procurement), but mostly these interventions have been unsuccessful or have reinforced the autonomy of member states and of the utilities.

Certainly there has been little in EC policy on electricity prior to the IEM which would indicate such a transformation. While the Commission indicated that an integration and liberalization of the ESI was desirable, the idea did not receive any serious consideration. Policy has for the most part been developed in the 1970s and was largely informed by the need to diversify fuel types in power production by discouraging and encouraging various forms of power generation. The use of gas and oil was limited in 1975 (although it was a measure that was largely honoured in the breach), while incentives for coal, nuclear fuel and renewables were also devised.

The Commission's view of how the IEM should affect electricity has sought to balance the special characteristics of the sector with the drive to integrate and liberalize its structure. Integration of the electricity market is the Commission's principal objective. The Commission believed the development of international interconnection in Europe to be very limited by comparison with the potential of an EC-wide electricity pool. The system of interconnection was balkanized between different groupings of countries; none of these had any executive power. Within each grouping, moreover, trade was conducted on a bilateral basis on terms agreed by the utilities. The Commission viewed the structure of the system as a major constraint in the emergence of more competitive pressures in electricity production, failing not only to take advantage of the potential downward pressure on costs which a more competitive market might provide, but also, and more importantly, to exploit the comparative advantages of a mix of supply sources and the economies of a fully integrated system.

The Commission's view implicitly criticized the dominance of national systems in the ESI by identifying a number of distortions and barriers to trade within and between these systems. According to the Commission, these differences in treatment of the industry between countries were key obstacles to an economically efficient ESI: divergences proliferated in such areas as fiscal and financial treatment, planning procedures and standards. In terms of the industry's operation, the critical factor which has distorted the emergence of a market has been the influence of governments on utility purchasing, affecting the purchase of new power plant and the options available in fuel supply.

According to the Commission, the main obstacle to these developments has been the organizational structure of the ESI in most member states. The close organizational links between production on the one hand and transmission and distribution on the other have tended to favour national supply solutions for electricity. A change in the relationship between these constituent parts of the ESI would help to foster the development of trade in power. The Commission hinted at a radical transformation of the industry when it suggested that 'a change in the operational (as distinct from the ownership) system would be conducive to further opening of the internal market' (CEC, 1988b, p. 72). Although the Commission was aware of technical and security of supply issues associated with the development of open access or common carriage, it chose to push for such policies on the basis of what it believes to be the benefits to be derived from opening the market up to both large consumers and co-generators.

In 1989, the Commission took the first steps to creating a single electricity market. The first element of this was a revival of its pricing policy proposals aimed at increasing the transparency of electricity prices. In a review of transparency in the energy sector (CEC, 1989a), it considered the lack of publishable information on prices to large consumers as unacceptable. It sought to devise reference tariffs against which consumers across the EC can assess and compare their own prices. The measure was accompanied by moves to increase the scope for trade (or transit) and to foster investment co-ordination between the utilities. After nearly two years of negotiations, the Council agreed to the transparency and transit directives but not to the Commission's plans for investment co-ordination, committing themselves to a better use of existing agreements in this area.

The Commission's next step was to consult with governments and industry on the feasibility of greater competition. After an inconclusive series of reports, which would probably have rejected the idea of competition were it not for the support of the British government and electricity industry, a prolonged debate within the Commission took place, the result of which was a set of limited proposals for reform. These called for an extension of market access to independent power producers, distribution companies and large consumers, with the possibility of a complete market opening some time in the future. The directive was, however, drawn up as a proposal to the Council; the Commission did not use Article 90 to force the proposals through (although its use had been debated). Moreover, the directive itself was framed in a way that emphasized gradual implementation, concessions to supply security and maximum national autonomy in applying the directives (COM (91) 548; Argyris, 1993).

An agreement to liberalize the electricity market was eventually reached in 1996 after further watering down of the original proposals: competition will only be introduced for the largest consumers, with a gradual opening of the market over nine years. Countries will be able to opt for either 'negotiated third party access' or a 'single buyer' system (the latter preserving to some extent the position of the single vertically integrated utilities which enjoy a near monopoly in some member states), although in both cases the different components of the market (production, transmission and distribution) will have to be 'unbundled' (a separation of accounts for each component – see Klom, 1996). While the agreed reforms fall short of outright deregulation, it is clear that many member states are considering (and some such as the UK and Sweden have already implemented) more radical reforms. Nevertheless, on 4 May 1999, the Commission noted, in its report on the application of the internal market to electricity under the IEM, that more than 60% of the EU market had been liberalized and expressed satisfaction since the minimum expected was 25%.

14.3.5 Non-fossil sources: nuclear, renewables, conservation

Growing concern over supply security and latterly the environment has fuelled an interest in non-fossil fuel sources of energy in many member states. In the 1970s and early 1980s nuclear power was the main focus of interest. More recently, however, the potential of renewables and energy conservation measures has been recognized.

The growth of nuclear power in the EU has been rapid but not dramatically so (see Table 14.8). Its contribution to electricity input in the EU has risen from almost zero in 1960 to almost 36% by 1997. The position varies widely from country to country, reflecting the different political climates within which the industry has developed: some such as France obtain 80% of electricity from nuclear power while others such as Denmark have none. The industry has been badly shaken by scandal (Transnuklear) and crisis (Chernobyl) and characterized by highly variable operating record and cost levels (Thomas, 1988). Now nuclear power is promoted less for its economic than for its environmental benefits (since it does not emit greenhouse gases). Nonetheless, not even its proponents stick to the optimistic forecasts made in the 1950s and which persisted into the early 1980s.

The EU nuclear industry is broadly composed of utilities, national authorities and fuel agencies. In almost every case the industry is predominantly publicly owned. Advanced nuclear technologies (such as the fast breeder reactor and fusion) are even more the preserve of the public sector. As part of the ESI, and given its special characteristics, the industry has not been subject to competitive pressures. Commission policy on the sector has never lived up to the expectations of the Euratom Treaty. Too many countries have endeavoured to maintain autonomy over the industry. Yet the Commission has sought to sustain the industry as much for its industrial policy implications as for energy concerns (CEC, 1970b). Considerable resources have gone into promoting nuclear power and particularly joint ventures on advanced technologies: of the 1200 million ECUs proposed for energy research in the third Framework Programme, over 75% was allocated to the nuclear sector.

The Commission's treatment of nuclear power and the IEM is separate to that of electricity, and as a result focuses less on the economics of nuclear power as a source of electricity than on the characteristics of nuclear fuel, plant and services. As in the case of coal, the Commission notes the wide disparities in policy and practice across the EC and the relative weakness of Euratom, the Treaty guiding the sector's development and the obstacles facing the development of a European and competitive market for nuclear fuels and equipment. In the first case, the long-term nature of

Table 14.8 Nuclear energy

	Production (Mtoe)	% of total energy production
1973	17.9	5.1
1983	97.8	21.8
1990	187.8	33.6
1995	210.9	35.1
1996	221.4	35.4
1997	224.1	35.8

contracts for enrichment and reprocessing means that any moves towards an internal market will have to wait for their expiry (CEC, 1988e).

Aside from very significant levels of research support, the Commission has scarcely addressed the nuclear issue since the mid-1980s, confining itself to reviews of the current status of the industry. The divisions between member states have persisted, effectively preventing any Community policy to emerge (though the inertia which grants almost all Community energy R&D funds to nuclear persists). There have been four developments which may allow a policy to develop in future, however. The first is the greenhouse debate. For many in the nuclear industry, the fears surrounding global warming may rekindle interest in nuclear investments although it has not so far led to a formal declaration of Community support. The second issue is industrial policy: supporters of the sector in member states and the Commission have stressed the importance of the sector as a 'high technology' sector (see Chapter 10). A related issue is the potential for rebuilding the nuclear industry in the former socialist bloc: poor safety and performance records in East Europe and the former Soviet Union have presented the European nuclear industry with new opportunities for investment and maintaining industrial capabilities (Defrennes, 1997). The final issue is market liberalization. As part of its attempts to apply the competition rules to the energy sector, the the Commission scrutinized British attempts to protect the nuclear industry during the privatization of the electricity industry. In this case, the Commission was able to limit the level and duration of support given by the British government, justifying the exception on the grounds of supply security. If the development of an internal energy market exposed more market distortions relating to nuclear energy, this mechanism could be used again.

It may be, however, that the uncertain economics and the controversial politics of nuclear power will continue to rule it out in future EU energy strategy. In that context more and more attention and resources will have to be given to the other non-fossil options: renewables and conservation.

The most established renewable energy industry is hydroelectric power, which accounts for a sizeable proportion of electricity (most major sites are in use and new developments face considerable opposition). The 'new' renewables such as mini-hydro, solar, wind and wave have largely developed in the aftermath of energy crises and growing environmental concerns. While still small in terms of power contribution, they are a fixture in many utilities and their role is set to grow in most, as their reliability and competitiveness improve. The sector's industries largely consist of joint ventures between governments, utilities and manufacturers.

The importance and structure of conservation industries are even harder to discern. While advisory, architectural and control systems companies (each offering ways to reduce energy consumption) proliferate, their impact is difficult to assess (given that they are aiming to help consumers to forgo energy usage). The overall improvement in energy efficiency must be partly due to these companies but also to other factors such as economic restructuring and price effects. Largely private, these companies have received varying degrees of support from governments while the energy industries have for the most part been lukewarm, perceiving conservation as a threat to growth of their market. More recently, however, some large energy companies have adopted a higher profile on conservation issues as a means of developing their market and diversifying.

Policy initiatives have also intensified largely as a result of the pressure of environmental concerns. On renewables, the Commission announced in 1988 a recommendation to allow favourable access for such supplies (on the basis of their environmental benefits) to public grid systems. Further measures were proposed in the wake of the Commission's greenhouse strategy. The four-part initiative, Altener, tabled in 1992, involving the promotion of a market for renewables, fiscal and economic measures, training and information, was formally adopted in 1998 (see section 14.2.4) while recently the Commission published a Green Paper on renewables and set the objective of doubling the share of renewables in the Community's energy balances (COM (96) 576). On conservation, the Commission has developed a number of programmes, the most recent of which – SAVE II – sets out a variety of measures including labelling of appliances, third party finance, audits and inspections (see section 14.2.4). Given parallel interests in member states, these options have been taken more seriously than previous energy strategies. However, an attempt to overcome the regulatory barriers to the development of these options looks unlikely to be accepted. In recent years the Commission has sought a new approach to energy investment – so-called integrated resource planning is designed to factor in 'externalities' (most importantly, impact upon the environment) to investment choices. Such techniques have been used in the USA and some member states to support renewable and conservation options. The measure is opposed by the larger utilities across the Community as well as by a number of governments.

14.4 Conclusion

It is more than forty years since the first Community initiatives on energy policy were proposed, yet, in spite of the Energy Charter Treaty and its supporting programmes, a *coherent* policy remains elusive. As is clear, each of the energy sub-sectors has been affected by Community policies, largely invoked on the back of the internal market and environmental protection. While not all policy proposals are agreed to or implemented successfully, there is no longer any doubt that what the Commission proposes should be taken seriously by member states and the energy industries. In a sense, however, its relative success with certain initiatives has meant that the Community has many policies for the energy sector, but no overall policy.

The absence of such a policy means that there is a danger of conflicting objectives. This is not a new problem. From 1951 to 1973, energy policy efforts tried to balance the goal of a single and open energy market with the need to maintain security of supply. For the next ten years, the security goal predominated. Now the balance of policy is even less clear. The tone of many debates and the nature of proposals suggest that the IEM agenda is in the ascendant, with a corresponding emphasis of policy towards free markets. At the same time, however, the growth of the environment as a policy concern highlights rather different priorities, casting doubt on a purely market-driven approach. Nor has the 'old' agenda of supply security disappeared, and the temptation to use the energy sector for industrial, regional and social policy objectives also persists. The problems of such a multidimensional 'policy' would be considerable if any institution had the task of co-ordinating them. Given that there is no remit for such a role to be played, how much greater are the risks of contradictory signals to governments, energy suppliers and consumers and how much more difficult are the intra-Commission disputes (i.e. those between different directorates)?

It may be that the pressures of different policy objectives and the need both to reconcile these and to rationalize and regulate derogations from them will push the Community towards a *de facto* energy policy. This, however, raises a number of questions about accountability and democracy which are all too apparent in a range of EU policy areas. The irony is that such problems as do arise from the absence of energy policy or an *ad hoc* approach will be the result of a failure by member states to consider and debate a coherent and common energy policy for the Community.

15 Tax harmonization

A. M. EL-AGRAA

Tax harmonization has turned out to be a very thorny issue for the EU: witness the vehement utterances during 1988–9 by Baroness Thatcher when she was British Prime Minister (see Chapter 26), and by both the then German Chancellor Helmut Kōhl and Jacques Delors when he was President of the EU Commission, when she flatly declared that tax harmonization was not EU business, only to hear the other two announce that it was indispensable for EU integration. Such a bold statement cannot be treated lightly since tax harmonization still remains an area where new EU legislation requires unanimity; hence a single EU member nation can frustrate any new initiatives within this domain. The purpose of this chapter is to clarify what tax harmonization means before going on to assess the progress the EU has achieved in this field.

15.1 Tax harmonization in the context of fiscal policy

Very widely interpreted, fiscal policy comprises a whole corpus of 'public finance' issues: the relative size of the public sector, taxation and expenditure, and the allocation of public sector responsibilities between the different tiers of government (Prest, 1979). Hence fiscal policy is concerned with a far wider area than that commonly, but arguably, associated with it, namely, the aggregate management of the economy in terms of controlling inflation and employment–unemployment levels.

Experts in the field of public finance (Musgrave and Musgrave (1976) rightly stress that 'public finance' is a misleading term, since the subject also deals with 'real' problems) have identified a number of problems associated with these fiscal policy issues. For instance, the relative size of the public sector raises questions regarding the definition and measurement of government revenue and expenditure (Prest, 1972), and the attempts at understanding and explaining revenue and expenditure have produced more than one theoretical model (Musgrave and Musgrave, 1976; Peacock and Wiseman, 1967). The division of public sector responsibilities raises the delicate question of which fiscal aspects should be dealt with at the central government level and which aspects should be tackled at the local level. Finally, the area of taxation and expenditure criteria has resulted in general agreement about the basic criteria of *allocation* (the process by which the utilization of resources is split between private and social goods and by which the 'basket' of social goods is chosen), *equity* (the use of the budget for achieving a 'fair' distribution of income), *stabilization* (the use of the budget as an instrument for achieving and maintaining a 'reasonable' level of employment, acceptable inflation and economic growth rates and for achieving equilibrium and stability in the balance of payments), and *admin-*

319

istration (the practical possibilities of implementing a particular tax system and the cost to the society of operating such a system). However, a number of very tricky problems are involved in a consideration of these criteria. In discussing the efficiency of resource allocation, the choice between, for example, work and leisure, or between private and public goods, is an important and controversial one. With regard to the equity of distribution, there is the problem of what is meant by equity: is it personal, class or regional equity? In a discussion of the stabilization of the economy, despite the controversy between 'Keynesians' and 'monetarists', there still exists the perennial problem of controlling unemployment and inflation and, in spite of the relative demise of the Phillips curve (see Chapter 6), the trade-off between them. A consideration of administration must take into account the problem of efficiency versus practicality. Finally, there is the obvious conflict between the four criteria in that the achievement of one aim is usually at the expense of another; for example, what is most efficient in terms of collection may prove less (or more) equitable than what is considered to be socially desirable.

These complex considerations cannot be tackled here, given the level of generality of this chapter. The interested reader is, therefore, advised to consult the very extensive literature on public finance.

The above relates to a discussion of the problems of fiscal policy in very broad national terms. When considering EU fiscal policy, there are certain elements of the international dimension that need spelling out and there are also some interregional (intra-EU) elements that have to be introduced.

Very briefly, internationally, it has always been recognized that taxes (and equivalent instruments) have similar effects to tariffs on the international flow of goods and services – non-tariff distortions of international trade (generally referred to as non-tariff trade barriers, NTBs – see Baldwin, 1971 and Chapter 8). Other elements have also been recognized as operating similar distortions on the international flow of factors of production (Bhagwati, 1969; Johnson, 1965a, 1973).

In the particular context of the EU, it should be remembered that its formation, at least from the economic viewpoint, was meant to facilitate the free and unimpeded flow of goods, services and factors (and the other elements discussed in Chapter 1) between the member nations. Since tariffs are not the only distorting factor in this respect, the proper establishment of intra-EU free trade necessitates the removal of all non-tariff distortions that have an equivalent effect. Hence, the removal of tariffs may give the impression of establishing free trade inside the EU, but this is by no means automatically guaranteed, since the existence of sales taxes, excise duties, corporation taxes, income taxes, etc. may impede this freedom. Indeed, this is precisely what happened in the EC: the removal of tariffs in the 1960s immediately highlighted the significance of NTBs. This is also the reason why the Commission was able to persuade the member nations to adopt the Single European Act (SEA) to enable the creation of one internal market free of such distortions from the end of 1992 – see below and Chapter 8. The moral is that not only tariffs, but all equivalent distortions, must be eliminated or harmonized.

At this juncture it becomes necessary to emphasize that there are at least two basic elements to fiscal policy: the instruments available to the government for fiscal policy purposes (i.e. the total tax structure) and the overall impact of the joint manoeuvring of these instruments (i.e. the role played by the budget). The aim of this chapter is to discuss the meaning of and the need for tax harmonization, and to assess the progress made by the EU in this respect. The other element of fiscal policy, the general budget of the EU, is discussed in the following chapter. Hence, the two chapters complement each other in that, taken together, they cover the two basic elements of EU fiscal policy.

15.2 The EU tax structure and its implications

In case it is not obvious why taxes should give rise to trade distortion (Swann, 1978), it may be useful to examine the nature of taxes before the inception of the EU (see Table 15.1), as well as to consider the treatment given at the time to indirect taxation on internationally traded commodities.

Before considering these aspects, however, it may be useful to remind the reader that there are two basic types of taxation: direct and indirect. Direct taxes, such as income and corporation taxes, come into operation at the end of the process of personal and industrial activities. They are levied on wages and salaries when activities have been performed and payment has been met (income taxes), or on the profits of industrial or professional businesses at the end of annual activity (corporation taxes). Direct taxes are not intended to play any significant role in the pricing of commodities or professional services. Indirect taxes are levied specifically on consumption and are, therefore, in a simplistic model, very significant in determining the pricing of commodities, given their real costs of production.

Historically speaking, in the EC there existed four types of sales, or turnover, taxes (Dosser, 1973; Paxton, 1976): the *cumulative multistage cascade system* (operated in West Germany until the end of 1967, in Luxembourg until the end of 1969 and in the Netherlands until the end of 1968) in which the tax was levied on the gross value of the commodity in question at each and every stage of production without any rebate on taxes paid at earlier stages; *value-added tax* (VAT), which has operated in France since 1954 where it is known as TVA – *Taxe sur la Valeur Ajoutée* – which is basically a non-cumulative multistage system; the *mixed* systems (oper-

Table 15.1 Percentage composition of tax receipts and tax burdens in the EC, 1955

	Income and property taxes	Turnover taxes	Consumption taxes	Tax receipts as % of GNP
Belgium	50.7	26.5	22.8	17.1
France	38.4	41.5	20.1	19.6
West Germany	52.4	26.9	20.7	21.9
Italy	32.3	21.1	46.6	22.9
Luxembourg	66.4	15.4	18.2	23.6
Netherlands	60.0	20.1	19.9	26.6

Source: Balassa (1961).

ated in Belgium and Italy) which were cumulative multistage systems that were applied down to the wholesale stage, but incorporated taxes which were applied at a single point for certain products; finally, *purchase tax* (operated in the United Kingdom) which was a single-stage tax normally charged at the wholesale stage by registered manufacturers or wholesalers, which meant that manufacturers could trade with each other without paying tax.

Although all these tax systems had the common characteristic that no tax was paid on exports, so that each country levied its tax at the point of entry, one should still consider the need for harmonizing them.

A variety of taxes also existed in the form of excise duties, the main purpose of which is to raise revenue for the governments. The number of commodities subjected to these duties ranged from the usual (or 'classical') five of manufactured tobacco products, hydrocarbon oils, beer, wine and spirits, to an extensive number including coffee, sugar, salt, matches, etc. (in Italy). The means by which the government collected its revenues from excise duties ranged from government-controlled manufacturing, e.g. tobacco goods in France and Italy, to fiscal imports based on value, weight, strength, quality, etc. (Dosser, 1973, p. 2).

As far as corporation tax is concerned, three basic schemes existed, and still exist in a slightly disguised form, but not in any single country at all times. The first is the *separate* system which was used in the United Kingdom – the system calls for the complete separation of corporation tax from personal income tax and was usually referred to as the 'classical' system. The second is the *two-rate* or *split-rate* system which was the German practice and was recommended as an alternative system for the United Kingdom in the Green Paper of 1971 (HMSO, Cmnd 4630). The third is the *credit* or *imputation* system which gives shareholders credit for tax paid by the company, and this credit may be used to offset their income tax liability on dividends; part of the company's tax liability is 'imputed' to the shareholders and regarded as a prepayment of their income tax on dividends – this was the French system and was proposed for the United Kingdom in the White Paper of 1972 (HMSO, Cmnd 4955) and adopted in 1973 – see Kay and King (1983) for a full explanation of how the system works within the United Kingdom context; in the appendix to this chapter, a bare skeleton of the system is provided.

Generally speaking, corporation tax varied from being totally indistinguishable from other systems (Italy) to being quite separate from personal income tax with a single or a split rate which varied between 'distributed' and 'undistributed' profits, to being partially integrated with the personal income tax systems, so that part of the corporation tax paid on distributed profits could be credited against a shareholder's income tax liability (Dosser, 1973, p. 2).

The personal income tax system itself was differentiated in very many aspects among the original six, as regards not just rates and allowances, but also administration procedures, compliance and enforcement.

Finally, the variety in the para-tax system relating to social security arrangements was even more striking. The balance between sickness, industrial injury, unemployment and pensions was very different indeed, and the methods of financing these benefits were even more so – see Chapter 19.

In concluding this section, it is useful to discuss certain problems regarding these taxes. Since VAT is the EU's turnover tax (see the section below on EU progress on tax harmonization), I shall illustrate the problems of turnover taxes in the context of VAT.

The first relates to the point at which the tax should be imposed. Here, two basic principles have been recognized and a choice between them has to be made: the 'destination' and 'origin' principles. Taxation under the destination principle specifies that commodities going to the same destination must bear the same tax load irrespective of their origin. For example, if the United Kingdom levies a general sales tax at 8% and France a similar tax at 16%, a commodity exported from the United Kingdom to France would be exempt from the United Kingdom's 8% tax but would be subjected to France's 16% tax. Hence, the United Kingdom's export commodity would compete on equal terms with French commodities sold in the French market. Taxation under the origin principle specifies that commodities with the same origin must pay exactly the same tax, irrespective of their destination. Hence, a commodity exported by the United Kingdom to France would pay the United Kingdom tax (8%) and would be exempt from the French tax (16%). Therefore, the commodity that originated from the United Kingdom would compete unfairly against a similar French commodity.

The choice between the destination and origin principles raises a number of technical issues which cannot be tackled here. Those interested should consult the voluminous literature on the subject (Shoup, 1966, 1972; Dosser, 1973; Paxton, 1976; Pinder, 1971).

The second problem relates to the range of coverage of the tax. If some member countries are allowed to include certain stages, e.g. the retail stage, and others made allowances for certain fixed capital expenditures and raw materials, the tax base will not be the same. This point is very important, because one has to be clear about whether the tax base should be consumption or net national income. To illustrate, in a 'closed' economy:

$$Y = W + P = C + I$$

where Y = gross national product (GNP), W = wages and salaries, P = gross profits, C = consumption and I = gross capital expenditure. If value-added is defined as $W + P - I$ (i.e. GNP minus gross capital expenditure), then consumption will form the tax base. If instead of gross capital expenditure one deducts only capital consumption (depreciation), then net national product will become the tax base. Obviously, the argument holds true in an 'open' economy. It is therefore important that members of a union should have a common base – see Table 15.2 for variations in the percentage of GDP devoted to domestic investment in the EU member states.

The third problem relates to exemptions that may defeat the aim of VAT being a tax on consumption. For example, in a three-stage production process, exempting the first stage does not create any problem, since the tax levies on the second and third stages together will be equivalent to a tax levied at all three stages. Exempting the third stage will obviously reduce the tax collection, provided of course that the rates levied at all three stages were the same. If the second stage is exempt, the tax base will be in excess of that where no exemptions are allowed for, since the tax on the first stage cannot be transferred as an input tax on the second stage, and the third stage will be unable to claim any input tax from items bought from the second stage. The outcome will be a tax based on the total sum of the turnover of stages one and three only, rather than a tax levied on the total sum of the value-added at all three stages.

With regard to corporation tax, a proper evaluation of any system raises national as well as interregional (intra-EU) questions. The national questions relate to the standard criteria by which a tax system can be judged: its effects on budget revenue and

Table 15.2 EU gross domestic investment as a percentage of GDP

	1960	1970	1982	1990	1998
Austria	28	30	22	25	24
Belgium[a]	19	24	16	21	18
Denmark	23	26	16	17	17
Finland	30	30	25	27	17
France	24	27	20	22	17
Germany[b]	27	28	21	22	21
Greece	19	28	22	19	19
Ireland	16	24	23	21	18
Italy	24	27	17	21	17
Netherlands	27	30	18	21	20
Portugal	19	26	29	32	24
Spain	21	27	25	26	21
Sweden	25	25	17	21	15
United Kingdom	19	20	17	19	16

[a] Includes Luxembourg.
[b] The figures up to 1990 refer to the Federal Republic only.
Sources: Collected from various Eurostat publications and issues of the World Bank's *World Development Report*.

aggregate effective demand, on income distribution, on the balance of payments, on the rate of economic growth, on regional differences and on price levels. It is obvious that what is very efficient for one purpose need not be so for the other purposes.

The intra-EU questions relate to the treatment of investment, since, if capital mobility within the EU is to be free from restrictions as guaranteed by the Maastricht and Amsterdam treaties and encouraged by the EEC Treaty of Rome before that, investors must receive equal treatment irrespective of their native country (region). Here, Dosser recommends highly the separate system since it is 'neutral' in its tax treatment between domestic investment at home and abroad, and between domestic and foreign investment at home, provided that both member countries practise the same system (Dosser, 1973, p. 95). Prest (1979, pp. 85–6) argues that even though a separate system does not discriminate against partner (foreign) investment, it does discriminate between 'distributed' and 'undistributed' profits, and that the imputation system, even though it is neutral between 'distributed' and 'undistributed' profits, actually discriminates against partner (foreign) investment. Prest therefore claims that neither system can be given 'full marks'.

Again, at this level of generality, one cannot go into all the complications raised by such questions. The interested reader is therefore advised to consult Dosser (1966, 1971, 1973, 1975), Dosser and Han (1968), Paxton (1976) and Pinder (1971), or the vast and growing literature on this subject.

As already mentioned, excise duties are intended basically for revenue-raising purposes. For example, in the United Kingdom excise duties on tobacco products, petroleum and alcoholic drinks account for about a third of central government revenue (Kay and King, 1996). The issues raised by the harmonization of these taxes are specifically those relating to the function of these taxes as raisers of revenue and to the equity, as opposed to the efficiency, of these methods.

Finally, the income tax structure has a lot to do with the freedom of labour mobility. Ideally, one would expect equality of treatment in every single tax that is covered within this structure, but it is apparent that, since there is more than one rate, the harmonization of a 'package' of rates might achieve the specified objective.

15.3 The meaning of tax harmonization

Having discussed the problems associated with taxes in the context of economic integration, it is now appropriate to say something about the precise meaning of tax harmonization.

In earlier years, tax harmonization was defined as tax co-ordination (Dosser, 1973). Ideally, in a fully integrated EU, it could be defined as the identical unification of both base and rates, given the same tax system and assuming that everything else is also unified. Prest (1979, p. 76) rightly argues that 'co-ordination' is tantamount to a low-level meaning of tax harmonization, since it could be 'interpreted to be some process of consultation between member countries or, possibly, loose agreements between them to levy tax on a similar sort of base or at similar sorts of rates'. It is therefore not surprising that tax harmonization has, in practice, come to mean a compromise between the low level of co-ordination (the EU is much more than a low level of integration – see Chapter 1) and the ideal level of standardization (even if the Maastricht and Amsterdam treaties are fully implemented and without the opt-out protocols, the EU will come close to but will not become a complete political entity – see Chapter 2). However, the SEA asks for the creation of one internal market, and this has been interpreted to mean a market without fiscal frontiers which the Commission insists must be one where taxes are near equal – see below. The Maastricht and Amsterdam treaties have reinforced this decision.

15.4 The EU's experience with tax harmonization

To discuss the experience of the EU with tax harmonization meaningfully, it is sensible to consider the developments before the adoption of the SEA separately from those after it.

15.4.1 The period leading to the SEA

During this period, the main driving force was Article 99 of the EEC Treaty of Rome, which specifically calls for the harmonization of indirect taxes, mainly turnover taxes and excise duties. Harmonization here was seen as vital, particularly since the removal of tariffs would have left taxes as the main source of intra-EU trade distortion. However, given the preoccupation of the EU with the process of unification, the Treaty seemed to put very little stress on the harmonization of its initial tax diversity. Moreover, the Treaty is rather vague about what it means by 'harmonization': for example, in Article 100 it does not specify more than that laws 'should be approximated' with regard to direct taxation. The whole development of tax harmonization during this period was influenced by the work of special committees, informal discussions, etc., i.e. the procedure detailed in Chapter 2. This, however,

Table 15.3 Taxes and actual social contributions, VAT and corporation tax

	Taxes and actual social contributions (% of total), 1980				Effective rates of VAT (%), 1982[c,d]				Corporation tax[e,f]		
	Taxes linked to production and imports	Current taxes on income and wealth	Capital taxes	Actual social contributions	Standard	Reduced	Increased	Rate (%)	System	Imputation credit (%)
Belgium	27.1	41.8	0.8	30.3	17.0	6.0	25.00	48.00	Imputation	49.8
Denmark	41.5	56.3	0.4	1.8	22.0	–	–	37.00	Imputation	25.5
France	35.5	20.4	0.6	43.6	18.6	5.5/7.0	33.30	50.00	Imputation	50.0
West Germany	32.0	32.7	0.2	35.1	13.0	6.5	–	56.36	Imputation	100.0
Ireland[a]	49.1	35.6	0.4	14.9	30.0	0.0/18.0	–	45.00	Imputation	52.4
Italy[b]	30.9	32.3	0.2	36.6	15.0	2.0/8.0	18.35	36.25	Imputation	58.6
Luxembourg	27.2	43.5	0.2	29.1	10.0	2.0/5.0	–	40.00	Separate	None
Netherlands	25.6	34.5	0.5	39.5	18.0	4.0	–	45.00	Separate	None
United Kingdom	43.6	38.5	0.5	17.6	15.0	0.0	–	52.00	Imputation	39.6

[a]1979. [b]1978. [c]The effective VAT rate is that on the price net of tax. [d]Greece was still to introduce VAT. [e]Proposals were made in August 1982 for increasing Italy's to 35–38%. [f]The West German system is a two-rate one.

Source: Eurostat, 1982 (various publications) and Bulletin of the European Communities, Supplement 1/80.

should not be interpreted as a criticism of those who drafted the Treaty. On the contrary, given the very complex nature of the subject and its closeness to the question of political unification, it would have been short-sighted to have done otherwise.

Given this general background, it is now appropriate to describe the progress made by the EU with respect to tax harmonization during this period.

In the area of indirect taxation, most of the developments were in terms of VAT, which the EU adopted as its turnover tax following the recommendations of the Neumark Committee in 1963, which was in turn based on the Tinbergen study of 1953 (CEC, 1953) – particularly since it was realized that the removal of intra-EU tariffs left taxes on traded goods as the main impediment to the establishment of complete free trade inside the EU. Between 1967 and 1977, six directives were issued with the aim of achieving conformity between the different practices of the member countries. These related, apart from the adoption of VAT as the EU sales tax, to three major considerations: the inclusion of the retail stage in the coverage of VAT; the use of VAT levies for the EU general budget (see the following chapter); the achievement of greater uniformity in VAT structure. These directives were later supplemented by several minor ones and by a series of draft directives.[1]

What, then, was the state of play? (See Table 15.3 for information covering this period.) Having adopted the VAT system and having accepted a unified method of calculating it, the EU also acceded to the destination principle which, as we have seen, is consistent with free intra-EU trade. It was agreed by all the member states that the coverage of VAT should be the same and should include the retail stage (now the normal practice), that crude raw materials, bought-in elements and similar components were to be deductible from the tax computation, and that investment stock and inventories should be given similar treatment by all member nations. There was agreement about the general principle of VAT exemptions, but the precise nature of these seemed to vary from one member country to another, thus giving rise to the problems concerning the tax base discussed earlier.

On the other hand, this similarity of principles was, in practice, contradicted by a number of differences. The tax coverage differed from one member country to another, since most of them had different kinds, as well as different levels, of exemptions. For example, the United Kingdom applied zero rating for foodstuffs and children's clothing (zero rating is different from exemptions, since zero rating means not only tax exemption from the process, but also the receipt of rebates on taxes paid at the preceding stage – see Dosser, 1975; Paxton, 1976; Prest, 1979). There was a wide difference in rate structure.

With respect to corporation tax, the Neumark Report of 1963 (CEC, 1963) recommended a split-rate system, the van den Tempel Report of 1970 (CEC, 1970c) preferred the adoption of the separate or classical system, and the draft directive of 1975 went for the imputation system. Moreover, the method of tax harmonization which was accepted was not the ideal one of a single EU corporation tax and a single tax pattern, but rather a unified EU corporation tax accompanied by freedom of tax patterns. Hence, all systems were entertained at some time or another and all that can be categorically stated is that by 1986 the EU limited its choice to the separate and imputation systems – see Table 15.4.

As far as excise duties were concerned, progress was rather slow, and this can be partially attributed to the large extent of the differences between the rates on the commodities under consideration in the different member countries – see Tables 15.5 and 15.6 for information during this period. This is a partial explanation, however, because, as was pointed out earlier, these taxes are important for government revenue purposes and it would have been naïve to have suggested that rate uniformity could have been achieved without giving consideration to the political implications of such a move.

The greatest progress was achieved in tobacco, where a new harmonized system was adopted in January 1978. The essential elements of this system were the abolition of any duties on raw tobacco leaf and the adoption of a new sales tax at the manufacturing level, combined with a specific tax per cigarette and VAT. Prest (1979) argues that the overall effect of this would have been to push up the relative prices of the cheaper brands of cigarettes.

It has been suggested (Prest, 1979) that the harmonization of tax rates here is misguided, since the destination principle automatically guarantees fair competition. This is a misleading criticism, however, since the harmonization of the tax structure should be seen in the context of the drive in the EU for monetary inte-

Table 15.4 Corporation tax structure and rates, 1986

	System	Corporation tax rate (%)	Imputation credit (%)
Belgium	Imputation	45.0[a]	40.87
Denmark	Imputation	50.00	25.00
France	Imputation	45.00	61.11
West Germany	Imputation	56.00/36.00[b]	100.00
Greece	Imputation[c]	34.00 to 47.20	100.00
Ireland	Imputation	50.00[a]	53.85
Italy	Imputation	46.368[d]	100.00
Luxembourg	Separate	40.0[a]	0.00
Netherlands	Separate	42.00	0.00
Portugal	Imputation[c]	42.20 to 47.20	100.00
Spain	Imputation	35.00	18.57
United Kingdom	Imputation	35.0[a]	75.81

[a] Reduced rates are applied to low income.
[b] The 36% is levied on distributed profits.
[c] Greece and Portugal have no corporation tax on distributed profits – this is tantamount to a 100% imputation credit.
[d] This is the sum of both central and local taxes.
Source: various publications by the Commission and national sources.

Table 15.5 Excise duty application in each member state as a percentage of EU average (July 1979 = 100)

	Cigarettes	Spirits	Wine	Beer	Petrol (high grade)	Gas–oil
Belgium	86	62	69	46	99	85
Denmark	299	289	240	272	132	51
France	42	89	4	7	127	156
West Germany	118	63	0	29	92	203
Ireland	74	147	218	289	76	72
Italy	57	18	0	34	140	27
Luxembourg	54	34	34	33	74	44
Netherlands	77	62	69	46	91	82
United Kingdom	92	136	265	144	68	180

Source: *Bulletin of the European Communities,* Supplement 1/80.

gration (see Chapters 6 and 17) and political unification (see Chapter 2), processes which become increasingly difficult without tax harmonization – see next section.

Some progress was achieved with regard to stamp duties. Harmonization here was necessary for promoting the freedom of intra-EU capital flows. The 1976 draft directive recommended a compromise between the systems existing in the member countries. This recommendation was accepted, with the proviso that time would be allowed for adjustment to the new system.

Nothing was attempted in the area of personal income taxation and very slight progress was achieved in social security payments, unemployment benefits, etc.; the only exception was the draft directive of 1979 which dealt with equity in the taxation of migrant workers, but this did not have any serious impact. These issues are discussed in some detail in Chapter 19.

15.4.2 The period beginning with the SEA

The SEA was to have transformed the EC into a single internal market by the end of 1992, i.e. the EC should have become 'an area without internal frontiers in which the free movement of goods, persons, services and capital is ensured' (see Chapter 8); thus, the SEA reiterates the original objectives of the EEC Treaty of Rome, but is more explicit on NTBs. The Commission emphasizes the 'Europe without frontiers' since it is convinced that frontiers are the clearest symbol of divisions within the EU. It is adamant that, if frontiers persist, they will be used as convenient locations for practising some protectionist measure or another.

Table 15.6 Excise duties, proposed and current in 1985 (ECU)

Excisable goods	Proposed rate	EU average		1985 rates in the member states[a]											
		Arithmetic	Weighted	B	D	WG	F	Gr	Ir	It	L	N	P	S	UK
Alcoholic beverages															
Pure alcohol (1 hl)	1271.0	1271.0		1252	3499	1174	1149	48	2722	230	842	1298	248	309	2483
Intermediate products (1 hl)	85.0	103.0		61	292	70	6	2	404	10	41	63	0	0	286
Wines (1 hl)	17.0[b]	58.0		33	157	20	3	0	279	0	13	33	0	0	154
Beers (1 hl)	17.0	22.5		10	57	7	3	10	81	17	5	20	7	3	49
Mineral oils															
Petrol, leaded (1000 l)	340.0	340.0	336	261	473	256	369	349	362	557	209	340	352	254	271
Diesel (1000 l)	177.0	153.0	177	123	236	213	190	106	279	178	100	109	162	124	229
Heating gas/oil (1000 l)	50.0	62.0	50	0	236	8	53	109	48	178	0	44	23	38	15
Heavy fuel oil (1000 kg)	17.0	26.0	17	0	266	7	25	93	10	7	2	15	11	1	11
LPG (1000 l)	85.0	85.0	61	0	163	160	138	40	222	96	21	0	17	27	1353
Cigarettes															
Specific excise (per 1000)	19.5	19.5		2	77	27	1	1	49	2	2	26	2	1	43
Ad valorem duty + VAT (%)[c]	52–4.0	53.0		66	39	44	71	60	34	69	64	36	65	52	34
Other manufactured tobacco[c]															
Cigars (%)	34–6.0	35.0		22	40	26	50	31	56	39–63	23	20	40	21	50
Cigarillos (%)	34–6.0	35.0		27	40	29	54	31	56	39–63	23	25	40	21	50
Smoking tobacco (%)	54–6.0	55.0		37	58–83	36–54	65	63	70	71	38	56	26	31	65–70
Other (%)	41–3.0	42.0		37	41–57	20	37–59	64	20–70	42	38	56	30	36	13–50

[a]Rates are as on 1 April 1987, in ECU.
[b]Sparkling wines: 30 ECU/hl.
[c]Ad valorem duty + VAT, as a % of the retail price.
Source: EU Commission's Europe Without Frontiers (Information 1987, p. 51); COM (87) 325–8.

The most significant feature of frontiers is the customs posts, and, as we have seen, these crucially relate to taxes. Of course, as Baroness Thatcher has persistently claimed, and both her successors (Major and Blair) have reiterated, they may be very important for controlling the movement of terrorists and drug trafficking; but our concern here is with the free movement of licit goods and factors of production. As our earlier discussion has demonstrated, customs controls protect the indirect taxes of one EU member country from relative tax bargains which are obtainable elsewhere within the EU. Moreover, customs controls guarantee that governments can collect the VAT that belongs to them. A frontier-free EU would undermine these factors unless the rates of indirect taxation within the EU were brought much closer to each other. They do not have to be equalized, not only because of the 'package' nature mentioned above, but also because the experience of the United States indicates that contiguous states can maintain differentials in sales taxes of up to about 5 percentage points without the tax leakage becoming unbearable. The Commission would ideally like to see an equalization of the rates, but given the United States' experience and the subsidiarity principle (see Chapter 2), it has decided to aim for a position similar to that of the United States.

Given the brevity of this chapter, it is unjustifiable to devote space to the development of the position that the Commission would have liked the member nations to adopt. Those interested in a full description and some analysis of this development are advised to consult Guieu and Bonnet (1987), Bos and Nelson (1988) and Smith (1988). Here, due to its major significance, we shall concentrate on the position adopted by the Commission in 1985.

In the 1985 White Paper, the Commission reached the conclusion that, to treat EC transactions crossing frontiers within the EC in exactly the same manner as transactions within an EC member state, certain measures would have to be adopted with regard to VAT and excise duties. For VAT, these were as follows:

1. The replacement of the system of refunding tax on exportation and collecting it on importation by a system of tax collection by the country of origin.

2. The introduction of an EC clearing mechanism to ensure that revenues would continue to accrue to the EU member nation where consumption took place so that the destination principle would remain intact.

3. The narrowing of the differentials in national VAT rates so as to lessen the risks of fraud, tax evasion and distortions in competition.

With regard to excise duties, three conditions were deemed necessary:

1. An interlinkage of the bonded warehouse system (created to defer the payment of duty since, as long as the goods remain in these warehouses, duties on them do not have to be paid; recall that excise duties are levied only once on manufacture or importation).

2. Upholding the destination principle.

3. An approximation of the national excise duty rates and regimes.

The initial recommendations advanced by the Commission regarding how to achieve these requirements were examined by an *ad hoc* group invited by the Council of Ministers for Foreign Affairs (ECOFIN). The group reported (Council of the European Communities, 1986) that some of its members did not endorse the need for abolishing fiscal frontiers. However, they felt that, if frontiers had to be removed, the proposals put forward by the Commission were necessary, but inadequate: the group advanced a number of serious problems with respect to the clearing mechanism and the system of interlinked bonded warehouses.

The Commission responded in August 1987 (CEC, 1987b) by mainly elaborating on the proposals put forward in the White Paper and by advancing different recommendations concerning the VAT clearing mechanism and the approximation of excise duties; thus, it responded in precisely the way it had been instructed. These recommendations were as follows:

1. The creation of a central account, in ECUs, to be administered by the Commission and to which net exporting member nations would contribute on a monthly basis and from which net importing member countries would receive payment.

2. The settlement of accounts on the basis of statements made by each member state about its net position (the balance of its VAT on intra-EU input and output).

The new clearing mechanism differed from the one suggested by the *ad hoc* group in that, apart from the proposal that the Commission should administer it, it asked for a clearing of net VAT flows, not a clearing of claims based entirely on input VAT data. The Commission justified this new proposal by stating that it is soundly based; guarantees each member nation its correct VAT allocation; minimizes the extra burden on traders; ensures the system's compatibility with the existing VAT administrative structure; bases clearance on data on individual transactions; and ensures that the mechanism is self-financing.

The Commission was also of the opinion that the removal of fiscal frontiers was impossible unless the approximation of VAT rates was achieved first. It therefore put forward proposals for both the number and level of rates and the allocation of products to the rates. Being well aware that the SEA did not extend the system of majority voting to taxation (see Chapter 1), owing to the obsession with national sovereignty, the Commission stuck closely to the prevailing system: it suggested a dual-rate structure consisting of a standard (normal) and a reduced rate. The reduced rate was to cover basic necessities such as foodstuffs, energy products for heating and lighting, water supplies, pharmaceuticals, books, newspapers, periodicals and passenger transport. To discourage excessive tax-induced distortions on competition, it proposed a six-point band for the standard rate (14–20%) and a five-point band for the reduced rate (4–9%) – see Figure 15.1.

Precise rates were also proposed by the Commission for excise duties. These rates were fixed amounts, specified in ECUs, for the various excises (on alcoholic beverages, mineral oils and tobacco products). Only for the sum of the *ad valorem* elements of excise duty and VAT (on tobacco products) was an optional margin allowed, the impact of which on retail prices would equal the VAT band for non-excisable products – see Table 15.6. The approximation of excise duties was tantamount to an equalization of rates which the Commission deemed to be necessary because VAT was also charged on excisable products, and the combined effect of differentials in excise and VAT rates might otherwise result in unreasonably high tax-induced differences in prices.

Of course, as mentioned above, some of these developments were not necessary if all that was being sought was an internal market. For example, the factors that influence prices are both numerous and diverse, and differentials in tax rates are only one such factor. That is why some authorities argue that it is only when fron-

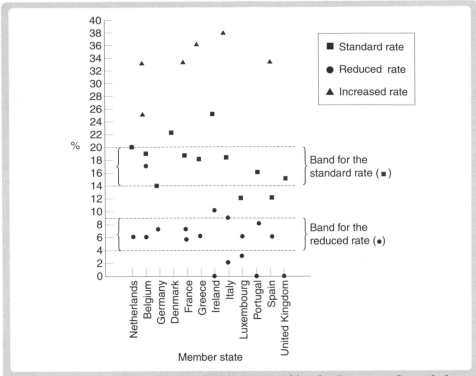

Figure 15.1 VAT rates in the EC – bands proposed by the European Commission and current rates in the member states (1987)

Source: CEC, *Europe Without Frontiers* (Information 1987, p. 51); COM (87) 325–8.

tiers are abolished, without prior harmonization of tax rates, that the distortions arising primarily from fiscal factors can be measured. We have also seen that, even in a federation as strong as the United States, the equalization of tax rates has not been necessary. Moreover, in the case of excise duties, the system prevailing after 1986 ensured that duties were charged where the goods were sold since exports were duty free; thus, for those dutiable goods mainly purchased by consumers, such as alcoholic drinks and tobacco products, that system provided fiscal neutrality with respect to the location of production, even though the member states applied very different levels of duty (Smith, 1988, p. 154). Be that as it may, the relevant criterion for judging the position of the Commission is the dynamic one concerning where the EC wanted to go after 1992, and the EU has since then adopted the Maastricht Treaty which was supposed to lead to, *inter alia*, an EMU, a common defence policy and closer political co-operation, but the Amsterdam Treaty of June 1997, although it confirms EMU, now a reality for the 11 member nations using the Euro as their single currency, says nothing specific on the last two (see Chapter 2). Thus it was perfectly in order for the Commission to have asked for an approximation of rates. The piecemeal analyses carried out by most economists seem to centre around what is happening at a particular time, but the Commission is entrusted with introducing measures consistent with EU policies as well as with initiating efforts for the further integration of the EU, even though this role has formally been taken over by the European Council; hence its perspective is, rightly, much wider and goes further into the future: reaching the summit requires looking out for the precipices.

Given this background, one needs to ask about what has actually been happening. It would be both tedious and unnecessary to provide here every single directive or communication that has been passed by the EU in this respect. Therefore, all that I intend to do is to go through the latest developments; those interested in knowing every single detail can do so by simply following the appropriate directives by glancing at the latest issue of the *Bulletin of the European Union*, the *Official Journal of the European Union* and the *Annual General Report of the Activities of the European Union*, and then tracing back to the year in question.

Since the late 1980s, the EU has made considerable progress with tax harmonization. With regard to VAT, on 19 October 1992, the Council adopted a directive (92/77/EEC) on the approximation of rates, which is a follow-up to an earlier directive (91/680/EEC) supplementing the common system, setting the standard rate of VAT at no less than 15% and the optional and reduced rates at no less than 5%, and abolishing the increased rates. Provision has also been made for certain zero and extra-low rates to be retained for a transitional period.

As to turnover taxes, on 2 July 1992, the Commission adopted a proposal for a directive designed to abolish certain derogations in Article 1(1) of Directive 77/388/EEC of 1977 and the second subparagraph of Article 1(1) of Directive 89/465/EEC of 1989. The aim of this proposal for amending the sixth directive on VAT is to revise and generally to limit the derogations from the common system granted to the member countries in respect of the basis of assessment in order to move closer to a uniform basis of assessment.

In the case of excise duties and other indirect taxes, major progress was also achieved. On 25 February 1992, the Council adopted a directive (92/12/EEC) on the general arrangements for products subject to excise duty and on the holding and movement of such products, which lays down the rules for movement within the EU of products subject to excise duty (fuel, tobacco and spirits) and the arrangements for the collection of excise duties once border controls have been abolished. As regards trade, the new arrangements are based in particular on the movement of products via tax warehouses established throughout the EU. Under the directive, from 1 January 1993, individuals should have been able to purchase in other member countries dutiable products for their personal use at the rates obtaining there. In contrast to the harmonized VAT system, these general arrangements are definitive. On 14 December 1992, the Council adopted a directive (92/108/EEC) designed to clarify the previous one, but without altering its content or substance.

On 19 October 1992, the Council also adopted directives (92/78/EEC to 92/84/EEC) on the harmonization of excise duty structures and on the approximation of excise duty rates on cigarettes and other manufactured tobacco, on mineral oils and on spirits and other alcoholic beverages, together with a decision (92/510/EEC) authorizing member countries to continue to apply to certain mineral oils, when used for specific purposes, existing reduced rates of excise duty or exemptions from them.

On 19 February 1992, the Commission adopted a proposal for a directive on the excise duty rates applicable to motor fuels from agricultural sources (biofuels) with a view to bringing about an EU-wide reduction in the rates applied to such products. The proposal is based on the principle that biofuels can help to improve the EU's security of energy supplies, that they are more environmentally friendly than other fuels and that they will encourage the growing of non-food crops on land subject to compulsory set-aside in line with the reform of the CAP initiated by the MacSharry package (see Chapter 11).

In the case of corporation taxes, the Commission submitted a communication on guidelines on 24 June 1992 (CEC, 1992l). This was based on the report by the Committee of Independent Experts on Company Taxation, chaired by the ex-Finance Minister of Denmark, Onno Ruding, which was submitted on 18 March, and which endorsed the Commission's own position as indicated in its April 1990 report. Those guidelines were approved by the Council on 23 November and by the Economic and Social Committee on 24 November. The gist of these guidelines is that priority should be given to the abolition of double taxation of cross-border flows as a means of eliminating the competitive distortions stemming from tax disparities between the member countries.

In addition to the recommendation for eliminating double taxation, the Commission examined the Ruding Committee's proposals relating to the rates, the base and the systems of corporation tax. Although the Commission felt that some of these suggestions went beyond what is strictly necessary at the EU level (the subsidiarity principle suggests that there is no need to harmonize the system itself), it agreed that the idea of a minimum EU rate of 30% for corporation tax is worth thorough examination. It felt that the same sentiment applied to their recommendations regarding the tax base for company profits and tax incentives for promoting research and environmental protection.

Between 1992 and 1996, there were no fundamental or major changes; the developments were in the nature of refinements, adjustments, adaptations or fine-tuning. These can be followed in the manner suggested above. However, Table 15.7 gives the picture with regard to corporation tax and VAT rates and Table 15.8 somewhat duplicates the corporation tax rates for 1996, but demonstrates their real complexity; there were very minor variations in excise duties relative to those given in Table 15.6, so all one needs here is a specification of the EU minimum standards, i.e. a member nation's excise duty may not be lower than this rate:

1. *Cigarettes and other manufactured tobacco products.* The overall minimum duty (specific duty plus *ad valorem* duty excluding VAT) is fixed at 57% of the retail selling price, inclusive of all taxes for cigarettes in the most popular price category, while the specific duty (per unit of product) must be between 5% and 55% of the total tax burden (total excise duty plus VAT) on cigarettes in the most popular price category.

   The rates fixed for cigars and cigarillos and for smoking tobacco may be *ad valorem*, specific or composite rates. The overall excise duty inclusive of all taxes, expressed as a percentage or for a given number of items, may not be lower than:
   – 5% of the retail selling price, or 7 ECUs per 1000 items or per kilogram (kg), for cigars and cigarillos;
   – 30% of the retail selling price, or 20 ECUs per kg, for fine-cut smoking tobacco intended for the rolling of cigarettes;
   – 20% of the retail selling price, or 15 ECUs per kg, for other smoking tobaccos (pipe tobacco).

2. *Alcohol and alcoholic beverages.* The minimum rates of duty are:
   – 0.748 ECUs per hl/degree Plato or 1.87 ECU per hl/degree of alcohol for beer;

Table 15.7 EU corporation tax and VAT rates, 1996

	Corporation tax (%)	VAT (%) Standard	Reduced
Austria	34	20	10
Belgium	39	21	12, 6
Denmark	34	25	0
Finland	28	22	6, 12, 17
France	36⅔	20.6	5.5, 2.1
Germany	45, 30	15	7
Greece	35	18	4, 8
Ireland	38	21	0.25, 12.5
Italy	37	19	4, 10, 16
Luxembourg	33	15	3, 6, 12
Netherlands	35	12.5	6
Portugal	36	16	5
Spain	35	16	7, 4
Sweden	28	25	0
United Kingdom	33, 35, 25	17.5	8

The rationales for the different rates are explained in the text.
Source: Various EU.

- 0 ECU per hl for still and sparkling wine;
- 45 ECUs per hl for intermediate products;
- 550 ECUs per hl of pure alcohol and alcohol contained in other beverages.

However, member nations which apply to the last category of products a rate exceeding 1000 ECUs per hl of pure alcohol may not reduce their national rate. In addition, member states which apply to those products a rate exceeding 1000 ECUs per hl of pure alcohol may not reduce their national rate below 1000 ECUs.

3. *Mineral oils*. The minimum rates are:
   - 337 ECUs per 1000 litres on leaded petrol;
   - 287 ECUs per 1000 litres on unleaded petrol;

Table 15.8 EU taxes on company earnings in 1996 (%)

Member state / CT system	CT (on retained profits)[a]	Dividend relief — Particulars	Dividend relief — As a percentage of classical tax burden[b]	Ordinary top PT[a]	CT + PT on distributed profits[c]	Top PT on interest[d]	Top PT on capital gains[e,f] — Ordinary shares	Top PT on capital gains[e,f] — Substantial holdings
		Tax credit as a fraction of net dividend						
Imputation system								
Finland	28	$\frac{7}{8}$	100	57.5	28	28**	28	28
France	36⅔	½ (basic CT)	91	60.2	61.5	19.4*	19.4	19.4
Germany	56[g]	⅗ (CG/CT)	59	57	64.4	57*	–	π[h]
Ireland[i]	38 (10)	$\frac{23}{77}$ ($\frac{1}{18}$)	49	48	58.1 (50.6)	42*	40	40[j]
Italy	53.2	$\frac{9}{63}$ (CG/CT)	66	51	58.7	12.5**	15	25
UK	33	¼	51	40	49.8	40*	40	40
Tax credit method		*Tax credit*						
Portugal	39.6	60% of CT[k]	91	40	42.2	20**	–	–
Spain	36	40% of net div.[l]	71	56	60.6	56*	π[m]	π[m]
Special PT rate		*PT rate*						
Austria[n]	34	22	109	50	48.5	22**	–	Half of PT
Belgium[n]	40.2	25[o]	135	60.6	55.1	15**[o]	–	–
Denmark	34	40[p]	105	61	60.4	61	40	40
Greece	35	0	152	45	35	15**	–	–
Luxembourg[n]	40.3	Half of PT	62	51.3	55.6	51.3	–	25.6
Sweden	28	30	152	56	49.6	30	30	30
Classical system		*No relief*						
Netherlands	35	–[q]	0	60	74	60	–	20

Abbreviations have the following meaning:

CT = company income tax; PT = personal income tax; CG = central government; π = reduced rate.

Some information may be incomplete or out of date.

Percentages have been rounded to one decimal place.

[a] Rates include surcharges, surtaxes or profit (income) taxes levied by local governments (if different, an average or representative rate has been chosen). Net wealth or capital taxes – levied in Germany, Italy and Luxembourg – are not included.

[b] Measured against the combined CT+PT under the classical system, according to the formula

$$\text{Dividend relief} = \frac{\text{CT+PT without relief} - \text{Actual CT+PT}}{\text{CT+PT without relief} - \text{CT+PT with full relief}}$$

[c] Calculated as CT + [(1 − CT)PT] *minus* any tax credit, if available. Under the dual income tax in Finland, the top PT rate on capital income equals the CT rate of 28%. In countries with special PT rates on dividend income, obviously the special PT rate is taken as the top PT rate in calculating the CT+PT on distributions. Dividend payments to residents are subject to withholding tax in Austria (22%), Belgium (25%), Denmark (25%), Germany (25%), Italy (12.5%), Luxembourg (25%), the Netherlands (25%), Portugal (12.5%) and Spain (25%).

[d] An asterisk (*) denotes that interest payments are subject to a withholding tax; a double asterisk (**) means that the withholding tax is final. Generally, royalty payments to residents are not subject to withholding tax, except in France (15%) and the UK (25%).

[e] Usually, capital gains realized by companies are subject to CT at the normal rate; generally, the tax is deferred if the gain is reinvested.

[f] Capital gains are adjusted for inflation in Ireland, Italy, Luxembourg and the UK. Alternatively, short-term and long-term gains are taxed at different (effective) rates in Denmark, France and Spain as well as in Ireland. PT rates shown are for long-term capital gains. Various countries exempt small amounts of capital gains.

[g] A lower rate of 30% applies to distributed profits. This rate is 42% if the 7.5% surcharge and the 17% tax-exclusive, deductible, local tax are included. This form of partial dividend relief at company level is called the split-rate system. Overall, however, imputation is the dominant feature of Germany's CT/PT system.

[h] Capital gains up to DM 30 million on substantial holdings (more than 25% of the share capital) are taxed at reduced rates.

[i] The rates/fractions given in parentheses apply to profits/tax credits of qualifying manufacturing and processing companies.

[j] In Ireland, the capital gains tax rate is 27% on the disposal of shares in unquoted trading companies held for at least five years.

[k] In Portugal, 60% of the underlying CT is creditable against the PT without gross-up. Alternatively, a special (final) PT rate of 12.5% applies to net dividend income. This provides dividend relief at 70%, distributions being taxed at a CT+PT rate of 47.2%.

[l] In Spain, 40% of the net dividend is grossed up and credited against the PT. However, there is no compensatory tax on distributions out of profits not subject to CT.

[m] Reduced rates are related to the length of the holding period and the amount of other income.

[n] Austria, Belgium and Luxembourg permit a (limited) deduction from personal income of expenditures on the purchase of new shares.

[o] In Belgium, the PT rate is 15% on dividends paid on shares issued after 1 January 1994 and 25% on interest paid on bonds issued before 1 March 1990.

[p] Share income not exceeding DKr 33 800 (DKr 67 600 for married couples) is taxed at 25%.

[q] Df 1000 dividend income is exempt from PT (Df 2000 for married couples).

Source: International Bureau of Fiscal Documentation, *European Taxation* (Amsterdam: loose-leaf).

- 245 ECUs per 1000 litres on gas oil used as a propellant;
- 18 ECUs per 1000 litres on gas oil used for other purposes;
- 18 ECUs per 1000 litres on heating gas oil;
- 13 ECUs per 1000 kg on heavy fuel oil;
- 100 ECUs per 1000 kg on LPG and methane used as a propellant;
- 36 ECUs per 1000 kg on LPG and methane used for other purposes;
- 0 ECU per 1000 kg on LPG and methane used for heating purposes;
- 245 ECUs per 1000 litres on kerosene used as a propellant;
- 18 ECUs per 1000 litres on kerosene used for other purposes;
- 0 ECU per 1000 litres on kerosene used for heating purposes.

Since 1996 refinement and fine-tuning have continued. Following the recommendations in 1997 of a Taxation Policy Group, chaired by Mr Mario Monti, a package was introduced in 1998 with the aim of tackling harmful tax competition between the member states and, in particular, of reversing the trend towards higher taxation of labour as a means of compensating for the lower tax burden on more mobile factors of production. The package had three elements:

- a code of conduct on company taxation (this was established by the Primarolo Group in April 1999);
- an EU solution to the taxation of income from savings; and
- measures to eliminate withholding taxes on cross-border payments of interest and royalties between firms.

The Helsinki Council reiterated that all citizens resident in an EU member state should pay the tax due on all their income from savings and appointed a high-level working group to study the most effective way of implementation and report by June 2000.

Also, the Council decided, within the context of the SEM, that tax- and duty-free sales for intra-EU travellers should be abolished as from 1 January 1999; this policy came into effect on 1 July of the same year. Moreover, on 5 May 1999 the Council set the threshold for the standard VAT rate at 15% until 31 December 2000, and on 25 October adopted a directive which makes it possible, subject to certain provisos, for member states so wishing to reduce VAT rates on highly labour-intensive services as from 1 January 2000.

15.5   Conclusion

In conclusion, it should be emphasized that the lack of fundamental progress with tax harmonization in the EU, especially during the period prior to the adoption of the SEA, should not come as a surprise. There are three basic reasons for this. First, lest it be forgotten, the EU stands for the harmonized integration of some of the oldest countries in the world, with very diverse and extremely complicated economic systems, and this diversity and complexity is increasing with the enlargement (and potential enlargement) of the EU. Second, tax harmonization is intimately connected with the role played by the government in controlling the economy (a role subject to great debate and controversy, with the neo-Keynesians and mone-tarists standing poles apart; the latter not only completely dismissing the import-ance of the government's role in this respect, but also claiming that it is actually detrimental) and, since this role depends on a complicated package of taxes, it should be apparent that the separate harmonizing of the different components of the package is not only extremely difficult, but also misguided. Finally, and more importantly, tax harmonization, or at least the complex and sensitive elements within it, is very closely linked with the question of monetary integration and pol-itical unification – see Chapter 6 for a technical argument on the inseparability of these issues. It would therefore be naïve to expect substantial progress in tax har-monization, without similar progress in these other fields. The full implementation of the Maastricht Treaty on European Union and its endorsement by the Amsterdam Treaty, leading to the adoption of economic and monetary union (EMU), with the Euro as the single currency, by 1999, for 11 member countries, one common EU defence policy and closer political co-operation, will bring the EU closer to becoming a 'United States of Europe'. As we have seen, this process has-tened the need for fiscal harmonization, but not necessarily for tax-rate equaliza-tion, something that does not exist, and need not prevail, even in the United States.

Note

1. The first (67/227/EEC – this is the official notation where '67' refers to the year, '227' to the number, and 'EEC' to the legislating authority, but in this note I shall provide only the number) and second (228) VAT directives (all the directives mentioned in this note are issued by the Council) were issued on 11 April 1967; they are related to the harmo-nization of legislation in the EU member states – see *Official Journal of the European Communities* (*Union* from the end of 1993; hereafter, *OJ*), no. L 71, 14 April 1967. The sixth (388) VAT directive of 17 May 1977 was also concerned with harmonization in the member states (*OJ*, nos. L 145, 13 June 1977 and L 149, 17 June 1977).

    The minor directives include the eighth (1072), of 6 December 1979, which is con-cerned with foreign taxable persons (*OJ*, no. L 331, 27 December 1979) and the tenth (386), of 31 July 1984, concerning the application of VAT to the hiring out of movable tangible property (*OJ*, no. L 208, 3 August 1984).

    The latest issue of draft directives is rather complex, and thus the following is just a sample:

    – Proposal (referred to as 'COM' for communication) for a twelfth VAT directive con-cerning a common system of VAT, expenditure on which tax is not deductible (pro-fessional and private usage), COM (82) 870, 25 January 1983 and COM (84) 84, 16 February 1984 – *OJ*, no. C 37 of 10 February 1983 and no. C 56 of 29 February 1984.

    – Proposal for a thirteenth VAT directive relating to the refund of VAT to taxable persons not established in EU territory (in parallel to the eighth VAT directive), COM (82) 443 of 15 July 1982 and COM (83) 413 of 24 June 1983 – see *OJ*, no. C 223, 27 August 1982 and no. C 196, 23 July 1983.

    – Proposal for a seventh VAT directive concerning a common system of VAT for used goods, COM (78) 735 of 6 January 1978 and COM (79) 249 of 4 May 1979 – see *OJ*, no. C 26, 1 February 1978 and no. C 136, 31 May 1979.

    – Proposal for a sixteenth VAT directive concerning the implementation at the EU level of the ruling by the EU Court of Justice regarding the avoidance of double taxation and of used goods imported by a consumer in one EU member nation from a consumer in another, COM (84) 318 of 18 July 1984 and COM (86) 163 of 25 March 1986 – see *OJ*, no. C 226, 28 August 1984 and no. C 96, 24 April 1986.

- The eighteenth VAT directive concerning the abolition of certain derogations, which are still authorized within the framework of the sixth VAT directive, by 1 January 1992 at the very latest, COM (84) 649 of 30 November 1984 – see *OJ*, no. C 347, 29 December 1984.
- Proposal for a nineteenth VAT directive regarding clarifications to the sixth directive, COM (84) 648 of 22 November 1984 and 6 December 1984 – see *OJ*, no. C 347, 29 December 1984.

Appendix   An illustration of the imputation system

To illustrate how the system works, consider a shareholder who has received a cheque for £100 as his/her annual dividend. With a corporation tax rate of 52%, the company has had to use £208 of pre-tax profits to pay this dividend, with the balance of £108 (52% of £208) going to the United Kingdom's Department of Inland Revenue (UKDIR) in corporation tax. Part of this corporation tax bill is in fact prepayment of income tax at the basic rate on dividends which is deducted at source, and this component is paid to the UKDIR when dividends are distributed. Since this is usually before the date when the companies are called upon to pay corporation tax on the year's profits, this element of tax is called 'advanced corporation tax' (ACT), but in fact it is more properly regarded not as a company tax but as deduction at source of standard rate income tax on dividends. The remaining tax payments to the UKDIR are described as 'mainstream' corporation tax. It is these payments which constitute the effective corporate tax burden, since the amounts which are described as ACT would be paid, as income tax, even if corporation tax were completely abolished.

The essence of the imputation system is that when the shareholder receives his/her dividend cheque for £100 (s)he is deemed to have already paid income tax at the basic rate on the dividend. If all shareholders paid income tax at the basic rate that would be the end of the matter. However, some shareholders have higher marginal tax rates, and others lower, and this complicates matters somewhat because one has to calculate the amount of extra tax, or of refund, which is due. To do this, one should ask the question: what dividend before tax would I need in order to finish up with £100 after payment of the basic rate of income tax? Suppose the basic rate of income tax is 33⅓%. Then to end up with £100 after tax, one would need £150 before tax. This is the notional pre-tax dividend which the shareholder receives, the 'grossed-up' dividend, and £50 is the notional tax which one has paid.

If all this seems rather abstract to the shareholder, then (s)he should think again, for with the dividend cheque for £100 will come a piece of paper representing tax credit of £50, exactly equal to the notional tax that has just been described. On the tax form, the shareholder must enter the notional pre-tax dividend of £150 (which is equivalent to the value of the dividend of £100 plus the tax credit of £50) which will then be added to the shareholder's other income to calculate his/her total income tax bill. But since (s)he is deemed to have already paid the notional tax, (s)he can use the tax credit as an offset against his/her income tax liability. If our shareholder pays tax at the basic rate, the credit eliminates his/her liability and (s)he can forget about the imputation system of corporation tax. If the shareholder's marginal income tax rate is 60%, then his/her tax liability on the dividend is £90 minus the tax credit of £50. The shareholder will have to send a cheque for the balance of £40 to the UKDIR. However, if the recipient of the dividend cheque were a charity or pension fund, and hence not liable to tax, the boot would be on the other foot and the UKDIR would have to refund the tax credit of £50 to the shareholder. Of the pre-tax profit of £208, a basic rate taxpayer would receive £100, an effective rate of 52%, a charity would receive £150, a tax rate of 28%, and an individual with an income tax rate of 60% would receive £60, an effective tax rate of 71.2%.

16 The General Budget

A. M. EL-AGRAA

As stated in the previous chapter, the General Budget of the European Union (EU Budget hereafter but EC Budget where appropriate) forms an integral and very important part of the EU's fiscal policy. Recall that, very widely interpreted, fiscal policy comprises a whole corpus of public finance issues, and that there are at least two basic elements to fiscal policy: the instruments available to the government for fiscal policy purposes (the total tax structure) and the overall impact of the joint manoeuvring of the instruments (the role played by the budget). The former was tackled in the previous chapter; the purpose of this chapter is to explain briefly the nature of the EU Budget, to discuss recent developments concerning it, to demonstrate why it has been inequitable and to suggest ways in which it could be made less so.

Before doing so, however, one should provide an answer to an often asked question: why does the EU need a general budget? The answer is that it is natural for any group of economically integrated countries to have one. For example, since the revenues from the common external tariffs (CETs) are the property of the Union (see Chapters 5 and 6), then the methods for both their collection and disposal should be the collective responsibility of the Union. Also, any scheme that decides to create joint institutions needs to finance them on a communal basis. Moreover, when such a scheme opts for common policies, it must also collectively provide for them. Given what is stated in Chapters 1 and 2, it should be apparent that all such elements apply to the EU; hence the need for the EU Budget.

16.1 Budget rules and procedure

The EU has laid down a set of rules (see Articles 199–280 of the Amsterdam Treaty, which include amendments to the original Part Five, Title II of the EEC Treaty) to be followed with regard to the preparation and administration of its budget. The first of these is one which since 1957 has distinguished the EU Budget from most national budgets: revenues and expenditures must be in balance. Although this rule may appear to have been flouted, careful consideration will show otherwise. For example, by the end of 1986, the ECSC had extended lending to member countries, through borrowing in the open market, to the total of 12 billion ECU, Euratom lent a total of 2.4 billion ECU and the EIB engaged in activities needing 50 billion ECU. Also, the EU borrowed to assist those members in balance of payments problems during the oil crises. However, all of these were in the nature of capital transactions and financially self-supporting; hence they did not breach the principle of a balanced budget.

The EU has a very strict procedure and timetable to be followed for the adoption of the budget for each financial year. The financial year (hereafter, simply year) begins on 1 January and ends on 31 December. Before 1 July, each EU institution is obliged to draw up estimates of its expected expenditure for the year. The Commission then consolidates these and, together with revenue estimates, presents them as a 'preliminary draft budget' to which it attaches its own opinion, which may include different estimates. The presentation should be made to the Council which must receive it by not later than 1 September of the year immediately preceding that of implementation. If the Council wishes to make changes to the draft budget, it must consult the Commission and, where appropriate, the other institutions. Acting by QMV, the Council then forwards it to the European Parliament (EP), which must receive it not later than 5 October of the same year. If the EP either approves the budget as presented or simply does nothing with it within 45 days of its receipt, the budget becomes final.

However, the EP has the right to make amendments (see Chapter 2), provided they are supported by the majority of its members. It can also propose to the Council modifications to expenditures emanating from the Treaty or from acts adopted in accordance therewith if they get the absolute majority of votes cast. Then, within the 45 days, the draft budget, together with the amendments and/or modifications, should be sent back to the Council.

After discussions with the Commission and, where appropriate, the other institutions concerned, the Council can, by QMV, modify any of the amendments adopted by the EP. With regard to EP modifications, the Council has three options: if the modification does not increase the expenditure by an institution (increase in one area being matched by a decrease elsewhere), the Council, by QMV, can reject it, otherwise it stands; if the modification increases such expenditure, the Council, by QMV, can accept it, otherwise it stands; and if the Council rejects both options, it can, by QMV, either retain the amount specified in the original draft budget or fix another.

If, within 15 days of the receipt of the draft budget by the Council from the EP, the Council has not modified any of the EP's amendments and has accepted all EP modifications, the budget becomes final. The Council is obliged to inform the EP of the positions it has taken over the amendments/modifications. However, if the Council has modified one or more of the EP's amendments or modified or rejected the EP's modifications, the modified draft budget should go back to the EP within 15 days. The Council is obliged to let the EP know of the results of its deliberations. Also, within 15 days, the EP may amend or reject the modifications made by the Council to its own amendments, provided it gets the majority vote of its members and 60% of the votes cast. The EP may then adopt the budget accordingly. If the EP has not acted within this period, the budget becomes final.

When this procedure is completed, the President of the EP is to declare that the budget has been finally adopted. However, when important justifications exist, the EP may, by the majority vote of its members and 60% of the votes cast, reject the draft budget and ask for the submission of a new one.

One may ask: what happens if the budget is not finalized by the end of December? The answer is to be found in Article 273 of the Amsterdam Treaty, but its origin goes further back: 'If, at the beginning of a financial year, the budget has not been voted, a sum equivalent to no more than one-twelfth of the budget appropriations [see below] of the preceding financial year may be spent each month in respect of any chapter or other subdivision.' This is tantamount to the adoption of a budget of the same size as the previous year.

16.2 Expenditures

The EU Budget expenditures are grouped into two categories: compulsory and non-compulsory. The former is the expenditure emanating essentially from commitments in the treaties (such as the price support provided by the European Agricultural Guarantee and Guidance Fund – EAGGF – and certain types of foreign aid to third countries), while the latter arises from the operational areas of the EU Budget (such as some of the expenditures of the European Regional Development Fund – ERDF – and the European Social Fund – ESF). Compulsory expenditures have a priority claim, which is why the EU Budget is necessarily 'functional', i.e. the EU has been endowed with revenues to discharge certain specific functions arising from well-defined activities it was required to undertake either in the original treaty or as subsequently agreed by the EU Council, including, of course, any financial commitments arising from the adoption of the SEA and the Maastricht and Amsterdam treaties.

It should also be pointed out that the EU Budget expenditures are classified into two other types: payment appropriations and commitment appropriations. Payment appropriations define expenditure to be actually incurred during the financial year under consideration. Part of the payment may be in settlement of commitments made previously. Commitment appropriations define the ceiling on resources to be pledged in the current financial year. Part of the payment of commitment appropriations may be spread over subsequent years. As one would expect, the 'commitments' have always been in excess of the actual 'payments'. Note that the distinction originated in the Euratom Treaty (Article 176), but was not applied to other areas of expenditure until Regulation 76/919/ECSC, EEC, Euratom of 21 December 1976 was approved. Even then it was agreed as applicable only in some areas of expenditure, with many other areas dependent on a single set of 'undifferentiated' appropriations for payment during the year under consideration. In addition, special exemptions from the payment rules apply, for example to the EAGGF guarantee section in case there are difficulties in disbursing actual payments within the financial year.

The EU Budget provides for two types of expenditure. First, there are the administrative expenses (staff salaries, costs of providing and disbursing information, etc.) of the institutions of the EU: the Commission, the Council, the European Parliament, the Court of Justice, the European Coal and Steel Community (ECSC), the ESF, the ERDF, etc. (see Chapter 2). Second, there are the operational expenditures of the EU Commission, such as the intervention and guidance expenses of EAGGF, ERDF support grants and 'food aid'. The EU Budget also provides for a miscellaneous collection of 'minor' expenditures.

In 1985, when the White Paper introducing the internal market was issued, the EC Budget amounted to about 28.4 billion ECU (see Table 16.1), which was roughly equivalent to 18 billion pounds sterling (then, 1 ECU £0.567748) or \$21 billion (then, 1 ECU = £0.734949) or ¥5,206 billion (then, 1 ECU = ¥183.113). The total for 1986 was 31.8 billion ECU for the EC of nine and 35 billion ECU for the EC of 12, with the expenditure on the EAGGF guarantee section of the CAP falling to

Table 16.1 The EU Budget, 1986–99

Year	Total appropriations (million ECU)	Total payments (million ECU)	EAGGF guarantee (% of payments)
1986	36 052	35 174	62.9
1987	37 415	36 313	63.2
1988	45 344	43 820	62.8
1989	47 268	45 690	56.2
1990	49 047	46 790	53.6
1991	59 370	56 085	56.3
1992	66 118	62 827	49.7
1993	69 058	65 523	52.0
1994	73 444	70 013	52.1
1995	80 892	76 527	49.6
1996	86 525	81 888	49.9
1997	89 137	82 366	49.5
1998	94 744	90 581	47.8
1999	99 401	94 032	46.9

Sources: Various issues of the *General Report of the Activities of the European Communities* and *General Report of the Activities of the European Union* supplemented by data from various Eurostat publications.

62.9%; the 59.7% for 1982 was by then the smallest ever expenditure on this section of the EAGGF. Note that the figures are in current, not constant, prices, but this does not matter since no analysis of growth rates is being considered here, especially since the total actual EU Budget is less than 1.2% of EU GDP (see below), its growth rate in nominal terms has been low and the number of member countries over the relevant period covered in the table has increased from nine to 12 (1986) to 15 (1995). The reader who is particularly interested in data at constant prices may note that, for example, the figure for total appropriations for 1988 (45.3 billion ECU) would have increased to only 52.8 billion ECU in 1992 instead of the nominal figure of 66.1 billion ECU. However, some pertinent points, such as the accumulation of commitments which had to be paid and some disturbing developments in the EC Budget itself are considered in detail in section 16.7.

The total size of the EU Budget in 1999 is of the same order of magnitude as that of a large UK department such as Education and Science. In US terms, it is equivalent to about 90% of state and local expenditure on higher education. In terms of Japan, it is equal to about 80% of the expenditure by the Ministry of Posts and Telecommunications. The allegations regarding a very powerful EU Commission are thus ill-founded. Moreover, the suggestion that the EU has a large bureaucracy is also incorrect since only about 5% of the EU Budget is expenditure on administration and the EU Budget itself is limited to a maximum of 1.27% of EU GDP until 2006 (see section 16.7.3; the maximum was 1.2%, but the Edinburgh European Council of 11/12 December 1992 decided to raise this gradually, starting in 1993 and reaching the limit by 1999 – more on this below). However, one should add that this is not a justification for the vast number of translators and interpreters employed by the EU to assist with its official publications and meetings; it is high time the EU decided to reduce its official languages to a sensible number instead of the present system of using all the main EU languages.

16.3 Revenues

Turning to the financing side, the EU Budget revenues come from gross contributions termed 'own resources', i.e. the EU has its own independent and clearly defined revenue sources such that the EU member nations pay to it what actually belongs to it. This principle of 'own resources' was adopted after the Council Decision of 21 April 1970, and in 1980 fully replaced the previous system which was entirely based on national contributions determined largely in accordance with the member nations' relative economic strength.

Before the introduction of more radical changes in the EC Budget in 1987 (see section 16.6), there were three basic categories of own resources:

1. Agricultural and sugar levies.

2. Customs duties, i.e. the proceeds from industrial tariffs on imports from third countries.

3. Until 1984, up to 1% of the common VAT base yield (see Table 16.2).

If more than 1% of the VAT base yield is required, further legislation ratified by all the member nations becomes necessary – see below.

These revenues are collected by the member states, through their appropriate national authorities, on behalf of the EU. It has been the practice to allow the member states to retain 10% of the revenues collected as a charge for their services for the EU, but this percentage has recently been raised to 25% – see section 16.7.3.

16.4 Net contributions

Table 16.3 gives gross contributions and gross receipts in 1980, together with net receipts for the period 1979–81, broken down by member nation; the choice of this period is to highlight the reasons for the budgetary battles during the early 1980s (later developments are considered below). It should be clear from the table that the United Kingdom and West Germany provided the largest share of gross contributions with regard to all three categories of the EC Budget revenues; the levies and tariffs categories are easily explained in terms of the two countries' large extra-EC

Table 16.2 Revenues of the EU General Budget, 1982–99 (%)

Revenue	1982	1983	1984	1985	1986	1987	1988	1989	1990	1991	1992	1993	1994	1995	1996	1997	1998	1999
Agricultural and sugar levies	12.2	11.7	9.1	7.4	6.8	8.6	6.0	5.5	4.5	4.9	3.8	3.3	3.5	2.9	2.5	2.4	2.2	2.5
Customs duties	31.6	34.6	30.1	30.2	24.3	24.7	21.4	23.3	24.7	22.7	21.1	18.7	18.9	18.5	16.1	16.9	14.8	15.5
VAT	54.6	52.0	55.2	54.4	66.1	64.7	55.1	59.5	59.3	54.0	58.1	54.3	55.2	52.9	43.9	43.2	40.9	35.5
Financial contributions	0.9	0.8	–	–	0.6	0.6	0.5	–	–	–	–	–	–	–	–	–	–	–
GNP-based own resources	–	–	–	–	–	–	14.0	6.5	0.2	13.2	14.0	25.3	28.1	19.3	26.0	34.1	43.0	45.9
Miscellaneous revenue	0.7	0.9	1.8[a]	1.0	0.9	1.1	0.9	0.8	0.9	0.8	0.8	0.8	0.9	0.8	0.9	1.1	0.8	0.8
Advances from member states	–	–	3.8	7.0	–	–	1.2	–	–	–	–	0.0	0.0	0.0	0.0	0.0	0.0	0.0
Balance of VAT and GNP-based own resources from previous years	–	–	–	–	1.3	0.3	0.9	1.8	3.7	2.1	0.1	–1.7	–5.9	–1.1	1.0	–1.4	0.0	0.0
Budget balance from previous year	–	–	–	–	–	–	–	2.6	9.6	5.1	4.6	1.5	1.5	8.8	11.4	5.5	0.0	1.6
Own resources collection costs	–	–	–	–	–	–	–	–	–2.9	–2.8	–2.5	–2.2	–2.2	–2.1	–1.8	–2.0	–1.7	0.8
Total	100.0	100.0	100.0	100.0	100.0	100.0	100.0	100.0	100.0	100.0	100.0	100.0	100.0	100.0	100.0	100.0	100.0	100.0

[a] The figure includes the surplus from 1983 (307.1 million ECU) and VAT/GNP balances corrections (–111.7 million ECU).
Sources: Bulletin of the European Union, various issues; General Report on the Activities of the European Union, various issues; and various Eurostat publications.

Table 16.3 EC Budget, 1980

	Gross contributions, 1980 (% share)	Gross contributions by source, 1980			Gross receipts 1980 (% share)	Net receipts (million ECU)		
		Agricultural levies	Industrial tariffs	VAT		1979	1980[a]	1981[a]
Belgium and Luxembourg	6.1	11.0	7	5	11.9	+394	+250	+351
Denmark	2.4	2.0	2	3	4.4	+246	+174	+157
France	20.0	13.0	15	24	20.0	−50	+41	+102
West Germany	30.1	20.0	30	31	23.5	−924	−1177	−1260
Ireland	0.9	0.5	1	1	3.8	+352	+372	+340
Italy	11.5	20.5	9	14	16.8	+345	+329	+215
Netherlands	8.4	15.0	9	6	10.5	+186	+215	+81
United Kingdom	20.5	19.0	27	16	8.7	−549	−203	−56

[a] The 1980 and 1981 'Net receipts' allow for refunds to the United Kingdom (see Table 16.4 for further details).
Source: Wallace (1980), and various publications by the EC Commission.

trade. The table also shows West Germany and the United Kingdom to have been the only net losers with regard to net receipts; this was the main reason for the UK budgetary battles with the EC, particularly since the United Kingdom was the second largest net contributor when its position in the league of EC GDP was third from the bottom. This anomaly arose simply because a large percentage of the EC Budget expenditures falls on agriculture when the size of the agricultural sector is not strictly related to GDP (Denmark with a large agricultural sector had the highest per capita income within the EC) and because VAT contributions, which are to a large extent related to GDP (see the previous chapter and Nevin, 1988), form only just over half of the total EC Budget revenues.

16.5 Budgetary transfers

If the EU Budget is to be regarded as the 'embryo centre of a federal system' (Brown, in the first two editions of this book), its size relative to EU GDP (just over 1%) means that it is at a very early stage in its development – more on this below. However, because the EU Budget expenditures are still dominated by agricultural spending, it does play a significant role in the transfer of resources between the member nations; hence the British budgetary quarrels with the rest of the EC during the early 1980s. Discussion of this aspect has been very disappointing indeed; it concentrated on the CAP when a 'proper' evaluation of the extent of transfers should have included a similar treatment of industrial products. For example, if a member nation ceases to import a manufactured product from outside the EU and replaces it with imports from a partner nation, that country will contribute less to the EU Budget revenues (reduced proceeds from industrial tariffs); but since this act is one of 'trade diversion' (see Chapter 5), the country will pay more per unit of that product in comparison with the pre-membership situation. This element of transfer of resources must surely be included in any proper evaluation – simply to allege that, on balance, this element is 'mutually advantageous' to all the member nations (Cambridge Economic Policy Review, no. 5, April 1979) and hence that it is appropriate to ignore it, is to bypass the intricate issues raised with regard to the elimination of such effects – see El-Agraa (1989a), Mayes (1982) and Chapter 7. In short, in order to assess the budgetary effects of the transfer of resources between the member nations, one needs to take into account *all* the elements that enter into such calculations.

16.6 Developments prior to the SEA

The inequity of the EC Budget was the main reason for the heated quarrels between the United Kingdom and the rest of the EC during the early 1980s. Through protracted discussions and compromises, the United Kingdom managed to reduce its net contribution (see Table 16.4) – note that 2.0 billion ECU was equivalent to £1.1 billion, $1.5 billion or ¥366 billion. The 24–25 June 1984 Fontainebleau settlement, which asked for the raising of VAT to 1.4% in 1986, included paying the United Kingdom 1.0 billion ECU in 1984 and 66% of the *difference* between its VAT contribution and the EC Budget expenditures in the United Kingdom in subsequent years. This was later interpreted to mean rebates of 1.0 billion ECU for 1985 and 1.4 billion ECU for 1986. These provisions were conditional on agreement regarding some changes in the CAP. First, the agriculture ministers agreed on 31 March 1984 on a package which reduced the EC's common farm prices by 0.5% and relied on a system of quotas to restrict milk production from 103 million tonnes in 1983 to

Table 16.4 UK net contribution to the EC Budget before compensation, compensation and net contribution after compensation, 1980–3 (million ECU)

Year	Net contribution before compensation	Compensation	Net contribution after compensation
1980	1512	1175	337
1981	1419	1410	9
1982	2036	1079	957
1983	1900[a]	750	1150[a]

[a]These figures were approximate.
Source: Kindly supplied by Commissioner Christopher Tugendhat.

99.2 million and 98.4 million tonnes in 1984 and 1985 respectively; thereafter it was to be pegged for a further three years. Ireland, whose dairy production was equivalent to 9% of its GNP, was awarded a special dispensation in that its quota was actually increased (see Table 16.5); Greece (which was undergoing transition at the time) was the poorest EC member nation and was awarded treatment better than that of Ireland. Moreover, the quotas which already applied to sugar beet were extended to other surplus products such as cereals, oilseeds and processed tomatoes. In order to reduce wine production, new vines were banned until 1990. Finally, various production and consumption subsidies to livestock, butter, fruit and vegetables were reduced and the MCAs were to be phased out over four years (see Chapter 11).

The EC Commission felt that for 1985 the prices for most agricultural products should be kept unchanged, or, if they were to change, that the changes should be modest and not exceed 2%. For certain items, the Commission proposed significant reductions in prices, particularly for products where the guarantee threshold was exceeded. Indeed, the agreed package for 1985–6 included reductions in the prices of butter, beef/veal, sheepmeat and olive oil, with the target price for milk kept at the 1984–5 level.

These changes affected countries such as West Germany, the Netherlands and the United Kingdom by the full impact of the price cuts since they had positive MCAs. Countries with weak currencies found that the price cuts actually led to price rises ranging from 1.5% for Denmark to 17.6% for Greece (see Table 16.6). According to

Table 16.5 EC changes in milk production, 1984 (%)

	Milk quota
Belgium	−3.0
Denmark	−5.7
France	−2.0
West Germany	−6.7
Greece	+7.2
Ireland	+4.6
Italy	0.0
Luxembourg	+3.5
Netherlands	−6.2
United Kingdom	−6.5

Source: CEC (1984a).

Table 16.6 Price changes for the 1984–5 farm year

	Change in ECU (%)	Change in national currency (%)	1985 inflation forecast
Belgium	−0.6	+ 2.7	+5.8
Denmark	−0.7	+1.5	+4.9
France	−0.6	+5.0	+7.1
West Germany	−0.6	−0.6	+2.8
Greece	+0.4	+17.6	+19.8
Ireland	−0.6	+2.7	+7.8
Italy	−0.4	+6.4	+11.0
Luxembourg	−0.5	+2.8	+7.4
Netherlands	−0.5	−0.5	+2.0
United Kingdom	−0.6	−0.6	+5.3

Source: CEC (1984a).

The Economist (7–13 April 1984), the outcome of the MCA changes 'is to turn the apparent 0.5 per cent cut in the ECUs into an average rise of 3.2 per cent in national currencies, which are the ones farmers get paid in'. Note that in all EC countries farmers experienced a fall in their real earnings when the 1984 inflation rates were taken into consideration; British farmers suffered the largest fall (5.9%) and French farmers the smallest (2.1%).

It may come as a surprise to learn that the agreed package did not reduce costs but actually raised them in 1984 and 1985. The package cost about 0.9 billion ECU in 1984 and about 1.4 billion ECU in 1985. However, in the longer term, relative costs are bound to decline, provided other things remain the same (the fall in the percentage of the EU Budget expenditure on EAGGF guarantee since then could be advanced in support, but that would be overstretching the point).

All these changes were formally adopted and ratified by the European Parliament and the EC member nations. The British government was pleased with them since a tightening of expenditures on the CAP was necessarily beneficial to countries like the United Kingdom. Moreover, as pointed out in Chapter 11, these reforms in the CAP were being continuously pursued by the EU, the MacSharry package on which has been described as marking a watershed in the reform of the CAP. However, as we shall see in the final section of this chapter, there is no reason for elation over this matter.

16.7 Most recent developments

16.7.1 The 1988 Council decision

The most recent major developments in this area are three. The first, referred to as the Delors I package, arises from the decisions reached in the 11–12 February 1988 Council meeting. The second and third arise from the Delors II package and *Agenda 2000* (CEU, 1997a), dealt with respectively in the following two sub-sections. In order to appreciate the first fully, it is necessary to have some background information. This background is set out fully in the Commission's submission to the Council and Parliament on 28 February 1987 (COM (87) 101 final).

In that report, the Commission drew attention to some disturbing developments concerning the EC Budget. First, although the own-resource system was meant to provide financial stability so as to enable the Commission to concentrate on policy decisions, it had failed to do so, owing to the following:

1. The erosion in the traditional own resources (customs duties and agricultural levies) because of tariff reductions and increasing self-sufficiency in the EC.
2. The VAT base growing at a slower rate than economic activity because of the reduction in the share of consumption in total GNP.
3. The Fontainebleau mechanism actually decreasing the resources available in so far as the ceiling on VAT rates applied to the individual member nations which financed the abatement, not to the EC as such.

Second, as a consequence of the reluctance to provide additional finance to the EC, budgetary practices had arisen which disguised the real impact of expenditure decisions. These practices had to continue because new own resources were insufficient even by the time they were finally adopted. Thus, for the 1984 and 1985 EC Budgets, intergovernmental advances were needed to cover legal expenditure obligations, equivalent to an increase in the VAT rate of 0.14% and 0.23% respectively. For 1986 and 1987, underbudgeting of expenditure took place owing to the exhaustion of the own resources then available, equivalent to 0.10% and 0.23% respectively. For all the years under consideration, the EC failed to provide a proper financial depreciation of agricultural stocks. The Commission argued that these, and similar, developments led to a heavy burden weighing on the own resources in future years. Third, apart from the above, the system had not been adapted to more fundamental developments in the EC. This was because, at best, VAT revenue produced little, if any, redistributive effect in relation to the relative prosperity of the member nations; the system as such provided no buffer for a structural decline in one of the components once the VAT ceiling had been reached – several types (not just two) of own resources are required to make the system sufficiently flexible; and VAT own resources were not in reality own resources of the EC, rather contributions by the member states – as such, EC expenditure was not subject to direct taxpayer control; the Commission argued that, had the actual collection of VAT in member states been made on the harmonized VAT base, it would have been impossible for taxpayers to identify the EC share, and taxpayers would have been able to react similarly to other directly collected revenue by the EC.

The detailed analyses supporting these considerations cannot be tackled here, but it should be stressed that the Commission argued strongly that agricultural stocks represented a considerable potential liability on the EC Budget (their values for later years are given in Figure 11.10). Moreover, it pointed out an additional liability consisting of what had come to be known as the 'cost of the past'. This concerned in particular the EC's structural funds, but also related to development aid. Because of the marked increase in structural expenditure in those years, mainly due to the two enlargements, the volume of outstanding commitments had risen rapidly. Indeed, the rapid build-up of commitment appropriations had been stated policy as reflected in the annual EC Budget procedure. However, given the regulations and management practices, the scale of the rise had created some problems. First, the underestimation of the time needed to complete the political, administrative and technical aspects of the operation had meant that commitments had translated into payments at a slower rate than had been expected. There had also been a tendency to inflate annual commitment appropriations to levels beyond the Commission's management capacity and the absorption capacity of the potential beneficiaries. Second, the failure to keep sufficient watch on the progress of operations had meant that a certain volume of commitments no longer had any real equivalent in terms of projects. These commitments should have been cancelled; but this was not always possible under the existing rules.

In short, one has to agree with the Commission's conclusion that to contain the growth of the 'cost of the past' and to return to proper EC Budget management, including its enactment in good time before the beginning of the fiscal year, the payment appropriations provided should flow from the commitments decided. Therefore, it was appropriate to apply budgetary discipline only to commitment appropriations and to do this only with due respect given to the political undertaking by the competent authority in the EC prior to the annual EC budgetary process.

Given this background, the Commission put forward its own proposals for new EC own resources. These were largely endorsed by the Brussels Council of 29–30 June 1987. However, the finer details were left to the Copenhagen Council which met later, in December; but since that Council ended in disagreement, the final decisions were left to the February 1988 Council. However, this is not the place to discuss the actual differences between the proposals suggested by the Commission and the final Council decisions.

The Council decided (Council, 1986) that there would be both an overall ceiling on own resources and annual ceilings for the period 1988–92. This would be done by laying down a ceiling for commitment appropriations in 1992 and determining an orderly evolution for them, maintaining a strict relationship between commitment appropriations and payment appropriations to ensure their compatibility and to enable the achievement of the ceilings for subsequent years as expressed in payment appropriations.

It also decided that the annual growth rate of EAGGF guarantee expenditure should not exceed 70–80% of the annual growth rate of EC GNP. The expenditure on EAGGF guarantee was defined as that chargeable to Section III, Part B, Titles 1 and 2 (EAGGF Guarantee) of the EC Budget, less amounts corresponding to the disposal of ACP (the Afro-Caribbean–Pacific group – see Chapter 23) sugar, food aid refunds, sugar and isoglucose levy payments by producers and any other revenue raised from the agricultural sector in future years. For the financial years 1988–92, systematic depreciation costs for newly created agricultural stocks, commencing at their time of establishment, were to be financed from these allocations. The Council was to enter each year in its draft EC Budget the necessary appropriations to finance the costs of stock depreciation. Moreover, Council Regulation 1883/78 was to be modified so as to create a legal obligation to proceed to stock depreciation over the specified period in order to arrive at a normal stock situation by 1992.

The costs connected with the depreciation of existing agricultural stocks would be kept outside the guidelines; 1.2 billion ECU would be inscribed in Title 8 of the EC Budget for this purpose for 1988, and 1.4 billion ECU per year, at 1988 prices, for the period 1989–92. Spain and Portugal would be treated in this respect as if their depreciation had been entirely financed by the EC in 1987; an appropriate restitution would be entered in Title 8 of the EC Budget for this purpose.

The reference basis for the definition of the annual allocations for EAGGF guarantee expenditure would be the 1988 figure of 27.5 billion ECU, at 1988 prices, adjusted in accordance with the points specified above regarding sugar, food aid, etc. The annual maximum allocation for any year after 1988 would be this figure multiplied by 70–80% of the growth rate of EC GNP between 1988 and the year in question, again, given the above proviso.

In addition to this, new agricultural 'stabilizers' would be introduced – these are mentioned briefly in Chapter 11; details are provided here because of their direct bearing on budgetary expenditure. For example, the threshold for cereals would be set at 155–160 million tonnes per year for the period 1988–91, and an additional co-responsibility levy of 3% would be provisionally charged at the beginning of each marketing year to ensure that agricultural expenditure stays within the specified limits. Similar quotas were set for oilseeds and protein products, existing stabilizers would continue for olive oil and cotton, the quota system for milk would be extended for another three years, etc. What is significant, however, is that the Council agreed to adopt provisions to limit supply by withdrawing agricultural land from production. This 'set-aside' programme was devised to complement market policy measures, and would be compulsory for member countries but optional for producers. Exceptions to compulsory application would be possible for certain regions 'in which natural conditions or the danger of depopulation militates against a reduction in production'. In the case of Spain, the exceptions may also relate, on the basis of objective criteria, to 'specific socio-economic circumstances, pursuant to the relevant' EC procedure. In the case of Portugal, the set-aside arrangements would be optional during the transition period. The set-aside period is a minimum of five years, but farmers may be allowed to terminate it after three years. The area involved must be at least 20% of arable land used for cultivating products covered by the common market organization, and the premium should cover the income lost by the farmer, the minimum level being 100 ECU/ha and the maximum 600 ECU/ha, rising to 700 ECU/ha in exceptional circumstances to be determined by the Commission. Farmers opting to set aside 30% of their equivalent land would also be exempted from the basic and additional co-responsibility levy for 20 tonnes of cereals marketed. The EU contribution to the premiums would be 70% of the first 200 ECU, 25% for ECU between 200 and 400, and 15% for ECU between 400 and 600. The member states may grant farmers the possibility of using the land set aside for fallow grazing by means of extensive cattle farming or for producing lentils, chick peas and vegetables, but the conditions for these were still to be determined. The essential point, however, is that the EU undertakes to be responsible for only 50% of the amount granted, with its contribution being 70% for the first 100 ECU, 25% of the next 100 ECU and 15% of the third 100 ECU; hence, the responsibility rests with farmers and the EU as well as the member nations. The EU contribution would be 50% financed from the EAGGF guarantee section and conversion would be introduced on a trial basis for three years; after that the Commission was asked to report to the Council and to submit appropriate proposals. In addition, the Council agreed to introduce optional EU arrangements for promoting the cessation of farming (early retirement). As we saw in Chapter 11, special incentives have been provided for this in the latest package of CAP reforms.

In order to promote efficient budgetary management, the Council decided that EAGGF expenditure should be controlled by operating an efficient 'early warning' system for the development of the individual EAGGF expenditure chapters. Before the start of each budget year, the Commission is asked to define expenditure profiles for each budget chapter based on a comparison of monthly expenditure with the profile of the expenditure over the three preceding years. The Commission will then submit monthly reports on the development of actual expenditure against profiles. Given this early warning system, if the Commission finds that the rate of development of real expenditure is exceeding the forecast profile, or risks doing so, it will be entitled to use the management measures at its disposal, including those which it has under the stabilization measures, to remedy the situation. If these measures prove insufficient, the Commission is asked to examine the functioning of the stabilizers in the relevant sector and, if necessary, to present proposals to the Council calculated to strengthen their action. The Council is then required to act within a period of two months in order to remedy the situation.

To enable the Council and the Commission to apply the above rules, it was agreed that measures shall be taken to accelerate the transmission and treatment of data supplied by the member countries on agricultural expenditure within each marketing organization in order to ensure that the rate at which appropriations in each chapter are used is known with precision one month after the expenditure has occurred. Existing agricultural legislation will be adapted to ensure this. The special provisions concerning the financing of the CAP decided for 1987 will continue to apply. However, the delay of the advances by the Commission to member states shall be extended from two to two and a half months. The existing system for payment of interest will be continued, but payment of EC advances is made conditional on member states complying with their obligation to make available to the Commission the information given above justifying EC payment.

The above decisions, together with the statement that the agricultural price proposals should be consistent with the specified limits and the provision of a 'monetary service' of 1 billion ECU to cater for movements in the ECU/US dollar rate, can be broadly described as decisions consistent with the Commission proposals for 1987, as are the latest proposals in this area – see below.

With regard to non-compulsory expenditure, the Council reaffirmed its 1987 Brussels decision that budgetary discipline must be applied to all EC expenditure, both to payment appropriations and to commitment appropriations, and this must be binding on all the institutions which will be associated with the implementation. The Council, for its part, decided to apply the provisions of Article 203(9) of the Treaty in such a way as to ensure that two guidelines will be respected:

1. Progression of the non-compulsory expenditures which have been the subject of a multi-annual financing decision by the Council for the period 1988–92 (structural funds, IMP – integrated Mediterranean programme – and research) ensuring that such decisions will be honoured.

2. Progression of non-compulsory expenditures other than those referred to in (1) equal to the maximum rate of increase communicated by the Commission.

The results of these guidelines should be considered as a maximum by the member states during all the budget procedure.

It was also decided that, in the interest of better budgetary management, carry-overs of differentiated appropriations shall no longer be automatic. However, it was also decided that the size of any future negative reserves in the EC Budget should be limited to 200 million ECU.

As to the structural funds (which in 1989 integrated the various structural aspects: ERDF, ESF, the guidance section of the EAGGF and since 1994 the FIFG), it was agreed that the member states shared the broad outlines of the Commission's general approach on the reform of the funds: they confirmed the conclusions of the Brussels Council concerning renationalization of the funds' objectives, concentration of their measures in accordance with EC criteria, due account being taken of the relative underdevelopment of certain regions or of regions in industrial decline and recourse to the programme method (see below and Chapter 18). It was reiterated that the EC operations under these funds, the EIB (European Investment Bank) and the other financial instruments should support the achievement of the general objectives set out in Articles 130(A) and 130(C) of the Treaty by contributing to the achievement of five priority objectives:

1. Promoting the development and structural adjustment of the less-developed regions.
2. Converting the regions, border regions or part regions (including employment areas and urban communities) seriously affected by industrial decline.
3. Combating long-term unemployment.
4. Facilitating the integration of young people.
5. Speeding up the adjustment of agricultural structures and promoting the development of rural areas, all within the context of reforming the CAP.

The funds' finances are to be increased in a manner consistent with these objectives. The details of these increases are too elaborate to state here.

As to own resources, a limit of 1.25–1.30% of EC GDP was adopted but, before the end of 1991, the Commission was asked to report on the operation of the system and the application of the budgetary discipline. It was also affirmed that the EDF will continue to be financed outside the EC Budget. It was further agreed that the correction of budgetary imbalances would be carried out in such a way that the amount of own resources available for EC policies was not affected.

With regard to the details of own resources, the Council has decided to continue to use the agricultural levies and sugar and isoglucose duties as a source, together with the addition of ECSC duties, but has refused the Commission's suggestion regarding the elimination of the 10% refund for collection costs in both cases – it can be seen from Table 16.2 that these have been close to 5% of revenues but were 3.8% in 1992. The Council also offered the Commission two options for the remaining sources. The first option includes:

1. The application of a rate of 1.4%, valid for all member states, to the assessment basis for VAT which is determined in a uniform manner for member states according to the EC rules.

2. The application of a rate to be determined under the budgetary procedure in the light of the total of all other revenue, but not exceeding 1.4%, to an additional base representing the difference between the sum of GNP at market prices and the sum of the bases for VAT as stated in (1) of all member states. It was added that for each member state this additional base may not exceed 55% of GNP at market prices.

The second option included:

1. The application of a rate as in the first option, but with the specific rate being 1.4% in 1988, 1.3% in 1989, 1.2% in 1990 and 1.1% in both 1991 and 1992, and a limitation on the assessment basis for VAT, which may not exceed 60% of GNP at market prices for each member state.

2. The application of a rate to be determined under the budgetary procedure in the light of the total of all other revenue to an additional base representing the sum of GNP at market prices.

No logical explanation has been provided to justify these formulae. Note that Table 16.2 provides all the information that is needed for a comparison of what the EU has been doing in order to meet these commitments. The table does not include the facts that the 1989–92 budget outlays amounted to between 1.01% and 1.08% of EC GDP; the commitments were for 1.17–1.12%.

As to the compensation mechanism for the United Kingdom, it was decided to continue with the Fontainebleau mechanism.

16.7.2 Delors II package

With regard to the second package of recent developments, on 11 February 1992 the Commission adopted a communication entitled 'From the Single Act to Maastricht and beyond: the means to match our ambitions', the aim of which was to give shape to the policies arising from the Maastricht Treaty, either by adjusting old policies or by creating new ones. As we have seen, especially in Chapters 2 and 6, these include the following:

1. The creation of a Cohesion Fund by 31 December 1993 to help the poorer nations of the EU (defined as those with a per capita GDP of less than 90% of the EU average, i.e. Greece, Ireland, Portugal and Spain).

2. The adoption of a new approach to competition policy.

3. The introduction of a common industrial policy.

4. The promotion of research and technological development.

5. The taking of steps to strengthen social policy and to promote vocational training.

6. The developing of infrastructure networks.

In short, the communication contains the Delors II package, which concentrates on three major aspects: expanding external action in a manner consistent with the EU's new responsibilities in world affairs, which has been interpreted to mean promoting balanced economic and political relations with the rest of the world and assisting people faced with exceptional situations; strengthening economic and social cohesion, which was an essential condition for the acceptance of the

Maastricht Treaty, and which the Commission believes is an essential basis for political union; the creation of an environment conducive to improving the competitiveness of EU business, not by helping EU companies directly, but by anticipating and cushioning change.

One should emphasize that the package is based on the two fundamental principles now governing EU activities. The first is that of subsidiarity which, as we saw in Chapter 2, has been defined to mean that action at the EU level should be limited to areas where the EU is most effective, i.e. do not do at the EU level what can best be done at the individual member country level. The second is that of solidarity, which is reflected in the objective of promoting economic and social cohesion.

With the above in mind, the Commission proposed a doubling, between 1992 and 1997, of the financial resources allocated to external action. It also proposed increasing by two-thirds the funds allocated to the structural funds for the poorer EU nations, while other funds were to be increased by 50%. These, together with the funds needed to meet the third objective, amount to a raising of the ceiling on EU own resources from 1.20% to 1.37% of Community GDP between 1992 and 1997. This would represent an annual growth in the EU budget of about 5% in real terms.

However, the Edinburgh Council, which extended the period by two years (to 1999), reached agreement on different figures. It was decided that the ceiling on own resources will gradually rise from 1.20% of Community GDP in 1993 to 1.27% in 1999. Payment appropriations will rise from 65.9 billion ECU in 1993 to 80.1 billion ECU in 1999. The proportion of these amounts devoted to the poorer regions will increase by 72%, and a further 15.15 billion ECU is allocated to the Cohesion Fund, which will double the commitments made to the four poorer nations of the EU to date. Expenditure on external action will increase to 5.6 billion ECU in 1999 from 3.9 billion ECU in 1993, while that on internal policies will rise from 3.64 billion ECU in 1993 to 5.1 billion ECU in 1999, and this is despite the fact that the Commission had argued strongly in favour of the provision of adequate resources to cover the cost of internal priorities, such as research and trans-EU networks.

It should therefore be clear that the EU Commission continues to put forward proposals consistent with the policies adopted by the EU member countries, while the member nations continue to shy away from providing the full resources needed to carry out what they commit themselves to.

16.7.3 *Agenda 2000*

The very latest developments originate from *Agenda 2000* (CEU, 1997a), but are adjusted by the Berlin summit of 24–25 March 1999. They amount to four commitments:

1. To subject to stricter discipline overall EU expenditures.
2. To ensure that existing ceilings on EU revenues are not raised as a consequence of enlargement, to include the Countries of Central and Eastern Europe (CEECs), beginning in 2002.
3. To raise the levels of efficiency and control of expenditure on the CAP and ERDF.
4. To introduce modifications to ensure consistency between the ability to pay and contributions by the member states (see Table 16.7 for a comparison of the two dimensions in 1992, 1996 and 1999).

Table 16.7 Percentage shares in the financing of the Union and in total GNP

	1992		1996		1999	
	Budget	GNP	Budget	GNP	Budget	GNP
Belgium	4.0	3.1	3.9	3.1	3.8	3.0
Denmark	1.8	1.9	1.9	2.0	2.0	2.0
West Germany	30.2	28.2	29.4	27.4	27.7	26.2
Greece	1.3	1.4	1.5	1.5	1.6	1.6
Spain	8.6	8.2	6.3	6.8	6.7	6.7
France	18.7	18.6	17.5	18.1	17.5	17.5
Ireland	0.8	0.7	0.9	0.7	1.0	0.8
Italy	14.7	17.0	12.5	14.1	13.4	14.3
Luxembourg	0.2	0.2	0.2	0.2	0.2	0.2
Netherlands	6.3	4.6	6.2	4.6	5.9	4.6
Austria	–	–	2.7	2.6	2.6	2.5
Portugal	1.5	1.3	1.3	1.2	1.4	1.3
Finland	–	–	1.4	1.4	1.4	1.4
Sweden	–	–	2.6	2.9	2.9	2.8
UK	11.9	14.8	11.6	13.4	11.9	15.1

Source: CEU, 1997a.

These commitments are reflected in the 'financial perspectives' (meaning agreements between the member nations regarding the upper ceilings for EU expenditures) for the years 2000 to 2006 as shown in Table 16.8. The figures clearly indicate that agricultural guarantee expenditure will reach a peak in 2002 then decline steadily thereafter. Also, the structural funds are to be reduced by about 8% over the period, but, as mentioned in Chapter 18, actual spending will become more concentrated on the poorer regions. Moreover, funds have been earmarked to assist with enlargement by six new members, beginning in 2002, as well as to finance pre-accession preparations by the candidates. Finally, for the entire period, the ceiling on appropriations for payment falls short of the 1.27% of EU GNP available for revenues, providing a safety net of some significance, given the relative magnitudes involved.

Although the ceiling of 1.27% has been maintained, changes in own resources were introduced with the purpose of achieving a better balance in the contributions by member states. First, they will reduce as of 1 January 2001 the maximum call-in rate for the VAT resource from 1% to 0.75%. Second, they will raise from 10% to 25% starting on 1 January 2001 the proportion of traditional own resources kept by the member states to cover their collection costs and related activities. These changes are expected to lead to a corresponding increase in the proportion of the GNP resource, which is regarded as a better reflector of ability to pay. Finally, they maintain, with minor adjustments to avoid windfall benefits due to the changes in own resources and future enlargement, the 1984 Fontainebleau settlement, extending the special compensation for the UK government (see above), but they reduce the contribution to it by Austria, Germany, the Netherlands and Sweden.

Table 16.8 EU financial perspective for 2000–6

	2000	2001	2002	2003	2004	2005	2006
Agriculture	40 920	42 800	43 900	43 770	42 760	41 930	41 660
Structural funds and cohesion fund	32 045	31 455	30 865	30 285	29 595	29 595	29 170
Internal policies	5 930	6 040	6 150	6 260	6 370	6 480	6 600
External action	4 550	4 560	4 570	4 580	4 590	4 600	4 610
Administration	4 560	4 600	4 700	4 800	4 900	5 000	5 100
Reserves	900	900	650	400	400	400	400
Pre-accession aid to applicant countries	3 120	3 120	3 120	3 120	3 120	3 120	3 120
Total appropriations for commitments	92 025	93 475	93 955	93 215	91 735	91 125	90 660
Appropriations for payments reserved for possible new member states after accession	–	–	4 140	6 710	8 890	11 440	14 220
Total ceiling on appropriations for payments	89 600	91 110	98 360	101 590	100 800	101 600	103 840
Ceiling on appropriations for payments as % of GNP of the EU countries	1.13%	1.12%	1.18%	1.19%	1.15%	1.13%	1.13%

Source: CEU, 1997a.

16.8 A proper budget?

Before concluding this chapter, it is of interest to ask whether the EU Budget can be made to perform proper fiscal policy functions, i.e. can it be used to reduce income disparities between the member nations? Can it perform stabilizing functions? Even with the new and increased own resources, the budget will not do much in this respect, given the recommendation of the MacDougall Report (CEC, 1977c) for a minimum budget of about 2.5% as a necessary precondition for EC monetary integration. However, even the MacDougall recommendations are in the nature of a compromise since a proper system must necessarily incorporate progressivity (rather than the somewhat arbitrary structural fund allocations) in order to ensure a narrowing of income disparities between the member nations and an equitable distribution of any possible gains and losses. In El-Agraa and Majocchi (1983) it was demonstrated how a progressive income tax method can gradually be introduced in such a way that the EU Budget eventually approximates to the ideal. This section is devoted to a brief consideration of this vital issue.

To describe the nature of the proposed mechanisms, an exercise can be developed with regard to fiscal year 1980 when the principle of own resources (a decision on which was taken on 21 April 1970) was fully operational – see above and Wallace (1980, pp. 54–8). This is a convenient year to use since at that date Greece, Portugal and Spain were not parties to the inequity issue. However, the original figure given for that year (24.8 billion ECU) has in reality come closer to the 1983 payment appropriations. The main hypothesis is that the size of the EC Budget is to be made equal to 2.5% of EC GDP, in accordance with the recommendations of the MacDougall Report. EC Budget expenditures are, therefore, to increase to 49.6875 billion ECU. These expenditures are to be financed by the traditional resources plus an income tax. The first two sources of revenue (agricultural levies and customs duties) are provided according to the factors determining them. The differences between these receipts and payments appropriations is covered by VAT and income tax.

The burden of income taxation must fall among the member states in a progressive way. To achieve this, the EC establishes at the beginning a proportional rate that can be fixed, say 50% of the share of EC expenditures in EC GDP. The total yield of the proportional income tax is, therefore, 24.8438 billion ECU (see Table 16.9). The yield for each country is obtained by multiplying the common rate (1.25%) by the national GDP and is equal, as a share of the total yield, to the proportion of each country's GDP in EC GDP (see Table 16.10, columns 1 and 2).

Table 16.9 Financing an EC budget equal to 2.5% of the EC GDP in 1980

	Million ECU	% of total
Agricultural levies	1 535.4	3.09
Sugar levy	466.9	0.94
Customs duties	5 905.7	11.89
VAT	16 324.1	32.85
Miscellaneous	611.6	1.23
Indirect taxation	24 843.7	50.00
Income taxation	24 843.8	50.00
Total	49 687.5	100.00

Source: Fourteenth General Report of the Activities of the European Communities (Brussels, 1981), p. 57.

Table 16.10 National distribution of income tax burden

	1[a]	2[b]	3[c]	4 (= 1 × 3)	5[d]	6[e]	7[f]	8[g]
Belgium	1 048.4	4.22	1.1188	1 172.95	4.47	1 110.5	1.32	1.059
Denmark	598.8	2.41	1.2260	734.13	2.80	695.6	1.45	1.162
France	5 868.1	23.62	1.1489	6 741.86	25.71	6 387.4	1.36	1.088
West Germany	7 373.6	29.68	1.2597	9 288.52	35.42	8 799.7	1.49	1.193
Ireland	159.0	0.64	0.4915	78.15	0.30	74.5	0.58	0.469
Italy	3 547.7	14.28	0.6536	2 318.77	8.85	2 198.7	0.78	0.620
Luxembourg	42.2	0.17	1.1903	50.23	0.19	47.2	1.43	1.145
Netherlands	1 508.0	6.07	1.1219	1 691.83	6.45	1 602.4	1.33	1.063
United Kingdom	4 698.0	18.91	0.8824	4 145.52	15.81	3 927.8	1.04	0.836
Total	24 843.8	100.0		26 221.96	100.00	24 843.8		

[a] $T_i = t_a Y_i$ with $\sum_{i=1}^{9} T_i = T = t_a Y$, $t_a = 0.0125$.

[b] $Y_i/Y = T_i/T = y_i$.

[c] $k_i = (Y_i/N_i)/(Y/N)$.

[d] $t_i = (k_i T_i)/(\sum_i k_i T_i)$.

[e] $T_i^* = t_i T$.

[f] $t_{ai}^* = t_a(t_i/y_i) = (T_i^*/Y_i)$.

[g] t_i/y_i.

Y is GDP, t the tax rate, and T the total tax yield.

The parameter chosen for a progressive distribution of income taxation among EC countries is per capita income. Column 3 of Table 16.10 shows the ratio between each country's per capita income and the EC average. The amount of income tax attributed to each country under a progressive scale is determined in two stages. First, multiply the proportional yield for each country (column 1) by its per capita income relative to the EC average (column 3). This is given in column 4. Then divide each country's relative per capita income (column 3) by the sum of column 4.[1] Thus, the new share for each country of the total yield is established (column 5). By multiplying such a share by the total yield to be provided, the amount of income tax is determined for each EC nation (column 6). The per capita burden of income taxation is thus different in each country and a scale of rates follows, ranging from 0.58 for Ireland to 1.49 for West Germany (column 7). The effective rate for each country equals the proportional rate multiplied by a progressivity coefficient (column 8), represented by the ratio between the effective share of each country in total yield (column 5) and the share of each country in EC GDP (column 2).

If the chosen size of the EC Budget is different, the effective rate for each country can be established by multiplying the proportional rate, fixed with regard to the level of expenditure to be covered by income taxation, by the progressivity coefficient of column 8.

The degree of progressivity, as measured by the elasticity of the yield with regard to the change in income, is very high and near 2%. The implicit tax function, estimated by normal cross-section regression, has in fact the following exponential shape:

$$\log T/N = -13.407 + 2.004 \log Y/N$$
$$(0.04463) \quad (0.00501)$$

where the values in parentheses are the standard errors of coefficients.

The distribution among the member states of the burden of income taxation is thus defined, and the target (of a progressivity hitting the richer countries more heavily than the poorer) is attained. The second step is the distribution within each country among its own citizens. In the proposed scheme, this is left for each country to determine in accordance with its income-tax progressivity scale. The distributive formula among the citizens is therefore considered to be beyond the boundaries of EC competence: what is important, from an EC viewpoint, is only the levelling of economic conditions for the member states such that a true economic and monetary union can be realized.

The gap between the amount of payments appropriations and the revenue accruing from income taxation, agricultural levies and customs duties is filled by VAT collections; hence VAT plays a residual role. The expected yield is divided by the VAT base to determine its rate.

The distribution of the total burden of financing an EC Budget equal to 2.5% of EC GDP among the member nations is represented in Table 16.11. The share computed for each country by the Commission for fiscal year 1980 is adopted with respect to agricultural levies, customs duties and VAT. The values for the income taxation are taken from Table 16.10.

The result is shown in column 1, where the global share for each country of the total yield from the proposed scheme can be compared with the effective share in fiscal year 1980 (according to the Commission calculations) – column 2 – and with the share of each country's GDP in EC GDP – column 3. From the revenue side, a redistribution-oriented budget emerges, which should support a more balanced growth of the EC economy.

One should ask at least two questions about the proposed scheme. Is it a just and efficient one? Is it a feasible one? From the point of view of justice, it seems difficult, at first sight, to accept that the per capita burden of income taxation differs in the member states according to the level of average income in each state. It is important to recall here that the national income-taxation quota is distributed among the citizens according to the progressivity scale applied in domestic taxation. It is therefore unlikely that the poor in a richer country will pay more than the rich in a poorer country. In any case, the difference in the burden of income taxation can be justified if one also takes into account the fact that the poor citizens of a richer member state can exploit many opportunities and enjoy benefits that are unavailable to those of a poorer member nation.

Table 16.11 National distribution of the total income tax burden

	Agricultural levies, etc.	VAT	Income tax	Total	1	2	3
Belgium	660.2	723.2	1 110.5	2 494.0	5.02	6.00	4.22
Denmark	168.7	419.5	695.6	1 283.8	2.58	2.40	2.41
France	1 238.7	3 943.9	6 387.4	11 570.0	23.29	20.00	23.62
West Germany	2 319.9	5 259.7	8 799.6	16 379.2	32.96	30.10	29.68
Ireland	81.8	140.4	74.5	296.7	0.60	0.90	0.64
Italy	1 153.6	1 905.0	2 198.7	5 257.3	10.58	11.60	14.28
Luxembourg	5.1	34.4	47.2	86.6	0.17	0.10	0.17
Netherlands	874.1	1 025.2	1 602.4	3 501.7	7.05	8.40	6.07
United Kingdom	2 017.4	2 873.0	3 927.8	8 818.2	17.75	20.50	18.91
Total	8 519.6	16 324.1	24 843.8	49 687.5	100.00	100.00	100.00

Source: Eurostat Review, 1971–80.

With regard to efficiency, this type of taxation introduces a strong fiscal incentive to reduce disequilibria within the EC. In particular, the stronger countries take an interest in the growth of per capita income in the weaker member nations insofar as, if convergence ensues, their own burden of income taxation is reduced. Indeed, if a perfect equalization of per capita incomes is attained, the coefficient of progressivity will become one for all the member nations, and the distribution of income taxation among them will become proportional. Meanwhile, the weaker member nations have no incentive to slacken their efforts in reducing disparities in the level of income since, with a progressive income taxation, the elasticity of disposable income is less than unity, but considerably larger than zero.

Concerning the political feasibility of the proposal, it is important to stress the need to clearly define an overall strategy relating to the growth of the budget. A plan for economic and monetary union involves a whole series of co-ordinated decisions spread over a long period of time. Since such decisions have to be taken at different times by more than one decision-making body, they are unlikely to be effective if there is no stated general frame of reference. If the Maastricht Treaty is fully implemented so that the EC will introduce a common central bank and one currency before the end of this century, this proposal will have to be discussed seriously and immediately; the introduction of a cohesion fund, though to be applauded, will not take care of this problem.

16.9 | Conclusion

It should be apparent from the foregoing that a proper analysis of the future prospects for the EU Budget cannot be confined to its present structure. The EU Budget must be seen not only in its proper context of public finance, but also in the wider context of the ultimate objectives of the Community as a whole. Given its existing structure and the present stage reached in the EU integrative process, an equitable EU Budget, in the absence of a more *fundamental* reform of the CAP, must aim at increasing the non-compulsory expenditures (regional, social and industrial aspects including employment generation, not just the so-called structural expenditures). This would require more than the mere strengthening of the recent changes in the EU Budget (as agreed in the Edinburgh and Berlin summits in December 1992 and March 1996 respectively) since the introduction of a progressive income tax facility for revenue-raising purposes (recall that VAT, which is still prominent in the new EU Budget structure, is regressive), especially now that the majority of the EU member nations have endorsed full EMU and a single currency. The proposal put forward in El-Agraa and Majocchi (1983) is a practical one with very clear guidelines, since it has a well-defined framework for reference. Moreover, it is not beyond the reach of the EU, given the Maastricht and Amsterdam treaties, and recalling that before the own resource system was introduced in 1970, the EC Budget was financed by national contributions determined according to each member nation's relative prosperity within the EC.

Note

1. With the introduction of the progressivity coefficient, the yield of income taxation does not change unless:

$$[t_a \sum_{i=1}^{6} Y_i(Y_iN/N_iY) + t_a \sum_{j=1}^{3} Y_j(Y_jN/N_jY)] - [t_a \sum_{i=1}^{6} Y_i + t_a \sum_{j=1}^{3} Y_j] = 0$$

where countries i have an above-EC average per capita income, and countries j a per capita income lower than the EC average. Rearranging the terms, the condition can be expressed as:

$$\sum_{i=1}^{6} Y_i(Y_iN/N_iY - 1) - \sum_{j=1}^{3} Y_j(1Y_jN/N_jY) = 0$$

Thus, the condition shows that the yield increases if a progressivity coefficient larger than 1 is applied to countries i with a large (in absolute terms) cumulative national income and a progressivity coefficient lower than 1 to countries j with a small cumulative national income, the final result depending also on the values of the progressivity coefficients. This is what is happening in the numerical example in Table 16.10.

17 The European Monetary System

D. G. MAYES*

As a result of the implementation of the provisions of the Maastricht Treaty, monetary policy in the EU is the responsibility of the European System of Central Banks (ESCB). Since 1999 the European Monetary System (EMS) has been composed of two parts: the Eurosystem, which consists of the European Central Bank (ECB) and 11 national central banks (NCBs) that have adopted the Euro as their currency, and the remaining four NCBs that are thus far running their own monetary policies with their own currencies. This is a transitory arrangement. The Eurosystem adopted the Euro for monetary operations and 'wholesale' financial markets at the beginning of 1999 but will only phase in the notes and coins during the first half of 2002, after which the national currencies will be withdrawn.

When the membership of the Eurosystem was decided by the European Council in June 1998, Austria, Belgium, Finland, France, Germany, the Irish Republic, Italy, Luxembourg, the Netherlands, Portugal and Spain were deemed to have met the criteria for membership (see Chapter 6). Denmark, Sweden and the UK decided that they did not want to apply at that juncture and Greece was deemed not yet to have qualified. Each of the four countries can be considered for membership if they so wish. Greece exercised this option in 2000, was successful and will join at the beginning of 2001. Sweden may also consider applying if the political mood is favourable. Denmark and the UK seem to be rather farther away from such a decision and are not under an obligation to do so at any stage.

In this chapter we look at the development of the EMS through to the present day and at its current plans for further development. Chapter 6 sets Economic and Monetary Union (EMU) in the context of closer economic integration.

17.1 Founding and inception of the system

With the current focus on the prospects for economic and monetary union (EMU) in the EU, the EMS is sometimes presented as if it was from the outset intended as the route to EMU. Although some undoubtedly hold that view, its original aims were more limited, and part of the difficulties over recent years stem from the way it has evolved or more accurately failed to evolve. The EMS began operation on 13 March 1979 following a decision of the Council of Ministers meeting in Brussels in December 1978. The short delay between the Council's favourable decision and the actual inception of the EMS accommodated the negotiation of additional assistance

---

* A previous edition of this chapter was written by Michael Artis. His text has been updated and extended in subsequent editions.

to Italy and Ireland, both of which were thought likely to encounter some difficulties in adjusting to the EMS. The initiative for the establishment of the EMS came, not from the EC Commission, but from the Chancellor of Germany, Helmut Schmidt, and the French President, Valery Giscard d'Estaing. Their decision was in turn guided by a perception that the United States was not capable at the time of exercising a responsible leadership in global monetary affairs and the proximate aim of the EMS was to create a zone of monetary stability in Europe – see Chapter 6. This aim accorded well with the strong, historically based aversion to inflation which governed German economic policy and the German interest in shielding its currency from the effects of irregular speculation against the US dollar together with the long-standing desire of successive French governments to break away from the global dominance of the United States in monetary affairs. The initiative also revived what had been perceived as a disturbing deceleration in the momentum of political development of the EC and corresponded closely to a call made by the Commission's President in his speech at Florence in October 1977 for a corrective initiative along just these lines.

Preparations for the establishment of the EMS involved extensive discussions among the potential members from the moment when the idea was first floated in the Council of Ministers meeting at Copenhagen in April 1978 and in these the United Kingdom played a full role, although it was clear from the start that the British side had substantial reservations about the idea. (Ludlow, 1982, gives a very ample account of the negotiations involved.) When the time for decision came, the EMS, although involving all the other members of the EC at the time, was launched without the full participation of the United Kingdom.

17.2 Provisions of the EMS

The most significant provisions of the EMS relate to the so-called parity grid of bilateral exchange rates or what is called the 'exchange-rate mechanism' (ERM). This is the vital aspect of the operation of the EMS and is the part to which the United Kingdom decided not to adhere on inception of the system. Although the United Kingdom 'shadowed' the ERM for a period in the mid-1980s, it did not join until October 1990. Even so, its membership was short lived since it left in September 1992 when market pressures pushed sterling out of the grid.

Under the provisions of the parity grid, member countries – aside from Portugal, Spain and the United Kingdom – undertook to maintain their exchange rates with each other within ±2¼% of a central rate of exchange.[1] Italy and Ireland negotiated a wider ±6% band for its currency to enable it to achieve a smoother transition from outside the previous snake arrangement, and in June 1989 Spain followed the Italian precedent, joining the ERM with a similar ±6% band. Portugal and the United Kingdom also entered with these wide bands while Italy moved to the ±2¼% band in 1990 (although it too left the ERM in the September 1992 collapse). When the EU was expanded in January 1995, Austria immediately joined the ERM. Finland joined in October 1996 and Italy rejoined the following month.

Central rates of exchange were denominated for convenience in terms of a composite currency, the European currency unit (ECU), and could be changed by collective decision in a formal 'realignment'.[2] Table 17.1 shows the composition of the ECU which, as can be seen, comprised literally so many French francs, so many deutschmarks, so many pounds sterling, etc. These components were selected so as

Table 17.1 Composition and weighting of the ECU

Country (currency)	Composition of the ECU (units of national currency) 13 March 1979– 14 September 1984	17 September 1984– 18 September 1989	From 21 September 1989	Percentage weight from 25 February 1993	Percentage weight from 31 December 1996
Belgium–Luxembourg (franc)	3.80	3.85	3.431	8.61	8.64
Denmark (krone)	0.217	0.219	0.1976	2.70	2.69
France (franc)	1.15	1.31	1.332	20.26	20.62
Germany (mark)	0.828	0.719	0.6242	32.24	32.41
Greece (drachma)	–	1.15	1.44	0.60	0.49
Ireland (punt)	0.00759	0.00871	0.008552	1.10	1.07
Italy (lira)	109.000	140.00	151.8	8.09	7.96
Netherlands (guilder)	0.286	0.256	0.2198	10.10	10.13
Spain (peseta)	–	–	6.885	4.94	4.20
Portugal (escudo)	–	–	1.393	0.78	0.71
United Kingdom (pound sterling)	0.0885	0.0878	0.08784	10.58	11.08

Source: Bank of Finland; *Financial Times*.

to provide a weighting of currencies in the ECU in accord with relative GNP and trade and were subject to review every five years. It may be noted that representation of a country's currency in the ECU and its participation in the ERM are *not* coterminous, as, for example, neither the pound sterling nor the drachma belonged to the ERM. Until September 1989 the Spanish peseta and the Portuguese escudo were not included in the ECU. After the revision in September 1989 the weights remained fixed until the Euro came into operation and replaced it on a one for one basis. When the EU was expanded to include Austria, Finland and Sweden in January 1995 the definition of the ECU was not changed and hence these countries' currencies were not included in the weights.

The use of a composite currency in which to denominate the central rate is not strictly necessary to the operation of the parity grid – participants in the ERM could simply have announced their adherence to a consistent set of bilateral central rates and bands. But the use of the ECU had useful symbolic connotations and gave the EMS an identity over and above that which would be commanded by a mere agreement to stabilize exchange rates – the identity, in fact, of a potential monetary union. EU transactions were denominated in ECU, as were the debts acquired by central banks intervening to support their currencies in the framework of the EMS.

In addition, the ECU did provide a necessary basis for what appeared at the time to be the most innovative technical feature of the EMS, that of the 'divergence indicator' (DI). The essential role that the DI was designed to perform was that of enforcing timely and symmetrical adjustment. The idea of the indicator was that it should be designed so as to signal when a currency was becoming out of line with the rest of the system. Coupled with the injunction that the 'flashing' of the indicator gave 'a presumption' of corrective policy action on behalf of the country whose currency was singled out in this way, the DI would – it was hoped – enforce adjustment equally on a strong-currency country or on a weak-currency country, provided that the currency in question stood out from the pack. Combining this role with that of providing an early warning, the DI was to be triggered when a currency crossed a threshold set at 75% of its permitted $\pm2\frac{1}{4}$% movement against all other currencies in the EMS. Because each currency is itself a component of the ECU, the DI threshold in terms of the ECU is less than $\pm(0.75 \times 2.25 = 1.6875\%)$ of the currency's central rate by an amount which is larger the larger is that currency's weight in the ECU.

Flanking these exchange-rate provisions, with the obligation to intervene at the bilateral limits and the 'presumption of action' created by a triggering of the DI threshold, the EMS also provided for credit mechanisms to enable weak-currency countries to borrow in order to defend their currencies. The principle of such a mechanism, called the VSTF (very-short-term financing facility), provides for the extension of credit from one central bank to another, repayable over a term initially of 45 days; at the bilateral limits one central bank can call on another for credit in the partner's currency without prospect of a refusal, the amount being repaid under this mechanism. In the extensions to the EMS negotiated in Nyborg in September 1987 (frequently referred to as the Basle–Nyborg agreement), the term of repayment under the VSTF was increased to 60 days and, more important, the provision for 'automatic' borrowing for intervention at the limits was extended to cover intervention *within* the limits (so-called intramarginal intervention). In association with its credit mechanisms the founding of the EMS called for the central banks concerned to pool 20% of their gold and dollar reserves in exchange for ECUs in a central fund, the EMCF (European Monetary Cooperation Fund).

17.3   Precursors of the EMS

The provisions and aspirations of the EMS reflected in part lessons felt to have been learned from past endeavours among EC members to stabilize their currencies.[3] The recurrent failures marking these endeavours contributed to the absence of high aspirations to European monetary union (EMU) in the stated objectives of the EMS: by contrast, the Werner Report of 1972 had projected the achievement of EMU by 1980 – for a fuller discussion of this, see Chapter 6. Recent practical experience embodied in the failure of the so-called snake also contributed to the design of the DI and to a greater degree of self-consciousness about the need for multilateral decision making on such issues as realignments.

The snake took shape in April 1972 as a response to the acceptance by the EC of the Werner Committee's optimistic goal setting, and more immediately as a response to the Smithsonian Agreement of the previous December. That Agreement sought to extend the life of the Bretton Woods system by reinstating a global system of fixed but adjustable exchange rates on the basis of wider bands than had prevailed during previous decades; the dollar, although undergoing a discrete devaluation of its price in terms of gold, remained the *numéraire* key currency of the new system. Since the exchange rates of individual European currencies against the dollar were to be confined under the Smithsonian Agreement to ±2¼%, this implied that European currencies could move against each other by ±4½%. The European countries sought to correct this and the snake agreement, which involved all six of the founding members, joined shortly after its inception by the United Kingdom, Ireland, Denmark and Norway (all countries which at that time expected to become members of the EC), simply suggested that exchange rates between participating countries should also be limited to ±2¼% bands of fluctuation. It was from this period that the system earned the sobriquet 'snake in the tunnel', in that while the snake currencies were pegged within the Smithsonian margins against the dollar (the 'tunnel'), their variation against each other was more tightly constrained by the provisions of the snake agreement. The provisions of the snake continued to be pursued even after generalized floating against the dollar took place (in 1973), whereupon it became known as the 'snake outside the tunnel'. Just the same analogy can be applied to the EMS as the system as a whole floats against third currencies such as the US dollar.

The snake agreement was a failure. Sterling left it as early as June 1972 and the lira left in February 1973. The French franc left the snake, rejoined it and left again. There were several other changes. It ended as a collection of smaller currencies heavily dominated by the deutschmark and including some non-EC currencies – a 'worm' or small deutschmark zone – and even within this grouping there were several changes of parity. The goal of establishing EMU by 1980 was officially abandoned by December 1974 – see Chapter 6.

One reason diagnosed for the calamity of the snake was that German dominance of the system was excessive and the invention of the DI was in part a result of this apprehension. Another was that decision making was unilateral (as it had been in the Bretton Woods system), so countries could change their parity agreement without feeling any restraining influence from other members of the system.

The EMS benefited from lessons learned from this period to emerge as a better-founded arrangement with more modest immediate objectives than its predecessor. Nevertheless, when it was launched, scepticism was widespread that the EMS could succeed where its precursors had failed. It was not difficult to greet the inauguration of the EMS as yet further evidence of the triumph of hope over experience.

17.4   The EMS in operation: the overall balance sheet in summary

The survival of the EMS belied this early scepticism and there is little dispute that the EMS was something of a success. There was, however, a period from 1992 onwards when it looked as if the EMS might collapse altogether, just at the time that the final push to EMU was being agreed upon (see below). This success can be seen as embodied in three principal achievements.

First, despite occasional realignments and fluctuations of currencies within their pre-set bands, it seems that the EMS succeeded in its proximate objective of stabilizing exchange rates – not in the absolute sense but in the relevant and realistic sense of appearing to have brought about more stability than would have been enjoyed without it. Moreover, up till 1992 this was done without provoking periodic speculative crises such as marred the demise of the Bretton Woods system.

Second, the claim is made for the EMS that it provided a framework within which member countries were able to pursue counterinflationary policies at a lesser cost in terms of unemployment and lost output than would have been possible otherwise.

Third, while it is claimed that nominal exchange-rate stability was secured, it is also argued that the operation of the EMS prevented drastic changes in *real* exchange rates (or 'competitiveness'). This is contrasted with the damaging experience in this respect of both the United Kingdom and the United States over the same period.

Finally, while not an immediate objective of the EMS as such, it is well worth mentioning that the ECU became established as a significant currency of denomination of bond issues, which can be viewed as some testimony to the credibility of the EMS and the successful projection of its identity.

These achievements – which we detail and examine below – have not been without some qualifications. The DI mechanism does not appear to have withstood the test of time, for example, while sceptics would charge that the counterinflationary achievements of the EMS in fact amount to little more than a bias against growth and expansion.

The enforced changes to parities in and after September 1992 considerably reduced the credibility of the system and called into question the validity of the idea of approaching monetary union through increasingly fixed exchange rates while having no controls over capital flows. Although the widening of the bands to ±15% in August 1993 appeared to remove much of the effective distinction between the ERM and freely floating exchange rates, the practice has been for very considerable convergence and for a system which takes only limited advantage of the flexibility that has been offered.

What we have seen since 1993 has effectively been pressure on member states through the convergence criteria for EMU (see Chapter 6). The requirement to keep inflation close to that of the least inflationary member states, the need to follow a prudent fiscal policy and the requirement for longer-term interest rates to converge will also tend to lead towards exchange rate stability. As a result the goal of EMU gained increasing credibility and took over as the anchor of the system.

17.5 Exchange-rate stability

As the EMS allowed for realignments and for fluctuations of its currencies within the bands, absolute exchange-rate stability was not achieved. However, realignments were few in number, did not always involve the major currencies, were usually small and did grow less frequent with the passage of time. The exception of course is the period between September 1992 and May 1993. The large realignments that took place then and indeed the wider fluctuations that took place when the band was widened to ±15% in August 1993 are in part a reflection of failure to adjust earlier. Thus to some extent the apparent stability in the five years from February 1987, when there were no realignments, was in fact disguising an unsustainable build-up of pressure. Table 17.2 details all the realignments that have taken place, from which the support for these contentions is obvious. A particular feature of the realignment process is that, until the second half of 1992, it was largely free from speculation. When the speculative crises which dogged the end of the Bretton Woods system are recalled, this is a remarkable achievement. An innovation of the EMS in this regard was the practice of carrying out a realignment in such a way that the central rate and bands were changed without disturbing the market rate. This device was introduced to rob the market of the opportunity to make a one-way bet. The difference is illustrated in Figure 17.1. The one-way bet realignment is sketched in Figure 17.1(b): the discrete disturbance of the market rate, if correctly anticipated, affords huge gains to speculators.[4] For example, if a currency is allowed to drift to the bottom of its band so that it can only be expected to be devalued by, say, 5%, the gross gains from correctly anticipating the day on which this takes place substantially exceed, in annual interest rate terms, a rate of 1500% (5% × 365). Speculators could take advantage of this situation by borrowing the weak currency to buy the strong one in anticipation of the devaluation, thereafter redeeming the loan in cheaper currency: clearly interest rates in the weak-currency country

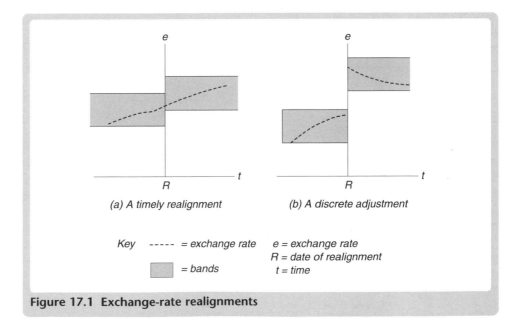

(a) A timely realignment   (b) A discrete adjustment

Key   ----- = exchange rate   e = exchange rate
                      R = date of realignment
        = bands   t = time

Figure 17.1 Exchange-rate realignments

Table 17.2 Realignment of EMS currencies (% changes)

Dates	Belgian–Luxembourg franc	Danish krone	DM	Drachma[a]	Escudo	French franc	Dutch guilder	Punt	Lira[c]	Peseta	£[c]
24 September 79	–	–3.00	+2.00	–	–	–	–	–	–	–	–
30 November 79	–	–5.00	–	–	–	–	–	–	–	–	–
23 March 81	–	–	–	–	–	–	–	–	–6.00	–	–
05 October 81	–	–3.00	+5.50	–	–	–3.00	+5.50	–	–3.00	–	–
22 February 82	–8.50	–	–	–	–	–	–	–	–	–	–
14 June 82	+1.50	–	+4.25	–	–	–5.75	+4.25	–	–2.75	–	–
21 March 83	–1.90	+2.50	+5.50	–	–	–2.50	+3.50	–3.50	–2.50	–	–
18 May 83[b]	–	–1.90	–1.90	–	–	–1.90	–1.90	–1.90	–1.90	–	–
17 September 84	–	–	–	–	–	–	–	–	–	–	–
22 July 85	+2.00	+2.00	+2.00	–	–	+2.00	+2.00	+2.00	–6.00	–	–
07 April 86	+1.00	+1.00	+3.00	–	–	–3.00	+3.00	–	–	–	–
04 August 86	–	–	–	–	–	–	–	–8.00	–	–	–
12 January 87	+2.00	–	+3.00	–	–	–	+3.00	–	–	–	–
08 January 90	–	–	–	–	–	–	–	–	–3.68	–	–
14 September 92	+3.50	+3.50	+3.50	–	+3.50	+3.50	+3.50	+3.50	–3.50	+3.50	+3.50
17 September 92	–	–	–	–	–	–	–	–	–	–5.00	–
23 November 92	–	–	–	–	–6.00	–	–	–	–	–6.00	–
30 January 93	–	–	–	–	–	–	–	–10.00	–	–	–
13 May 93	–	–	–	–	–8.00	–	–	–	–	–6.50	–
06 March 95	–	–	–	–	–7.00	–	–	–	–	–3.50	–

[a] Not participating in ERM.
[b] Technical realignment of £.
[c] Suspended participation in ERM 17 September 1992.

Source: Eurostat; The Economist; Banco de España Economic Bulletin.

would have to be very high indeed to challenge the huge gains in prospect. The EMS technique of changing the central rate and thus the bands *around* the current market rate in a 'timely' realignment (Figure 17.1(a)) robs the speculator of the incentive of such large gains. In practice, EMS realignments have not always been 'timely' – Kenen (1988) estimates the proportion to be just over 70% – and exchange controls have also played a role in deterring speculation. The demise of these controls will put a higher premium on the exercise of the non-provocative realignment procedure described; a premium which turned out to be too high to bear in the autumn of 1992.

Given that realignments have taken place and that currencies have fluctuated within the permitted bands, it cannot be assumed that the EMS has necessarily imparted stability to nominal exchange rates. This question can, however, be examined statistically. Investigators who have done this have taken to assuming as a counterfactual (or *anti-monde*) that, in the absence of the EMS, exchange-rate stability would have evolved in the same way for the EMS currencies as it did for non-EMS currencies. Thus the examination proceeds by comparing a measure of exchange-rate stability for the EMS currencies with a similar measure for non-EMS currencies before, and after, the EMS period itself. By varying the precise measure of the exchange rate used (bilateral or effective; (log) level or (log) change), the data frequency (weekly, monthly, quarterly), and the precise measure of stability

Table 17.3 Exchange-rate variability against ERM currencies, 1974–85[a]

	Period means			
	Levels		Log changes	
	1974–1978	1979–1985	1974–1979	1979–1985
France	31.6	15.9	16.8	7.6
West Germany	29.2	16.3	14.7	7.0
Italy	36.0	19.3	19.3	8.8
Average ERM[b]	28.4	15.1	14.8	7.3
Japan	44.5	48.1	21.1	21.7
United Kingdom	32.7	37.8	16.8	20.9
United States	34.7	55.7	18.8	27.4
Average non-ERM[c]	34.5	35.9	17.2	17.9

[a] Weighted average of variability of bilateral nominal exchange rates against ERM currencies (their log change), monthly data, IMF MERM weights. Variability is measured by the coefficient of variation for levels, and by the standard deviation for (log) changes (in both cases × 1000). Period means are unweighted.
[b] Including all ERM countries.
[c] Includes Japan, United Kingdom, United States, Australia, Canada, Norway, Sweden and Switzerland.
Source: H. Ungerer *et al.* (1986), table 7, p. 35.

employed, this basic counterfactual assumption has supported a variety of estimates. From them, however, a strong consensus has emerged that the EMS has exerted a stabilizing influence on the bilateral nominal exchange rates of its members and on their effective nominal rates.

An authoritative example of this kind of approach is provided in a study for the IMF by Ungerer *et al.* (1986), an excerpt from which is shown in Table 17.3. The results quoted in this table are for nominal bilateral exchange rates against ERM currencies, the exchange rates being weighed together according to the pattern of weights implied by the IMF's multilateral exchange-rate model (MERM), which is standard for this type of application. Two concepts of stability are then explored – stability of the actual level and stability of the (log) change. The latter thus allows for some regular change as the norm against which variability is to be assessed. For levels, the authors use the coefficient of variation (the standard deviation divided by the mean) and for log change the standard deviation itself (both scaled by 1000) as a measure of month-to-month variability. As can be seen, for both levels and log changes, the index of variability rises for the three main non-ERM countries and falls for the three main ERM countries. Including in addition the smaller ERM countries in the coverage and a set of other developed countries in the non-ERM average, the conclusion remains the same: where volatility falls sharply for the ERM countries between the pre-EMS and the EMS period, it rises for the non-participant countries. Weber (1991) extends this analysis to 1988.

17.6   A framework for counterinflationary policy

The inception of the EMS coincided with the second oil shock. Following a meeting in December 1978, the OPEC countries raised oil prices in several stages through 1979 by some 130%. On the fact of it, such a shock, coming so soon after the founding of the EMS, might have been supposed to ensure its early demise. After all, the failure of the snake in the 1970s followed the disruption created by the first oil shock in 1973–4, in the aftermath of which countries followed different adjustment policies incompatible with maintaining fixed exchange rates between themselves. It could well have been apprehended that the second oil shock would expose the EMS to similar strains. In fact, the EMS not only survived the shock but, in the eyes of some observers, proved to have some added advantages in providing for its members a framework within which to prosecute efficient counterinflationary policies.

The first advantage the EMS proved to have over the snake was the provision for realignment. As Table 17.2 shows, the realignments at the beginning of the life of the EMS were quite frequent. It was important for the survival of the EMS that it should have been able to accommodate exchange-rate realignments at this stage and still to continue as a system. This contrasted with the snake, where countries changing their exchange rates were deemed to 'leave' the snake. In the early period, then, as countries accommodated the inflationary shock of the oil price rise in different ways, the EMS displayed sufficient flexibility to survive. Later on, countries in the EMS converged in their attitudes towards the inflationary problem, tending – in common with developments in other countries outside the system – to give first priority in their economic policy objectives to the defeat of inflation.

The claim is made for the EMS that it provided a particularly advantageous framework in this respect. The analysis of that claim is based on the modern theory of the value of reputation in economic policy and the important role played by expectations in the inflationary process. Both features are to an extent controversial and the empirical value of the claim made for the EMS is a matter of controversy. To take the two elements in the claim in reverse order: it is well known from work in the late 1960s by Phelps and Friedman that inflationary processes are capable of being sustained by self-fulfilling expectations. One of the things that a government intent on reducing inflation has to do is to break the climate of inflationary expectations. One way of doing this, of course, is to reduce demand so drastically that, despite the impetus given by strong expectations of inflation, actual inflation winds down and, as it does so, so also does the expectation of inflation. Such a process is potentially very costly in terms of the output which will be lost and the unemployment which will be created by the deflationary demand policy. The more stubborn the expectations are, the higher these costs will be. Another way of breaking the climate of inflationary expectations is for a government to find a direct means of persuading agents that inflation really will fall. In the 1960s and 1970s the device of incomes policies was popular for this purpose but these policies fell out of favour and in the 1980s the principal counterinflationary policy commitment was provided by the publication of targets for the reduction of the rate of growth of the money supply.

At this point we must take account of the theory of 'reputational' policies. This theory points out that the credibility of a government's commitment cannot just be taken for granted. For electoral and other reasons a government may be led to cheat on commitments it makes; if the apprehension of cheating is sufficiently widespread the commitment will be distrusted. If a government's announcements about its counterinflationary intentions and policies are distrusted, perhaps because of a poor reputation acquired by past behaviour or simply because the electorate considers this to be the way of governments, the government will be unable to influence expectations directly. Inflation can then be brought down only by the costly route of demand deflation. But a government may be able to secure greater credibility in various ways: in particular, by committing to policies which are easy to monitor and by raising the visible costs to itself of cheating. The policies must, of course, be plausibly related to the goal. Membership of the EMS offered three important advantages in these respects for the control of inflation. First, the dominant economy in the EMS was Germany, which has a very secure and well-known record of low inflation; targeting exchange rates in the EMS involved targeting against the deutschmark and to the extent that exchange rates reflect relative inflation, a stable deutschmark exchange rate must imply low, German-like, rates of inflation. Second, an exchange-rate commitment is exceptionally easy to monitor; exchange rates are quoted every minute of the day and it is clear what an exchange rate is. Third, by committing itself to the EMS, a government puts its credibility on the line, not only with its own electorate but also with foreign governments; the commitment was the more credible for this reason.[5]

This is the theory. What are the qualifications and what is the evidence? An immediate qualification is that the argument takes for granted that EMS membership puts a heavy premium on exchange-rate fixity: yet, as we saw earlier, realignments are a part of the EMS and were not infrequently used in the early years. How do agents know that the rules have changed from permissiveness to a more disciplined approach and how can they be sure that their government will not go back to the earlier ways of the system?

The evidence does not really help to give a decisive verdict on the claim. It is not, of course, true that the EMS countries alone have brought inflation down; as Table 17.4 shows, inflation has fallen in the United States and the United Kingdom as well even though the United Kingdom was outside the ERM for much of the period. The claim that the EMS provides a superior counterinflationary framework does not deny that other countries could bring inflation down – only that the costs of doing so are higher for them. A 'quick' indicator of the costs of disinflating is the ratio of the cumulative rise in unemployment to the reduction in inflation – the so-called sacrifice ratio.[6] Table 17.4 gives estimates at four intervals for this ratio. It can be seen from this that Germany has the highest sacrifice ratio of all. However, this is not necessarily inconsistent with the hypothesis at issue in as much as it is the non-German members which are supposed to reap the benefit of Germany's extreme inflation aversion by targeting the deutschmark. Indeed, it can be seen that the sacrifice ratios for France and Italy were lower than those for the United Kingdom, consistent with the hypothesis. More recently, the ratio for France has risen. It is

Table 17.4 Inflation and the 'sacrifice ratio'

| | Consumer prices – inflation (% pa) | | | | |
	United States	West Germany	France	United Kingdom	Italy
1980	13.5	5.4	13.6	18	21.2
1981	10.3	6.3	13.4	11.9	19.3
1982	6.1	5.2	11.8	8.6	16.4
1983	3.2	3.3	9.6	4.6	14.9
1984	4.3	2.4	7.4	5	10.6
1985	3.5	2.1	5.8	6.1	8.6
1986	1.9	−0.1	2.7	3.4	6.1
1987	3.7	0.2	3.1	4.1	4.6
1988	4.1	1.3	2.7	4.9	5
1989	4.8	2.8	3.6	7.8	6.6
1990	5.4	2.7	3.4	9.5	6.1
1991	4.2	3.6	3.2	5.9	6.5
1992	3	5.1	2.4	3.7	5.3
1993	3	4.5	2.1	1.6	4.2
1994	2.6	2.7	1.7	2.5	3.9
1995	2.8	1.8	1.7	3.4	5.4
	Sacrifice ratios[a]				
1980–84	0.64	4.43	1.40	1.51	0.42
1980–86	0.51	3.82	1.55	2.00	0.63
1980–88	0.36	6.73	2.29	2.69	1.01
1980–92	0.05	117.33	3.41	2.99	1.76
1980–95	−0.20	14.7	4.64	3.58	2.47

[a]The ratio of the cumulative increase in unemployment to the difference between inflation in 1980 and inflation in the terminal year (1984, 1986, 1988, 1992, 1995).
Source: OECD, *Economic Outlook*, December 1996.

the United States, on the other hand, which seems to do best of all (there was no cumulative rise in unemployment by 1992). While this might be treated as a special case, it is obvious that the evidence is far from unambiguous. A position on the agnostic side of the question is probably the safest.

Whatever the position on the differential advantage of using the EMS as a counterinflationary framework, it must certainly be acknowledged that it was, in fact, used as such. The DI was an inevitable casualty of this, for a simple reason. Whereas the DI was designed, as explained above, with the intention of inducing symmetry of adjustment – and, in particular, of inducing adjustment by Germany – the counterinflationary policies of the period ran counter to this conception. It was not desirable to induce Germany to raise its inflation to the EMS average (even supposing this could have been done); rather, the point was to bring the average down to the German level.[7]

In the last four years of the EMS the process of counterinflationary policy was dominated by convergence towards meeting the criteria for membership of Stage 3 of EMU laid down in the Maastricht Treaty. Again this was asymmetric as the target was set by the three lowest inflation countries, whoever they might be at the time.

17.7 Competitiveness

The real rate of exchange, the nominal rate corrected for relative prices, provides an index of competitiveness. Although the formal provisions of the EMS focused on nominal exchange-rate agreement, in a customs union exchange-rate arrangements must ensure a degree of stability in real rates of exchange. The reason is that because the real rate of exchange governs an economy's competitiveness, a sharp change – say a large appreciation in the real rate producing a large fall in competitiveness – will arouse protectionist pressures and thus threaten the reversal of the customs union's achievements in removing internal tariff barriers. Other, non-tariff barriers may be promoted and progress slowed on the removal of these and other obstacles to intraunion trade. Whether reflecting this 'inner logic' or not, the evidence does confirm that whereas the real rates of exchange of both the United Kingdom and the United States underwent changes in the 1980s and 1990s, changes in competitiveness of the EMS economies were more muted. Thus it appears that among the achievements of the EMS might be included that of reducing the extent of exchange-rate 'misalignment', deviations of real rates of exchange from equilibrium levels.

A qualification must be entered at this stage. It is one thing for the real exchange rates of EMS countries to show less evidence of misalignment than those of some key non-EMS (or non-ERM in the case of the United Kingdom) countries. It is another thing to be sure that the record of the EMS in stabilizing real rates of exchange was adequate. A reason why it might not have been adequate is the fact that, as argued above, countries have used the EMS as a counterinflationary framework. Among other things, this has meant that realignments, although always changing central rates in the direction indicated by relative inflation, have been deliberately tardy and niggardly in doing so. The object was to ensure that realignments did not accommodate and encourage inflation. A consequence of this is that an economy which persistently inflated above the EMS average rate would undergo prolonged pressure not to adjust its exchange rate to accommodate this and so would gradually lose its competitive edge. Because of the 'inner logic' of real rate stabilization referred to earlier, such a situation could not be regarded as sustainable. The position of the United Kingdom and to a lesser extent Italy shows this clearly. In 1992 the system broke down and these currencies were forced to devalue along with Nordic and Iberian countries.

17.8 The popularity of the ECU

As described above, the ECU was simply a 'composite currency', with no necessary role in the critical parity grid of the EMS. It had no central bank of issue and even its role as the foundation for the DI mechanism seems unimportant in light of the proven weakness of that mechanism.

Nevertheless, the ECU proved quite popular as a currency of denomination of international bond issues; in 1985 it became the fifth most used currency of denomination of such issues outside the US dollar, its share rising to nearly 11.5% (see Table 17.5).[8] While the official transactions of the EC itself were denominated in ECU, the ECU was barely used as a means of payment by the private sector.[9] Its attraction was that of a 'currency cocktail', in that it offered some 'hedging' properties that agents found worth while. Thus, a trading company whose activities are concentrated in, say, three different markets may find that the best way of hedging its liabilities, if it needs to borrow, is to issue bonds which are denominated in a cocktail of the three different currencies used in those markets. The alternative of issuing bonds in one currency only (one of the three used in the markets where it trades or a fourth, outside currency) inevitably involves the company in taking on the risk associated with changes in the exchange rates between the currency of denomination of the bond and the currencies used in the markets it operates in. While the risk, in itself, is as much a risk of gain as of loss, the trading company may not be interested in speculating in this way, or be able to do so. For this reason,

Table 17.5 Non-dollar international bond issues by currency of denomination (%)

	1981	1983	1985	1987	1990	1995
Swiss francs	44.7	42.7	23.0	21.2	18.5	10.0
Sterling	7.3	8.8	10.1	13.2	9.2	7.1
Deutschmark	13.4	19.6	17.4	13.2	7.7	22.9
Yen	16.2	12.4	18.9	22.0	23.1	30.3
ECU	1.3	4.9	11.4	6.5	13.8	3.0
Others	17.1	11.7	19.2	23.8	27.7	26.8

Sources: Computed from data shown in Walton (1988) and from the Bank of England Quarterly Bulletin.

a demand for currency-cocktail borrowing arises from traders who are averse to risk. ECU-denominated bond issues appealed to businesses whose activities were concentrated in the EU for this reason. In a similar fashion, a demand for assets of this denomination arose from firms and institutions whose liabilities were of a similar nature. In fact, most of the bond issues were made by EC organizations and national governments, although more recently corporate ECU borrowings became significant. Both the Italian government (between 1987 and 1993) and the British government (since 1988) have issued short-dated ECU-denominated debt instruments, helping to correct a deficiency in the market for short-term ECU assets. In addition to the ECU bond market there was also a development of bank lending and borrowing in ECU.[10]

The apparent success of the ECU depended on something more than its currency-cocktail quality, however, since modern financial procedures readily allow cocktail mixing to take place and it does not seem difficult to imagine that for many purposes cocktails containing slightly different mixes of EU currencies (and perhaps including the Swiss franc, for example) would be preferable. Two main points should be mentioned.

One is that ECU borrowing could be seen in some countries of the EMS (France and Italy) as a reflection of exchange control. Certainly, the largest sources of ECU borrowing were Italy and France, where the special status accorded to the ECU permitted residents, in effect, to borrow from overseas in a way that would not have been allowed if the borrowing were done in a single currency or, indeed, any other currency cocktail. At the same time, the comparatively high interest rates available on ECU-denominated loans made these loans quite attractive to residents of some low interest rate countries. Viewed in this light, the prevalence of ECU-denominated borrowing and lending was a rather ambiguous advertisement for the EMS. However, it does seem clear that the volume of private sector ECU issues was well above what can be attributed solely to such features and in itself this counts as a highly positive declaration of the credibility established by the EMS. So the second point to make is that the fact that the ECU was chosen rather than some other cocktail testifies to a perception of the credibility of the EMS and paved the way for the ECU to become a genuine EC currency, albeit renamed as the Euro.

The all-time high for ECU bond issues was reached in 1991. Although, in total, new issues of ECU bonds had recovered to their 1988 levels by 1997, the big difference lay in the composition of issuers. Up till 1992 the issue of bonds from outside the EU was considerably higher than that from inside. From 1993 the balance was the reverse. By 1997 external issues had still not recovered to their 1985 level.

17.9 The position of the United Kingdom

The United Kingdom declined to participate in the operation of the EMS, to begin with, out of a belief that the system would be operated in a rigid way which would threaten the United Kingdom, with its high 'propensity to inflate', with a decline in its competitiveness, especially *vis-à-vis* Germany. This concern for the United Kingdom's freedom to determine or preserve its competitiveness still marks one strand of oppositional thinking on the question of British membership of EMU today. The problems of September 1992 in many ways served to reinforce the views that had led to the initial reluctance to join the ERM and hence were not wholly uncongenial.

While opposition to full membership of the EMS was voiced on these grounds by the Labour government of Mr Callaghan, opposition on different grounds was voiced by the incoming Conservative government headed by Mrs Thatcher. The Thatcher government wished to run an experiment in monetary policy in order to bring inflation down and reasoned, correctly, that if the instruments of monetary policy (principally interest rates) were to be directed at reducing the rate of growth of the money supply, they could not simultaneously be used to target the exchange rate. Technically, this dilemma could be avoided by maintaining a suitably strong set of exchange controls; such controls would allow a government some freedom to maintain two different targets for monetary policy but the Thatcher government was keen to remove these controls in any case and did so not long after taking office.

Events were to turn out somewhat paradoxically. The first phase of the Conservative government's monetary experiment was associated with a very marked *appreciation* of the exchange rate – so competitiveness would have been *better* preserved inside the EMS – and the deep recession that soon set in was attributed by many observers to this cause. The view took root that while the Thatcher government was correct to say that membership of the EMS was incompatible with pursuit of an independent monetary policy and would involve a loss of sovereignty in this respect, better results would nevertheless be attained by adhering to the EMS. In particular, the exchange rate would be steadier and competitiveness more assured, while inflation would be dragged towards the modest German level (we have already described the claims made for the EMS as a counterinflationary framework).

This view gained momentum as official British policy towards the exchange rate as a target changed and as it became clear that monetary policy was no longer aimed in single-minded fashion solely at controlling the supply of money. In fact, with practice preceding the public statement, the Chancellor of the Exchequer made this very clear in his 1983 budget speech. A House of Lords report on the question of entry into the EMS, published a little later in the same year, favoured 'early, though not necessarily immediate' entry into the system.

That report referred to four problems that the United Kingdom had had in relation to the EMS and noted that in each case events had moved in a favourable fashion. The first problem was the apprehension that the EMS would prove rigid and inflexible: the committee noted that the EMS had allowed a number of realignments. The second problem was that the United Kingdom had wanted to put the control of the money supply ahead of the goal of stabilizing the exchange rate – where, as described, policy had already retreated somewhat. The third problem was related to the UK position as an oil exporter, with sterling subject to quite a different response from that of the EMS currencies to oil price shocks. The committee saw this as less problematic as the oil market had become less disturbed. The fourth problem arose from sterling's still persistent role as a vehicle currency, i.e. one widely held by agents other than those solely concerned with UK trade. The committee acknowledged that this might mean that it would not be so easy to stabilize sterling in the ERM.

The viewpoint of the House of Lords report appears to have been representative of a wide range of opinion. Although the later report of a subcommittee of the House of Commons Select Committee on the Treasury and Civil Service revived some of the earlier arguments against entry, the general climate of opinion had changed markedly in a favourable direction by the early 1980s. With the passage of time the lingering reservations over the exposure of sterling to oil shocks and over the problem of speculation diminished still further, while the case for exchange-rate management became more widely and firmly accepted. The initiative launched by the United States in 1985 to secure the co-ordinated actions of its major partners to bring the dollar down substantially reinforced the latter process.

In September 1986, at the meetings of the IMF, the Chancellor of the Exchequer advertised the non-speculative realignment process of the EMS and not long afterwards followed this up with a policy of 'shadowing the EMS', keeping the sterling exchange rate closely in line with the deutschmark. This policy initiative lasted for just over a year; by the end of February 1988, following a well-publicized exchange of views between the Chancellor and the Prime Minister, sterling was uncapped. Higher interest rates, invoked as a means of dampening monetary growth and in response to forecasts of inflation, caused the exchange rate to appreciate through its previous working ceiling. The incident underlined the inconsistency between an independent monetary policy and an exchange-rate policy and at the same time served to confirm that sterling was unlikely to participate in the ERM during the prime ministership of Mrs Thatcher. Even when sterling ultimately went into the ERM in October 1990 it appeared to be with considerable reluctance.

Membership of the ERM only lasted until September 1992, when markets pushed sterling out of the system. It did not rejoin, even when a government with a more favourable attitude was elected in May 1997. The issue has now been overtaken by whether the UK should join EMU. While a close shadowing of the Euro, as has been followed by Denmark, could make sense in its own right to help acquire greater stability, the main reason for such a policy would be as part of the preconditions for membership of the Eurosystem. UK monetary policy was immediately focused on an explicit inflation target of 2.5% a year in May 1997. Pursuit of this target with only narrow bands of 1% either side almost inevitably means that UK monetary policy will vary from that of the ECB, with its medium-term target of inflation less than 2%.

With the advent of the Euro, bond issues have leapt up. Member government borrowers have naturally switched to the new currency, but the private sector has also changed its behaviour. Borrowers from inside the area issued 76% of their debt in Euros between July 1998 and December 1999, compared to 50% in their own currencies between January 1990 and June 1998. Outsiders have doubled their issues in the later period, with a quarter of their new international issues being in Euros.

17.10 The challenge of the Single Market

Full participation in the EMS was not a requirement of membership of the EU nor was it implied in the original Rome Treaty. The SEA, however, did add a section to the Treaty calling for member countries to take steps to ensure the convergence of economic and monetary policy, prefiguring the emergence of monetary union from the EMS and the ECU. However, the provisions of the Single Market which are of immediate consequence to the EMS were those that required the dismantling of exchange controls. The consequences of this for the functioning of the EMS were profound and could have been fatal, as was demonstrated during the last part of 1992.

Exchange controls of the type maintained by Italy and France throughout the first ten years of the life of the EMS have as their immediate object the prevention of the short-run export of capital. Controls of this type therefore forbid the direct export of financial capital, restricting or forbidding portfolio investment overseas, the holding of foreign-currency-denominated bank deposits and lending (and borrowing) overseas. These restrictions are not watertight but they are effective. They have two important effects. First, they prevent or slow down speculation. Agents anticipating a devaluation of a currency cannot, if they are residents of the country concerned, simply sell the currency for foreign exchange in the expectation of making a quick gain when buying it back after the devaluation; nor can they lend the currency to non-residents who could carry out the same speculative raid. Second, the controls break the link that holds currencies together when there are no obstacles to perfect arbitrage. The interest parity link states that the interest differential between two currencies is equal to the expected rate of change in the exchange rate between them. Thus, taking two countries, say France (F) and Germany (G), interest parity would have $r_F = r_G + d_{F/G}$ where r_F, r_G are interest rates on similar-maturity, similar-risk instruments denominated respectively in the French and German currencies and $d_{F/G}$ is the expected rate of depreciation of the French franc against the German mark.

The removal of exchange controls therefore posed two problems for the EMS. First, a protection against speculation was lost. Second, because interest parity was no longer prevented, interest rates everywhere were tightly linked as the amount of expected depreciation was confined by the bands of permissible fluctuations of the currencies against one another. Because Germany was by far the largest economy in the EMS, this meant that interest rates, and hence monetary policy, everywhere in the system were dominated by Germany. Unless Germany in turn tempered its monetary policy by concern for the economic situation in other countries this could turn out to be an unacceptable state of affairs, as indeed proved to be the case in 1992–3.

These problems were realized and various solutions proposed. First, as regards the problem of speculation the mechanisms of the EMS were improved by measures to accommodate automatic lending by a strong-currency country to a weak-currency country in the event of need; whereas previously this automaticity applied only when intervention was taking place at the edge of the band, since the deliberations of the EMS finance ministers in Nyborg in September 1987, it applied also to so-called intramarginal intervention, i.e. foreign exchange operations taking place to support a currency before it has reached its limit. These new provisions were tested by a speculative run on the French franc in the autumn of 1987 and proved successful; the Bundesbank lent heavily to the Banque de France but the lending was rapidly repaid once the speculation subsided and confidence returned. The second problem – that of excessive German dominance – was only resolved by moving on to full EMU. The Nyborg provisions called for much closer monetary co-operation, implying more continuous exchange of information, and interest rate movements within the EMS after that time displayed a high degree of synchronization. However, the co-operation called for also seemed to imply a degree of common decision making going beyond simply following a German lead in a prompt and well-prepared way. Progress on this front is less evident. The anxiety of France on this score, however, led to important initiatives. First, France called upon Germany to discuss economic policy on a regular basis and an economic council was set up for this purpose. Second, it was on French initiatives that the EC was led to call for an investigation into the requirements of full monetary union, an investigation subsequently carried out by the Delors Committee, the recommendations of whose report were endorsed by all 12 nations of the EC in June 1989, leading to the Maastricht Treaty on European Union.

The path which the EMS participants agreed to follow thus called for increasing intervention resources and other devices to combat the threat of speculation and for increased economic and monetary co-operation between member countries, eventually leading to the creation of the European Central Bank. But we should note that there were alternative short-run solutions. One way in which countries could recover a greater measure of independence from the dominant power would be to enlarge the bands of exchange-rate fluctuation, which is what they did in 1993; another would be to compromise on the Single Market by retaining a measure of exchange control. Either device has obvious counterspeculative advantages too. If maintained over the long term, these alternative solutions would be in effect a defeat for the higher aspirations of the EMS. But either one could, in principle, be adopted on a purely monetary basis until such time as the political prerequisites for greater co-operation were met. The second mechanism was not used but it is not difficult to think of circumstances in which it might have been, given the increasing popularity in the late 1990s of the idea of putting 'sand in the wheels' of international financial transactions in order to limit their volatility.

The removal of exchange controls undoubtedly posed problems for the future of the EMS. Following the delicate path to which the member countries agreed exposed the system to the hazards of speculation and posed political problems relating to the acceptance of German dominance in monetary affairs. The alternative short-run solutions had the disadvantage of taking the pressure off the search for a solution to the political problem, or perpetuating an obstacle to the integration of the European financial area.

The forecast threat to the system duly occurred in September 1992. Uncertainty about the outcome of the French referendum on the Maastricht Treaty contributed to speculation against the weakest currencies in the ERM, sterling and the lira. Both were unable to resist the pressure despite substantial increases in interest rates. By the summer of 1993 not even the French franc could survive the pressure and the bands had to be widened to allow it to devalue.

Other currencies also came under pressure, such as the Irish punt and the Swedish krone (which was shadowing the ERM), and have been forced to devalue (see Table 17.2). There was considerable pressure on the French franc in September 1992 but it survived, aided by substantial intervention by the Bundesbank on its behalf. It is arguable that all the currencies which were devalued were in some sense overvalued in terms of their long-term sustainable values. (One interpretation of this is the Fundamental Equilibrium Exchange Rate, FEER, the rate at which the balance of payments is sustainable in the long run.) However, the problem was not merely one of great domestic inflation by the devaluing countries but of the special problems of the dominant German economy leading to a divergence from the domestic objectives of the other countries.[11] German interest rates were driven up by the need to finance unification over and above the willingness to raise taxes. With the tight linkage of EMS interest rates other states also had to have rates that were high in real terms.

In the case of the United Kingdom it was clearly a relief that the constraints of the ERM could be broken. Interest rates had already been progressively cut to the point that sterling was close to its lower bound. A domestic recession was being exacerbated by the inability to use monetary policy to alleviate it. On exit, interest rates were lowered by four percentage points in virtually as many months. There was no immediate prospect of sterling re-entering the ERM and indeed its fall of over 15% is no larger than that suggested by the FEER, and its subsequent rise as the economy recovered was predictable.

The EMS suffered considerably through being unable to organize an orderly realignment of exchange rates. The mechanisms existed but political pressures meant that the member states could not agree among themselves. Blame has been placed in a number of quarters – on the Bundesbank for not taking greater account of the impact of its policy on other countries and on the United Kingdom for not being sincere in trying to maintain parity within the bounds – but the basic weakness of the system remained: that trying to have narrow bands without exchange controls is really not sustainable when there are substantial shocks to the system. This was admitted in practice by widening the bands.

17.11   From EMS to EMU

The EMS took a back seat after the devaluations of September 1992 and the widening of the band to ±15% in August 1993. However, the system remained intact and slowly regained credibility. Despite three devaluations of the peseta and the escudo between November 1992 and March 1995 the participating currencies moved back into closer alignment. At the end of 1996 all bar the Irish punt were within the 2.25% band. Although sterling and the drachma have remained outside the ERM and the Swedish krone did not join, Italy rejoined in November 1996 and Finland (October 1996) and Austria (January 1995) also became participants.

The EMS survived through to its replacement by the Eurosystem at the start of 1999 primarily because of the determination of EU governments to qualify for EMU under the Maastricht criteria (see Chapter 6). The restraints on fiscal policy from needing to keep deficits below 3% of GDP and debt below 60% (or make credible progress towards 60%) simultaneously helped inflation to converge and the member states to get their business cycles in line. The steady development of the internal market has integrated them further. The Maastricht Treaty offered two possible dates by which monetary union could start. The member states could decide by mid-1996 which of the states that had met the criteria should join Stage 3 at the beginning of 1997. If Stage 3 was not started then it would begin on 1 January 1999 with whichever states had qualified by mid-1998.

Initial progress was not, however, very promising and during 1995 and 1996 the countries diverged. It became clear that by the initial qualifying date for the member states to decide whether Stage 3 should be started on 1 January 1997 there was no serious chance of EMU taking place. Only Luxembourg met all the criteria on a strict interpretation. Indeed, New Zealand was the only other OECD country that would have 'qualified'. In part the convergence period after the shocks of 1992–3 was just too short, particularly for countries like Sweden and especially Finland for which the shocks were greatest, but the evolution of the general economic cycles was not favourable. From then onwards, however, convergence was easier and all member states except Greece could have qualified. However, just as the adverse circumstances in the mid-1990s were bad luck so the EU was extremely lucky that 1996–8 was a period of very considerable stability. Even the Asian crisis did not have a marked effect and decreased the chance of importing inflation from the rest of the world.

Once financial markets felt that fiscal convergence and EMU were likely, this expectation brought the required convergence in real interest rates. Had it not been possible for some of the countries that had experienced the greatest difficulty in converging to join then, it is likely that they would have experienced considerable pressures in the period immediately after the decision. The loss of credibility involved would then have made joining at a subsequent date much more expensive than it was for those who were successful earlier on.

The creation of the Eurosystem has created three groups of countries within the EMS: those who are in the Euro area, those who are outside but hope to join in the reasonably near future and those who are outside but have no immediate plans. The third group, Denmark and the UK, are free to pursue their own independent monetary policies just as they could outside the ERM of the previous EMS. The Eurosystem has, however, created an extension of the ERM labelled ERM2 for those countries that wish to try to converge. The rules are similar to those that faced the new members, Austria, Finland and Sweden under the original ERM. Their currencies did not form part of the ECU basket and hence if their exchange rate moved with respect to the other members it did not affect the value of the ECU itself.

A central value is agreed between the ECB and the member state for the exchange rate with the Euro. The intention is then for the rate to remain within the same 2.25% range that prevailed within ERM. Realignments are possible and indeed have already happened for Greece (upwards). Only Sweden and Greece are currently participating but this mechanism will be open for all of the new members of the EU when enlargement takes place. Some like Estonia, however, already have a much tighter arrangement with the Euro, through having a currency board. There is therefore no variation at all with respect to the Euro.

All member states are members of the ESCB and the governors of their central banks sit on the General Council along with the President and Vice-President of the ECB. The President of the ECB is the chairman. The General Council reviews the progress of ERM2 and other matters not related to the Eurosystem. Conduct of the Eurosystem is the responsibility of the *Governing* Council, composed of the ECB Executive Board and the governors of the participating central banks, this time excluding those who are not in Stage 3.

ERM2 is thus a rather one-sided affair, very much reminiscent of the early days of the original ERM. It is for the applicants to adjust to the behaviour of the Euro area. Euro monetary policy is run without regard to their problems, it is the ECB that determines the parities. The ECB will offer an opinion on whether convergence has occurred. In the case of Greece, the government was keen to go ahead with membership of the Euro area as soon as possible. It was accepted for membership in June 2000 and will join the Eurosystem at the beginning of 2001.

Sweden is still to make up its mind as to the exact date but its decision not to seek membership in 1998 was on the basis that the timing was not yet right, not that membership was not desirable in principle (Calmfors, 1997). Even if the EU were to expand to accept all of the 12 current applicants and they were to join ERM2, the system would be highly unbalanced in favour of the Eurosystem in terms of relative economic size. In some ways dependency will actually be a strength to the system as it makes stable alternatives substantially more costly for the applicants. Thus not only will they have a strong incentive to try to remain in the system and not follow policies that are likely to lead to downward realignments, but the existence of these incentives will be obvious to everybody else as well, thereby increasing the credibility of the commitment.

However, the applicant countries are likely to find ERM2 a much more difficult proposition than the four other members of the ESCB, who are currently not in the Eurosystem as they are still undergoing a major process of structural change and have not in most cases achieved sustainably low inflation. It is therefore likely that, as with the original ERM, the weaker members will experience real exchange rate increases that will ultimately force them into realignments. Adopting a currency board based on the Euro may offer greater credibility. Ironically one element of convergence to the behaviour of the Eurosystem may be easier than for some of the existing ESCB members as the applicants are in the main heavily integrated with the Euro economy already, even though geography might have led one to expect closer links with third countries. Particularly in the case of the former Soviet bloc countries, the economic ties further east have been thoroughly broken. It is thus the problems of transition that are likely to present the greatest strains rather than worries about asymmetric shocks that have affected countries like the UK with substantial economic linkages outside the Euro area.

Transition is likely to be slow in many cases, so ERM2 is also likely to be a relatively long-lived arrangement. However, in many cases the applicants will feel that they would rather complete the process of adjustment within EMU than outside. The credibility and hence much lower real interest rates offered by membership may very well be thought to outweigh the gains from exchange-rate flexibility. Massive changes in their labour markets are known to be inevitable, so there may be a willingness to accept the pressures on non-monetary and non-fiscal routes to adjustment, a process that has presented considerable difficulties for many of the current EU members.

The combination of the single market and the absence of exchange controls has clearly added to the risk from speculative pressures for the EMS. It is not surprising therefore that there was very strong pressure to move to Stage 3 of EMU despite the costs of transition. This will still apply.

Notes

1. As from 2 August 1993, this became ±15% for all participating countries, although the Netherlands maintained a ±2.25% fluctuation limit with respect to the deutschmark.
2. Realignments in the EMS have only gradually become collective decisions (see Padoa-Schioppa, 1985).
3. The reader should refer to Swann (1988) for a useful summary and to Kruse (1980) for a detailed account of these past endeavours.
4. This is excellently illustrated by the huge gains reported for speculators against sterling in September 1992.

5. The title of the paper by Giavazzi and Pagano (1986) on this issue is indicative. However, the deutschmark itself experienced problems after the unification of Germany which could not, from then on, be regarded as the least inflationary country in the ERM.

6. The sacrifice ratio is normally computed on a cyclical basis (see Mayes and Chapple, 1995, for example). The fall in inflation is thus contrasted with the rise in unemployment over the period up to the point that the economy gets back to its trend growth. However, other factors also affect unemployment both positively and negatively over the period and it has been argued that there has also been a strong secular upward movement in unemployment in Europe over the period.

   Extending the calculation beyond 1995 would therefore continue to generate high figures for the sacrifice ratio in the Euro countries, as, although inflation did not fall much further, except in the UK and Italy, unemployment continued at high levels in the continental European countries. However, unemployment has continued to fall in the United States, amid claims that this reflects the emergence of a 'new economy', and also in the UK but not to such low levels.

7. Thus a strong currency country should in these circumstances revalue, not inflate. This is very clear in the European Commission's evidence to the House of Lords (1983). This is precisely what Germany did not do in the immediate aftermath to unification in the early 1990s. Here the obvious response would have been a revaluation but suitable changes were only achieved by devaluation of many of the other currencies outside the process of agreed realignment within the ERM.

8. The crisis of September 1992 brought new issues in the ECU market to a grinding halt, and it did not regain the same level of popularity. The focus turned back towards the deutschmark.

9. Walton (1988) notes that ECU invoicing accounted for 1% of all foreign trade in Italy and France, where it was most popular.

10. The reader is referred to Bank for International Settlements (1989) for a detailed account.

11. Cobham (1996) provides a helpful exposition of the different possible explanations of the crisis.

18 Regional policy

H. W. ARMSTRONG

> Member states of the European Community are 'anxious to ensure their harmonious development by reducing the differences existing between the various regions and the backwardness of the less favoured regions'. (Preamble to the Treaty of Rome 1958)

> In order to promote its overall harmonious development, the Community shall develop and pursue its actions leading to the strengthening of its economic and social cohesion. In particular the Community shall aim at reducing disparities between the various regions and the backwardness of the least favoured regions, including rural areas. (Article 130a, Single European Act 1986. Reaffirmed as Article 130a of the Treaty of Union 1992)

These two quotations, more than thirty years apart, illustrate the strength of the EU's commitment to regional policy. The commitment to regional policy is, at first sight, a curious one. The EU has aspirations to become a federal system. Regional policy of the type we know in Europe is, however, rarely found in long-established federal countries such as the USA, Canada and Australia. To understand EU regional policy requires an understanding of the uniqueness of the European situation, with a patchwork of independent nation states seeking to move step by step towards closer economic, social and political relationships.

This chapter examines EU regional policy at an important moment in the step-by-step process of European integration. With the EU on the verge of full economic and monetary union (EMU), at least for the majority of the member states, and with the looming accession of a number of Central and Eastern European countries, a radical new regional policy programme has been introduced for the period 2000–6.

The chapter begins with an examination of the case for having an EU regional policy running alongside the regional policies operated by each of the member state governments. This is followed by an overview of the ways in which economic integration can affect regional disparities. Attention will subsequently be concentrated on the EU regional policy which emerged from 1989 onwards in the aftermath of the Single Market and the 1992 Treaty on European Union. Finally, the key issues which confront EU regional policy in the first decade of the new millennium will be examined. In particular, the EU's response to the challenge posed by Eastern Enlargement in the form of the *Agenda 2000* reforms of regional policy for the period 2000–6 will be considered.

18.1 The case for an EU regional policy

Regional policy has always been controversial. It is undeniably interventionist. Those who distrust the competence of governments fear that regional policy penalizes successful businesses in prosperous regions while simultaneously encouraging unsuitable economic activities in the depressed regions. To those who hold this opinion regional disparities are the inevitable outcome of the market system – something to be tolerated until market forces such as labour migration, capital investment and expanding trade combine to automatically revitalize low-wage depressed regions.

Supporters of regional policy are much more sceptical of the ability of market forces to solve long-standing regional problems. An array of arguments is marshalled in support of an active government-led regional policy. The main arguments are as follows:

1. *Equity and 'fairness'*. Regional policy is seen as a way of ensuring that all parts of society can share in the benefits of a modern, growing economy.

2. *Extra income and production*. Regional policy is portrayed as being essential if underutilized resources – particularly unemployed labour – are to be drawn into productive use.

3. *Lower inflation and faster growth*. The concentration of economic activity in a few, already prosperous regions means that during periods of economic upturn markets in regions such as South-East England tend to quickly 'overheat'. The resulting surge in wage levels, house prices, rents etc. sends a wave of inflationary pressure rippling across the remainder of the economy and also results in a rise in imports to meet the growing demand, thus worsening the balance of payments position. Regional policy, by spreading economic activity, eases bottlenecks in the market economy. This in turn allows the economy to enjoy lower inflation and more sustained growth over time, to the benefit of all.

4. *Fewer urban problems*. Economic activity in Europe is heavily concentrated in the big metropolitan areas and capital cities of the member states. The quality of life in these cities is a cause of great concern. Traffic congestion, pollution, crime and overcrowding are serious problems. Regional policy offers a way of easing the pressures on the big cities by diverting part of the economic activity elsewhere.

These are powerful arguments and most are as valid now as they ever were. They do not in themselves, however, constitute a case for an *EU regional policy*. In the past they have been used to justify individual member states' regional policies. In Britain, for example, the national government has had its own regional policy since 1928, a policy which has survived a succession of governments of widely differing ideologies (Armstrong, 1991; Armstrong and Taylor, 2000). The crucial question from an EU point of view is why a separate EU regional policy is required *in addition to* the regional policies of the individual member states. The individual regional policies of the member states have continued alongside EU regional policy over the years since 1975 (when the European Regional Development Fund was established). There is no suggestion that they should be laid down in favour of a single EU regional policy.

Several distinct arguments can be advanced in support of a regional policy operated at EU level. Each argument will be considered in turn.

18.1.1 The 'vested interest' argument

The nation states of Europe are becoming increasingly integrated economies. Rapidly expanding trade links, together with much freer capital mobility and more slowly growing cross-border labour migration, are being stimulated by EU initiatives such as the Single Market. Increasingly, the economic well-being of citizens of one member state depends on the prosperity of the economies of other member states. The presence of disadvantaged regions experiencing low incomes and high unemployment is in the interests of no one. Put another way, the citizens of one member state have a *vested interest* in ensuring that the regional problems in *other* member states are reduced. An EU regional policy can therefore be justified as a mechanism which allows one member state to become involved in policies which stimulate economic activity in regions of other member states.

Why do citizens in a prosperous member state such as Germany have a vested interest in helping to solve regional problems in, say, Greece or Spain? They have a vested interest because the solution of regional problems elsewhere generates *spillover benefits* – benefits which spread across member state boundaries. The more integrated the EU becomes, the bigger are the spillover effects of one member state on another. At present they are significant, but still relatively small, and comprise:

(a) equity spillovers;

(b) efficiency spillovers;

(c) spillover of non-economic benefits.

Equity spillovers arise because there is a widely held view in the EU that the benefits of integration should be 'fairly' distributed across regions and member states. Residents in more prosperous EU member states derive utility gains from helping citizens of poorer regions and member states to improve their economic status.

In addition to the pervading desire for 'fairness', reducing regional problems in the EU also generates *efficiency spillover* gains in already prosperous regions and member states. Lower unemployment increases income and production for the EU as a whole, and also stimulates tax receipts (e.g. VAT) for the EU while simultaneously reducing the pressure on EU spending programmes such as social policy. An EU regional policy also has the potential to create gains for everyone in the form of lower *overall* EU inflation and easing the urban problems in the big cities at the heart of the EU.

Some of the benefits of EU regional policy are in the form of *non-economic spillover* gains. Reduced regional disparities can help in achieving greater social, economic and political 'cohesion' in Europe. Areas which feel left out of the benefits of integration are unlikely to co-operate or to fully embrace the concept of a more united Europe. Some would go further and argue that a strong EU regional policy is vital if the EU is to survive and to progress towards a fully fledged federal political system as well as full EMU. If this is true, the citizens of already prosperous regions will support an EU regional policy as a means of protecting and extending the existing EU. In doing so they may also reap additional non-economic benefits in the form of extra security, the preservation of local languages and cultures and the extraordinary socio-cultural diversity for which Europe is famous.

18.1.2 The 'financial targeting' argument

The second main argument in support of an EU regional policy is concerned with the effectiveness with which regional policy is operated in Europe. Regional policies are expensive to operate and resources must be found from public sector budgets. The disadvantaged regions of the EU are not evenly distributed among the member states of the EU. Some member states carry such a burden of disadvantaged regions that they constitute depressed regions in their own right. This is particularly the case with some of the member states in the Mediterranean south of the EU.

Given the inevitable pressure on public sector budgets, it is not surprising to find that it is precisely those member states with the most severe burden of regional problems which have the greatest difficulty in financing an active regional policy. Leaving regional policy wholly to the member states is not therefore effective from an EU perspective. Member states such as France and Germany, with fewer regional problems, have been best able to afford an active regional policy. Those with the most severe regional problems such as Greece and Portugal already have severe budget deficits and find it difficult to fund their domestic regional policies adequately.

The difficulties faced by member states in ensuring that the most disadvantaged EU regions receive the greatest volume of assistance represent a powerful case for an EU regional policy. Member states on their own are simply unable to target regional policy funds on the most disadvantaged regions. Only the EU, it can be argued, is capable of drawing resources from more prosperous parts of the EU and ensuring that they are allocated to the most heavily disadvantaged regions.

18.1.3 The co-ordination argument

The third argument which can be made in support of an EU regional policy concerns the advantages of a co-ordinated approach. The EU has immense potential to improve the effectiveness of the regional policy effort by acting as a supra-national co-ordinating agency. Regional development initiatives within the member states are offered by a bewildering array of organizations. As well as the member state governments, typically also involved are regional governments, local councils, non-elected development agencies and, increasingly, private sector organizations and joint venture schemes between private and governmental bodies.

Lack of co-ordination can be very wasteful. Firms seeking assistance in the disadvantaged regions may be bewildered and deterred by the complexity of the types of help on offer. Different regions may compete, using regional policy subsidies as a weapon, for one another's firms or for inward investment projects of Japanese or USA firms. In addition, valuable development opportunities (e.g. cross-border transport links) may not be implemented as a result of co-ordination failures. The co-ordination agenda for an EU regional policy is clearly a wide one.

In exercising its supra-national co-ordination role the EU must simultaneously attempt to link together:

1. EU regional policy with *other EU policies* (e.g. agriculture, social).

2. EU regional policy activities within a given member state with the regional policy of the member state government.

3. Member states' regional policies one with another, particularly where the member states share a common border.

4. EU regional policy, member states' regional policies and the initiatives being operated by regional and local level organizations.

This is an enormous and difficult task, but one which only the EU has the potential to perform.

18.1.4 The 'effects of integration' argument

This is the most controversial of the arguments advanced in support of an EU regional policy. EU involvement in regional policy, it is argued, is necessary to overcome the adverse regional impact of the integration process. This argument rests upon two suppositions. The first is that economic integration, if left to its own devices, tends to cause a worsening ('divergence') of regional disparities. The second is that it is the EU, rather than the member states, which is best placed to tackle the regional problems which develop as integration proceeds. Both suppositions have been the subject of fierce debate. The effect of integration on regional disparities is an issue of immense importance and will be considered further in section 18.2.

18.1.5 The 'effects of other EU policies' argument

A further argument frequently advanced in support of EU regional policy is that it is needed to help to mitigate the adverse regional effects of other EU policies. A number of EU policies are known to have particularly severe effects on the disadvantaged regions. Value added tax, for example, a major source of EU revenues, has long been known to be a regionally regressive tax (CEC 1979g). Other EU policies also have their own distinctive patterns of regional effects (Franzmeyer *et al.*, 1991; CEU, 1996a). The adverse regional effects of the EU agriculture price guarantee policy – a major item in the EU budget – have been a source of particular concern. The concentration of EU agriculture policy help on products such as cereals, milk, oilseed and beef (products of the more prosperous northern EU farming regions) means that despite repeated reforms of agriculture policy, more prosperous regions continue to benefit most.

The ideal solution, of course, to policies with adverse regional impacts such as EU agriculture policy would be to alter the nature of the policies themselves. This is, however, only occasionally possible and may not, in any case, be desirable. The EU, therefore, has adopted a twofold approach as part of its regional policy effort. First, regular research studies are made of major EU policies to identify, and where possible rectify, policies with adverse regional effects. Second, EU regional policy initiatives are designed, wherever sensible, to mitigate adverse regional effects of other EU policies.

18.1.6 The 'further integration' argument

This argument centres upon the incomplete nature of the EU integration process. An EU regional policy, it is argued, is necessary to ensure that the benefits of integration are more fairly spread. Only if this is done will all member states be willing to countenance further steps towards full integration. This argument too is a controversial one. Even if one accepts, post-Treaty of European Union, that economic and political union is an acceptable goal, there is little hard evidence that *regional* disparities prevent *member states* from agreeing to further integration.

The list of arguments in favour of a separate EU regional policy is a long one. The case is a strong one too. It should be noted, however, that there is no case for a *com-*

plete transfer of regional policy powers from member states to the EU. The EU's own commitment to 'subsidiarity' – the maximum devolution of powers – requires that member states, regional and local governments and organizations all have a role. The vast majority of modern types of regional policy initiatives (e.g. advice to firms, training policies) also require an active local input to be effective. The remoteness of Brussels from many of the problem regions, the lack of specialist local knowledge and experience at the centre, and the virtue of allowing variety and experimentation in regional policy all suggest that partnership and not dominance is the appropriate EU role.

18.2 The effects of integration on EU regional disparities

The implications of economic integration for EU regional disparities are still poorly understood. The economic processes at work are extremely complex and long lasting. The regional effects even of the creation of the original customs union have not yet been fully experienced, and the regional implications of the Single Market process are still really only in their early stages. Add to these the regional ramifications of the 1996 enlargement (which saw the accession of Austria, Finland and Sweden), together with the geographical effects of the stage-by-stage progress towards EMU since 1992 and one can see just how complex the effects of economic integration are. Each of these steps in the process of economic integration has its own very distinctive 'regional footprint' and each has set in train effects which will take decades fully to emerge. Nor will the system have time to draw breath in the decade ahead, for the final completion of monetary union in 2002, combined with a wave of new accessions of countries in Central and Eastern Europe, will trigger yet more complex regional impacts right across the existing EU.

An examination of the existing pattern of regional disparities in the EU reveals an array of problems which are formidable by comparison with those in other parts of the world such as the USA. Figure 18.1 shows regional GDP per capita for the EU at 1996. The most affluent ten regions in the EU have GDP per capita values 3.1 times higher than the bottom ten (CEC, 1999e). These GDP per capita disparities are more than twice as great as those found in the USA. Figure 18.2 shows the extent of EU regional disparities using another popular indicator, the regional unemployment rate. In 1997, the best ten regions had an average unemployment rate of just 3.6%, compared with an average rate of 28.1% in the ten worst performing regions – almost eight times higher (CEU, 1999e).

The regional problems confronting the EU are extremely diverse as well as being severe. The EU itself in the period 1994–9 identified four main types of problem region. These have been, respectively, Lagging Regions (or 'Objective 1' regions), whose GDP per capita falls below 75% of the EU average; Declining Industrial Areas (or 'Objective 2' regions); certain Rural Regions (or 'Objective 5b' regions); and some sub-Arctic regions in Sweden and Finland ('Objective 6 regions'). The Objectives referred to here are those laid down for the EU's Structural Funds in a set of reforms introduced in 1989 and subsequently amended in 1994 and 1996 in the aftermath of the Treaty on European Union.

These broad categories of disadvantaged regions hide within them an extraordinary array of different types of problem region. Some are rural in nature, others urban. Some regions are suffering from problems arising from their geographical

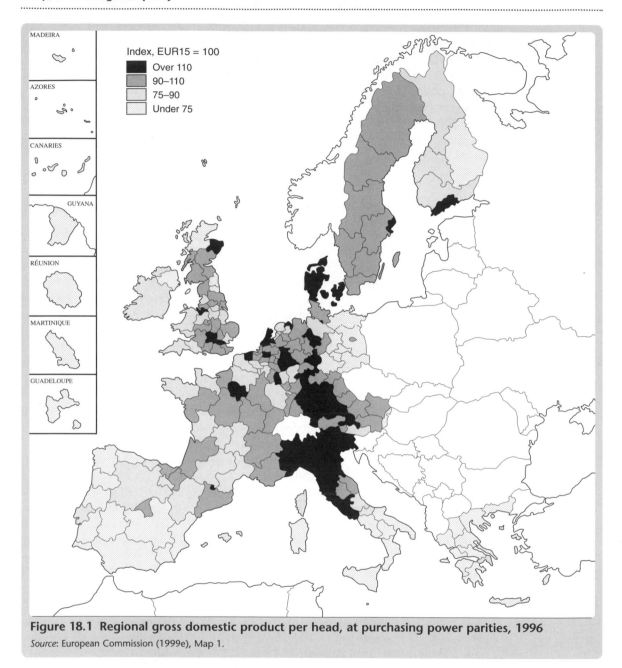

MADEIRA

AZORES

CANARIES

GUYANA

RÉUNION

MARTINIQUE

GUADELOUPE

Index, EUR15 = 100

Over 110
90–110
75–90
Under 75

Figure 18.1 Regional gross domestic product per head, at purchasing power parities, 1996
Source: European Commission (1999e), Map 1.

isolation from the main EU markets. Yet others suffer from economic dislocation caused by the removal of internal frontiers (disrupting their traditional trade patterns), or because they lie along the external borders of the EU. Another distinctive category of problem region is represented by the large number of island economies, many in very isolated locations.

Despite the great variety of EU regional problems, the overwhelming impression which one obtains from statistics such as those presented in Figures 18.1 and 18.2

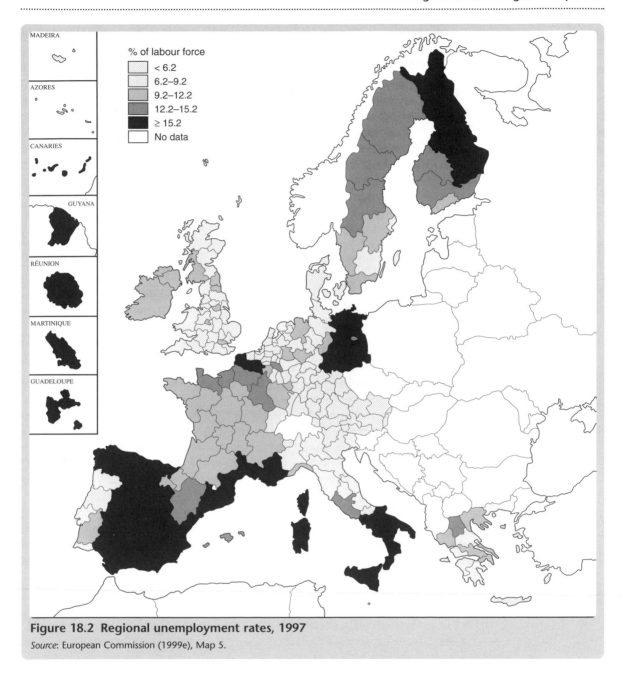

Figure 18.2 Regional unemployment rates, 1997

Source: European Commission (1999e), Map 5.

is that there appears to be a well-established 'core-periphery' pattern to EU regional disparities. A high proportion of the more prosperous regions lie at the geographical centre of the EU, whereas disadvantaged regions tend to be grouped around the periphery, particularly but by no means wholly, in the Mediterranean 'south'. Accession of countries from Central and Eastern Europe in the first decade of the new millennium will greatly reinforce the core-periphery pattern of regional disparities in the EU by bringing many low-income and high-unemployment regions in along the eastern periphery. The traditional prosperous core of the EU stretches from the South-East of England to Northern Italy. There is some evidence of the possible emergence of a new growth belt from Northern Italy through the south of France and into North-East Spain. This will not, however, alter the overall conclusion that a 'core-periphery' situation prevails in the EU.

The 'core-periphery' nature of EU regional problems has existed for many years. It is the outcome of economic processes which predate the existence of the EU, and others that have come into existence as a result of the EU. Economic integration is a process which is progressing continuously on a worldwide scale. Improvements in transport infrastructure and transport technology have gradually reduced freight cost barriers to trade. So too have general improvements in production technology, which have had the effect of reducing the transport inputs required to assemble materials and distribute the output of manufacturing industry. Moreover, in the post-war period there has been a consensus in favour of freer trade which has led to successive international steps (e.g. GATT/WTO agreements) designed to reduce the barriers to trade. The member states of the EU have participated in these worldwide processes of integration, and the pattern of *intra-EU* regional disparities which we observe today has been affected by them. Many of these processes predate the creation of the EU in 1958. In addition to these broad integration processes common to all countries, the EU has acted to trigger its own distinctive 'accelerated' integration programme. The current maps of regional disparities (Figures 18.1 and 18.2) will have been affected by these too. The regional effects of the Single Market process have not yet been fully experienced, partly because the complete Single Market has yet to be implemented and partly because the effects are extremely long term in nature. The effects of the convergence process leading up to EMU in 2002 are already being felt, but here too longer-term regional impacts are to be expected. Existing regional disparities moreover continue to be affected by the creation of the EU customs union in 1958, and by the successive widening of the customs union to include new member states in 1973 (Denmark, the UK and the Republic of Ireland), 1981 (Greece), 1986 (Spain and Portugal), 1991 (East Germany) and 1996 (Austria, Finland and Sweden).

No two rounds of economic integration ever have an identical effect on regional disparities. Each round in the integration process can be thought as having two groups of effects: a unique regional imprint or pattern of effects, combined with a 'core-periphery' effect in common with other rounds. The creation of the original customs union, for example, involved the removal of tariffs which had previously provided most protection to *manufacturing* industries. The most severe effects of this act of integration were therefore experienced in regions most heavily dependent on manufacturing industries. The creation of a Single Market between 1989 and 1992 involved the removal of an array of non-tariff barriers. In this round of integration both manufacturing and service industries were affected. It is thought that a distinctive group of some forty manufacturing sectors have been most affected by the Single Market, along with certain types of services such as banking and finance (CEC, 1990b; Quévit, 1992, 1995; Begg, 1995). Some regions are clearly more at risk than others, giving rise to a distinctive regional imprint.

While it is obvious that each round in the integration process has its own distinctive regional impact, why integration in the EU should exhibit systematic core-periphery effects as well is less clear. Evidence to date suggests that integration tends to favour the central core regions of the EU. In practice, this 'centralizing' tendency is probably the outcome of two sets of countervailing forces, one set tending to cause regional *convergence* while the other tends to bring about regional *divergence*. Which set of forces will predominate in the years to come is an issue of first importance to the EU.

The forces which tend to bring about *convergence* of regional disparities within the EU are predominantly a series of automatic equilibrating processes which occur whenever a system of freely functioning markets is in operation. Free trade in goods and services will, it is argued, lead to regions specializing in the production and export of goods and services in which they have a comparative advantage. Under traditional trade theory such as the Heckscher–Ohlin model all regions benefit from this process and regional differences in wage rates and capital rentals are also eliminated (Armstrong and Taylor, 2000). The convergence effects of freer trade are reinforced by the effects of freer factor mobility. Where wage rates differ significantly between regions, there is an incentive for labour to migrate from low-wage to high-wage regions, a process which reduces regional wage inequalities. Capital investment in the meanwhile is attracted to the disadvantaged regions by the low wages and excellent labour supply available there. This too reduces regional inequalities. The combination of freer trade and large-scale factor mobility offers real hope for the convergence of regional disparities in the EU. It is thought, however, that these processes operate only very slowly and that decades will be required before their full effects are felt. Moreover, there are forces leading to divergence of regional disparities. It is to these that we now turn.

At the heart of the economic integration process set in motion by the EU has been a desire to achieve free trade and the free movement of labour and capital. In order to enjoy the benefits of integration (Emerson *et al.*, 1988; CEC, 1988i, 1990b), it is essential that major restructuring of industry should occur. The various static and dynamic gains from integration require regions to switch production and concentrate on those goods and services for which there is a comparative advantage. The greater the integration envisaged, the greater are the potential benefits, but the greater too are the restructuring implications. Painful though the restructuring process is for those involved, in principle it should be experienced by all regions. The crucial question, therefore, is why integration seems in the EU to be associated with systematic core-periphery effects. A series of different divergence forces are thought to accompany the integration process:

1. *Economies of scale.* These represent a potent source of benefit from integration. The concentration of production at larger plants can lead to great efficiency gains. Firms seeking to exploit economies of scale are likely to be attracted to regions at the geographical core of the EU. Input assembly costs are lower, and access to the whole EU market is much easier from central locations. Moreover, the core regions are already the most prosperous regions and therefore represent the strongest markets.

2. *Localization and agglomeration economies.* Localization economies arise when firms in the same industry locate close to one another (e.g. access to labour with appropriate skills, information flows, ability to subcontract work, etc.). Agglomeration economies occur when firms from many different industries locate close to one another (e.g. transport facilities, financial facilities, etc.). These 'external economies of scale' effects tend to strongly favour the core regions of the EU. Firms are drawn towards existing successful agglomerations of

economic activity. The core regions of the EU contain almost all of the main financial, industrial and capital cities and are a potent magnet for new activity.

3. *Intra-industry trade and dominant market positions.* Modern trade theory is increasingly sceptical of the ability of all regions to share equally in the growth associated with freer trade. There is evidence that intra-industry trade in similar products has shown the most rapid growth among the more prosperous core regions and member states of the EU (Neven, 1990). Regions in the Mediterranean south of the EU have fallen behind in participation in this important and fast-growing type of trade. Similarly, much trade in manufactured goods in the EU is now dominated by large multinational enterprises. These firms are already concentrated in the core regions of the EU and it is thought that they may exploit their ability to dominate markets in ways which disadvantage peripheral regions. Opening up peripheral regions to competition from large multinational firms could have serious effects for the smaller and less powerful firms more frequently found there.

4. *Lack of competitiveness in peripheral regions.* Research commissioned by the EU (IFO, 1990) has provided powerful evidence that many firms in the EU's peripheral regions face severe problems in meeting the competitive challenges posed by integration. The lack of competitiveness is based on a combination of factors largely outside the control of the firms themselves. These include poor location, weak infrastructure facilities (e.g. transport, telecommunications), low-skill labour forces, and local tax and financial sector problems.

5. *Selective labour migration.* The peripheral regions are also weakened, as integration proceeds, by the loss of migrants. The freeing of labour mobility stimulates migration from peripheral to core regions. Migration is highly selective. It is the young, the skilled and the economically active who migrate. Their loss is a severe blow to peripheral regions seeking to compete in an integrated EU.

6. *The loss of macro-policy powers in peripheral member states.* This is a particular problem with the next stage of integration – EMU. Those member states committed to EMU have already lost control of their exchange rates as a result of the adoption of the Euro. Most of the others have lost some control as a result of their membership of EMS. Full monetary union in 2002 will mean the complete loss of powers to try to protect a weak local economy by way of currency devaluation. With interest rates tending to equalize across the EU and with a single currency the member states will have lost the power to use monetary policy to stimulate a weak local economy. Even fiscal policy will be increasingly constrained under EMU. Peripheral member states face a future of very limited macro-policy powers. This will restrict their ability to protect their local economies.

The divergence forces set out above seem convincing and strong. There has been considerable discussion of the possibility that the divergence forces may interact and reinforce one another in such a way that *cumulative causation* occurs. This is where the loss of firms and a continuous outflow of migrants so weakens a peripheral economy that it can no longer attract new economic activities and hence goes into a downward spiral of decline. This is by no means a theoretical possibility. A number of rural regions of the EU (e.g. the west of Ireland, parts of southern Italy) have experienced depopulation on a large scale.

Evidence from federal countries with a long history of being fully economically integrated suggests that in the long term integration is associated with convergence

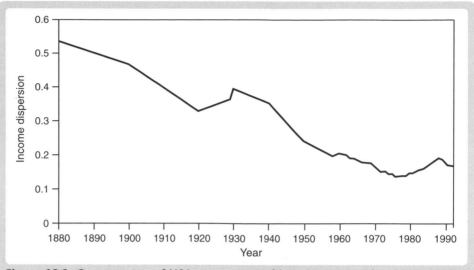

Figure 18.3 Convergence of USA state personal incomes per capita, 1880–1992
Source: Sala-i-Martin (1996), Figure 2.

of regional disparities rather than divergence, as Figure 18.3 shows for the USA (Barro and Sala-i-Martin, 1991; Sala-i-Martin, 1996). This evidence implies that the convergence forces at work eventually come to predominate over the divergence forces. The resulting balance of forces results in a process of convergence which is slow (2% per annum in the USA), but is also sustained over a long period.

The evidence for convergence among EU regions is more contested, partly because good statistics do not exist for the long periods of time necessary to check whether or not convergence is occurring. The balance of the evidence that is available suggests that cumulative causation has not occurred in the EU. Most researchers have found that prior to the mid-1970s regional disparities in the EU had experienced quite a long period of narrowing. This was followed by a period of widening of disparities in the late 1970s and early 1980s. The EU's regional disparities now seem to have stabilized or perhaps are even very slowly narrowing (Armstrong, 1995a, 1995b; CEU, 1999e; Sala-i-Martin, 1996). However, this evidence remains rather controversial, for some analysts have also found evidence for *divergence* among EU regions, at least for certain periods of time (Dunford, 1996; Magrini, 1999). What can be said, however, is that those spells of divergence which have been observed tend to have been recent and apparently short-lived. Economic integration does appear, on the whole, to be associated with a narrowing of regional disparities, although at a painfully slow rate.

18.3 EU regional policy from 1989 to 1999

18.3.1 The reforms of 1989 and 1994

EU regional policy traces its origins to the decision in 1975 to create a European Regional Development Fund (ERDF). The policy subsequently underwent minor reform in 1979 and 1984 (Armstrong, 1978, 1985). The current EU regional policy, however, owes most of its distinctive features to the major reform of the EU's structural funds which took place in 1989. This reform was specifically designed to accompany the introduction of the Single Market and, like the Single Market itself, was phased in gradually between 1989 and 1992. The 1989 reform integrated a number of previously separate EU funding mechanisms, renaming them the 'structural funds'. The EU's structural funds comprise the ERDF, together with the European Social Fund (ESF), the Guidance Section of the European Agricultural Guidance and Guarantee Fund (EAGGF) and, since 1994, a Financial Instrument for Fisheries Guidance (FIFG).

The budget period for EU regional policy which has recently ended (i.e. 1994–9) was operated in all of its essential characteristics on the basis of the reform to the structural funds introduced in 1989. As noted earlier, this reform was deliberately designed to coincide with the implementation of the Single Market legislation. The Single Market represented a major step towards integration in the EU and one which has gradually brought about massive structural changes in the economies of the member states and their constituent regions. The 1989 reform package represented the most significant turning-point in EU regional policy since the origins of the ERDF in 1975 (see CEC, 1989e, for a summary of the reforms). The 1989 reforms established the ERDF as an integral part of the EU's policy for dealing with the effects of structural changes which inevitably accompany integration. The reformed policy was designed not only to accompany the Single Market process, but also to provide the basis for further minor reforms (subsequently brought in during 1994) designed to accompany steps towards EMU (see CEU, 1996b, for a summary). While the 1994 reform was minor in the sense of leaving the system largely intact, 1994 did see the announcement of a major new infusion of funds for the ERDF and the other structural funds for the budget period 1994–9.

The outcome of the major 1989 reform package and the various minor amendments in the 1990s was the creation of a comprehensive and co-ordinated delivery system for regional policy in the EU; one which is now very well funded by Brussels. By 1999 the structural funds' share of the full EU budget had risen to 36%. The structural funds (ERDF, ESF, EAGGF (Guidance), and FIFG) were given the task of attempting collectively to attain six priority objectives in the 1994–9 budget period. These priority objectives were as follows, with the EU funds involved in each objective shown in parentheses:

1. Development and structural adjustment of the regions whose development is *lagging behind*, defined as having GDP per capita under 75% of the EC average (ERDF, ESF, EAGGF and FIFG).

2. The conversion of regions in *industrial decline* (ERDF and ESF).

3. Combating long-term unemployment (more than 12 months) and facilitating the integration into working life of young people (under 25 years of age) and of persons exposed to exclusion from the labour market. This was a 'non-regional' objective (ESF only).

4. Facilitating the adaptation of workers of either sex to industrial changes and to changes in production systems. This too was a 'non-regional' objective (ESF only).

5. Promoting rural development by:

(a) speeding up the adjustment of agricultural structures in the framework of the reform of the common agricultural policy (a 'non-regional' objective relying on EAGGF and FIFG); and

(b) facilitating the development and structural adjustment of rural areas (ERDF, ESF and EAGGF).

6. Promoting the development and structural adjustment of regions with an extremely low population density (ERDF, ESF, EAGGF and FIFG).

As can be seen, the four objectives of particular importance to EU *regional* policy were (1), (2), (5b) and (6). It must be borne in mind, however, that the disadvantaged regions of the EU contain disproportionate numbers of long-term unemployed and unemployed young people and therefore have also always benefited substantially from the activities of the ESF which alone has had responsibility for objectives (3) and (4). Indeed, the 1989 reform sought to strengthen further the deliberate regional bias built into the way in which the ESF has always operated. The structural funds between 1994 and 1999 were also reinforced by the activities of the Cohesion Fund, introduced in 1994, to help Greece, Spain, Portugal and Ireland to cope with EMU.

The 1989 reform represented a clear break with the past in that for the first time, in 1989, the EU drew up its own map of areas eligible for assistance. Prior to 1989 the ERDF had, in allocating help, simply relied upon the areas designated as eligible for regional policy assistance by the member states (as part of their own domestic regional policies). The 1994–9 map of EU assisted areas (for the 'regional' objectives (1), (2), (5b) and (6)) is shown as Figure 18.4. Detailed quantitative criteria were used to identify eligible assisted areas under each of the four regional objectives. The Objective (1) regions were by far the most important of the four categories of assisted areas and they cover 25.0% (or 92.151 million persons) of the combined population of the 15 members of the EU. As can be seen from Figure 18.4, the main Objective (1) areas were in the Mediterranean (Greece, Portugal, Spain and southern Italy), Ireland and East Germany. Objective (2) assisted areas in the period 1994–9 were based upon smaller regional units, but still encompassed 16.4% of the EU's population. They were scattered widely throughout the EU, as Figure 18.4 shows. Objective (5(b)) regions in the period 1994–9 formed a category of assisted areas much less important than the first two. They encompassed only 8.8% of the EU's population, while the highly specific Objective (6), introduced only in 1996 (targeted on the remoter northern areas of Sweden and Finland), encompassed a mere 0.4% of the combined EU population. In total, the four types of assisted areas covered no less that 50.6% of the EU population.

The EU has deliberately concentrated the bulk of its financial assistance on the very poorest areas: in practice the Objective (1) regions. During the budget period 1994–9 the allocations for the four structural funds, by objective, were as follows (all at 1994 prices):

Objective (1)	93.972 billion ECU
Objective (2)	15.360 billion ECU
Objectives (3) and (4) (non-regional)	15.180 billion ECU
Objective (5(a)) (non-regional)	6.916 billion ECU
Objective (5(b))	6.862 billion ECU
Objective (6)	0.697 billion ECU

401

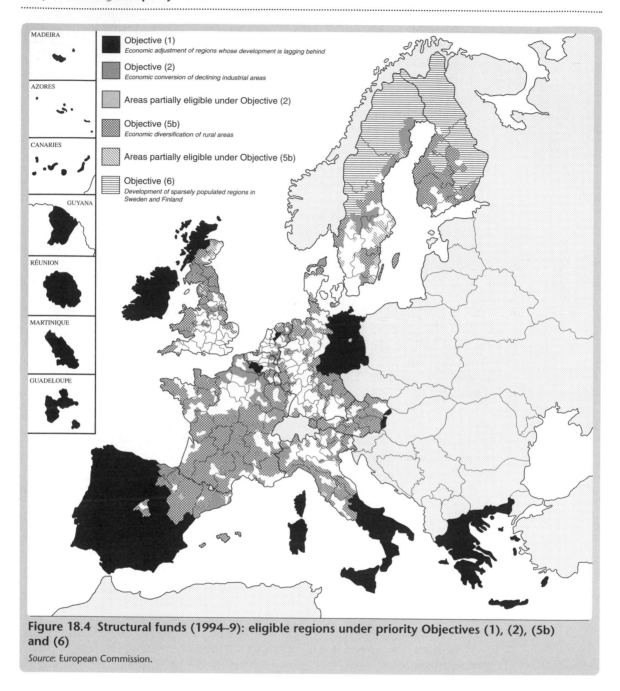

Figure 18.4 Structural funds (1994–9): eligible regions under priority Objectives (1), (2), (5b) and (6)

Source: European Commission.

In addition, some 14.051 billion ECU was set aside for the period 1994–9 for Community Initiatives (CIs), although in practice not all of this was subsequently spent. These are initiatives designed to tackle specific cross-country and pan-EU problems. The 13 CIs have been wide-ranging and have included RECHAR (for coal mining areas), RESIDER (for iron and steel areas), PESCA (for fishing communities), INTERREG (for cross-border initiatives) and STRIDE (for research and technology).

Taking all of the monies allocated to regional policy (i.e. including the CIs), there was a doubling in the real value of the structural funds between 1989 and 1993, followed by a further doubling again between 1994 and 1999. This is an indication of the rapidly growing importance of regional policy within the EU.

The ERDF, as one of the four structural funds, has, of course, shared in this large increase in the funds' operations. The ERDF directs the vast bulk of its operations towards the Objective (1) regions, with most of the remainder being allocated to Objective (2) regions. This was certainly the case in the period 1994–9 and, as will be shown, this will also be the case for the budget period 2000–6. Table 18.1 shows how the 1994–9 structural funds were targeted by member state and by regional objective. The overwhelming size of the funds directed towards the Objective (1) regions and Objective (2) regions can be clearly seen.

The structural funds are *grant-awarding* instruments, as is the Cohesion Fund. ERDF grants are essentially designed to assist industrial and infrastructure development. ESF grants are targeted on labour market initiatives such as training and mobility policies. The Guidance Section of the EAGGF and the FIFG assists a range of initiatives designed to facilitate the restructuring of the agriculture and fisheries sectors and the economic regeneration of the communities experiencing structural change. The post-1989 delivery system also strongly encourages a close co-ordination of the structural funds with *loan-awarding* EU instruments. Most important of these are the European Investment Bank (EIB), together with the European Coal and Steel Community (ECSC). Both the EIB and the ECSC are long-established EU instruments and have always operated with a deliberate bias towards the disadvan-

Table 18.1 ERDF allocations, 1994–9 (1994–6 for Objective (2) regions) (million ECU at 1994 prices)

Member state	Objective (1) Lagging regions	Objective (2) Industrial areas	Objective (5b) Rural areas	Objective (6) Low population density areas
Belgium	730	342	195	0
Germany	13 640	1 566	1 227	0
Greece	13 980	0	0	0
Spain	26 300	2 416	664	0
France	2 190	3 774	2 238	0
Ireland	5 620	0	0	0
Italy	14 860	1 463	901	0
Portugal	13 980	0	0	0
United Kingdom	2 360	4 581	817	0
Denmark	0	119	54	0
Luxembourg	0	15	6	0
Netherlands	150	650	150	0
Austria	162	99	403	0
Finland	0	179	190	450
Sweden	0	157	135	247
Total	93 972	15 360	6 862	697

Source: EU Commission.

taged regions. The EIB makes loans (often on advantageous terms) right across the EC, but makes a special effort to help the disadvantaged regions. In 1997, for example, 70% of the EIB's loans within the EU were made in the EU's assisted areas for regional development purposes (European Investment Bank, 1998). The ECSC, by concentrating on the coal and steel industries, is inevitably active in some of the most disadvantaged parts of the EU. The ECSC makes direct loans to the coal and steel industries themselves, but also helps other types of industries to set up in the coal and steel areas in order to create new jobs and diversify the local economies. The ECSC also gives grants to help with retraining and mobility of workers in the coal and steel areas. The EIB and ECSC have, since 1989, worked very closely with the structural funds.

18.3.2 Strategic planning, programming, partnership and additionality

As well as the commitment to much closer co-ordination of the activities of the EU's financial instruments, the regional policy which emerged in the aftermath of the 1989 reform placed great emphasis on four further principles. These four great principles continue to underpin EU regional policy. They are the use of a system of *multi-annual progammes* of assistance, the need for a close *partnership* between all of those involved in regional policy, a commitment to *subsidiarity* (the retention at EU level of the minimum necessary powers) and a desire that EU money should be a genuine supplement to regional policy spending by the member states (*additionality*). None of these principles was entirely new to the 1989 reform package, but the 1989 reform represented the first comprehensive attempt to create a regional policy 'delivery system' which would allow the principles to be achieved. The principles themselves have withstood the test of time and remain at the heart of the reforms for the 2000–6 budget period.

The delivery of structural funds assistance through multi-annual programmes is now well entrenched. Key to the development of each programme is the drawing up of a Single Programming Document – SPD (or Community Support Framework – CSF – in some regions). These documents are effectively strategic plans for the region and are the responsibility of the regional and local partnership organizations delivering the programme, although the SPDs are subject to national and Commission involvement too. The role of the regional and local partners in the SPD is important since these partners are the ones with the local knowledge and expertise needed for effective planning. Their role also emphasizes the EU's commitment to subsidiarity in its regional policy. Each SPD contains an analysis of the strengths and weaknesses of the region, together with a development strategy and an analysis of how it is to be financed. EU structural funds can only be used in conjunction with matched funding from the member states. This whole medium-term planning process is supplemented by research and analysis of regional problems at the EU level. In particular, a system of regular periodic reports is employed to disseminate results of technical analysis of regional problems from an EU perspective (see CEU, 1999e for the most recent of these). There is also a very active programme of research of a high standard on regional issues.

The multi-annual programmes introduced in 1989 represented a major break with previous practice for EU regional policy. The original ERDF set up in 1975 awarded grants on a project-by-project basis, in much the same way as some member states' initiatives still do today (e.g. Regional Selective Assistance in the

UK). From 1979 onwards, however, the EU began to experiment with a small number of programme-based initiatives. This approach has come into its own since 1989. As well as being multi-annual, programmes are essentially collaborative ventures (partnerships) between the EU, member state governments and the array of 'delivery organizations' at regional and local level involved in actually implementing the programme. A typical SPD is a group of projects (usually several hundred in number) designed to achieve pre-designated objectives in a co-ordinated manner. As has already been noted, a distinctive category of programmes are the Community Initiatives (CIs). These are programmes which span the member states and are designed to tackle common problems. As their name suggests, they are initiated at the discretion of the EU rather than the member states.

The 1989 reform package and subsequent reforms in 1994 and 1999 have contained new commitments to two other long-held principles of EU regional policy – partnership and additionality. The concept of *partnership* is essential in an EU committed to the maximum devolution of power (*subsidiarity*). The reforms since 1989 have embodied ever-stronger procedures to encourage a strong dialogue between partners at all levels (i.e. EU, member state, regional and local), and an ever-wider range of types of organization has been drawn in (most recently voluntary organizations and trade unions). The SPDs, as well as the formal procedures for monitoring and evaluation of the policy, all include a requirement for close consultation with the partners. *Additionality* has proved to be an exceptionally thorny issue in the EU's relationship with member state governments. Some member states have been accused of responding to increases in EU regional policy expenditures by cutting back on their own domestic regional policy budgets. Successive reforms to the structural funds since 1989 have sought to ensure that member states do not continue with this practice, although pressures on budgets in the 1990s resulting from attempts by member states to get within the EMU convergence criteria have not made the task any easier. The issue of additionality continues to be a delicate one for EU regional policy. Repeated attempts in the 1990s to use increased disclosure of funding statistics, moral persuasion and outright conflict with the members states (as in 1991 with the freezing of UK RECHAR funding as the result of an additionality dispute) have all proved to be only partial solutions.

18.4 Some key issues for the new millennium

EU regional policy has shown itself to be capable of evolution and change over the years since its introduction in 1975. Some of the key issues that EU regional policy must confront in the new decade are legacies of the past (e.g. additionality and the underfunding of the policy). Others, such as the response of the policy to the full implementation of monetary union and eastern enlargement, are wholly new issues. Each will be considered in turn, beginning with the fundamental challenge posed by eastern enlargement and the EU's initial response to this.

18.4.1 New accessions and the challenge of eastern enlargement

The EU has always found it necessary to make changes to its regional policy whenever new accessions have occurred. In most cases this has taken the form of an increase in the budget for regional policy and a redesignation of the map of the assisted areas, but without the fundamental principles of the policy itself being disturbed. This happy state of affairs has now come to an end. The reason for this is the impending accession of a series of (mostly) former Communist countries from Central and Eastern Europe. Six countries are currently actively engaged in accession negotiations – Cyprus, the Czech Republic, Estonia, Hungary, Poland and Slovenia. These will form the first wave of accessions well within the first decade of the new millennium. Behind these is a queue of other countries with economies even weaker than those in the first wave. This second wave includes Bulgaria, Romania, Latvia, Lithuania, Slovakia and Turkey. Precisely when, if ever, these additional countries will be allowed to accede remains a matter of conjecture. The first wave alone, however, has posed enormous challenges for an EU which has been shaken by the cost and difficulty of to date absorbing only one of the former Communist states, East Germany.

Eastern enlargement poses two distinctive challenges to the regional policy of the EU:

(a) The challenge to the EU budget

The EU budget is dominated by two items: the common agriculture policy (CAP) and the structural funds. Between them they command the majority of the full EU budget (see Chapter 16). The economic decline in many of the Central and Eastern European countries (CEECs) which followed the collapse of Communism in the early 1990s, together with the decision to encourage them to seek early accession, triggered an enormous debate on how the challenge could be met. The main threats to the ability of the EUR15 countries to meet the costs of enlargement were quickly identified as being via the structural funds and CAP.

The challenge to the structural funds arises from the fact that virtually all of the regions in the CEEC countries are eligible for the highest rates of structural funds assistance (i.e. Objective (1)). Figure 18.5, for example, shows that on the evidence for 1996 only two small regions (Prague and Bratislava) would have had GDP per capita values in excess of the 75% of EU average GDP, the critical value for Objective (1) membership. Hence accession even of the relatively prosperous CEECs such as Poland and the Czech Republic implies that virtually all of their constituent regions will become automatically eligible for Objective (1) status (on the basis of the 1994–9 regulations). The challenge to the CAP budget arises from the fact that countries such as Poland and Hungary are both large producers of agricultural products and also tend to specialize on the types of commodities (e.g. dairy products, cereals) that attract high levels of intervention by the EU.

Preliminary estimates of the likely additional burden on the EU budget as a result of eastern enlargement raised the alarming prospect that the existing 15 member states of the EU would be unlikely to cope with the additional demands. Applying the 1994–9 structural funds and CAP regulations to the countries seeking to accede produced estimates of additional structural funds costs of between 13 billion ECU and 27 billion ECU per annum in the new millennium. Additional CAP costs were thought likely to be between 10 billion ECU and 37 billion ECU per annum. 'Best estimates' placed the structural funds at an extra 13 billion ECU per annum and the CAP at 10 billion per annum (Baldwin et al., 1997), figures still much too large to be borne by an EU budget already under pressure from the main net contributor countries such Germany and the UK.

Faced with estimates of this kind, the Berlin meeting of heads of state in March

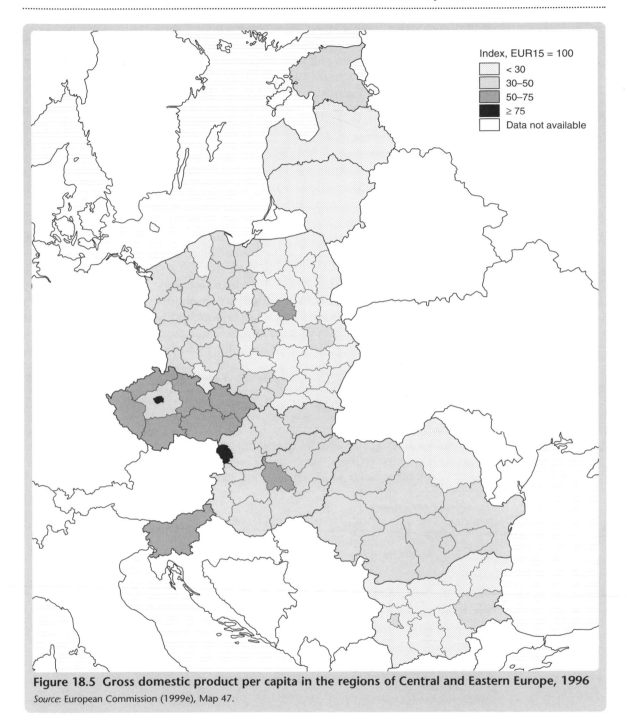

Figure 18.5 Gross domestic product per capita in the regions of Central and Eastern Europe, 1996
Source: European Commission (1999e), Map 47.

1999 (European Council, 1999b) found itself with some very difficult decisions to take in setting the budget allocations for the period 2000–6. The solution adopted, as Table 18.2 shows, was to spread the pain around. The countries seeking accession were allocated rather less money than they had hoped for, spread over a longer period. With new member states likely to accede in a stepwise manner, pre-accession aid is to be continued at a constant 3.12 billion ECU per annum through until 2006. This pre-accession aid will be mostly in the form of the existing PHARE programme, but there will also be 1.04 billion ECU per annum from the structural funds and 0.52 billion ECU per annum from CAP. As can be seen from Table 18.2, post-accession allocations to the new member states will start at a mere 6.45 billion ECU per annum in 2002, but rise rapidly to 16.78 billion ECU by 2006, the vast majority of which will be in the form of Objective (1) structural funds allocations. It has been argued that these structural funds levels are pretty much the maximum that it would be safe to assume the new member states could safely absorb in such a short period of time. They do not in any sense represent the kinds of investment levels that would be necessary to solve the economic problems there.

Where are the extra monies for the new entrants to come from? In part the answer lies in continued economic growth in the existing EUR15. This growth, combined with the decision to hold the EU budget at roughly 0.46% of the combined GDP of EUR15, generates some of the extra funding needed. As Table 18.2 shows, however, the rest of the money is to be found from cuts *in real terms* from the structural funds, from the cohesion fund and from the CAP budget in the existing EUR15 member states. The structural funds alone in EUR15 are scheduled to be cut from 32.045 billion ECU in 2000 to 29.170 billion ECU in 2006.

Table 18.2 EU budget commitments, 2000–6 (billion Euros at 1999 prices)

	2000	2001	2002	2003	2004	2005	2006
EUR15 – Structural funds and Cohesion Fund	32.045	31.455	30.865	30.285	29.595	29.595	29.170
EUR15 – Agriculture policy	40.920	42.800	43.900	43.770	42.760	41.930	41.660
EUR15 – Other internal policies	5.900	5.950	6.000	6.050	6.100	6.150	6.200
EUR15 – External policies	4.550	4.560	4.570	4.580	4.590	4.600	4.610
Admin. and reserves	5.460	5.500	5.350	5.200	5.300	5.400	5.500
Pre-accession aid: structural funds	1.040	1.040	1.040	1.040	1.040	1.040	1.040
Pre-accession aid: other	2.080	2.080	2.080	2.080	2.080	2.080	2.080
Post-accession aid: structural funds	–	–	3.750	5.830	7.920	10.000	12.080
Post-accession aid: other	–	–	2.700	3.200	3.700	4.200	4.700
Total commitments	91.995	93.385	100.255	102.035	103.085	104.995	107.040

Source: European Council (1999b).

How to share out the pain of the cutbacks in the structural funds (and CAP) in the existing EUR15 countries has proved to be extremely difficult despite the Commission's best attempts to produce a 'soft landing'. In its *Agenda 2000* proposals the Commission has sought to preserve the fundamental features of the 1989–99 structural funds system (e.g. programming, partnership, etc.) while at the same time reining back spending in the EUR15 countries (CEU, 1997a, 1998b). Two main changes have been made to bring this about:

1. *Reduction in the areas eligible for assistance.* The six priority objectives of the 1994–9 budget period have been cut back to only three for the 2000–6 period. The New Objective (1) (Lagging Regions) is very similar to the old Objective (1) in that it encompasses regions with GDP per capita under 75% of the EUR15 average, although the former Objective (6) (Low Population Density) areas in Sweden and Finland have also now been granted Objective (1) status, as have a number of remote territories (the Canary Islands, the Azores and the French overseas departments). Figure 18.6 shows the map of areas eligible for the New Objective (1). The areas shown as eligible for transitional support are those regions which obtained Objective (1) help in 1994–9 but which are now having it slowly withdrawn over the period 2000–6. In the British Isles, for example, large parts of Ireland, the whole of Northern Ireland and the Scottish Highlands and Islands are no longer eligible, whereas South Yorkshire and parts of Wales and South-West England become newly eligible in 2000–6. The use of transitional funding is one of the main methods being used to bring about a 'soft landing' for regions earmarked to lose their Objective (1) status. So too are devices such as the special programme to assist coastal areas of Sweden (see Figure 18.6). Taken together, the changes in Objective (1) eligibility imply a cut in the populations eligible for Objective (1) status from 25% to 20% of the EUR15 combined population. Objective (2) is a similar story, but with even bigger cuts being set in train to reduce coverage from 25% to 18% of the EUR15 population. The New Objective (2) (Economic and Social Conversion of Regions in Structural Crisis) effectively rolls together the previous Objectives (2) (Industrial Decline) and (5)b (Rural Areas), with disadvantaged urban areas and fishing communities also invited to make a case. The New Objective (3) (Human Resources) effectively rolls together the former ESF 'non-regional' Objectives (3) and (4). Although still purely an ESF objective, the New Objective (3) has now effectively become a 'regional' objective since it is applicable only in regions *not* covered by Objectives (1) and (2). It is clear therefore that, despite the safety net of transitional funding, many areas which obtained structural funds help in the 1994–9 period will lose substantially in the 2000–6 period.

2. *Reduction in the community initiatives in the EUR15 countries.* Community initiatives have also been radically cut back from 13 to a mere three and there has been a reduction in the CI share of the structural funds budget from 9% (1994–9) to 5% (2000–6).

While the *Agenda 2000* reforms have also been used as a vehicle to try to simplify bureacracy, and to draw in more partner organizations (e.g. trade unions and voluntary organizations) at the regional and local level, it is the cuts in budgets and eligible areas that are clearly the most important feature. These have arisen directly from the need to free up resources to meet the challenge of eastern enlargement.

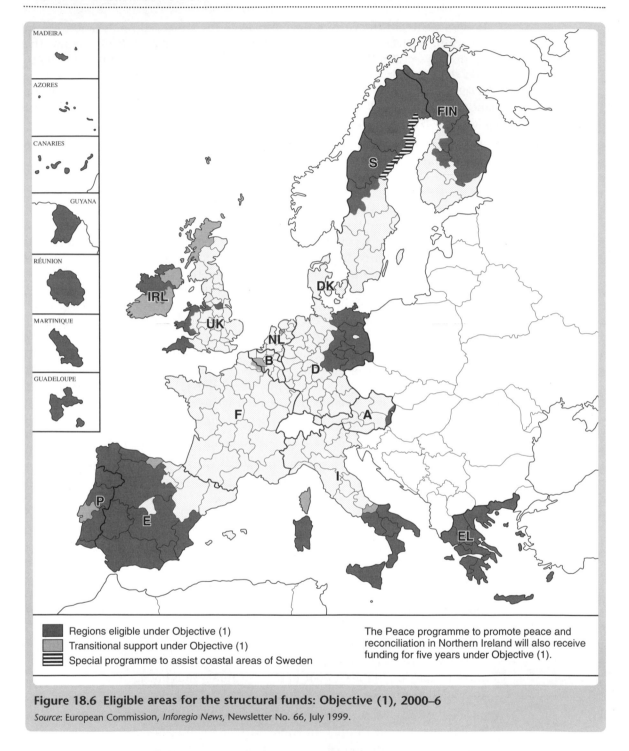

Regions eligible under Objective (1)
Transitional support under Objective (1)
Special programme to assist coastal areas of Sweden

The Peace programme to promote peace and reconciliation in Northern Ireland will also receive funding for five years under Objective (1).

Figure 18.6 Eligible areas for the structural funds: Objective (1), 2000–6

Source: European Commission, *Inforegio News*, Newsletter No. 66, July 1999.

(b) The challenge posed by the regional impact of eastern enlargement.

Eastern enlargement poses a further challenge to the structural funds. As has been noted earlier, each act of economic integration tends to produce a set of broad core-periphery effects within the EU, but also a distinctive geographical pattern of losing and gaining regions. Eastern enlargement is also thought likely to have its own distinctive set of regional impacts within the EUR15 member states. Estimates of these impacts remain rough and ready, but it is thought that it is the new entrants themselves that will gain most (up to 20% extra GDP) while the EUR15 countries will enjoy an expansion of perhaps one-quarter of 1% on their combined GDP (Baldwin *et al.*, 1997). However, within the EUR15 countries, simulations predict that it is the relatively prosperous regions of the north of the EU (especially in Germany, France and the UK) that will gain the most from eastern enlargement, particularly in Germany (Baldwin *et al.*, 1997). The structural funds within the existing EUR15 countries will therefore have to cope not only with budget cuts and restricted eligible areas, but also with a new set of strains on the existing regional disparities.

18.4.2 EU regional policy and full monetary union

The Treaty on European Union of 1992, with its commitment to full EMU (see Chapter 6), stimulated a debate which continues to this day on what the appropriate EU regional policy response should be to the prospect of full monetary union. The attainment of the formal 'convergence conditions' by the majority of the member states in January 1999, and the subsequent decision of a majority of the member states to lock their exchange rates and push on to full monetary union in 2002, have important implications for EU regional policy which have yet to be confronted. EMU is effectively a further step in the long process of economic integration. As with previous rounds such as the customs union and the Single Market, EMU will almost certainly result in a distinctive regional imprint combined with some general core-periphery effects. Moreover, all regions will experience structural change as the full implications of EMU work their way through the economic system (CEC, 1990c; Emerson *et al.*, 1991). Precisely what the regional impacts will be remains a controversial issue and one made more uncertain by the fact that some member states such as the UK have not yet decided when (if ever) they will join the Euro currency area.

It was realized at the time of signing of the Treaty on European Union in 1992 that the step-by-step process of moving towards the attainment of the convergence criteria, and then on to the single currency, would trigger new strains within the EU and could exacerbate regional problems. These strains, it was argued, would occur immediately since the convergence criteria themselves (e.g. restraining public sector deficits) would affect the poorer regions more than the prosperous regions. The Edinburgh Summit of EU Heads of State on 11–12 December 1992, therefore, took a decision to increase the structural funds budget from 19.8 billion ECU in 1993 to 27.4 billion ECU in 1999 (both at 1992 prices). In addition, a newly constituted cohesion fund was allocated a budget of 1.5 billion ECU in 1993, rising to 2.6 billion ECU in 1999 (at 1992 prices). The effects of EMU have not, however, stopped in 1999. The structural funds in the new millennium will have to cope not only with the regional impacts of eastern enlargement, but also with the lingering after-effects of the Single Market and the new strains imposed by full monetary union among member states whose economies have not yet fully converged.

18.4.3 The issue of under-funding

Despite the increases in EU budget resources devoted to the structural funds, there is a lingering concern that the EU regional policy remains seriously underfunded for the tasks which it has set itself. This issue is a difficult one to examine since no one knows how much would need to be spent and over what time period for EU regional problems to be eliminated. At 0.46% of the combined GDP of the EU member states, the structural funds remain small. The experience of Britain in the 1960s, when the member state government operated a regional policy with better funding (relative to GDP) than the current EU regional policy and still failed to eliminate relatively narrow regional disparities, suggests that EU regional policy is still significantly underfunded. The proposed additional funds following the Treaty on European Union will not help much since they will be needed to meet the *new* regional problems which EMU will create.

The underfunding issue is made more serious in the EU compared with federal systems elsewhere (e.g. USA) by the inadequacies of the EU's system of *interpersonal* and *intergovernmental* fiscal transfers. On average, the four federal countries of Australia, Canada, Switzerland and the USA, for example, have redistributive transfer systems which eliminate some 40% of regional income differentials (O'Donnell, 1992). Such transfers are extremely weak within the EU and there would be considerable resistance by member states to a major expansion of them.

18.4.4 Equalization of disparities or equality of opportunity?

Although the current EU regional policy has taken great care in defining its priority objectives (in terms of the *types* of regions to be helped – lagging, industrial decline, etc.), there remains the issue of what the final overall objective of EU regional policy should be. The complete elimination of regional disparities within the EU is unattainable – particularly in view of the underfunding problem. From time to time in the EU discussion emerges of the possible goal of 'equality of opportunity' for the disadvantaged regions rather than 'income equality' or 'unemployment rate equality' (NIESR, 1991). This goal would imply that the disadvantaged regions would be given regional policy help such that their infrastructure, labour-force skills and financial markets were of roughly equal quality to those found in the prosperous regions. Regional policy, it is argued, would thus be transformed from a policy designed to prop up depressed areas, to a policy designed to allow the depressed areas to compete on a level footing with other regions in the open trading system of the 1990s. Such a policy would need to have an explicit social welfare aspect (e.g. help for education, health and direct transfers to poor families) to provide a safety net for those who lose out in such a competitive environment.

18.4.5 Additionality and subsidiarity

Despite the new initiatives in the reforms for the new millennium, it is clear that additionality remains a serious problem for EU regional policy. Member states faced with domestic public sector budget problems will always be tempted to cut their local regional policy efforts as EU regional policy is expanded. Similar comments apply to subsidiarity, where some member states remain reluctant to release powers to the regional and local partners. This remains the case in the UK despite the creation of elected regional governments in Scotland, Wales and Northern Ireland. English regions do not have elected assemblies.

18.4.6 The final division of policy powers

Perhaps the most fundamental issue that continues to face EU regional policy in the new millennium (as it did in the 1990s) is the division of regional policy responsibilities among the different tiers of government involved. The commitment to subsidiarity is useful, but does not answer the crucial question of what the final assignment of regional policy powers is to be. This is particularly important in an era of *multi-level governance* in which the powers of the member states appear to be waning. What is to be the final role for the member states? What is to be the role of the EU and the regional governments? Until this is decided, the EU will continue to find itself in a series of conflicts with the other partners in the regional policy effort.

19 Social policies

C. D. E. COLLINS

19.1 Introduction

By the time of the Treaty of Amsterdam, the EU had acquired a broad responsibility in the social field. The emphasis had shifted somewhat from the original concentration on the labour market to embrace modern concepts of citizenship and equality. Nevertheless, the central core of Community social policy is to be found in questions relating to employment, industrial health, the social costs of industry, labour mobility and the role of social spending in social affairs. In the early years of the EC, broader issues of social welfare seemed of little relevance but the subsequent growth of its social competences has been remarkable. There are a number of reasons for this. Social affairs now form a large component of national public policy which, in turn, has to be fitted into a European framework and more problems have a transnational element. Community policies have also matured and as they reach into detailed areas of life, as in the equal opportunities policy, so they become more visible. In consequence, many people and organizations now recognize that their interests may be as well served by lobbying in Brussels as in the national capitals. The history of the EU also shows that the Commission, normally backed up by the European Parliament, has always believed it should play an active and positive role in social affairs and, particularly during the 1980s, it stepped up the social momentum as part of the drive to strengthen the political legitimacy of the EC in the move towards European union. It is hardly surprising that the Commission has clashed with national governments which still wish to claim credit with their citizens for their work to improve the conditions of life. Differences of view have surfaced, notably over the 'social dimension' of the Single Market. Here the biggest single issue has been whether the Community needs a common framework of employment law and certain rules relating to working conditions in order that the Single Market may work effectively. Subsequently, the argument from Brussels has been that the EU must become 'closer to its citizens', a view that encourages an ever more important social role. The result of these pressures is that social policy now covers a wide range of individual policies with no less than five Commissioners and their Directorates having direct responsibilities for the items covered by this chapter.

The legal foundations for social policies are to be found in the Treaties of Rome (EEC), Paris (ECSC) and Rome (Euratom) as modified by subsequent developments. The Single European Act brought changes thought necessary because of the move to the Single Market while the Maastricht and Amsterdam treaties both widened responsibilities and sharpened up existing ones. Some treaty provisions are clear-cut but others are of a very general nature and do not require legislation so much as political programmes, with the result that at any moment there is a wide variety of social activities which demand a different degree of commitment from member states. One consequence is the growing overlap of interest with that of national authorities which leads both to co-operation and to conflict. Although national governments remain primarily in charge in matters such as mainstream education, personal health care, the value of social security benefits and housing provision and national sources of finance are overwhelmingly important, it is routine for ministers to attend specialist Council meetings to agree both Community policy initiatives and joint activities in this matters. It is important, however, to retain a sense of perspective. Community interest is often marginal to the main body of work carried out nationally since it derives in the first instance from economic objectives and the current emphasis upon subsidiarity suggests this division is intended to remain. An example is in education, where the EU accepts that member states are primarily responsible for fulfilling educational needs but sees a role for a 'European dimension' through supporting language teaching, mobility of staff and students and co-operation between educational establishments in different member states.

19.2   The Treaty of Rome

Although the Treaty of Rome was relatively weak on the social side it was sufficient to allow much development. First, it had general objectives of a broadly social character, such as a high level of employment and social protection and a raised standard of living. Second, it contained a recognition by member states of the need to improve living and working conditions and of their expectation that social policies would gradually align under the impact of the new system. There was agreement to collaborate in specific fields such as labour legislation, working conditions, vocational training, social security, industrial health and welfare and trade union and collective bargaining matters. Here the Commission was given the responsibility of promoting collaboration. In this way, scope for joint action was left open should the evolution of the EC require it but common policies were not considered inevitable. Third, the question of the effect of social costs on competition was raised in 1957. The sensitivity of French industry on this point led directly to the principle of equal pay for men and women. This has proved the basis for some significant policy developments. Fourth, the belief that manpower was ineffectively utilized led to the setting up of the European Social Fund (ESF), the aim of which was to help both occupational and geographical mobility. In addition, the treaty included an agreement to establish the common principles of vocational training.

The fifth item of great social significance was the adoption of the principle of the free movement of wage earners, along with rules to give it practical effect and to ensure the equal treatment of such migrants with indigenous workers. It was agreed, also, that rules would be necessary to allow the free establishment of the self-employed and for services to be provided across frontiers. These clauses have given rise to programmes of great complexity.

The free movement policy, together with its supporting policies of employment exchange collaboration, maintenance of social security rights and protection of equal working rights for migrants, was a major EC success although it owed much to the buoyant economic conditions of the time. Subsequent attempts to move the policy into the much more difficult area of social integration and social equality

415

and to evolve a policy towards migrants from outside have been far harder to accomplish.

Sixth, special protective measures, which derive from the appropriate treaties, were set up in the coal, steel and nuclear sectors. Not only is there a special concern for health and safety matters but, in coal and steel, pioneering work was done to operate a system of cash benefits and services for workers who lost their jobs as the industries lost their pre-eminence in the economy.

19.3 The Single European Act and the Social Charter

The prime social aim of the SEA was to develop the provisions made necessary by the internal market although there were disagreements as to what these were. It also began the process of widening the concept of social policy. It made an important statement of principle in its preamble affirming the fundamental civil, political and social rights of citizens, drawing on the work of the Council of Europe for this. By doing so, it strengthened the EC's moral base and thus the hands of those who wished to see the EC play a more positive social role. A special section of the SEA supplemented the Rome Treaty. It agreed to pay special attention to better health and safety standards at work and to harmonizing standards while maintaining existing high ones. This reflected the fear that firms would be tempted to cut standards as they entered a more competitive situation. Minimum standards were to be introduced gradually by directives and passed by Qualified Majority Voting (QMV) in the Council of Ministers. At the same time, a cautious note was sounded by stressing that the conditions in member states must be taken into account and the needs of small business considered. A dialogue between management and labour at the EC level, which might, in turn, lead to formal agreements between the two sides of industry, was to be set up.

Certain reservations about the use of QMV continued. In the social field, unanimity was still required for free movement rules, the rights and interests of employed persons and for the passing of directives which would require alteration in the methods of training for, and practice in, some professions. The treaty referred to the need for the Commission to use high standards when regulating health, safety and environmental issues and when dealing with consumer protection.

Underlying these legislative provisions were considerable uncertainties. Some member states feared that, by having EC standards imposed upon them, their goods with be unable to compete; others feared pressure to lower their standards to meet competition from members with lower labour costs; yet others feared the import of goods, livestock and plants that would introduce new forms of disease. Denmark added a special declaration to the SEA designed to ensure it could continue with its own high standards. The United Kingdom was anxious to prevent the imposition of labour regulation which would damage the upsurge of small businesses and thought the social dialogue provisions would encourage the revitalization of trade union power which the Conservative government had been attacking at home. No solutions were found to these conflicts of interest but the SEA, by introducing clauses to satisfy everyone, made future conflict inevitable. This soon began to occur.

A new subsection introduced the concept of economic and social cohesion. Primarily concerned with regional policy and the support of the most backward

Community members, it affected the use to be made of the ESF. Environmental issues were also brought under the EC umbrella for the first time.

The SEA gave a boost to the development of social policy. New initiatives to encourage language teaching, student exchanges and better vocational training and to establish health and safety norms soon began to appear and were broadly acceptable to member governments. However, the Commission was less successful in mobilizing support for proposals relating to working conditions. The opposition was led by the United Kingdom whose government disliked such formal controls over business and was suspicious of the opportunity offered by some of the proposals for the growth of trade union power. The UK government also objected to what she considered a misuse of treaty powers in that directives were being proposed under cover of the implementation of the Single Market when they were not really necessary for this purpose. In consequence, they could be passed by QMV. The matter received great publicity when the Commission produced a Charter on the Fundamental Social Rights for Workers (the Social Charter) setting out the proposed actions thought necessary in consequence of the Single Market. There were 47 initiatives in all, many of them non-controversial and some already agreed, but others moved on to contested ground. In December 1989, the Social Charter was accepted by all governments other than the British and it became, not a legally binding document, but a statement of proposed action which the Commission subsequently used as a document to organize its work.

19.4 The growth of social policy

Given the rather incoherent guidance of the early years, it is not surprising that the development of social policy was patchy. The first decade saw major steps taken to implement the policy on labour movement, a formal adoption of the equal pay policy, a narrow exploitation of the ESF and considerable study of, and research into, labour questions but there was a sense of social policy hanging fire. However, a new impetus can be detected by the end of the 1960s when hopes in Western Europe were high for social improvements and the EC benefited from this optimism. Widespread unease existing over environmental pollution, the problems of the disadvantaged, social inequalities and the increasing distance between the citizen and the services run by big bureaucracies originally developed to help the ordinary man and woman. There was a certain vacuum in social policy which enabled the EC to establish a role. The Hague conference in December 1969 agreed that the EC needed to go further in the pursuit of common economic and political goals in which a 'concerted social policy' would have a part. This line was continued by the Paris summit of 1972 which asserted the importance member states attached to vigorous action in the social field. Specifically, it referred to the need to widen participation in decision making and action to lessen inequalities and to improve the quality of life. The political momentum thus established led to the first Social Action Programme (SAP). Its hopes were, however, quickly dashed by the onset of recession and the burden of large-scale unemployment and it was this that began to dominate social concerns as the EC experienced structural changes in employment patterns, including a rapid growth in part-time and shift work, together with formidable problems of long-term and youth unemployment. A major preoccupation for the EC became the need to analyse unemployment issues, encourage co-operative action by member states and support programmes to help to overcome specific problems such as lack of training.

By the 1980s, a new momentum in the EC can be discerned, in which social policy had an important role. In 1981, the newly elected French socialist government had proposed a programme for a 'social space' for the EC and the following year the European Parliament called for a reform of the treaties and the achievement of a European union which would require a new policy for society. The entry of Greece, Portugal and Spain added another dimension by turning attention away from the urban problems of the more developed North to the importance of devoting resources to the characteristic problems of agricultural inefficiency, disguised unemployment in rural areas and lack of training for industrial work. The later entry of Austria, Sweden and Finland maintained the interest in social policy and brought the strong Scandinavian welfare tradition into the counsels of the EU.

The urge to establish the Single Market and the insistence that this must be accompanied by some steps towards cementing European union drove the Community towards a fresh consideration of citizens' rights. The European Council accepted two reports from the *ad hoc* Adonnino committee in 1985 which included a host of recommendations for building 'The People's Europe'. Some were new, others asked for current policies to be pursued more rigorously. Although some were implemented, others ran into difficulties.

19.5   The Treaty of Union

Subsequent to the passing of the SEA, controversy in social matters revolved round questions raised by the Single Market and, in particular, over possible extensions of European employment law. The Maastricht negotiations led to a totally unexpected result. Amended Articles 2 and 3 reiterated the social goals of the Treaty of Rome but in a broader, often more explicit, form. They now included respect for the environment, a high level of employment and social protection and the raising of the standard of living and the quality of life. Subsequent purposes included the free movement of people, measures concerning the entry of people, a continuation of the ESF and the policy of cohesion, a contribution to a high level of health protection, to education and training and to the flowering of culture as well as to consumer protection and to measures in the sphere of tourism.

Most importantly, the treaty established the legal concept of Union citizenship 'to strengthen the protection of the rights and interests of the nationals of the Member States'. Citizens were given the right to move and reside freely, to vote and stand as candidates in municipal and European Parliamentary elections in all member states on the same terms as nationals (each right being subject to certain limitations). Citizens, when outside the Community, received the right to diplomatic protection from the services of any member state. They may now petition both the European Parliament and the European Ombudsman. Directives are in place to give effect to these political rights and the Ombudsman has been appointed.

The novelty was that 11 (later 14) states, excluding the United Kingdom, signed an attached Protocol and Agreement, popularly known as the Social Chapter (now fully incorporated in the treaties, see below). This affirmed their wish to continue with the Social Charter and clarified the goals. Article 1 of the Agreement included 'the promotion of employment, improved living and working conditions, proper social protection, dialogue between management and labour, the development of human resources with a view to lasting high employment and the combating of exclusion'. The Agreement made explicit that the Community is competent to act in the fields of the working environment, working conditions, equality of men and women concerning opportunities and treatment at work, the social integration of excluded groups and with regard to the information and consultation of workers. It established the right of the Council to pass directives on minimum standards by the use of QMV for matters of health and safety, working conditions, information and consultation, equality at work and the integration of those outside the labour market. The Council may also act, by unanimity, on social security and protection, protection of redundant workers, the defence and representation of workers' and employers' interests, employment conditions for third country nationals, financing of measures for employment and job creation (but not the use of the ESF, which is in the main treaty). Pay, the right of association and the right to strike and impose lock-outs are specifically excluded, while states may continue to provide specific advantages for women in order to equalize their working opportunities.

The Agreement strengthened the corporatist element in decision making through a stronger role for management and unions. First, member states may delegate to the social partners the task of implementing directives relating to the above goals; second, the Commission must consult them before submitting any formal social policy proposals; and third, the Agreement recognized that the social partners may be in a position to agree on actions themselves. In addition, they can agree to ask for the formal structures to implement agreements they have reached. Some analysts see the clauses relating to the social dialogue and the role of the social partners as very significant, arguing that they signal a new way of applying doctrines of partnership, consultation and openness and of implementing the principle of subsidiarity. The protocol was concerned with the use of the Community's institutions by the signatories to the Agreement.

The effect of the Agreement on social policy was tiresome rather than significant since it was always the intention to get all members to agree if possible and only to use the Agreement as a last resort. British employers' and union organizations were represented through the European umbrella organizations, so Britain's voice was not entirely excluded. However, it is just as well that the new Labour government announced in 1997 that it was ready to accept the Agreement which thus became incorporated into the legal structure with the Amsterdam Treaty.

The Union treaty also brought changes regarding the entry of migrants. Most member states are under pressure from nationals of third countries at present and, in consequence, immigration and asylum policies are being re-examined. The Council of Ministers obtained the duty to determine the third countries whose nationals must be in possession of a visa, at first by unanimity but, from January 1996, by QMV. Emergency arrangements may be made to deal with a sudden inflow of people. Migratory movements also affect the Community role in ensuring co-operation in the fields of justice and home affairs (see section 19.6 below).

All in all, the Union treaty gave the EU more standing in social affairs, tidied up existing policies and made explicit where the Community had arrived in the execution of its work. This, in itself, helped to avoid future arguments about the legal basis of proposals. The more significant developments are to be found in the broadened objectives and enhanced role of the social partners, developments which have been consolidated through the Treaty of Amsterdam.

This chapter now turns to examine individual policies in more detail, reflecting the fact that unemployment is the major preoccupation of the moment. Since policies are run by the European Community but citizenship is a matter for the European Union, the terms EC and EU are used as appropriate.

19.6 European citizenship

It is logical to begin with the notion of European citizenship. The concept is a mixture of ideas about the provision of legal rights and the development of policies to improve well-being. The reasoning behind it was that political union requires an assumption of responsibility for the social condition of the people who are unlikely to support a union which appears uninterested in their needs. The argument appeared justified when the unpopularity of the European project surfaced during the debates on ratification of the Maastricht Treaty. This experience heightened the belief that the EU must not only do more for the general public but be seen to be doing so. A greater transparency of action, more efforts to inform the public of what was happening, taking decisions closer to the people and involving them more in decision making became aims to be met through greater publicity, closer relations with voluntary organizations and the use of procedures under the Social Agreement. Of course, if the social dialogue is to be a means of reaching out to the citizen and to be a channel of influence on broader issues than at present then it, in turn, must broaden its membership. This remains for the future but it is worth noting that, in 1996, the Commission argued that the social dialogue could well be promoted at sectoral level, leaving the European discussions to concentrate on strategic priorities. The more broadly these are defined, the stronger becomes the case for admitting representatives of voluntary organizations, the churches and local authorities to membership.

Political rights having been covered in the TEU, discussion moved on to human and social rights. The commitment in Article 6 (EU) is to respect the European Convention on Human Rights and Fundamental Freedoms, and the possibility of suspension of membership in the case of violation has been added to the treaty. The question is still raised whether the EU should formally subscribe to it. The ECJ has studied the question more than once, concluding that to do so would require a full-scale treaty revision (Opinion 2/94 28.3.96). There are further references to the importance of human rights in the treaties, including their significance for the common foreign and security policy. The Commission set out its views on the protection of human rights in the EU and the priorities for action in 'The European Union and human rights: from Rome to Maastricht and beyond' (COM (95) 567). It is also usual to find that contractual ties with third countries make 'respect for democratic and human rights' an essential part of the text and the Commission is particularly watchful in the case of aspiring Union entrants and the recipients of development aid. An innovation was the declaration adopted at Amsterdam noting the fact that most member states have now abolished the death penalty and that it has not been applied in any of them for many years.

At the start of 2000, elections in Austria brought a challenge to the EU's position on democratic and human rights. The Freedom Party, from the far right, became eligible to join the government but its leader had expressed intolerant views, widely reported and disapproved of across the EU, notably with regard to immigrants. The

EU President, on behalf of the remaining 14 members, informed Austria that bilateral relations between them would be frozen if the Freedom Party were to be a part of the government. Whatever the result of this diplomatic quarantine, it has created some form of precedent for the EU to act in future against member states in danger of developing xenophobic attitudes and perhaps, therefore, was intended as a warning to states now seeking entry.

While the Amsterdam Treaty has strengthened the social commitments of the EU there is still a view that the EU needs its own charter of civil and social rights to be protected by the ECJ. This demand has so far been met by a reference to the European Social Charter of the Council of Europe now to be found in Article 136 (EC) although a year-long convention began work in 2000 on a formal Charter.

The development of co-operation by judicial systems and police forces has an obvious relevance to the idea of citizenship. Extradition can be difficult in the absence of common definitions, for example of alleged political offences or membership or a proscribed organization, and if the conditions are tighter when a state is asked to extradite its own nationals. Simplified procedures were agreed in 1995. Proceedings and sentences in criminal matters may require greater harmonization across the Union if they are not to create anomalies. Control over entrants to the EU and the extent of their ability to move freely within the Union were identified at Maastricht as requiring common rules.

At the Dublin summit meeting in December 1996, a programme to fight organized crime, terrorism and the drugs trade was agreed and moves taken to curtail drug production and addiction. A European Drugs Unit has joined Europol, the police agency created under the TEU. The latter has extended its remit to cover trafficking in human beings, and common definitions of paedophile crime have been agreed. Although a single travel area for citizens has not yet been fully achieved, the Schengen Agreement has now been brought into the treaty structure, making for ease of travel over large parts of the Union territory. Although it will be some time before these agreements become fully operative they begin to mould the concept of European citizenship in a meaningful way, clarifying the rights of qualifying individuals (see section 19.16 below).

19.7   Free movement

An essential element of citizenship is the ability to move freely through the territory to which one belongs but, although great strides have been made, this does not apply fully in the EU and it seems generally accepted that it will be a long time before it does. The policy reflects the original economic objectives, growing out of the need to establish the free movement of workers. Piecemeal extensions have been made which have brought in more categories of people but it is not yet possible to say that free movement of persons can be taken for granted.

The 1957 provisions were primarily concerned with the mobility of unskilled labour and, in practice, were mainly of benefit to Italy. Today, matters look different. Movement within the Community takes place for many reasons. It may be a way of escaping local unemployment, of filling skill shortages, of a temporary posting from one branch of a company to another or of a firm fulfilling a contract elsewhere in the EU. Movement for non-economic reasons such as joining a breadwinner, study, holidays or the wish to live elsewhere is growing in importance.

The essential structure to ensure free movement of wage earners within the EC of six members was in place by 1968 or settled not long afterwards. The rules protected the right to move for work and to remain in a country subsequently, gave entry rights to families and elaborated a complex system for the maintenance of social security rights. They also confirmed the right to join a trade union and stand for office, the right of access to vocational training and to use the employment services. In this way, the principles of equal treatment and of ensuring non-discrimination were accepted. Broadly speaking, these rules were applied without undue difficulty. Individual cases of discrimination continue to find their way to the ECJ, eligibility to social security benefits being a particularly complex area, but, gradually, the rules have become better understood and observed.

It is necessary, of course, constantly to develop the rules as gaps are found or as the nature of migration changes. Social security for the self-employed as possibilities for movement were opened up, and rules concerning the right of families to move and to receive certain benefits soon required attention. In later years, the movement of skilled persons, managerial staff and professional people became more important. These groups can be more affected by occupational benefits than by statutory social security systems, especially for pension entitlement or by the quality of housing, availability of schools and leisure facilities and, although the EC has not become involved in all these matters, questions of transferability of occupational pension schemes, the incidence of taxation on the transfer of monies and variations in taxation methods are all ones in which it has expressed interest.

An action programme to modernize the free movement arrangements was begun in 1997, not only with the aim of rationalizing the rules but because the EU can now start from the principle of the right of free movement for EU citizens, developing the minimum number of rules for special groups as required (COM (97) 586 final). The passing of the SEA had already led to rules to establish the right to residence for students and their families during the period of education (Directive 90/366); employees and the self-employed were given the right to remain after working in a country (Directive 90/365); and other groups were covered by Directive 90/364). In all cases, the right was made subject to the possession o adequate financial resources. There is now a drive for new legal rules, means to overcome administrative difficulties and known obstacles, a more modern interpretation of eligibility of family members, as well as to cater better for third country nationals who are resident in one member state but to whom free movement rules may not apply. As part of this policy, a proposed revision of the basic Regulation on social security (Regulation 1408/71, see OJ L28, 30.1.97 and OJ C325, 23.10.98) is intended to improve and clarify the rules of the application of social security schemes to ensure all persons eligible for benefits are covered (i.e. to include the non-active), to aggregate periods of entitlement, to ensure effective co-ordination of the rules and to cover newer types of benefit, for example early retirement benefit. Further rules are expected.

Bringing vacancies and workers together was recognized as a necessity from the start but proved a tremendously difficult project. It is much affected by the efficiency of national employment services and by the existing procedures for job descriptions, methods of achieving qualifications and the content of skills expected by such qualifications. Great efforts have been made by the EC to bring some uniformity into these matters so that expectations on both sides match reasonably well. Gradually, agreed European norms are being introduced into national qualifications and into job descriptions without bringing standardization. The latest attempt at a mechanism for matching up jobs and applicants was launched in 1994 (EURES); handling the exchange of information between social security systems has also been greatly developed (TESS).

There are, however, still problems to overcome to ensure that workers benefit as they should from EC policies. Problems are still reported, for example concerning access to training or the application of the principle of equal opportunity while in the host country. In practice, the right to obtain work in the public sector is often restricted, for example by applying a nationality rule to areas of work which are unconnected with the exercise of public authority in any way. The tax treatment of those who live in one country and work in another or the workings of an early retirement scheme may penalize a migrant. There is also a general need for co-ordination between the rules for occupational and supplementary pension schemes, especially now that these are becoming more important. A start was made with Directive 98/49 to protect supplementary rights for the employed and the self-employed who are on the move by ensuring that pensions can be paid in another member state, contributions are maintained and workers properly informed of the situation. The directive must be in force by 2001. Technical formalities, too, are often formidable but there are plans for a standardized EC Resident card for the automatic renewal of a residence permit, including for those whose work is interrupted by unemployment or ill-health.

Free movement of the self-employed and the ability to supply services across frontiers were both written into the original treaty but were very hard to apply due to differences of standards of training, in its content and in the way services are provided in different states. Sometimes the right to supply services has been traditionally qualified by rules concerning nationality, place of origin or where qualifications were obtained, and dismantling such barriers without damage to standards is a highly technical matter. The application of rules to ensure conformity of national qualifications can take many years and in the meantime other barriers can be used to avoid letting non-nationals practise. Disputes, such as that of non-French ski instructors barred from access to work on French ski slopes, can rumble on for years.

The EC has, therefore, always been interested in the comparability, and mutual recognition, of qualifications as a necessary precondition for the mobility of working people. In 1985 the Council of Ministers agreed that the mutual recognition of qualifications must be speeded up and directions were provided on how to establish comparability (OJ C264/83; OJ C208/84). A ruling from the ECJ made it clear that many university courses could be considered as vocational training and that students from all member states must be admitted on the same terms as nationals. This ruling also helped to open up the issue of the content of professional courses. It is generally accepted, however, that it is a field of great complexity and there is a long way to go before a full transparency and understanding of qualifications is obtained.

The health sector saw some of the early work since basic training could be harmonized to a degree to allow for movement for some doctors, nurses, dentists, veterinarians, midwives and pharmacists. Other professions followed but it became necessary to adopt a general directive for the recognition of professional standards of university level and above, other than those already recognized by existing sectoral directives (Directive 89/48). This established a general right to practise, subject to the right of the state to apply limited tests to ensure competence. This was complemented by a second directive (Directive 92/51, OJ L209/92) designed to cover a wide range of education and training courses, including on-the-job training in some instances, but where specific qualifications are not laid down (CEC 1991e).

19.8 Employment

There have been striking changes in the labour force of the EU since 1957 (see the latest issues of Eurostat *Review* and EC *Employment in Europe* (annual)). It is very much bigger as the population of working age has grown, women have come into the workplace and the EC has enlarged to become the EU. Further increases in membership are foreseen. At the same time, the employment structure has altered. One of the most dramatic changes has been in the growth of information and communications technology both as a new industry and as a business tool. Often, however, the new growth is not geographically well placed to absorb redundant workers who, in any case, would need new skills, while the jobs it offers are frequently part-time or temporary, taken by women rather than men. Overall, the EU does not generate new jobs at a rate comparable with that of the USA and Japan and the European rate is inadequate to absorb the larger labour force. It is always hoped that the major economic policies of the Union, such as the Single Market and EMU, either directly or indirectly will create jobs but, often, taking advantage of developments means that workers must be more mobile and more highly trained than heretofore. It is obvious that there are great linguistic and cultural barriers in the EU to worker mobility and, meanwhile, there is a serious mismatch of jobs and workers which implies high unemployment rates in certain areas. European policies have paid particular attention to unemployment amongst young people, women and the long-term unemployed but there is a growing realization of the difficulties faced by older people in finding and keeping a job although they still have skills to offer. Furthermore, the changing demographic structure suggests that the EU needs to keep an open mind on the need for younger, migrant labour to replenish its labour force in the future. A great deal of time is devoted to these questions by European policy makers.

It has proved hard for states to grapple with the changes and particularly difficult for the EU to find a positive role since it operates at one remove. Nevertheless, employment is so central to the work and significance of the EU that it has found ways of developing a wide range of policies to deal with particular employment issues. In 1957, the Treaty of Rome referred to the promotion of a high level of employment and at a time of prosperity the Community could devote itself to specific tasks, such as the free movement and equal pay policies. As the pace of change accelerated and unemployment seemed composed of a number of difficult sub-issues, doubts were expressed as to whether Western Europe would ever again experience very low unemployment rates. Voices were heard suggesting that the treaty required a new goal with a definite commitment to promote employment and in 1997 a new chapter on employment was written into the Treaty of Amsterdam. This requires the Community to promote high employment through a co-ordinated strategy which includes training a more highly skilled workforce, guidelines for member states to follow, encouragement to best practice and annual assessment of the situation. Employment considerations should, in the future, influence new policy decisions. Limited financial support is now available for experimental initiatives and the EIB has been asked to encourage small and medium-sized businesses and new technological activities which are the main job creators. A new employment and labour market committee was created under Art. 130 (EC) and discussion with the social partners given more attention while the Employment Observatory links national organizations together in a mutual support structure and provides regular information on employment trends and on developments in national structures.

The 1990s saw a steady growth of the EU's interest in employment and what might be done to help with the supply of jobs and to assist individuals to obtain the necessary training and qualifications to fill them. Amongst them the White Paper on Growth, Competitiveness and Employment of 1993 (COM (93) 700 final) was something of a turning-point, helping to elevate employment to a place in the highest EU counsels. It referred to a necessary reorientation of labour market policies to meet new competitive requirements and stressed the significance of the arrival of a knowledge-based information society and the new jobs it was bringing. Subsequently, the Essen Council meeting of December 1994 agreed major policy lines. There was a marked policy shift, away from the traditional approach of income support for the unemployed as the main service available, to the belief that far more had to be done to match people's qualifications to the jobs of today and tomorrow. It stressed that individuals must be actively encouraged to enter, or return to, the labour market.

At the Essen meeting states agreed on the need for more investment in education and vocational training, the importance of increasing the employment intensity of growth, notably through the reorganization of working time, moderate growth in wages and through opening up new areas of employment. They accepted the need to reduce indirect labour costs and to increase the efficiency of labour market policy by moving towards active measures and by targeting services on to specific groups of job seekers.

Studies show that, even today, the so-called passive benefits cost states more than the active, individualized measures. Nevertheless, the European effort is put into the support of schemes for the unemployed which encourage job seekers to (re)train, actively look for work, persist in job applications and help to make themselves more attractive to employers. Traditional employment services need to change themselves if they are to provide these new types of assistance.

If growth itself does not provide a sufficiency of jobs, then governments have to consider what they can do to support more labour-intensive work. Society has a significant demand for service jobs, notably in environmental improvement, child care and social services, and it may be necessary for some time to ensure some vacancies remain for unskilled workers. Since it is small and medium-sized firms that have the better record in job creation it is worth while considering how to help them prosper. A main theme for the Commission has been to encourage local initiatives, employment-intensive growth, help with training and extra costs, and help firms to overcome legal obstacles which face those that wish to take on someone who has been unemployed for some time.

Subsequent summits have continued to stress the importance of job creation and effective measures to help the unemployed. At the Luxembourg summit in 1997, four pillars for employment strategy were laid down. These are improving employability, encouraging entrepreneurship, promoting adaptability and equal opportunities amongst the working population, aims which permeate the current guidelines adopted by Council Resolution in February 1999. These embrace a broad spectrum of activities ranging from improved education and skills, encouragement to small and medium-sized enterprises, upgrading the skills of existing workers and a constant examination of working patterns to ensure a necessary flexible and family-friendly environment. A possible development for the future is that the Community should introduce rules to forbid discrimination in employment in conformity with Art. 13 (EC). The overall approach remains one of an employment strategy primarily based on investment in physical and human resources, promoting knowledge and skills and ensuring an entrepreneurial environment quite different from earlier objectives relevant to previous working patterns.

19.9   The European Social Fund

The principal weapon the EC possesses to combat unemployment directly is the ESF which operates through grant aid to approved schemes of vocational training and employment support (Art. 146 (EC)). It has undergone several reforms and extensions so that today it is part of a more co-ordinated effort to fight unemployment and to deliver a highly skilled and adaptable workforce. However, it has never been entirely clear how widely its remit should be drawn as it soon became obvious that many of the unemployed required, for example, help with social skills, child care facilities and the like. Recently, the ESF was placed squarely in the context of the employment strategy of the Amsterdam Treaty but this enables it to contribute to a number of social goals since social integration and the pursuit of equal opportunities can come through enabling people to work. Thus a variety of measures may need support. Specialized help for the long-term unemployed, assistance in developing education and training systems, the promotion of life-long learning, assistance to schemes to improve the skills of the existing workforce and to aid women's participation in the labour force are all examples of the Fund's support activities. Its remit is now very wide, covering, for example, aid to help people set up in self-employment, to improve the training of teachers, to modernize employment services as well as to aid 'accompanying measures' such as child care, facilities for dependants, health care and legal assistance for those who, without such help, could not work. Although there has always been a school of thought that would like the ESF to undertake support of schemes with specific social aims, it seems clear that these must be viewed as subordinate to the main objective of helping people into employment or to move to higher skilled work. Considerable interest attaches to the question of which schemes actually receive funding, and competition is intense.

In recent years, the work has been primarily concentrated in poorer regions and countries as part of a targeted effort by all the structural funds. However, a reference to the past may help in understanding the complicated arrangements; a constant cry of reform is for simplification and clarification.

The ESF started in a limited way and primarily assisted migrants form the Italian South to move north into the industrial areas but a subsequent reform, in 1971, created a larger and more flexible fund which could be used to help with training and which gave special attention to the needs of particular groups of workers or regions. By the 1980s it was felt that the fund needed further adaptation. It began to concentrate upon work to promote the employment and training of young people under 25 years of age and, subsequently, of the long-term unemployed. By 1985, grants were also available to members of both groups wishing to set up in self-employment. Grants to special groups such as the handicapped, women workers and migrants continued, as they still do, but were no longer earmarked. Employment in small and medium-sized businesses was encouraged and special grants introduced to aid vocational guidance and placement. The most deprived regions continued to receive special aid but otherwise the fund directed its efforts to areas of persistently high unemployment and where large reconstruction projects were required.

Much of this work was formalized following the passing of the SEA. Perhaps the most important effect was the recognition of the need to pursue economic and social cohesion as a goal which would offset the possible disadvantageous effects of the Single Market in some areas. A master Regulation was agreed (2052/88) which established that the European Regional Development Fund (ERDF), the European Agricultural Guidance and Guarantee Fund (EAGGF) (Guidance section) and the ESF, now known jointly as the structural funds and later joined by the Financial Instrument for Fisheries Guidance (FIFG), should co-ordinate their work and should work closely with the European Investment Bank (EIB) as well.

Objectives applicable to all funds were laid down. Regional definitions have recently been reduced to three (see Chapter 18). Objective (1) areas of low GDP and generally high unemployment will receive about two-thirds of structural funds monies and cover about 20% of the EU's population. This objective includes the very remote regions which may be sparsely populated. Objective (2) covers areas undergoing major economic and social restructuring and includes those where there are special problems, for example areas dependent upon fishing or suffering from industrial decay or rural decline. About 18% of the EU's population should be covered. In both Objectives (1) and (2) transitional arrangements will help those areas which will no longer be eligible. Objective (3) is concerned with the development of human resources and tackling unemployment generally and is the domain of the ESF (COM (98) 131 final, OJ C176, 9.6.98, amended COM (99) 4 final, OJ C74, 18.3.99).

The Fund has been given five broad tasks. It is to contribute to the development of active labour market policies, including the prevention of unemployment; it must promote social inclusion; it is to aid life-long learning and training to promote employability; it must help workers anticipate and respond to economic and social change and it must aid equal opportunities for men and women. It places much emphasis upon the importance of local initiatives and also provides support for back-up measures such as care and health services. While these aims are drawn up in the light of the overall employment strategy, in the past the greater part of the ESF's finances has been spent in the poorer regions and therefore integrated with projects falling under Objectives (1) or (2).

The budget of the ESF for the years 2000–6 should be nearly 70 billion ECU, 35% of the structural funds monies. In most cases, its aid is limited to half the cost of an approved scheme. Of the structural funds monies, 5% is handled directly by the Commission and used to support transnational, cross-frontier and inter-regional schemes, and 1% is earmarked for a variety of innovative schemes and local projects. Here the Commission may provide total funding. It is in this area that experimental schemes, often run by voluntary organizations and working on a small scale, are to be found. The *Leader* programme is for rural areas, *Urban* for deprived city areas and *Equal* for equality promotion projects.

The search for an improved administrative structure continues. It is generally agreed that grant procedures are cumbersome and administration is opaque but successive changes seem to make little difference. The post-1988 system brought important changes with a shift towards making schemes find their place in an overall national plan which can then be approved in Brussels. The emphasis was on partnership between the Commission, member governments, local authorities and other representatives who should together formulate multi-annual programmes to their mutual satisfaction and which should give a necessary stability of finance to individual schemes. The Commission, instead of being involved in the minutiae of scheme approval, was expected to develop its monitoring, control and evaluative functions. This arrangement put far more control into the hands of the central national agency, usually a Department for Employment or its equivalent, which became a channel for the submission of applications and disbursement of grants. Administratively, this arrangement worked much more smoothly than when the Commission was involved in the detail of schemes and it can, of course, be argued that national authorities know their own needs best. One obvious danger of national control is that the Commission is less able to impose its views on how grant aid should be used. Since it tends to be forward looking and has an interest in the spread of new skills and in grasping the opportunities of technological change the Commission may clash with national representatives who are often under pressure to maintain jobs in declining industries or to support new schemes of job creation as an immediate method of reducing unemployment irrespective of long-term viability. However, great importance is currently attached to these issues, to find more effective methods of monitoring schemes and ensure financial efficiency. Current emphasis continues on the importance of partnership with regional and local authorities, economic and social partners and others, with a stress on local development initiatives. Importance is given, too, to the work of voluntary organizations, with authorities being encouraged to help them obtain a place in Community programmes. Clashes of priorities will clearly continue as not all these bodies have the same interests, the Commission has its own agenda and national governments wish to be major players in policy at home and to obtain the maximum possible share of the grants available. Evaluation and monitoring of schemes is clearly difficult for the Commission but a new monitoring committee, with a balanced male/female membership, is another innovation.

A further difficulty facing the Commission is to ensure the principle of additionality. The intention has always been that the Commission, by insisting upon matching grants from member states, ensures that more work is done than would otherwise have been the case but whether it truly does so often remains a mystery.

The ESF has become a significant part of the EU structure, especially now that its mandate has broadened to enable it to play a role in delivering a highly skilled and adaptable workforce. It has begun, in a small way, to reach out beyond the immediate confines of work by recognizing social factors which inhibit potential workers from coming forward and thus it is beginning to play a part in the prevention of social exclusion and to reflect the view that disadvantaged people must be helped to become self-supporting. It is, however, a long way from becoming a true social, as opposed to a work-related, fund but it is not impossible to imagine it moving further in that direction.

<table>
<tr><td>**19.10**</td><td>**Education and vocational training**</td></tr>
</table>

19.10 Education and vocational training

From the start, the EEC had certain responsibilities in the field of vocational training and these have led to its gradual move into educational work. The dividing line between training and education is increasingly hard to draw since it is now believed that, in the past, educational systems were too divorced from economic reality so that many young people left school ill-prepared for the world of work. A further impetus has come from the need to reconsider the content of training in order to equip the labour force with the higher skills that industry requires. The Community, no less than its member states, is in the process of adapting to these new requirements and trying to make its services appropriate for current needs. At the same time, more attention to education and training provides an opportunity to encourage greater awareness of the EU and its objectives amongst the rising generation (see COM (97) 256 final, *Teaching and Learning: towards the Learning Society* (CEC, 1995f); *Living and Working in the Information Society: People First*, COM (96) 389 final (CEC 1996u); and *Towards a Europe of Knowledge*, COM (97) 563 final).

The legal base for action in the fields of education and vocational training is now in Articles 149 and 150 (EC). These refer to the Community's role in contributing to quality education while fully respecting the responsibilities of member states for educational services and their cultural and linguistic diversity. Educational action aims to develop a 'European dimension' through helping to improve language skills, increase mobility and exchanges amongst students and staff, through work to ensure the recognition of qualifications, to promote co-operation between educational establishments and long-distance education. Similar phraseology surrounds the vocational training policy which is designed to support and supplement national efforts through encouraging adaptation to industrial changes, improved training and retraining, and facilitating access to it, and greater mobility and co-operation between instructors, training establishments and trainees.

The new drive on education and vocational training policy began in 1995. Objectives were linked to the need for a better quality of education, a spread of qualifications throughout the population and work to make national systems more comparable. Since states themselves are actively recasting educational and training systems, the Commission's role is to act as a stimulus, to help to set up schemes and to encourage their development in ways which help to cement the EU. A special interest is to foster innovation and the effective use of technology through the encouragement it can give to young people, the learning of new skills and the transfer of knowledge.

Following its White Paper of 1995 the Commission regrouped its many programmes into three main groups. Its *Youth* programme supports youth exchange schemes, short visits and voluntary participation in common projects in order to increase European awareness (see OJ C309, 9.10.98; OJ C311, 10.10.98; OJ C314, 13.10.98 for details). *Leonardo da Vinci* is concerned with vocational training. Like the *Youth* schemes it includes Norway, Iceland and Liechtenstein and is extending to cover Central and Eastern Europe, Cyprus and Malta. By 2000, there should be 31 participating countries. Placement and exchange schemes enable those in training or on university courses to obtain work placements in another member state with the aim of improving vocational training and promoting vocational skills. A particular interest is in placements in the use of information technology (Council Decision OJ L146, 11.06.99).

It was as early as the 1970s that the Commission became aware of the problem of young people leaving school inadequately prepared for work and it began to encourage schemes to provide better pre-training preparation for them. At the same time, it established the European Centre for the Development of Vocational Training (CEDEFOP), now in Thessaloniki, to encourage greater awareness of training needs and learning opportunities and to act as an information and resource centre. The Centre has a series of agreements with other European states to ensure a basic compatibility between all training developments. In similar vein, a European Foundation for Training, in Turin, maintains links with CEDEFOP and acts as a channel offering similar support to the countries of Central and Eastern Europe, the ex-Soviet states and Mongolia. One particular problem is that some states need to prepare their training systems for the hoped-for closer association with the EU and this aim requires considerable change and a great deal of effort to improve fluency in at least one EU language.

Third, the *Socrates* programme, which again includes Norway, Iceland and Liechtenstein, has responsibilities in higher education. Student exchanges figure prominently, with a special interest in language studies, joint courses and teacher exchanges. The aim is still to have 10% of the student population spending some time abroad so as to create a growing pool of graduates with EU experience for the future. A new venture is to support university courses which wish to introduce a European element into courses which are not formally joint or exchange schemes but which will, nevertheless, contain a measure of joint co-operation. A system of Course Credit Transfer is being developed which should make student mobility easier over time and this, in turn, may well lead to a greater uniformity in course content, with the benefit of making it easier for courses followed to be recognized. Recently, the *Socrates* programme has agreed to support alternative educational pathways to higher education, to promote the use of multi-media techniques and to encourage innovative schemes.

The *Comenius* programme, with similar aims, covers the secondary school years. It is based on the need to foster partnership between schools which may co-operate in language and other subject teaching; this is made easier by the growth of computer networks and fast communications. Children of migrants and itinerants have been able to benefit for many years from language and introductory courses which are now operated through *Comenius*.

Language teaching at all levels is today supported more strongly than ever with the aim of seeking proficiency in three Community languages for younger generations. This depends critically on being able to offer opportunities in other member states for language teachers and teachers in training. Improved teaching material is always being sought and the use of open learning techniques encouraged. Support for courses in European studies in adult education is beginning.

All these schemes are now asked to support the EU's broader social aims of equal opportunities and combating inequality. The *Eurydice* network exists specifically to provide information on the range of schemes, an office for educational statistics has been created and the *Iris* network handles the exchange of information on women's education.

A particular effort is being made towards Central and Eastern Europe, including the ex-Soviet states and Mongolia, to aid the reform of higher education. For the relevant states, this is believed to be a necessary preliminary to membership of, or association with, the EU. The projects are becoming more varied as different national needs are identified but it is considered important that universities, in general, should open up to outside influences. A rough division can be made between the group of states from the ex-Soviet area and Mongolia, the group preparing for membership of the EU or at least some form of pre-membership, for whom the need for change in educational and training systems is in known, specific ways, and a third group. Their membership is a very long way off but their geographical position demands sympathy for their aspirations. These include the states of ex-Yugoslavia (other than Slovenia which falls into the second group) and Albania. Contacts with the universities of Western Europe, the provision of teaching materials and an increased mobility for students and staff are all important.

A clause in the EC Treaty decreed that the Community should contribute to the flowering of the cultures of the members. Its particular tasks are to concentrate upon encouraging co-operation between member states, improving knowledge about European culture and history and conserving the cultural heritage of European significance. As a result, the Commission has a range of initiatives relating in particular to the last-mentioned goal, and has a new framework of programmes starting in 2000. One of the most contentious issues has been the use of television and, with the increase in the number of channels, whether transmission should give some priority to European programmes. Despite efforts to make it mandatory to devote half of all viewing time to European productions it appears likely that the EU will persevere with voluntary quota systems. Financial assistance is given through 'incentive measures' to these various schemes.

19.11 Consumer policy

The Maastricht Treaty gave consumer protection the status of a full policy (Article 153 (EC)). It now covers an obligation to promote the interests of consumers, ensure their protection and promote their right to information and education and to better organization to safeguard their interests. The Single Market raised the problem that consumers simply would not know how to judge the quality of goods bought unless minimum standards were applied, would have difficulty in obtaining redress for faulty goods or would not understand what was being offered by a service. The public has, indeed, to have full information about goods and services on offer but recent worries over food safety and the lack of information provided through labelling (e.g. in relation to genetically modified ingredients) suggest that a good deal more needs to be done. The Consumer Committee gives direct access to the Commission for national consumer groups but consumer representation is poorly developed in the southern states and in Central and Eastern Europe. Consumer protection has now been combined with health to form a Commission portfolio.

A directive and recommendation on direct selling and an improved directive on misleading advertisements are slowly moving through the EC procedures. A time share directive was adopted in 1994 and the general product safety directive of 1992 is now in the hands of states to implement. A database on home and leisure accidents has been set up and some protection is given on the use of computer-held personal data. A directive covering the periods of guarantee on goods bought must be in force by year 2002.

19.12 Working conditions and industrial relations

Collective bargaining remains a matter handled within member states and it is only gradually that industrial relations acquired a European dimension, although some of the Commission initiatives have met with fierce opposition. From the Community's point of view, three themes stand out which, in day-to-day affairs, are often tangled together. There is, first, the belief that it is important to involve employers' associations and unions in the operation of European affairs; second, that consultation, or even cross-Community negotiation, may be necessary in some cases; and third, that an integrated market may require some changes in traditional national arrangements.

The Paris and Rome treaties established certain formal structures, notably the ECSC Consultative Committee and the EEC Economic and Social Committee, to associate representatives of employers, workers and other groups with EC affairs. Subsequently, advisory committees, such as those for the ESF, were constituted with joint representation: many joint committees meet to consider the problems of a particular industry as required and a number of attempts have been made to establish a meeting place for the two sides of industry, with or without representatives of governments. However, none of these methods proved satisfactory and tension grew with the rise in unemployment. The then Commission President, Jacques Delors, was a prime mover in attempts to give the 'social dialogue' more prominence, seeing it as one way in which trade union and business opinion might be mobilized behind the process of European integration.

The theme of consensus between the social partners, leading to agreed policies to improve working conditions and social security benefits, is a long-standing one in some Continental systems of industrial relations but alien to others. The British government, particularly in the 1980s, disliked both the attempt to give the social dialogue a formal place in Community affairs and the greater legal regulation of industrial matters to which it can give rise. Nevertheless, the UK agreed that the SEA should give the Commission a duty to develop the dialogue between management and labour at European level and, with the Amsterdam Treaty, political objections have been removed. Not only is the dialogue supported but the Commission has a duty to consult the social partners prior to any social policy initiative and, if a further development is decided upon, management and labour may handle the matter through their own procedures for agreements (Articles 138, 139 (EC)).

A recent addition to the machinery is the European Industrial Relations Observatory set up in 1997 primarily to study questions of the workplace, establish a database and keep national centres in touch with developments across the Union.

How far regulation of working conditions by the Community is made necessary on moral grounds, on economic grounds to ensure competitive fairness or simply on political grounds to meet demands from powerful interests has never been resolved. Although in recent years it has been a major bone of contention, there now exists a body of European legislation which is in process of being bedded down. It is not expected to grow a great deal during the next few years. Some of this legislation is extremely precise and detailed but some is more of an outline which member states are expected to apply themselves. This is particularly true in health and safety measures.

In the early 1970s, a particular form of job loss came through a spate of takeovers and mergers, often connected with the growth of multinational companies. Here the EC felt it could claim a particular interest and successfully passed directives on the procedures to be followed in the case of collective dismissals (now Directive 98/59 OJ L225, 12.8.98), the maintenance of employee rights when companies merged (now Directive 98/50 OJ L201, 17.7.98) and the protection of rights when a firm became insolvent (Directive 80/987). Subsequent attempts by the Commission to pursue higher standards of employment law proved less successful and a succession of proposals were either dropped or postponed. However, more recently, there have been signs of agreement on a number of regulatory matters. Limits on working time were the subject of a proposed directive in 1990, being agreed in principle by the Council of Ministers in 1992 and finally adopted in November 1993 (Directive 93/104 OJ L307/93). The directive ensures a weekly rest period of one complete day, that rules for annual holidays had to be a minimum of four weeks by 1999, the need for a break after six hours work, a maximum working day of 11 hours and night shifts with an average maximum of eight hours. Revisions are under discussion to try to limit the large number of exempted posts which include workers in transport, sea fishing and doctors in training and some amendments have been proposed (COM (98) 662 final). Managers may be exempt, apart from the annual holiday clauses, and governments can find ways of shielding some industries, including the media, agriculture and the utilities. Collective agreements may be used to modify the rules. Workers can volunteer to work for longer hours (at least until 2003) and some flexibility exists in working out the 48 hours by averaging out the hours worked over a period from four months to one year. The impact appears to be variable and the rules are so elaborate that to get round them is probably not too difficult. Small firms reported administrative difficulties in fulfilling the requirement at first (*The Economist*, 16 November 1996; *Financial Times*, 2 November 1996).

A proposal on the protection of pregnant women at work became law as Directive 92/85 (OJ L348/92). A directive on the provision of proof of an employment contract (Directive 91/533) was agreed but a proposal to safeguard the conditions of workers temporarily posted elsewhere in the Community dragged on until 1996 (Directive 96/71 OJ L18/97, 21.1.97). It applies to firms which post workers to another member state and to temporary employment agencies engaged in hiring out labour in another member state. Its aim is to allow workers to benefit from the working conditions operative in the state to which they are posted, subject to certain exemptions.

A long-drawn-out project has been to ensure information for, and consultation of, workers in Europe-wide firms through the setting up of works councils or their equivalent. Apart from disagreements about the substance of the proposals there have been practical difficulties about how to implement them. Real differences of national practice and interest appeared to be involved, as well as a clash between the conception of a single market as one of deregulation and free enterprise or one in which the future requires the prior agreement of the social partners and a framework of European employment law. The quarrel led to the first directive under the Social Agreement (Directive 94/45 OJ L254/94) which became operative in

December 1996. It covers firms with at least 1000 employees, operating across borders and with at least 150 employees in each of two countries or more. It aims to give employees a degree of information about, and influence on, operations. British companies with staff elsewhere in the EU had to comply if they fell within the rules, as did non-EU firms. Some affected British companies included their British staff as it was simply more convenient to do so and most companies which believe in consulting their workforce do so in ways which conform to the rules. Existing arrangements registered by 22 September 1996 were acceptable and many British firms met this deadline. An advantage of a voluntary agreement was that the details could be more varied but, in the last resort, eligible firms may have the form of agreement imposed upon them. The directive seems to have been accepted without much difficulty and employer hostility diminished sharply when it became clear that voluntary agreements, which many firms had anyway, were acceptable and now, of course, it is applicable to Britain in the normal way. In 1997, the rules were extended to countries in the EEA.

The Commission has proposed that similar consultative procedures should be applied to all companies, excluding only those with but a handful of employees. The idea has met with some opposition and it is unclear what the outcome will be. The proposal comes in a very flexible form with a list of minimum requirements (COM (98) 592). Consultation procedures will also be found in the long-awaited statute for a European company.

A directive on parental leave (Directive 96/34 OJ L145/96) was also originally produced under the Social Agreement on the basis of a framework produced by the Union of Industries of the European Community (UNICE), the European Centre for Population Studies (CEEP) and the European Trade Union Confederation (ETUC) and subsequently submitted to the Commission to be put up to the Council of Ministers for adoption in June 1996. Men and women are entitled to three months unpaid leave to be taken before the child's eighth birthday and to time off for urgent family reasons. It sets out minimum standards only and stresses the importance of not using the directive to level down or to indulge in discriminatory practices, makes states responsible for compliance and allows them to fix penalties for infringement. This directive is now operative in the UK (from December 1999), although in a rather limited way.

The encouragement of employee asset holding and profit sharing was done through a recommendation (COM (91) 259 final) and a directive to give better health and safety protection for part-time workers (Directive 91/383) was adopted in June 1991.

Employment difficulties are acute for the disabled and handicapped. The Council passed a recommendation in 1986 stressing the importance of providing fair opportunities for training and employment and setting out a model code of action. A proposed directive (COM (90) 588 final, amended by COM (91) 539 final) lays down rules to assist workers with motor disabilities with travel to and from work in employer-provided and public transport (see also section 19.15).

Another long-standing issue is the question of whether European controls are needed over the conditions of part-time workers and those on temporary contracts. The Commission had long held the view that they should be employed on the same terms as full-time employees, on a *pro rata* basis including the same chances of promotion and access to the same range of benefits. The social partners began to negotiate on flexible working time and worker safety, looking at the many new forms of work now offered. This in itself is a more modern and flexible approach to a difficult subject which accepts that atypical employment has become the norm for many people and can, if handled carefully, even produce a better balanced lifestyle as long as it can be developed without exploitation. A framework agreement on contractual rights for part-timers (whether on permanent, temporary or fixed contracts but not casual workers) was thereby reached to cover occupational pensions, paid occupational sick leave, staff discounts and paid holidays (Directive 97/81 OJ L14, 20.1.98). The control of abuse of fixed-term contracts through the repeated issue of very short-term contracts which escape the rules is also being discussed.

Nevertheless, the pros and cons of employment regulation by the EC continue to be hotly debated. The benefits to workers are contrasted with the possible impediment to business creation, to worker recruitment and thus to labour mobility – all of which are desirable social goals.

19.13 Health and safety

The protection of industrial health and safety stretches back to 1951 when the ECSC established a programme of research and standard setting. Special commissions were created for the steel industry and for mining, the latter including off-shore oil wells, and a large number of recommendations have been issued. The Euratom treaty gave the Commission power to establish precise standards of protection in the nuclear industry while monitoring of the amount of radioactivity in the environment is carried out under Article 36. Industrial health and safety was included in the Treaty of Rome as one of the matters on which the Commission might encourage collaboration and it developed an active programme of research and recommendations as a result.

Over the years, EC interest broadened. Its span extended to include environmental pollution and issues of protection and conservation. Meanwhile, the EC edged towards a clearer role in community health with an emphasis on preventive programmes, interesting itself in questions such as the effect of modern industrial lifestyles on human welfare, the social costs of night work, the incidence of alcoholism and drug abuse and of social scourges such as cancer and Aids. The ever-increasing cost of social security, of which health care forms a large part, pushed the EC into taking a greater interest in the specific question of the costs of personal health care.

Much of the work reflected the fact that there are many problems which can no longer be dealt with in a national context. Thus basic standards to protect both the general public and workers against ionizing radiation were published in 1980 and updated following the Chernobyl accident. An outline directive on the protection of workers against the use of dangerous substances was agreed the same year and was followed by one concerned to protect against the hazards of a major accident, this following the chemical disaster at Seveso, Italy. This directive was replaced by Directive 96/82 OJ L10/97. All such factors meant that health ministers found it advantageous to meet together and set up co-operative and joint programmes.

The drive to the internal market renewed interest in industrial health and safety standards if only because of their possible effect upon the new policy. The Act took the path of agreeing to minimum standards, to avoid placing an excessive burden on small and medium-sized businesses and accepted that no state should be forced to lower its existing standards. A framework directive was passed to cover all main sectors of activity and to set out the duties of employer and employees. This provided the context for more specialized directives dealing with particular industries. However, it remained a difficult field, in which industrial change required a faster momentum of work in order to keep pace; control and monitoring had to be made effective and the growing number of public complaints handled. It became clear, too, that interpretations differed as to what subjects should be included in terms such as 'the working environment' and 'health and safety'. The Maastricht Treaty made explicit that the EC has a duty to contribute towards ensuring a high level of health protection (Articles 3(0) and 152 (EC)) and singles out disease prevention, including drug dependence, as a main field of interest through encouraging research and information and educational programmes. However, these can lead to awkwardness. It is often pointed out, for example, that support of research into the ill-effects of nicotine and the drive to discourage consumption sit ill with subsidies to tobacco-growing under the CAP. However, a ban on tobacco advertising, albeit with a long lead time, was agreed in 1998.

Community health problems are constantly changing and the EU, by virtue of its responsibilities in both health and the free flow of goods, necessarily takes on new subjects, as demonstrated by the question of the import of American products containing genetically modified maize and of British beef exports once bovine spongiform encephalopathy (BSE) had been identified. Such safety worries have led to the demand for an independent European Food and Public Health Authority. The need for better data and informational programmes seems set to grow and a five-year programme for health action was established despite arguments over its financing (see COM (95) 282 final, Medium Term Action Programme for Health and Safety at Work 1996–2000).

There have been a number of cases concerned with the supply of drugs and the need to reconcile confidence in them with the maintenance of a single market. A European agency collects and analyses data on drug use while a monitoring centre analyses drug addictions. The European Agency for the Evaluation of Medicines is part of the regulatory framework. The Amsterdam Treaty has given fresh prominence to a drug action programme both in the sense of control over new, synthetic drugs and with measures to control illegal supply and drug trafficking.

Although some enthusiasts would like to see minimum standards of health care established, the EU does not have a responsibility for personal health care but it does have an effect on service provision. The free movement policies have meant the need to establish the mutual recognition of the qualifications of health professionals, some of whom now have the right to practise anywhere while others still do not. EU citizens who trained outside the EU are not normally covered although bilateral arrangements may overcome this problem. In practice, movement is on a small scale for administrative barriers abound, hidden discrimination is reported and linguistic difficulties are genuine.

The free movement of citizens policy may have a greater impact on the patients than the staff should they begin to move to obtain treatment. For some years people have been entitled to treatment if they fall ill when visiting another member state, special schemes cover some groups of workers (e.g. transport workers or students) and cross-frontier services have become acceptable although in a controlled way. There is, as yet, no explicit right for people to travel to seek help but such travel can be arranged, and there are examples of cross-frontier agreements with hospitals to supply surgery where there is pressure on beds. Two recent cases heard by the ECJ raised the question of reimbursement from the state health insurance scheme of Luxembourg for the cost of goods and services obtained outside the home country. The Court held that prior authorization could be necessary in some circumstances but that the principles of Community law, notably the principle of the free movement of goods and the freedom to supply services, must be respected (*Kohll* and *Decker* judgment, 28 April 1998, Cases C–120/95 and C–158/96). There are other interesting questions looming, for example whether the growth of private health insurance should develop to cover care in another member state and whether a prescription issued in one country should be honoured in another. Although the legal basis for action is limited, there are considerable pressures towards seeing EU health policy expand in the future.

19.14   Equal treatment of men and women

Work to improve the position of women, both socially and economically, has proved one of the most positive of EU policies. Starting from a limited legal base, the EC was able to exploit the absence of effective national policies and to become an important influence on their development. Unusually in social affairs, it had a relatively clear field which allowed it to adopt a leadership role for which its position makes it well suited.

An equal pay policy was written into the Treaty of Rome at French insistence. France already had a legal requirement for equal pay and French industrial costs were assumed to be generally high. There remained, however, a noticeable lack of enthusiasm about the enforcement of the treaty until the 1970s. Some publicity had been attracted to Article 119 (now Article 141 (EC)) by the problem of a Sabena air hostess who had lodged a complaint in Belgium concerning the inequality of her conditions of service. The question of her pay, which was less than that of a male steward, led ultimately to a consideration by the ECJ which made clear its view that the article was meant to be taken seriously and properly applied. One result was to spur the Commission to produce a directive on equal pay in 1975 (Directive 75/117 OJ L45/75). This included a definition of equal pay, to include both identical work and work of equal value, established certain controls and required an effective appeals system. It therefore provided a much stricter framework within which member states had to apply the policy.

It soon became clear, however that by itself this was a reform of limited value if women were to achieve equality at work. Apart from the need to clarify the concept of equal pay, which is gradually being done through court judgments, men and women had very different social security coverage and Directive 79/7 (OJ L6/79) required the progressive implementation of the principle of equal treatment in statutory schemes over a six-year period. There were still certain exclusions to the rules, notably for family and survivors' benefits, and member states could retain some different provisions if they wished. The most important was the right to retain different ages for retirement pensions although, in practice, this difference is slowly disappearing. Since the *Marshall* case, women have had the right to retire at the same age as men from the public sector (Case C–152/84 [1986] OJ C79). In 1986, the principle of equal treatment was extended to cover occupational schemes and provision for the self-employed (Directive 86/378 OJ L225/86 and 283/86). This directive was intended to ensure equal rights in the private sector by 1993 subject to some latitude allowed for differences in life expectancy. An important ECJ judgment in 1990 (Case C–262/88) held that occupational pensions were to be considered as part of pay and, therefore, that the rules of equal pay must apply. Different ages for eligibility for such pensions could no longer be used, although the judgment was not retrospective. Directive 96/97 (OJ L46/97) has incorporated this rule although differences in life expectancy still affect actuarial calculations and the self-employed are not yet covered.

The Commission has been anxious, for some time, to see a new directive on social security to include benefits still outside the scope of EC directives, notably to include equal treatment for the sexes in retirement and in claiming benefits for dependants. It would also like to move the legal basis for entitlement to that of an individual's rights rather than deriving rights from the concept of dependency and this would put many women workers in a very different position from the one they hold today. Progress on these two moves is slow.

Underlying questions of pay and social security is the whole question of women's position in the labour force, which is still much less favourable than that of men. Women in practice earn less, often because they are concentrated in low-skilled and low-paid work and form the bulk of part-time workers. The unemployment rate for working women is disproportionately high, partly because their work is particularly vulnerable. These factors may result in an indirect discrimination, which is much more difficult to remedy through Court rulings.

Recognition of the lack of equal opportunities to obtain work and of equality of treatment at work opened the way to a variety of EC support programmes. These have ranged from a consideration of the types of education offered to girls to the importance of effective support for the working mother through more flexible hours and the development of child care facilities and the need to encourage men to take on more household chores. Thus EC policy has, for some years, followed twin paths. On the one hand have been measures to ensure legally enforceable rights and, on the other, programmes to encourage a fuller social and working role for women. Equality of treatment for men and women in the labour market and the need to pay more attention to the balance between employment and family responsibilities received a modest priority in the first Social Action Programme and resulted in a directive to establish equal opportunity with regard to employment, job recruitment, promotion and training (Directive 76/207 OJ L39/76, a draft amendment is COM (96) 93 final OJ C179/96). A start on rules for equal treatment in self-employment was begun by Directive 86/613 (OJ C113/84).

Attempts to strengthen, and equalize, the position of workers taking parental leave, or leave for family reasons, were blocked for a long time but they are a useful reminder that an equal treatment policy may sometimes require more rights to be given to men. These issues are covered in section 19.12. A Council recommendation on the need to develop child care facilities for working parents and for those taking courses was passed in 1992 (OJ L123/92).

The ESF has always been interested in grant-aiding schemes which help women at work and these have been important in raising the level of understanding about women's needs. Upgrading of women's opportunities through better education and more appropriate training has been encouraged; grant aid has been given to help women return to work after child rearing, to enter posts normally filled by men, to train for work using new technologies and to finance child care facilities and to give help to the female entrepreneur. In recent years, the Community Action programmes on equal opportunities for men and women have put a stress on treating equal opportunities as an objective which should run through all Community policies, and equality issues began to receive a higher profile in the Commission's work in general. Particular concerns have been to promote measures to reconcile working and family life for both men and women, to promote equality in decision making and in opportunities for education, vocational training and in the labour market. Information and research projects in culture, education and the media to raise awareness, schemes enabling the exchange of information and knowledge of good practice and a special scheme to assist in preventing violence to women have also received grant aid.

A directive on the burden of proof in sex discrimination cases before industrial tribunals is now operative and must be in force by 2001 (Directive 97/80 OJ L14/98). No longer will the complainant have to carry the entire responsibility to prove a case but will be required to submit evidence of direct or indirect discrimination which the employer will then be required to rebut.

For some years, the Commission has attempted to set an example in recruiting women to posts of greater responsibility, hoping states will follow suit in their public sectors. Targets have been set for directors, heads of units and administrators in the Commission staff but the real boost to the equality goal came with the Treaty of Amsterdam. Not only did this elevate equality between men and women to a major principle, it made it necessary for all Community activities to aim at eliminating inequalities and promoting equality, made a special mention of the importance of equality in the labour market and, in maintaining the provision on equal pay, made explicit that states might pursue affirmative action in job sectors where either sex is under-represented (Articles 2, 3, 137 and 141 (EC)). The Council of Ministers has also the right to act to combat discrimination whether based on sex, racial or ethnic origin, religion or belief, disability, age or sexual orientation (Article 13 EC)).

19.15 Social exclusion

The limited social responsibility of the early treaties and the emphasis upon economic integration left the EC open to the charge of weakness in social policy. Criticism mounted in the 1960s as the darker side of affluence was exposed. The marginalization of many groups, including the inhabitants of the inner cities, migrants, the elderly and disabled people, made clear that the EC itself had small scope for action to ameliorate the conditions of the most disadvantaged although it pursued active policies of encouragement to member states. The more generous wording of the Treaty of Amsterdam is meant to go some way to remedying this situation although it appears unlikely that much money will be available for supporting schemes.

An important factor in clarifying the role of the EC arose through the strain put upon social security policies as unemployment rose, the number of retired people grew rapidly, pressures on health care mounted and governments attempted to restrict social security expenditure. At the same time, schemes needed to adapt to the growth of part-time and flexible working, the changing position of women and to new health needs. A considerable study programme was launched by the Commission which included consideration of the argument that the Single Market would require an alignment of social security costs and benefits. Although this is not accepted as a necessary goal, the EC has accepted a recommendation (COM (91) 228 final) on the ultimate convergence of objectives and policies in view of the similarity of many of the social problems now faced by member states. At present, these include the funding of long-term care, early retirement and sustaining pension commitments. It continues to report on the trends in social security and is anxious to maintain the debate on the wider subject of social protection (COM (95) 457; COM (95) 466).

There has been some interest in the proposition that the EC should seek to establish a basic minimum resource level but this has, so far, proved impossible to define and is far from being politically acceptable. The Council of Ministers did, however, accept a recommendation in 1992 that states should provide a guarantee of basic assistance with effective administrative measures (Recommendation 92/442 OJ L245/92).

An anti-poverty programme was included in the first SAP as a result of an Irish initiative. This gave rise to interesting experiments and drew attention to the need for, and difficulties of, cross-national research. Grant aid for projects helping groups in poverty concentrated on new, and sometimes unorthodox, procedures and drew the Commission into close, direct contact with social reform movements and local authorities and associations. Innovation has been a watchword which has led to an encouragement of a multidimensional approach, the use of partnerships to ensure effective co-operation between local actors, active participation of excluded groups themselves and trans-national research, but in recent years funding has been seriously curtailed. The Amsterdam Treaty brought the aim of fighting social exclusion firmly within the EU's remit (Articles 13, 136, 137 (EC)) but funding is likely to remain on a very small scale.

For some years, disabled people have been a group eligible for aid from the ESF for training and, in addition, action programmes with their own modest budgets have been established. These have meant that grants were available for tasks such as access to creative activities, sport and tourism, integration in nursery schools and functional rehabilitation. An emphasis was placed on the use of new technology as an aid to integration, to independent living and to education and training and in recent years the programmes have been brought under the umbrella of the broader goal of equal opportunities and full participation in social life for all. Member states are encouraged to bring their support for the disabled into equal opportunities programmes through the use of the structural funds, mobilizing the work of non-governmental organizations (NGOs), improving access to employment opportunities and through using information technology to pursue equal opportunities.

Elderly people, too, have become a group in which the EC expresses interest. They are, of course, affected by many general EC policies, notably the extension of the free movement policy to allow retired people to spend their later years anywhere in the Community and rules to control atypical work. Problems connected with ageing have figured in the health research programmes and a small action programme was set up to exchange knowledge, ideas and experience. At present, the Commission is very involved in setting up networks and encouraging a dialogue between itself, NGOs and independent experts. A new support programme was submitted to the Council in 1995 but ran into difficulties similar to those facing the anti-poverty programme and at present the Commission seems to be concentrating on the insertion of an 'age dimension' into other, more established programmes as a means of highlighting issues concerning the elderly.

19.16   Migration and asylum

The creation of the EEC, and more particularly the passing of subsequent treaties, progressively distinguished three groups of residents who might be on the move. Those with the nationality of a member state, those entering the EU as migrants and those resident 'third-country nationals' who wished to move within the EU's borders all needed their own arrangements. The first group was to be covered by the free movement policy and a brief outline of the issues relating to the second group is attempted here. The third group constitutes rather a mixed bag. It covers, for example, a non-EU spouse married to a mobile EU national and long-resident non-EU residents who wish to move to take up work elsewhere, and the EU has special rules covering these categories. Many groups will be covered, too, by the rules written into the special relationship treaties which the EU has signed, for example nationals of the EEA. The Amsterdam Treaty has now laid down the elements of an EU policy in Article 63 (EC) to which states will conform in dealing with asylum seekers, refugees and displaced persons and immigration policy but these need further elaboration.

As far as the second group is concerned, there have been two waves of concern. In the early years, it was the question of large numbers of unskilled workers entering the EU to fill job vacancies and, more recently, the flows of refugees and asylum seekers.

Although people fall into different legal categories, the reasons for movement are often similar and may present similar problems of family reunion, new working patterns, finding adequate housing and schooling as well as language difficulties. The scale of migration, from whatever source, during the 1960s brought anxieties about social integration but member states were wary about allowing the EC a competence in some of the more sensitive areas of domestic policy. As migrants came from further afield, cultural gaps became more evident and pressures on local services increased in congested urban areas. By the late 1970s, the Commission had begun to question the value of large-scale, uncontrolled migration. Stress began to be laid on the ill-effects for regions and countries losing manpower, the pressure on the urban infrastructure, the slowing down of capital development in industry and the uncertain benefits for countries of emigration. The situation became further confused as unemployment grew, member states began to ban the entry of non-EC nationals, work permits expired and many third-country migrants decided to stay in the EC illegally rather than risk the possibility they would not be allowed back when conditions improved again.

EC policy made uncertain progress at this time, with the Commission limited to encouraging states to extend to all the improvements resulting from the free movement policy. It made all migrants eligible for grants from the ESF and tried to improve the education of children through grants for induction courses, language teaching and special training for teachers. These attempts remained on a small scale and it was in any case difficult to see the lines of an effective policy when settlement policies were so different, ranging from that of the UK which received migrants from the Commonwealth expecting to stay for permanent settlement to Germany with a great influx from Turkey whose workers were originally expected only for a short while and for whom issues of family settlement were, at first, of less importance.

Current estimates suggest that there are between 12 and 14 million legally resident 'third-country nationals' in the EU. By no means all of them are in a vulnerable position; their legal rights will vary from state to state and according to country of origin. It is clear, nevertheless, that many of them are still not fully part of the society in which they now live and that problems are being inherited by the second and third generations. A variety of national policies have emerged to encourage, or insist upon, assimilation but no overall EU policy exists.

A European Migrants Forum now exists to lobby in the EU, while the Council of Ministers has set up a Consultative Committee to monitor the expression of racism and xenophobia which have seen a disturbing rise in recent years. The European Parliament, in particular, has urged the EU to take a stand against such phenomena and a number of declarations have been issued. The Amsterdam Treaty has given the EU the capacity to act against discrimination, including that based on nationality, racial or ethnic origin (Articles 12, 13 (EC)) and for some time the Commission has been urging states to provide legal protection against discrimination. Meanwhile the Justice and Internal Affairs Council, meeting in March 1996, reached agreement on legal co-operation in order to prevent infringements of national rules against public incitement and the circulation of racist literature.

New immigration on a large scale is no longer thought of as desirable and the Commission's view is that emigration needs to be controlled through co-operation with sending countries and that it will lessen if jobs can be created in the home country and, with this, Community policies can help. The EU is still likely, however, to attract better qualified migrants, people who wish to set up in business, students in training and, no doubt, other special groups and the question remains of what EU action is necessary. Now that member states have accepted that immigration is a matter of common interest, a greater rationality in rules concerning entry and movement may be expected and an interesting point was made in a Council resolution in 1996 which dealt with the factors, such as income and health, to be considered when states authorize long-term residence. It has been suggested that such residents, not holding EU citizenship, should have preference over third-country nationals when it comes to recruitment and the EP argues that such populations should have the same rights as EU citizens.

Recent moves towards common rules have also been seen in asylum policy. These have become acceptable not just because of the very large number of recent applicants whose claims are often confused but with the realization that the existence of a Single Market means that all states can be affected. Sudden large influxes of refugees have thrown great burdens on services in receiving states but also mean that states are now more reluctant to grant refugee status, while the long delays in processing asylum applications have led to distress and difficulty. The 1990 Dublin Convention made a single state responsible for examining an application for asylum on the basis of objective criteria (subject to the rights of other states if they are particularly affected) and allows for the exchange of information on asylum activities. In 1995 the Council agreed on a harmonized definition of a refugee, minimum guarantees for asylum procedures and a resolution on burden sharing to help with temporary problems, and these matters are now set out in treaty form. The

Commission, naturally enough, would like a budget to help to co-finance schemes set up to cover the many costs for maintenance, health care, schooling and legal representation that arise as well as for integration or voluntary repatriation.

The abolition of internal border controls raises the question of the effective policing of the external frontier and no subject has required more soul searching in recent years. If the state of first entry is lax then criminal elements, terrorists and unwanted migrants gain easy access and can pass anywhere within the EU. As a forerunner of a single system, a group of neighbouring states signed the Schengen agreement in 1985, then outside the EU treaties but now incorporated within. Although not yet fully operative. it has created a frontier-free zone for a core group of members within which people can move freely. The essential elements of the system are effective controls at the external frontier and close police and judicial co-operation in criminal matters (see Articles 29–42 (EU)). The UK and Ireland are not bound by these rules since the former still wishes to operate its own border controls. However, they are entitled to 'opt in' to arrangements made under this section of the treaty and a request was made to do so on some aspects of frontier controls, police and judicial co-operation in criminal matters, anti-drug procedures and the Schengen Information system. Special rules also apply to Denmark; Iceland and Norway are associated with the arrangements and any new members of the EU will be expected to accept the rules in full.

19.17 An overall view

The range of topics discussed here shows how diverse the social concerns of the EU now are. At first sight, they can appear as a miscellany rather than a single coherent policy but this is inevitable given the range of modern social policy. A hard core of matters relating to employment is the bedrock of Community social policy. Although there is agreement that some minimum standards are necessary to support the Single Market policy, there is strong suspicion that some proposals are covert measures to protect national markets from the competition the Single Market is designed to bring and it is unlikely that there will be a swift resolution of this difference of view.

One difficulty in standard setting is that precision is often impossible and all that can be achieved is agreement on a general principle which then must be interpreted and applied in a host of different circumstances. It is undoubtedly difficult to ensure that such agreements are effectively applied and do, in fact, achieve a comparable result. Often it is a case of changing attitudes, encouraging developments in similar directions and explaining current best practice; the Commission is in a favourable position to carry out such tasks. A further noticeable feature is the support it gives to research, investigations and pilot schemes which normally have cross-national elements and attempt fresh approaches to old problems.

During the 1970s, it was agreed to set up three European institutes for study and research. In 1977, CEDEFOP began work to give new impetus to a common policy of training through the harmonization of national systems and to promote new initiatives. In 1975, a Foundation for the Improvement of Living and Working Conditions was set up in Dublin. Finally, the Council agreed to support a project of the European Trades Union Confederation (ETUC) to set up a European Trades Union Institute for the study of union affairs. A more recent development has been to set up Observatories to monitor and analyse social policies and to encourage mutual understanding of national policies and cross-national networks. Observatories exist for family policies, ageing and older people, policies to combat social exclusion and employment. A recent addition is the Industrial Relations Observatory to work closely with the Dublin Foundation.

Many of these activities may be classified as educational and promotional. For the specialist circles that are involved they play an important part in enhancing mutual understanding. Grant aid in the social field may still be small compared with the scale of national spending but for some of the poorer countries it is very significant, for example the ESF grants for training. Even in countries where it is less important in amount, it is, nevertheless, money that governments like to have and, however grudgingly, they do adapt their activities to conform to EU ideas.

Social policy has developed in the shadow of economic policies. Even with the passing of the SEA it was described as a flanking policy to the introduction of the Single Market and the obvious need to deal with the social consequences of intended action provides a strong argument for the development of social standards. However, this view has never satisfied everybody, especially those wanting a full-blown political union and who have therefore always argued for free-standing social goals and responsibilities. The Amsterdam Treaty suggests some movement towards this view; a glance back to the early days of the ECSC shows how far social policy has come. It is now accepted that there is a European dimension in health, social security, equal pay, working conditions and other social fields even though there is always disagreement about how far policy should go. There is no reason to suppose this process will come to a halt.

Supranational social responsibilities are constantly clarified through the activities of the EC. It is in an excellent position to identify the processes of economic and social change occurring in Western Europe and to suggest responses to them. Thus at the start the exodus from agriculture and the development of industry led to the free movement policy and the ESF, the prosperity of the 1960s and early 1970s to recognition of discrimination and inequalities and the response of the women's policy. Later on, unemployment led to special programmes for vulnerable groups and retraining whereas today the globalization of markets, the impact of new technology and ageing populations are giving new emphasis to education, skill development and pension issues. Often such changes require similar national reactions but these do not always have to be standardized. In so far as major economic policies of the EU bring adverse social consequences for some people, it seems only fair that the EU should shoulder the responsibility of mitigating them. However, arguments are as lively as ever as to how far its actions need to go, whether EC legislation is necessary and what should be left to national governments.

A fruitful source of disagreement over respective functions is likely to come in the future as the Commission works out its ideas of subsidiarity, participation and partnership since it is evident that, in many social matters, both national governments and the EU have valid concerns. The Commission needs to be in touch with local and regional authorities, voluntary organizations and citizens' groups and may easily tread on national sensitivities as central governments try to hold on to their position as the conduit through which relations with the Community are handled.

The growth of an international society is also affecting the methods of handling social policy. The EEC was originally directed to work closely with the ILO and the Council of Europe and these links are growing closer. The 1996 version of the

Council of Europe's Social Charter embodies ideas also to be found in ILO conventions and bears a strong resemblance to the moves towards equal opportunities, more information for workers, greater participation in relevant decisions and protection for the elderly which are so much part of the EU's current interests. Contacts with Central and Eastern Europe through the Phare agreements, educational bodies and outlying agencies referred to in the text bring awareness of other social priorities and methods of approach, while developing countries often find it helpful to discuss with the Commission their plans for social security and educational development. Multilateral and bilateral co-operation are now widely practised but have grown in an *ad hoc* way which might now benefit from systematization. Discussions in recent years on international trade agreements have raised moral issues which both influence, and are influenced by, the EU and this again suggests that there is an international element in social policy today.

It is clear that the EU does not have a social policy whose *raison d'être* is large-scale resource redistribution but one that depends on many relatively small-scale programmes, framework agreements, legal rules and a multiplicity of efforts to align attitudes, share experiences and generally encourage social progress. It is increasingly difficult to envisage an EU which has developed politically without some commitment to ensure citizens a place in society, in which human rights are protected and institutions effectively democratized. The 1994 White Paper on Social Policy pinpointed the values which are shared between members and which are at the basis of the EU's social policy as democracy, individual rights, free collective bargaining, the market economy, equality of opportunity, welfare and solidarity. It is still struggling to determine what, in practical terms, it needs to do in order to promote these values on the grounds that member states are no longer fully competent to do so alone.

20 Environmental policy

A. MARIN

Background

For a long time it was not clear whether there was any legitimate basis at all for an EC policy on the environment. In the 1950s there was no influential generalized concern for the environment. Occasionally, a specific particularly harmful episode of pollution would give rise to remedial action to deal with the specific problem, but no more. For example, in the winter of 1952–3 there was an even denser than usual smog in London, leading to a dramatic increase in mortality among the elderly and bronchitic. As a result, following an inquiry, new laws were introduced to allow the control of domestic coal fires. But the episode did not lead to a more widespread concern with air pollution generally. The same attitude was prevalent in other countries at that time. Hence, the Treaty of Rome made no provision for any joint EU policy on controlling pollution, let alone more general environmental conservation.

By the end of the 1960s, however, a new attitude which led to demands for new policies had become widespread. Although, perhaps, not initially as strongly as their counterparts in the United States, noticeable numbers of people in Western Europe had begun to express concern over degradation of the environment. There were various strands, not always compatible, within the burgeoning 'environmentalist' movement, in terms both of the issues of concern and of the political outlooks of those most prominent.

There were various organized groups who had an effect on EC environmental policy, especially where they gave a stronger crusading force to the aspects of environmental concern which had most influence on policy. Some were the groups who stressed ecology and preservation. It is not simply that they have eventually succeeded in getting enough votes to have some 'Green Party' members in the European Parliament (MEPs), as well as representatives at national and lower levels; some national governments have felt obliged to be seen to be responsive to public opinion on environmental issues, in order to try to keep the Greens from gaining enough seats to be a threat to the government majorities. These governments, initially primarily the German and Dutch, have an extra incentive to support EU environmental policies.

The areas which seem to be of general concern to the wider public (and where the Green movements have sometimes provided the impetus) are partly the preservation of natural amenity and wildlife, and, more importantly for EU policy, pollution. The change from 1957 is that pollution is seen to be a general, ongoing, problem. Concern may be heightened by particularly harmful and/or well-publicized cases, for example the disposal of toxic waste from Seveso, but it is now considered that action should not be limited to reacting to such cases but should be introduced to control harm before blatantly dangerous situations occur.

As a result of the changes in attitudes just outlined, in October 1972 the heads of government (prompted by a report from the Commission earlier that year) called for an EC environmental programme, which led to approval in November 1973 of the First Environmental Programme 1973–78.[1] This has been followed by subsequent programmes up to the Fourth Programme 1987–92. The Fifth Programme has no formal concluding date, but is supposed to cover the period up to 2000. During 2000 the Commission is supposed to present proposals for a new programme.

Despite the agreement of the heads of government to an EC programme, and thus to a commitment to joint policies, for some years there was doubt as to whether there really was a legal basis for issuing directives in this area. The doubts were particularly strongly expressed within the United Kingdom.[2] On several issues (as will be detailed later), the UK approach to pollution control differed sharply (or so it seemed in public statements) from the majority view among the other member states. There were some who proposed a challenge to the legality of the directives – although a recourse to the ECJ was never, in fact, pursued.

The official basis for actions that were clearly not foreseen in the Treaty of Rome was twofold. First, a few of the types of pollution dealt with could result from the use of goods, for example noise and exhaust emissions from vehicles, or packaging and labelling of solvents. In these cases, joint EC standards could clearly be justified as part of product harmonization to prevent different national standards acting as a non-tariff barrier to inter-state trade.[3] However, many of the directives concerned types of pollution and environmental standards that could not constitute a hindrance to inter-state trade on any reasonable criterion, such as the quality of bathing (i.e. swimming) water or the hunting of wild birds.

The second basis claimed for EC environmental policies would justify joint policies on all types of environmental concern, even where trade is unaffected. Article 2 of the Treaty of Rome stated that 'The Community shall ... promote throughout the Community a harmonious development of economic activities, a continuous and balanced expansion ... an accelerated raising of the standard to living.' It was claimed that measures to protect the environment could be considered to further a balanced expansion and raised standard of living, given the importance now attached to the environment by public opinion and the extent to which people's sense of well-being was threatened by pollution and environmental degradation.[4]

No legal challenge was ever mounted to the Community's right to make decisions on the environment; the matter is now beyond dispute. In 1986, Articles 130R–130T were inserted into the Treaty by the SEA (Articles 174–6 of the Consolidated Treaty (CT)). These Articles are explicitly devoted to the environment; see Chapter 19 for more on this and other developments. Furthermore, according to Article 100A (95 (CT)), actions taken to further the 'completion of the internal market' are supposed to take as their base a high level of environmental protection. In addition, allowance is made for individual member states to set higher environmental standards, provided that these do not constitute barriers to trade – though the acceptable boundaries can be contentious. Conflicts did arise over whether particular directives should be treated as relating to product harmonization (therefore falling under Article 100A concerning the internal market) and thus subject to majority voting or as environmental protection (therefore falling under Article 130S) and requiring unanimous agreement.

Decisions by the ECJ in several disputes about the correct Article which should have been used seem to be somewhat contradictory. The amendment of Article 130S (175 (CT)) at Maastricht and Amsterdam further extended majority voting to most aspects of environmental policy, so that in general it does not now matter which Article is used.[5]

The SEA, Maastricht and, especially, Amsterdam treaties increased the power of the European Parliament. This increase in power can also lead to stronger EU policies on the environment and the adoption of stricter standards. The European Parliament is generally considered to be more concerned about environmental issues than the Council. This is partly because of the presence of the Green MEPs, but MEPs of other parties also seem to be more affected by environmental concerns. One early case where pressure from Parliament clearly helped to push the Council to take stronger action was Parliament's amendment in April 1989 of the Council's proposal on exhaust emissions, which resulted in more stringent limits that could be met only by using catalytic converters on all cars. Given the general movement towards environmental consciousness in the preceding year, the previous opponents of stringent limits (especially the United Kingdom) were not prepared to face the odium of no action at all as a result of rejecting the Parliament's amendment.[6]

Whatever the legality according to the unamended Treaty of Rome of EC directives on issues affecting the environment, there still remains the question of why the governments of the member states wanted a *joint* environmental policy at all, on those aspects where individual national policies would not be a barrier to trade and where transfrontier flows of pollution were not a problem. (As already indicated, the small group which could lead to barriers could be dealt with under the procedures on product harmonization.) It is never possible to be completely sure what is in people's minds, but discussions at the time and subsequently suggest two primary motivations.

First, statements by EC leaders often stressed that it was felt to be important that, if there were to be public support for the European ideal, the EC should be identified in the minds of the public with issues with which they were concerned. It should not be thought to be limited to 'boring' technical issues, whether product standard harmonization or the minutiae of calculating transport costs between Rotterdam and Duisberg. Joint EC policies on an issue which had recently become the focus of much media discussion and campaigning would help to convince the public that the Community was relevant to them and responsive to their worries.

Second, it was clear to governments in member states that they would have to respond to public pressures over pollution and environmental preservation. This was especially true of the German and Dutch governments among the original six, but the others were not immune either. Many of the measures which would be required were likely to raise production costs. For example, firms would have to install new equipment rather than just pouring noxious waste into rivers or sewers, or would have to buy the more expensive low-sulphur fuels to limit emissions of sulphur dioxide. If some countries were to have tighter standards than others, then their firms would face 'unfair competition' from firms that had lower production costs just because they were located in countries that had laxer requirements on pollution abatement.[7] Uniform emission standards (referred to as UES in the literature) would prevent this threat to competitiveness. Hence the desire of governments for joint EC environmental policies which would affect all member states equally.

20.2   Economic (or economists') assessment of environmental policies

In order to judge the appropriateness of EU environmental policies, it is necessary to have criteria. The criteria used elsewhere in this book are primarily (although not exclusively) those of standard neoclassical welfare economics.

For the policies examined in this chapter, equity – at least in terms of income distribution – has not been a major consideration.[8] However, it is worth noting that one difference between the approach of many environmentalists and that of many economists is related to the standard assumptions of welfare economics. Economists tend to judge policies and institutions by their effects on the welfare of individuals.[9] Environmentalists, however, often feel that some things are worth while even if no humans are affected. They place a value on the diversity of natural habitats and the continuation of species, even where there is no benefit to humans. By their training, many (although not all) economists are resistant to such a view.[10]

There have been few EU policies which deal with protection of species *per se*.[11] One exception was the 1979 directive on the conservation of wild birds, augmented by a 1992 directive on habitat protection and a 1999 directive on zoos, the purpose of which is to protect wild fauna and conserve biodiversity. Some have argued that the directives on water quality for rivers and estuaries containing fish or shellfish are not just to protect human health, but also to protect the fish *per se*. Another, limited, exception is the 1985 directive requiring an environmental impact assessment before certain large development projects are undertaken. This exception is limited, both because the types of project requiring the assessment are largely left to national governments and because, once the assessment has been made, there is no requirement for any weighting to be given to adverse environmental effects in deciding whether the project should proceed. There are also EC directives concerning other endangered species (seals and whales), but, although motivated by environmental concerns (and the repugnance at the methods of killing seal pups), these formally deal with trade in the products of the species.

20.2.1   Externalities

Most of the EC environmental polices have concerned pollution in some form. For economists, pollution is a problem that cannot be solved by the market mechanism because it is an externality. Indeed, most textbooks on microeconomics use pollution as the classic example of an externality. One way of viewing externalities is that they are cases where the actions taken by one economic agent (individual or firm) affect others, but where there is no feedback mechanism leading the agent to take correct account of the effects on others. It is not the existence of an effect on others that constitutes an externality, but the lack of incentive to take full account of it. Every economic action may affect others, but in a well-functioning system the price mechanism provides incentives to take account of the effects.

For example, when deciding whether to drive my car to the shops or walk, in reaching my decision I use my car only if the benefit is greater than the price I have to pay for the petrol. If the price equals the marginal cost (the usual criterion for Pareto optimality), then I will use my car only if the benefit is greater than the cost to society of the scarce resources used up in providing me with the petrol. Hence the price system provides me with the correct incentive to take account of the effects of my action (driving my car) on others (using up scarce resources, which are therefore not available to provide somebody else with that petrol). However, if the use of my car pollutes the air and causes annoyance, or more serious harm, to others, there is no incentive for me to allow for this. I could be said to be using up another scarce resource (quiet and clean air), but I do not have to pay for it. Hence, there will be times when I use my car even though the benefit to me is less than the true cost to society, i.e. the sum of the costs of which I take account (the petrol) plus those of which I do not (the pollution); the result is therefore not optimal. Thus another, exactly equivalent, way of expressing an externality is to define it as when the marginal private cost is not equal to the marginal social cost.[12]

There are two diagrams which are often used to analyse the problem of pollution and to indicate possible policy solutions.[13] The first one concentrates on the divergence between social and private cost, usually in the context of a competitive industry which causes pollution during the production of some good. In Figure 20.1 the supply curve of the industry is, as always, equal to the sum of the marginal (private) costs (MPC) of the firms. Given the demand curve, Q_0 is produced and sold at a price of P_0. This is not optimal. If the pollution emitted during production is allowed for, the true sum of marginal social costs for the firms is given by MSC, and the optimal output is where $P = MSC$, i.e. at Q_1 and P_1.

Figure 20.1 has the advantage of stressing that part of the result of pollution in production is that the price to consumers is too low and therefore consumption is too high. Conversely, any policy to achieve efficiency will involve a higher price and less output and consumption. It is therefore not surprising that both employers and trade unions in the industries affected are sometimes among those opposing particular EU policies to control pollution. Nor is it surprising that, in some countries of the EU (possibly in contrast to the United States), the importance attached to environmental policies declined in the second half of the 1970s and early 1980s. The rise in unemployment led to more stress on the reduction in output that might result from pollution control measures,[14] an example of the more general point that if displaced workers are not confident of finding alterna-

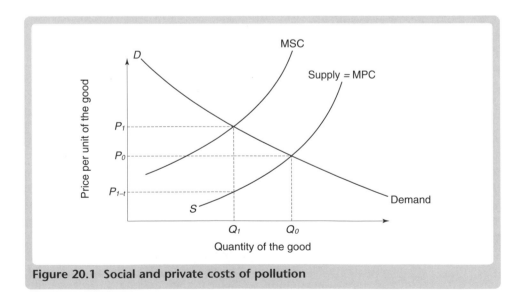

Figure 20.1 Social and private costs of pollution

tive jobs easily, then employment becomes an aim in its own right and policies are not judged solely by the total consumption of goods (even allowing for the 'consumption' of 'bads' involved in pollution).[15]

As a means of analysing policies to control pollution, Figure 20.1 has the disadvantage of neither explicitly showing what happens to pollution nor showing whether pollution can be reduced by means other than a drop in production of the final output of the industry. For these reasons, an alternative diagram is now often used, which draws attention to these aspects, although it has the disadvantage that the implications of Figure 20.1 to which we have drawn attention are left implicit, and may therefore be inadvertently downplayed.

In Figure 20.2, the pollution is measured explicitly. For convenience, we have drawn the diagram with the abscissa measuring pollution abatement from the level that would occur with no policy controls. Some authors use pollution emissions instead. This is equivalent to Figure 20.2 working leftwards from the 100% abatement (zero remaining pollution) point. The diagram shows the abatement of some particular form of pollution for some particular industry. The marginal benefits (MB) of pollution abatement are the avoidance of the external costs placed on others – health, annoyance at noise, loss of amenity, etc. The marginal costs (MC) of pollution abatement to the firms in the industry are the costs associated with various abatement techniques, such as the treatment plant for noxious effluents in our earlier example, as well as the loss of profits if emissions are reduced by cutting back on the level of output of the final product sold. The approach in Figure 20.2 draws explicit attention to the possibilities of using other resources (labour, capital) to reduce emissions (unlike Figure 20.1 which is usually drawn on the assumption that the externalities associated with each level of output are fixed).

The shapes of the marginal benefit and cost curves in Figure 20.2 follow from what is known for many types of pollution – some abatement is often easy but, when 95% of potential emissions have already been removed, removal of the remaining 5% is usually much more expensive. On the benefit side, the marginal curve is usually drawn downward sloping, although the justification is less well

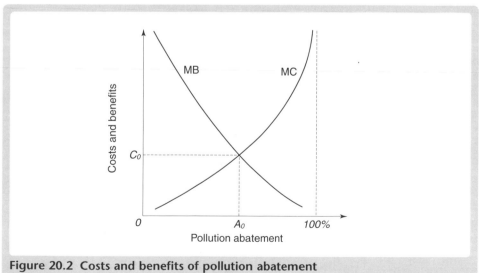

Figure 20.2 Costs and benefits of pollution abatement

founded and there may be some forms of pollution (especially affecting amenity) where the downward slope is not correct; for example, once a line of pylons has been put over a previously unspoiled mountain range, any further developments do less marginal harm. However, most of the EU pollution policies deal with worries about effects of pollution on human health, and for this the downward MB curve is usually reasonable (as it is for the policies on sulphur dioxide and some car exhaust emissions where the motivation is also partly human, partly the effects on forests).

In some cases it is suspected that there may be thresholds of pollution below which the body can cope, but above which harm may start. In these cases, the MB curve may have the shape in Figure 20.3.

Returning to the more general case of Figure 20.2, one important policy implication of this way of analysing pollution is that there is an optimum level of pollution. Except in very special cases, it is not optimal to aim for the complete elimination of pollution.[16] Less than 100% abatement is desirable. The optimum level, which maximizes welfare, is where the marginal costs of further abatement just equal the marginal benefits, level A_0 in Figure 20.2. This is an implication of the economists' approach which is uncongenial to some in the Green movement.

EU policies have followed the economists' approach on the whole. In the early years of EC action there were some clashes between member states. The United Kingdom, in particular, advocated its traditional policies, summed up in such expressions as 'best *practicable* means' of pollution control. The notion of 'practicable' involves a weighing up of costs and benefits – although this balancing seems always to be implicit rather than explicit and to rely on the intuition of the relevant inspectorates. The United Kingdom feared that at times the other member states were proposing the approach of best *available* technology, i.e. pushing as far as technically feasible towards 100% abatement, irrespective of costs. Ultimately, although some directives still mentioned that best available technology should be adopted, there was no time limit set for adoption, or else the phrase was qualified by saying that the adoption should be provided if it did 'not entail excessive cost' – which reduces it to practicable – or else some other let-out was included. It is

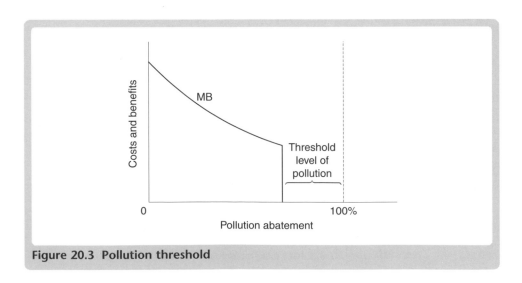

Figure 20.3 Pollution threshold

actually doubtful that the other states were completely unconcerned with costs. In reality, the apparent disagreements seem to have been rather over how much abatement was desirable, with the other countries saying in some cases that the United Kingdom tended to overestimate the costs of abatement, to underestimate the benefits and urgency of reductions in pollution, and often to claim that more evidence was needed before action should be taken. One example is the UK position on sulphur dioxide, where for a long time the United Kingdom delayed reductions, partly because of claims that the evidence failed to show that UK emissions contributed significantly to forest damage elsewhere in West Europe. The new 'Environment' title inserted by the SEA specifically refers to the need to take account of 'the potential benefits and costs of action or lack of action' (Article 130R (174 (CT)), 3). From the other side, in an attempt to appear to bridge the gap, at least superficially, UK legislation has now adopted the principle of 'BATNEEC', which stands for 'best available technology not entailing excessive cost'. But the 'NEEC' implies that there has been no real change in the approach.

20.2.2 Control of pollution by regulations or taxes

If the problem is that of externality, the 'obvious' solution might seem to be to 'internalize the externality'. It is often suggested that an implication of the economists' analysis is that polluters should have to pay a tax equal to the external costs imposed on others. In terms of Figure 20.2, if a tax equal to C_0 were levied for each unit of pollution emitted, firms would abate up to level A_0. At abatement levels less than A_0, it is less costly for them to abate than to pay a tax of C_0. From A_0 onwards, the marginal cost of further abatement is higher than the tax, and hence it will be more profitable to continue to pollute and pay the tax. A tax will therefore achieve the optimum. The idea of controlling pollution by taxation rather than by quantitative regulations imposed on firms also seems to fit economists' predilection for relying on price (here the 'price' of using up clean air, etc.) rather than quantitative controls. The latter are supposed to require information rarely possessed by the central authorities.

In the early 1990s it became popular to argue that there is another advantage of taxes to control pollution. This argument is often called the 'double dividend' advantage. The first 'dividend' is the benefit from the reduction in pollution that is induced by the tax. The second 'dividend' is that the revenue from the pollution taxes can be used to reduce other taxes in the economy that are themselves distortionary from a welfare economics viewpoint, e.g. income tax (distorting the choice between working and leisure) or employers' taxes (distorting labour demand choices). An alternative jargon was that pollution taxes were thus 'win-win'.

A particularly strong version of the 'double dividend' was sometimes advocated: a pollution tax would be desirable because of the second dividend even if it turned out there were no net benefits to reducing the pollution *per se*. For example, at the time of the proposed EU carbon tax discussed below, there was some residual scepticism over whether global warming was really occurring at all and even if it were occurring, whether the results would be harmful enough to justify the sacrifices required to have a noticeable effect on the warming. Some of the statements in favour of the carbon tax said that even if the doubts were eventually proved correct, the tax would still be worth while because of the second dividend from the use of the revenue.

However, the double-dividend argument came under attack from other economists.[17] The essence of the attack is that the idea of the double dividend inherently relies on a 'second-best world' with existing distortions, in addition to the distortion of possibly uncorrected externalities. However, the existing distortions are likely to mean that there is too little paid work (too much leisure) because of taxes that impinge on labour supply and demand. Any imposition of a pollution tax will raise the price of some products (those whose output or use involves the pollution), and thus further reduce the real return to working. This increased disincentive to employment will reduce welfare. It is quite possible to find situations where this second effect could outweigh the second dividend of using the revenue to reduce distortionary taxes – thus pollution taxes would reduce welfare if there is no 'first dividend' and possibly reduce it even if there is a 'first dividend'.

Another way of putting this is that, because of existing distortions, there is too little of most goods being produced, including too little of some goods which also cause pollution.

As often in 'second-best' analyses, all sorts of things could happen, depending on particular combinations of substitution/complementarity links. However, there is probably a consensus emerging (see the summaries referred to in note 17) that in many of the cases investigated, both theoretically and empirically, the following results are typical:

1. If the question is whether a particular level of pollution emissions should be reached via quantitative regulations or taxes, the second dividend of using the tax revenue to reduce other distortionary taxes is a reason for pollution taxes rather than regulation.

2. When there are other distortionary taxes, the optimum level of pollution taxation is higher when the revenue is used to reduce those distortionary taxes than when the revenue is used in a lump-sum way.

3. Even if the revenue is used to reduce other taxes, the optimum level of a pollution tax is often lower in a second-best world of distortionary taxes than the level of the Pigovian tax (P = MSC, or MB = MC of abatement) that would result if there were no other distortions in the economy; but this optimal level is still often positive (i.e. some abatement is desirable) if there are benefits to the abatement.

4. The strong double-dividend argument outlined above is generally wrong – i.e. if there are no net benefits at all from 'pollution' abatement, then the second dividend does not give a valid reason to impose a 'pollution' tax.

Despite the common view that analyses such as Figure 20.2 show the desirability of controlling pollution by taxes, even if we abstract from the second 'dividend' of the use of the revenue,[18] and that all (respectable?) economists agree, there is a serious flaw in the argument.[19] To achieve the optimum level of pollution, a government needs to know the size of the correct tax, C_0. But to know C_0 requires knowing the marginal costs and benefits of abatement and where the curves intersect. But this information is the same as is required to know, and directly to impose, A_0. Hence a government that can achieve optimality via taxes can achieve it via regulation as well.

Although it is easy to draw diagrams for hypothetical cases of unspecified pollutants and industries, to estimate reliable MB and MC curves quantitatively in real-life cases is much more difficult.[20] Very often the MB curves are little more than guesses. There is a two-stage problem:

1. Working out the physical relationship between varying levels of the pollutant and the harm caused (the dose–response relationship).
2. Putting a monetary valuation on the harm.

It is not just the economic problem of the latter stage – although that is often contentious enough – but that scientists usually have only sketchy and controversial evidence on the first stage, i.e. the way that the damage changes with different levels of the pollutant. The experts sometimes disagree over whether a substance is harmful at all, and often disagree over whether there is a safe threshold or whether even the minutest dose has some small chance of doing some harm to somebody; for example, whether there are any safe levels of lead absorption or nuclear radiation.

As a result, the level of pollution aimed at – often called the 'standard' in the EU literature – is often at best a very rough guess. However, perhaps surprisingly, once it is accepted that the aim is not an optimal level of pollution, there is then a strong argument for achieving the fairly arbitrary standard by the use of taxes, rather than by simply telling all firms contributing to the pollution to abate by some particular percentage, or telling all firms that they can each emit only some particular amount of pollution. The reason is that typically some polluters have lower abatement costs than others. To minimize the costs of achieving any given arbitrary level of aggregate abatement, more of the abatement should be done by firms which can abate more cheaply. Normally, the abatement should be spread between firms in such a way that the *marginal* cost of abatement is equal for each firm. But the argument given above as to how firms will react to a pollution tax shows that, in response to a given tax, each firm will abate up to the point where the tax equals its marginal cost of abatement. Since each firm faces the same tax, they will all end up where they have equal marginal costs of abatement. Hence taxes will minimize the cost of abatement.

Despite this cost-minimization argument, until recently pollution taxes have hardly been used in most EU countries, and although their use has been increasing, they are still relatively rare (Sweden and Denmark are probably the EU countries with most use).[21] Among the minor exceptions is the reduced tax in some countries on lead-free petrol as compared with leaded petrol, during the period when both were available. In terms of Figure 20.1, a tax differential equal to t has been imposed on petrol containing lead.[22] Ironically, however (in the year preceding the final Council agreement of 1989), the Commission – at the urging of the French and UK governments – had been threatening to take the Dutch to the ECJ for offering tax concessions to purchasers of cars fitted with catalytic converters which reduce exhaust pollution. This was said to be a distortion of trade – the British and French car makers not having moved as fast as the Germans and some others in adapting their production towards cars which can be easily fitted with converters.

However, the EU itself has tried taking pollution taxes more seriously. In 1989 the Council of Environmental Ministers requested the Commission to draft proposals on environmental taxation. Specific proposals by the Commission emerged with the debate on global warming, and the need to reduce emissions of carbon dioxide.[23]

In 1991 the Commission proposed an energy tax in two parts: one part related to the carbon content of fossil fuels and the other part on all non-renewable energy. Thus, for example, nuclear power might be taxed at a rate which would be about half that levied on electricity from oil-burning power stations. The proposal also allowed for possible exemptions for some industries which are particularly energy intensive, such as steel, in order to preserve international competitiveness – such exemptions could be removed if other competitor countries agreed to tax such industries in a similar way.

The proposals aroused considerable opposition, especially from fuel producers and many industrial groups. The result was that the Commission effectively agreed to make implementation contingent on the acceptance of carbon taxes in the major competitors, especially Japan and the United States. At the Earth Summit in Rio de Janeiro in June 1992, US opposition ensured that no binding international agreement was reached on controlling carbon dioxide emissions (at that time the US government still claimed that lack of evidence on carbon dioxide emissions and global warming meant that the costs of controlling the emissions were unjustified). As a result, the Commission did not push its energy tax proposal with much urgency, and the Council could not come to an agreement on the tax. Eventually, UK refusal to agree to directives which could be seen as giving the EU power over member states' taxation forced the abandonment of any EU-wide carbon tax, irrespective of its other merits or drawbacks. (Ironically, at the time of writing, there has been a major controversy in the UK, with industry lobbying hard against government proposals to introduce a tax on the industrial use of energy to induce abatement of carbon dioxide emissions.) Currently, EU directives merely 'encourage' member states to use environmental taxes.

Some interesting economic issues are raised by the episode as it developed. One is the justification for the non-carbon part of the energy tax. The Commission mentioned encouragement of energy efficiency. This is only justifiable if there are other externalities which are due to the use of energy, which are not fuel specific and which cannot be taxed directly; but the case has not been made. It is probable that the aim was really to avoid substitution by nuclear power, because of its own risks, but that it was considered politically more acceptable to achieve this as part of a new tax ostensibly aimed at global warming rather than as a control of nuclear power in its own right. The general economic issue is the interrelatedness of environmental impacts – as with any other aspect of resource allocation (e.g. the discussion above of the double dividend), affecting one input or output will have repercussions on others, and an overly partial analysis will miss these interconnections. The EU is now explicitly attempting to deal with such interrelatedness by its 1996 directive (96/61) on integrated pollution prevention and control, which will be applicable to some heavily polluting installations.

20.2.3 Competitiveness and pollution policy

Another issue raised by the EU energy tax proposals is that of international competitiveness and distortion of trade, as exemplified both by the initial exemptions on energy-intensive industries and by the reluctance to impose carbon-content taxes unless competitor nations do the same. From an economic efficiency perspective, it is precisely the most energy-intensive industries that should either be induced to substitute other inputs for energy usage or else raise their prices and cut back production the most, as they are the heavy users of a resource with what is now considered to be a high social cost. As seen in Figure 20.1, the relative prices of their products should rise and their outputs should therefore fall. Furthermore, if there are any possibilities for a move away from energy use in production, then the cost-minimization argument implies that they should not be exempt from the tax, at least at the margin.[24]

The reluctance to impose any carbon-related tax unless other countries do confuses a valid and an invalid argument. Since the benefits of any reduction in carbon dioxide emissions in the EU would accrue globally, it is reasonable to argue that the EU should not abate at all unless other countries do the same – it is a classic free-rider problem, since the pollution is a public bad at the global level. However, if other countries were to agree to cut back their emissions, but decide to do so by means other than economic incentives, this should not affect the EU's decision on using taxes. For any cutback that the EU wishes to achieve, it will be better off if it achieves that cutback at the minimum cost – precisely the argument in favour of pollution taxes that has been outlined above. As always in arguments over international trade, there is a conflict between the employment impacts of changes that alter the pattern of production, and the efficient allocation once employment has adjusted to the new pattern.[25]

The issue of competitiveness brings us back to the underlying justification of having any *joint* EU policy at all. As mentioned above, a major (in my judgement, the major) reason was because otherwise some member states might suffer a loss of competitiveness *vis-à-vis* other member states with laxer controls on pollution. This was, and is, considered to be unfair, or distorted, competition.

Although the avoidance of 'unfair' competition (and subsequent loss of sales and employment) has always been a fundamental principle of the EU (e.g. Articles 92–3 of the Treaty of Rome (87–8 (CT)), standard economic analysis generally implies that this principle may be unnecessary. In the case of imposing uniformity of environmental standards, it may even reduce social welfare in the long run.

Left to themselves, different countries may well want different levels of environmental purity and exposure to pollutants. These choices could result from differences in culture, 'tastes' or income levels. For example, it might be expected that those with a higher level of income will demand (and be prepared to pay more for) higher levels of amenity and health.

Living standards fully defined will comprise both goods and services bought by individuals and also those provided publicly but not paid for by individual consumers. The latter include environmental quality. At any given level of national productivity and resources (i.e. a given production possibility frontier), if more publicly provided goods are consumed then less privately purchased ones can be consumed, and vice versa. Conventional measures of net real wages and real personal incomes only account for privately purchased consumption possibilities. Thus if a country wishes to have a higher standard of environmental quality, the level of real wages (as conventionally measured) will have to be below that possible with lower environmental standards.

If one country raises its environmental standards, one path that could lead to the fall in real wages is that, at existing initial levels of real wages, but with higher costs of meeting the more stringent pollution controls, firms will try to raise prices and thus become uncompetitive. They would then have to lay off workers.[26] As unemployment begins to rise, wage reductions will be needed to restore full employment. Wage cuts will enable firms to cut prices and to compete again. The final equilibrium will be one of full employment and capacity output. Although there will be lower incomes than initially when defined in terms of privately purchased goods, there should be higher living standards when these are viewed as including enjoyment of environmental amenities and reduced pollution.

In general, since not all industries pollute equally, a country which wants less pollution will also need an industrial structure which comprises less production in industries which are heavily polluting per unit value of output, and more of its production in industries which emit less pollution. Again, a path by which the reallocation could occur would be the changes in relative prices of goods that result from the more heavily polluting industries being uncompetitive at the initial prices (plus more stringent pollution controls), as well as the direct closing down of some of the now uncompetitive polluting firms. In order for those who were employed in the more heavily polluting industries to be deployed into other industries, their wages may have to fall, which should happen as a reaction to their temporary unemployment.

In the process that has been indicated here, the interim period of 'unfair competition' is part of the market mechanism leading to the correct result. The problem is that if (as some believe) wages in EU countries are rigid downwards even in the face of protracted high unemployment, the unemployment may last a long time, together with its attendant social and economic troubles.[27] Hence the pressure for common EU emission standards.

The analysis in this section applies both to the issue of unfair or distorted competition between EU states and to international competitiveness between the EU as a whole and the rest of the world. As indicated, the problems arise because the 'short run' during which wages would be too high, and thus unemployment also be too high, might last a long time. The long-run result of differing national environmental standards (where each country chooses the levels that reflect its own wishes) would eventually be higher social welfare, but it may take too long to be waited for passively. In Keynes' famous phrase, 'In the long run we are all dead.'

20.2.4 Tradeable permits and the EU position on global warming

As stated in section 20.2.2, one advantage of taxes over regulations is that they achieve the minimization of the aggregate cost of reaching any particular pollution reduction, when governments are ignorant of firms' abatement cost functions. However, this same attribute can lead to what may be a major drawback. If the government does not know the firms' marginal costs of abatement, it cannot be sure what aggregate level of abatement will be induced by any particular tax level. The tax it chooses may lead to more or to less abatement than it expects.

For some pollutants the failure to hit the standard exactly is not crucial – the target itself is only a rough guess. In other cases, however, this can be a major disadvantage. This is especially in cases (like Figure 20.3) where there is thought to be a threshold of pollution above which serious effects become apparent. For example, no government is likely to use taxes to control radioactive emissions, because overshooting the target would be unacceptable.

There is an instrument that ensures that the target is met, and yet minimizes the aggregate cost of abatement. This instrument is the use of tradeable emission permits (or quotas). The aggregate volume of permits equals the maximum pollution target, but the permits can be bought or sold by firms. Trading will establish a market price per permit. Each firm will abate up to the point where its marginal cost of abatement equals the price of a permit. For example, if initially it is at a point where its marginal cost of abatement is less than the price, it would be profitable to abate more and sell its surplus permits. Conversely, if its marginal cost is above the price, it would be cheaper to buy permits and to abate less (pollute more). Since each firm sets its marginal cost equal to the same (market) price of a permit, all will have equal marginal costs – which is the condition for minimizing the cost of abatement. (There may be other problems with permits; for example, if permits are initially 'grandfathered', i.e. handed out to firms, rather than being auctioned, there is no government revenue to provide the 'double dividend'.)

Tradeable pollution permits are currently under discussion in several EU countries, but are not yet functioning in the EU, although they are in the USA. They have, however, become of practical importance in one EU pollution policy issue – global warming. In 1997, an international agreement was reached in Kyoto, Japan, on controlling emissions of 'greenhouse gases' (primarily, but not exclusively, carbon dioxide). The EU has agreed that by 2010–12 its emissions will fall to 8% below those in 1990. The EU is to be a 'bubble', i.e. the reduction applies to the EU as a whole, not to individual countries. Within the total EU reduction, the Council agreed on an allocation in which the poorer member states (which currently emit less per capita) will actually be allowed to increase their emissions, in order not to inhibit their economic growth. (See Table 20.1.)

One of the bitterly contested issues in the negotiations leading to the Kyoto agreement was that the USA insisted that internationally traded permits should be incorporated. Countries which emitted less than their targets would be allowed to sell their excess to other nations, which could then emit more than their targets. The EU was among those opposed to such trading, though eventually trading was conceded in order to obtain US participation in the agreement.

Table 20.1 Greenhouse gas emission changes from 1990 to 2010

Country	%
Austria	−13
Belgium	−7.5
Denmark	−21
Finland	0
France	0
Germany	−21
Greece	+25
Ireland	+13
Italy	−6.5
Luxembourg	−28
Netherlands	−6
Portugal	+27
Spain	+15
Sweden	+4
UK	−12.5

Source: EU press document 9402/98 (Presse 205), C–98/205.

There were various reasons why the EU and some others opposed pollution trading. One was the fear that because the ex-Communist countries had suffered a large drop in their industrial production after 1990, they would automatically undershoot their targets. If they then sold their surplus allowances to others who thereby did not have to meet their own targets, the aggregate cutback would be less than would otherwise be achieved.

Another basis of opposition was almost a moral one. It was considered wrong that the USA would be able to use its wealth to buy permits, and thus continue to use energy profligately and not share in the 'pain' of controlling its energy use or constraining its economic growth.[28]

The distrust of international trading still continues. In May 1999 (to the disapproval of the USA) the Commission proposed that at least half of the EU's target reduction of 8% must be achieved by internal abatement. The accompanying press release by the Environment Commissioner included the statement, 'Everybody needs to contribute . . . We must reduce our carbon dependency.'

However, the same Commission proposal also advocated serious consideration of emissions trading by firms *within* the internal market of the EU. Some member states, especially the UK and Germany, are already considering the use of tradeable permits – US experience shows that they can achieve large savings in aggregate abatement costs.[29] It is therefore possible that tradeable pollution permits will become an acceptable instrument of pollution control within the EU.

20.3 Further implications for EU policies

Despite the cost-minimization argument discussed in section 20.2.2, as stated above, pollution taxes are currently rare in the EU. Nevertheless, the theory outlined in section 20.2 does have important implications for some other controversies over EU environmental policies.

In the course of the discussion of the standard economic analysis of pollution control, we have already noted in passing a few of the implications for EU policies. There are other important aspects of the policies which can also be usefully examined in the light of the analysis.

20.3.1 Polluter pays principle (PPP)

The EU has followed the rest of the OECD in accepting the polluter pays principle (now incorporated in Article 130R (174 (CT), 2 by the Maastricht Treaty). At first, many commentators mistakenly thought that the PPP was an acceptance of the taxation approach ascribed to economists, in which polluters pay taxes on unabated pollution. However, this was not the meaning of the PPP. It was instead an agreement that governments should not subsidize firms for the costs imposed upon them by anti-pollution regulations. The PPP is satisfied if the polluters bear the cost of achieving the prescribed standards.

The PPP is thus a way of making firms 'internalize the externality'. If the standards they have to meet are correctly chosen, then, given the constraints placed on them, individual firms' own choices of abatement techniques and of output will be correct from a social standpoint.

It might also be noted that from the point of view of the first-order conditions for achieving efficiency, a subsidy per unit abated would achieve the same result as a tax per unit emitted (though in the long run the size of the industry might differ because of the different profitability). The opportunity cost to the firm of continuing to pollute would include subsidy forgone. Thus the rationale for PPP is not to enforce efficiency, but rather fears of 'unfair competition', as discussed above.

Within the EU, although PPP (as well as the general limits to state aid in Articles 92 and 93 of the Treaty of Rome (87 and 88 (CT); see Chapter 9) has meant that subsidies for pollution abatement are generally forbidden, this has been applied very strictly only for the higher running costs associated with operating equipment to reduce emissions. Transitional costs may be subsidized. Its new guidelines also allow some temporary operating cost relief to avoid harming international competitiveness when new environmental taxes are first introduced.

At times the Commission has allowed some help with initial investment costs to install abatement equipment in order to adapt to new mandatory standards, to speed the implementation of agreed standards prior to the final compliance date or to encourage firms to go beyond the mandatory standard. In the latter case the maximum limits are higher at 30%, as compared with 15% for the adaptation to new standards (40% more in each case for SMEs).[30] Similarly, in 1998 when car emission limits were tightened (Directive 98/69), tax concessions on purchases of new cars were allowed for, in order to expedite the purchase of new cars meeting the revised standard and the scrapping of older, more polluting cars.

20.3.2 Thresholds and standards

As stated above, it is very difficult to get convincing evidence about the dose–response relationships of pollutants. The problems of obtaining evidence make the techniques used much closer to those of econometricians than those of laboratory-based science testing.[31] Where human health is concerned, it is simply unethical to conduct laboratory tests, for example taking very young babies and giving them feeds containing different levels of nitrates to observe the level which causes serious damage. Most EU policies are concerned with potential health effects. But even where only amenity is at stake, the number of possible interactions and natural variations in them still make it difficult to gather conclusive evidence. The arguments over the cause of forest die-back are a case in point. There are various possible pollutants which may interact in causing damage, damage may depend on soil and weather, and the route taken between emissions of sulphur dioxide and nitrogen oxides on the one hand and the precipitation of acid rain on the other is difficult to forecast.

One result of this is that it is important to try to obtain reliable data on a range of pollutants, over many years and at a sufficient number of locations, so as to enable statistical studies relating various aspects of health to pollution to be based on enough observations to be significant (in a statistical sense). One of the focuses of EU environmental policy has been to require monitoring of pollutants. The earliest requirements were for smoke and sulphur dioxide (from 1975 onwards), water pollution (from 1977 onwards) and, more recently (from 1987), there has been an attempt to gather systematic data on damage to trees. The European Environment Agency, established by the EU in 1993, is similarly concerned with collecting and assessing data.

More fundamentally, the lack of definitive knowledge on the damage caused by different levels of pollution means that any standards adopted are done so largely by a political process disguised as a scientific one. Different groups put pressure on governments to be more or less lax, and the governments then take stands in the Council according to the balance of their feelings; often, possibly the position they have previously taken domestically is then taken with respect to EU policy. Each government will claim scientific backing for its stand, usually refusing to admit the uncertainty. Those pushing for the laxest standard will tend to claim that there is no conclusive evidence of harm, while not admitting that there is no conclusive evidence of lack of harm either; the UK position on sulphur dioxide mentioned above is one example. Others will mention the studies which suggest that there could well be serious damage caused by the current levels of pollution. As part of the process, there is the temptation to look for a threshold, as in Figure 20.3, even where there are no strong grounds for expecting one. If a threshold did exist, it would often make sense to adopt it as the standard – the marginal cost curve would have to cut the marginal benefit curve to the left of the threshold to justify less abatement (higher pollution).

A large number of medical scientists are doubtful that overall thresholds exist for many pollutants. The levels of a pollutant, such as smoke, that may be harmless to a healthy person may be deleterious to somebody already vulnerable, such as a bronchitic old-age pensioner living in a damp flat. Thus, a threshold which would be applicable to all might well be at so low a level of pollution as to be useless for policy.

Once a standard has been decided upon, by whatever process of bargaining based on whatever motives and justifications, it is then too often treated as though the agreed standard were really a well-defined threshold.[32] On the one hand, governments may use the fact that an EU standard exists to try to allay public anxiety over the potential harm from some pollutant and to claim that because levels are below the accepted standard there is nothing at all to worry about – even if new evidence has since emerged to suggest that low levels are more harmful than was thought before. On the other hand, environmentalists and other pressure groups may use the breach of a standard as an indication that the health of the public is being seriously damaged and argue that pollution must be immediately reduced to the standard, whatever the cost.

In most cases, the EU has laid down that member states must notify the Commission if they cannot reach the agreed standard by the required date. The Commission then has to decide whether the failure can be condoned or not. At this stage, the pressures mentioned in the previous paragraph come into play again: is the standard just a rough guess at the level at which marginal costs equal marginal benefits, so that less abatement is justified if a particular country can plausibly claim that its costs are especially high, or is it a well-defined threshold of pollution above which completely unacceptable harm is caused? The decision is complicated by the worry that, if some member states are granted exemptions too readily, others will in future not comply because of fears of 'unfair competition' from those given exemptions.

20.3.3 Emission versus ambient standards

In Figures 20.1, 20.2 and 20.3 we followed most of the literature in simply linking pollution to damage. However, on closer examination it becomes apparent that there are various stages of pollution. There is the initial emission at the point where the pollution is produced, such as the factory chimney or waste pipe outlet. The pollution may then flow through various media; for example, it may be carried by wind through air, then deposited on plants, then eaten by animals which are then slaughtered. During the processes, the pollution from any one source is added to by pollution from other sources and simultaneously diluted by fresh air, water, etc. mixing with the carrying medium, and much of the substance may be deposited where it does no harm. The ultimate stage to be considered is where the pollution finally directly affects humans.

From the economist's, anthropocentric, viewpoint, the pollution that matters is that which affects human beings. Typically, therefore, we are concerned with the ambient levels of pollution – i.e. the concentration in the medium which affects health, such as micrograms per cubic metre of lead particles in the air or milligrams per litre of nitrates in drinking water.

In setting standards for pollution, a standard could be applied at any of the stages of the process. At the final stage, one could set standards of acceptable levels of absorption of pollution by people; for example, there was at one time a Commission proposal to set a maximum limit for the level of lead in people's blood. Obviously one would hardly fine or imprison people with more lead in their blood than the standard. Instead, the idea was that if tests showed that anybody was above the limit, then the government of their country should take agreed action to reduce their lead intake. In fact, governments do use monitoring of human exposure or absorption as a trigger for action, and occasionally set standards in this form, such as radiation exposure limits for workers. In the EC case, partly as a result of UK pressure, the directive on blood lead levels was watered down somewhat and became one for an EC-wide screening programme, primarily for information gathering and with a member state required to take only such actions as the government itself thought were appropriate measures if too many people were above the specified values.[33]

The next stage back is that mentioned above, i.e. the concentration in the medium that directly affects people. In the EU standards defined for this stage are sometimes called 'exposure standards' or 'primary protection standards'. Another example of such standards, in addition to those for drinking water or air, would be the bacteria content of bathing water.

Sometimes the standards are somewhat further back in the process, but still concern ambient levels. These are often called 'environmental quality standards'. The standards applying to water, in rivers or lakes, which could be taken for drinking, or those applying to water with shellfish, are examples.

Standards may also be set at the initial emission stage. These are usually called 'emission standards'. A similar stage is when the pollution is caused by the use of products which are sold, such as car exhaust pollution or noise from lawnmowers. A somewhat similar stage is where the EC mandates labelling or other aspects of products to avoid *potential* danger from misuse, for example the controls on the shipment of toxic waste.

As already stated, from an economist's viewpoint it would seem that, if the standards are to be used at all, the relevant standard should be as far down the chain as is technically possible – exposure standards where possible or at least environmental quality standards. The only cases for EU standards on emissions would be either where they were also product standards (to allow unhindered trade) or where there was some reason why even environmental quality standards were not feasible. Otherwise, it should be up to the relevant government inspectorate/agency to find the least-cost way of achieving the environmental quality or exposure standard. If pollution taxes (or tradeable permits) were not used, then the requirement for pollution abatement should be shared between the various sources of emissions in the most efficient way possible.[34] As explained earlier, the aim would be (subject to information/enforcement limitations) to require abatement by each polluter up to the point where the marginal cost of abatement was equal.

In the 1970s there was a heated controversy over whether the EC should define its policies by environmental quality standards (EQSs) or UESs, with the latter defined as maximum 'limit values' so that member states could have stricter emission limits if they wished. The issue arose over a linked series of directives on water quality aimed at rivers and estuaries – there was a framework directive, finally passed in 1976, on the approach to 'Dangerous substances discharged into the aquatic environment', followed by subsequent directives on specific pollutants/industries.[35] The contestants were the UK on the side of EQS and the other member states, plus the Commission, on the side of UES.

The reasons for the attachment of the Commission and other member states to UES were partly explicable in terms of one of the motivations for having a joint EC policy at all: the fear of 'unfair competition' if different countries had different emission standards for a set of pollutants which were primarily industrial effluents. Countries such as the UK, which has a long coastline with relatively fast-flowing estuaries and rivers, would be able to achieve any given EQS with much higher emissions than their trade partners (rivals?). In addition, countries which shared river systems (as along the Rhine) would find it difficult to allocate individual polluters' emission levels to achieve an EQS: upstream countries would have little incentive to impose severe cutbacks on their industries. The issue of trans-frontier pollution is of less importance for the UK, which not only is primarily an island (ignoring Northern Ireland and its border) but has the fortune to be mainly upwind of its nearest neighbours. The other member states felt that the co-operation that should underlie the Community ought to lead to policies in a form which would help, not hinder, the solution of joint problems, including trans-frontier pollution.[36]

On the other side of the debate, the UK put views which are close to part of the approach taken by most economists and outlined above. Since it is the damage to humans that is the problem, an EQS is what matters, not emissions *per se*. Emissions need only be limited to the extent that they lead to unacceptable damage. In terms of a traditional British statement: 'There are no harmful substances, only harmful concentrations.' On the question of unfair competition, the UK government said that it was no more unfair that the United Kingdom should benefit from its coastline and estuaries than that Italy could benefit from its sunshine: it would be absurd to require the Italians to grow tomatoes in greenhouses just to stop them having an 'unfair' advantage over the Dutch. Although not stated in those terms, this was an application of the theory of comparative advantage, applied to polluting industries.

In the end, a typical EC compromise was reached. Countries could choose *either* to accept UES in the form of limit values *or* to establish EQS, provided that they could show the Commission that the quality standard was being met. Only the UK chose the latter. The subsequent directives for particular dangerous and persistent pollutants followed the same compromise of a choice of either approach, although within the EQS approach it is odd that separate directives should be issued for separate industries.[37]

Despite the strong disagreements over UES or EQS, it could be argued that neither side was really consistent. The UK, despite the type of statement mentioned above, had in many cases applied UESs to whole industries (in some cases only to new pollutants, but the EC also made a similar distinction). For example, the old Alkali Inspectorate typically applied its notion of best practicable means to the whole of an industry it supervised and the same applies to the new Pollution Inspectorate (now part of the UK's Environment Agency) and BATNEEC. Conversely, other EU policies set EQSs without any fuss from the member states, for example the air quality standards for nitrogen dioxide, sulphur dioxide and particulates. It could also be argued that the dispute forced the UK to be much more rigorous about the EQSs that were needed.

In view of the economic assessment of 'unfair competition' discussed in section 20.2.3, one could go even further than the UK argument that unfair competition considerations should not impose UES. In the absence of trans-frontier effects of pollution, there may not even be a case for an EU-level EQS. As noted, however, the strong dismissal of the 'unfair competition' criterion would completely undermine not only much of EU environmental policy (e.g. on drinking water standards, where typically there are virtually no trans-frontier effects), but many other EU policies as well.

20.3.4 Damage and designated areas

One last issue in EU environmental policy that we shall examine is also linked to the economic analysis. The stress on the costs and benefits of abatement implies that it is not merely the dumping itself of something into water, air or earth that matters, but the harm done relative to the benefits from the activity. The harm done will depend on the potential use by people (directly or indirectly) of the medium. It therefore makes sense to vary the desired standard of pollution according to its use. Water used for drinking could well require stricter standards on its nitrate concentration than water used only for boating. The EU has followed such a policy.

In some cases the use of the medium is obvious; in other cases, less so. In the latter cases there may be some decentralization so that countries are allowed to designate particular areas for the application of particular standards. For example, the standards for bathing water apply to stretches of water where bathing is traditionally practised by large numbers of people. Similarly, member states can designate areas where water standards need to be set to protect shellfish.

Although the approach seems sensible, the application has not always been so. In particular, in so far as governments have discretion over the areas designated, they can use this as a way of avoiding the effective implementation of EU policies that they feel are unnecessary. This has indeed happened. In the case of standards for water supporting different sorts of freshwater fish, and for the shellfish case already mentioned, some member states simply did not designate any waters at all. Similarly, those readers who are familiar with English seaside resorts might be interested to know that the UK government originally used its discretion over how to assess where 'large numbers' traditionally bathed to exclude both Blackpool and Brighton. At that time the UK government was worried about public expenditure, and any improvement in water quality of beaches would require new sewerage works. Later on though, in 1987, in response to threats from the Commission over infringement, as well as strongly adverse comments from the Royal Commission on Environmental Pollution (and the beginning of a changed attitude by the UK government to its poor reputation on environmental issues), many more beaches were added to the list.

A final example is a 1975 directive on the sulphur contents of gas/diesel oil, which is a medium-grade oil used for heating of commercial, light industrial and domestic buildings, as well as for diesel fuel for vehicles. The directive is interesting partly because it was a mixture of UES and EQS, although it is also concerned with product harmonization. It set two limits on the sulphur content of the oil, and the higher sulphur type could be used only in areas designated by member states. The aim was that the higher-sulphur-content oil should only be used where air pollution from sulphur dioxide was not a problem. In the event, the UK government decided that the whole of the United Kingdom was to be designated for the use of the higher-sulphur-content oil *except for roads*. The road network would therefore be designated for the lower-sulphur-content oil – since diesel for vehicles was already low sulphur compared with other gas/diesel oil.[38]

20.4   Conclusions

In some ways the EU policies on the environment can be counted as a success story. Despite the fact that it may not be clear that common policies are required at all in many cases, nevertheless a set of policies has emerged. Furthermore, despite some of the problems mentioned above and despite the failure to move quickly on some other policies because of the conflicting interests of the member states, as compared with other common policies (such as for transport or agriculture), progress has been fairly steady and not too divisive, acrimonious or blatantly inefficient.

In the 1990s there has been a revival of public interest in the environment, even in those member states where interest waned in the decade after 1974. Those in favour of stronger environmental policies may well feel divided about EU actions. Those who live in those member states where Green pressures are strong will feel that they are held back, as compared with what their governments could achieve (or be pressured into achieving) without the requirement to carry other member countries with them. Conversely, environmentalists who live in those countries whose governments tend only to move on these issues when really compelled can be grateful both for the more stringent standards set by EU policies and for the possibility that the Commission will enforce compliance.[39]

In the second half of 1992, during the British presidency, it seemed as though EC environmental policy might be put into reverse. Following the problems in summer 1992 with ratification of the Maastricht Agreements, the UK (especially) stressed the notion of subsidiarity that had been incorporated into the proposed Treaty amendments. To various extents, the other member states, and even the chastened Commission, also said that subsidiarity should be taken seriously, and that EC policies should be scrutinized to see whether joint action was really necessary. As indicated at various points in this chapter, the justification of EU-level environmental policies is often debatable. It was possible, therefore, that the movement on subsidiarity might lead to the reconsideration of some existing EU environmental directives.

However, subsidiarity has not made a major difference as far as existing policies are concerned. It is difficult to judge whether new EU-level joint actions on the environment have been as readily adopted as previously, even where there is no strong reason for an EU, rather than a national, policy. My own subjective judgement is that any diminution has been minimal or even non-existent, and I do not expect this to change despite the new Articles on subsidiarity in the Amsterdam Treaty.[40] Not only do they include transnational problems as a reason for joint actions, but they also include the correction of 'distorted competition'. As explained above, however misguided it may be from an economist's viewpoint, the standard interpretation of 'distorted competition' has always been a prime reason for EU-level environmental policy.

Notes

1. For earlier years, references to the Official Journals (OJ) for the environmental programmes and various directives can be found in the Economic and Social Committee (1987) outline, Haigh (1989), or Press and Taylor (1990). Many of the documents up to 1994 have been reprinted in the seven-volume *European Environmental Legislation* published by DGXI (updated edition, 1996 – CEU 1996t). The Fifth Programme was published separately by the Commission under the title *Towards Sustainability* (CEC, 1993c) with a progress report on it in COM (95) 624 and a further review in COM (97) 471 with an agreed assessment by the Council and Parliament in OJ L275/1, 10.10.98. The annual *Reports* and *Monthly Bulletins* by the Commission have brief sections on the Environment. A useful summary is in the semi-annual series of UK Government Reports, *Recent Developments in the EU*.
2. Including reports during 1977–80 by the House of Lords Select Committee on the European Communities.
3. Some of these directives predate the proposal for an EC Environmental Programme.
4. Once it was accepted that environmental policy could be fitted in as an objective of the Community, Article 235 then gave legal power for binding actions.
5. See Kramer (1998) for a thorough discussion.
6. It is not always the case that MEPs are inevitably more environmentalist than the Council. In debates on a tough new proposal for recycling cars in late 1999, it seemed very likely that the EP would relax the Council and Commission decision (*Financial Times*, 22 November 1999). This may be due to the more conservative political composition of the EP following the 1999 elections and/or the vulnerability of some MEPs to sophisticated lobbying by producers (though in the end the attempted weakening was not carried through).
7. As in other applications of this notion of 'unfair competition', or 'distortion of competition' as it is often called in EU documents, it contains implicit assumptions about the fixity of wages, prices and exchange rates. These assumptions are often not realized and their validity may or may not be dubious. This point will be amplified in section 20.2.3 and will also be relevant to controversies discussed later in this chapter.
8. Although some of those opposed to action on the environment have alleged that concern about environmental issues is a middle-class luxury, which is not shared by the working class or the poorer members of society.

    The agreement on sharing the burden of carbon dioxide reduction within the EU 'bubble' does make special provision for poorer EU member states. See section 20.2.4.
9. Formally, the arguments in the social welfare function are the individual welfares or utilities, even if the functional form (weighting of individual welfares) may reflect egalitarianism or some other values.
10. Theoretically, in formal treatments, there would be no obstacle to putting concern for

endangered species into somebody's utility function, even where the person does not know of the existence of some of the species. Conversely, environmentalists sometimes appeal to the possible future uses to man of endangered species of plants, which would be forgone if the species were destroyed before the discovery of their uses.

11. The EU environmental policies primarily comprise regulations and directives imposing implementation requirements on member states. Unlike some other policy areas (e.g. the CAP, regional policy) there is little spending on the environment out of the EU's own budget. The only EU spending specifically on the environment (though funds in the Cohesion part of regional spending can be spent on the environment) is the LIFE programme. The priority in this programme is the protection of habitats and preservation of nature, rather than simply control of pollution. However, compared to other EU spending, the amounts are trivial: the current LIFE2 programme covering 1996–9 has a budget of 450 million ECU.

12. An externality also occurs when marginal private benefit is not equal to marginal social benefit. Pollution is a negative externality, i.e. private cost is less than social cost. Some older microeconomic textbooks sometimes use the term 'social cost' to refer only to the *excess* cost imposed on others, which is a different usage from that followed here.

13. For further detailed discussion, there is now a wide range of textbooks on the economics of pollution control, e.g. Baumol and Oates (1988) or Perman *et al.* (1999) for more advanced treatment.

14. According to the *Financial Times* (4 December 1996) even Germany, previously viewed as an EU pacesetter in environmental protection laws, has reacted to its recent rise in unemployment by a reluctance to introduce new anti-pollution measures which might raise costs. There were even moves to reduce existing measures as part of the drive to deregulation.

15. Another way of putting the same point is to say that the MPC curve in Figure 20.1 is too high because the true opportunity cost of labour is below the wage rate. Hence the MSC, which should measure the cost of resources by the value of their alternative use, includes some components which make it lower than the MPC – see Chapter 5. Note also that if the industry is not perfectly competitive, the output may be too low for the usual reasons, despite the externality – it depends on the balance between the strength of the externality (output too high) and the imperfection (output too low).

16. A possible exception is the case of pollutants which are cumulative (non-degradable) and highly toxic – see Pearce (1976) or Chapter 11 in Perman *et al.* (1999).

17. Many of the articles are technically advanced, especially for those who have not studied public finance. A less technical useful summary is Goulder (1997), with even more accessible accounts in Parry (1997) and Parry and Oates (1998).

18. That is, even if the revenue is not used to reduce distortionary taxation elsewhere.

19. A more detailed discussion of this and other problems of using pollution taxes is in Marin (1979) or, in a US context, in Arnold (1994), Chapter 11. Also see Kelman (1981) for a study of some other reasons for the hostility of non-economists to the idea of pollution taxes, and various articles by Frey, e.g. Weck-Hannemann and Frey (1997).

20. For a (rare) EU attempt at using a cost-benefit study, but to find the desirable *maximum* level of pollution concentrations, see COM (97) 500.

21. A summary of EU countries' pollution charges can be found in OECD (1997a) and European Environmental Agency (1996). In many of those cases where pollution charges are used in the EU they are part of a package of measures, not the sole instrument.

22. This case is suitable for Figure 20.1, as once the leaded petrol has been put into the fuel tank, the motorist has no realistic options for varying the total emissions of lead for each gallon bought. The same applies to the carbon content fuel tax discussed below.

23. A brief account and assessment of the Commission's proposals can be found in Pearson and Smith (1991). More detailed analyses are in the papers in Carraco and Sinisalco (1993). The EC had already agreed to aim at stabilizing CO_2 emissions at the 1990 level by the year 2000.

24. If we concentrate on the cost-minimization argument only, and (for the reasons already discussed) ignore overall optimality, imposing the pollution tax but giving lump-sum subsidies to these industries (to avoid a large rise in their average costs) might be acceptable.

25. The argument here and in the remainder of this section is made within a framework which assumes perfect competition inside countries. To what extent it still holds within the framework of the 'New Trade Theory' of oligopolistic competition is currently the subject of research.

26. Firms may also have to accept lower profits. Whether or not this happens depends on how internationally mobile capital is. In the EU now, it may well be that profit rates cannot be forced down.

27. If the country is one of those EU member states not in EMU, the change in the aggregate real wage could be hastened by changes in nominal exchange rates, provided that money wages do not respond fully to the changes in the price of imports – the usual 'money illusion' condition for devaluations to have any real effects. However, the relative sectoral reallocations of resources cannot generally just be achieved by this route (the exception would be if all traded goods were uniformly more polluting than non-traded goods).

28. This objection parallels some of the early popular opposition to economists' advocacy of pollution taxes. Many felt it wrong that firms or wealthy consumers could continue to pollute if they were prepared to pay. See the Kelman and Frey references in note 19.

29. See, for example, 'Symposium on SO_2 Trading', *Journal of Economic Perspectives* 12(3), Summer 1998.

30. The Commission's original position is briefly restated in CEC (1991c), paragraph 284, and given in greater detail in CEC (1987d), paragraph 159. The new guidelines were published in OJ C72, 10.3.94 and summarized in CEU, 1996e.

31. The examples in this and the following paragraphs are taken from EU environmental policies.

32. Jordan (1999) shows in the context of water purity the way that, once a standard has been agreed, it can inhibit further adjustment.

33. The debates over this directive (77/312) illustrate not only the monitoring function of the EC mentioned above, but also the sensitivity to thresholds. Part of the objection to the original proposal was that it would suggest that the standard was a threshold which, if exceeded by anybody, would mean they were in danger.

34. Whether pollution taxes or quantitative regulations are used to apportion the necessary abatement between emitters, allowance should be made for the different contributions of emissions in different places to the pollution measured as environmental quality, e.g. because of prevailing wind or tide patterns. Tradeble pollution permits should similarly allow for differential contributions (which is one practical difficulty of using them for pollutants for which the location of emissions matters).

35. An excellent detailed account of the controversies is given in Guruswamy *et al.* (1983). As pointed out in this article, although originally the term 'environmental quality objective' meant something else, the EQS is now sometimes referred to as a 'quality objective'.

36. The well-known 'Coase Theorem', Coase (1960), implies that optimum levels of pollution can be achieved by bargaining between the polluter (upstream country here) and the pollutee (downstream). If the polluter would otherwise have the right to pollute, then the pollutee will have to pay compensation to the polluter for the abatement. Since EU countries bargain over a wide range of issues, concessions by the pollutee country on other issues of interest to the polluter may enable an optimal level of pollution to be reached in circumstances where direct pecuniary payments would be unacceptable.

37. Mercury from the chloralkali industry. The directive for the titanium dioxide industry had already been foreshadowed in the First Environmental Action Programme, together with controls for the pulp and paper industries (the latter has never been enacted).

38. In 1992 the Council agreed on a new directive setting a uniform limit on the sulphur

content of all gas/oils. More recently, diesel fuels for road transport have been included in the same directives as petrol.

39. A politically important example in the UK was the Commission's threat to prosecute over the failure to meet the standards for nitrates in water (other countries besides the UK were also threatened). In the absence of these threats, especially given UK official scepticism over the levels of the EQS actually laid down in the directive, there would have been an even greater lack of urgency over an issue which was so adverse for the privatization process. (In 1992 both the UK and Germany were found by the ECJ to be in breach of the directive.)

40. Others may disagree, e.g. Golub (1996b) states that there was a fall in the number of Commission environmental proposals during the period 1992–5.

21 Factor mobility

D. G. MAYES

Although the freedom of mobility of labour and capital were objectives enshrined in the Treaty of Rome itself, only fairly limited progress had been made by the early 1980s in turning this into a reality. Most countries had capital controls of one form or another and labour faced considerable constraints on movement through lack of recognition of qualifications and other problems over establishment and transfer of benefits. The slow progress stemmed from two sources. In the case of capital, member states were worried that having free movements would lead to destabilizing flows which would disturb the running of the domestic economy. The main fear was a capital outflow which would depreciate the currency, drive up the rate of inflation and require monetary and fiscal contraction to offset it. Labour controls, on the other hand, were more concerned with inflows. Employees in the domestic economy feared that an inflow from other countries would lose them their jobs – countries would export their unemployment. Much of this was dressed up as a need to have certain skills, standards and local knowledge for the protection of consumers. A closer examination reveals that only some of this was necessary. However, much of the fear stemmed from ignorance of what others' qualifications meant and overcoming this required a long and tedious process of determination and negotiation.

The 1985 White Paper on completing the internal market and the 1986 Single European Act (SEA) signalled the determination to break through this complex of restrictions and move to a much more open market, with freedom of movement of capital and labour being two of four basic 'freedoms' set out as the objective of the market (the other two being freedom of movement of goods and of services). In the case of capital, this was to be achieved by 1 July 1990. This target was largely not met for the EC of 9 and Portugal and Spain managed to participate in 1992 only for the ERM crisis of September 1992 (see Chapter 17) to require some controls to be reintroduced by member states in the hope of stabilizing their exchange rates. The setback proved to be short-lived. The Maastricht Treaty, which came into force in 1993, had advanced progress further and capital markets have become even more open with the introduction of the Euro at the beginning of 1999. There is still considerable segmentation of markets, which may be perpetuated for small firms and households, especially where there are limitations to information. However, the mergers between financial institutions and the ease with which electronic linkages between markets are taking place suggest that capital will continue to become even more mobile for some time yet.

The legislative programme for the Single Market measures was intended to be complete by the end of 1992. While this was largely achieved, some of the labour mobility measures are still to have their full effect. The Maastricht Treaty also covered labour through the 'Social Protocol'. However, the fact that the UK was not prepared to participate and the fact that the other 11 member states felt it necessary to introduce further requirements for minimum standards at work suggest that the actual exercise of labour mobility, and indeed capital mobility if it has consequences for employment, is still feared within the EU rather than being viewed as an unambiguous benefit. Even though the UK has now signed the protocol, progress on further legislation has been limited. Failure to make much progress in reducing unemployment in the 1990s heightened concern about the workings of the labour market and worries about possible immigration when the EU is enlarged to include Central and Eastern European countries.

The logic behind achieving a 'free movement' of capital and labour is elementary if the full opportunity for exploiting efficiency gains within the EU is to be achieved. The practice in the case of capital movements was that those countries frightened of an uncontrollable outflow realized that with the increasing ease of international capital transactions they were both making their own firms pay a higher price for capital and making themselves a less attractive location for mobile investment. The increasing stability of the EMS may also have acted as an incentive, although this provides somewhat of an irony as the removal of capital controls itself served to destabilize the EMS (see Chapter 17).

In the case of labour there were also two main factors involved in easing the decision to remove barriers. The first is simply that with the exception of Greece, Portugal and Spain there were no great pressures for major destabilizing labour flows; hence their removal would not have major consequences. Indeed, migration had fallen from its levels in the 1960s and early 1970s. Second, in the professions and more skilled jobs it was proving possible to find a way round the impasse and to move forward much more rapidly by countries accepting mutual recognition of each others' qualifications, rather than attempting the extremely difficult task of agreeing a common standard. However, it still remains to be seen in practice how well such recognition will work (Brazier *et al.*, 1993). Even in highly internationalized professions such as the academic one, employment of foreigners tends to be more on the basis of work they have published than by qualification alone. Furthermore, the EU is now finding itself threatened by migration problems, not from within, but from Eastern Europe and North Africa.

21.1 The historical perspective

As illustrated by the North American Free Trade Agreement (NAFTA), most of the emphasis and interest in negotiations and assessments concerning integration tends to concentrate on products rather than inputs. However, freedom of movement of products within the EU does not necessarily entail the absence of protection or completely free competition if there are still constraints on inputs; this was recognized by the Single Market programme. In the case of imported produced inputs, intermediate goods and services, the subject has been extensively explored with the measurement of effective protection. The differences between nominal rates and effective rates can be quite striking. If the EU's Common External Tariff (CET) were 5% on a particular product, while the CET on the main produced inputs (which form 50% of the production costs) were zero, then the effective rate of protection would be double the nominal rate (all other influences such as differential transport costs for the finished and intermediate products being ignored). Effective protection is thus the rate of protection of the value-added in the production of the final product – see El-Agraa (1989b).

Similar considerations apply to the non-produced inputs of labour and capital in the productive process. If there are restraints on the mobility of labour, then differences in the price of labour can exist between countries in the same way that differences between product prices can exist when the mobility of products is restricted. Thus, for products with a high labour content, considerable competitive advantages could accrue to the country with the lower wage levels even if trade in the products were completely free. This separation of labour markets is not, of course, just an international phenomenon. It occurs widely within individual countries and hence a range of wages is to be expected.

It might be possible to get round some of the problems of immobility of labour if capital were mobile. Thus, instead of labour moving to take up opportunities elsewhere, firms could set up new plants and hence remove much of the differential in wages. Where capital mobility is also restricted, differences can persist across the EU.

It is important to recall that if a firm in one country wishes to sell a product to a consumer in a second country, there are three ways in which it can go about it (assuming there is just one step in the productive process). It can export the finished product, it can set up a manufacturing plant in the second country or it can set up a manufacturing plant in a third country. The first of these thus involves trade flows, the second capital flows and the third both. The development of trade patterns will be crucially affected by the degree of factor mobility. *Ceteris paribus*, the greater the factor mobility, the smaller trade needs to be for any particular pattern of consumption.

Although the Single Market programme will remove many of the remaining restrictions on factor movements, it is unlikely that capital, let alone labour, will be as mobile as it is within individual member countries. Factors reducing mobility include differences in tastes and customs, and variations in risk. Having a single currency is an important step in removing one source of risk and reducing transition costs.

The 1992 programme enables integration; it does not compel it. Thus, in the same way that the idealized total specialization of trade in economic theory is rarely realized, we would not expect total perfection in capital markets and nothing like it in labour markets where many other factors lead to continuing segmentation. To quite some extent this is affected by the nature and treatment of the services in which the labour is embodied which have national diversity in the same way as there is diversity in the demand for goods.

If factors and products can move between countries freely, then, neglecting any transport or transfer costs, the whole trading area can be treated as a single market with a uniform reward right across the area to each factor, and uniform product prices. However, such a system is not only very far from a description of the reality of the EU after 1992, but is also indeterminate and does not tell us the extent to which the products rather than the factors move – a typical problem of under-identification (see Mayes, 1988). The imperfections of the real world, however, are actually an aid in this case as they increase the chance of being able to identify the determinants of the various movements.

Although there are some differences in the way in which labour can move from one country to another, particularly when countries have common land frontiers, the movement of labour usually involves the person concerned moving to and living in the new country. However, in some cases it may be possible to commute across the border and to work in a foreign country while continuing to be resident in the home country. Movements can be long or short term and the worker may or may not bring his or her family along too. Nevertheless, there is fairly straightforward behaviour involved in most movement of labour.

Capital, on the other hand, can be moved in a variety of ways. While the basic distinction lies between direct investment, which involves the setting up or acquisition of a 'subsidiary' in a foreign country, and portfolio investment, involving the purchase of shares and bonds or the making of other forms of loan to a company in a foreign country, other, more complicated, arrangements exist which involve the effective transfer of capital between countries even if this is not recorded as such in the statistics on capital movements. 'Back-to-back' loans are a simple example whereby exchange control can be evaded. In such a case, although the parent company can use only domestic currency while wanting to invest in foreign currency in the foreign country, it can make the domestic funds available to a foreign borrower who is essentially in the same position – his or her funds are in his or her own currency while he or she wishes to use foreign currency. The exact matching process may be much more complicated than this simple one-to-one swap. (The problem is more complicated if the investment abroad is financed solely by a loan raised abroad. In such a case, there is not really any international movement of capital.) In a single capital market, a firm can raise debt or equity anywhere in the market by having access to all financial services on the same basis as all other borrowers. In the same way, of course, providers of capital would have equal opportunity to offer services. Simple removal of exchange controls also does not necessarily achieve this.

In the case of labour movement, individuals physically move from one country to another and then provide their labour services in the second country. Capital, on the other hand, in the sense usually considered, involves the transfer of claims through a financial transaction and not the transfer of capital goods themselves in the form of plant, machinery and vehicles. If existing physical capital is exported, then the financial transfer is lowered. If new physical capital is purchased from the home country, there is an additional export but the net inflow of physical capital is smaller. The net flow is largest when the new physical capital is all produced in the country where the new plant is set up.

Some of the distinctions between types of capital movement may not be very important from the point of view of actual output and trade patterns. Portfolio investment resulting in control of the foreign enterprise may be largely indistinguishable from direct investment, for example. However, the major distinction normally lies in the type of investor.[1] Direct investment is undertaken by firms on their own behalf (or by governments). Portfolio investment, on the other hand, is more usually undertaken by financial companies of one form or another, although cross-share holdings by commercial companies are common in some parts of the EU. Much of this latter investment may therefore not seem particularly relevant to the problem in hand as it relates to a change in the ownership of existing assets rather than the direct financing of the creation of new physical assets used for the production of goods and services. However, this is mistaken from two points of view:

474

direct investment may also be purely a change in ownership, this time involving control; second, we need to enquire what subsequent use the funds released to the seller were put to. The ability to exchange domestic debt for foreign equity can affect the range of options open to a firm. Moreover, even if the purpose of capital inflows into a country is to 'enable' the foreign government to run a deficit which cannot be financed fully by its private domestic sector, such lending may permit a higher level of investment in physical capital in that country than would otherwise be the case.

Clearly, the latter form of capital flow is of more than passing interest in a group of countries which are attempting some co-ordination of their economic actions. When exchange rates are relatively fixed between member countries through the snake or the European Monetary System (EMS), balance of payments surpluses/ deficits on current account may open up rather wider than would otherwise be the case. In so far as these imbalances are not met by official movements (or reserves), they must be eliminated by countervailing capital movements, encouraged in the main by differences in covered interest rates.[2,3] With freely floating exchange rates, the exchange rate can take rather more of the burden of adjustment between countries and capital flows rather less. Co-ordination of fiscal or monetary policies between countries will also affect the ways in which capital flows have to balance the remaining transactions.[4] Now with the Euro, there is no more concern about the private financial flows between the participating countries than there is about the flows between regions of the same member state. The burden of adjustment falls largely on the labour market (see Chapter 17).

These considerations raise many issues which lie outside the scope of this chapter; but it must be borne in mind that capital transfers take place between countries for reasons that are not necessarily related to the essentially microeconomic decisions of the individual firm. To invert the argument, wider issues influence the values of the macroeconomic variables which affect firms' decisions over their overseas investment and these wider issues themselves form part of the way in which the members of the EC choose to conduct the handling of economic policy, both jointly and independently. Since direct investment abroad and borrowing of foreign funds by enterprises in foreign countries may both involve not just the same size capital inflow but also the same increase in capital formation within the country, it is not possible to set aside either long-term or short-term portfolio investment as being irrelevant to the purpose in hand.

As is clear from Table 21.1, portfolio investment from abroad had usually been much less important for the United Kingdom than direct investment until the mid-1980s.[5] The lifting of exchange controls in 1979 resulted in a similar switch in the composition of the outflow of capital, with portfolio investment replacing direct investment as the most important category. The issue is complicated by the activities of oil companies which are separately covered in the table. Fortunately, the more detailed statistics (available in *Business Monitor MA4*) also distinguish non-oil investment, and in the discussion that follows we shall also try to omit oil investment as the movements of capital are largely unaffected by any considerations relating to the EC. The other EC countries do not exhibit these distortions to the pattern of capital flows in a manner which confuses their changes in response to the formation and development of the EC to the same extent as those of the United Kingdom. As the 1994 figures make clear, there can be striking readjustments in the portfolio.

Table 21.1 Inward and outward investment in the United Kingdom, 1972–98 (£ million)[a]

	1972	1976	1980	1984	1988	1992	1994	1998
Overseas investment in UK								
Direct investment	408	799	2 541	−181	12 006	9 184	6 103	40 792
Investment by oil companies[b]	78	819	1 714	–	–	–	–	–
Portfolio investment	290	438	1 499	–	15 564	24 616	33 221	20 206
Miscellaneous investment[b]	−4	35	100	1 288	–	–	–	–
Total	772	2 091	5 854	1 107	27 570	33 800	39 324	60 998
Private investment overseas								
Direct investment	−737	−2 145	−3 371	−6 036	−20 944	−10 850	−22 208	−64 077
Investment by oil companies and miscellaneous investment[b]	−61	−214	−1 495	–	–	–	–	–
Portfolio investment	−604	90	−3 150	−9 753	−11 239	−27 346	21 799	−34 380
Total	−1 402	−2 269	−8 016	−15 789	−32 183	−38 196	−401	−98 457

[a] Assets and liabilities are shown from the point of view of the United Kingdom: increase (decreases) in assets +(−), increases (decreases) in liabilities −(+), both net of investment.
[b] After 1983 included in direct investment.
Source: UK Balance of Payments.

21.2 Capital movements

Exchange controls were eliminated in the United Kingdom in October 1979, but the reasons for that move had little to do with membership of the EC. At that stage, the remaining Community countries all had restrictions on capital flows, although these varied in their degree of tightness. After the start of the Single Market programme, these restrictions were steadily removed and there has been effective freedom of capital movements since the start of stage 2 of EMU. With the exception of the new members, freedom throughout the Community was in place by July 1990, the start of stage 1 of EMU. In most cases there was a distinction between controls applied to residents and those applied to non-residents, with the restrictions being lighter in the latter case. However, interestingly enough, such restrictions as did apply to non-residents usually applied equally to all such non-residents, regardless of whether they were residents of another EC country or of a third country. There is thus no counterpart to the preference system applied to trade through differential tariffs as far as capital movements are concerned, nor, it seems, was there any intention of taking the opportunity of introducing discrimination against third countries by making this freedom of movement only in respect of fellow members.[6] To a large extent this is a practical matter, because it is difficult to control some transactions when others do not have to be vetted. However, 'reciprocity' is an argument which has been used in other parts of the Single Market programme in order to obtain concessions for the EC in third-country markets. In one sense, therefore, this simplifies the analysis as one potential source of substitution, and encouragement of capital flows does not in the main exist. However, the restrictions that matter are not in the capital movements themselves but in how those funds can be used to purchase physical assets. Constraints, or indeed incentives, apply to inward investment, to mergers and acquisitions and to the operation of multinational companies. Thus, freedom of capital movements is to some extent a myth if there are further constraints on how the funds can be used. Nevertheless, it is clear that restrictions are being progressively eliminated.

Of the other EU countries, Germany has probably had the most liberal capital controls. The controls in the Netherlands were also mainly intended to facilitate the inflow and outflow of capital (which was largely free) in the short run. There were, for example, restrictions on deposits from non-residents during the period 1972–5 to ease the pressure from high capital inflows. The Netherlands has been a net capital exporter in most recent years.

The situation in Belgium and Luxembourg, which can for the most part be treated as a single unit, has been complicated by a two-tier exchange-rate system. This comprised a 'free' capital market and a controlled market for current transactions. It is in France and Italy that the greatest controls have been found, although in the French case direct investment was one of the two main exceptions to the tight controls on the export of capital. As is to be expected, inflows by non-residents were less controlled than outflows by residents. However, inwards direct investment has been subject to control by the French government when the foreign control of the companies entailed has been thought unsuitable. In Italy also, restrictions related to flows other than direct investment, although, since import and export financing were exempted, it has been possible to get round many of the regulations.

The general direction of changes in controls on capital movements over the period has, of course, been for reduction, with final elimination for all but Spain, Portugal and Greece taking place in July 1990. Thus, as for trade flows, we would expect to observe a more rapid increase in direct investment abroad than in GDP itself. This duly occurred in the second half of the 1980s, but was not confined to the EU. However, the distribution of that investment by country of investor is unlikely to have been affected by any changes relative to the EU as such because liberalization has almost entirely been non-discriminatory. The influence of the EU on capital flows is as a result likely to be in changes in discrimination in the traded goods and services market. Increased trade flows are likely to involve changes in capital flows – to set up distribution networks and to establish local production as market penetration increases – although the direction of the change is still problematic as we cannot tell *a priori* the extent to which trade and direct investment might be substitutes rather than complements.

21.3   The determinants of direct investment

Investment flows between countries cannot really be treated in the same manner as investment within the economy because, although total investment can be explained through well-known relationships, the split between home and foreign expenditure, on an economy-wide basis, is not so clear. In the first place, magnitudes are sufficiently small for a limited number of decisions by individual companies to have a noticeable effect on the final outcome. Second, we are concerned in this case not just with what resources firms are prepared to put into capital for future production, but where they are going to site it. Most consideration, therefore, has been devoted to the problem at the level of the firm itself rather than through modelling of the components of the capital account of the balance of payments. Even within the confines of aggregate explanation there has been a tendency to avoid modelling direct investment flows directly, modelling them indirectly through the determination of the exchange rate as a sort of reduced-growth approach. (See Cuthbertson *et al.* (1980) for a discussion of this work.)

Such an approach may be appropriate for the explanation of portfolio investment, particularly since much short-term portfolio investment is usually described as speculative in nature, but it is much less useful for direct investment because of the degree of permanence embodied in the existence of physical capital held abroad. Such capital will tend to generate profits, which themselves form direct investment if they are not remitted to the investing country. Furthermore, such productive facilities have costs of closure and require a continuing stream of new investment to remain profitable, thus reflecting rather different considerations from those that might be thought appropriate to portfolio investment decisions and allocations.[7]

Perhaps the easiest route into the problem is to consider what the position of a supplier of a good on a world-wide scale would be. Other things being equal, sales to any particular foreign market would be affected by market size. Divergences from this simple position would occur as costs between the supplier and its competitors varied and according to the tastes in the particular market. Thus, in the case of the EU, one would expect greater trade between partner countries, first because of the discriminatory tariff and second because the countries tend to be near neighbours. Elaborating this to consider the problem from the point of view of the country rather than the firm, shares in markets will tend to be affected by the economic size of the supplying country as well. Such an approach leads to the sort of gravity models of trade put forward by Linnemann (1966) and Bluet and Systermanns (1968), and discussed in the context of the EU by Aitken (1973) and Mayes (1978). Here trade flows are primarily determined by the size of the supplying country, the size of the destination country, the transport cost between them and any special factors discriminating against or in favour of that specific flow. In these models the effects of the EU on trade flows can be measured as the ex post discrepancy between trade patterns observed for the EU and patterns seen for the rest of the world (allowing for distortions from other trading areas).[8]

The pattern of direct investment might be revealed by the other side of this same relation, namely, the trade model can show what desired trade is in a non-discriminatory world. The extent of the barriers and the degree to which actual trade diverges from this 'desired' level might then give an indication of the market that could be reached by production inside the trade barriers of the foreign country, hence giving the demand for direct investment abroad to set up the facilities to achieve the desired output. The distance between countries, since it contributes to transport costs, would also lead to direct investment rather than trade.

By this simple model, direct investment abroad among the EU countries would decrease as their tariffs on mutual trade fell, but that from (and in) third countries would increase: it would become increasingly difficult for these third countries to compete through trade as the costs of their partner competitors were reduced by the size of the tariff cut (although producers might choose to offset all or part of the gain). From this simple point of view, direct investment 'creation' and 'diversion' as a result of the lowering of tariff barriers on mutual trade by the EC would be of opposite sign to that of the corresponding trade creation and trade diversion. However, as with the two trading concepts, direct investment creation and diversion would be static effects lasting for a transitional period only.[9]

There is, moreover, a major distinction between investment and trade which would blur the relation just outlined, even if it were correctly identified. Previous direct investment results in the accumulation of capital in the form of a foreign subsidiary or associated company. Although, like all domestic companies in the foreign country, it will face increased competition for its products from companies in the other EC countries as tariffs are removed, the subsidiary may continue to make profits and to invest. Although no transfer of funds takes place with the parent company, any increase in assets of this form will be classified as direct investment according to the definition we have outlined. The foreign subsidiary is thus operating like any other domestic firm and it will participate in market growth like the other firms, thus continuing the upward path of direct foreign investment.

The behaviour of multinational companies is a reflection of variations in costs of inputs in various locations as well as the structure of markets they wish to serve. The pressure for the European Single Market came just as strongly from European multinationals as it did from political sources. Wisse Dekker, then head of Philips and the European Round Table of major companies, put forward a plan in January 1985 to achieve a single market in five years, i.e. by 1990, thus anticipating the White Paper. This globalization of markets reflects the nature of technology and the pace of change. New products have to be exploited quickly round the world rather than by tackling individual country markets one at a time.

These technical changes are complex, as, with just-in-time manufacturing and other improvements to reduce inventory costs and improve quality, links between companies have to be closer and quicker to execute. One facet of this is to cut down on the number of suppliers. This may actually lead to a concentration of production, disturbing some of the simpler trends of direct investment.

However, the simple model disguises a further facet of investment abroad. The development of foreign sales will normally follow an evolutionary pattern which starts with trading (unless the barriers are insurmountable) and is only followed by direct investment once the potential market looks worth while. Initial investment is more likely to be in distribution rather than manufacturing, as an agency is replaced by a more direct arrangement. Once the market is adequately covered, then production in the local market may follow.

Since there are economies of scale in production in many industries, the number of overseas subsidiaries may be strictly limited on a regional basis. Thus, US and Japanese firms may wish to invest in only one EU country and supply the rest of the EU from that base. Similarly, for the multinational company, it may be advantageous to split various parts of the manufacturing operation to take advantage of particular resources which are available in different countries – raw materials, cheap hydroelectricity, etc.

While there were technical, customs and other barriers between the member states, there was an incentive to invest in several member states rather than to concentrate in a single location. This pressure is weakened in the Single Market and there is some continuing incentive to reorganize.

This multinational structure of production and pressures to expand it have consequences for trade. The existence of subsidiaries rather than purely domestic firms tends to create trade between various parts of the multinational company. In 1980, 30% of exports covered by the Department of Trade inquiry across a sample of over 7,000 enterprises went to related enterprises abroad.[10] While this trade would not be zero if there were no related enterprises, one would expect it to be much smaller. Unfortunately, the statistics do not refer to related imports, so we cannot build up a symmetric picture. Almost two-thirds of motor vehicle exports went to related enterprises and US-controlled UK enterprises had over half their exports going to related enterprises.[11] On any basis, it is clear that the level of related exports is considerable when direct investment has taken place. The consequences for the structure of trade are therefore complex.

Most early empirical work on direct investment flows in the EU concentrated on inflows from the United States, partly because of the quality of data available. However, attention then turned towards Japan, whose direct investment increased dramatically in the second half of the 1980s. Japan replaced the United States as an investment 'threat', with a heavier political overtone, as the US economy has always been fairly open to return investments and acquisitions. Indeed, the level of recent direct investment in the United States has been so great that concern is being expressed, while Japan is a much more difficult economy to enter through either export or investment. Traditionally, US investment in Europe has had a strong element of takeover of existing enterprises. Japanese investment, on the other hand, tended to be greenfield. Arrangements with existing European firms tended to be joint ventures without Japanese majority control. This generated worries about technology transfer, the greenfield sites often being assembly operations of established products, while the joint ventures were sometimes accused of being more effective in transferring technology to Japan.

However, with the collapse of Japanese asset prices in the mid-1990s the pressure has changed. It has been outward investment by the EU, particularly in the United States in the face of better growth performance and prospects, that has caught the headlines. There has also been a substantial growth in cross-border investment within the EU.

It is noticeable that most modelling of inward investment relates to flows into the EU from outside, not to the flows within the EU itself. Yet it is these internal flows that should be of prime interest in the case of the Single Market. The studies of external flows suggest that there are three basic mechanisms at work. First, investment tends to increase with sales to the EU, i.e. supporting trade rather than substituting for it (Scaperlanda and Balough, 1983). Barrell and Pain (1993) suggest, following Vernon (1966), that there is an initial level of exports that is required before it becomes worth while setting up dealer networks and other downstream services. Second, investment takes place to overcome trade barriers (Culem, 1988; Heitger and Stehn, 1990) or anti-dumping duties (Barrell and Pain, 1993). However, overseas investors having a choice of locations and flows are also affected by relative costs and relative barriers. Thus, when anti-dumping actions were at their height in the United States in the mid-1980s, this acted as a spur to Japanese investment there. Finally, investment flows are crucially affected by the availability of funds in the investing country.

We can approach the problem of the effect of changes in relative trade barriers by examining the development of direct investment flows into and out of the EC over the period of UK accession. These flows are shown in aggregate in Table 21.2, from which it is immediately clear that the patterns of outward and inward flows for the United Kingdom are very different. In the period before accession to the EC, around two-thirds of direct investment in the United Kingdom came from the United States; but over the same period, UK investment in the United States varied between only one-tenth and one-quarter of total outward investment. However, outward investment itself was more than twice as large as inward investment, and thus simple proportionate comparisons give little idea of bilateral balances. The United Kingdom invested widely abroad in both the developed and the developing world whereas, not surprisingly, it is mainly the developed world which has invested in the United Kingdom. (As countries gain increasing maturity they tend to move through a number of phases of direct investment flows. Initially they have difficulty in absorbing investment, then the ability to absorb inward investment increases while outward investment is negligible. Eventually, although the ability to absorb inward investment increases, outward investment exceeds inward investment as overseas locations of production offer increasing advantages and sales networks are expanded. See Chapter 3 of El-Agraa (1988a) for a fuller explanation.)

As is clear from Tables 21.2 and 21.3, the United Kingdom has been the largest investor overseas in the EU and is the second largest in the world after the United States.[12] Only the Netherlands among other EU countries has been a net direct capital exporter over the last ten years, although West Germany had substantial net exports between 1975 and 1990. There was a clear surge in inward investment in the EU in 1973 and 1974, and more strikingly so in West Germany over the longer period of 1971–4. It was only in those four years that investment in Germany was greater than that in the United Kingdom. Investment in France, however, shows a strikingly different pattern, with France attracting the highest investment of all the EC countries in 1975 and 1981, and the second highest after the United Kingdom

Table 21.2 Direct outward and inward investment in the United Kingdom, 1970–85 (£ million)

	1970	1972	1974	1976	1978	1980	1982	1985
Outward								
Total	546	737	1 576	2 145	2 740	3 492	2 122	8 994
United States	134	105	401	378	969	1 784	1 414	3 187
% share	24.5	14.2	25.4	17.6	35.4	51.1	66.4	35.4
EU	88	256	367	497	579	482	−173	2 553
% share	16.1	34.7	23.3	23.2	21.1	13.8	−8.2	28.4
Belgium and Luxembourg	13	31	49	85	37	19	−5	295
Denmark	2	9	25	5	15	23	3	15
France	27	62	74	79	69	109	45	248
West Germany	20	64	109	176	113	376	47	290
Ireland	14	12	49	40	169	93	34	245
Italy	8	24	26	39	47	32	23	120
Netherlands	10	42	35	73	130	−168	−321	1 340
Inward								
Total	354	405	854	799	1 292	2 576	1 137	4 331
United States	223	266	410	550	807	1 678	372	2 323
% share	63.0	65.7	48.0	68.8	62.5	65.1	32.7	53.6
EU[a]	51	38	76	177	310	153	167	1 313
% share	14.4	9.6	8.9	22.2	24.0	5.9	14.7	30.3
Belgium and Luxembourg	6	3	6	22	42	15	13	81
Denmark	0	0	2	19	15	13	28	7
France	1	17	25	85	155	48	21	226
West Germany	15	5	34	34	69	34	58	44
Ireland	0	1	−7	37	23	24	20	6
Italy	4	8	6	11	−4	−16	6	73
Netherlands	25	6	11	−31	9	35	20	856

[a] Includes all eight countries shown throughout, although Denmark and Ireland were not members until 1973.

for the period 1977–80. At the other end of the scale is the very low level of direct investment in Italy. Thus, despite any attractiveness which may have existed from surplus and cheaper labour in Italy, this factor advantage has been met by labour outflow rather than capital inflow. Italy similarly has a low level of direct investment abroad, although it is still sufficiently large to show net capital exports over the last four years.

There is no uniform pattern of investment flows among the EU countries.

Table 21.3 Direct investment flows of EU countries, 1984–93 (ECU million)

	1984 Intra	1984 Extra	1984 Total	1987 Intra	1987 Extra	1987 Total	1990 Intra	1990 Extra	1990 Total	1993 Intra	1993 Extra	1993 Total
Outward												
BLEU	−635	60	−575	−1 655	−545	−2 200	−3 077	−1 175	−4 252	−2 698	−1 469	−4 167
Denmark	−122	−222	−344	−278	−219	−497	−649	−415	−1 064	15	−1 234	−1 219
Germany	−1 168	−2 978	−4 146	−1 610	−5 266	−6 876	−9 577	−5 369	−14 946	−8 869	−4 440	−13 309
Greece	−9	−48	−57	−1	−9	−10	−16	−3	−19	−3	−4	−7
Spain				−270	−227	−497	−1 023	−733	−1 756	−836	−796	−1 632
France	−827	−1 747	−2 574	−3 639	−3 483	−7 122	−11 409	−6 864	−18 373	−4 575	−4 644	−9 219
Irish Republic	−25	−100	−125	−65	−86	−151	−548	−22	−570	−353	32	−321
Italy	−642	−1 512	−2 154	−998	−495	−1 493	−3 250	−1 031	−4 281	−3 316	−1 530	−4 846
Netherlands	−1 262	−1 011	−2 273	−1 998	−3 607	−5 605	−6 459	−4 497	−10 956	−4 118	−3 155	−7 273
Portugal	−3	−11	−14	8	−6	2	−83	−26	−109	−151	−3	−154
UK	554	−9 627	−9 073	−1 730	−16 728	−18 458	−3 100	−392	−3 492	−5 935	−4 609	−10 544
EU12	−4 213	−17 407	−21 620	−12 344	−30 670	−43 014	−39 295	−20 527	−59 822	−30 844	−21 854	−52 698
Inward												
BLEU	749	64	813	1 265	693	1 958	6 454	1 355	7 809	5 749	3 343	9 092
Denmark	−8	32	24	−127	151	24	269	567	836	308	911	1 219
Germany	694	115	809	250	215	465	4 235	2 187	6 422	2 181	1 410	3 591
Greece	15	−27	−12	102	87	189	229	79	308	300	60	360
Spain				1 976	1 338	3 314	6 062	2 956	9 018	4 028	1 846	5 874
France	1 316	1 387	2 703	1 654	2 056	3 710	4 009	3 365	7 374	5 652	2 929	8 581
Irish Republic	141	−30	111	160	327	487	2 233	964	3 197	1 804	1 291	3 095
Italy	867	927	1 794	1 310	1 745	3 055	2 085	3 020	5 105	2 266	1 410	3 676
Netherlands	−1 098	139	−959	1 315	664	1 979	4 542	3 013	7 555	4 977	809	5 786
Portugal	99	135	234	230	97	327	1 135	586	1 721	758	284	1 042
UK	559	1 996	2 555	4 085	5 619	9 704	8 327	14 661	22 988	2 825	7 260	10 085
EU12	3 334	6 512	10 365	12 344	12 991	25 335	39 295	32 753	72 048	30 844	21 090	51 934

'Intra' refers to flows to or from other EU countries, 'Extra' to flows to or from the rest of the world.

Source: Eurostat, *European Union Direct Investment, 1984–93.*

However, what is clear in general is that outward direct investment has been rising considerably faster than in the United States, while inward investment has risen more slowly. Thus, while in 1981 and 1982 the United States was a net capital importer, the EU was a substantial exporter. Much of EU direct investment must therefore be directed outside the EU rather than to other EU countries, as is clearly the case for the United Kingdom.

Direct investment abroad, like domestic investment, is substantially affected by trade cycles. Thus the peak in 1973–4 coincided with the peak of a cycle and the sharp fall in 1975 with the consequence of the first oil crisis. Of course, 1980 is an exception, for although there was a sharp downturn in UK activity (preceding that of the world in general), it coincided with the removal of exchange controls, the effect of which we have already discussed. Accession to the EC may thus have its effects obscured by the trade cycle, as total direct investment could have been expected to increase at the same time as the transition period, purely because of the trade cycle. Looking at proportions may help to reduce this confusion. The most striking facets are, first, that there is no proportionate surge of investment by the other EU countries in the United Kingdom immediately following accession. There is some increase in 1976–8, but it is by no means clear that this represents any particular change in behaviour as wide year-to-year fluctuations have been observed earlier.

Outward investment by the United Kingdom in the EU, on the other hand, shows a very considerable surge *before* accession, in 1971–2, a process which is ended by 1974. Since the benefits from investment are usually not immediate, some anticipatory investment might have been expected to take full advantage of membership when it occurred. There is thus some change which could be viewed as evidence of an initial investment effect of membership in this one respect. Since we are dealing with proportions, changes in one area necessarily entail relative changes elsewhere. In the case of outward investment, the short-run decline was taken by the residual (non-EC, non-US) category – the same category that absorbed much of the surge in UK investment in the United States after 1977.

It is also not realistic to treat the EU as a largely homogeneous unit from the point of view of direct investment. For example, direct investment flows between the United Kingdom and the Netherlands were far larger than relative economic size would suggest both before and after accession to the EU. This presumably reflects, among other things, the number of Anglo-Dutch multinational companies. However, the nature of the relation is not clear as the major sectors of disinvestment in 1977, 1979 and 1980 were different (the disaggregate tables – tables 3.3 and 4.3 in *Business Monitor MA4*, 1980 – are rather difficult to interpret, as the sum of the parts is very different from the total, despite the existence of 'other' categories in both manufacturing and non-manufacturing industry).

Other differences between EU countries can readily be observed. Although Germany is economically larger than France and the United Kingdom, outward investment has followed that relation and inward investment has followed a different pattern, with French investment tending to be the larger. However, in both cases UK investment has been larger than the reverse flow. Irish investment in the United Kingdom, which was negligible before accession to the EU, has picked up substantially since. This is perhaps more difficult to explain than geographical nearness might imply, as the easy movement of funds was possible prior to accession. The total picture is thus rather confused, but it suggests that there has been no dramatic switch in the nature of direct investment in the United Kingdom as a result of its accession to the EU.

As noted earlier, between one-half and three-quarters of net investment abroad by the United Kingdom is composed of profits by overseas subsidiaries and associated companies which are not remitted to the United Kingdom. Net acquisition of overseas companies' share and loan capital is, partly by consequence, around one-sixth to one-third of the total, except for the two years 1970 and 1980 when it was about half. Unfortunately, these same figures are only available for EC countries for the period 1975–80, so we cannot make any contrast of the position 'before' and 'after' accession to the EU.[13]

The scale of net inward investment has meant that over the period 1973–9 there has been a steady increase in foreign ownership of UK firms, from 15% to 20% of net output in manufacturing. Not surprisingly, direct investment tends to be concentrated on larger firms, for reasons of information if for no other, and this 20% of output was produced by 2.5% of the total number of establishments in the United Kingdom. These firms also have a below average labour intensity (14% of total employment) and about average investment flow (21.5% of the total). This, however, gives us little indication about the nature of changes in investment flows which could be expected, although it does suggest that foreign-owned firms make an important contribution to productivity and investment for future growth, thus emphasizing the role that freedom of capital movement can play in increasing EU competitiveness.

It seems likely, therefore, that if we were to apply the same form of analysis as Scaperlanda and Balough (1983) to other flows of direct investment among the EU countries which involve the United Kingdom, we would not find any strong effect from changes in relative trade restrictions. Thus, while there may be some short-run effects, it does not appear likely that there are major changes in capital movements in the EU which involve the United Kingdom as there have been in trade patterns, as shown in Mayes (1983a), for example.

As mentioned earlier, figures on US direct investment are rather more detailed and hence we can get some idea of whether the United States changed either the extent of its investment in the EC relative to other areas, after the expansion of the EU in 1973, or the pattern of it among the member countries.

Prior to accession, the United Kingdom had a much larger proportion of US direct investment (Table 21.4) than its economic size alone would suggest. In the first few years after accession, although investment was still large in comparative terms, it was sufficiently lower to allow the United Kingdom's share of the existing stock of US investment in the EU to fall by nearly 4%. However, since 1977 the share of investment has been running ahead of the stock share again: hence the stock share has more than recovered its previous loss. The shares of other EU countries in the total stock have also changed only slowly. This is partly because of the scale of the change in the flow (investment) required to make any substantial change in the capital stock over a short period. Nevertheless, Germany and France have seen a substantial change in share, the Netherlands being the main 'gainer'. Changes are nothing like as striking as for trade flows. Again, it must be remembered that this evidence is very limited in itself, but it contributes to the overall picture.

Now that the Single Market is well developed, one might have expected to see a change in behaviour, but the position is largely unchanged. There has been no major diversion of US foreign direct investment to the EC. In fact, the share has

Table 21.4 US direct investment in the EU[a], 1973–98

	1973	1977	1980	1984	1987	1993	1995	1998
Total stock ($ million)	18 501	27 747	41 476	69 500	118 614	564 283	711 621	980 565
% of total stock in individual countries								
United Kingdom	35.7	31.9	33.9	41.2	38.0	45.42	39.95	41.78
Belgium and Luxembourg	8.1	9.4	8.6	7.2	6.6	7.20	8.47	7.92
Denmark	0.4	0.5	0.5	1.7	0.9	0.72	0.75	0.61
France	15.9	14.9	14.3	9.3	9.8	10.11	10.87	9.16
West Germany	24.0	25.3	23.3	21.4	20.8	15.31	14.32	10.02
Greece	–	–	–	–	–	0.17	0.15	0.15
Ireland	1.7	3.4	3.9	4.2	4.7	3.75	3.65	3.73
Italy	7.6	7.1	8.0	6.6	7.2	5.30	5.57	3.42
Netherlands	6.5	7.4	7.5	8.4	12.0	8.70	12.46	18.57
Portugal	–	–	–	–	–	0.53	0.57	0.34
Spain	–	–	–	–	–	2.78	3.23	3.00
US investment in EC as % of total US direct investment abroad	39.2	38.3	51.7	0.0	46.1	42.61	42.91	43.61
US investment in UK as % of US investment in the EC	29.7	39.2	58.5	[b]	17.6	–	–	–

[a] EC (9).
[b] Total investment in EC, $8 million; investment in UK, $891 million.
Source: US Department of Commerce, *Survey of Current Business*, Department of Industry.

remained remarkably stable. Expansion of the EC(9) to EC(12) shows little impact and investment is still flowing to traditional destinations.

Some of the most interesting evidence for a change in behaviour comes from the 1990 Special Edition of *European Economy* which explores the impact of the Single Market by industrial sector. Table 21.5 shows that there was a marked increase in mergers and acquisitions in the late 1980s in the EU. Of these, the proportion emanating within the EU but across the borders of the member states increased sharply in the final year.

The picture is weakened somewhat by the fact that this was part of a world-wide merger boom, but it is interesting that while joint ventures and minority investments also rose over the period it was on the whole nothing like the same scale.

More recently the European Commission has put together a database called AMDATA that provides a more detailed list of merger and acquisition activity involving EU enterprises. This increases the scale of activity markedly to an average of around 7000 transactions each year from 1989 to 1998. Not surprisingly since this picks up smaller transactions the proportion relating to purely national transactions is higher at around 60% in the years up to 1996. In 1996 to 1998 the proportion has fallen to around half, with the remaining 50% being split almost equally between cross-border transactions in the EU and cross-border transactions involving inward and outward flows with firms outside the EU altogether. Cross-

Table 21.5 Mergers and acquisitions

Year	Total (no.)	National (%)	EC (%)	International (%)
1983–84	155	65	19	16
1984–85	208	70	21	9
1985–86	227	64	23	13
1986–87	303	70	25	5
1987–88	383	56	29	18
1988–89	492	47	40	13

Source: European Economy.

border activity within the EU is thus still the smallest area of activity. During 1998 and early 1999 there was another boom in mergers and acquisitions, particularly in the financial and other services sector. Some transactions were extremely large, making the use of counts of numbers of transactions a very misleading indicator of activity. At least one of these, a hostile bid for Mannesmann of Germany by Vodaphone of the UK, has been viewed as a path-breaking entry into markets that were hitherto closed. If this turns out to be correct then direct investment across borders in the EU may increase substantially.

There has certainly been an increase in the cross-border movement of capital since the start of the 1992 programme. However, not all is due to that programme. Research by Molle and Morsink (1990) shows that foreign direct investment does respond to exchange rate changes, while the dramatic fall in share prices in Japan has led to a substantial reduction in the pace of their investment throughout the world including the EU. The pattern of this investment still strongly reflects the traditional pattern of ease of entry. It is by no means clear that entry by acquisition has become particularly harmonized or, indeed, greatly eased thus far. The market for capital has thus become freer, but linkages between commercial firms and the providers of capital remain which are little affected by the Single Market regulatory changes.

21.4 Labour movements

Although in the abstract economists tend to talk about the two main factors, capital and labour, in one breath, the differences in their behaviour from a practical point of view in the EU are enormous. At a simple level, it was noticeable that the total direct investment statistics for the United Kingdom in any one year were substantially affected by the behaviour of a single company. (For flows between any particular pair of countries, a single company can dominate the total effect.) Labour flows, on the other hand, are the result of the decisions of a large number of independent households (although actions by companies and communities can have a strong influence on these decisions). With some limited exceptions involving transient staff and actions in border areas, movement of labour simply involves a person shifting his residence from one country to another to take up a job in the second country. There is not the same range of possible variations as in the case of capital movements. There is also the great simplification that there is no equivalent problem of the relation between the financial flows (or retained earnings) and the physical capital stock. The number of foreign nationals employed will be the sum of the net inflows, without any revaluation problems and only a relatively limited difficulty for 'retirements' (through age, naturalization, etc.).

A major incentive to move is an income differential in real terms. However, it is not merely that the same job will be better paid in the second country; it may mean that the person moving will be able to get a 'better' job in the second country (in the sense of a different job with higher pay). There are severe empirical problems in establishing what relative real incomes are, not just in the simple sense of purchasing-power parities, but in trying to assess how much one can change one's tastes to adapt to the new country's customs and price patterns and what extra costs would be involved if, for example, the household had to be divided, and so on. This is difficult to measure, not just in precise terms for the outside observer, but even in rough terms for the individual involved. This sort of uncertainty for the individual is typical of the large range of barriers that impede the movement of labour, in addition to the wide range of official barriers that inhibit movement. Ignorance of job opportunities abroad, living conditions, costs, ease of overcoming language difficulties, how to deal with regulations, etc., is reduced as more people move from one country to another and are able to exchange experiences. Firms can reduce the level of misinformation by recruiting directly in foreign countries.

Even if it were possible to sort out what the official barriers are and to establish the relative real terms, there would still be a multitude of factors which could not be quantified but perhaps be given some implicit costs. These other factors involve differences in language, differences in customs, problems of transferring assets (both physical and financial), disruptions to family life, changing of schooling, loss of friends, etc. Of course, some of these factors could work in a favourable direction: it might be easier to find accommodation abroad, and setting up a new household and finding new friends might be an attractive prospect. All this suggests that margins in labour rewards between countries may be considerable in practice, even if free movement of labour is theoretically permitted. It should thus be no surprise to find that many differences in labour rewards exist among the EC countries. However, it would also be a mistake to think that there are no barriers in practice to employment in other EC countries. In the first edition of this book, El-Agraa and Goodrich (1980) set out the barriers which existed for one particular group: accountants. Skills and methods of working vary among the EC countries. There is a natural reluctance to accept those with different qualifications and experience, and considerable effort has gone into trying to make movement easier between countries.

Bourguignon *et al.* (1977) identify two other main determinants of the ease of movement in addition to the income differential (which they interpret in the narrow terms of monetary difference), namely, age and the attitude to risk. Their model, however, relates to the nature of the people who move: younger people, with less responsibility, who are willing to take risks. This is not very useful in the current context, where we wish to deal with the flows among the EU countries and the flows from non-members in aggregate. In our case, we need to consider variables which are of a similar aggregate nature: average per capita income, distance between countries, language differences, common land boundaries, etc. These factors, like those influencing capital movements, can be classified into three general groups which we could label 'push' factors, 'pull' factors and impediments. 'Push' factors relate to the tendency to emigrate – from poor living conditions, etc. – without regard to the destination; 'pull' factors correspondingly relate to the features attracting immigrants – availability of jobs, etc. – without regard to origin. The impediments are both general – applying to all migrants (both to exit, as in the East European countries before 1989, and to entry) – and specific: lifting of restrictions on members of other EU countries, for example.

It is clearly much more difficult to set out a model of labour flows when many of the restraints are not on a price basis (like a tariff), nor on a simple quantitative basis (like a quota). If, as appears to be the case for many non-member countries, there is excess supply of willing migrants at the prevailing income differentials and associated social difficulties of movement, we merely need to examine what determines demand (assuming, that is, that 'workers' cannot move without a work permit and that work permits are issued only in respect of specific jobs). In most cases this will be a combination of the wishes of firms as employers and governments as regulators. The British experience of regulation of inflows from the new Commonwealth is one example of the operation of the quantitative restrictions. However, movements of nationals of member states are not so readily determined. It may very well be that there is still excess supply in that flows take place when there is a job to go to. (Returning home, however, does not necessarily occur immediately a job is lost as some unemployment benefits will probably have accrued.) With unemployment averaging 10% or more in recent years and much higher in some member states, it is clear that in general there are few examples of excess vacancies that might encourage major flows of migration within the EU. Differences in benefits for the unemployed and indeed initial income losses from lost benefits in the home state are such that, in the face of the other language and cultural barriers, no major movements have taken place. Thus to a large extent the previous barriers had little effective impact. The position may change on further enlargement. In general we see an EU labour market in which mobility is permitted but does not occur readily, even within member states.

21.5 Labour flows in the EU

The official position in the EU is straightforward. Freedom of movement of labour was part of the framework of the Treaty of Rome itself. However, the original six EU member nations had to start from a position of considerable restrictions of labour movement, and it was not until 1968 that work permits were abolished and preferences for home country workers no longer permitted. The Single Market programme involved a range of measures to try to eliminate those fiscal barriers, not just for the worker but for the accompanying family as well. However, even within member states, changing jobs and location results in the loss of privileges: the number of days leave may increase with length of service, golf clubs may have waiting lists, etc. However, merely permitting labour mobility does not in itself either facilitate or encourage it. It is readily possible to make mobility difficult through measures relating to taxes and benefits which make a period of previous residence or contribution necessary for benefit.

The actual path of labour migration is heavily affected by overall circumstances. If an economy is growing and able to maintain 'full employment', it is likely to attract more labour from abroad for two reasons: first, because there are more job opportunities; and second, because there is less domestic opposition to immigration. In the period after the first oil crisis, when unemployment rose sharply and the EU economies moved into recession, there was much more resistance to the flow of labour between countries and an encouragement to reverse the flow. Although the position improved somewhat in the second half of the 1980s, unemployment is still a major problem and is likely to remain so for some time. The fall in the numbers of young people has eased the overall problem. Indeed, the problem for the future is the increasing dependency ratio as people live longer. Thus, there are simultaneous pressures to retire early in response to unemployment and higher real incomes, and to work longer as accumulated pension rights and wealth need to sustain a longer period of retirement.

There are several examples – Finland and Sweden, and Australia and New Zealand, for instance – where regular ebbs and flows in labour migration have been observed. Ebbs and flows in the EU seem to be less common to all countries with the exception of Ireland, where emigration has been common both to the United Kingdom and to the United States. Indeed, one of the main factors permitting the very rapid growth of the Irish economy in the 1990s has been a reversal of some of the previous outflow. While, as might be expected, the number of foreign workers fell after 1974 with the economic cycle in West Germany and the Netherlands, it rose in Belgium and Denmark. (There was little change in Italy and Luxembourg; suitable statistics on the same basis were not available from the Statistical Office of the EU for the remaining countries.)

The clearest feature of the development of the permitted mobility of labour among the EU countries was that restrictions were lifted on workers from other member countries rather than non-members. Nevertheless, as is clear from Table 21.6, only Belgium and Luxembourg have had a higher proportion of their foreign workers coming from within the EU than from outside it. The position has changed relatively little in recent years (see Table 21.7) with the exception of Germany, where there has been a small rise, and Luxembourg, where there has been a small fall in the number of non-nationals in the workforce. Looking at it from the point of view of country of origin, Table 21.8 shows that in all cases except Ireland only a very small percentage of the labour force had moved to other countries. (Those who have moved and changed their nationality will be excluded, but that is unlikely to make more than a marginal difference to the total.) With the exception of Denmark and Italy, it appears that size and percentage of working population abroad have an inverse relation. Looking at the same figures from a different point of view, with the exception of Luxembourg it is the EU countries with the lowest incomes that had the highest outward mobility. Greece, Spain and Portugal alter the picture fairly considerably. They all had above average numbers of people working elsewhere in the EU even before they joined, particularly Portugal. Thus, it might be expected that as restrictions were removed there would have been some expansion in movement. However, despite high levels of unemployment, there are no obvious signs of this.

Table 21.6 Foreign employees by nationality (thousands)

	West Germany		France			Netherlands			Belgium			Luxembourg			United Kingdom		
	1974	1986	1975	1986	1990–1	1974	1986	1990–1	1974	1986	1990–1	1974	1986	1990–1	1975	1981	1986
Total member countries[a]	718	498	305	590	608	51	76	72	130	187	231	31	52	53	323	313	398
of which:																	
Belgium	na	7	na	12	20	22	22	10	–	–	–	na	9	5	na	na	3
West Germany	–	–	na	15	21	na	16	21	na	6	11	na	6	4	na	na	18
Italy	341	188	230	85	90	na	7	na	83	61	101	11	8	9	na	na	57
Ireland	na	1	na	1	2	na	1	na	na	1	1	na	0	0	232	228	268
Total non-member countries[a]	1 613	1 048	1 595	583	696	66	92	104	77	46	96	17	3	6	468	447	423
Algeria	na	2	440	190	199	na	0	na	na	2	3	na	0	0	na	na	0
Morocco	na	14	130	132	152	9	25	na	na	17	35	na	0	0	na	na	4
Portugal	82	35	475	351	352	3	3	na	3	4	7	13	0	22	3	8	2
Spain	159	65	265	111	84	11	7	na	16	15	22	2	1	1	21	15	15
Tunisia	na	8	70	47	62	na	1	na	18	2	2	na	0	0	na	na	1
Turkey	618	499	25	23	52	22	36	40	11	10	24	na	0	0	4	6	7
Yugoslavia (former)	473	283	na	31	25	na	5	na	na	2	3	1	1	1	na	na	4
Total	2 331	1 547	1 900	1 173	1 304	117	169	178	207	233	327	48	55	59	791	760	821
As % of employees	9.0	6.9	9.2	6.4	na	2.5	3.6	na	5.4	6.2	7.8	31.2	37.4	na	3.2	3.2	3.8

[a] In 1986 and 1990–1 Spain and Portugal are included as members and not as non-members. Greece is treated as a member in 1990–1.

Sources: Eurostat, OECD, Labour Force Statistics, 1970–81.

Table 21.7 Labour force by nationality in EU member states, 1990 and 1995 (% share)

	National		Other EU		Non-EU	
	1990	1995	1990	1995	1990	1995
Belgium	94.6	92.2	5.2	5.4	0.2	2.5
Denmark	98.0	98.1	0.5	0.8	1.5	1.1
Germany	91.5	91.0	2.8	2.8	5.7	6.2
Greece	99.3	98.3	0.2	0.2	0.5	1.5
Spain	99.8	99.2	0.1	0.3	0.1	0.5
France	93.5	93.7	3.0	2.5	3.5	3.7
Ireland	97.4	97.0	2.1	2.4	0.5	0.6
Italy	na	99.6	na	0.1	na	0.4
Luxembourg	66.6	61.0	31.5	36.2	1.9	2.8
Netherlands	96.3	96.1	1.4	1.7	2.3	2.2
Portugal	99.4	99.6	0.1	0.2	0.5	0.2
United Kingdom	96.6	96.4	1.6	1.6	1.8	2.0
Austria	–	90.4	–	1.1	–	8.5
Finland	–	99.3	–	0.2	–	0.5
Sweden	–	95.9	–	2.0	–	2.1
EU	95.2	95.3	2.0	1.7	2.8	2.9

Source: *Labour Force Survey*, 1991, 1995.

Turning to inward flows, the picture is a little more complex. Luxembourg stands out with around a third of the working population coming from foreign countries. France, Germany and Belgium form a second group with a little less than 10% of their workforce from abroad; and the remaining countries have smaller proportions, down to negligible numbers in the case of Italy. Since Italy is a major exporter of labour to West Germany, France and Belgium, it is not surprising to find that it is a negligible importer since these flows do not represent an exchange of *special* skills, but a movement of workers with *some* skills towards countries with greater manufacturing employment opportunities.

Table 21.8 Foreign employees in the EC, 1976 (thousands)

	Nationals working in other member states	Domestic working population	(1) as a percentage of (2)
	(1)	(2)	(3)
Belgium	68	3 713	1.8
Denmark	7	2 293	0.2
West Germany	137	24 556	0.5
France	114	20 838	0.5
Ireland	455	1 021	44.6
Italy	694	18 930	3.6
Luxembourg	6	148	4.1
Netherlands	83	4 542	1.8
United Kingdom	61	24 425	0.2
Total EC	1 625	100 464	1.6
Spain	447	12 535	3.5
Greece	239	3 230	7.4
Portugal	569	3 279	17.4
Turkey	587	14 710	4.0
Yugoslavia	458		
Algeria	447		
Morocco	183		
Tunisia	85		
Others	1 392		
Total non-EC	4 407		
Total	6 032		

Source: Emerson (1979).

As only principal flows are shown in Table 21.6, it is difficult to make any generalizations across the whole range of behaviour. Some special relationships are apparent which relate to previous history rather than the EC as a determinant of the pattern of flows: former colonies in the case of France and the United Kingdom and, to a lesser extent, in the case of Belgium and the Netherlands; and the relationship between the United Kingdom and Ireland. The West German policy of encouraging foreign workers is clearly shown with the large numbers coming from Turkey and (the former) Yugoslavia. What is perhaps surprising is that despite the recruitment ban on countries outside the EU in 1973 the shares of member and non-member countries in number of foreign nationals employed in West Germany remained at approximately the same levels after 1974, the share of non-members falling only as some of the countries became members. The more recent data, provided in Table 21.7, show a fall in foreign labour in most countries by 1990 and stabilization thereafter. However, the switch is much larger for those from non-member states than for those from the other members.

At first glance it appears that labour, in proportionate terms, is rather less mobile than capital, particularly if one takes the United Kingdom as an example. The balance of labour and capital flows tends to be in opposite directions according to the development of the various economies. However, there are many specific factors overriding this general relation. The wealthier countries have attracted labour and invested overseas at the same time, thus helping to equilibrate the system from both directions. However, there is little evidence inside the EU that there are large labour movements purely as a result of the existence of the EU. Some movement between contiguous countries is to be expected, especially where they are small, and also movements from those countries with considerable differences in income, primarily Greece, Italy, Ireland, Portugal and, to a lesser extent, Spain. However, the major movements have been the inflow of workers from outside the EU, primarily into Germany and France. Thus, despite discrimination in favour of nationals of member countries, the relative benefits to employers (the ability to offer worse conditions, readier dismissal, lower benefits, etc.) and to employees (the size of the income gain and the improvement in living standards for their families) make flows from the lower income countries more attractive to both parties.

Worries about competitive exploitation of employees through reducing social protection (known colloquially as 'social dumping') have led the Community to develop the social dimension of the Single Market programme, expressed through the Charter of Fundamental Rights for Workers and the action programme for its implementation (see Chapter 19). The measures are specifically designed to ensure a 'single market' for labour in the EC. This does not necessarily mean that labour will be more mobile or labour markets more flexible as a consequence. Indeed, the UK government has argued forcefully that these actions might make it more difficult to eliminate pockets of unemployment and hence harm some of these workers whom it is designed to protect. As a consequence, the United Kingdom did not sign the Social Charter and would not accept the Social Chapter proposed for the Maastricht Treaty. As a result the Social Chapter was appended as a protocol to the treaty signed by the other 11 members. In practice the 'social dimension' has led to relatively limited changes in labour market legislation and the Social Charter has not yet been fully adopted. Even the Working Time Directive, which caused a major debate, was ultimately watered down to the point where it did not change much existing behaviour (see Chapter 19).

It should be no surprise that international mobility is limited when one sees the extent of reluctance to respond to economic stimuli for movement within countries. The existence of sharply different regional unemployment levels and regional wage differentials reveals the reluctance. In the United Kingdom the system of public sector housing is thought to aid labour rigidity. Possession of a council house in one district does not give any entitlement to one elsewhere. However, even for private sector house owners, negative equity and the very considerable transaction costs of sale and purchase act as a substantial restriction on mobility. Many of the social restraints also apply: disruption of the education of children, loss of friends, for example. The differentials in rewards or other incentives to move, therefore, have to be very considerable to induce international movement once a person has a family and a home. Mobility in the United States, on the other hand, is much greater, showing that the level of EU mobility is a facet of European society, not a necessary part of economic behaviour. Indeed, if movement had been more common it is unlikely that the member states would have been willing to permit a free flow under the 1992 programme.

21.6   Capital and labour movements combined

As was noted at the outset, factor movements cannot legitimately be examined without looking at the behaviour of the markets for internationally traded goods and services at the same time. Nor are the two factor markets independent. While the capital market has little of the characteristics of discrimination in favour of fellow members of the EU that form the basis of trading relationships between the countries, the decision over whether to invest abroad or at home is related to decisions over whether or not to export from the domestic market. Other things being equal, investment at home will generate more domestic employment, and indeed it may encourage an inflow of labour from abroad. Investment abroad, on the other hand, will tend to encourage employment in that country and a transfer of labour abroad as well.

The final outcome will depend very much upon whether there is full employment. When there is a shortage of skilled employees, or indeed a shortage of unskilled employees, at wages consistent with successful international competition, investment abroad, especially where costs are lower, may be a preferable substitute for labour-saving investment at home.

Clearly, within the EU there is less incentive to invest abroad where product prices are not subject to tariffs and hence no big gains in competitiveness can be made. Indeed, one would expect investment from non-members to increase because of the increased size of the common market. Thus, capital flows could be expected to change in the opposite direction to trade flows, with both an investment-reducing equivalent of trade creation and an investment-increasing switch from third countries as an equivalent to trade diversion. Controls on labour movements have been removed in a manner that favours inflows from EU members rather than non-members.

Running across these considerations are two other factors. Labour can be expected to move from where rewards are lower to where they are substantially higher (to cover the costs of moving), as is evidenced by the outflow from Italy. Second, capital investment could be expected to move to areas where labour costs are much lower, but this movement has been much less marked. Instead, capital movements have tended to follow sales opportunities and other locational advantages rather than just labour cost. In so far as labour and capital movements do not take place, factor price differentials will continue to persist, assuming they are not eliminated by trade flows, and the allocation of resources among the EU countries, and indeed between them and non-members, will be inefficient.

In recent years Krugman and Venables (1993) *inter alia* have argued that the pattern of location of industry will be rather different from that initially expected, as there are several factors that lead to increasing economies of scale and agglomeration, at least over a range above the position applying in the early 1990s. Proximity to the main markets, networks of suppliers, skilled labour, etc. may actually attract firms to the main centres of existing industry even though costs may be higher, thus encouraging labour and capital to move in the same direction and exacerbate rather than ease existing disparities.

This idea of clustering of activity both in terms of location and in range of industrial activity has a long history, although it has been heavily popularized by Porter (1990) more recently. Porter offers not so much an explanation of why activity concentrates, as an encouragement to governments to reorient their policies to encourage the process so that they can reap a competitive advantage. The key to this comes from the exploitation of the immobile and less mobile factors of production such as land, physical and business infrastructure and services and, particularly in the case of the EU, highly skilled labour. The increasing returns occur because the process feeds on itself – endogenous growth.

EU structural policy has followed this line of argument (see Chapters 18 and 19) using this policy as a means of helping disadvantaged regions compete through improving public and private infrastructure and human skills. Thus there have been counter-forces to those of increasing concentration in existing centres that market forces alone might have fostered.

This process of concentration has clearly been followed in practice in the EU but it is by no means the only force for development, as the Irish economy demonstrates. Here high technology and IT-based industries have been able to flourish where their location was not very important, aided by favourable macroeconomic, wage bargaining and other direct incentives. High-value, low-weight items, with a world-wide market, are not so dependent on location but do require skilled labour. Similarly call centres, internet services and computer software can be located in any lower-cost region and their results transmitted electronically immediately. The 'new economy', widely talked about for the United States, enables a society to change much more rapidly and hence grow faster without hitting traditional inflationary pressures from the labour market.

While there are only limited signs that the 'new economy' has taken hold in the EU, except perhaps in Ireland and Finland (with the phenomenal development of Nokia), there is the potential for it to do so. If it does we can expect that there will be a further reason for labour to remain fairly immobile.

Until the downturn in the European economy, inefficiency would have been expected to take the form of insufficiently capital-sensitive investment, with a labour inflow being used to avoid restructuring. This would shift some more labour-intensive processes abroad to more labour-intensive EU members, or even outside the EU. Limits on labour mobility decrease this tendency, but with high levels of unemployment currently, and for much of the foreseeable future in the EU, it seems unlikely that much further encouragement to move will take place. Indeed, the pressures are the other way round. There is a danger that protectionism will apply not just to goods but to factor movements as well. The failure to start a new round of multilateral negotiations on reducing protection in Seattle in late 1999 may be indicative of a gap between the liberalizing rhetoric and the more restrictive actions. In so far as the EU increased the ease of factor mobility, it may be able to maintain a competitive advantage over other countries which resort to this form of protection. It is not surprising, therefore, that third countries have been keen to operate inside the EU and are using just that freedom of capital movement to achieve it.

The experience with migration from Central and Eastern Europe since 1989 has increased the caution over opening up the labour market more widely. It reinforces the suspicion that labour movement has been widely regarded as a key ingredient of European union largely because it has not occurred on a substantial scale.

Notes

1. Indeed, it is the concept of control that distinguishes direct from portfolio investment. The technical definition adopted by the IMF (Balance of Payments Manual, fourth edition, 1977) is 'Direct Investment refers to investment that adds to, deducts from or acquires a lasting interest in an enterprise operating in an economy other than that of the investor, the investor's purpose being to have an effective voice in the management of the enterprise'. Clearly, this distinction can be made only by asking companies themselves about their overseas investment – by the Department of Trade, the Bank of England and the British Insurance Association, in the case of the UK.

2. 'Covered' in the sense that the forward exchange rate premium or discount is taken into account in the computation of the difference in interest rates between countries.

3. This description of capital flows 'balancing' trade flows could equally be phrased as trade flows 'balancing' capital flows. They are two sides of the same coin. If there is a differential in rates of return capital will be attracted into a country, and this will raise the exchange rate, thereby tending to encourage imports and lower exports and hence balancing the capital movement.

4. As was pointed out by Padoa-Schioppa *et al.* (1987), it is not possible to run a stable system with fixed exchange rates, free capital movements, free trade and independent fiscal policies. One or other of these must be constrained (the last in the case of an integrated single market).

5. In each case the transactions shown are the net transactions of the particular category of investor. Thus, outflows are net investments by UK firms abroad or by UK residents in foreign securities, and inflows are net investments by foreign companies in UK companies, etc. A positive value for net portfolio investment overseas from the UK thus means that the portfolio of foreign assets has been run down (net disinvestment).

6. There are, of course, differential restraints on the activities of financial institutions depending upon whether or not they are registered within the EU.

7. The data on capital flows (and stocks) are notoriously unreliable, which inhibits empirical work. For example, the distinction between debt and equity can sometimes be blurred when there are tax advantages in following one form of finance rather than another.

8. The analysis would be more effective if the nature of the barriers to trade and the size of the distortion through preferential tariffs could actually be inserted in the equations as well.

9. The analogy between trade diversion and creation, and investment diversion and creation, should not be pushed too far as the trade concepts are welfare changes, not just changes in trade patterns.

10. *Business Monitor MA4* (1980), table 6.3 (oil and diamond companies are excluded). The equivalent figure in the 1976 survey was almost identical.

11. But the number of firms in the sample is very small in some cases, so the results should be treated with care.

12. On an annual basis, the UK was overtaken by Japan, but the UK's outstanding stock of foreign direct investment was still larger.

13. Unremitted profits as a percentage of total net outward investment by the UK in the EU (all countries) were in 1975 74 (40)%, 1979 112 (71)%, 1982 40 (80)% and 1985 122 (55)% (*Business Monitor*).

22 External trade policy

M. BRÜLHART and D. McALEESE*

The external trade policy of the EU impinges on over one-fifth of world trade. Hence, an understanding of the principles and practice of the Union's trade policy, the Common Commercial Policy (CCP), is of vital importance to any student of the global trade environment. The World Trade Organization's (WTO) biennial publication *Trade Policy Review of the EU* provides insight into how trade specialists view the EU and, no less important, how the EU sees its own role. Ongoing research on the CCP has addressed both broad themes and detailed aspects of the Union's trade policy (Heidensohn, 1995; Sapir, 1998; Memedovic *et al.*, 1999).

Some special features of the CCP should be mentioned at the outset. First, trade policy touches on an ever-wider range of economic issues. In the early years of the CCP, discussions concentrated almost uniquely on the level and structure of the common external tariff (CET). These questions could be analysed within the established framework of trade theory. As tariffs were reduced in successive rounds of multilateral trade negotiations to near insignificance, other policy areas have become increasingly relevant to international trade: non-tariff barriers, implicit export subsidies, intellectual property, taxation, competition policy, labour standards, consumer protection and environmental policy, to mention but a few.

Second, the CCP is inherently complex, being the outcome of different national legacies and numerous compromises at Council and Commission level. The Union is still in the process of defining its identity and forging solidarity among its members. Change in the CCP involves hard bargaining, not just between the EU and non-member states but between member states as well. The Union's approach to trade matters can therefore appear piecemeal, and its untidy collection of regional and national trade agreements makes generalization difficult. For example, traditional ties with former colonies go far towards explaining the complex series of preferential trade arrangements with African, Latin American and Mediterranean countries.

Third, EU policy makers frequently remain more concerned with the interests of their particular member state than with those of the Union as a whole. Hence, the impact of trade on the constituent national economies and regions weighs more heavily in determining trade policy than in a unitary system. For example, in the United States, an employee who moves to San Francisco after being made redundant in Dallas enters the national statistics as a happy example of internal mobility. An Italian who moves to Munich after losing a job in Milan is seen in a different light. To the Italian government, emigration would have overtones of domestic policy failure and, to the German government, the inflow of Italian workers might be seen as exacerbating Germany's unemployment problem. Any analysis of the

---

* The authors are grateful to Carol Boate for valuable research assistance.

EU's trade regime therefore has to take account of the particular political priorities and sensitivities prevailing in the Union.

The background to EU trade policy is different in many respects from the trade policy of other major trading groups. For this reason alone, it constitutes a worthwhile subject of study. The evolving nature of the EU in a context of continuous globalization of the economy makes such a study even more challenging and important. In recent years, the CCP has been subject to far-reaching changes, induced both by initiatives within the EU, such as the completion of the Single Market and the establishment of the Euro, and by initiatives on a multilateral stage, related to the implementation of the Uruguay Round (1995) and to preparations for a Millennium Round.

This chapter is divided into five sections. The first presents an overview of the principles and policy instruments of the CCP. The second describes the pattern of trade between the EU and the outside world. The third considers EU trade policy specifically towards its main trading partners. The fourth contains an analysis of trade policy issues which are coming to the forefront in ongoing trade negotiations. The concluding section considers the future development of the CCP.

22.1 The CCP

The EU is an association of states with a particular legal character. It is regarded as a community in international law, not as a nation, although it possesses some features of 'nationality'. Many EU laws and regulations are enforceable in member states without requiring ratification by national parliaments. These transferred sovereign powers include foreign trade and the right to conclude trade agreements with different countries (see Chapters 1–3).

A common trade policy for the EU is *necessary*, because in its absence the purpose of a common market will be frustrated. For instance, if member states had different tariffs, third countries would export to the member state with the lowest tariff. Once inside the Union, the goods would then enjoy free passage to states with higher tariffs. High-tariff member states would of course object and would be tempted to impose restrictions on imports from the low-tariff member state. But such barriers would frustrate the whole concept of a single market. A similar situation would arise if one member state applied trade rules, or provided export assistance, more liberally than another member state. Hence, a common market needs to be complemented by a single commercial policy. A common trade policy, moreover, can be *desirable* in so far as it strengthens the bargaining power of the Union in negotiating with its trading partners. Small member states in particular benefit from this: on their own they would be more vulnerable to pressure from larger countries.

22.1.1 EU decision-making procedures and WTO constraints

The key provisions of the CCP are contained in Articles 110–16 of the Treaty of Rome. Article 110 contains the well-known aspiration:

> By establishing a customs union between themselves member states aim to contribute, in the common interest, to the harmonious development of world trade, the progressive abolition of restrictions on international trade and the lowering of customs barriers.

The cornerstone of the CCP is Article 113. It sets out the important rule that:

> the CCP shall be based on uniform principles, particularly in regard to changes in tariff rates, the conclusion of tariff and trade agreements, the achievement of uniformity in measures towards the liberalisation of export policy and in measures to protect trade such as those to be taken in the case of dumping or subsidies.

Article 113 functions on the basis of qualified majority voting in the Council (see Chapter 2). Subject to the Council's approval, the Commission is empowered to conduct negotiations in consultation with a special committee appointed by the Council for this purpose, the 'Article 113 Committee', and within the framework of such directives as the Council may issue to it. Association agreements concluded with third countries must in addition be ratified by the European Parliament. The EU has observer status at both FAO and the United Nations and negotiates on behalf of member states at the WTO.

The evolution of the CCP has been marked by continuing efforts by the Commission to centralize power over external relations policy in Brussels. The objective is to make the conduct of the CCP easier to adjust, quicker to implement and more efficient overall. The establishment of the Single Market marked a serious erosion of individual member states' power over trade policy. The free *internal* circulation of goods and services that the Single Market promised could be viable only if there were uniform and transparent procedures governing *external* trade. And who more appropriate to determine such procedures than the European Commission? In 1994, the European Court of Justice confirmed the Commission's exclusive competence to conduct international negotiations on trade in goods (see Chapter 3). The Commission's position, however, was considered less clear in the case of negotiations related to services and intellectual property, where decisions require a unanimous instead of a majority vote. This division of competencies was confirmed by the Amsterdam summit in 1997.

Paradoxically, at the same time as the Commission's power was increasing in relation to member states, its discretion over trade policy was becoming progressively more circumscribed by the terms of successive multilateral trade agreements. The latest such agreement, which resulted from the Uruguay Round, committed the EU to an extensive range of trade-liberalizing measures and other obligations, which are monitored and enforced by the newly established WTO. The three most visible trade-liberalizing measures were:

- an average 38% tariff reduction on imported manufactures;
- the conversion of import barriers on agricultural goods into equivalent tariffs, and the gradual reduction of these agricultural tariffs by 36%;
- the phasing out of quantitative restrictions on textile and clothing imports.

But the Union's international commitments go well beyond removal of import barriers. Membership of WTO binds it to wide-ranging codes of conduct dealing with such matters as export subsidies, intellectual property, rights of establishment and disputes settlement and imposes many other obligations. As the world trade system has become increasingly subject to rules, the EU's discretion to dictate the terms on which third countries can trade with it has diminished. A topical example would be the conditions a regional trade agreement between the EU and a third party must satisfy if it is to obtain WTO approval. The balance of power in trade matters has tended to shift over time from Brussels to Geneva (where the WTO has its headquarters).

The Commission is legally obliged to defend the commercial interests of the EU. Under the Trade Barriers Regulation (1994), any EU firm, industry or member state can request the Commission to conduct an investigation against third countries which are believed to be in breach of WTO rules, and, if necessary, to initiate a dispute-settlement procedure at the WTO. The Commission also plays a proactive role. As part of its 'Market Access Strategy', launched in 1996, the Commission has sought information on trade barriers facing EU products in non-EU markets (over 700 'obstacles' have been identified so far). This information has been assembled in a market access database, made publicly available on the Internet (http://mkaccdb.eu.int).

22.1.2 Instruments of the CCP

The principles of the CCP are put into effect by means of *trade policy instruments* and *trade agreements*. First, we survey the principal instruments of EU trade policy, while trade agreements with non-EU countries are discussed in section 22.1.3.

We can distinguish four main policy instruments which the Commission can employ to influence external trade: (a) tariffs, (b) quotas, (c) voluntary export restraints (VERs) and (d) anti-dumping measures (see Table 22.1). This list is by no means exhaustive. *Export promotion* measures might also be included, such as the Japan export promotion programme (WTO, 1997), though most of them have been phased out. Also *trade sanctions* can be imposed on countries for political reasons. *Countervailing duties* can be imposed where there is evidence of export subsidies in third countries. *Safeguard clauses* under WTO provisions allow signatories to take special measures in order to protect certain overriding interests. *Rules of origin* determine the proportion of the value of a product that must be added locally for a product to qualify as originating from a particular country. Such rules are important in the context of preferential trade agreements. The higher the required local content, the lower is the degree of preference granted to an exporting country. Finally, it is important to note that the boundary between trade measures and other economic policies has become increasingly blurred. Direct trade interventions, therefore, comprise only part, albeit a highly visible and significant one, of the EU's policies influencing external trade.

(a) Tariffs

The most visible element of EU trade policy is the *common external tariff* (CET). In 1995, the overall average EU tariff rate stood at 9.6% of import values (WTO, 1995b). Tariffs on agricultural imports were higher (26% on average); and tariffs on manufactured imports were lower (6% on average). These average rates have since been reduced by roughly one-third under the terms of the Uruguay Round. The revenues from import duties flow into the general EU budget, after a 10% deduction retained to cover the costs of customs administration by the importing country (see Chapter 16).

Tariff averages mask substantial variation of tariff levels across commodities. For example, most EU industrial imports enter the EU market free of tariffs. Also, following the Information Technology Agreement signed in March 1997, the EU phased out remaining tariffs on most computer and telecom-related goods. Extension of the product coverage and inclusion of non-tariff barriers (NTBs) are likely to follow in the next such agreement. At the other extreme, 'sensitive'

Table 22.1 Major instruments of EU trade policy

Policy instruments	EU policy	WTO regime
Tariffs	• *overall* average: 9.6% of import value in 1995 • average for *industrial goods*: 6% of import value in 1995, 3% in 2000 • most industrial imports free of tariffs • average for *agricultural goods*: 26% of import value in 1995, 18.4% in 2000 • peaks on some food products in excess of 50% of import values • tariffs on computer and telecom-related goods phased out	• non-discrimination (equal tariffs for all WTO members, except for regional integration agreements and preferences granted to developing countries) • average tariffs on manufactures to be reduced by 38% in 2000 and average tariffs on agricultural goods by 36% in 2001
Quotas	• no national quotas since Single Market • Multifibre Arrangement: quota restrictions on clothing and textiles to be phased out between 1995 and 2005 • quotas on bananas; iron and steel from former Soviet Union; various manufactures from China	• banned in principle under WTO rules (Article XI) • exceptions for agricultural goods and balance-of-payments considerations
Voluntary export restraints	• car imports from Japan (expired in 1999) • VERs no longer a feature of EU trade policy	• banned under WTO rules if negotiated or enforced by governments • to be phased out under Uruguay Agreement
Anti-dumping measures	• imposed if dumping margin and material injury to domestic industry are detected • 141 measures in force end 1997 • cover 0.3% of total EU imports	• allowed under WTO rules

Sources: WTO (1995b, 1997), CEU (1997b).

imports such as trucks, cars, clothing and footwear continue to attract high tariffs, in excess of 10% *ad valorem*. The peaks are even more pronounced in the agricultural sector. Tariffs on meat, dairy products and cereals were greater than 50% in 1997.

The restrictiveness of a tariff system depends not just on the level of tariffs but also on the degree of tariff escalation. A tariff structure is escalated when tariffs on imports of raw materials and intermediate products are lower than those on finished goods. Such escalation affords downstream activities higher effective protection than the nominal rates suggest. Under the Uruguay Round, tariff cuts were generally larger on high tariffs, so that the degree of escalation was reduced substantially. Nevertheless, significant escalation remains in textiles and clothing as well as in agricultural and food products (WTO, 1997).

(b) Quotas

Theory teaches that import quotas give rise to particularly severe welfare costs. The EU is phasing out these restrictions, but they still apply to some products such as textiles, clothing, bananas, and iron and steel imports. The most important quotas are those imposed on imports of clothing and textiles, under the Multifibre Arrangement (MFA, 'Agreement on Textiles and Clothing' since 1995). These products have effectively been exempted from GATT disciplines since 1974 (Hoekman and Kostecki, 1995). The Single Market has forced EU members to replace national quotas by Union-wide restrictions, since monitoring of national quotas was no longer possible after intra-EU border controls were dismantled. This has led to a considerable streamlining and easing of quantitative restrictions (Pelkmans and Carzaniga, 1996).

Also, the EU is committed to phasing out all MFA quotas by 2005. Import quotas on the EU's eastern neighbours which have signed Europe Agreements have already been eliminated. However, quotas remain in place for imports from non-WTO countries such as textile-related and other basic manufactures from China and steel products from Russia, Ukraine and Uzbekistan.

(c) Voluntary export restraints

A VER is an agreement between an exporter and importer whereby the former 'voluntarily' undertakes to limit the quantity of goods consigned to the importing country. Such agreement can be obtained through political pressure from the importing country (e.g. with the threat of initiating anti-dumping procedures), or it can be genuinely voluntary, when import demand is sufficiently inelastic to increase the exporter's profits after a reduction in the quantity of exports (Tharakan, 1995). Although VERs negotiated or enforced by government are illegal under WTO law, no case has as yet been brought before the WTO dispute-settlement panel. Perhaps this is because VERs, by allowing an increase in price, create rents which the two key players, exporters and import-competing domestic producers, can each enjoy at the expense of consumers. A point often made in trade policy discussion is that the interests of the consumer are difficult to organize and often tend to be under-represented in trade negotiations.

An example of a VER was the 'consensus' on EU car imports reached with Japan in 1991 (WTO, 1995b). Under this regime, ceilings for Japanese car exports were set annually, based on 'supply forecasts' and on the principle that Japanese exports may account for no more than two-thirds of market growth or for no less than two-thirds of any market shrinkage. This VER expired at the end of 1999. In the past, imports of video recorders, cotton fabrics and forklift trucks have also been subject to VERs (see El-Agraa, 1995).

(d) Anti-dumping measures

As visible trade barriers are being dismantled, other ways of restricting imports in 'sensitive' sectors are resorted to. Excessive recourse to anti-dumping measures is an example of such practice. Dumping is defined as the selling in export markets below some 'normal' price. The 'normal' price of a good is commonly defined as the price prevailing in the exporter's home market. Such divergences could arise for several reasons: predatory pricing and government subsidies to export activities among others. The imposition of countervailing measures is permitted under WTO rules, if dumping 'causes or threatens material injury to an established industry ... or materially retards the establishment of a domestic industry'. Complex pricing policies and adjustment for indirect cost factors leave a degree of arbitrariness in the calculation of dumping margins and 'material injury'.

The EU has had frequent resort to anti-dumping measures. Over the period 1988 to 1997, the number of anti-dumping measures in force fluctuated between 139 and 177 (CEU, 1997b). Anti-dumping actions take one of two forms: (a) anti-dumping duties equivalent to the dumping margin or (b) undertakings by exporting countries not to sell to the EU below an agreed price.

Probably the most high-profile anti-dumping actions currently in force relate to imports from non-market and transition economies, notably China and Russia, and to a select group of Asian developing countries. Views differ as to the protective impact of anti-dumping measures. Defenders of EU anti-dumping practice point out that the number of actions taken has fallen slightly over the 1990s, and that these measures affected a mere 0.3% of imports to the EU in 1997 (WTO, 1997). Some European industrialists would argue that the anti-dumping procedures are expensive to invoke and reach conclusions on the need for action only when irreparable injury has been done to the import-competing industry. Critics, however, have accused the Commission of bending the figures in favour of anti-dumping complaints (see Tharakan and Waelbroeck, 1994). They argue that the mere threat of anti-dumping procedures can act as a deterrent to exporters. Frequent investigations, even if they result in no definitive measures, can amount to a form of harassment of exporters, because they create uncertainty and costs, sometimes referred to as a 'trade chilling' effect (Tharakan, 1999). These effects cannot be quantified, but anti-dumping policy contains at least the potential for protectionist abuse and therefore needs to be monitored carefully. This is all the more true since there is growing use of anti-dumping measures by countries such as Mexico, South Africa, Korea and Turkey that traditionally were the targets rather than the initiators of such measures. In 1997, the EU accounted for 137 of the total of 880 anti-dumping actions notified to the WTO, well below the US figure of 302 (WTO, 1998).

22.1.3 Regional trade agreements

The EU has developed an elaborate web of preferential trade agreements, mainly with neighbouring countries and former colonies. WTO rules allow the formation of such regional trade agreements (RTAs) as long as trade barriers on average do not rise after integration, tariffs and NTBs are eliminated within the area on 'substantially all' intra-regional trade and the project is notified to the WTO in time for it to determine whether these conditions are satisfied (see Chapter 1, especially its Appendix).

The EU's penchant for RTAs is apparent from Table 22.2. The most favourable treatment is given to the 121 countries that fall into the least developed category, or are members of Lomé (see below and Chapter 23), or have completed bilateral trade agreements with the EU. Countries at the top of the hierarchy (Turkey, the Europe Agreement countries) enjoy free access to the EU market for industrial goods. Next come the middle-income and poor countries that benefit only from the

Table 22.2 The EU's preferential trade system

Trading partners	EU preferences
Turkey	Customs union for industrial products since 1996; preferential access for some agricultural products
European Economic Area, EEA (Norway, Iceland, Liechtenstein)	Extension of most aspects of the Single Market since 1994; free trade area (rules of origin necessitating some continuation of customs checks)
Europe agreement countries (Bulgaria, Czech Republic, Estonia, Hungary, Latvia, Lithuania, Poland, Romania, Slovak Republic, Slovenia)	Abolition of tariffs and quotas on industrial products since the mid 1990s; preferential access for some agricultural products; creation of bilateral free trade areas
Switzerland	Reciprocal abolition of tariffs and quotas on industrial products since 1973; bilateral treaty on liberalization of transport markets, agricultural trade, public procurement and labour markets to enter into force in 2001
Israel	Reciprocal abolition of tariffs and quotas on industrial products since 1975; free trade area with Mediterranean countries envisaged for 2010
Cyprus and Malta	Partial abolition of tariffs and quotas on industrial products since 1973/1970; customs union envisaged with Cyprus for 2002
Mediterranean countries (Algeria, Egypt, Jordan, Lebanon, Morocco, Palestine, Syria, Tunisia)	Non-reciprocal free access for most industrial products, raw materials and 'traditional' agricultural exports; free trade area envisaged by 2010
African, Caribbean and Pacific (ACP) countries (70 countries covered by Lomé Convention)	Non-reciprocal free access for industrial products and agricultural goods not covered by CAP; preferential access for agricultural goods covered by CAP
Generalized System of Preferences (GSP) beneficiaries (145 developing countries)	Reduced tariff rates depending on the 'sensitivity' of products, subject to safeguard clause; tariff-free access for industrial and some agricultural goods from 45 'least developed countries'

Sources: WTO (1995b, 1997), Pelkmans and Brenton (1999).
Note: Free trade areas envisaged with MERCOSUR (target date 2005), Mexico (for completion in 2007) and South Africa (for completion in 2012).

non-contractual discretionary preferences of the standard Generalized System of Preferences (GSP). Further down the hierarchy are countries which are members of the WTO but not of the GSP (such as the United States and Japan), while the EU's markets are least accessible to countries that belong to none of these groups (such as China and Russia). The EU's appetite for regional trade deals seems nowhere near its saturation point yet. In 2000, there were advanced projects for free trade areas with Mexico (to be completed in 2007), South Africa (to be completed in 2012) and with the countries of MERCOSUR (target date of 2005).

Messerlin (1999) has argued that the institutional set-up of the EU has resulted in a bias of trade policy towards bilateral or regional agreements rather than multilateral liberalization. Two reasons stand out. First, the EU authorities have only limited competence to conduct foreign policy; hence trade agreements tend to be used as a substitute for foreign relations of the EU. Second, the organization of the Commission also used to favour bilateral trade deals, since the breakdown of the trade portfolio along geographical lines provided incentives for Commissioners to arrange specific agreements with 'their' preferred countries. However, in the current Commission, revamped under Romano Prodi in September 1999, the responsibility for trade relations is concentrated in a single directorate, which should be less biased in favour of bilateral trade deals.

Why do the EU's trade partners participate in these RTAs? The question is relevant, since, for many partner countries, losses from trade diversion cannot be ruled out. Their level of industrial protection remains high (average tariffs of around 30% are found in the Mediterranean countries) and, as tariffs are reduced under the RTAs, EU products could replace lower-cost imports from third countries. Yet, fear of trade diversion has not deterred countries from seeking RTAs with the EU. There are three possible reasons for this. First, Europe is often their main export market and RTAs are perceived as providing much greater security of market access than a multilateral agreement. Member countries see themselves as having an inside track on policy changes that could impact on their exports. Another important attraction of RTAs is that they can act as a means of 'locking in' domestic policy reforms. RTAs bind partner governments to trade rules, outlaw the arbitrary subsidization of favoured industries and make possible better economic policy governance. The gains from this can vastly outweigh any trade-diversion losses. Third, the trade aspects of RTAs are often seen as the first step in a long path towards closer integration with the EU, in some cases leading to full membership and involving major dynamic gains (Pelkmans and Brenton, 1999).

As world trade becomes more liberalized, the preferential value of RTAs will diminish. All WTO members will enjoy relative freedom of access to Europe's market. EU products might, however, suffer from discrimination created by other RTAs. To avert this danger the EU will seek conformity across the board to WTO rules. As a result, its own RTAs are becoming less discriminatory, more insistent on reciprocity from the partner country and more broadly focused than in the past. They address regulatory issues, right of establishment, foreign investment, competition policy, financial aid and technical co-operation as well as standard tariffs and import barriers *per se*. Thus, opposition to RTAs on the grounds of their breaking the non-discrimination principle of the GATT has diminished considerably over the years.

22.1.4 Estimated welfare effects of the CCP

Traditionally, there are two methods of estimating the restrictive effects of trade policy. One way is by measuring the extent to which trade barriers raise the domestic selling price of imported goods. In the case of tariffs we estimate average tariff levels; in the case of non-tariff barriers we estimate the tariff equivalent or else the share of imports subjected to such barriers. The greater the incidence of such barriers, the higher the price of imports relative to domestic substitutes. This offers a crude indicator of the restrictiveness of a particular trade regime (see Chapter 7).

Another, more sophisticated, method is to supplement information on price effects by an analysis of quantity effects, based on elasticity estimates. This allows us to quantify the effects of trade barriers on import and export volumes and, with suitable assumptions, the consequential effect on economic welfare and real incomes. A good example is a study by Messerlin (2000), which estimates that the total cost to the EU of its remaining external trade barriers is equivalent to around 7% of GDP, or $600 billion. It is no surprise, therefore, that the estimated benefits from liberalization of the CCP are also significant. According to simulations carried out by economists of the GATT (1994), EU income in 2005 will be higher by US$164 billion in 1990 prices, as a result of the Uruguay Round. When compared to an estimated total world gain of US$510 billion, this implies that the EU will obtain fully one-third of the global gains. Clearly the EU is a major beneficiary of the trend towards global trade liberalization.

22.2 EU trade and specialization patterns

22.2.1 The structure of EU trade

The EU constitutes the largest trading bloc in the world. Excluding intra-EU trade, exports of the Union accounted for 20% of world exports in 1998. The United States and Japanese shares were 17% and 10% respectively (see Table 22.3).

External trade has tended to grow about twice as fast as GDP in most parts of the world and the EU is no exception. During the 1990s, EU trade volumes increased by 5.5% annually compared with 1.9% GDP growth (CEU, 1998c). A useful aggregate measure of trade dependence is the export of goods and services/GDP ratio. For the EU this now stands at 13%, slightly higher than that for the USA (11%) and Japan (12%).

About 45% of extra-EU trade is directed towards *developed countries*. Within the developed countries group, the United States is the largest trading partner, followed by Japan and Switzerland (see Table 22.4). If intra-EU trade is added to extra-EU

Table 22.3 The EU in world merchandise trade, 1998

Exports from	Value	
	(US$bn)	%
EU (excluding intra-EU trade)	814	20.3
United States	683	17.0
Japan	388	9.7
Other	2133	53.0
Total world (excluding intra-EU trade)	4018	100.0

Source: WTO *Focus*, April 1999.

Table 22.4 EU merchandise trade by area, 1997

	Imports		Exports	
	US$bn	%	US$bn	%
Developed countries[a] of which:	363.6	17.6	343.6	16.3
United States	163.34	7.9	157.74	7.5
Japan	72.94	3.5	39.86	1.9
Switzerland	50.8	2.5	60.0	2.8
LDCs[b]	310.5	15.0	323.3	15.4
Central and Eastern Europe[c]	94.6	4.6	117.7	5.6
Other	18.3	0.1	41.1	2.0
Extra-EU	787.0	38.0	825.6	39.2
Intra-EU	1283.5	62.0	1279.8	60.8
Total EU	2070.4	100.0	2105.4	100.0

[a] Western Europe, North America and Japan.
[b] Africa, Latin America, Middle East and Asia (excluding Japan).
[c] Central and Eastern Europe, Baltic States, Commonwealth of Independent States.
Source: Computed from Table A10 in WTO, 1998, vol. 2.

trade with developed countries, we find that almost 80% of the Union's trade is with countries of broadly similar income levels. This is a familiar empirical phenomenon world wide, but it runs counter to the expectation that trade flows should be greatest between countries that are most different in economic structure. It has given rise to much new theorizing about the causes of trade (Krugman, 1994).

Developing countries (LDCs) account for 40% of extra-EU trade but for only 15% of total EU trade. Generally one observes a strong asymmetry in trade relations between individual LDCs and the EU. Most LDCs rely far more on the EU as an export market than the EU does on them. For example, 27% of India's exports go to the EU, but only 1.3% of EU exports go to India, and India's exports account for only 1.5% of total EU imports. African countries in general are even more dependent on the EU market. The asymmetry in bargaining positions is modified somewhat by the strategic importance of some LDC primary product exports, oil being an obvious case in point, but this factor has not carried much weight over the past two decades. The most dynamic element in EU–LDC trade has been the growth in manufactured goods trade with South-East Asian countries. This repeats the general pattern: as countries become more industrialized (i.e. more similar) they trade more with one another.

The commodity structure of EU trade varies greatly by geographical area (see Table 22.5). Trade with developed countries consists predominantly of trade in *manufactured goods*. In 1997, these goods accounted for 86% of the Union's exports to developed countries and 80% of its imports from them. Trade with LDCs has a different composition. Primary products figure more prominently in their exports to the EU. Agricultural products comprise 18% of the total and fuels and other

Table 22.5 Commodity composition of EU trade with major trading groups, 1997 (% shares)

	Manufactures		Agricultural products		Fuels and other products	
	Exp.	Imp.	Exp.	Imp.	Exp.	Imp.
Developed countries[a]	86.4	79.9	7.0	7.4	6.6	12.7
LDCs[b]	87.4	59.9	7.9	17.9	4.4	22.2
Central and Eastern Europe[c]	83.7	57.7	11.8	9.6	5.5	32.7

[a] Western Europe (excluding intra-EU trade), North America and Japan.
[b] Latin America, Africa, Middle East and Asia (except Japan).
[c] Central and Eastern Europe, Baltic States, Commonwealth of Independent States.
Source: Computed from Table A10 in WTO, Geneva, 1998, vol. 2.

products a further 22%. However, the share of manufactured goods in total imports from the LDCs has grown dramatically in recent decades (up from 18% in 1980 to 60% in 1997).

The EU's *balance on extra-EU merchandise trade* has been in modest surplus since 1994. It amounted to 0.1% of GDP in 1999. So far, the Union's trade balance has not elicited much comment; in contrast with the analytical and political angst surrounding the United States deficit (2.6% of GDP) and the Japanese surplus (2.4% of GDP). Nevertheless some bilateral trade imbalances have been perceived as troublesome, in particular the persistent deficit with Japan. The trade balance's economic importance derives from its being both a lead indicator and the largest component in the *balance of payments on current account*. This balance includes services trade and other current transactions. Trade in *commercial services*, comprising travel, transport, royalties and business services corresponds to one-quarter of the EU's total trade with third countries.

The EU's current balance of payments account has been in surplus since 1993 and during the intervening period has averaged 1.2% of GDP. This position is important for two reasons. The first reason derives from the mercantilist fallacy of interpreting a trade surplus as a sign of economic strength gained at the expense of other countries. A variant of this argument is that countries with a balance of payments surplus are automatically guilty of 'beggar my neighbour' behaviour because they generate more employment through exports than they lose through imports. This upside-down economics confuses the welfare gains from trade with the balance of trade in goods and services. From a welfare point of view, exports to foreigners are a 'bad' (we could consume them ourselves instead) and this bad has to be weighed against the benefits of being able to consume imports. A more valid reason for concern is that a persistent balance of payments surplus or deficit can affect the exchange rate. Up to now there has been little reason for concern with the EU's overall balance of payments. With the advent of the Euro and the establishment of the European Central Bank, however, the linkage between the balance of payments account and the Euro's value *vis-à-vis* other currencies will become the focus of increasing scrutiny. And, as we have seen, shifts in exchange rates have a way of impinging on trade policy.

In trying to work out the effect of a customs union such as the EU on partner and third countries, customs union theory focuses on the share of intra-union versus extra-union trade (see Chapter 5). The growth of intra-union trade could be due to either trade creation (a good thing) or trade diversion (a bad thing). As a general rule, the greater the absolute growth of extra-union trade, the less the danger of trade diversion. In the EU's case, two facts stand out. First, the share of *intra-EU trade* in total trade has risen markedly from 42% in 1961 to 63% in 1998, though it appears to have stabilized after 1990 (Brülhart and Elliott, 1998). As integration among EU members outpaced liberalization with the rest of the world, this relative expansion of intra-EU trade is in line with the predictions of theory (see Chapter 5). Second, the increase in intra-EU trade share was accompanied by a rapid absolute growth of *extra-EU trade*. This indicates a preponderance of trade creation over trade diversion. Further analysis suggests that, with the exception of agricultural trade, the rise in intra-EU trade has not been at the expense of non-EU countries (Sapir, 1996).

Fears of increasing trade diversion were raised in the late 1980s by the implementation of the Single Market. Some argued that the liberalization of the internal market would divert energies away from liberalizing external trade and give EU firms an unfair competitive edge over third-country exporters. However, *ex post* evaluation has shown that these fears of a 'Fortress Europe' were unfounded. Extra-EU manufacturing imports increased their share of consumption over the period 1980–93 from 12% to 14% (CEU, 1996a). Looking specifically at LDC exporters, Buigues and Martínez (1999) found that between 1989 and 1995 the LDC share of EU imports increased both in absolute terms and in comparison with the United States. This increase was particularly pronounced in the sectors most affected by the Single Market programme.

All this suggests an important conclusion. As a general rule, the process of European integration has not created problems for other trading countries. This conclusion is likely to continue to hold following the introduction of the Euro. While the single currency will facilitate trade among member states, it will equally assist those countries not participating in the single currency that export to the Euro area. Indeed the Euro will most likely enhance the openness of the EU market generally and hence reinforce the rapid expansion of trade with third countries observed during the 1990s.

A final consideration is the *terms of trade*. This is defined as the price index of exports over the price index of imports. If, say, the price of imported oil or coffee declines, this would represent an *improvement* in the EU's terms of trade. The European consumer can consume more oil or coffee with the same nominal income and is clearly better off as a result. Likewise, a fall in pharmaceutical export prices would lead to deterioration in the EU's terms of trade. Unlike the gains from trade, the terms of trade is a zero-sum game: your loss is my gain and vice versa.

EU-wide indicators of the terms of trade are difficult to compute. We do know that the price paid for primary goods imported from the LDCs has fallen over the past two decades, in some cases very steeply. African exporters have been particularly hit by declining terms of trade. Clearly, the LDCs must try to diversify their exports into more profitable lines. A case on equity grounds can also be made for the EU to provide compensating aid to LDCs, given that the European consumer has been a prime beneficiary of the decline in LDC export prices.

22.2.2 Intra-industry versus inter-industry trade

Much academic interest has focused on the composition of international exchanges in terms of intra- and inter-industry trade. *Intra-industry trade* (IIT) refers to the mutual exchange among countries of similar goods. This type of trade runs against the predictions of neoclassical trade theory, according to which countries would export one set of products – those in which they have a comparative advantage – while importing an entirely different set of products – those for which the comparative advantage is enjoyed by other countries. IIT is based not on country-specific advantages, but on determinants such as consumers' taste for variety, increasing returns in production and the international dispersion of various stages in the production process of advanced industrial goods. IIT therefore typically dominates trade among diversified high-income economies.

Trade within the EU exhibits generally high shares of IIT. Brülhart and Elliott (1998) have shown that, on average, the share of IIT trade among EU countries rose from 48% to 64% over the period 1961–92. Given that the definition of an 'industry' in that study is very narrow (SITC 5-digit), this is strong evidence that intra-EU trade is driven by forces other than the type of comparative advantage once emphasized in the textbooks.

The IIT share of extra-EU trade has also been growing, but less rapidly than in the case of intra-EU trade. Countries with the largest and most diversified industrial bases (Germany, France and the United Kingdom) have the highest levels of IIT with third countries (OECD, 1994). Greece and Portugal have lower IIT levels – their extra-EU trade relations are still predominantly *inter-industry*. The proportion of IIT in the EU's trade with developed countries such as the United States is high, as one would expect, and with developing countries it is low. IIT with Japan, however, is surprisingly low, a fact often interpreted as a symptom of the impenetrability of the Japanese market to manufactured exports from the west (Lincoln, 1990). The EU's trade with Central and Eastern European countries (CEECs) also displays comparatively low IIT values, but for different reasons from those that apply in relation to Japan. Hoekman and Djankov (1996a) show that IIT with the CEECs has been increasing, albeit from a low level. Low IIT levels could imply that further trade liberalization with these countries might involve substantial structural adjustment costs for both parties (see Brülhart, 1994, 1998). This may explain in part the insistence on a certain minimum level of economic development being achieved by applicant countries before accession to full membership of the Union is agreed.

22.2.3 External trade and economic specialization: high-tech industries and low-skill workers

Changes in the EU's trade structure and trade policy regime have stimulated corresponding changes in the pattern of specialization of member states. The share of agricultural employment in EU total employment has fallen from 12% in 1970 to 4% in 1999. There has been a massive expansion of the services sector, and a fall in the share of industrial jobs from 41% to 31% in the same time period. Some industrial sectors were particularly hard hit. Employment in the EU12 coal industry, for instance, declined by 65% (329 000 jobs) between 1984 and 1993 (Eurostat, 1997). Since 1984, employment has also shrunk significantly in iron and steel (down 36%

or 184 000 jobs by 1997), in textiles (down 44% or 776,000 jobs by 1997) and in clothing (down 47% or 625,000 jobs by 1995).

Of course, specialization pressures induced by external trade are not the only forces that shaped the observed changes in the EU's production structure. Even if the EU had existed in autarky, changes in technology, incomes, tastes and demography would have led to structural adjustment. For this reason, it is difficult to isolate and quantify the impact of external trade liberalization on observed specialization trends. However, recent empirical analysis has yielded some insights into the processes at work. We concentrate here on two sectors, for which the role of extra-EU trade has been subject to particularly intensive debate and substantial research: *high-technology* industries and *low-skill intensive* industries. Both have been identified as losers from the EU's trade liberalization; the former due to insufficient R&D efforts in the EU, the latter due to the inexorable law of comparative advantage.

Trade performance in *high-tech products* has been a source of concern to the EU for many years. The concern focuses on Europe's perceived poor performance in high-tech sectors relative to the USA and Japan. One way of measuring this is by the *technology balance of payments*, i.e. the difference between exports of technology (such as international licensing contracts and technical assistance) and imports (such as purchases of foreign patents, know-how and R&D). According to OECD estimates for 1997, the EU had a deficit in technology of $4.4 billion in contrast with an American surplus of US$24.3 billion (*The Economist*, 21 August 1999). A second indicator examines patterns in high-tech merchandise trade, such as (a) the share of high-tech products in total exports, (b) the ratio of exports to imports in high-tech compared with low-tech products (the trade coverage ratio), and (c) the export market shares. These statistics need careful interpretation. One, the share of high-tech exports in total manufacturing exports, shows the EU (12%) falling well below the United States (24%) and Japan (25%). Other trade statistics provide less conclusive results. Thus, the EU has a negative trade balance in some key high-tech sectors such as office and telecom equipment but enjoys a surplus in others such as machinery and transport equipment (see Table 22.6). France Germany, Italy and the UK have much lower export/import ratios in high-tech products than Japan, but all except Italy have a higher ratio than the USA (OECD, 1999). Notwithstanding this, the Second European Report on Science and Technology Indicators (CEU, 1997i) warned of a 'stagnation' in European research compared with its competitors.

The problem of high-tech industries relates to the strategic positioning of the EU economy. Low-skill intensive industries give rise to a different type of concern. In the latter case, it is generally accepted that the EU will lose market share to third countries. What is at issue is the pace of change and its effects on the incomes of *low-skill workers*, particularly against the backdrop of the EU's high unemployment. Some argue that the law of comparative advantage has been working to the detriment of European blue-collar workers and, in an unholy combination with institutional labour-market rigidities, has fuelled unemployment.

Trade economists have conducted numerous analyses with the aim of isolating trade-related determinants of structural change. Two concepts of structural change have been used: changes in wage differentials across industries and changes in unemployment rates. The starting hypothesis is that liberalization of trade *vis-à-vis* labour-abundant developing countries, particularly the South-East Asian 'tiger

Table 22.6 Extra-EU trade in selected products, 1980 and 1997 (US$ billion)

		Exports	Imports	Trade balance	Change in balance 1980–97
Chemicals	1980	35.7	17.2	+18.5	
	1997	101.9	59.1	+42.8	+24.3
Machinery and	1980	115.9	58.0	+57.9	
transport equipment	1997	361.8	268.4	+93.4	+35.5
Electrical machinery	1980	11.9	5.7	+6.2	
	1997	40.5	35.7	+4.8	−1.4
Office and telecom	1980	11.3	17.2	−5.9	
equipment	1997	65.9	110.4	−44.5	−38.6
Automotive products	1980	27.5	8.2	+19.3	
	1997	75.6	35.8	+39.8	+20.5

Source: Computed form Table A10 in WTO, 1996, 1998, vol. 2.

economies', has depressed demand for unskilled labour in industrialised countries. Trade liberalization therefore contributes either (a) to the widening gap between skilled and unskilled wages, as in the United States and the UK, or (b) to rising unemployment of unskilled workers, where union power and labour legislation impede United States-style flexibility of wages. In the EU case, attention primarily focuses on whether increased imports from low-wage countries have exacerbated the unemployment problem.

Most available studies cover the United States or the entire OECD, rather than just the EU, and a number of different methodologies are used. Some studies estimate average factor contents of imports and exports, and infer net effects on domestic factor demands (see Sachs and Shatz, 1994). Other studies regress changes in factor demands over various determinants including import penetration (see Larre, 1995). A majority of analyses find that trade liberalization accounts for some of the fall in demand for blue-collar workers in developed countries. However the contribution of trade to the rise in the skill premium is at most 20%; by far the bigger culprit is trade-independent technological change (Slaughter, 1999).

A contrary conclusion was reached by Wood (1994, 1995), who argued that import penetration from the LDCs is a major cause of falling demand for low-skill labour in the OECD. He refined the standard factor-content analysis and found empirical evidence that manufactured imports of OECD countries tend to have higher low-skill labour contents than similar goods produced locally, and that imports thereby crowd out low-skill jobs in developed countries. Furthermore, he detected a tendency for OECD industry to engage in 'defensive innovation', substituting capital for low-skill labour in order to survive competition from low-wage exporters, and he pointed to the (often ignored) surge in service exports from those countries. He concluded that demand for unskilled labour relative to skilled labour in OECD countries in 1990 fell by about 20% compared to what it would have been had prohibitive barriers been imposed on trade with the LDCs. Neven and Wyplosz

(1999) also found evidence of defensive innovation by EU industries in response to competition from LDCs, but the magnitude of their estimated employment and wage effects is very small.

The nature of the trade–employment link is likely to remain a controversial topic for some time. As the EU reduces its external trade barriers under WTO commitments, and as the exporting capacity of developing countries increases, the pressures for trade-induced specialization will also intensify. Underlying the empirical debate about the significance of trade liberalization for EU labour-market adjustment there is a strong *normative* consensus against a return to protectionism. Even though trade liberalization is acknowledged to produce losers, gainers are still in the majority. The appropriate policy response is not to reimpose trade barriers to non-EU imports, but to deregulate EU labour markets, to subsidize employment of low-skill workers (in the short term), and to invest in education (in the long term).

22.3 Trade relations with the main partners

22.3.1 The LDCs

In spite of their relative economic weakness, the LDCs are a key trade partner for the EU (see Table 22.5). The present pattern of trade agreements owes as much to history and proximity to the EU as to economic rationale. The Mediterranean countries, for instance, are bound to the EU by many ties. Fear of excessive immigration from these areas has given the EU an added incentive to assist their economic development through strong trade preferences. Following the 1995 Barcelona Declaration, the EU and 11 Mediterranean countries agreed to form a Euro-Med free trade area by the year 2010. Also contained in this programme are pledges to abolish obstacles to trade in goods and services on a reciprocal basis. Bilateral FTAs incorporating these principles have already been signed with several Mediterranean countries (Stevens *et al.*, 1998).

The EU's trade preferences on industrial goods have provided a stimulus to outward contracting foreign investment in Tunisia and Morocco. Security of access to the EU market has also been helpful to natural resource based investment in these countries. In Morocco, the 'lock-in' factor in its domestic liberalization programme also played a role in securing the government's endorsement of the FTA. Most Mediterranean countries have a small, weak and (until recently) heavily sheltered industrial base. Tariff revenues are a significant source of government revenue, amounting to 36% in Jordan, 28% in Tunisia and 18% in Morocco (Hoekman and Djankov, 1996b). Much remains to be done to ensure that they are able to withstand competition from EU firms, develop export capabilities and generate the dynamic gains from trade in terms of foreign investment and technology.

Prior to the Barcelona programme, the Lomé Convention was the EU's most preferential agreement with LDCs (see Chapter 23). Signed in 1975, and renewed at regular intervals thereafter, it gives a group of African, Caribbean, and Pacific (ACP) countries free access to EU markets for manufactures and a substantial range of primary goods (76 such countries were included in the latest agreement, signed in 2000). The Lomé accords encompass more than tariff reductions. They include commodity protocols which provide preferential prices to ACP exports of bananas, sugar and beef, the relaxation of NTBs, more flexible application of safeguard clauses, rules of origin and exemption from MFA restrictions. Trade preferences are supplemented by special aid and technical co-operation arrangements.

So much for the good news. The bad news is that, in spite of the preferential access, the ACP countries' export performance in the EU market has been disappointing. Their market share has been declining in most of the post-war period and accounted for only 3.4% of EU imports in 1995 (2.7% if oil is excluded). Their share of other markets has also fallen, even faster than in the EU market (Auboin and Laird, 1999). It would be hard to dispute the Commission's conclusion that the impact of trade preferences has been 'disappointing by and large' (CEU 1996d). Preferential arrangements have certainly contributed significantly to the exports of some ACP countries (Ivory Coast, Jamaica, Mauritius and Zimbabwe), but generally these countries have lacked the economic policies and the domestic conditions needed to develop trade.

Another group to which especially favourable preferences are given is the least developed countries (LLDCs). In the EU's case, this is of only limited relevance because the majority of LLDCs happen to be ACP countries and hence already qualify for preferential treatment.

For most non-ACP developing countries the *Generalised System of Preferences* (GSP) dictates the degree of preferential access for their exports to the EU. Initiated in 1971 by UNCTAD, the purpose of the GSP was to help LLDCs to industrialize through exports to the developed world. Most developed countries have adopted some version of the GSP, in the case of the USA and the UK not without some initial reluctance (MacBean and Snowden, 1981). The GSP provides substantially weaker trade preferences than the Lomé convention. Some GSP countries also participate in special agreements with the EU. An example is the EU-India Enhanced Partnership agreement (1996) set up with the aim of facilitating trade and investment links, speeding up implementation of WTO agreements and encouraging closer understanding.

Prior to 1995, the GSP provided duty-free access for industrial products, subject to ceilings, classified by country of origin and member state of destination. This regime has been replaced by a 'modulation mechanism' which assigns trade preferences according to the 'sensitivity' of import goods without quantity ceilings (WTO, 1995b). The list ranges from 'very sensitive' products (textiles, clothing and ferro-alloys), which are subject to 85% of the regular tariff, to 'non-sensitive' products, which benefit from duty-free treatment. This modulation system is complemented by a 'graduation' mechanism under which preferential treatment is gradually reduced once GSP countries have reached a certain level of economic development. Graduation also applies to specific sectors. For example, textiles and leather exports from India were 'graduated' from the GSP in 1997 because India's share of the total EU market in these sectors had reached the threshold level.

The EU's multiplicity of agreements and special arrangements with LDCs is undergoing considerable reassessment. First, as global trade liberalization gathers pace and trade barriers crumble, the practical usefulness of trade preferences has diminished. Preference erosion is likely to accelerate markedly over the next decade. This will pose special problems for the ACP countries that have benefited for many years from advantageous access to the EU market. Second, attention is likely to focus more on issues such as the right of establishment in services markets, the attraction of foreign investment, rights to tender for public sector contracts in partner countries and competition law. We will hear less about trade preferences and more about development programmes. Third, LLDCs will have to provide reciprocity in future RTAs if they are to be acceptable under WTO rules. This means they will have to reduce their own import barriers as well. For some there will be a serious loss of government revenues as a result and some (small) danger of trade diversion. While some LLDC governments tend to see the reduction in tariffs as a 'concession', trade theory suggests the opposite conclusion. Properly managed, the liberalization of imports can bring considerable benefits to their economies.

22.3.2 The United States

The United States is the EU's largest trade partner, accounting for 16% of combined extra-EU imports and exports (see Table 22.4). Although trade with industrial countries is in principle governed by the rules of the WTO, this has not prevented controversy arising on many specific issues.

EU economic relations with the United States have been based on strong political and cultural ties as well as common economic interests. Yet, at times, it appears as if the two partners are locked into a state of perpetual crisis. In the past, trade wars have threatened to erupt because of disputes over steel, pasta, citrus fruit, agricultural exports to Egypt, and the Mediterranean enlargement. More recent sources of discord are hormone-treated beef, aircraft noise, subsidies to Airbus, genetically modified crops and bananas. The EU has complained about unilateralism in United States trade legislation, 'Buy American' restrictions, discriminatory taxes, public procurement and restrictions on non-nationals in the service industries. Some European grievances were vindicated in September 1999, when a WTO Panel confirmed that US export subsidies covering approximately US$250 billion worth of US exports were in violation of the WTO rules and had to be abolished by October 2000. Europeans feel rather defensive about the American lead in high-technology goods. For its part, the United States feared a protectionist 'Fortress Europe' arising from the Single Market programme and continues to accuse the EU of unfairly subsidizing high-tech sectors such as aviation. The most acute and enduring cause of friction, however, has been trade in agricultural products. The growing United States trade deficit with the EU has been ascribed to the domestic price support given by the CAP. The United States has further objected that growing EU food surpluses are being sold at subsidized prices on third markets thereby creating difficulties for United States exporters to these markets. The EU retorts, with some justification, that agricultural subsidies are applied on both sides of the Atlantic. This illustrates the problems that arise when all countries try to subsidize the same product.

The disputes over aircraft noise and beef illustrate how easily trade and environment/welfare issues overlap. From an EU perspective, the proposal to reduce aircraft noise and to ban hormone-treated beef addresses issues relating to the environment and public health. It may have adverse effects on US exports, but this is an incidental side-effect, not its objective. Adjudication on these disputes is clearly difficult.

Although full-scale trade wars have threatened to break out on many occasions, the strong mutuality of interests between the United States and the EU has, on each occasion thus far, saved them from the brink. Trade relations are characterized by constant levels of minor friction rather than a deep-seated divergence of interest. Certainly, a tit-for-tat series of retaliations would leave both Europe and the United States worse off, a fact which both sides appreciate. There is talk of eliminating all trade barriers, thereby creating a 'new transatlantic marketplace' of 700 million affluent consumers. A transatlantic free trade agreement could yield welfare gains in the range 1–2% of GDP for Europe and 1.6–2.8% for the United States (see Stokes, 1996; and Boyd, 1998).

22.3.3 Japan

Trade policy towards Japan has been marked by resistance to what is perceived as excessively rapid import penetration in a narrow range of product markets. It is also marked by internal disunity within the EU (see O'Donnell and Murphy, 1994). Some member states, such as the United Kingdom and Ireland, have become important hosts to Japanese investment. Naturally, these member states have tended to view sales by Japanese firms more benignly than those with a small presence of Japanese-owned production facilities. Also, countries whose domestic industries compete directly with Japanese goods tend to take a tougher line in the trade policy debate than those for which Japanese sales compete only with other imports. Thus, the high share of Japanese passenger car imports in Ireland (43%) and Denmark (34%) aroused little concern, whereas Italy and France were highly resistant to any easing of restraints on Japanese imports despite having much lower import shares (5% and 4% respectively in the mid-1990s) (WTO, 1995b).

The EU's persistent trade deficit with Japan has been a bone of contention. It has been attributed to the combined effects of the strong competitive performance of Japanese firms, of Japan's high savings rate and, controversially, of Japan's reluctance to open its market to EU exporters. In 1997, 9% of total extra-EU imports came from Japan, while the Japanese market absorbed only 5% of EU exports. The main problem with this unbalanced trade was that Japanese exports tended to be highly focused on a small number of sectors (automobiles, consumer electronics).

On the basis of explicit barriers to trade, the Japanese market appears relatively open. Japan has committed itself in the Uruguay Round to a trade-weighted tariff average on industrial goods of 1.7%. This is the second-lowest average of all countries (only that of Switzerland is lower). However, there are important implicit barriers to imports. First, access to the Japanese market is restricted by regulatory obstacles such as the arbitrary specification of technical standards for electrical appliances and conditions for participation in the financial services market. Japanese non-acceptance of international standards and European certification procedures hamper trade in areas such as the agro-food sector, pharmaceuticals and construction. Second, the existence of tightly connected business groups ('keiretsu'), built upon interconnected manufacturers and distributors, makes it particularly difficult for European firms to sell to Japan.

The EU has exerted pressure on Japan to liberalize access to its market, albeit in a less confrontational strategy than that of the United States. Consultation is the keyword in EU trade diplomacy with Japan. Annual summit meetings have been held between the Japanese Prime Minister, the President of the European Council and the President of the Commission since 1991, and a permanent dialogue was established in 1993 between MITI, the Japanese ministry for international trade and industry, and the corresponding Commission Directorate. In addition, export-enhancing schemes such as assistance for marketing in Japan and special visit and study programmes have been initiated to facilitate access to the Japanese market for European business. Notable successes in EU–Japanese trade diplomacy include the 1991 'consensus' to phase out VERs on Japanese car exports by the year 2000, and Japan's agreement in February 1997 to end discriminatory taxation of imported spirits.

Partly as a means to circumvent European VERs and anti-dumping action, Japanese firms have invested heavily in production facilities within the EU (see Dent, 1997). This investment has been eagerly sought by the less developed regions of the Union and does much on the ground to counter the accusation that Japanese imports are 'destroying' jobs in the EU. On the other hand, competition from Japanese subsidiaries was seen as a threat to established industry. ('Established' industry includes subsidiaries of non-EU firms such as Ford whose only claim to preferment is that they got into the EU market first.)

Concern over Japanese import penetration has quietened down in recent years. One reason is that the Japanese economy has proved to be weaker and more vulnerable than was believed a decade ago. Another is that despite the deficit with Japan, the EU enjoys an overall trade surplus. Hence, to object too strenuously to Japan's surplus might give ammunition to countries which had a deficit with the EU! Third, following the major reforms of its financial sector in the late 1990s, access to Japan's market has become much easier for European investors. More European companies now have a stake in good relations with Japan. Fourth, EU manufacturing companies have raised productivity by copying Japanese techniques. 'Just in time' techniques are now commonplace. Fifth, as Europeans have gained in confidence, they are more ready to acknowledge that failure to obtain market share in Japan could partly be due to their poor knowledge of the Japanese market. One piece of evidence on what has been called this 'knowledge deficit': the population of Japan is one-third that of the EU but there are five times more Japanese people living in Europe than Europeans in Japan. Finally, Japanese companies are becoming more open and more prepared to engage in co-operative ventures than in the past. The Nissan-Renault merger is an exemplar of this kind of co-operation. Clearly, the EU strategy of encouraging exports to Japan and promoting investment between the two countries is superior to protectionism. One must remember that the EU consumer has gained enormously both from access to Japanese goods and from the efficiency improvements forced on European industry by exposure to Japanese competition.

22.3.4 The CEECs

The political upheaval and ensuing economic reforms in Central and Eastern Europe have raised formerly isolated neighbours to the top the EU's list of candidates for trade integration. The EU has concluded Association Agreements and started accession negotiations with ten former Soviet-bloc countries. Most CEECs have enjoyed duty-free access for industrial products since 1995. Removal of remaining obstacles on sensitive sectors such as steel and textiles has also been agreed along with improved access for agricultural goods. A feature of the arrangements is 'linkage' between trade liberalization and market conditions. To reassure EU competitors that free trade will also be 'fair' trade, the CEECs have had to implement competition policies and reduce state subsidies.

The effects on trade policy of closer economic relations with the CEECs are difficult to predict. The starting-point is one of low trade volumes. In 1989, EU trade with these countries, including the Soviet Union, accounted for some 6% of total EU trade in industrial products with third countries. Their lack of hard currency made the CEECs poor markets for EU exports, while many of their own goods carried little attraction in Western markets. At the bottom of the EU's preferential ranking up to the late 1980s, and with even the small amount of trade riddled with interventions on both sides, past trade trends are an unreliable guide to the future. Yet, research based on gravity models suggests the potential for a dramatic (six-fold) increase in trade between the EU and the CEECs (Baldwin *et al.*, 1992).

Evidence on trade changes in the 1990s points towards a gradual process of trade reorientation by the CEECs towards the EU. Yet, most of the increase in these exports has consisted of new products rather than a diversion of products previously exported to the Soviet bloc. Hoekman and Djankov (1996a) estimated that at most 20% of increased CEEC exports to the EU were 'diverted' flows. The bulk of the remainder were produced by subsidiaries of foreign firms or by outward contracting. East European firms have pursued a strategy of upgrading and differentiating 'traditional' exports, relying upon EU firms for new machinery, components and know-how.

The prospect of eastern enlargement means that free trade in manufactures is only a matter of time. Also, the huge agriculture potential of the CEEC bloc has given the EU another powerful incentive to speed up the liberalization of the CAP. The specialization pattern that will emerge between the EU and the CEECs once the remaining obstacles are fully removed is hard to predict. Pressure will undoubtedly be placed on the EU's protected agriculture, steel, textiles, clothing and footwear industries and other semi-skilled activities. However, given the CEECs' relatively high educational standards, they are unlikely to specialize in low-skill, low-tech sectors in the long run. IIT in advanced manufactured products and services is likely to increase. Furthermore, the need for capital and intermediate goods in the reconstruction of many CEEC industries will continue to provide attractive opportunities for EU exporters, particularly those in countries located close to the border.

22.4   Trade policy in a globalizing world

Expanding volumes of international trade and investment are the clearest indicators of economic globalization. The typical large firm in the globalized economy has subsidiaries in several countries, switches among sub-contractors and suppliers in many others, deals in intangible assets, engages in intra-firm trade among subsidiaries and competes with its rivals not in segmented national economies, but in regional or even global markets. In such a context, exports and imports are intertwined and the 'nationality' of goods and services is difficult to identify. The advent of e-commerce makes this task even harder.

The closer integration of the international economy has broadened the scope of trade policy. Expanding international trade flows imply that trade measures impact on an ever larger part of economic activity, and the growing complexity of international economic relations dictates a widening remit for trade negotiators. The two major EU trade liberalization projects of the 1990s, the Single Market and participation in the Uruguay Round, have brought into focus several new issues with relevance to trade policy:

● rules regulating cross-border provision of services;

● international protection of intellectual property rights;

- linkages between trade and environmental policy;
- linkages between trade and labour standards;
- rules relating to foreign direct investment;
- international competition policy;
- harmonization of product standards; and
- the opening of public procurement to foreign suppliers.

This section concentrates on the first four of the new issues listed above. Each of them will be likely to feature prominently on the agenda for future rounds of trade negotiations.

22.4.1 Services

So far, this chapter has dealt primarily with merchandise trade. Services have traditionally been perceived as non-traded, but this perception is no longer valid. Technological improvements and policy liberalization have led many service providers to compete on foreign markets. There are thriving international markets in tourism, travel, financial services and software. Unfortunately this trade is notoriously difficult to measure empirically. Services differ from merchandise, because they are intangible, cannot be stored and often involve the movement of the provider to the consumer (e.g. transport, consulting) or vice versa (e.g. tourism, education). Measuring such trade by origin and destination is especially problematic. Considering that services account for over 60% of GDP in OECD countries, there seems to be enormous potential for trade expansion in this sector.

EU trade in commercial services was estimated at 25% of the value of merchandise trade in 1997 (WTO, 1998). For most member states, exports of travel and transport amounted to around 40% of their total services exports, with the remaining 60% spread among financial services, computer and information services and miscellaneous business services. The EU has traditionally held a strong competitive position in services.

Extra-EU services trade has received a multilateral legal base through the General Agreement on Trade in Services (GATS), which was negotiated during the Uruguay Round. The scope of this agreement encompasses both the right to do business across countries and also the right to establish, since it also applies to services provided by foreign affiliates of multinational firms. The GATS extends the non-discrimination rule to all service sectors, except those listed in the Annex to the agreement by each signatory (the 'negative list'). *National treatment* (i.e. equivalent treatment to that given to domestic suppliers of a service) is granted to foreign suppliers in the sectors listed in each signatory's schedule of commitments (the 'positive list').

Like other developed countries, the EU was an enthusiastic proponent of freer trade in services. Such is invariably the case for sectors in which countries enjoy a decided comparative advantage. Where such an advantage is less clear, e.g. in the case of audio-visual services, where Europe is a major net importer from the USA, free trade was seen as posing a threat to European cultural identity. The EU's position in the GATS negotiations was complicated by the European Court ruling whereby competence to conclude the GATS was shared between the Union and the member states (see Chapter 3). As a consequence, some service activities (e.g. air transport) were not covered by the CCP. However, a common stance was found, and GATS commitments made in several others, notably financial services.

The GATS provided limited coverage of service sectors, but it contained provisions for continued negotiations. As already noted, an agreement was reached on telecommunications in 1997, according to which 69 WTO members granted each other (and most other WTO countries) national treatment in all forms of telecommunication services, thus covering over 90% of global telecommunications. The information technology agreement (ITA I) complements the services agreements while a second ITA is being prepared. The WTO estimated that telecom liberalization could mean cumulative global income gains of some one trillion dollars over the next decade or so, which represents about 4% of world GDP (WTO *Focus*, February 1997). Negotiations on financial and professional services were also completed successfully, but proposals for maritime transport were blocked by the USA.

Quantification of the effects of liberalizing services trade is subject to a wide margin of error. However, the GATS has placed access to service markets firmly on the multilateral trade-policy agenda. The EU has an obvious interest in promoting this agenda. In addition, its own experience of liberalization under the Single Market programme teaches one important lesson. Strong central action is needed to break down regulatory impediments that segment different national markets. International agreements alone are not enough without powers of enforcement. Consistent implementation of rule changes at the national level can be more difficult to attain than declarations of intent at international fora.

22.4.2 Trade and intellectual property rights

Services are not the only kind of intangible commodity whose share in trade as well as in economic output at large is increasing. 'Knowledge goods', ranging from computer programs to pop songs, and 'reputation goods' such as trade marks or appellations of origin, account for an unquantifiable but undeniably growing share of the value embodied in traded products. The nature of trade policy with respect to such knowledge and reputation goods differs radically from policy aimed at liberalizing merchandise trade, since the main concern is not to abolish obstacles to imports (as countries are generally keen to attract knowledge goods), but to safeguard owners' property rights. Negotiations on intellectual property rights therefore do not consist of bargaining on abolition of barriers, but agreements to set up minimum standards of ownership protection.

From a theoretical viewpoint, the enforcement of intellectual property rights is a double-edged sword (see Primo Braga, 1995). In the short run, protecting owners of knowledge goods (e.g. through patents) violates the rule that public goods, whose marginal usage cost is zero, should be free. Static efficiency considerations therefore advocate a lax implementation of such property rights, to allow maximum dissemination. In the long run, however, the generation of additional knowledge goods is costly: resources have to be invested in research and development, and this will only occur if a future pecuniary return on such an investment can be safely anticipated. A zero price of knowledge goods is therefore socially sub-optimal in a dynamic sense, because it discourages innovation.

Property rights on reputation goods also have their advantages and drawbacks in equity terms. Trade-mark protection on the one hand increases the monopoly power of owners, and thereby restricts competition, but on the other hand it can increase consumer welfare by allowing product differentiation and facilitating product information.

Both sides of the theoretical argument have been advanced in multilateral negotiations on intellectual property rights. Since developed countries, including the EU, tend to be the owners and exporters of intellectual property, while developing countries are net importers, the former generally argue in favour of stricter property-right enforcement than the latter. This was particularly evident during the Uruguay Round. These negotiations culminated in the Agreement on Trade-Related Aspects of Intellectual Property Rights (the TRIPS Agreement), which, alongside the GATT and GATS, forms one of the three pillars of the WTO. TRIPS negotiations were championed mainly by the United States and the EU against much initial opposition from developing countries.

Under the TRIPS accord, signatories have to establish minimum standards of intellectual property right protection, implement procedures to enforce these rights and extend the traditional GATT principles of national treatment and most-favoured-nation practice to intellectual property. It was agreed that 20-year patent protection should be available for all inventions, whether of products or processes, in almost all fields of technology. Copyright on literary works (including computer programs), sound recordings and films is made available for at least 50 years. Under the agreed transition period, most countries had to take on full TRIPS obligations by 2000, while some of the LLDCs may postpone application of most provisions until 2006.

The TRIPS Agreement impinges on competencies held by the EU as well as by national authorities. Both the EU and member states therefore had to ratify the agreement and were subsequently responsible for the required legal adaptations. Relatively few changes were necessary for the EU, since all member countries had long been signatories to the Paris Convention on patents and trade marks and the Berne Convention on copyright, which constitute the basis of the TRIPS framework.

The EU, being one of the main beneficiaries of the TRIPS Agreement, remains one of its most committed promoters. It has a particular interest in the protection of geographical labelling and has sponsored ongoing negotiations on a multilateral registration system for wines and spirits. (An example is its vigorous defence of the champagne label; sparkling wine produced outside France cannot call itself champagne even if it is produced by the same method.) Exporters of technology-intensive goods as well as owners of high-street brand names stand to gain substantially from stricter patent protection and a clampdown on trade in counterfeit goods.

22.4.3 The environment

Environmental policy moved to a prominent position on the trade agenda during the 1990s (see Chapter 20). Up to then, virtually the only environmental concern to affect trade policy was the protection of endangered species. With the rise of ecological awareness and transfrontier pollution problems such as ozone depletion, acid rain and global warming, trade policy came to be seen as a significant element in a country's overall environmental policy.

The main trade policy issue in this debate relates to the use of import restrictions on goods whose production creates negative trans-border environmental externalities. Economic theory suggests that in such circumstances the most efficient remedy is to apply direct environmental policy at the source of the externality (e.g. through pollution taxes, eco-subsidies or regulation; see Chapter 20). This is termed the 'first-best' policy (see Corden, 1997). However, environmental policies are often difficult to enforce, so the first-best option may not be feasible. In that case, import restrictions may be the only practicable policy tool. The main drawback of import restrictions against polluting countries is that they provide protection to domestic producers of the importable good, and ecological arguments are therefore vulnerable to abuse by domestic protectionist lobbies. For this reason, trade measures should be temporary and accompanied by efforts to implement environmental policies in the polluting countries.

Even if the externalities are dealt with by environmental policies adopted at the source, new problems can still emerge. Environmental policies affect the competitiveness of open economies. Thus, countries with lax environmental legislation are blamed for 'ecological dumping', and import-competing industries in countries with stringent laws may lobby for protection to ensure a 'level playing field'. As before, the first-best way of ensuring a level playing field is by achieving some degree of co-ordination in environmental policies across countries. This does not necessarily mean that all countries must adopt exactly the same environmental regime, but it provides a powerful rationale for seeking agreement on environmental policies on a multilateral basis. Even if no agreed way of eradicating 'ecological dumping' could be found, it remains questionable if trade restrictions are the most appropriate remedy. Restricting imports can be counterproductive as it promotes the domestic activities which the environmental policy is attempting to restrain.

On another tack, some environmentalists argue that the rising volume of international trade in itself is causing serious damage to the environment. Oil leakage from tankers and pollution from increased road haulage are classical examples. They recommend reduction in trade, if necessary by protection, as a solution. Neoclassical economists respond that trade restrictions will be inefficient and that policy should instead be aimed at the source of the problem (e.g. taxation of oil shipments and on the use of polluting fuels by lorries). One could agree with this while pointing out that such correct policy action may not be politically feasible. Witness, for example, the way in which the EC's proposals for a carbon tax have been resisted by business interests.

Some controversy has arisen in this context between the EU and Switzerland. In bilateral negotiations about extending parts of the Single Market to Switzerland, the EU has pressed for free Alpine road haulage transit. The Swiss, concerned by air and noise pollution from increased freight traffic in narrow mountain valleys, are pursuing the strategic policy of redirecting all transit freight traffic on to railways, both by increasing rail transport capacity and by levying high taxes on road transit. The EU counters that the restrictive Swiss policy diverts traffic on to Austrian and French routes. Ideally, this problem should be solved through international co-ordination of environmental rules. The withholding of Single Market freedoms from Switzerland, or the use of a blanket ban on road freight transit by the Swiss, are sub-optimal ways of dealing with this issue.

We conclude that trade policy is not the appropriate instrument to protect the environment. International dialogue and agreed domestic policy measures are more efficient alternatives. The main platform for such negotiations is the WTO Committee on Trade and Environment, which was established in 1995. Discussions in this committee have so far been a mere stocktaking exercise, and its report to the Singapore WTO Ministerial Conference in December 1996 contained no specific proposals. The EU, like everybody else, supports the case for multilateral environmental agreements, but the difficulty lies in getting countries to agree.

22.4.4   Labour standards

Just as there are concerns that lax environmental rules can be used as a strategy to secure economic competitiveness in traded industries, it is often feared that countries neglect the protection of workers' rights to attain a cost advantage ('social dumping'). This argument has sometimes been invoked in trade relations among developed countries, for instance after the UK's opt-out from the Social Chapter in the Maastricht Treaty (a policy which was reversed by the Labour government in May 1997), but it appears with much greater frequency in relationships between developed and developing countries. Trade unions in developed countries have been particularly vocal in urging sanctions against exports from Asian countries that employ child labour and have restricted labour rights.

The theoretical implications of this issue resemble closely those discussed in the context of 'ecological dumping'. The first-best policy is to seek agreement on minimum international labour standards directly rather than via the detour of trade sanctions. It is therefore often suggested that the issue should be left to the International Labour Organization (ILO) and kept separate from the trade talks at the WTO (OECD 1996a). The pragmatic counter-argument is that the ILO has only moral powers to enforce its rules, and that trade sanctions might be the only source of leverage over countries offending against core labour standards (Oxfam, 1996).

The issue of labour standards was introduced in the final stages of the Uruguay Round at the insistence of France and the United States. Strong resistance from LDCs obstructed a 'social clause' in the WTO legal code, but agreement was found that signatories would abide by 'core labour standards' as defined by the ILO. These core standards include:

- the elimination of child labour exploitation;
- prohibition of forced labour;
- freedom of association;
- the right to organize and bargain collectively; and
- non-discrimination in employment.

These aspirations, however, are not backed by any WTO rules allowing countries to impose trade restrictions on exporters who are deemed to be violating the core labour standards. The EU continues to press for the inclusion of labour standards issues and social goals in future trade negotiations.

22.5   Conclusions

An 'open' market is an elusive goal. Despite much liberalization, the EU continues to maintain strong defences against sensitive imports. It is unlikely that the gates will be opened completely in the near future. Even under an optimistically liberal scenario, it will be some time before Australia and New Zealand will be able to sell agricultural produce or India textile and clothing products into the EU market without let or hindrance. However, this chapter concludes that the direction of change has leaned, and will continue to lean, towards easier access. The 'Fortress Europe', which some had feared would be erected around the Single Market, has happily not materialized. Instead we are moving towards a free trade area embracing all of Western and Eastern Europe, the Mediterranean countries and sub-Saharan Africa.

A dynamic European economy will have to be an open one. The EU continues to promote trade with extra-EU countries because it is in its interest to do so. Its economic gains from the Uruguay Round were estimated as equivalent to almost one-half those derived from the Single Market.

The scope for further *negative integration*, in the sense of reduction of tariff and non-tariff trade barriers, is approaching exhaustion, but in its place there will be greater emphasis on *positive integration*. That means requiring governments to adapt domestic policies and institutions so as to ensure that the scope for expanded trade is not frustrated by differences in regulation, market institutions, technical standards and taxes. Linkage between trade issues and other policy areas once considered exclusively in the national domain will grow in importance over time.

The precise form of the EU's future external policy will depend on several factors. First, the maintenance of strong economic growth remains crucial. Enthusiasm for integration gathers momentum when an economy is doing well. To some extent European integration and external liberalization are 'fair weather phenomena'. It is also true that the process of liberalization itself tends to improve the weather! A prime concern at present is the EU's high rate of unemployment. Free trade and unemployment are uneasy, even incompatible, bedfellows. The welfare gains from increased imports do not impress the unemployed. It is remarkable how effective the Commission has been in forwarding its trade liberalization agenda. One reason may be that many EU countries have a significant balance of payments surplus; when exports exceed imports, it becomes difficult to blame unemployment on excessive imports.

Second, within the context of a strong EU economy, the maintenance of regional balance is important. The long-run effects of European integration on the EU's less developed regions seem more favourable now than they did in the past (see Chapter 18). Despite this, a large variance in regional performance still remains. The advent of the single currency is posing another challenge for the internal cohesion of the Union. From a trade perspective, it is likely to make the EU market more open and accessible to third-country exporters, and thus more vulnerable to external economic shocks. This strengthens the case for regional and national counter-balancing policies as well as for enhancing the flexibility of EU labour markets.

Third, the growing heterogeneity among EU members is likely to increase the difficulty of reaching consensus on trade policy. Such heterogeneity can be expected to result from the staggered adoption of the single currency, from the 'opt out' clauses in the 1997 Amsterdam Treaty and from the accession of new members in Central and Eastern Europe with long transition periods in key policy areas. To keep these divergent interests in line, the EU will have to deepen its relations with its trade partners to ensure that trade is seen as fair as well as free. In so doing, the Commission will enhance its own standing and power with neighbouring non-member states, an attractive political plus that it will be unlikely to overlook.

Fourth, awareness of the benefits from international integration has increased. New trade theories stress the importance of economies of scale, product variety and competition, all of which require large, open markets for their full realization. This is particularly relevant to fast-growing dynamic sectors of industry and services. The advent of e-commerce presents as yet unquantifiable opportunities that will be best exploited on an international scale. Extensive though the EU market already is, economic efficiency requires continuing extension of the global market, just as Adam Smith predicted over two hundred years ago.

23 EU–ACP development co-operation beyond Lomé

E. GRILLI

23.1 EU–ACP development co-operation in retrospect

Development co-operation between the EC (now EU) and the countries of Africa, the Caribbean and Pacific (ACP) has a long history. It was born of necessity as an appendix of European colonialism. In 1957 several of the signatories to the Treaty of Rome still had colonies, which had somehow to be linked to the new European Economic Community (EEC). Modified into an 'association' of independent states after decolonization, extended to all sub-Saharan Africa and a few countries outside it in the mid-1970s in the aftermath of the United Kingdom's entry into the European Community (EC), the special co-operative relationship with this sub-group of developing countries has continued until today. Enshrined in a succession of 'Lomé Conventions' (from the name of the first one signed in 1975 in the capital of Togo), hailed as a new model of development co-operation and assigned lofty, at times almost extravagant, objectives, the relationship between the EC and the ACP countries has continued to aim at the social and economic development of sub-Saharan Africa, and at keeping it closely tied to Europe.

Over time, some of the forms and the rationale of EC-ACP development co-operation were modified and made more suitable to the new circumstances in which it was called to operate. Its basic scope, however, has remained virtually intact since 1975. It always reflected the strong regional preference by Europe for Africa, the consequence of history, economic choices and political realities of the post Second World War era, and the concomitant recognition by newly emerged countries in Africa that even colonial trade and investment relationships established over a long period of time, deeply rooted as they had become in domestic economic realities, could not be changed overnight. Given existing patterns of production and exports, which for the African (and Caribbean) countries were largely dominated by primary commodities, the continuation of a privileged access to European markets for these products, plus the assurance of multilateral aid flows of some magnitude from the Community (in addition to those of the members), were quite valuable to them, despite the unpleasant legacies that such privileges recalled and the new goals of production and export diversification being entertained at that time in line with prevalent development thinking. Ideally, a preferred access to European markets could have preserved the old side of the economic relationship with the former colonial centres, while aid could have helped to pave the way for the development of new ones, built around industrialization and exports of manufactures first to Europe and then (after the necessary learning) to the rest of the industrialized world.

The formal framework of this trade-aid-development relationship also remained

527

unchanged after the mid-1970s: a quasi-contractual agreement 'negotiated' between two equal parties for given periods, containing the specific terms and conditions of the development co-operation to be pursued during each of them. The forms and motions of 'coopération paritaire' served the purpose of making it politically more palatable to the associates, when this was an issue of some relevance (especially in the 1960s and 1970s), and to make the Community look 'progressive' and 'innovative' in the eyes of developing countries. But the inherently uneven nature of this relationship could never be altered, by rhetoric, preambles to conventions enshrining 'common objectives' or public relations efforts by either side. Some political analysts have gone as far as to characterize it as 'collective clientelism' (Ravenhill, 1985b). Others have called it an Euro-African 'entente cordiale' based on an implicit, but clear, exchange: international political support to Europe from the African states against economic support to them by Europe (Lister, 1988). At least from the economic standpoint, there could be no doubt that the Community was the 'giving', and the ACP countries the 'receiving', side. The relationship was thus basically asymmetric, and such it remained ever since the start. The only point of economic strength in favour of the Africans was the capacity to offer raw materials to Europe, but it materialized only sporadically, when security of supply became an issue. Otherwise, Europe could supply itself elsewhere (in Asia, North and South America), and advancements in handling and transport technology[1] made alternatives also more competitive. The other aspect of European economic interest in Africa – exports to that region – had too little a weight to be significant at any time for Europe at large.

On the political side, the support to Europe coming from Africa, quite valuable when the cold war was on, became progressively less so with the toning down of the East–West political-military confrontation in the 1980s, and virtually disappeared in the 1990s with the demise of the former Soviet Union. In fact, the marked shift in the EU's attention from Africa to Eastern Europe that occurred in these years is the clearest sign of the changing balance of political interests taking place inside Europe. Long accustomed to being courted, the ACP countries are now in the new position of having to struggle to maintain even an adequate level of European attention on them. Much of this change has its origins in the end of the Soviet 'empire' and in the disappearance of the threat to Europe that emanated from it. But part of it also derives from the negative backlash effect that Africa's failure to develop economically and politically during the past two decades has created in Europe.

23.2   The changing rationales of EU–ACP co-operation

Finding a solid justification for the regional approach taken from the start in co-operating with developing countries has never been easy for the Community. While the roots of the choice made in the late 1950s and confirmed in the 1960s are clear, French-inspired associationism standing on the notion of a common-wealth of interests between Europe and Africa based on geographical proximity and economic complementarity (Lister, 1988), the model chosen never acquired a generally credible economic or political rationale (Grilli, 1993). In fact, no serious attempt to articulate it directly has ever been made by the Brussels authorities.

In its first memorandum on Community development policy, the EC

Commission justified the choice made by the constituent members in 1957 simply by referring to 'history, geography and [the Community's] limited means' (CEC, 1971c, p. 4). A few years later, in the so-called 'Fresco Memorandum' (CEC, 1974c) on development aid, the Commission was content to briefly sketch a 'grand' design of co-operation that would 'combine the [developing countries]' wealth in raw materials, population and area with the technology and the vast markets of the industrialized countries' (EC Commission, 1974c, p. 8). The design was unmistakably similar to the original EC conception of relations with Africa, but its rationale was again assumed by the Commission, rather than persuasively argued. The second development decade which had just been launched by UNCTAD and the growing emphasis then put on poverty by McNamara's World Bank made heeding the call for more development aid politically opportune for the Community as well. The Commission, moreover, eager to legitimize its position of autonomous agent and of significant player in the development co-operation arena at large, could not pass up the chance then being provided to emphasize the merits of its own model of North–South co-operation and its extendability beyond the core of privileged associates maintained until then. One cost of such generalization was, of course, some diffusion of the regional priority placed on Africa, but this could be met rather easily under the circumstances of the time with a more general use of food aid and the extension of limited financial aid to 'non-associated' developing countries. Some other developing countries could be made slightly better off without making the associates worse off. The first important statement of the Council on this subject was in fact issued in the early 1970s, when this need to go more general was more keenly felt by Europe at the political level.

A few years later, the oil crisis and the related fears, particularly strong in Europe, of insecurity of supplies of raw materials came, at least for a while, to vindicate the wisdom of the original priority put on Africa. It could then be argued that only an Africa solidly tied to Europe, not only by history and proximity, but also by a network of economic interests, could be relied upon as a trustworthy supplier of essential industrial inputs. The preservation of this access was then considered worth a substantial extension, in content and area of application, of the original framework of development co-operation. This was done with the first Lomé Convention, that extended 'associationism' practised on a more limited scale through the previous two Yaoundé conventions to the whole of Africa and slightly beyond it (to some areas of the Caribbean and the Pacific). The originality of this framework of development co-operation was also worth stressing at that time, as it appeared almost providential in the circumstances of possible shortages of raw materials created by producer 'cartels' which it was feared were in the making everywhere.

As to the motives of its co-operation policies, the EC could now be more explicit than in the past. The Pisani Memorandum of 1982[2] openly recognized the selfish interests of the Community, which 'as a political and mercantile power, [had] a fundamental interest in the existence of a stable, well regulated and predictable system of international relations' (CEC, 1982d, p. 12). In addition, being not the emanation of 'a multilateral developmental institution, but the expression of a European identity', its development policies 'embodied a geographical preference' (ibid., p. 14). As for aims, EC development policy 'though an expression of solidarity with certain developing countries' also reflected the 'Community's economic interests in the organization of its relations with countries on which it depended for the security of its supplies and markets' (ibid., p. 14, italics added).

Yet, security of raw materials supplies, in addition to maintenance of export markets, were used as justifications well beyond their worth in time and weight, for Europe's giving priority to Africa. As late as 1988 they were still publicly touted by the Commission as vital economic interests for Europe.[3] By then the share of imports of minerals coming from Africa had dropped to 7% of the total and that of non-ferrous metals to 2.5%. Even imports of fuels from Africa had dropped to just above 20% of the total. On the export side, while non-OPEC developing country markets accounted for about 25% of total EC exports, exports to Africa were just 3% of it (see Table 23.1). Oil prices had collapsed in the 1980s, real commodity prices had resumed their secular (slow) downward trend, and security of supplies had long ceased to be an issue. The problem was the glut, not the shortages, of raw materials in world markets. The traditional justification of the importance of Africa to Europe had completely lost its credibility.

Moreover, in the late 1980s most developing countries were still in the throes of a debt crisis of major proportions and lasting consequences that had broken out at the beginning of that decade, and the countries of Africa associated to the EC were facing a true economic crisis. Production in sub-Saharan Africa was lagging, exports were declining, public finances were in disarray in many countries, critical infrastructure was no longer being maintained, supplies of basic services had broken down, banking systems and public sector enterprises were in distress.[4] By then, if there was a new rationale for EC–ACP co-operation, it lay in fostering structural adaptation and a greater role of the private sector in the associated countries, confronted with a growth crisis that stemmed largely from grossly inadequate public policies, fraying social fabrics, poor institutions, weak economic incentives to production and wrong development priorities pursued for too long.[5] What had appeared as insufficient gains in the 1960s and 1970s in Africa (and elsewhere in the developing world) now looked almost like 'paradise lost'. Growth of per capita income had in fact collapsed in most of sub-Saharan Africa during the 1980s (see Table 23.2).

However, a Community policy dialogue with Africa over core changes (in ownership structures, trade strategies, exchange rate regimes, taxation of agriculture, financial systems and the like) meant necessarily the advocacy of macroeconomic and structural reforms, the conditioning of financial assistance and systematic verification of results, which did not fit well in either the past political rhetoric of 'co-

Table 23.1 Relative importance of Africa in EU trade

	1965	1970	1980	1990	1996
Share of Africa in EU exports					
Total exports	6.2	4.9	6.1	3.0	2.2
Share of Africa in EU imports					
Total imports	7.1	6.6	5.6	3.1	2.1
Imports of minerals and ores	14.9	11.0	9.1	7.3	5.1
Imports of non-ferrous metals	19.3	16.2	5.2	2.5	2.4
Imports of fuels	18.6	29.3	16.7	22.3	16.9

Source: UNCTAD, *Handbook of International Trade and Development Statistics*, various issues.

Table 23.2 Growth in per capita income in developing regions*

	1950-60	1960-70	1970-80	1980-90	1990-95
			(% per annum)		
Asia	2.8	2.5	3.5	6.1	7.7
Latin America	2.5	2.6	3.2	−0.4	1.4
Africa North of Sahara	2.1	1.7	4.3	1.2	−0.4
Africa South of Sahara	1.7	1.2	0.9	−1.6	−1.4

*Weighted averages.
Source: Grilli and Salvatore, (1994).

opération paritaire' or the historic patterns of EC–ACP development co-operation largely built until then around traditional project and programme financing, with priorities chosen in addition by the recipients. It also meant deep changes in the practice of 'no strings attached' to the resources provided to the associates, revisions of the method of joint administration of the aid granted by the Community, and necessary adjustments in country aid flows on the basis of performance. Since a strong dimension of entitlement had been built into the EC aid relationship with the ACP countries, changing it was clearly difficult for both sides. In addition, a good portion of EC aid was by then automatically disbursed, as commodity export earnings fell. STABEX aid (aimed at compensating export shortfalls) and SYSMIN aid (ostensibly devoted to keeping up mining capacity in associated countries) shared these basic characteristics.[6] Introducing a logic of performance in the allocation of such aid was in practice tantamount to destroying its original rationale. Conditionality, moreover, appeared to be the very negation of the 'coopération paritaire' enshrined in the preamble of Lomé III, and often underlined as a defining trait of the EC development co-operation model. The ACPs did not want conditionality in Community aid, and the Commission had little political stomach for it, aside from having prior technical experience in administering it.[7]

Under these circumstances, adapting the rationale for EC aid and development co-operation to the important changes that had taken place and continued to occur was quite difficult. Resorting to time-tested, if trite and rather misleading, notions such as security of supplies and export markets thus retained an appeal, at least as a way to postpone facing the issue of reform. Yet it appears that no new thoughts concerning development co-operation were being entertained by the Commission or at least being publicly expressed by it. At the time, the 'novelties' being debated were largely limited to the 'duration' of the new convention between the EC and the ACP countries, with some wanting to make its duration unlimited.[8] The Community seemed to have become prisoner of a development co-operation model without a clear rationale, cast in unchangeable forms and no longer suited either to its needs or to those of the countries it wanted to help (Grilli, 1993).

A thorough review of the sense and purpose of Community development policies had to wait for the conclusion of the Maastricht Treaty on European Union, which made development co-operation an official Community policy, and explicitly defined its objectives and methods (Articles 130U, 130V and 130X). Once again, as in the case of the EEC Treaty of Rome, the political decision came first and led the way. The technical arguments came later (at least as far as one can tell from the outside), and started with a review of the Commission's development co-operation record over the previous three decades. This review, for the first time, took a global perspective, and addressed the problems of all developing countries.

The general objectives for the EU policy of development co-operation, introduced in the Treaty, were in part traditional, and previously articulated, such as 'the social and economic development of the developing countries' with emphasis being placed on the poorest among them. In part, they were traditional, but newly specified as priorities, such as 'the smooth and gradual integration' of the developing countries into the world economy. Some of them were even rhetorical and redundant, such as 'the campaign against poverty', which was an aim already clearly subsumed in the priority placed on the poorest developing countries. The Treaty, nonetheless, did contain genuine innovations, such as the contribution that the EU now intended to make with its development co-operation policy to 'consolidating democracy, the rule of law, and the respect of human rights and fundamental freedoms' in developing countries (Article 130U2). The political element built into EU development co-operation, based on explicit values, could not have been more authoritatively and clearly highlighted than in the new treaty. The problem now was to explain it and make it acceptable to the other parties.

The explanation of the rationale for such a 'political' reorientation of EU development policy came with the Commission's 'Run-up to 2000' paper (CEC, 1992m), which not unexpectedly departed in a significant way from past thinking. The paper finally acknowledged that there had been a major growth crisis in developing countries, and that some had done much better than others, even within the same global economic context. Not all differences in performance could thus be attributed to the differences in starting-points or in the natural endowments of countries.[9] The lessons of three decades of development co-operation were that domestic policy performance mattered and that aid was important for some groups of developing countries, but not critical for all. Aid could help, but could not substitute for a lack of good domestic policies. Flows of private capital were assuming prominence for a growing number of developing countries. The globalization of the world economy was proceeding at a fast pace, creating for all categories of countries – developed and developing – new interdependencies and new adjustment needs. The paper noted that other critical changes were also occurring in the international context. After the collapse of the Soviet Union and the waning of ideological differences and related enmities, the geostrategic importance of many developing countries was diminishing rapidly, as was their political bargaining power. Economic performance was now becoming the issue, and the key to continued external support to all emerging countries.

Up to this point, the analysis presented in the 'Run-up to 2000' paper was largely conventional in content. The Commission was just embracing (and with some delay) the consensus that had emerged in the 1980s about development policies and development co-operation, thus updating itself in light of realities that it could no longer ignore. The major novelty for the Union lay in its acceptance of the notion that the performance of developing countries would be considered and evaluated in both the economic and the political domains. In order to benefit fully from EU development co-operation, developing countries would now be expected to make strides in reforming their economies and in behaving in conformity with the fundamental values that underpinned the Union's very existence: the promotion of peace, the peaceful resolution of conflicts, the development and con-solidation of democracy, the observance of human rights and the respect of funda-mental freedoms. This was a tall order for countries long accustomed to political and economic arbitrage between the East and the West, and used to considering internal political choices as their exclusive and unobjectionable right. For the ACP countries in particular, the new political position assumed by the EU represented in practice a unilateral change of principle on non-interference in basic domestic decisions fully accepted until then by both parties.[10]

The European Union was now saying, and emphatically so, that solidarity with the developing world would be reinterpreted in the light of its own core political values, and not in conformity with those of the recipients. Thus, the need for a con-tinuing 'political dialogue with developing countries with a view to the adoption of political and economic reforms' (CEC, 1992m, p. 1, Conclusion). To paraphrase Mr Pisani's Memorandum of 1982 (CEC, 1982), the Union was stating that 'not being a multilateral development institution, but a political entity, it was pursuing political goals'. The technical arguments could well be 'delegated' to the World Bank, to the regional development banks and to the International Monetary Fund (IMF). The political objectives, however, would not only be given first priority (in the Commission's language the adjective 'political' came ahead of 'economic' in characterizing reforms), but also be retained in the exclusive domain of the Union, its member states and the other world political democracies. The corollary of this was that, to be fully credible, this new type of political-economic dialogue with developing countries would have to be backed by the actions of all industrialized countries (*ibid.*, p. 1). Making what was once a privileged and partial relationship more general now concerned not only the goals, but also its actors.

23.3   The lasting instruments of EU–ACP co-operation

Since its beginning, EC development co-operation with the countries of Africa, and later also with those of the Caribbean and the Pacific, employed two instruments: trade preferences and direct aid. Preferential entry into the Community of the exports of the 'associated countries and territories' was the main legacy of col-onialism, incorporated in the EEC Treaty of Rome. Free access to the markets of the respective colonial centres became in practice free access to the markets of the whole Community. This privilege was kept – with some restrictions – by the colonies when they became independent states. As associates of the Community they kept a highly preferential access to its markets, relative not only to developed countries, but also to other developing countries.[11] Bilateral aid to the colonies was also a reality in the 1950s – this was particularly important for the colonial posses-sions of France. The addition of EC multilateral aid to the bilateral aid of the mem-bers was a modest innovation at the time of the Treaty of Rome. It was a sign of solidarity from those members of the Community that had no colonial possessions to those that still did, rather than an innovation in the development armoury of the new community of European nations that was being formed. The addition of EC aid to the bilateral aid of members, characterized later on as important testi-mony to the enhanced development awareness of the Community, was at the start only a way to ensure some internal burden sharing in dealing with the legacies of colonialism.

The trade preferences granted to the associated countries were initially significant for some of their exports (coffee, bananas, groundnut oil, palm oil, cocoa), but were eroded over time by reductions in benchmark import tariffs – the most-favoured nation (MFN) tariffs of the Community – (Grilli, 1991), and in part by the concession of preferences to other developing countries – those of the Maghreb and the Mashreq, for example, and by the generalized system of preferences (GSPs) granted in 1971 to all developing countries (Langhammer and Sapir, 1987). Preferences for manufactures never became significant (with some notable exceptions such as Mauritius), given the very limited manufacturing capacity that emerged within Africa. Exports of some agricultural commodities that competed with domestic productions were nonetheless granted only limited access privileges by the Community. Despite some additional liberalization of the import regimes applied to associates, these remained the fundamental characteristics of the trade preferences of the EU (Cosgrove, 1994).

Multilateral aid to developing countries became progressively more important in total size and as a share of overall EC aid (bilateral and multilateral), but within it aid to ACP countries, which was dominant until the late 1980s, declined drastically in the 1990s as EU aid priorities shifted markedly towards Central and Eastern

Table 23.3 Distribution of European Aid[a] (%)

	1976–1977[b]	1986–1987	1991–1992	1996–1997
Total European aid (ODA)				
Bilateral	87.0	85.0	82.0	80.0
Multilateral	13.0	15.0	18.0	20.0
Bilateral EU-15 aid				
Sub-Saharan Africa		43.6	43.4	42.5
North Africa			10.8	9.1
Middle East			5.5	4.9
Asia			18.4	17.5
America			12.1	14.1
Oceania			3.8	5.1
Europe			6.1	6.7
European Commission aid				
ACP	91.7[c]	63.1	50.7	34.4
South Asia		0.5	1.2	0.8
Asia	2.5[d]	7.4	6.2	9.3
Latin America		3.5	4.7	5.8
Mediterranean and Middle East	5.8	13.5	16.7	12.5
CEECs	0.0	0.1	9.3	21.1
NIS	0.0	0.0	5.5	8.2
Unallocable	0.0	12.2	5.7	8.2

[a] Aid disbursed.
[b] Includes Middle East
[c] Includes Oceania.
[d] Includes South Asia.

Sources: Cox and Chapman (1999); Grilli (1993); OECD (1998); *Geographical Distribution of Financial Flows to Aid Recipients*, Paris, various issues.

Europe (see Table 23.3). Aid was adjusted for the growing totals of recipients in the associated countries. In nominal terms, it therefore increased substantially from the 1970s to the 1990s, but in real terms it remained constant.

The Community long maintained that the quality of its aid was as important as its quantity. It stressed that its aid to ACP countriess was specified in advance, covered a number of years (to ensure greater predictability of flows), assigned to associates through an interactive and co-operative process, 'jointly-administered' by the two parties, gave concessions and mostly comprised grants. Yet, when Lomé conventions were negotiated, it was the quantity of aid that was often the point at issue. Quality considerations remained in the background.

The Community also made changes in both the instruments and the functional destination of its aid to ACP countries. Beginning with Lomé I, special loans and European Investment Bank (EIB) credits became significant components of EC aid packages, in addition to outright grants. Risk capital became important with Lomé II (see Table 23.4). Structural adjustment aid, as part of programme aid, became important with Lomé IV. These changes reflected in part the struggle faced by the Commission to find resources to cover the aid requirements of an increasing number of associates (which eventually became 71 in number), and in part redirections in the focus of EC aid co-operation.

On the whole, the terms and conditions of Community development assistance to ACP countries were kept highly non-reciprocal. The Community was extending trade preferences to its associates, without reciprocal concessions from them, and aid, which by its very nature was a one-way flow. Nonetheless, internal constraints

Table 23.4 Evolution of EDF and EIB resources

	1957 Rome Treaty EDF 1	1963 Yaoundé I EDF 2	1969 Yaoundé II EDF 3	1975–80 Lomé I EDF 4	1980–85 Lomé II EDF 5	1985–90 Lomé III EDF 6	1990–95 Lomé IV EDF 7	1995–2000 Lomé V EDF 8
EDF total	581	666	828	3 072	4 724	7 400	10 800	12 967
Grants[a]	581	620	748	2 150	2 999	4 860	7 995	9 592
Special loans	–	–	–	466	525	600	–	–
STABEX	–	–	–	377	634	925	1 500	1 800
SYSMIN	–	–	–	–	282	415	480	575
Risk capital	–	46	80	99	284	660	825	1 000
EIB own resources[b]	–	64	90	390	685	1 100	1 200	1 658
Total EDF plus EIB	581	730	918	3 462	5 409	8 500	12 000	14 625
Per capita EDF								
Current[c]	10.7	9.7	10.5	12.3	13.5	17.9	21.9	23.6
Constant[d]	62.9	50.3	41.2	31.5	22.6	24.2	24.3	23.6

[a] This includes assistance for regional co-operation, interest rate subsidies, structural adjustment assistance (Lomé IV), emergency and refugee assistance (Lomé IV) and other grants.
[b] This is a ceiling set by the board of the EIB which has never been reached.
[c] Total current value of EDF divided by associate country's population (millions) at the beginning of each convention period.
[d] EDF totals expressed in 1997 terms: current values deflated by the EC GDP deflator index centred in the mid-year of each convention (1961 for EDF 1; 1965 for EDF 2; 1971 for EDF 3).
Sources: Grilli (1993); Cox and Chapman (1999).

such as the Common Agricultural Policy (CAP), on the policy side, and the reluctance of Community members to contribute ever larger resources to the EDFs, on the budget side, always tempered the generosity of the Commission towards the associates.

23.4 The ACP countries' limited gains from EU aid and trade preferences

Trade preferences and aid granted to associated ACP countries had a limited impact on their trade and development. The gains derived by ACP countries from Community concessions in both these areas were small and insufficient to generate significant and self-sustaining growth. This much the Commission finally accepted in its Green Paper on relations with ACP countries on the eve of the twenty-first century (CEU, 1997f), with the admission that its co-operation policies in ACP countries had not worked.

However, limited success could have resulted either from the fact that the 'privileges' effectively granted to the ACP countries were too limited or from their inability to maximize the full potential of the concessions obtained, or both. The two reasons for the failure, which was noted by outside experts much earlier than by the Commission, are obviously connected to each other. But one may surmise that the size problem might have been the more important in the area of trade preferences, while the problem of domestic policies and conditions might have predominated in the case of aid.

Community trade preferences to the ACP countries never amounted to much[12] (apart from a few specific sectoral exceptions such as the special regimes for sugar and bananas) and were progressively eroded by GSPs granted to all developing countries and generally by multilateral trade liberalization. What remained of them after all this was not enough to offer the ACP countries a significant competitive advantage over non-associated developing countries.[13] Yet, even if this were the main explanation of the ineffectiveness of EC preferences, the size argument could not have applied to nearly the same extent to aid. Total European aid to ACP countries – both bilateral and multilateral aid – was substantial. As already noted, Community aid had remained at least constant in real per capita terms for the recipients since Lomé II (see Table 23.4) and total aid to sub-Saharan African countries, which constitute the bulk of the ACP countries, had been similarly constant since 1980.[14] Its lack of effectiveness (again with few country and sector exceptions) had to do with the ways in which aid was utilized, either as the consequence of weak donor practices or recipients' bad habits (especially in framework policies). The general problems of external aid are well known: external resources can substitute for domestic ones, and above all lead to reduced domestic efforts, thus leaving recipients' fortunes indeterminate (better or worse than in the absence of aid, depending on the degree of substitution).

The specific problems of EU aid had to do with poor project implementation, and above all with inadequate project sustainability, as the Court of Auditors of the EC amply documented in its first large-scale evaluation of project aid to ACP countries (Court of Auditors, 1982). Perhaps the major obstacle to the effectiveness of aid in ACP countries was, nonetheless, the poor policy framework within which aid was utilized. Much of the aid went to economic and social infrastructure (18.8% and

7.5% respectively in the 1986–98 period).[15] Substantial amounts went to agricultural production (see Table 23.5). But, even when projects financed in these critical sectors are effective in themselves, they do not lead to permanent or general developmental gains in the absence of appropriate incentive policies, dynamic sectoral institutions and sufficient or efficient national funding. The necessary framework conditions – both sectoral and macroeconomic – were often not in place in ACP countries during the years in which Lomé aid was disbursed. This is what the Commission also found in its review of aid effectiveness and openly recognized in its Green Paper (1997f, p. 7).

Another important explanation for the limited effectiveness of EU aid to ACP countries had to do with the weak distribution criteria used by the Commission. Much of the aid was allocated according to the perceived needs of recipient countries, and not on the basis of their capacity to use it or their actual performance in doing so (Grilli and Riess, 1992). Disagreements with recipients over policy priorities and the inability of the Commission to use aid conditionality effectively also reduced the effectiveness of the aid given. Finally, EU aid did not succeed in fostering much private sector development in recipient countries.

Project aid, available evaluations indicate, had mixed results. It was more effec-

Table 23.5 Sector distribution of total Community aid to the ACP countries[a]

	Average 1986–1998 (% of total)
Programme aid	25.4
Structural adjustment assistance	11.7
STABEX	11.6
SYSMIN	2.1
Food aid (development)	8.9
Humanitarian aid	7.3
Agriculture[b]	6.2
Industry[c]	8.1
Economic infrastructure[d]	18.8
Social infrastructure[e]	7.5
Multisector	8.9
Other aid	3.3
Unallocable by sector	5.6
Total	100.0

[a] Aid committed.
[b] Includes forestry and fishery.
[c] Includes mining, trade and tourism.
[d] Includes transport, communications, energy and finance.
[e] Includes education, health, water supply and other social infrastructure.
Source: Cox and Chapman (1999).

tive in transport than in agriculture and rural development. Structural adjustment assistance, introduced with some fanfare in Lomé IV, had little effect, being hampered by the Commission's problems with defining its policy conditions and its ambiguity towards the conditions demanded by other aid suppliers, such as the World Bank in the IDA programmes it financed in sub-Saharan Africa. Commodity-based aid, given through STABEX and SYSMIN, proved to be totally ill-suited to the objective it was supposed to serve: diversification out of primary commodity production and maintenance of production capacity in mining. Much, if not all, was used by recipient country governments for general purposes, often to finance current budget expenditure, instead of sector investments. The fact that its allocation was automatic (once called 'objectivity') and the lack of enforceable conditions over its domestic use led almost inevitably to these outcomes.

While the developmental ineffectiveness of aid to poor countries in sub-Saharan Africa and elsewhere is now widely accepted (see Killick, 1991; Mosley and Hudson, 1995)[16] and the basic reasons for this failure are well documented (World Bank, 1998), there is still a surprising amount of disagreement in the literature over the value of EU trade preferences to ACP countries and thus over the benefits of retaining them.

Ex ante, the average trade-enhancing effects of EU tariff preferences could never but be presumed to be large under any reasonable set of price elasticities that could apply to the existing exportable product they effectively covered. Preferences were also too low to generate new export potential. *Ex post* analysis, largely based on market shares at different levels of product disaggregation, has systematically confirmed the overall presumptions that could be made *ex ante*. ACP countries' trade figures over time are rather depressing, no matter how one reads them. The importance of ACP countries in world trade has waned: from 3.5% in 1975 to about 1% today. Over the same period, other developing countries increased their share of world trade steadily and substantially. The importance of ACP countries as suppliers to the EU has also declined drastically. In 1974, 8% of total EU imports came from ACP countries. In 1998, the equivalent figure was 2.9%. Over the same period, imports from non-ACP developing countries went from 14% to 24%. Thus, the importance of ACP countries as exporters (and importers) shrank not only *vis-à-vis* the rest of the world, but also relative to other developing countries in both world and EU markets. ACP countries lost shares also in their most privileged market and *vis-à-vis* other developing countries that had less favourable entry conditions (see Figure 23.1). In addition, ACP countries' exports have done comparatively better in terms of growth in US and Japanese markets, where they competed with other developing countries on the basis of parity of access, than in the EU market where they enjoyed special treatment. All this leads one to think that it was not relative market access that mattered in determining the relative market share performance of ACP countries, but other comparative conditions regarding the supply of exportable goods, especially manufactures.

Many non-ACP developing countries, particularly those of Asia, by virtue of better incentive policies (initiated in some cases well before 1975) had established more conducive domestic conditions for the production of goods exportable to Europe than had ACP countries, and were taking advantage of these conditions,[17] despite more limited entry for textiles and clothing exports, a great number of NTBs imposed on them by the Union and the lack of special import regimes for certain commodities such as sugar, for which ACP countries also enjoyed preferential

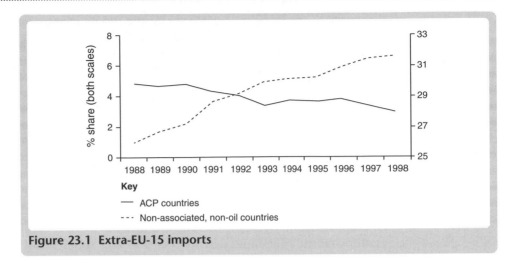

Figure 23.1 Extra-EU-15 imports

import prices.[18] Examination of the composition of ACP exports to the Community (overall and in comparison with exports from other developing countries) indicates that the key to their unfavourable export performance had in fact to do with manufactures, i.e. with the overall failure of ACP countries to develop them as a major export item (again with some exceptions such as Mauritius and Kenya). Despite some improvement in the quota of manufactures in total exports to the EU, the bulk of ACP exports remained primary commodities.[19] But the explanation for the failure of ACP countries to develop exports of manufactures lies not in the details of the preferential access that they enjoyed (such as EU rules of origin), but in the inadequate export incentives offered by these countries to domestic and foreign producers. Overall, it was supply conditions that mattered the most in ACP countries (Agarwal *et al.*, 1985). This is shown not only by the scarcity of new supplies of exportable manufactures, but also by the systematic deterioration in the conditions of production of traditional exportable commodities: copper in Zambia and Zaire, cocoa in Ghana, sisal in Tanzania and so on. There has in fact been a strong and fairly continuous correlation between declines in domestic production and exports of most primary commodities from ACP countries in the post-1975 period (Grilli, 1993).

By themselves, trade preferences made very little difference in stimulating ACP country exports to European markets. No amount of quibbling over the details (by country, product and time) can obfuscate this reality. At the margin one can always find some positive results, but when the results remain marginal they matter very little. There is a striking negative correlation between the extent of preference enjoyed by different groups of developing countries and the overall export performance in EU markets: the ACP countries that had (relatively speaking) the highest preferences did the worst in market share terms, while the Asian countries that had the least favourable access did the best. This result is consistent not only with the observation of specific differential supply conditions prevailing in ACP countries *vis-à-vis* both large and small Asian countries (real exchange rates, import regimes, infrastructure, quality of administrative support, etc.), but also with the general story of common trade preferences (the GSP schemes, for example), the benefits of which have been shown to go to a handful of beneficiary countries:

those able to ensure better conditions for the supply of manufactures for export.[20] One may be more charitable, and say that ACP countries under-performed other developing countries in EU markets because 'they were simply less successful at diversifying into products with a better market outlook than have other LDCs' (Stevens, 1992), but the core issue remains the why, which has to do with policies, internal political and social circumstances (as they affect foreign investments, for example) and to a lesser extent with the initial conditions.[21]

One may ask why it took so long for the Commission to reach the conclusion that trade preferences did not have much effect on ACP countries, but not question the conclusion itself, which had been quite evident for at least a decade. The next logical question is what to do with the preferences. And this is turning out to be a much more difficult question than probably the Commission itself had anticipated, given its own long-standing inclination for differentiated trade regimes across developing country groups, the EU 'institutional' bias in favour of regional integration and the punctilious defence, made by ACP recipients of the 'residual' value of the preferences. They seemed to think, individually and collectively, that even a very small privilege is worth preserving (ACP Heads of State, 1997; ACP Group, 1998; ACP Group, 1996).

23.5 The African preference in EU development policies

In the early part of the 1990s the Commission was apparently engaged in a difficult balancing act: correcting past shortcomings, updating its views and trying to reshape the rationale, if not yet the geographical focus, of EU development co-operation. By casting its analysis in a global perspective, addressing the problems of the various classes of developing countries and attempting to draw general implications for the Union's policies, it appeared to be trying to extricate Europe from the straitjacket of special relationship with a single developing region and from historical models of co-operation (above all associationism) that had not produced many positive results and had become rather outmoded. Remarkably, the 'Run-up to 2000' document never mentioned the ACP countries by name.

Yet, the Commission was also clearly mindful of reality. Powerful business and political interests still lay behind the *status quo*. In fact, the Commission did not advocate, as would have been logical, a radical redirection of trade and assistance across country groups and developing regions.[22] As for EU aid, it limited itself to noting that the distribution of European multilateral aid resources, being the result of history and proximity, was geographically 'unequal' and would 'be likely to remain so'. As for regional focus, according to the Commission, EU assistance should have aimed at supporting economic restructuring in sub-Saharan Africa, but without disregarding traditional priorities such as food security, population growth and basic infrastructure, which past action had often missed and which, in addition, could be pursued only through project or programme assistance, i.e. using the traditional tools of EC/EU 'development trade'.

Implicit in this advocacy was a compromise position, perhaps an intermediate one in terms of strategy: the affirmation of the objective of a global development co-operation policy, driven by a common vision and general goals, but without too immediate a threat to the *status quo*, and thus a policy compatible, at least for a while, with a continued aid focus on sub-Saharan Africa. The logical consequences stemming from this position could be drawn later. Significantly, the Commission document did not specifically address trade policies, which could be reshaped more easily than aid policies to satisfy specific development needs of other priority areas, such as North Africa or Central and Eastern Europe.[23]

The Commission returned to the EU–ACP relationship in the context of the Lomé negotiations, first with the mid-period review of Lomé IV, and then when preparations for its successor began. Both were mandated occasions for rethinking regional strategies and repositioning options. At the mid-period review of Lomé IV, a major goal pursued by the Commission seems to have been the 'normalization' of ACP–EU co-operation: transformating it from a special to a regular relationship, incorporating into it new principles and objectives concerning development co-operation as well as the new realities faced in sub-Saharan Africa. The substantial amendments to Lomé IV introduced in 1995[24] were, therefore, in the political field, and came with the explicit recognition that application of democratic principles, the consolidation of the rule of law in ACP countries and good governance were essential dimensions of the European–African relationship. Violation of these principles could lead to the suspension of the Convention's application (Art. 366a). ACP–EU development co-operation was being increasingly justified, *de jure* and *de facto*, as an avenue for extending democracy, good government and the rule of law in the world. Gone were the days when the Community prided itself on the apolitical nature of its development assistance and when even dialogue about development effectiveness was thought to be highly controversial in the context of the European–African relationship (CEC 1982d and 1984e; Pisani, 1984). The ACP countries, at least in the political domain, were now being treated like the rest of the developing countries and asked to conform to the general political goals being pursued by the EU if they wanted to continue to benefit from its solidarity.

In the economic domain the ACP countries were still treated in a privileged way. Yet, appearances differed from realities. The trade preferences that the ACP countries enjoyed, for whatever they were worth, were only marginally increased. Aid granted to them in the second half of the period covered by Lomé IV (1995–2000) was also marginally upgraded. Yet, tangible signs of the decline in the relative importance that these countries were given in the overall framework of EU development co-operation were clearly emerging. Revealed EU preferences were speaking more loudly than political or policy pronouncements to the contrary. Commission-administered aid was progressively concentrated in Europe, both in Central and Eastern European Countries (SEECs) and in south eastern European countries. The ACP share in EU aid actually disbursed dropped below 35% in the late 1990s, from over 60% of ten years before, while the share of the CEECs increased from zero to 20% of the total (see Table 23.3). As total aid to ACP countries was still going up, although only slightly, in both nominal and real terms, aid deflection, strictly speaking, cannot be said to have occurred. But aid to other regions, especially Eastern Europe and the Balkans, grew much more rapidly than aid to ACP countries, indicating the direction in which EU preferences were rapidly shifting. In the 1990s the Union was in fact redressing the global 'terms of trade' of its African relationship: it was clearly demanding much more of them in terms of political commitments and supplying just about the same in terms of real resources. The African preference was on the wane.

23.6 EU–ACP development co-operation today: going beyond Lomé?

Despite a history of 35 years of co-operation, a remarkable variety of instruments used to keep it going, considerable attachment to it from both parties and powerful forces created during this period in favour of the maintenance of the *status quo*, the EU–ACP relationship could not escape a major critical scrutiny in the 1990s and is emerging from it much changed. This change was overdue and difficult to bring about.

With the Green Paper the Commission prepared the ground for changes to be made and aimed at a normalization of its development co-operation with the ACP countries in both ends and means. The general starting-points were the 'changed political and economic conditions for development and the changed attitudes in Europe' (CEU, 1997f, p. vi). The global backdrop of EU–ACP relations had changed. The collapse of the Soviet bloc had reshaped the international political context. The Union was feeling the obligation to provide major assistance to the emerging democracies of Central and Eastern Europe and to co-operate economically with Russia, to keep it at least minimally stable. Globalization of trade and financial systems required that even the poorest developing countries were not excluded. They all needed to be helped to meet the requirements of the global economy. One could no longer distinguish between poor associates and poor non-associates, as they faced the same challenge of participation and the same risk of exclusion. Official development assistance was suffering a crisis of legitimacy. It was too often becoming reactive (to crises and threats, be they migratory, religious, medical), instead of proactive and development driven, as Commissioner Pinheiro was no doubt reminding the associates in the middle of the Lomé V negotiations (CEU, 1999a). Conditions in Europe, especially public attitudes towards immigration, the perceived threat of Islamic fundamentalism and the continuing instability in the south-eastern part of Europe, were pushing its development assistance in that direction. Development co-operation, especially that with ACP countries, which had for so long held the centre stage, thus needed to be reshaped and rethought. This was the central political message of the Green Paper.

In the economic domain, the specific building-blocks of the paper came from the lessons of four decades of co-operation with the ACP countries, the most important of which were that the association had 'lost its substance', 'the bulk of ACP countries [had] lacked the economic policies and the domestic conditions for developing trade' and, as far as financial assistance was concerned, 'the state of the institutions and economic policy in the recipient countries [had been] a major constraint, making Community aid less effective'. Moreover, 'financial resources granted automatically and the EU's tendency . . . to take the initiative away from its weaker partners, had not encouraged ACP governments to display genuine political commitment'. Thus, 'there was a tendency for development instruments to dictate policy rather than the other way around' (Green Paper, CEU, 1997f, p. vii). The Commission was saying for the first time, and in plain and forceful language, that one had to start from reality: trade preferences and EU aid had not worked to foster growth and development in ACP countries because in most cases they had exerted their effects in inhospitable policy and institutional environments. These were lessons drawn long before by many field observers and economic development analysts, which the Commission was finally acknowledging as essential in shaping its future policies.

The negotiations for the successor to Lomé IV became for the Union the right occasion for starting to make at least some of the desired changes. The offer that the EU made to its associates was in the end a tactical one, embodying a compromise, but it served to advance the strategic objective it pursued. The proposal envisaged the transformation of the association agreement with the ACP countries into a partnership agreement based on political dialogue, trade co-operation and support for development. Aid would remain a critical feature of the partnership, but trade relations would change from one-way to two-way preferential and be somewhat differentiated. They would be based on a series of WTO-compatible free trade agreements between the Union and different groups of ACP countries. The main compromise involved the length of the phasing-in period for the changes in trade relations, which would begin only five years after the signature of the partnership agreement, and be subject to a previous review process. All the least developed countries, associates and non-associates, would be given free entry into the Union for practically all their exports beginning at the latest in 2005. In the area of aid, assistance would continue and be multi-year, but it was to be reshaped and rebased. Need and the performance of the recipients were to be the joint criteria for allocating it.

The conceptual novelties of the offer lay first in the transformation of ACP countries from associates to political and economic partners. This implied new obligations from them, particularly in the political sphere, including the acceptance of core EU political values such as democracy and respect of human rights, in addition to enhanced co-operation in promoting good governance and in fighting corruption at home. The other conceptual novelty was the introduction of differentiation among former associates. Trade preferences would be kept for only the poorest of them, on a par with those for most poor non-associates, and free trade areas could be set up with different groups of ACP countries.[25] Non-discrimination by the Union among ACP countries was in fact being dropped as a guiding principle. Another novelty was the introduction of performance in the criteria for the allocation of financial assistance to the new partners. The practical novelties were more numerous. They had to do, for example, with the elimination of automatic aid allocations, such as those of STABEX and SYSMIN, the periodic review of aid performance in recipient countries and co-operation between the EU and the partners in matters such as migration and the control of illegal immigration.

A new Partnership Agreement between the EU and the ACP states, with a twenty-year duration, was in fact reached on 3 February 2000. It will be officially signed in May 2000. Since its terms are not yet public, one must remain somewhat guarded about it. The devil often lies in the details. However, from what is officially known at the moment,[26] it seems the Union had to make some additional compromises to bring the negotiations to a conclusion. One had to do with the phasing in of the free trade areas. The period during which this will happen is now 2000–7. The trade *status quo* will thus be maintained for seven years, instead of five.[27] The Ninth EDF will be worth 13.5 billion Euro.[28] In addition there will be 1.7 billion Euros in EIB loans. Total financial assistance of 15.2 billion Euros for the period 2000–7 contrasts with an original EU offer of 14.3 billion Euro covering the 2000–5 period, which was in turn higher than the allocation made for the Eighth EDF.[29] The ACP countries clearly sought and obtained assurances on extended financial assistance from the Union.

Whether the agreement and the related architecture will represent the beginning of a new era in EU–ACP co-operation, instead of a simple adaptation of the old Lomé model, will depend on many factors, some endogenous and some exogenous to the partnership. An important step seems to have been made, nonetheless. ACP countries haggled over terms, but accepted a 'global' relationship with Europe, clearly encompassing both a political and an economic dimension. They have assumed obligations in sensitive areas, such as the control of illegal migration, good governance, defined as 'the transparent and responsible management of public resources for the purposes of equitable and sustainable development', in the context of 'a political and institutional environment that [would] uphold human rights, democratic principles and the rule of law'.[30] They have accepted the objective of integrating themselves more fully and rapidly in the global economy, even if this is through the protective shield of free trade arrangements with the EU. Many of them have renounced, even if more reluctantly than one would have expected, given their very limited worth, trade preferences and opted for a non-discriminatory trade regime *vis-à-vis* the Union. They have also undertaken, at least in practice, to push on with the development of the private sector in their economies and to achieve substantial improvements in their use of the development aid they will receive.

Are we moving beyond Lomé? We do not know yet. But the new agreement seems to be a significant step in the direction of a more productive development co-operation between Europe and Africa than was possible under Lomé. Naturally, the undertakings it contains must be followed through and steadily implemented in order to bear positive results. This will take time and effort. The risks that this process may be derailed remain high. Past experience is not reassuring. The Union can help its new partners, but the main choices and the major burdens are with them. In the end, it is up to the ACP countries to shape their own future.

Notes

1. Particularly in bulk handling and transport of ores and basic metals.
2, Named after the EC Commissioner who drew it up.
3. CEC (1988m), pp. 10–13.
4. In launching its agenda for action in sub-Saharan Africa, just seven years earlier, the World Bank had observed that 'for most African countries, and for a majority of [the] African population, the record is grim and it is no exaggeration to talk of a crisis. Slow overall economic growth, sluggish agricultural performance coupled with rapid rates of population increase, and balance of payments and financial crises are dramatic indicators of economic trouble' (World Bank, 1981, p. 2). In 1984, the same institution, in presenting its joint programme of action in sub-Saharan Africa, was noting how the consensus had become that African problems were 'structural and just to be tackled by a range of policy measures' (World Bank, 1984, p. 4). The situation was, unfortunately, quite clear.
5. The most important factor was perhaps excessive statism, and consequent lack of incentives to domestic entrepreneurship and risk taking. Another was limited openness, which resulted in a slow pace of factor productivity growth, in both absolute and relative terms, as shown by the comparative growth accounting of Bosworth *et al.* (1995).
6. In the jargon of the Community, the main instrument of Lomé financing was 'programmable' aid, allocated in advance to associated countries and used to finance projects, while 'non-programmable' aid was not pre-allocated, being used to finance STABEX, SYSMIN and emergency aid and was subsequently risk capital. Resources allocated to STABEX and SYSMIN accounted for about 15% of total Lomé conventions' finances, while risk capital made up another 7–8%. Both 'programmable' and 'non-programmable' aid

came from a special extra-budget fund (the European Development Fund, or EDF), replenished periodically with direct contributions from member states). Only a relatively small portion of humanitarian aid was financed using EDF resources. Most of it came directly from the EC budget and in recent years from the Community's Humanitarian Office (ECHO).

7. In CEC (1988) *op. cit.*, n. 4, one finds references to 'unpalatable reforms' that the ACP countries had had to undertake since Lomé III, being 'in danger of financial strangulation'(*sic*), and to the fact that 'softening the hardness of "adjustment" could sometimes be essential' (*op. cit.*, p. 35). In envisaging the next convention (then about to be negotiated), the Commission signalled the possibility of 'some more organized form of support for ACP countries undertaking structural reform . . . [which] would demonstrate the ACP–EEC partners' capacity to come up with solutions to new problems without departing from their fundamental aim', which remained 'the encouragement of sustainable, long-term development in the ACP countries' (*ibid.*, p. 35). Support for structural adjustment was envisaged as a way to soften the 'unpalatable' consequences of the measures that the World Bank was demanding (by then about 30 ACPs had obtained structural or sectoral adjustment loans from the IDA and the IBRD), and not as a vehicle for redirecting EC–ACP development co-operation. The Commission appeared in the late 1980s to be still at pains to reassure the associates that the thrust of its development co-operation would not be changed with Lomé IV. In fact, as late as February 1989, the time of the Brazzaville meeting of the ACP-EC Ministerial Council, the issue of 'new forms of aid' (for which, read structural adjustment aid) was apparently still being treated very gingerly by the two parties (see Killick and Stevens, 1989).

8. The Commission entertained such a notion as a way 'to allay the fears of some ACP countries that their advantages under Lomé (were) being eroded or diluted' (CEC *op. cit.*, 1988, p. 35). This was hardly an indication of new thinking.

9. This was by no means a new finding, as it had emerged quite clearly from the growth experiences of many countries. Good natural resource endowments are neither a necessary nor a sufficient condition for growth. Exports of manufactures, moreover, a key stage in the growth process of most mature nations, are also not systematically tied to resource availability at home. For Africa in particular, this is shown to be the case, while also important are transaction costs and incentives, such as real exchange rates (Elbadawi, 1999).

10. The 'right of each state to determine its own political, social, cultural and economic policy option' had in fact been introduced in the 'objectives and principles' of Lomé III. This principle continued to be formally in force, being part of Article 2 of the revised Lomé IV, Article 5 of which concurrently stated that 'development policy and co-operation shall be closely linked to respect for and enjoyment of fundamental human rights and the recognition and application of democratic principles, the consolidation of the rule of law and good governance', without any apparent concern with the contradictions between the two sets of principles.

11. In this sense they were at the top of the so-called pyramid of trade privileges that the Community over time granted to different categories of developing countries. The ACP associates were, in other words, the most privileged of all.

12. Even at their most powerful, i.e. when first granted under the Treaty of Rome to the countries and territories still under the jurisdiction of the EC member states, tariff preferences did not amount to much except for coffee, ground nut oil and bananas. By 1975 (the year of the first Lomé Convention, when these preferences were extended to practically all sub-Saharan Africa) their weighted value had already reduced by almost half. Ten years later they had become virtually nil for the most important primary commodities that the associated countries exported, except for bananas, as the result of GATT-sponsored tariff cutting. Meanwhile, the extension of GSPs to other developing countries, and the privileges granted to North African countries in the framework of the co-operation agreements

signed with them by the Community, further reduced the tariff advantages enjoyed by ACP countries because of the free entry into the EC of exports of manufactures (see Grilli, 1991).

13. Cosgrove (1994) contains a careful review of the coverage of EC trade preferences to ACP countries and an analysis of their erosion over time. According to the author, in 1993 the duty-free access granted by Lomé IV did not afford the beneficiaries any significant preferential advantage for almost two-thirds of their exports. They would have had free access to EU markets under GSP or MFN trade regimes.

14. According to official figures, total net aid (bilateral and multilateral) disbursed by the EU to sub-Saharan Africa, calculated at 1995 prices and exchange rates, had increased from $6 billion in 1980 to $9 billion in 1994–5. In real per capita terms, aid received by sub-Saharan Africa was $16 in 1980 and $15.7 in 1994–5 (but with a peak at mid-period, when it reached $20).

15. See Cox and Chapman (1999) for detailed documentation and analysis of the sector distribution of Community aid to ACP countries.

16. A good review of the problems and evidence is contained in Tsikata (1998).

17. Asian countries, whose share of total EU imports in the mid-1980s was still around 3% (thus lower than that of ACP countries), had by 1996 6.6% of the overall EU import market (more than twice the share of the ACP countries), and made up 52% of all EU imports from developing countries (against the 10% accounted for by imports from ACP countries).

18. In looking at the relative export performance of ACPs and Asian countries in EU markets, the tariff preferences enjoyed by the former can in fact be assumed to have mattered little, since they were substantial only for primary commodities that the latter countries export only to a limited extent, while exports of manufactures from Asia under the GSP regime (with the exception of textiles and clothing) enjoyed tariff treatment substantially similar to that granted to ACP countries. In the specific case of manufactures, however, tariff exceptions and NTBs, which the EU did not generally use to limit ACP exports, were important. In comparing the export performance of ACP countries with that of other groups of developing countries – those of Latin America, for example – differences in tariff treatment should be relevant, because both exported mostly primary commodities, some – like tropical products – in direct competition with each other.

19. Primary commodities (including fuels) still accounted in 1993 for 76% of total ACP exports to the EU. The corresponding share for Mediterranean countries was 56%, for Latin American countries 69% and for Asian countries 13%. Detailed data show that in 1998 nearly half of total ACP exports to the EU were made up of six primary products: petroleum (16%), diamonds (8%), cocoa beans (7%), coffee beans (6%), sugar (4%) and wood (7%). See Eurostat (1998).

20. The observation of this pattern of effects begins with Baldwin and Murray (1977) and continues with Langhammer and Sapir (1987), Brown (1989) and others. All these studies also observe that trade preferences on beneficiaries in general had only limited effects.

21. The initial conditions in Korea and Taiwan in the 1950s, for example, were little different from those of ACP countries in terms of poverty, overpopulation, dependency on agriculture, lack of basic infrastructure, etc. If anything, many sub-Saharan African countries had a much better natural resource base than Korea and Taiwan (Grilli and Riedel, 1995).

22. See Wolf (1997) for an analysis of the effects of alternative (non-preferential) trade regimes.

23. The Council, however, was hardly moved. In its Declaration of 18 November 1992 on the 'run-up to 2000' it welcomed the Commission communication simply as 'an important contribution', limiting itself to reaffirming the Treaty's objectives, and expressing some innocuous generalities on development co-operation (Council, 1992). The *status quo* was alive and well.

24. CEU (1996f).

25. Naturally, there remained all the problems related to the effectiveness of free trade areas between groups of ACP countries and the Union, and the issue of integration among themselves.
26. *EU–ACP Negotiations, Information Memo No. 10* (February 2000) (CEU, 2000).
27. The extended trade preferences for all least developed countries will, however, start in 2005, as originally proposed by the EU.
28. Of which 10 billion Euros will constitute the long-term financial envelope, 1.3 billion Euros go towards regional co-operation and 2.2 billion Euros will fund the new investment facility to promote private sector development.
29. The Eighth EDF, covering the 1995–2000 period contained 13.1 billion Euros of financial resources.
30. *EU–ACP Negotiations, Information Memo No. 9* (December) (CEU, 1999b).

24 Enlargement

D. G. MAYES

Enlargement of the EU and its more effective operation as a larger unit are the key issues of the current policy agenda. In 2000 there is an intergovernmental conference (IGC) among the member states of the EU that has the more effective operation of the EU at its heart. The Helsinki summit at the end of 1999 expanded the scope for enlargement. Enlargement is now almost entirely a matter of looking eastwards.[1] Although the previous round of enlargement ended up with rather less than expected, as only Austria, Finland and Sweden of the EFTA countries joined on 1 January 1995, there are no immediate plans to explore closer relationships with the remainder – Switzerland, Liechtenstein, Norway and Iceland. Of these, only Switzerland is not in the European Economic Area (EEA), which effectively brings them into the 'internal market', with the exception of agriculture and fishing.

The next steps that are planned in enlargement were spelled out in the Amsterdam summit and in *Agenda 2000*, which was published in 1997 by the Commission (CEU, 1997a). In particular the appendices to *Agenda 2000* set out the Commission's opinion on the applications from ten central and eastern European countries (CEECs): Bulgaria, the Czech Republic, Estonia, Hungary, Latvia, Lithuania, Poland, Romania, Slovakia and Slovenia. The way forward for negotiation over membership was then opened for the Czech Republic, Estonia, Hungary, Poland and Slovenia – in addition to Cyprus, which was agreed earlier. The others on the list were for later consideration, as indeed was Turkey.

However, the picture has changed steadily since then. There was considerable outcry from the second group of countries and the Luxembourg Council in 1997 went out of its way to emphasize that all the applicant countries were to be included in the enlargement process from the start, although more active negotiations were to be confined to the first six. However, in 1999, the new Prodi Commission suggested that all the applicants should be considered actively for membership and admitted when 'ready'. This procedure was approved at the Helsinki Council in December and Malta, which had renewed its application after a change in government, was added to the list, making 12 countries who could join to swell the EU to 27 members. A further surprise in 1999 was the ending of the Greek outright opposition to Turkish membership, so that discussions could advance.

When the EFTA countries were being considered for membership, there was no real question as to whether they met the appropriate criteria, with the exception of the issue of political neutrality. The question was merely whether they were willing to accept the conditions of joining, and in the case of Norway and Switzerland the answer was negative. The negotiation process was very one-sided (see Chapter 9 in Mayes (1997b) by Brewin for an exposition). Now, since there have been real concerns over whether the Union could cope with the particular applicants, it has become necessary to spell out the criteria for membership much more explicitly.[2] Thus, it is now possible to explore the full political economy of the process of enlargement much more clearly. Furthermore, as the extent of enlargement has progressed, the EU has reached the point that it has to make changes in its administrative structure and finances if it is not to find the system becoming increasingly unworkable and the cost unacceptable. The 2000 IGC will address this, although past experience suggests there will be clear limitations to the member states' willingness to limit their powers of veto.[3]

24.1 The process of enlargement

Even from its earliest stages the European Community hoped to embrace the whole of 'Europe':

> The high contracting parties, determined to lay the foundations for an ever-closer union among the peoples of Europe, resolved to ensure the economic and social progress of their countries by common action to eliminate the barriers which divide Europe ... and calling upon the other peoples of Europe who share their ideal to join in their efforts. (Preamble to the Treaty of Rome)

However, it took 16 years from its foundation in 1957 before the Community was first expanded in 1973, with the addition of the United Kingdom, Denmark and the Irish Republic. The delay was not because others did not want to join. The UK applied unsuccessfully in both 1963 and 1967, but it was not until the beginning of the 1970s that a set of terms could be found that was acceptable both to the UK and to all the existing members.

This problem of achieving a balance between what the applicants would like and what the existing members are prepared to concede is inevitable in such circumstances. The expansions to include Greece in 1981 and Portugal and Spain in 1986 were not without their difficulties, but the problems of the applicants were dealt with by having extended periods of transition in sensitive areas and by having explicit arrangements to assist in the structural development of disadvantaged regions, which in the case of Portugal meant the whole country. Even at that stage, it was clear that the process of enlargement presented problems for the Common Agricultural Policy (CAP), which was (and still is to a lesser extent) the major area of expenditure in the EU. Since the structure of the CAP was aimed largely at Northern European temperate products, it did not offer an easy balance of gain for the applicants and new explicit expenditures were necessary to offset this (through the structural funds).

The fourth enlargement in 1990 offered no such problems as no new treaty was required. When the former DDR joined the Federal Republic of Germany, no constitutional change was required as the eastern *Länder* were viewed as in effect being temporarily under a different administration. The questions to be resolved related to assistance with structural change and the timing of the transition periods for applying Community law. The speed of change during that period meant that there was little time to consider any wider implications. The EC was in the middle of the main phase of implementing the completion of the internal market following the Single European Act of 1986 (SEA) and was considering the steps to be taken towards Economic and Monetary Union (EMU) and forming the EEA.

Until the collapse of the former Soviet Union and the regime changes in central Europe, the remainder of EFTA – following the exit of the UK, Denmark and the Irish Republic – faced various constraints in joining the EC or indeed in developing closer relations with it. Despite negotiating entry along with the UK, Denmark and the Irish Republic, Norway had rejected membership in a referendum, and hence there was difficulty in mobilizing political enthusiasm for membership. Iceland is not only very small in population, even compared with Luxembourg, but also has been relatively slow in participating in European integration and has an economy of a very different character, dominated by fishing. Austria, Finland, Sweden and Switzerland all had concepts of neutrality built into their policy or constitutions. In the last two cases it was largely a matter of independent choice, whereas in the former it was a consequence of the construction of Europe after the Second World War. These states were therefore either unwilling or unable to contemplate membership while the cold war continued. Liechtenstein has also followed a path very similar to that of Switzerland. The changes further east led to a major reappraisal. Finland in particular was very keen to find means of strengthening itself with respect to its eastern neighbour, first because the collapse of trade with the former Soviet Union (FSU) led to a drastic cut in Finnish GDP and second because of the political instability. Finland only gained full independence from Russia in 1917 and had been forced into losing territory at the end of the war.

However, economic motivation was appearing in addition to the political attractions. As it became clear that the completion of the Single European Act would mean a substantial step towards closer economic integration for the EC, there was an incentive, both for the EC and for EFTA, to try to deepen their relationship. Unless the EFTA countries adopted the conditions of the Single Market there was a danger that they could gain a substantial cost advantage through their free trade agreements with the EC. Hence the EC had a clear incentive for a closer agreement. By the same token, if the EFTA countries wanted equal access for services a new agreement was required.[4] This led to the formation of the EEA in parallel with the Treaty on European Union in 1993.

Whereas the free trade agreements between the EFTA countries and the EC had all been bilateral, the EEA agreement was a single document which applied to all of the countries. Or rather, almost all, as Switzerland rejected membership of the EEA in a referendum in December 1992.

One might have expected the EEA to be a very good compromise for the EFTA countries as it brought the gains of access to the Single Market without broaching the sensitive subject of agriculture and without the need to participate in the bureaucratic mechanisms of the EU. The Cohesion Fund which was set up to provide a transfer from the better-off parts of the EEA to the relatively disadvantaged regions was a relatively small price for the EFTA countries to pay. However, two facets of the process encouraged a different view. First of all the EU was simultaneously taking another step towards integration with EMU, which might again place the EFTA countries at a disadvantage. Second, the negotiation of the EEA had not been a very happy experience for the EFTA countries (see Brewin, in Mayes, 1997b).[5] The process had been very one-sided, with the EC only being prepared to discuss variations in the timetable for transferring the relevant parts of the *acquis communitaire* into the EFTA countries' domestic law. At the last moment the European Court added to the rather one-sided nature by insisting that jurisdiction over the agreement could not be shared as originally negotiated.

Thus the EFTA countries found themselves having not just to accept most of the EEA terms as a *fait accompli* but having relatively little opportunity to influence the development of future legislation. They thus had many of the responsibilities of the EU members but without the same rights. It was not even a matter of accepting the *status quo*. The EU was moving on. The Maastricht Treaty made it clear that deepening was to come before further widening of the EU. There would therefore be further steps which could put the EFTA countries at a disadvantage. Furthermore, there was even the danger that some of the central European countries, such as Hungary, Poland and the Czech and Slovak Republics, might overtake them in the process of achieving membership, as the focus of interest, in Germany in particular, had clearly moved towards the east.

From the EU side, membership by the well-off EFTA countries was likely to provide few problems and could result in clear benefits in terms of increased resources to deal with the concerns of structural change. They were likely to be net contributors to the EU budget, not net recipients, and if they were to accept all the existing *acquis communitaire* there was very little downside. The market would be widened and the usual range of efficiency and dynamic gains would be available. There was therefore no need to draw up detailed rules or justifications to determine which countries were to be admitted to membership. At the same time, the CEECs were undergoing such trauma in their transition to market economies that they were clearly not in a position to cope with membership; nor indeed could the EU have coped readily had they joined.

The process of enlargement was therefore divided rapidly into two streams, without outright negotiations for membership being undertaken with the four EFTA applicants, but a range of other agreements for a slower pace of integration being concluded with the CEECs. The Visegrad countries, Hungary, Poland and the Czech and Slovak Republics, were given the fastest initial track, with separate Europe Agreements in 1993–4, free trade agreements were concluded with the Baltic states of Estonia, Lithuania and Latvia in 1994 and new Partnership and Co-operation Agreements with Russia and Ukraine in the same year. The negotiations were shorter than for any of the previous enlargements, lasting only some 13 months, and Austria, Finland and Sweden joined in January 1995 after the referendum in Norway rejected membership, just 38 000 votes swinging the result. It is interesting to note that public enthusiasm in all of the applicants was not overwhelming, implying that the popular view did not coincide with either the idea of clear economic benefits or that of obvious political imperatives.[6] Perhaps the memory of the less than enthusiastic support for EMU in France, the rejection of the Maastricht Treaty at the first poll in Denmark and the reservations of the United Kingdom helped temper the deliberation.

The negotiations themselves, which followed those on the Maastricht Treaty with only a gap of a few months,[7] were relatively straightforward, with agriculture, fisheries, energy and regional problems being the main stumbling-blocks. A five-year phase-in period was agreed for the most difficult parts of the CAP, while a new Objective 6 on low population density regions was included for the structural funds to accommodate the Nordic countries' particular regional problems. Voting within the enlarged Council caused some debate among the existing members and it is interesting to note that the member states only agreed to let the total budget for agriculture expand by 74% of the rise merited by the increase in EU GDP, a prelude for the more difficult negotiations now envisaged.

The negotiations for the current enlargement are likely to be difficult for two main reasons. The first is the EU's concern that the changes they feel necessary are actually being implemented and that the applicants actually have the administrative capacity to make the changes. Not only have the applicants got to make more sweeping changes even to get to the same starting-point as previous applicants but the *acquis communitaire* itself has grown in size. Conversely, the applicants themselves will have worries over adjustment in sensitive areas, such as agriculture, inefficient industries from the previous regime, the social dimension requirements in terms of working conditions, etc. If the EU is unwilling to grant long transitional periods, this may contribute to delays in accession dates.

Many of the applicants may wish to move rapidly to membership of EMU as well, especially if their currencies could be fragile or if, like Estonia, they have a currency board based on the Euro. However, this is not on the table. Joining EMU will require separate consideration by the ECB and the Commission, which prepare convergence reports, and decision by the Council in the light of them. Only Sweden and Greece were considered in the reports for 2000, Greece being admitted as a result.

24.2 Deciding on a wider membership

Deciding upon admitting other applicants on this occasion was a much more difficult task than in the case of the EFTA countries, as in the short run admitting any of them would involve net costs for the existing members. It was therefore necessary to have some criteria which would help to keep the costs and difficulties within manageable bounds. In effect these were that the applicants should be economically and politically ready, in the sense that they could meaningfully adopt the principles of the Treaty on European Union and adapt their economies within a reasonably short timetable to the full rigours of the EU market. The Copenhagen Council in June 1993 adopted three key principles to express this by stating that membership requires that the candidate country:

- has achieved stability of institutions guaranteeing democracy, the rule of law, human rights and respect for and protection of minorities;
- the existence of a functioning market economy as well as the capacity to cope with competitive pressure and market forces within the Union;
- the ability to take on the obligations of membership, including adherence to the aims of political, economic and monetary union.[8]

Agenda 2000 took a step forward by assessing all the 10 CEECs listed at the beginning of this chapter in a single comparative framework. Thus it is possible to see not only the assessment of where the five countries first selected for negotiation lie, but where others would lie in the future. The individual country assessments were each around 120 pages in length. As negotiations have progressed so updates have been published.

The assessments try to go beyond a simple listing of the measures that have been adopted into a view of how they actually operate in practice. However, they do not represent an attempt to assess the costs and benefits to either the applicants or the existing member states. While this could have been done along the lines of, say, the *European Economy* (1996) evaluation of the internal market, the outcomes would depend upon which and how many of the applicants joined at any one time. It was, therefore, probably wise to neglect the cost–benefit approach and stick to assessment of a group of indicators. One consequence, of course, is that the assessment is relatively imprecise.

The countries not deemed ready yet for negotiation for membership (Bulgaria, Latvia, Lithuania, Romania and the Slovak Republic) were promised a further report by the end of 1998 and assistance with making the changes. Indeed, the countries recommended for membership negotiations were to get continuing assistance to prepare for membership during the period before accession (assuming the negotiation is successful) and these funds are built into the revised EU budgetary proposals in Part 3 of *Agenda 2000*.

Table 24.1 shows the extent to which factors beyond simple income per head were taken into account in making the judgements about readiness for membership.[9] The Slovak Republic, which had the third highest GDP per head in 1995 (after Slovenia and the Czech Republic) was not included in the first-round list, primarily because of lack of progress under the first, political, condition. Estonia, on the other hand, which had the second lowest GDP per head, was included because it has made good progress on all three fronts. With a GDP per head around a third of that prevailing in Portugal and Greece and less than a quarter of the EU average, clearly Estonia's adjustment process is likely to be long and could be dramatic. It is also the smallest applicant with a population of only 1.5 miilion.[10]

Not surprisingly, some of these decisions were controversial and some of the states relegated to the second round might have been the greatest potential gainers from membership. By 1999 the position had changed somewhat. The lead group was making steady but not necessarily uniform progress towards meeting the conditions for membership, while some of the following group made rapid advances as can be seen from Table 24.1.

The EU is progressing steadily with enlargement and is not at present having to face any awkward discussions over where the word 'European' reaches its technical or, more likely, political limits. From an economic point of view there is no particularly good reason why boundaries should be drawn on the basis of centuries old decisions by geographers as to where the continents should be thought to start and end. The Russian Federation spans the Urals and, although there are various divisions in the Federation, particularly in the south, there are strong economic links across the Urals. The economic resources in Siberia are such that European Russia attaches a very strong importance to the region and drawing that particular division would make little sense to them. The Far Eastern zone is already being drawn into the Asian economy and its development will probably be strongly influenced by the other parts of Asia and the Pacific (Bollard and Mayes, 1991).

Similarly, if we look southwards, in Roman times it made more sense to think of the Mediterranean as a region – a region based on sea rather than land mass. Travel was easier by boat than by land and there was considerable economic interdependence across the region. The same line of argument can be advanced for the Baltic. The links between Finland and Estonia are one of the reasons why Estonia has moved to a position suitable for membership rather more quickly than many other central European countries.

Most current definitions of 'Europe' therefore tend to depend on a combination of economic, political, cultural and geographic links and divisions.[11] However, it is only the eastwards definition that appears to have given the EU much of a prob-

Table 24.1 Basic data for applicant CEECs and EU member states, 1998

| | Area (1 000 km²) | Population (millions) | Population density (inhabitants/ km²) | GDP at current market prices | | | | GDP at purchasing power standard | | Agriculture (% of employment) |
| | | | | (billion ECU) | (ECU per head) | (ECU per head as % of EU average) | (billion ECU at ppp rates) | (ECU per head at ppp rates) | (ECU per head as % of EU average) | |
	1	2	3	4	5	6	7	8	9	10
Hungary	93	10.1	109	41.9	4 149	21	98.0	9 703	49	7.9
Poland	313	38.7	124	140.7	3 636	18	281.1	7 264	36	20.7
Romania	238	22.5	95	33.9	1 507	8	123.0	5 467	27	39
Slovak Republic	49	5.4	110	18.1	3 352	17	49.9	9 241	46	8.6
Latvia	65	2.5	38	5.7	2 280	11	13.5	5 400	27	18.3
Estonia	45	1.5	33	4.6	3 067	15	10.7	7 133	36	9.9
Lithuania	65	3.7	57	9.6	2 595	13	22.9	6 189	31	23.8[a]
Bulgaria	111	8.3	75	11.0	1 325	7	38.2	4 602	23	23.2[b]
Czech Republic	79	10.3	130	50.1	4 864	24	125.2	12 155	61	5.8
Slovenia	20	2	100	17.4	8 700	44	27.2	13 600	68	12.7
CE-10	1 078	105	97	337.0	3 547	18	796.7	7 588	38	
As % of EU-15	33	28	84	5	18		11	38		

Sources: [a] 1996, [b] 1994.

Table 24.1 (continued)

	Area (1 000 km²)	Population (millions)	Population density (inhabitants/ km²)	GDP at current market prices				GDP at purchasing power standard		Agriculture (% of employment)
				(billion ECU)	(ECU per head)	(ECU per head as % of EU average)	(billion ECU at ppp rates)	(ECU per head at ppp rates)	(ECU per head as % of EU average)	
	1	2	3	4	5	6	7	8	9	10
Belgium	31	10.2	329	223.7	21 920	110	229.9	22 538	113	2.3
Denmark	43	5.3	123	155.8	28 472	143	123.4	23 277	117	3.7
Germany	357	82.1	230	1 921.8	23 282	117	1 779.4	21 686	109	3.2
Greece	132	10.6	80	108.6	10 233	52	143.0	13 569	68	20.3
Spain	506	39.4	78	520.2	12 899	65	633.3	16 088	81	8.4
France	544	58.8	108	1 297.4	21 661	109	1 214.4	20 640	104	4.5
Ireland	70	3.7	53	75.8	20 479	103	79.4	21 384	107	10.4
Italy	301	57.6	191	1 058.7	17 837	90	1 160.4	19 774	99	6.8
Luxembourg	3	0.4	133	16.4	36 428	183	14.8	34 660	174	2.5
Netherlands	42	15.7	374	349.7	21 448	108	329.8	21 009	106	3.7
Austria	84	8.1	96	188.4	23 493	118	179.6	22 224	112	6.8
Portugal	92	9.9	108	97.6	9 615	48	142.3	14 293	72	13.7
Finland	338	5.2	15	114.8	21 621	109	102.6	19 882	100	7.1
Sweden	450	8.9	20	212	22 884	115	171.3	19 343	97	2.8
United Kingdom	244	59.2	243	1 252.8	20 599	104	1 171.0	19 765	99	1.9
EU-15	3 236	375	116	7 472.6	19 868	100	7 486.8	19 906	100	5

Source: Eurostat.

555

lem. Even westwards could have included Greenland had its inhabitants decided differently. In any case, non-European parts of France and Spain already form part of the EU. Turkey's application has been deferred, not because it is not 'European' – part of Turkey is clearly European in terms of traditional geographic definitions – but for political and economic reasons, particularly relating to human rights.[12] Turkey also poses a problem because of its size. It is more than half as large as all the CEECs considered in *Agenda 2000* and similar in size to the last two enlargements taken together. GDP per head is in the same league as that of most members of the CEECs which were originally not selected for the first round of negotiations. Furthermore, the very agrarian nature of Turkey, with around a half of the population still working in that sector, could pose major budgetary strains on the EU unless the basis of expenditure were altered. Calculations made by the UK Foreign and Commonwealth Office in 1992 suggested that Turkey would have been a recipient on the then rules of some 12 billion ECU a year, which would have been equivalent to 15% of its GDP and 5% of the total EU budget (House of Lords, 1992). The calculations by the Commission in *Agenda 2000* for all the potential applicants and the likely cost for those which become members is an order of magnitude smaller, reaching only 19 billion ECU per year in 1997 prices by 2006. Turkey is still likely to remain on a slow path to membership even though Greek objections to the principle of Turkish membership seem to have eased. Questions of human rights and the treatment of the Kurdish minority remain – to say nothing of the potential for migration to the existing member states.

The EU has, however, shown itself willing to tackle some of the hard political questions in enlargement by agreeing that accession negotiations with Cyprus should start without the prior requirement of a political solution to Cyprus's continuing divisions. This presents several problems, not least the lack of recognition of a legal authority for the Turkish-speaking north. So it is not fully clear with whom negotiations would be undertaken. The accession negotiations may themselves help to resolve some of the dispute. The issue of Malta becoming a member was removed from the agenda for a while when Malta withdrew its application in early 1997. Given the degree of integration already existing between Malta and the EU (some 75% of its trade is with the EU), and the fact that the level of GDP per head is similar to that of Portugal and Greece, it would have been difficult to exclude Malta from the next round of applications to be considered. With reactivation of the application, Malta has indeed joined the active negotiations.

Assuming that the negotiations succeed for at least a few of the next group, the point at which the fiscal and organizational issues highlighted in *Agenda 2000* have to be addressed will have been reached. However, difficult questions such as the position of Russia can be put on one side for the time being as Russia advances up the ladder of closer association.[13]

24.3   Coping with a larger Union

Somewhat surprisingly, *Agenda 2000* suggests that the EU will be able to absorb the budgetary consequences of enlargement reasonably readily and budgets are set out on an annual basis up to 2006. For example, the Commission concludes (*Agenda 2000*, vol. 1, p. 74): 'Maintaining the current agricultural guideline would not pose any difficulty in covering identified agricultural expenditure needs.' Initially this seems to be at variance with calculations about the impact of full membership by all ten countries on the EAGGF Guarantee section of 11 billion ECU per year by 2005 (*Agenda 2000*, vol. 2, p. 42). However, staggering membership and phasing in the introduction of the full CAP (as seems likely) and positing structural changes in the applicant countries enables this sum to be massively reduced.

Even the structural measures are an order of magnitude larger than can be accommodated without breaking through the current 'own resources' ceiling for EU expenditure of 1.27% of EU GDP (see Chapter 16). According to the Commission's calculations, the maximum, reached in 1999, is 1.25% and 1.22% is projected for 2002–6. These conclusions are of course based on a variety of assumptions and would be violated if, for example, economic growth in the existing EU-15 were slower than the 2.5% a year assumed. However, this is not a particularly optimistic assumption by comparison with the growth that has actually been recorded over recent years.

The new member states would, however, be absorbing around 30% of the structural funds by the end of the period. Reorganization of the funds would be required, with restriction in the current Objective 1 recipients and reduction in the expenditure on other Objectives (see Chapter 18). A review of the eligibility for the cohesion fund is also implied.

The Commission even concludes (vol. 1, p. 84) that it will not be appropriate to reappraise the rebates to the UK until after the first further enlargement. One might question the optimistic assertion – 'The next enlargement ... will inevitably provoke a deterioration in the budgetary positions of all the current member states. This cannot come as a surprise and should not give rise to claims for compensation.'

However, when it came to deciding upon the budgetary allocations up to 2006 at the Berlin Council in mid-1999, the member states were less prepared to change than the Commission had proposed. The progress in reducing the size of the CAP was slowed and the extent of the change in the structural funds was more limited, even though several of the Objective 1 regions had successfully made the transition towards the average levels of GDP per head and unemployment of the EU as a whole. There will now be a transition period until 2006 for them.

These slower budgetary moves place some question marks over the likely rate of progress of the enlargement process. The difficulties for the applicant countries may be underestimated and, if they are to adhere to the entire *acquis communitaire* quite quickly after admission, the starting date may prove to be later than anticipated in *Agenda 2000*.

The start of Stage 3 of EMU in 1999 and its likely completion before any enlargement takes place complicate the issue. Several of the applicants are almost keener to get into EMU than they are to take on various of the obligations of the *acquis*, since EMU offers them macroeconomic stabilization that might prove more difficult unaided – particularly if the difficulties of accession have been underestimated.

The budget agreed at the Berlin Council (see Chapter 16) gave annual figures for 2000–6. These were on two bases – an agreed budget for the current EU-15 and an outline for the enlarged EU-21. The additional expenditure on enlargement adds a little over 15% to the EU-15 budget by 2006 or 0.16% of EU GDP. Expenditure on the EU-15 is the same in 2006 as in 2000, having peaked in 2003. The current ceiling on EU spending of 1.13% of EU GDP is maintained, which means that the

Council could, if it wished, increase the budget by a further 0.14% of GDP without breaching the 1.27% ceiling. Thus it could cope with a virtual doubling of the costs of enlargement within that framework.

It is not at all clear that wider enlargement will not impose more substantial strains than those posed by the enlargements of 1981 and 1986 simply because of the extent of the income differentials. In the first place it is possible that the nature of the integration will exploit inter-industry trade rather than intra-industry trade as has been the case until now. There may be a tendency to concentrate more labour-intensive and lower value-added activities in Central and Eastern Europe. In these circumstances, differentials between the different parts of the EU may not converge quite as fast as they otherwise would have done.

The example of the difficulties of integrating East Germany is not a good one. For a start it occurred over a decade earlier, before any prior adjustment could take place. Second, it was decided, against the advice of the Bundesbank, to offer a very high rate of exchange for the Ost mark, thereby bringing wage levels much more rapidly into line than productivity would indicate reasonable.

An alternative scenario is that the extent of the differentials results in a degree of labour mobility that has hitherto not been too much of a concern for the EU. Substantial unemployment differentials have persisted in Europe (Mayes *et al.*, 1993, and Chapter 21) not just between member states but within them. The economic incentives to move are not as effective as they are in the United States, for example, where the population is much more mobile. In part this is a function of history. A large proportion of families in the USA do not have roots in the same location going back more than a short period. In Europe, on the other hand, many families have lived in the same place for centuries and therefore have much stronger ties.

With very large income differentials, the incentive to move, even if only for part of the working life, may be sufficiently strong to overcome the inertia which has prevailed in Western Europe. It is noticeable in Finland, for example, where urbanization has been largely a function of the present century, that many city dwellers still have family homes in the country or have built cottages there so as to be able to return.[14] Mobility from east to west to work may therefore be substantial by comparison with the past.

The Commission has already recognized its own need to restructure as the EU continues with a set of institutions designed for a Community of six. If the current round of negotiations is successful, several further countries will be added to the list. Almost all of them use at least one language that will be new to the EU. They will want their stake in the running of the Union. Despite suggestions to the contrary, the expansion to 15 member states occurred without major changes except the splitting up of portfolios. The Santer Commission proposed to restructure its own procedures, with decentralization, rationalization and simplicity as the three watchwords. It suggested that it should concentrate on the core functions and hive off the others to executive agencies which can be nearer the customers. It recommended that the number of commissioners be reduced to one per member state and that the Council needs to reconsider its voting rules. However, progress was in practice more limited. The new Prodi Commission that came in during 1999 has already introduced a range of changes, reorganizing the portfolios and the structures of the directorates-general. In many respects this is a response to the need to give a new face to the Commission following the forced resignation of the Santer administration, rather than just an attempt to create a body that can cope with enlargement. It remains to be seen whether the 2000 IGC will actually succeed in making major changes to the structure of operation of the Commission, Council or Parliament and their interaction. It has been suggested that a structure where it is difficult to introduce change might actually be appropriate given that the EU is reaching maturity, but this does not reflect everybody's agenda.

The structure of the ECB sets a precedent whereby it is possible to operate at the highest level without one person drawn from each member state. The Executive Board has only six members. However, the Governing Council, the primary decision-making body, also has one from each participating country. Thus it already has 17 members, with both the Commission and the Council presidency being able to attend (and speak but not vote). There will always be a reluctance both to give up any existing powers and to give up a seat at the table. Other institutions such as the World Bank and the IMF have had to handle this problem a long time ago to prevent administrative complexities getting out of hand, but experience in such organizations is not a particularly optimistic indicator of the likelihood of a very successful reorganization. The need for rationalization, of course, applies not just to the Commission but to all of the institutions.

24.4 Coping without enlargement

One question which is not well addressed in the existing literature is how well the aspiring applicant countries could cope without membership of the EU. Indeed, there might be benefits from staying out. The reason that the question is largely ignored is simply that these countries have found it very difficult to attract inward investment, whether from private sources or through governmental or intergovernmental agencies. Such investment usually requires considerable conditionality either explicitly or implicitly. The requirements for loans and project finance at the governmental or related level tend to include elements concerning fiscal and monetary prudence, the creation of market mechanisms, frameworks for property rights, etc. In the case of funds from the EU, the necessary framework is much more explicit and comprehensive. Furthermore, that framework does not usually conflict with that required by other public sector lenders or donors. There is therefore an incentive to adopt the framework irrespective of other considerations because it offers the fastest and most substantial route to achieving satisfactory structural change.

The private sector inflow, on the other hand, has a wide variety of motives (Nam and Reuter, 1992). While these will normally include an adequate infrastructure framework and some certainty about being able to enjoy the return on the investment, the same requirements for market openness may not be present, as the investor may well wish to gain from exploiting a monopoly position. In some respects, a less open and integrated market may appeal to the investor because it offers a greater certainty of maintaining cost advantages and privileged market access.

It might appear a rather short-sighted approach to permit such distortions to emerge, but the starting point is not an open market. The attraction of inward investment can be greater where there is the opportunity to buy existing incumbent firms with monopolies or near monopolies. This has been revealed very clearly in the case of New Zealand (Mayes, 1996), where inward investment over the years 1989–95 exceeded that of the whole of the Visegrad countries, despite the fact that their combined population is about twenty times as large. New Zealand sold a large range of public sector enterprises: an airline, a railway, telecoms, steelworks, banks, insurance, a hotel chain, forestry and many more as existing enterprises. Although the New Zealand competitive framework requires that industries be contestable (Mayes, 1997c), the practice is that the incumbents have a very strong position. Hence there is a good prospect of a strong profit stream. The domestic resources of the host country possess neither the financial capital necessary to make the investments to become internationally competitive nor the access to the necessary technological expertise and market contacts to make such investments successful.

As a result New Zealand has achieved a very rapid turnaround in just a decade, moving more swiftly into recovery than the CEECs, and experiencing a much smaller loss of GDP in the process. Of course, the circumstances are not directly comparable as the extent of distortions and lack of competitiveness were far greater in Europe. Nevertheless, there could be advantages in allowing the transformation of existing enterprises in a process of more measured transition (Mayes, 1997a) as the social costs need to be balanced against the rate of exploitation of the economic gains. Achieving this balance between 'cohesion' and competition has been a key feature governing the use of the structural funds inside the EU. There is a limit to which regional divergences are politically acceptable. Beyond that limit people vote against the process of change even though the longer-run outcome from change is clearly better, because they find the short-run costs too high.

The EU's approach as expounded in *Agenda 2000* seeks to address this point both by assistance to the countries not yet accepted for membership and by the transitional aid for those ready for membership. The irony in this arrangement is, however, that the further advanced in the process of integration a country is, then the greater assistance it receives from the EU. If, however, one were to take a view on the extent of need, then those furthest from being able to cope with membership might be thought to be those with the greatest need for assistance in the process of transformation. In part, this is a question of absorptive capacity (as the economy progresses so it is able to cope with more projects and faster structural change), but it is also a question of incentives. If less conditionality were to be attached to EU help, then the degree of transformation of the recipient economies might be lower.

Altering the process of adjustment to full membership of the EU, particularly by delaying the point at which labour mobility can be freer, may also affect the structure of the applicant economies. As discussed in Baldwin *et al.* (1995), it is not immediately clear which way a less integrated economy might develop. It will be less attractive to investors as a base for production for the whole market if there are barriers to export, but then it will need a wider range of production itself because of the same barriers. As there is a minimum time needed to establish viable firms with a higher value-added product, there may be some attraction in a more measured pace of change. However, the history of 'infant industries' and related arguments for slower transition is very mixed, with considerable success stories to point to in Asia and the Pacific region and much more disastrous experiences in much of the rest of the world. It is thus not clear whether there are any clear steps, other than the process of rapid opening towards the EU model, which would diminish the risk of getting locked into a rather unattractive form of inter-industry specialization.

Phinnemore (1999) poses the question of whether the aspiring applicants to the EU might not be better advised to stop one step further back in the process and settle for association agreements as longer-term arrangements. Under such agreements it is possible for the applicants to get a wide range of benefits from trade and investment if they adopt the *acquis* and yet avoid agreements on politically difficult subjects like fishing and agriculture. The EEA is the principal example. Iceland, Liechtenstein and Norway seem satisfied with the balance. However, in many respects this involves giving up more powers than if they were full members, as they do not have any say in any new EU legislation that falls in the areas covered by their agreements. In the case of the current applicants, they all have rather more to gain from membership than the EEA members, which had no aspirations under the structural funds. They would have been net contributors rather than beneficiaries.

24.5 Concluding remarks

One cannot help but be impressed with the rate of change in the EU over the last fifteen years and with the changes proposed for the coming five years: the enlargement to include Spain and Portugal, the Single European Act, the Maastricht Treaty, the European Economic Area, the agreements and programmes with Central and Eastern Europe, the enlargement to include Austria, Finland and Sweden, completion of Stage 3 of EMU with the founding of the ECB and the issuing of the Euro and a further enlargement ... One might have expected that something or other would have collapsed along the way, particularly given some of the political difficulties with agreeing the Maastricht Treaty.

Furthermore, this major expansion of programmes has been accompanied by a substantial budgetary expansion, but not one on the scale envisaged a decade or so earlier when the McDougall Report (1977), for example, looked at what would be the minimum size for a budget with a more federal feel to it (see Chapter 16). For more than two decades it has been thought that the CAP would have to change markedly, but while it has indeed changed it is still the dominant area of expenditure. It is merely that the structural funds have added a second major category. *Agenda 2000* suggests that the Union will be able to cope financially with the existing ceilings, despite the size of these programmes, through to 2006. The budgetary conclusions from the Berlin Council in 1999 repeat the view that enlargement can be accommodated within the existing ceiling of 1.27% of EU GDP but with somewhat less progress on agriculture and the realignment of the structural funds.

One must ask whether there is a stage at which the process will have to change its character. Taking a purely 'European' definition of the Union, the limits to size are beginning to come within the horizon for thought if not for actual long-term planning. Beyond Stage 3 of EMU the process of closer integration in other areas of economic, political and social affairs appears to be relatively slow (by comparison at least). However, it remains to be seen how much the member states will find that, for example, existing fiscal diversity is sustainable under monetary union. The temptation is always to think that the next stage in enlargement or indeed in 'deepening' the Union will be the one that triggers a more major change in the character of the institutions and the nature of the common policies and expenditures. To some extent such a change is likely within the next five years with another enlargement, but reluctance to change thus far suggests that the member states may prefer to accept the complexities and consequent inefficiencies for rather longer.

Any conclusion on this subject in this book is likely to be overtaken by history. The forces backing rapid progress to wider membership by all 12 main applicants are clear, through the new Commission and some member states. There are, however, signs that progress might be delayed. The Berlin agreement over the budget makes the financial arithmetic more difficult and reflects an increased reluctance on the part of donors to give more and on the part of existing recipients to receive less. The election of a controversial government in Austria in early 2000, with reservations about inward migration, may be another pointer. Enlargement requires unanimous assent. There are considerable opportunities for delay should the parties wish it. It might not be wise to bet the farm on any specific outcome.

Notes

1. This is not literally true in the sense of moving the easternmost point in the European Union. Currently that is in Finland (as is the northernmost point). Of those countries under current consideration for membership, it is only Cyprus which is further east. Otherwise the Union would have to include Belarus, Moldova, Russia, Turkey or Ukraine for it to stretch further eastwards. With the renewal of the application by Malta there is now a proposal to extend further southwards, although Spanish and French islands might make the claim for the boundary to be further south already.

2. The application from Turkey was not a real test either as Turkey is so large and at such a low relative income level that there was never any doubt that the Union would be unwilling to bear the cost. Similarly, Cyprus and Malta are sufficiently small that they would not pose a difficulty for the EU's resources. Any grounds for decision would be largely political rather than economic.

3. I notice I made a similar sceptical observation in the 1993 edition with a view to the IGC which was concluded with the Amsterdam Treaty in June 1996.

4. Baldwin *et al.* (1997) show that under imperfect competition the incentive to join a grouping of similar structured economies increases as the size of the grouping increases.

5. The Austrian application for membership was made in July 1989, antedating the EEA negotiations, while the Swedish application was made in June 1991 before the negotiations were complete. The Finnish, Swiss and Norwegian applications were made in March, May and November of 1992, respectively.

6. The Austrian result in June was clear, with 66.4% voting in favour, and support in Finland in October was 57%. However, the Swedish voted only 52.2% for and 46.9% against on 13 November and the outcome was in doubt right up to the end. The Norwegian vote came only a fortnight later but this time the 52.2% were against.

7. The Commission produced its favourable 'Opinions' on each of the applicants rapidly. (Norway's entry to the negotiations was officially delayed until April 1993 to allow the Opinion to be completed, although it had been involved in aspects of the negotiations earlier.)

8. The 'EFTA' group negotiations were already in progress at the time.

9. The accuracy of these GDP per head comparisons is of course limited but they are not so wrong as to invalidate the qualitative argument.

10. But with a land area bigger than Belgium, the Netherlands or Denmark. Malta is also considerably smaller in size but with a relatively high income per head and is likely to have more limited problems of adjustment. As a result, the reactivation of its application for membership probably means that it will be among the first countries to be admitted.

11. Sometimes the arguments over the appropriate boundary have been put in terms of the

limits of the former Austro-Hungarian empire, sometimes the extent of Christianity and sometimes the limits of Catholicism (Crouch and Marquand, 1992).

12. The 1964 Ankara Association Agreement with Turkey made clear that it was in principle eligible for membership. The question was merely when it would be ready. *Agenda 2000* makes it clear that Turkey will be judged on the same criteria as any other applicant. Turkey is receiving assistance from the EU to help it with the transition.

13. In Mayes (1993), I described the EU as having almost a series of concentric circles of closer affiliation for countries depending upon their geographic nearness. Since 1995 the EU has had a common border with Russia. If the negotiations with all of the next group of applicants succeed, that boundary will be increased and both Belarus and the Ukraine will then have common borders with the EU. The 'nearness' will thus continue to increase in geographic terms.

14. In part, this may be a special feature of the slow development of forests, where important proportions of rural family wealth can lie. It may take three generations to be able to reap the benefit from planting.

25 The development of the EU

A. M. EL-AGRAA

The aim of this chapter is to provide a brief review of the progress made by the EU in terms of establishing a true single market and moving towards full economic union. However, such a summary of events would not be complete without an adequate restatement of the most significant political developments that have taken place; indeed it could be argued that a list of EU accomplishments would be pointless without also explaining the political context within which they have been achieved. The first section of this chapter is therefore devoted to these developments while the remaining sections tackle the periods before and after the first enlargement of the EU, and the present. The future, being speculative and subject to many personal prejudices, is left to the final chapter.

25.1 Political developments

As stated in Chapter 2, at the beginning the EU (now that the reader has gone through the main aspects of the EU, no historical distinction between EEC, EC and EU will be made in this chapter) created a number of institutions to execute the tasks it had been entrusted with. These revolved around a legislative body (the Council of Ministers) and an initiator of policies (the Commission, which is also the administrator, mediator and police force of the EU), backed up by an advisory body (the European Parliament, with recently increased powers) and a guardian of the treaties (the Court of Justice). However, by the 1970s, it had become clear that the EU was entering a period of political change for which these institutions were less suitable than had initially been envisaged and for which they lacked adequate strength. Rather than promoting a strengthening of the existing institutions, a method was found to bring national political leaders more closely into EU affairs by the introduction of summit meetings. As we have seen, these were formalized under the name of the European Council in 1974.

The first major summit was held in The Hague in December 1969. At that summit, the original six member nations effectively recognized that they were so closely interdependent that they had no choice other than to continue as a united group. They were thus compelled to settle matters such as the Common Agricultural Policy (CAP) and changes in the financing of the General Budget from contributions decided annually to a system of own resources. A point of vital importance was the recognition that the EU possessed the political will to work for enlargement and hence had to confront the question of relations with the United Kingdom more positively.

The summit also recognized that the EU needed to reconsider its position in the

567

world. The EU's responsibilities neither matched its economic weight nor allowed effective consideration of the political aspects of its external economic relations. Individual member nations still conducted external affairs themselves and could, therefore, undermine EU interests. The attraction of bringing foreign policy into the EU sphere was the greater effectiveness this might bring in international affairs; but the idea raised such sensitive issues as relations with the United States and the USSR as well as defence matters.

In the end the Hague summit requested the foreign ministers to study the best way of achieving further political integration, within the context of commitment to EU enlargement, and to present a report. The later efforts made to achieve political co-operation, with emphasis upon international affairs, have been important in helping the EU identify its common aims and making the nature of the group coherent. Political co-operation has itself led to institutional innovation. This has occurred alongside the original institutions of the EU and not as part of them, although they are increasingly coming closer together.

In 1972 an important summit was held in Paris. This was attended by the three new members – Denmark, Ireland and the United Kingdom. The summit devoted considerable attention to the need to strengthen the social and regional aims of the EU. Furthermore, the deterioration in the international climate and the preoccupation of member governments with economic matters at home seemed to require frequent meetings of heads of government to ensure that the EU remained an effective economic unit.

The different philosophies and approaches of the governments of member countries to new problems made summit meetings essential for establishing the extent of common ground and for ensuring that this was used as the basis for action by the member nations. Initially, this seemed to strengthen the intergovernmental structure of the EU at the expense of the supranational element. However, it was also a reflection of the reality that the member nations had realized that their future aims were closely interdependent and required the formulation of joint goals and policies over a very wide field indeed. Informal discussion of general issues, whether economic or political, domestic or international, was a necessary preliminary to further, formal integration, and through the summit meetings and the political co-operation procedure the scope of the subject matter for the EU was steadily enlarged.

By the time of the Paris summit meeting in 1972 the member nations had laid down for themselves an ambitious programme of activity designed to lead to a 'European Union'. Much remained to be defined, but a number of external issues had been clearly identified. These included the following:

1. The need to maintain a constructive dialogue with the United States, Canada and Japan.
2. The need to act jointly in matters of external trade policy.
3. The need for member nations to make a concerted contribution to the 'Conference on Security and Co-operation in Europe'.

Foreign ministers were to meet more frequently in order to handle this last theme.

The global economic difficulties of the 1970s, triggered by the first oil shock, created a harsh environment within which the EU had to strive to establish its identity, future goals and executive responsibilities. It is easy to understand why progress was extremely slow during this period.

The Paris summit of 1974 formally agreed that the distinction between EU affairs and political co-operation was untenable, and in 1981 the foreign ministers agreed that political co-operation between the member nations had become central to their foreign policies. Proceedings became formalized and relations were established with the Commission.

The same summit asked the then Belgian prime minister (Leo Tindemans) to consult the governments of the member nations and to write a report on the concept of European union. This brought out into the open the long-standing question of whether the member nations did, or could, constitute an effective economic whole or whether progress as a two-tier EU might be preferable.

The concept of a two-tier EU means that those member nations which have the will and ability to forge ahead towards such a union should do so. The others would lag behind, but would not be relieved of the need to achieve the ultimate goal. As Swann (1988) has argued, this could be interpreted pessimistically: the fact that the concept is discussed at all suggests lack of cohesion between the member nations. It could also be interpreted optimistically: in the absence of majority voting, some member nations could still forge ahead despite the disagreement of the rest of the member nations – the European Monetary System (EMS) was launched on such a basis since the United Kingdom refused to take part in the exchange-rate aspect of the scheme (see Chapter 17) at the time. Although this question was avoided in favour of special measures (financed by the structural funds) within the EU to help the weaker member nations (see Chapter 16), it has surfaced again with respect to the single EU currency, the Euro and further developments.

A further proposition was that the EU should take steps towards making itself more of a citizens' Europe by including action in matters such as consumer rights, environmental protection and the safeguarding of fundamental rights – see Chapters 19 and 20.

Two further ideas were discussed:

1. A common stand in foreign policy, which could then be applied by the member states.
2. A tentative start on defence issues.

Institutional reform would be required in several directions. The interrelated issues of constitutional development and institutional reform continued to occupy the attention of those concerned with the EU, but for a number of years little progress was made. The EU appeared to be in danger of reaching a dead end:

1. The deepening of the integrative process required action that the member nations found controversial.
2. New member nations introduced their own problems and perspectives.
3. The recession meant that the attitudes of the member nations hardened towards the necessary compromise which is needed if co-operative solutions to problems were to be found.

A particular constraint was presented by the limits on EU finance (the size of the EU General Budget) which prevented the development of EU policies and led to the bitter arguments about the resources devoted to the CAP (see Chapter 16).

Internal divisions were compounded by fears of a lack of dynamism in the EU economy which threatened a relative decline in international terms. Such worries suggested that a significant leap forward was needed to ensure a real 'common market' and to encourage new growth. However, to move the EU in this direction and to modernize EU institutions so that they worked more efficiently proved a laborious process. While member nations could agree upon the aims, in practice they fought hard to ensure that the reform incorporated measures favourable to themselves.

As the debate continued, a major division emerged between those who were primarily interested in the political ideal of European union and who wished to see institutional reform which would strengthen the EU's capacity to act, and those who had a more pragmatic approach which stressed the need for new policies, especially those directed to stimulating the EU economy. The idea of European union was developed further by an Italian-German proposal for a European Act (the Genscher–Colombo Plan) and by the European Parliament which adopted a draft treaty on European union in 1984.

In the meantime a series of summit meetings was keeping the momentum going at the level of heads of state or government. The Stuttgart summit meeting of 1983 agreed on an impressive work programme of issues which needed solution, and produced a 'Solemn declaration on European union'.

The vehement discussions of the following two years, often complicated by the need to solve more immediate problems, meant that it was not until the Luxembourg summit meeting of 1985 that lines of the agreement could be settled. These were brought together in the Single European Act (SEA) which became operative on 1 July 1987 (see Chapters 2 and 8). They were reinforced and extended through the adoption of the Delors Report on Economic and Monetary Union (EMU) and, provided that the Maastricht Treaty of December 1991 is fully implemented, by the creation of an EU common defence policy, a single currency run by a common central bank for *all* member nations early in this century (see Chapters 2 and 6), and although the Amsterdam Treaty of June 1997 shied away from the idea of a common defence policy and institutional reform and settled for the membership of the expanded NATO, these matters are now being seriously discussed.

25.2 The period from 1958 to 1969

Between 1958 and 1969, when the transition period came to an end, the original six member nations were preoccupied with the construction of the 'community' envisaged in the Treaty of Rome. It is not necessary here to describe all the measures that were undertaken during this period since these have been fully discussed earlier in this book. It is enough to state that the basic elements of the customs union (i.e. the removal of the internal tariffs, the elimination of import quota restrictions and the creation of the common external tariffs (CETs)) were established ahead of schedule – see Tables 25.1 and 25.2. Initial steps were undertaken and measures proposed to tackle the many non-tariff barriers to the free movement of goods, services and factors of production so that by 1969 a recognizably common market could be said to exist.

Progress was uneven in the area of common policies. Because of French demands, sometimes bordering on threats, the CAP was almost fully operational by 1969. However, as Button clearly shows in Chapter 13, the common transport policy was

Table 25.1 EC intra-area tariff reductions (%)

Acceleration of reduction	Individual reductions made on the 1 January 1957 level	Cumulative
1 January 1959	10	10
1 July 1960	10	20
1 January 1961	10	30
1 January 1962	10	40
1 July 1962	10	50
1 July 1963	10	60
1 January 1965	10	70
1 January 1966	10	80
1 July 1967	5	85
1 July 1968	15	100

Source: CEC (1957), p. 34.

slow to evolve. Moreover, Collins has demonstrated in Chapters 2 and 19 that the European Social Fund (ESF) and the European Investment Bank (EIB) were duly established and were fully operational at an early stage. Furthermore, as Brülhart

Table 25.2 The establishment of the CET (%)

Acceleration of adjustment	Industrial products adjustment	Cumulative adjustment	Agricultural products adjustment	Cumulative
1 January 1961	30	30		
1 January 1962			30	30
1 July 1963	30	60		
1 January 1966			30	60
1 July 1968	40	100	40	100

Source: CEC (1957), p. 34.

and McAleese argue in Chapter 22, steps were taken to create a Common Commercial Policy (CCP), and, as Grilli clearly shows in Chapter 23, the original six undertook appropriate trade and aid arrangements in respect of their colonial and increasingly ex-colonial dependencies. A rudimentary system of macroeconomic policy co-ordination was also devised (see Chapter 6).

Although during this period progress was evident and optimism about the success of the EU was much enhanced, there were some disappointments. From a 'federalist' point of view, perhaps the greatest was the French refusal to accept the supranational element in the Treaty decision-making system, hence the 'Luxembourg compromise'. When the member nations signed the Treaty of Rome, they opted for an EU Council of Ministers which could take decisions on the basis of a supranational majority voting system, but the Luxembourg compromise meant that any member state could insist that nothing should happen unless it agreed that it should happen, i.e. a veto system was adopted.

25.3 The period from 1969 to the early 1980s

When the transition period came to an end in 1969, it would have been possible for the original six to state that their mission had been accomplished, given that their remit was only economic unity. However, there were several reasons why it was neither possible nor appropriate for the EU to stop there. First, the creation of common policies in such fields as agriculture and competition required an administration to operate them. This is because decisions regarding agricultural prices had to be taken on a seasonal or annual basis and markets had to be continuously manipulated in order that those prices should be received by farmers. The activities of businessmen and governments had to be continuously monitored in order that factors which would otherwise prevent, restrict or distort competitive trade should be eliminated. Second, although substantial progress had been made in achieving the aims listed in Article 3 of the Treaty, when the transition period was approaching its end it had to be admitted that substantial policy gaps still remained to be filled before it could be claimed that a truly common market existed.

Be that as it may, with memories of the Second World War still fresh in people's minds, it would have been possible for the member nations to state that, subject to the need to operate existing policies and to fill obvious policy gaps, no further economic integration or institutional development should be attempted. In fact the EU decided quite the contrary: new areas of economic policy were opened up and old ones were substantially changed.

In 1969, during the Hague summit, the original six decided that the EU should progressively transform itself into an EMU. Although important measures were subsequently introduced in order to achieve the EMU, the goal of reaching this aim eventually failed. This was due to the global economic difficulties of the early 1970s and to the first enlargement of the EU. Nevertheless, the idea did not go away since in the late 1970s a more modest scheme was successfully introduced – EMS. Moreover, in 1989, the member nations endorsed the Delors Report, committing themselves to achieving an EMU in three stages: as we have seen (Chapter 6) the first began on 1 July 1990, the second in 1994 and the third in 1999 for the 11 member nations which passed the strict conditions specified for this purpose and which had no opt-outs.

The EMU proposal was only one of a succession of new policy initiatives during 1969–72. Indeed, this period can be described as one of great activity. First, in 1970, the original six reached a common position on the development of a Common Fisheries Policy (CFP – see Chapter 12), although total agreement was not to be achieved until 1983. Second, at the Paris summit of 1973, agreement was reached on the development of new policies in relation to both industry and science and research. Third, the summit also envisaged a more active role for the EU in the area of regional policy, and decided that a European Regional Development Fund (ERDF) was to be established to channel EU resources into the development of the backward regions (see Chapter 18). Fourth, as we saw in Chapter 19, the summit also called for a new initiative in the field of social policy. Fifth, later in the 1970s, the relationship between the EU and its ex-colonial dependencies was significantly reshaped in the form of the 'Lomé Convention' (see Chapters 22 and 23). Finally, there was the series of institutional developments which we discussed briefly in the first section of this chapter (and, fully, in Chapter 2), especially the summit meetings and their formalization into the European Council.

It is obvious from all these developments that the EU needed financial resources not only to pay for the day-to-day running of the EU but also to feed the various funds that were established: the ESF, ERDF and, most important of all, the European Agricultural Guidance and Guarantee Fund (EAGGF). As we have seen, in 1970 the EU took the important step of agreeing to introduce a system that would provide the EU, and specifically the General Budget, with its own resources, thus relieving it of the uncertainty of annual decisions regarding its finances as well as endorsing its political autonomy (see Chapter 16). Another step of great importance was the decision that the European Parliament should be elected directly by the people, not by the national parliaments. In addition, the EU decided to grant the European Parliament significant powers over the General Budget; as we saw in Chapter 2, this proved to be a very significant development. Finally, but by no means least, was the development of the political co-operation mechanism. It is important not to forget that the dedicated Europeans had always hoped that the habit of co-operation in the economic field would spill over into the political arena, i.e. into foreign policy matters. As we have seen, that has indeed happened: the political co-operation that we see today can be said to date from the Hague summit of 1969 and was formally inaugurated in 1970, and, when the Maastricht and Amsterdam treaties are fully implemented, the EU will come very close to having a common defence policy (the 1997 Amsterdam summit's qualification, stressing NATO, cannot be the permanent reality); thus it will have to have a common foreign policy on defence and security matters.

Although there has been a series of institutional developments, the relationship between the member nations has undergone a significant change. When the member nations signed the Treaty of Rome, they opted for an EU Council of Ministers which could take decisions on the basis of a supranational majority voting system. However, the insistence of the French led to the Luxembourg compromise. In addition, and especially after 1969, the centre of gravity of decision making within the EU became the European Council.

The method of operation of the European Council is cast in the traditional intergovernmental mould. As Swann (1988) argues, the development of intergovernmentalism might have been expected to slow down the pace of progress within the EU: the unanimity principle would always force the EU to adopt the lowest common denominator and that might mean little or even no change whatever.

However, that was certainly not the case in the early 1970s: as we have seen, a number of new initiatives were launched and in the main those initiatives were designed to further the process of integration.

Intergovernmentalism was still strong in the 1980s, but the performance of the intergovernmental EU of the early 1980s was markedly less dynamic than that of the early 1970s. A good deal of activity within the EU then centred around quarrels over matters such as the reform of the CAP and the General Budget, especially the United Kingdom's contribution to it.

At this juncture it may be useful to stress two conclusions. The first is that, despite developments in foreign policy co-operation, unless the Maastricht and Amsterdam treaties are *fully* implemented, the EU would continue to lack two essential attributes of a state. These are responsibility for external affairs and defence. Thus, in spite of the serious discussions being conducted recently on these issues, as Collins argues in Chapter 2, the EU has a great gap in its competences, but its weight makes it highly significant in world economics and thus in world politics. The second is that the significant achievements of the EU during the post-1969 period made it very attractive. This attraction is demonstrated by:

1. Its first round of enlargement to include Denmark, Ireland and the United Kingdom in 1973.
2. The adhesion of Greece in 1981.
3. Its second round of enlargement to include Portugal and Spain in 1986.
4. Its third round of enlargement to include Austria, Finland and Sweden in 1995.
5. The recent applications for membership by several nations, including Cyprus, Hungary, Malta, Poland, Switzerland and Turkey, and most of the eastern European countries, especially the Czech and Slovak Republics.

Tables 25.3 and 25.4 give the timetable for the adjustments in the CETs and the dismantling of the internal tariffs for the three countries involved in the first enlargement: Denmark, Ireland and the United Kingdom. The tables do not cover all groups of commodities. For example, tariffs on coal imports were abolished from

Table 25.3 New members' intra-tariff reductions (%)

	Individual reductions made on 1 January 1972	Cumulative reduction
1 April 1973	20	20
1 January 1974	20	40
1 January 1975	20	60
1 January 1976	20	80
1 July 1977	20	100

Source: Bulletin of the European Communities, no. 8, 1978.

Table 25.4 Approaching the CET (%)[a]

	Individual adjustments made on 1 January 1972	Cumulative adjustment
1 January 1974	40	40
1 January 1975	20	60
1 January 1976	20	80
1 July 1977	20	100

[a] For products which differ by more than 15% from the CET.
Source: Bulletin of the European Communities, no. 8, 1978.

the day of accession, and tariffs on certain groups of commodities given in Annex III of the Treaty of Accession were abolished on 1 January 1974, etc. In the case of the CETs, those tariffs that differed by less than 15% were adjusted on 1 January 1974. Import quota restrictions were also abolished from the date of accession. Measures having equivalent effects to the import quota restrictions were eliminated by the deadline of 1 January 1975. All three new member nations had no difficulties in achieving these changes.

In the case of Greece's membership, a five-year period was agreed for the progressive dismantling of residual customs duties on Greek imports of products originating in the EU and for the progressive alignment of Greek tariffs to the CET. Customs duties on Greek imports from the EU were to be reduced in six stages commencing on 1 January 1981, with a reduction of 10 percentage points followed by a further reduction of the same percentage points on 1 January 1982 and four annual reductions of 20 percentage points so that all customs duties on Greek intra-EU trade should have been removed by 1 January 1986. Alignment of the CET was to follow the same timetable.

Quantitative restrictions between Greece and the EU were to be abolished on adhesion, with the exception of 14 products for which Greece was authorized to maintain transitional quotas. These quotas were to be progressively increased during the five-year transitional period and to be completely eliminated by 31 December 1985. As a general rule, the minimum rate of increase for such quotas was 25% at the beginning of each year for quotas expressed in value terms and 20% at the beginning of each year for quotas expressed in volume terms. Measures having equivalent effect to quantitative restrictions were to be eliminated upon adhesion, except for the Greek system of cash payments and import deposits which were to be phased out over three years (see *Bulletin of the European Communities,* no. 5, 1969, for these and further details).

In the case of Portugal and Spain, a ten-year transitional period was agreed. For Portugal, this is divided into two equal (five-year) stages for the majority of products and a basic seven-year period for other products, although some measures would apply for the full ten years. For Spain, there are some variations, but the essentials are basically the same.

It can be stated that Greece, Portugal and Spain have navigated their transition periods successfully. With regard to the three members joining in 1995, there is practically no transition period since they were members of EFTA, and, as we have seen, EFTA and the EU have had free trade between them for a very long time through the arrangement now known as the EEA. Indeed, the only derogation from immediate implementation of all EU legislation is a four-year transitional period during which the new members can maintain their higher than EU health, safety and environmental standards.

So far there has been one withdrawal. The position of Greenland was renegotiated in 1984 but it remains associated under the rules of 'Overseas countries and territories'. A special agreement regulates mutual fishing interests.

Of course, one should point out that, in contrast to this rosy picture, a number of non-tariff barriers remained. However, as we have seen (Chapters 2 and 8), the aim of the 'internal market' is to abolish these either directly or indirectly via the harmonization of technical specifications which will promote the right environment for getting rid of them. All these non-tariff barriers are fully set out in Chapter 8.

25.4 The present

The present begins in the mid-1980s. Without a shadow of doubt, its stars must be the SEA which now regulates all the activities of the EU and, provided that it is fully implemented, the Maastricht Treaty (since the Amsterdam Treaty of June 1997 does not incorporate major changes). In the section on political developments, we examined the factors which led to the birth of the SEA. As Collins has shown in Chapter 2, the SEA contains policy development which is based upon the intention of having a true single market in place by the end of 1992 with free movement of capital, labour, services and goods rather than the patchy arrangements of the past. The SEA also introduces, or strengthens, other policy fields. These include the following:

1. Responsibility towards the environment.
2. The encouragement of further action to promote health and safety at work.
3. Technological R&D.
4. Work to strengthen economic and social cohesion so that weaker members may participate fully in the freer market.
5. Co-operation in economic and monetary policy.

In addition, the SEA brings foreign policy co-operation into consideration and provides it with a more effective support than it has had hitherto, including its own secretariat to be housed in the Council building in Brussels.

Institutionally, as we have seen, it was agreed that the European Council would take decisions on qualified majority votes in relation to the internal market, research, cohesion and improved working conditions and that, in such cases, the European Parliament should share in decision making. These developments were followed later by agreement regarding the control of expenditure on the CAP (which, as we have seen in Chapters 11 and 16, has been a source of heated argument for a number of years) and, most importantly, a fundamental change in the EU General Budget (see Chapter 16).

Before turning to the other star, the Maastricht Treaty, recall that a three-stage timetable for EMU started on 1 July 1990 with the launching of the first phase of intensified economic co-operation during which all the member states were to submit their currencies to the exchange rate mechanism (ERM) of the EMS. The main target of this activity was the United Kingdom whose currency was not subject to the ERM discipline; the United Kingdom joined in 1991 while Mrs (now Baroness) Thatcher was still in office, but withdrew in 1992 when the UK could not maintain the ERM parity for the pound. During the second stage, which started in 1994, the EU created the European Monetary Institute (EMI) to prepare the way for the European Central Bank which started operating on 1 January 1997. As we have seen, the Treaty allows Denmark and the United Kingdom to opt out of the final stage when the EU currency rates were to be permanently and irrevocably fixed and a single currency (the Euro) floated.

Here is a sketch of the agreement:

1. The EC will be given an appropriate title: the 'European Union'.

2. A single currency, to be managed by an independent European Central Bank, will be introduced as early as 1997 if seven of the present 12 nations pass the strict economic criteria (see Chapter 6) required for its successful operation, and in 1999 at the latest.

3. The EC states are to move towards a joint foreign and security policy, but with most decisions requiring unanimity voting. The Western European Union (WEU; launched in 1954 as an intergovernmental organization to enable the ending of the occupation of Germany, but has been dormant ever since – see Chapter 2) will become the equivalent of an EC defence force. Thus for the first time the EC is set to have a common defence policy with the implication that the WEU will eventually be responsible for implementing the decisions of an inevitable EC political union. Appreciation for (or is it accommodation of?) NATO was reiterated by stating that the revival of the long-dormant WEU is to be linked to NATO, thus ensuring a continued alliance with the United States and Canada for the defence of Europe; an essential compromise for reaching agreement. The EC is given jurisdiction in specific areas with the member states voting to implement decisions. These areas include industrial affairs, health, education, trade, environment, energy, culture, tourism and consumer and civil protection. Also, social affairs will become an EC jurisdiction in all the member countries except the United Kingdom which rejected EC-imposed legislation on workers' rights on the pretext that this would undermine EC competitiveness. Increased political co-operation will be carried out under a new name: the European Union (EU). The EC will also create a permanent diplomatic network of senior political officials in the EC capitals. Finally, the European Parliament will get a modest say in the shaping of some EC legislation, but this falls short of their demand for 'an equitable sharing of the right to make EC laws with the EC governments'.

4. A European police intelligence agency (Europol), to fight organized crime and drug trafficking, will be created.

5. Greece, Ireland, Portugal and Spain, the less developed members of the EC, will receive increased support from the remaining partners to assist them in the process of catching up with the average level of development in the EC as a

whole. For this purpose, the EC will create a special fund (Cohesion Fund) in 1993.

To update on these aims, one should point out that the stipulated earlier (1997) floating of a single currency had to be waived, 11 member nations adopted the Euro on 1 January 1999, the British Labour government has decided to participate in the 'social chapter' and to run a referendum on the single currency, possibly after 2002, membership of NATO has been extended to the eastern European nations with the endorsement of Russia, which signed an agreement to that effect in May 1997, and serious efforts are being made towards the creation of a European army for defence in Europe.

25.5   Conclusion

The main conclusion is that the EU has been successful not only in achieving *negative* integration (see Chapter 1), but also in adopting a host of *positive* integration measures. Indeed, when the Maastricht and Amsterdam treaties become a reality, the EU would be heading towards the dream of its 'founding fathers', the creation of a United States of Europe, despite the vehement utterances, by *some* member nations, to the contrary.

26 The future of the EU

A. M. EL-AGRAA

To give a meaningful answer to the question of what the future will bring to the EU, one needs a specification of what the future means. Is it the immediate future? Or is it the indefinite future? Of course, the future is both of these, but, as will become apparent in this chapter, one needs to deal with these periods separately. However, the indefinite future is easy to tackle; hence it is discussed first and briefly in the following section.

26.1 The indefinite future

The long-term future of the EU is quite clear. As has been consistently and persistently indicated, the founding fathers, and more recently those who suggested a two-tier Europe, dreamed of the creation of a United States of Europe. The main reason for this is the achievement of eternal peace in an area with a long history of deep conflict and bloody wars. The political and economic dimensions came later and in a reinforcing manner: Europe stood no chance of being on a par with the United States and Japan in terms of economic excellence and say in world affairs without being united on both fronts. Thus, until a single European nation becomes a reality, the energies of those dedicated to this cause will still be devoted to finding ways of doing so. The continuing Franco-German efforts to speed up the unity process are consistent with this, and so is the statement by Mr Jacques Delors (ex-President of the EU Commission) that a two-speed Europe means that if and when those countries fit and able to make fast progress go ahead, this will not retard the integrative process, since the countries left behind will find themselves in a worse situation than before; hence they will hasten their catching-up process. Indeed, in doing so, they may actually enhance the speed of the integrative process for all the countries concerned.

This might sound like a bold and peculiar statement, given that the present Labour government of the United Kingdom, led by Mr Tony Blair, has clearly indicated that although it intends to play a full and co-operative part with its EU partner nations, it will do so within the clear context of independent, sovereign, states. However, this sentiment is certainly shared neither by the two largest countries behind the real drive for EU integration, France and Germany, nor by the Benelux countries, Italy or Spain; indeed, the closest ally to the UK in this respect is Denmark. Also, and as we have seen, it is consistent with the attitude adopted by Britain towards European integration throughout the post-Second World War period. Therefore, even if a multi-tier scenario became the reality, at least one substantial tier would continue with its pursuit of the cherished dream.

26.2   The new millennium

However, if by the future one is concerned with what will happen during the early part of the new millennium (i.e. will the opening up of the EU internal market and the full implementation of the Maastricht Treaty – the Amsterdam Treaty of June 1997 does not incorporate any major deviations – be ends in themselves or merely staging posts on the way to greater economic and political union?), then, as stated in the previous editions of this book, the answer requires a consideration of some interchanges that took place between British ex-Prime Minister Margaret Thatcher (now Baroness Thatcher), the President of the Commission during the late 1980s (Mr Jacques Delors) and Germany's ex-Chancellor Helmut Kōhl as well as the developments incorporated into the Maastricht Treaty. Let us examine these in turn.

During the middle of the summer of 1988, Mr Delors predicted that 'in ten years' time 80 per cent of economic, and perhaps social and tax, legislation will be of Community origin'. In early September of the same year, he followed this with a speech to the United Kingdom's Trade Union Congress (TUC) in which he spoke strongly of the 'social dimension' of the internal market, and called for a 'platform of guaranteed social rights', including the proposal that every worker should be covered by a collective agreement with his or her employer; a proposal which is close to the hearts of most, if not all, British trade unionists.

Later, during the same month (on 20 September), Mrs Thatcher, speaking in Bruges at the College of Europe (where else!), responded in very strong terms: 'We have not rolled back the frontiers of the state in Britain only to see them re-imposed at a European level, with a European super-state exercising a new dominance from Brussels.' Since then, she repeated the same emotive phrases regarding the 'nightmare of an EC government' on many occasions. She did this in Luxembourg and Madrid, alongside Lake Maggiore in Italy during a summit meeting, and before the Conservative Party Conference in Brighton in the United Kingdom. Nor did she confine her attacks to broad policy issues. She also did so with regard to every single practical measure by which her fellow EU leaders sought to achieve progress within the EU. She told a somewhat bemused Italian Prime Minister (then Ciriaco De Mita) at Lake Maggiore, 'I neither want nor expect to see a European central bank or a European currency in my lifetime or ... for a long time afterwards.' Recently, the Baroness has declared that she has regretted having signed the Maastricht Treaty, and backed Mr William Hague for the leadership of the Conservative Party simply because he had vehemently announced that qualification for membership in his shadow cabinet will require unwavering commitment to ensuring that the Euro will have no place in Britain. Choosing Michael Portillo as shadow chancellor soon after his return to politics is consistent with that since Portillo is a vehement opponent of the UK's adopting the Euro, and actually believes in its demise on the grounds that no single European currency has ever succeeded!

The first rebuttals of Mrs Thatcher's vehement utterances came not from the 'socialist' leaders of the other EC member nations at the time, such as President François Mitterand of France, Prime Minister Felipe Gonzalez of Spain or Prime Minister Andreas Papandreou of Greece. They sensibly kept their feelings to themselves, and left it to the more right-wing prime ministers, Germany's Chancellor Helmut Kōhl, Italy's Ciriaco De Mita, Holland's Ruud Lubbers and Belgium's Wilfred Martens, to respond to her.

The most outspoken was Chancellor Kōhl, hitherto Mrs Thatcher's closest ally. He declared flatly in Brussels in November of the same year that:

1. All internal frontiers within the EC must disappear by 1992.
2. Tax harmonization is indispensable.
3. A European police force is the answer to crime and terrorism.
4. By pooling sovereignty the EC states will gain and not lose.
5. The EC must have (in alliance with the United States) a common defence policy, leading to a European army.

He did not mention Mrs Thatcher by name, but every point he emphasized is one on which she is on record as taking the opposite view.

It should be stressed that Mrs Thatcher's stance on these matters suggests that she believes that the EU is predominantly a zero sum game: every increase in the EU's sovereignty is at the expense of that of the member nations, especially of the United Kingdom. However, most of the other EU leaders have fewer illusions about what the medium-sized member countries of the EU can achieve by themselves: they believe this is very little indeed. They reckon that by 'pooling sovereignty' they increase the range of possibilities for the EU as a whole and thus indirectly for their own countries as well. Hence, Chancellor Kōhl's carefully considered remarks on this subject should be much appreciated, particularly since Germany is not one of the smaller EU nations; indeed it is the largest country in the EU in terms of both population and GDP.

In short, it can be claimed that the other EC leaders saw Mrs Thatcher following the example of Charles de Gaulle, whose anti-EC policies in the 1960s held back the development of the EC, ironically including the admission of the United Kingdom. The comparison is almost certainly one which Mrs Thatcher herself may find flattering; but does she realize that de Gaulle's intransigence eventually did much to undermine French influence for a long time both within the EC and outside it?

Although Mrs Thatcher was in a minority of one within the EC, she put herself in that position entirely by her own doing – her isolation was self-inflicted. She had been in that situation before, when she fought her long and hard battle to reduce the United Kingdom's contribution to the EC General Budget, but then attracted much grudging admiration from the leaders of the other member nations. Although they objected to her tactics, they recognized that she was protecting a vital British interest and was seeking to remedy an evident injustice. However, their sympathy for the position she adopted in the late 1980s (and continues to espouse today) was non-existent. She was seen as acting out of sheer perversity or, at least, out of nationalism of the narrowest possible kind.

However, what is intriguing is the fact that being in a minority of one does not offer much hope for the majority. Although the other 11 member states were reasonably united in their opposition to Mrs Thatcher, there was little they could do to get their way without asking the United Kingdom to forgo its membership of the EC. As we have seen, majority voting does not extend to such vital issues as the admission of new member nations, tax harmonization, the creation, now a reality, of a common central bank and one currency, and banking in general; these are still subject to unanimity. Had Mrs Thatcher chosen to veto any proposed reforms in these fields, or any other moves towards a political union, there would have been no way to prevent her from doing so. I argued in the third edition of this book that the fact that she surprised everyone by endorsing the Delors Report, subject to some provisos (see Chapter 6), 'is neither here nor there since she may still drag her feet over the second and final stages of the EMU and may even slow down the first stage by making a real issue of every problem encountered over those innocent provisos' (p. 492). That prediction came true since, as we have seen, the UK obtained special protocols in the Maastricht Treaty for opting out of the single EU currency and the social charter (more on this below).

In the fourth edition, I added that the EC leaders could not have waited until Mrs Thatcher's retirement from the political scene. She told *The Times* (London) then that she would like to complete a fourth term of office, which could have taken her to 1997 or beyond. Given the divided state of Britain's opposition parties at the time, this could have been no idle boast; the results of the elections for the European Parliament then may have cast only a shadow of doubt on this (see Chapter 2). Few, if any, of the EC's other leaders had much hope of still being around then; two had already disappeared from the scene.

I asked: what could have been the way out of this impasse? To answer this question, I quoted from the third edition of this book:

> One may well ask who could change Mrs Thatcher's mind or coerce her into taking a different view? In theory, at least, her own political party could. The British Conservative Party led the United Kingdom into the EC and remained overwhelmingly committed when the Labour Party swung violently against. Moreover, the Conservative Party has a long tradition of being uncompromising in its choice of leader; therefore, if they agree that Mrs Thatcher is completely out of line, they are most likely to let her go. However, as discussed below, there is a recent twist to this argument.
>
> The irony now is that the Labour Party is at least warming to the EC (the Labour Party's manifesto for the 1983 general election contained withdrawal from the EC as one of its four major issues), and President Jacques Delors of the EC Commission was given a rapturous reception when he spoke to the TUC in September 1988. There is no reason to believe that the bulk of the Conservative Party has changed its mind about the EC, but there has been hardly a whisper of criticism of Mrs Thatcher's stance against the further development of the EC. Of course, it is still possible that the results of the recent (1989) elections for the European Parliament and one by-election in the United Kingdom may have a positive influence; indeed, it could be argued that Mrs Thatcher's endorsement of the EMU was entirely the result of this.
>
> The reason for this state of affairs was cruelly exposed by a recent satirical television broadcast in the United Kingdom, which reported that a man had crawled on his hands and knees for 27 miles just to get into the *Guinness Book of Records*. The TV commentator suggested that 'if he had crawled another three miles, he might have got into the Cabinet'. That Mrs Thatcher has surrounded herself with yes-men is one of Britain's worst-kept secrets. These yes-men now dominate the Conservative Party, and that is why the party is less likely to sack Mrs Thatcher from her position over the question of the future of the EC, or indeed any other issue. However, one of the future contenders (Michael Heseltine) for the leadership of the party has recently published a book fully endorsing the future envisaged for the EC by the most demanding of its advocates [see Heseltine, 1989]; but he is out of the Cabinet at the moment.
>
> As the years have gone by, there have [been] fewer and fewer people to whom she has been prepared to listen. One of them has certainly been ex-President Ronald Reagan, but he is now gone. Will Mr Bush command her attention and persuade this superpatriotic leader that in diminishing the EC she is also diminishing her own country? If not, the EC faces the dim prospect of another decade of lost opportunities. However, Mr Bush is not

likely to attempt to do so, given the present confrontation between the United States and the EC over agricultural and other matters, which is making progress very difficult indeed in the present round of GATT negotiations (see Baldwin *et al.*, 1988). Moreover, Mr Bush is more likely to be concerned with the Canada–US free trade area arrangement and the 'special relationship between the USA and Japan', i.e. he sees the centre of gravity to be increasingly moving towards the Pacific region, particularly with the USSR reducing its military forces in Europe and diverting them to the east. (pp. 492–3)

Given this background, I argued in that edition that, in spite of the endorsement of the EMU, all signs seemed to suggest either that the achievement of the internal market by the end of 1992 would be the final goal or that an EC without the United Kingdom would be the inevitable way forward. I saw this, and continue to see it, as a matter of vital importance, not only because it would have had to be contemplated if Mrs Thatcher had continued in office and insisted on her declared position, but also because the EC had no precedent on this matter and its constitution is completely silent on it. I urged that the legal implications of this had to be investigated, but in the meantime hoped that, if this issue became a reality, the United Kingdom would do the honourable thing and simply withdraw from the EC.

I did not leave this matter there. I added the following:

Of course, one should also consider what would happen if Mrs Thatcher managed to persuade some of the other member nations of the EC to adopt her position. If this did happen, the outcome then would most certainly be a two-tier EC. However, all the signs indicate that the majority of the member nations will forge ahead with political integration, with the second of the two tiers comprising no more than the United Kingdom. The result would be a United States of Western Europe minus the United Kingdom. That might not be a bad thing because the British would then have to consider their position seriously, and such a reconsideration would inevitably result in the United Kingdom applying to rejoin the EC, but then fully committed to a one-nation EC. Hence, in trying to prevent the further progress of the EC towards economic and political union, Mrs Thatcher may actually cause the EC to achieve this goal much sooner than its vehement supporters ever hoped for.

If the circumstances change so much as to enable the United Kingdom to secure the support of more EC member states, then the two-tier Europe would become a reality. Such an outcome would be most disappointing, given our discussion of the history of European unity. However, one cannot leave it there since as long as the European movement remains strong, the past suggests that a way out, and forward, will be found. Indeed, this may prove inevitable since the erosion of the illusionary sovereignty that Mrs Thatcher is worried about will certainly occur after the internal market has been achieved in 1992. By then:

1. The member nations of the EC will have to agree on a joint trade policy towards the rest of the world...
2. The ability of governments to set their own rates of VAT will become extremely limited...
3. The continued success of the EMS will ensure that the member states will move smoothly towards the second and final stages of the EMU (the complete fixity of exchange rates, the creation of an EC central bank and the adoption of a single currency). Putting it differently, the success of the EMS will force them to align their monetary policies more closely if they are to keep their promise of allowing capital to move freely across the borders of member nations; this may prove impossible without a common central bank.

Thus, whichever way one looks at it, the inevitable conclusion is that Mrs Thatcher is bound to fail and the EC is set to achieve the cherished aims of its founding fathers. The sovereignty that Mrs Thatcher is so reluctant to compromise has already been subjected to that process. Those who think in terms of absolute sovereignty live in an imaginary world. (pp. 493–4)

In the fourth edition, I stated that I need hardly add that although some of the detail in this argument may not have stood the test of the time between then and 1994, my main predictions came true. Mrs Thatcher was forced to resign by her own Conservative Party over the issue of the EC, and this was made possible because one of her closest allies in the Cabinet (Sir Geoffrey Howe) decided enough was enough by openly declaring his opposition to her attitude towards the EC. Although her recommendation for successor, Mr John Major, triumphed, he did not follow closely in her footsteps, and, apart from the challenge from a brand-new Labour Party (some would call it a neo-Conservative Party), his government's downfall was partly due to deep division within the Conservatives over the role of Britain within the EU; a division made starkly clear by the two who contested the final for his (Major's) replacement: Kenneth Clarke, a committed pro-European, and William Hague, a devout anti-European. Moreover, the EC has made great progress since Mrs Thatcher by ratifying the Maastricht and Amsterdam treaties, to which I now turn, albeit briefly simply because they have been covered in full in Chapters 2 and 6, and throughout the whole book.

I added that, as we have seen, the original Maastricht Treaty provided for the creation of a single EU currency by as early as 1997 if seven of the then 12 member countries passed the agreed strict, yet flexible, five criteria on price stability, interest rates, budget deficits, public debt and currency stability (see Chapter 6), or by 1999 at the latest. The earlier date was later waived, somewhat vindicating 'flexibility'. The Treaty also called for the establishment of a common central bank to be in charge of the common currency. These two plus the common defence policy, if it became a reality, although the Amsterdam Treaty of June 1997 seemed to suggest otherwise for the time being, would bring the EU much closer to a political union. Thus, the EU, but not in its entirety, seemed to be set on the road leading to the final destination.

I suggested that, against this rosy picture, one had to emphasize that full ratification became a thorny issue: Denmark had to have a second referendum in May 1993, and a favourable outcome there was needed to pave the way for approval by the United Kingdom. Ironically, what complicated the ratification process in the United Kingdom was the insistence of the Labour Party on British participation in the Social Act, one of the opt-out protocols negotiated by the British government. Moreover, some items of the Maastricht Treaty were watered down during the Edinburgh summit in December 1992 with the aim of pleasing the Danes in order to enable a positive outcome for their referendum (see Chapter 2), and some would argue that the resulting dilution ensured that political integration had been relegated to the distant future.

I did add that this pessimism could not be justified. First, the subsidiarity principle was not a diluting of the Maastricht Treaty since it simply clarified what should be attempted at the EU level (the central government) and at the national level (the local government). Second, as we have seen in the case of Mrs Thatcher, member countries such as France and Germany were not likely to adhere to this for long: they would go for a Delors-type two-tier EU, with the majority constituting one tier and Denmark and the United Kingdom as the other. Again, this could happen for only a short time because sooner or later, the Danes and the British would have no alternative but to return to the fold. A well-seasoned European,

Warner Ungerer, Rector, College of Europe at Bruges, tried to provide the rationale for this:

> if we had not had the European Community, the Danes, who have a large agricultural production, would have had great difficulty exporting agricultural products to the other European countries. In the Community there is a common market for agriculture. The Danes knew that, with their agricultural strength, they would be competitive in the common market. They did not want to join because of the ideas of European union. They wanted to join for economic reasons. This was predominantly the British motive as well. Those two countries have difficulties with European union because they never fully understood the concept of European union...
>
> The European union can live without Denmark ..., even without Great Britain. The Community existed before the British wanted to be part of it. The British did not join the Community at the beginning because they thought it would never work. They only joined when they saw that it works. If they left, the Community would continue to work. (Ungerer, 1993)

I reiterated that (as we have seen in Chapters 1, 2 and 25) this was no more than a very partial and distorted explanation. The British did not join from the start, simply because they were torn between their Empire and Commonwealth obligations and a commitment to a Europe determined to have a common policy for agriculture which ran against their own interests as well as against those of their partners in the Commonwealth. Of course, there was also another reason. At that time, Britain still thought of itself as a world superpower; hence it was equally torn between this delusion and the prospect of being relegated to one of three important nations in just Europe. Nevertheless, Britain did change its mind when it realized that its superpower status was no more than a figment of its own imagination and that the EC member countries were growing fast economically when Britain was hovering at the zero per cent level. Thus, the explanation is not purely economic; it is economic within the context of diminished international importance (see Young, 1998, for an excellent exposition). With regard to Denmark, the economic rationale is nearer to the truth, but, as we have also seen in the above chapters, Denmark simply followed in Britain's footsteps. These two countries seem to have a great deal in common, hence their insistence on the subsidiarity principle even though it has no direct bearing on the real substance of the integrative process, and their antics during the ratification of the Maastricht Treaty should be quite understandable.

I concluded that Ungerer's explanation left a lot to be desired. As has been emphasized again and again, the aim of the founding fathers is the creation of a United States of Europe. Thus, although it is true to argue that the EU can succeed without Britain and Denmark, such an argument misses this important dimension. In order to unite Europe, these two countries need to be accommodated, but not at the expense of the other EU nations. Attempts at such an accommodation may actually lead to the sacking of the British and the Danes from the EU, but the door must always be left open for them since, as argued above, they will have no alternative but to return, and then fully committed. This is especially so when one recalls (see Chapters 6 and 24) that any country which expects to join the EU must come fully committed not only to the Maastricht and Amsterdam treaties but to everything the EU stands and aims for at the time of joining: they must accept the *acquis communitaire*.

I repeat that although the above analysis, in its entirety, may not have stood the test of time, it remains essentially true. However, the real message from the inter-changes and developments is that because politicians, on the whole, stay at the helm for short durations, it should be understandable that their preoccupations are with their survival in office; hence they will endeavour to please the masses in accordance with the sentiments of the time. The ones who have the vision and commitment to its pursuit come once in a while, but they are the ones that really matter for European integration. Hence, one should not be distracted with petty squabbles between politicians at particular moments in time. However, Mr Blair seems to indicate a wider vision since in a speech in Ghent (next to Bruges!) on 23 February 2000, he said that he believes that by winning the argument for economic reform in Europe, he can mould the EU's agenda and in doing so simultaneously defuse much of the resentment Britons feel towards the EU. In short, he wants the UK to act from within the EU to the betterment of the EU itself and its attraction to Britons, adding that UK ties with the United States have been undermined by the failure of the UK to play an active role within the EU.

26.3 Conclusion

Thus, one seems to have gone round in a full circle: the immediate future led back to the indefinite future. However, although this is inevitable, it misses the real message that the road not only is long and winding, but also has ups and downs: the summit may be clear, but reaching it means not falling off the precipices. To put it differently, economics has never been the driving force behind European integration; it has been only a vehicle to that end. Economic problems are simply obstacles on the way, but the European movement will ensure that they are no more than that. Thus, it is inevitable that the two futures should come together.

Bibliography

Throughout this book, reference is made to numerous Communications by the Commission of the European Communities/Union to the Council. These are indicated by the official system adopted by the EC/EU, which is quite clear. For example, COM (88) 491 means Communication number 491, issued in 1988. Reference is also frequently made to the Treaties of the European Communities. Some of these are published by Her Majesty's Stationery Office (HMSO), now The Stationery Office (TSO), in the United Kingdom, but the most comprehensive set is issued by Sweet & Maxwell, which is listed here. Also listed is the Commission's Comprehensive Guide to the Maastricht Treaty (CEU, 1999g). See also the note on p. 48.

Throughout the book, *EU Bulletin* is used to refer to the Commission of the European Communities' *Bulletin of the Economic Communities/Union* (various issues), and *OJ C*, *OJ L* or *OJ CL* (where L stands for legal) refer to the Commission's *Official Journal of the European Communities/Union*. Again the EC/EU's own system of referencing is clear.

ACP Group (1996) *Information Note on Issues Pertaining to the Future of ACP–EU Cooperation Under the Lomé Convention*, Doc. ACP/26/068/96.

ACP Group (1998) *(Lomé) Negotiating Mandate*, Doc. ACP/28/028/98 Rev.2.

ACP Heads of States (1997) *The Libreville Declaration Adopted by the First Summit of ACPs Heads of State and Government*, 7 November.

Adams, W. and Stoffaes, C. (eds) (1986) *French Industrial Policy*, The Brookings Institution, Washington.

Agarwal, V. K., Dippl, M. and Langhammer, R. (1985) *EC Policies Towards Associated Developing Countries: Barriers to Success*, Mohr, Tubingen.

Agence Europe (pamphlet), various dates.

Aho, C. M. and Bayard, T. O. (1982) 'The 1980s: twilight of the open trading system?', *The World Economy*, vol. 5, no. 4.

Aitken, N. D. (1973) 'The effects of the EEC and EFTA on European trade: a temporal cross-section analysis', *American Economic Review*, vol. 68.

Albert, M. (1991) *Capitalisme contre Capitalisme*, Seuil.

All Saints Day Manifesto (1975) *The Economist*.

Allais, M., Duquesne de la Vinelle, L., Oort, C. J., Seidenfuss, H. S. and del Viscoro, M. (1965) 'Options in transport policy', *EEC Studies, Transport Series*, no. 1.

Allen, D. (1983) 'Managing the Common Market: the Community's competition policy', in H. Walllace, W. Wallace and C. Webb (eds), *Policy Making in the European Community*, Wiley, second edition.

Allen, G. H. (1972) *British Agriculture in the Common Market*, School of Agriculture, Aberdeen.

Allen, P. R. (1983) 'Cyclical imbalance in a monetary union', *Journal of Common Market Studies*, vol. 21, no. 2.

Allen, P. R. and Kenen, P. (1980) *Asset Markets, Exchange Rates and Economic Integration*, Cambridge University Press, Cambridge.

Alston, P. and Weiler, J. (1999) 'An "ever closer union" in need of a human rights policy: The EU and human rights', *European Journal of International Law*, vol. 9.

Alter, K. (1996) 'The European Court's political power', *West European Politics*, vol. 19.

Alter, K. (1998a) 'Who are the "masters of the treaty"?: European Governments and the European ECJ', *International Organization*, vol. 52.

Alter, K. (1998b) 'Explaining national court acceptance of European Court jurisprudence: a critical evaluation of theories of legal integration' in A-M. Slaughter, , A. Stone Sweet, and J. Weiler (eds), *The European Courts and National Courts: Doctrine and Jurisprudence*, Hart, Oxford.

Alter, K. and Meunier-Aitsahalia, S. (1994) 'Judicial politics in the European Community: European integration and the pathbreaking Cassis de Dijon decision', *Comparative Political Studies*, vol. 26.

Alter, K. and Vargas, K. (2000) 'Explaining variation in the use of European litigation strategies: EC Law and UK gender equality policy', *Comparative Political Studies* (forthcoming).

Alting von Geusau, F. A. (1975) 'In search of a policy', in M. Adelman and F. A. Alting von Geusau (eds), *Energy in the European Communities*, Sijthoff.

Anderson, M. and Liefferink, D. (eds) (1997) *European Environmental Policy – The Pioneers*, Manchester University Press.

Ardy, B. (1988) 'The national incidence of the European Community budget', *Journal of Common Market Studies*, vol. 26, no. 4.

Argyris, N. (1989) 'The EEC rules of competition and the air transport sector', *Common Market Law Review*, vol. 26, no. 1.

Argyris, N. (1993) 'Regulatory reform in the electricity sector', *Oxford Review of Economic Policy*, vol. 19, no. 1.

Armington, P. S. (1969) 'A theory of demand for products distinguished by place of production', *IMF Staff Papers*, March.

Armington, P. S. (1970) 'Adjustment of trade balances: some experiments with a model of trade among many countries', *IMF Staff Papers*, vol. 17.

Armstrong, H. W. (1978) 'European Economic Community regional policy: a survey and critique', *Regional Studies*, vol. 12, no. 5.

Armstrong, H. W. (1985) 'The reform of European Community regional policy', *Journal of Common Market Studies*, vol. 23.

Armstrong, H. W. (1991) 'Regional Problems and Policies', in B. F. Duckham *et al.* (eds), *The British Economy Since 1945*, Oxford University Press, Oxford.

Armstrong, H. W. (1994) 'Regional problems and policies', in B. F. Duckham *et al.* (eds), *The British Economy Since 1945*, Oxford University Press, Oxford.

Armstrong, H. W. (1995a) *Growth Disparities and Convergence Clubs in Regional GDP in Western Europe, USA and Australia*, Report for DG16, European Commission, Brussels.

Armstrong, H. W. (1995b) 'Convergence among regions of the European Union', *Papers in Regional Science*, vol. 40.

Armstrong, H. W. and Taylor, J. (1978) *Regional Economic Policy and Its Analysis*, Philip Allan.

Armstrong, H. W. and Taylor, J. (1993) *Regional Economics and Policy*, Routledge, London.

Armstrong, H.W. and Taylor, J. (2000) *Regional Economics and Policy*, Blackwell, Oxford, 3rd edition.

Armstrong, K. (1998) 'Legal integration: theorising the legal dimension of European integration', *Journal of Common Market Studies*, vol. 36.

Armstrong, K. and Bulmer, S. (1998) *The Governance of the Single European Market*, Manchester University Press, Manchester.

Arndt, H. W. and Garnaut, R. (1979) 'ASEAN and the industrialisation of East Asia', *Journal of Common Market Studies*, vol. 17, no. 3.

Arndt, S. W. (1968) 'On discriminatory versus non-preferential tariff policies', *Economic Journal*, vol. 78.

Arndt, S. W. (1969) 'Customs unions and the theory of tariffs', *American Economic Review*, vol. 59.

Arnold, F. (1994) *Economic Analysis of Environmental Policy and Regulation*, Wiley, New York.

Arnull, A. (1990) 'Does the ECJ have inherent jurisdiction?', *Common Market Law Review*, vol. 27.

Arnull, A. (1991) 'What shall we do on Sunday?', *European Law Review*, vol.16.

Arnull, A. (1996) 'The European ECJ and judicial objectivity: A reply to Professor Hartley', *Law Quarterly Review*, vol. 112.

Artis, M. J. (1981) 'From monetary to exchange rate targets', *Banca Nazionale del Lavoro Quarterly Bulletin*, September.

Artis, M. J. and Currie, D. A. (1981) 'Monetary targets and the exchange rate: a case for conditional targets', in W. A. Eltis and P. J. N. Sinclair (eds), *The Money Supply and the Exchange Rate*, Oxford University Press, Oxford.

Artus, J. R. and Crockett, A. D. (1978) 'Floating exchange rates and the need for surveillance', *Essays in International Trade*, Allen & Unwin, London..

Asch, P. (1970) *Economic Theory and the Antitrust Dilemma*, Wiley, Chichester.

Auboin, M. and Laird, S. (1997) 'EU import measures and the developing countries', mimeo, World Trade Organization, Geneva.

Auboin, M. and Laird, S. (1999) 'How important are trade defence measures and non-tariff barriers for LDCs – with particular emphasis on those of the EU?', in O. Memedovic *et al.* (eds), *Multilateralism and Regionalism in the Post-Uruguay Round Era: What Role for the EU?*, Kluwer Academic Publishers, Boston.

Audretsch, D. B. (1989) *The Market and the State: Government policy towards business in Europe, Japan and the United States*, Harvester Wheatsheaf, Hemel Hempstead.

Aujac, C. (1986) 'An introductiron to French industrial policy', in W. Adams and C. Stoffaes (eds), *French Industrial Policy*, The Brookings Institution, Washington, DC.

Babardine, O. A. (1994) *The Lomé Convention and Development*, Avebury.

Bacchetta, M. (1978) 'Oil refining in the European Community', *Journal of Common Market Studies*, vol. 11.

Bacon, R., Godley, W. and McFarquhar, A. (1978) 'The direct cost to Britain of belonging to the EEC', *Cambridge Economic Policy Review*, vol. 4.

Balassa, B. (1961) *The Theory of Economic Integration*, Allen & Unwin, London.

Balassa, B. (1967) 'Trade creation and trade diversion in the European Common Market', *Economic Journal*, vol. 77.

Balassa, B. (1974a) 'Trade creation and trade diversion in the European Common Market: an appraisal of the evidence', *Manchester School*, vol. 42.

Balassa, B. (1974b) *European Economic Integration*, North-Holland.

Baldwin, R. E. (1971) *Non-tariff Distortions of International Trade*, Allen & Unwin, London.

Baldwin, R. E. (1989) 'The growth effect of 1992', *Economic Policy*, no. 9.

Baldwin, R. E. (1994) *Towards an Integrated Europe*, Centre for Economic Policy Research, London.

Baldwin, R. E. *et al.* (eds) (1988) *Issues in US–EC Trade Relations*, University of Chicago Press, Chicago.

Baldwin, R. E. *et al.* (1992) *Is Bigger Better? The Economics of EC Enlargement*, Centre for Economic Policy Research, London.

Baldwin, R. E., Francois, J. F. and Portes, R. (1997) 'The Costs and Benefits of Eastern Enlargement: the Impact on the European Union and Central Europe', *Economic Policy: A European Forum*, vol. 24.

Baldwin, R., Haaparanta, P. and Kiander, J. (1995) *Expanding Membership of the European Union*, Cambridge University Press, Cambridge.

Baldwin, R. E. and Murray, T. (1977) 'MFN Tariff Reduction and the Developing Countries: Trade Benefits Under GSP', *The Economic Journal*, vol. 87, no. 345.

Ball, R. J., Burns, T. and Laury, J. S. E. (1977) 'The role of exchange rate changes in balance of payments adjustments – the UK case', *Economic Journal*, vol. 87.

Baneth, J. (1993) 'Fortress Europe and other myths about trade', *World Bank Discussion Papers*, no. 225.

Bangemann, M. (1992) *Meeting the Global Challenge: Establishing a successful European industrial policy*, Kogan Page, London.

589

Bangermann, M. (1994) 'Information Technology in Europe: The EC Commission's View', *European Information Technology Observatory*, p. 12, EITO, Frankfurt/Main.

Banister, D. and Button, K. J. (eds) (1991) *Transport in a Free Market Economy*, Macmillan.

Bank for International Settlements (1979) *Annual Report 1978*, Basle.

Bank for International Settlements (1989) *International Banking and Financial Market Developments*, February.

Bank of Canada (1983) 'The European Monetary System: the foreign exchange mechanism', *Bank of Canada Monthly Review*, August.

Bank of England (1979) 'Intervention arrangement in the European Monetary System', *Bank of England Quarterly Bulletin*, June.

Bank of England (1982) *Quarterly Bulletin*, March.

Barents, R. (1982) 'New developments in measures having equivalent effect: A reappraisal' *Common Market Law Review*, vol. 19.

Barker, E. (1971) *Britain in a Divided Europe*, Weidenfeld & Nicolson, London.

Barnard, C. (1995) 'A European litigation strategy: The case of the Equal Opportunities Commission' in J. Shaw and G. More (eds), *New Legal Dynamics of the EU*, Clarendon, Oxford.

Barnard, C. and Sharpston, E. (1997) 'The changing face of Article 177 references', *Common Market Law Review*, vol. 34.

Barrell, R. and Pain, N. (1993) 'Trade restraints and Japanese direct investment flows', mimeo, National Institute of Economic and Social Research, London.

Barro, R. J. and Sala-i-Martin, X. (1991) 'Convergence across states and regions', *Brookings Papers*, no. 1.

Barry, A. (1993) 'The European community and European government: harmonization, mobility and space', *Economy and Society*, vol. 22.

Barten, A. P. (1970) 'Maximum likelihood estimation of a complete system of demand equations', *European Economic Review*, vol. 1.

Barten, A. P. *et al.* (1976) 'COMET: a medium-term macroeconomic model for the European Economic Community', *European Economic Review*, vol. 7.

Baumol, W. J. and Oates, J. E. (1988) *The Theory of Environmental Policy*, Cambridge University Press, Cambridge, 2nd edition.

Bayliss, B. T. (1973) 'Licensing and entry to the market', *Journal of Transport Planning and Technology*, vol. 2, no. 1.

Bayliss, B. T. (1979) 'Transport in the European Communities', *Journal of Transport Economics and Policy*, vol. XIII, no. 1.

Bayliss, B. T. and El-Agraa, A. M. (1990) 'Competition and industrial policies with emphasis on competition policy', in the third edition of this book.

Begg, I. (1989) 'European integration and regional policy', *Oxford Review of Economic Policy*, vol. 5, no. 2.

Begg, I. (1992) 'The spatial impact of the EC internal market for financial services', *Regional Studies*, vol. 26.

Begg, I. (1995) 'The impact on regions of competition of the EC Single Market in financial services', in S. Hardy, M. Hart, L. Albrechts and A. Katos (eds), *An Enlarged Europe: Regions in Competition?*, Jessica Kingsley.

Begg, I., Cripps, F. and Ward, T. (1981) 'The European Community problems and prospects', *Cambridge Economic Policy Review*, vol. 7, no. 2.

Belcredi, M., Caprio, L. and Ranci, P. (1988) *The Aid Element in State Participation to Company Capital*, report to the Commission, Office for Official Publications of the European Communities.

Bellamy, C. and Child, G. (1987) *Common Market Law on Competition*, Sweet & Maxwell, London.

Bellamy, R. and Warleigh, A. (1998) 'From an ethics of participation to an ethics of participation: Citizenship and the future of the EU', *Millennium*, vol. 27.

Bellis, J. F. (1976) 'Potential competition and concentration policy: relevance to EEC antitrust', *Journal of World Trade Law*, vol. 10, no. 1.

Benvenisti, E. (1993) 'Judicial misgivings regarding the application of international law: An analysis of attitudes of international courts', *European Journal of International Law*, vol. 4.

Berglas, E. (1979) 'Preferential trading theory – the *n* commodity case', *Journal of Political Economy*, vol. 81.

Berglas, E. (1981) 'Harmonisation of commodity taxes', *Journal of Public Economics*, vol. 16.

Berglas, E. (1983) 'The case for unilateral tariff reactions: foreign tariffs reconsidered', *AER*, vol. 73.

Bergman, D. *et al.* (1970) *A Future for European Agriculture*, Atlantic Institute, Paris.

Berkhout, F., Boehmer Christiansen, S. and Skea, J. F. (1989) 'Deposit and repositories: electricity wastes in the UK and West Germany', *Energy Policy*, vol. 17.

Best, M. (1990) *The New Competition: Institutions of industrial restructuring*, Polity, Cambridge.

Beveridge, W. (1940) *Peace by Federation?*, Federal Tract no. 1, Federal Union, London.

Bhagwati, J. N. (1965) 'On the equivalence of tariffs and quotas', in R. E. Baldwin *et al.* (eds), *Trade, Growth and the Balance of Payments*, North-Holland.

Bhagwati, J. N. (1969) *Trade, Tariffs and Growth*, Weidenfeld & Nicolson, London.

Bhagwati, J. N. (1971) 'Customs unions and welfare improvement', *Economic Journal*, vol. 81.

Bhaskar, K. (1990) *The Effect of Different State Aid Measures on Inter Country Competition*, report to the Commission, Office for Official Publications of the European Communities.

Bieber, R. *et al.* (1988) *1992: One European Market? A critical analysis of the Commission's internal market strategy*, Nomos Verlagsgesellschaft.

Bishop, W. (1981) 'Price discrimination under Article 86: Political economy in the European Court', *Modern Law Review*, vol. 44.

Bishop, S. and Walker, M. (1999) *The Economics of EC Competition Law*, Sweet & Maxwell.

Black, J. and Dunning, J. H. (eds) (1982) *International Capital Movements*, Macmillan, Basingstoke.

Black, R. A. (1977) 'Plus ça change, plus c'est la même chose: 9 governments in search of a common energy policy', in H. Wallace, W. Wallace and C. Webb (eds), *Policy-Making in the European Communities*, Little Brown, London.

Blackoby, F. T. (1980) 'Exchange rate policy and economic strategy', *Three Banks Review*, June.

Blancus, P. (1978) 'The Common Agricultural Policy and the balance of payments of the EEC member countries', *Banca Nazionale del Lavoro Quarterly Review*, vol. 5, no. 3.

Bluet, J. C. and Systermanns, Y. (1968) 'Modèle gravitionel d'échanges internationaux de produits manufacturés', *Bulletin du CEPREMAP*, vol. 1, January (new series).

Boardman, R. *et al.* (1985) *Europe, Africa and Lomé III*, University Press of America.

Bodenheimer, S. (1967) *Political Union, a Microcosm of European Politics*, Sijthoff.

Boehmer-Christiansen, S. and Skea, J. (1990) *Acid Politics: Environmental and energy policies in Britain and Germany*, Pinter.

Bohme, H. (1983) 'Current issues and progress in European shipping policy', *The World Economy*, vol. 6.

Bollard, A. E. and Mayes, D. G. (1991) 'Regionalism and the Pacific Rim', *Journal of Common Market Studies*, vol. 30.

Bootle, R. (1983) 'Foreign exchange intervention: a case of ill-founded neglect', *The Banker*, May.

Booz, A. and Booz, H. (1989) *The Effects of the Internal Market on Greece, Ireland, Portugal and Spain*, a study carried out for the EC Commission.

Bork, R. (1978) The Antitrust Paradox: *A policy at war with itself*, Basic Books.

Bos, M. and Nelson, H. (1988) 'Indirect taxation and the completion of the internal market of the EC', *Journal of Common Market Studies*, vol. 27, no. 1.

Bosworth, B., Collins, S. and Chen, Y. C. (1995) 'Accounting for Differences in Economic Growth', *Brookings Discussion Papers in International Finance*, no. 115, Washington DC.

Boulding, K. E. (1966) 'The economics of the coming spaceship Earth', in H. Jarret (ed.), *Environmental Quality in a Growing Economy*, Johns Hopkins.

Bourgeois, J. and Demaret, P. (1995) 'European Industrial, Competition and Trade Policies: Legal Aspects', in P. Buigues, A. Jacquemin and A. Sapir (eds), *European Policies on Competition, Trade and Industry*, Edward Elgar.

Bourguignon, F., Gallais-Hamonno, G. and Fernet, B. (1977) *International Labour Migrations and Economic Choices: the European case*, Development Centre of the OECD.

Bovenberg, L. and Cnossen, S. (1997) *Public Economics and the Environment in an Imperfect World*, Kluwer.

Bowers, J. K. (1972) 'Economic efficiency in agriculture', in Open University, *Decision Making in Britain III*, Parts 1–6.

Bowers, J. K. (ed.) (1979) *Inflation, Development and Integration: Essays in honour of A. J. Brown*, Leeds University Press.

Boyd G. (ed.) (1998) *The Struggle for World Markets: Competition and Co-operation between NAFTA and the European Union*, Edward Elgar.

Brada, J. C. and Méndez, J. A. (1985) 'Economic integration among developed, developing and centrally planned economies: a comparative analysis', *Review of Economics and Statistics*, vol. 67.

Brander, J. (1981) 'Intra-industry trade in identical commodities', *Journal of International Economics*, vol. 11.

Brander, J. and Spencer, B. (1983) 'International R&D rivalry and industrial strategy', *Review of Economic Studies*, vol. 50.

Brander, J. and Spencer, B. (1984) 'Tariff protection and imperfect competition', in H. Kierzkowski (ed.), *Monopolistic Competition and International Trade*, Oxford University Press.

Brazier, M., Lovecy, J. and Morgan, M. (1993) 'Professional regulation and the single European market: a study of the regulation of doctors and lawyers in England and France', mimeo, University of Manchester.

Breckling, J. *et al.* (1978) *Effects of EC Agricultural Policies: A general equilibrium approach*, Bureau of Agricultural Research, Canberra.

Bredimas, A. E. and Tzoannos, J. G. (1983) 'In search of a common shipping policy for the EC', *Journal of Common Market Studies*, vol. 20.

Breton, A. and Scott, A. (1978) 'The assignment problem in federal structures', in M. S. Feldstein and R. P. Inman (eds), *The Economics of Public Services*, Macmillan, Basingstoke.

Brewin, C. (1987) 'The European Community: a union of states without unity of government', *Journal of Common Market Studies*, vol. XXVI, no. 1.

Brewin, C. C. (1992) 'Participation of non-member states in shaping the rules of the European Community's single market', Economic and Social Research Council report, Swindon.

Bribosia, H. (1998) 'Report on Belgium' in A-M. Slaughter, A. Stone Sweet, and J. Weiler (eds), *The European Courts and National Courts: Doctrine and Jurisprudence*, Hart.

Bright, C. (1995) 'Deregulation of EC competition policy: rethinking Article 85(1)', *1994 Annual Proceedings of Fordham Corporate Law Institute*, vol. 21.

Brittan, L. (1992) *European Competition Policy: Keeping the playing field level*, CEPS.

Britton, A. and Mayes, D. G. (1992) *Achieving Monetary Union*, Sage.

Brooks, M. R. and Button, K. J. (1992) 'Shipping within the framework of a single European market', *Transport Review*, vol. 12.

Brown, A. J. (1961) 'Economic separatism versus a common market in developing countries', *Yorkshire Bulletin of Economic and Social Research*, vol. 13.

Brown, A. J. (1977) 'What is wrong with the British economy?', *The University of Leeds Review*, vol. 20.

Brown, A. J. (1979) 'Inflation and the British sickness', *Economic Journal*, vol. 89.

Brown, A. J. (1980) 'The transfer of resources', in W. Wallace (ed.), *Britain in Europe*, Heinemann, Chapter 7.

Brown, D. K. (1989) 'Trade and Welfare Effects of the European Schemes of the Generalized System of Preferences', *The Journal of Development and Cultural Change*, vol. 37, no. 4.

Brülhart, M. (1994) 'Marginal intra-industry trade: measurement and relevance for the pattern of industrial adjustment', *Weltwirtschaftliches Archiv*, vol. 130.

Brülhart, M. (1998) 'Marginal Intra-Industry Trade and Trade-Induced Adjustment: A Survey', in M. Brülhart and R. C. Hine, *Intra-Industry Trade and Adjustment: the European Experience*, Macmillan, London.

Brülhart, M. and Elliott, R. (1998) 'Adjustment to the European single market: inferences from intra-industry trade patterns', *Journal of Economic Studies*, forthcoming.

Brülhart, M. and Elliott, R. (1998) 'A survey of intra-industry trade in the European Union', in M. Brülhart and R. C. Hine, *Intra-Industry Trade and Adjustment: the European Experience*, Macmillan, London.

Bruppacher, F. (1988) 'How European electricity trade is conducted', paper presented in the *Financial Times* World Electricity Conference.

Bryant, R. C. (1980) *Money and Monetary Policy in Independent Nations*, The Brookings Institution, Washington.

Buck, T. (1975) 'Regional policy and economic integration', *Journal of Common Market Studies*, vol. 13.

Buckley, P. J. and Casson, M. (1976) *The Future of the Multinational Enterprise*, Macmillan, Basingstoke.

Buckwell, A., Harvey, D. R., Thomson, K. J. and Parton, K. (1982) *The Costs of the Common Agricultural Policy*, Croom Helm, Beckenham.

Buigues, P. and Sapir, A. (1992) 'Community industrial policy', paper presented at an EIPA conference.

Buigues, P.-A. and Martínez Mongay, C. (1997) 'The European Union internal market in implementation: how single is the single European market for the LDCs?', mimeo, European Commission, Brussels.

Buigues, P.-A. and Martínez Mongay, C. (1999) 'Regionalism and Globalization: The LDCs and the Single European Market', in O. Memedovic *et al.* (eds), *Multilateralism and Regionalism in the Post-Uruguay Round Era: What Role for the EU?*, Kluwer, Boston.

Buiter, W., Corsetti, G. and Roubini, N. (1993) 'Excessive deficits: sense and nonsense in the Treaty of Maastricht', *Economic Policy*, vol. 16.

Bundesbank (1979) *Monthly Review*, March.

Burley, A.-M. and Mattli, W. (1993) 'Europe before the court: A political theory of legal integration', *International Organization*, vol. 47.

Burrows, B., Denton, G. R. and Edwards, G. (1977) *Federal Solutions to European Issues*, Macmillan, Basingstoke.

Butt Philip, A. (1981) 'The harmonisation of industrial policy and practices', in C. Cosgrove Twitchett (ed.), *Harmonisation in the EEC*, Macmillan, Basingstoke.

Butt Philip, A. (1988) 'Implementing the European internal market: problems and prospects', *Discussion Paper*, no. 5, Royal Institute of International Affairs.

Butt Philip, A. (1992) *Report to the European Commission*, presented to the Royal Economic Society Industry Seminar, Shell Centre, London.

Button, K. J. (1982) *Transport Economics*, Heinemann, Oxford.

Button, K. J. (1984) *Road Haulage Licensing and EC Transport Policy*, Gower.

Button, K. J. (1990) 'Infrastructure plans for Europe', in J. Gillund and G. Tornqvist (eds), *European Networks*, CERUM.

Button, K. J. (1992) 'The liberalization of transport services', in D. Swann (ed.), *1992 and Beyond*, Routledge.

Button, K. J. (1993a) *Transport, the Environment and Economic Policy*, Edward Elgar.

Button, K. J. (1993b) 'East-west European transport: an overview', in D. Banister and J. Berechman (eds), *Transportation in a Unified Europe: Policies Challenges*, Elsevier.

Button, K. J. (1998) 'The good, the bad and the forgettable – or lessons the US can learn from European transport policy', *Journal of Transport Geography*, vol. 6.

Button, K. J. and Gillingwater, D. (1976) *Case Studies in Regional Economics*, Heinemann, Oxford.

Button, K. J. and Gillingwater, D. (1986) *Future Transport Policy*, Croom Helm.

Button, K. J. and Keeler, T. (1993) 'The regulation of transport markets', *Economic Journal*, vol. 103.

Button, K. J. and Pitfield, D. (eds) (1991) *Transport Deregulation: An international movement*, Macmillan, Basingstoke.

Button, K. J. and Swann, D. (1992) 'Transatlantic lessons in aviation deregulation: EEC and US experiences', *Antitrust Bulletin*, vol. 37.

Button, K. J., Hayes, K. and Stough, R. (1998) *Flying into the Future: Air Transport Policy in the European Union*, Edward Elgar.

Byé, M. (1950) 'Unions douanières et données nationales', Economie Appliquée, vol. 3. Reprinted (1953) in translation as 'Customs unions and national interests', *International Economic Papers*, no. 3.

Bzdera, A. (1992) 'The ECJ of the European Community and the politics of institutional reform', *West European Politics*, vol. 15.

Cairncross, A. *et al.* (1974) *Economic Policy for the European Community: The way forward*, Macmillan, Basingstoke.

Calingaert, M. (1988) *The 1992 Challenge from Europe: Development of the European Community's internal market*, National Planning Association, Washington DC.

Callon, M. (1986) 'Some elements of a sociology of translation: domestication of the scallops and fishermen of St. Brieuc bay', in J. Law (ed.), *Power: action and belief: a new sociology of knowledge*, Routledge, London.

Callon, M. (1998) 'Introduction: The embeddedness of economic markets in economics', in M. Callon (ed.), *The Laws of the Markets*, Blackwell.

Calmfors, L. (1997) *EMU – A Swedish Perspective Report of the Calmfors Commission*, Kluwer, Dordrecht.

Cambridge Economic Policy Group (1981) *Cambridge Economic Policy Review*, vol. 7, no. 2.

Cameron, G. C. (1974) 'Regional economic policy in the United Kingdom', in N. M. Hansen (ed.), *Public Policy and Regional Economic Development*, Saxon House.

Camps, M. (1964) *Britain and the European Community 1955–63*, Oxford University Press.

Canenbley, C. (1972) 'Price discrimination and EEC cartel law: a review of the Kodak decision of the Commission of the European Communities', *The Antitrust Bulletin*, vol. 17, no. 1.

Cappelletti, M. (1987) 'Is the European ECJ "running wild"?', *European Law Review*, vol. 12.

Carraco, C. and Sinisalco, D. (eds) (1993) *The European Carbon Tax: An economic assessment*, Kluwer.

Carrier Licensing Report of the Geddes Committee, HMSO.

Cawson, A., Morgan, K., Webber, D., Holmes, P. and Stevens, A. (1990) *Hostile Brothers. Competition and Closure in the European Electronics Industry*, Oxford University Press.

Cecchini, P. (1988) *The European Challenge 1992: The Benefits of a Single Market*, Wildwood House.

Central Bank of Ireland (1979) 'A guide to the arithmetic of the EMS exchange rate mechanism', *Central Bank of Ireland Quarterly Bulletin*, Autumn.

Central Statistical Office (1981) *Britain in the European Community*, Reference Pamphlet 137, HMSO.

CEPS (1995) *European Telecommunications Policy – How to Regulate a Single Market*, Working Party Report 13.

Chalmers, D. (1993) 'Free movement of goods within the European Community: an unhealthy addiction to Scotch whisky?', *International and Comparative Law Quarterly*, vol. 42.

Chalmers, D. (1997a) 'Judicial preferences and the community legal order', *Modern Law Review*, vol. 60.

Chalmers, D. (1997b) 'Community trade mark courts: The renaissance of an epistemic community?', in J. Lonbay and A. Biondi (eds), *Remedies for Breach of EC Law*, John Wiley, Chichester.

Chalmers, D. (1998) 'Bureaucratic Europe: From regulating communities to securitising unions', CES, Baltimore.

Chalmers, D. (1999a) 'Europeanisation and differentiation within the practice of United Kingdom domestic law', Conference on Europeanised Politics, Nuffield College, Oxford.

Chalmers, D. (1999b), 'Accounting for "Europe"', *Oxford Journal of Legal Studies*, vol. 19.

Chalmers, D. (2000) 'Postnationalism and the quest for constitutional substitutes', *Journal of Law and Society*, vol. 27.

Choi, J.-Y. and Yu, E. S. H. (1984) 'Customs unions under increasing returns to scale', *Economica*, vol. 51.

Chard, J. S. and Macmillen, M. J. (1979) 'Sectoral aids and Community competition policy: the case of textiles', *Journal of World Trade Law*, vol. 13, no. 2.

Choufoer, J. H. (1982) 'Future of the European Energy Economy', address to the Conference of European Petroleum and Gas, Amsterdam.

Christiansen, T. (1997) 'Reconstructing European space: From territorial politics to multi-level governance', in K. Jørgensen (ed.), *Reflective Approaches to European Governance*, Macmillan, Basingstoke.

Clark, C. (1962) *British Trade in the Common Market*, Stevens.

Clark, C., Wilson, F. and Bradley, J. (1969) 'Industrial location and economic potential in Western Europe', *Regional Studies*, vol. 3, no. 2.

Clauvaux, F. J. (1969) 'The import elasticity as a yardstick for measuring trade creation', *Economia Internazionale*, November.

Cleutinx, C. (1996) 'Is there a future for coal in Europe?', *Energy in Europe*, no. 27, December.

Cmnd. 8212 (1981) *Statement on the Defence Estimates*, vol. 1, HMSO.

Cnossen, S. (1986) 'Harmonisation of indirect taxes in the EEC', *British Tax Review*, vol. 4.

Coase, R. (1937) 'The nature of the firm', *Economica*, vol. 16.

Coase, R. (1960) 'The problem of social costs', *Journal of Law and Economics*, vol. 3, October.

Cobham, D. (1982) 'Comments on Peeters and Emerson', in M. T. Sumner and G. Zis (eds), *European Monetary Union: Progress and prospects*, Macmillan.

Cobham, D. (1996) 'Causes and effects of the European monetary crises of 1996–93', *Journal of Common Market Studies*, vol. 34.

Cockfield, Lord (1986) Address to the International Management Institute, Geneva.

Coffey, P. (1976) *The External Relations of the EEC*, Macmillan.

Coffey, P. (1977) *Europe and Money*, Macmillan.

Coffey, P. (1979) *Economic Policies of the Common Market*, Macmillan.

Coffey, P. (1987) *The European Monetary System: Past, present and future*, Kluwer.

Coffey, P. and Presley, J. (1971) *European Monetary Integration*, Macmillan.

Cohen, B. J. (1981) 'The European Monetary System', *Essays in International Finance*, no. 142, Princeton University.

Cohen, C. D. (ed.) (1983) *The Common Market – Ten Years After*, Philip Allan.

Cohen, W. and Levin, R. (1989) 'Empirical studies of innovation and market structure', in R. Schmalensee and R. D. Willig (eds), *Handbook of Industrial Organization*, North-Holland.

Collier, P. (1979) 'The welfare effects of customs union: an anatomy', *Economic Journal*, vol. 89.

Collins, C. D. E. (1975) *The European Communities: the Social Policy of the first phase*, Martin Robertson.

Collins, C. D. E. (1980) 'Social policy', in A. M. El-Agraa (ed.), *The Economics of the European Community*, Chapter 15, Philip Allan.

Comanor, W. S. (1990) 'United States antitrust policy: issues and institutions', in W. S. Comanor *et al.*, *Competition Policy in Europe and North America: Economic issues and institutions*, Harwood Academic.

Comanor, W. S. *et al.* (1990) *Competition Policy in Europe and North America: Economic issues and institutions*, Harwood Academic.

Comité intergouvernemental créé par la conférence de Messina (1956) *Rapport des chefs de délégation aux Ministres des Affaires Etrangères*, Brussels.

Commission of the European Communities (various issues) *Bulletin of the European Communities Union*. (*EU Bulletin*).

Commission of the European Communities (various years) *Social Report*.

Commission of the European Communities (various issues and items) *Official Journal of the European Communities*.

Commission of the European Communities (three times a year) *Social Europe*. Also, Supplements.

Commission of the European Communities (annual) *Report on Social Developments*.

Commission of the European Communities (annual) *Employment in Europe*.

Commission of the European Communities (1953) *Report on Problems raised by the Different Turnover Tax Systems Applied within the Common Market* (the Tinbergen Report).

Commission of the European Communities (1957) *First General Report on the Activity of the Communities*, Brussels.

Commission of the European Communities (1960) *Community Energy Policy Objectives for 1985* (COM (74) 60).

Commission of the European Communities (1961) *Memorandum on the General Lines of a Common Transport Policy*.

Commission of the European Communities (1962) *Action Programme of the Community for the Second Stage*.

Commission of the European Communities (1963) *Report of the Fiscal and Financial Committee* (the Neumark Report).

Commission of the European Communities (1966) *Report on the Situation of the Fisheries Sector in the Member States and the Basic Principles for a Common Policy*.

Commission of the European Communities (1967) *Tenth Annual Report of the Activities of the Communities*, Brussels.

Commission of the European Communities (1968) 'Premières Orientations pour une politique énergétique communautaire', *Communication de la Commission présenté au Conseil le 18 Décembre 1968*, Brussels.

Commission of the European Communities (1969) 'Memorandum on the Report of Agriculture in the European Economic Community', *EU Bulletin*, Supplement, January.

Commission of the European Communities (1970a) 'Report to the Council and the Commission on the realisation by stages of economic and monetary union in the Community', *EU Bulletin*, Supplement, no. 11 (the Werner Report).

Commission of the European Communities (1970b) *Industrial Policy in the Community: Memorandum from the Commission to the Council*.

Commission of the European Communities (1970c) *Corporation Tax and Income Tax in the European Communities* (the van den Tempel Report).

Commission of the European Communities (1970d) *Industrial Policy in the Community*, Office of Official Publications of the European Communities.

Commission of the European Communities (1971a) 'Preliminary guidelines for a social policy', *EU Bulletin*, Supplement 2/71.

Commission of the European Communities (1971b) 'General regional aid systems', *OJ* C111 4.11.1971.

Commission of the European Communities (1971c), 'Memorandum on a Community Development Cooperation Policy', *Bulletin of the European Communities*, Supplement 5/71.

Commission of the European Communities (1972a) *Competition Law in the European Economic Community and in the European Coal and Steel Community.*

Commission of the European Communities (1972b) *First Report on Competition Policy.*

Commission of the European Communities (1973a) 'Proposals for a Community regional policy', *OJ* C68 16.10.1973, and *OJ* C106 of 6.12.1973.

Commission of the European Communities (1973b) *Programme of Action in the Field of Technological and Industrial Policy*, SEC (73) 3824 final, October.

Commission of the European Communities (1973c) *Communication from the Commission to the Council on the Development of the Common Transport Policy*, COM (73).

Commission of the European Communities (1974a) 'Social Action Programme', *EU Bulletin*, Supplement 2/74.

Commission of the European Communities (1974b) *Third Report on Competition Policy.*

Commission of the European Communities (1975a) 'Report and proposal decision on a programme of action for the European aeronautical sector', *EU Bulletin*, Supplement 11/75.

Commission of the European Communities (1974c) *Development Aid: Fresco of Community Action Tomorrow*, Bulletin of the European Communities, Supplement 8/74.

Commission of the European Communities (1975b) 'Council Regulation (EEC) 724/75 of 18 March 1975 establishing a European Regional Development Fund', *OJ* L73 21.3.1975.

Commission of the European Communities (1975c) *Report of the Study Group 'Economic and Monetary Union 1980'*, March (the Marjolin Report).

Commission of the European Communities (1975d) *Social Harmonization – Inland Waterways*, COM (75) 465 final.

Commission of the European Communities (1976a) *Fifth Report on Competition – EEC.*

Commission of the European Communities (1976b) 'Action Programme in favour of migrant workers and their families', *EU Bulletin*, Supplement 3/76.

Commission of the European Communities (1977a) *Guidelines for Community Regional Policy*, COM (77) 195 final.

Commission of the European Communities (1977b) 'Regional concentration in the countries of the European Community', *Regional Policy Series*, no. 4.

Commission of the European Communities (1977c) *Report of the Study Group on the Role of Public Finance in European Integration*, 2 vols (the MacDougall Report).

Commission of the European Communities (1977d) 'Community regional policy: new guidelines', *EU Bulletin*, Supplement, June.

Commission of the European Communities (1978a) 'Council Decision of 16 October 1978 empowering the Commission to contract loans for the purpose of promoting investment in the Community', *OJ* L298 25.10.1978.

Commission of the European Communities (1978b) *Twelfth General Report of the Activities of the European Communities in 1978.*

Commission of the European Communities (1978c) 'Regional aid systems', *OJ* C31 3.2.1979.

Commission of the European Communities (1978d) *Report on Some Structural Aspects of Growth.*

Commission of the European Communities (1979a) 'Regional incentives in the European Community', *Regional Policy Series*, no. 15.

Commission of the European Communities (1979b) 'The Regional Development Programmes', *Regional Policy Series*, no. 17.

Commission of the European Communities (1979c) 'Air Transport – a Community Approach', *EU Bulletin*, Supplement 5/79.

Commission of the European Communities (1979d) *Proposals for Reform of the Commission of the European Communities and its Services* (the Spierenburg Report).

Commission of the European Communities (1979e) *Eighth Report on Competition Policy.*

Commission of the European Communities (1979f), *Social Harmonization – Inland Waterways*, COM (79) 363 final.

Commission of the European Communities (1979g) *Report of Committee of Inquiry on Public Finance in the Community* (the MacDougall Report), Brussels.

Commission of the European Communities (1980a) *La Suisse et la Communauté.*

Commission of the European Communities (1980b) *Official Journal of the European Communities*, Legislation, no. C149.

Commission of the European Communities (1980c) *Tenth Report on Competition Policy.*

Commission of the European Communities (1980d) 'Commission Directive 80/723/EEC of 25 June 1980 on the transparency of financial relations between Member States and public undertakings', *OJ*, L195, 29 July.

Commission of the European Communities (1981a) *Communication to the Council on the Categories of Infrastructure to which the ERDF may Contribute in the Various Regions aided by the Fund*, COM (81) 38 final.

Commission of the European Communities (1981b) *Principal Regulations and Decisions of the Council of the European Communities on Regional Policy.*

Commission of the European Communities (1981c) 'Proposal for a Council Regulation amending Regulation (EEC) 724/75 establishing a European Regional Development Fund', *OJ* C336 23.12.1981.

Commission of the European Communities (1981d) *New Regional Policy Guidelines and Priorities*, COM (81) 152 final.

Commission of the European Communities (1981e) 'Deglomeration policies in the European Community – a comparative study', *Regional Policy*, no. 18.

Commission of the European Communities (1981f) 'Study of the regional impact of the Common Agricultural Policy', *Regional Policy Series*, no. 21.

Commission of the European Communities (1981g) 'Commission recommendation of 9.10.1981 on transfrontier coordination for regional development', *OJ* L321 10.11.1981.

Commission of the European Communities (1981h) *The Regions of Europe: First periodic report on the social and economic situation in the regions of the Community.*

Commission of the European Communities (1981i) 'The European Community's Transport Policy', Periodical 2/1981, EC Documentation.

Commission of the European Communities (1982a) *Fifteenth General Report of the Activities of the European Communities in 1981.*

Commission of the European Communities (1982b) *The Agricultural Situation in the Community – 1981 Report.*

Commission of the European Communities (1982c) *Ten Years in Europe.*

Commission of the European Communities (1982d) 'Memorandum on the Community's Development Policy', *Bulletin of the European Communities*, Supplement 5/82.

Commission of the European Communities (1983a) 'Memorandum of evidence to the House of Lords Select Committee on the European Communities', *House of Lords Report*, q.v.

Commission of the European Communities (1983b) *Twelfth Report on Competition Policy.*

Commission of the European Communities (1983c) *Seventeenth General Report on the Activities of the European Communities.*

Commission of the European Communities (1983d) *European Political Cooperation*, European File 13/83.

Commission of the European Communities (1983e) *Thirteenth Report on Competition Policy.*

Commission of the European Communities (1984a) *Eighteenth General Report on the Activities of the European Communities.*

Commission of the European Communities (1984b) *Review of Member States' Energy Policies*, COM (84) 88.

Commission of the European Communities (1984c) *Social Report*. Also, for other years.

Commission of the European Communities (1984d) *Civil Aviation Memorandum No. 2: Progress towards the development of a Community air transport policy*, COM (84) 72.

Commission of the European Communities (1984e) *The European Community's Development policy: 1981–1983*, Brussels.

Commission of the European Communities (1985a) *Completing the Internal Market* (White Paper from the EC Commission to the EC Council) – COM (85) 310.

Commission of the European Communities (1985b) *The European Community and its Regions*.

Commission of the European Communities (1985c) *Fourteenth Report on Competition Policy*.

Commission of the European Communities (1985d) *Community Energy Policy Objectives for 1985*, COM (74) 1960.

Commission of the European Communities (1985e) *Fifteenth Report on Competition Policy*.

Commission of the European Communities (1985f) *Nineteenth General Report on the Activities of the European Communities*.

Commission of the European Communities (1985g) 'Commission Directive 85/413/EEC of 24th July 1985 amending Directve 80/723/EEC on the transparency of financial relations between Member States and public undertakings', *OJ* L229, 28.8.1985.

Commission of the European Communities (1985h) *Progress Towards a Common Transport Policy, Maritime Transport*, COM (85) 90 final.

Commission of the European Communities (1986a) *Official Journal of the European Communities*, Legislation, no. C241.

Commission of the European Communities (1986b) *Communication on Natural Gas*, COM (86) 518.

Commission of the European Communities (1986c) *Twentieth General Report on the Activities of the European Communities*.

Commission of the European Communities (1986d) *Report Towards a High-speed Rail Network*, COM (86) 341 final.

Commission of the European Communities (1987a) *Efficiency, Stability and Equity* (the Padoa–Schioppa Report).

Commission of the European Communities (1987b) *Completion of the Internal Market: Approximation of indirect tax rates and harmonisation of indirect tax structure*, Global Communication from the EC Commission, COM (87) 320.

Commission of the European Communities (1987c) *European Environmental Policy*, Economic and Social Committee and Consultative Assembly.

Commission of the European Communities (1987d) *Sixteenth Report on Competition Policy*.

Commission of the European Communities (1987e) (Green Paper) *Development of the Common Market for Telecommunications Services and Equipment*, COM (87) 290.

Commission of the European Communities (1987f) *Seventeenth Report on Competition Policy*.

Commission of the European Communities (1987g) *Europe Without Frontiers* (Information 1987, p. 51).

Commission of the European Communities (1988a) *Bulletin of the European Communities*, Supplement 4/47.

Commission of the European Communities (1988b) *Review of Member States' Energy Policies – the 1995 Energy Objectives*, COM (88) 174.

Commission of the European Communities (1988c) *Proposal for a Council Recommendation to the Member States to Promote Cooperation between Public Electricity Supply Companies and Private Generators of Electricity*, COM (88) 225.

Commission of the European Communities (1988d) *An Internal Market for Energy*, COM (88) 234.

Commission of the European Communities (1988e) *The Internal Energy Market*, COM (88) 238.

Commission of the European Communities (1988f) *Review of the Community Oil Industry*, COM (88) 491.

Commission of the European Communities (1988g) *Report on the Application of the Community Rules for State Aid to the Coal Industry in 1987*, COM (88) 541.

Commission of the European Communities (1988h) *Completing the Internal Market: An area without internal frontiers*, COM (88) 650.

Commission of the European Communities (1988i) *Research on the Cost of Non-Europe: Basic findings*, 16 vols (the Cecchini Report).

Commission of the European Communities (1988j) *22nd General Report of the Activities of the European Communities*.

Commission of the European Communities (1988k) *Community R&TD Programmes*, special issue.

Commission of the European Communities (1988l) *Commission Directive on Competition in Telecommunications Terminal Equipment*, 88/301.

Commission of the European Communities (1988m), *The Europe–South Dialogue*.

Commission of the European Communities (1989a) *Transparency in Energy Prices*, COM (89) 123.

Commission of the European Communities (1989b) *Energy in Europe*.

Commission of the European Communities (1989c) *ESPRIT Workprogramme*.

Commission of the European Communities (1989d) *A Framework for Community R&D Actions in the 90s*.

Commission of the European Communities (1989e) *Guide to the Reform of the Community's Structural Funds*.

Commission of the European Communities (1989f) *Survey of State Aids*, Office for Official Publications of the European Communities.

Commission of the European Communities (1989g) *Communication on a Community Railway Policy*, COM (89) 564.

Commission of the European Communities (1989h) *Energy and the Environment*, COM (89) 369.

Commission of the European Communities (1989i) *First Report on State Aids*.

Commission of the European Communities (1989j) *Council Resolution on Trans-European Networks*, COM (89) 643 final.

Commission of the European Communities (1990a) *Second Survey on State Aids in the EC in Manufacturing and Certain Other Sectors*.

Commission of the European Communities (1990b) 'The impact of the internal market by industrial sector', *European Economy*, special edition.

Commission of the European Communities (1990c) 'One market, one money: an evaluation of the potential benefits and costs of forming an economic and monetary union', *European Economy*.

Commission of the European Communities (1990d) *Second Survey of State Aids*, Office for Official Publications of the European Community.

Commission of the European Communities (1990e) *Industrial Policy in an Open and Competitive Environment*, COM (90) 556.

Commission of the European Communities (1990f) *Commission Directive on Competition in the Markets for Telecommunications Services*, 90/388.

Commission of the European Communities (1991a) *The Regions in the 1990s: Fourth Periodic Report on the Social and Economic Situation and Development of the Regions of the Community*.

Commission of the European Communities (1991b) *Europe 2000: Outlook for the Development of the Community's Territory*, Communication from the Commission to the Council and European Parliament, Brussels–Luxembourg.

Commission of the European Communities (1991c) *Twentieth Report on Competition Policy.*

Commission of the European Communities (1991d) *Communication from the Commission to the Council on the European Energy Charter*, COM (91) 36.

Commission of the European Communities (1991e) *Opening up the Internal Market.*

Commission of the European Communities (1991f) *European Economy.*

Commission of the European Communities (1991g) *Amended Proposal for a Council Regulation (EEC) Establishing a Community Ship Register and Providing for the Flying of the Flag by Sea-going Vessels* (presented by the Commission pursuant to article 149(3) of the EEC Treaty, COM (91) 54/I final.

Commission of the European Communities (1992a) *Community Structural Policies: Assessment and outlook*, COM (92) 84 final.

Commission of the European Communities (1992b) *From the Single Act to Maastricht and Beyond: The means to match our ambitions*, COM (92) 2000 final.

Commission of the European Communities (1992c) *The Community's Finances Between Now and 1997*, COM (92) 2001 final.

Commission of the European Communities (1992d) *Third Survey of State Aids*, Office for Official Publications of the European Communities.

Commission of the European Communities (1992e) *Transport and the Environment – Towards sustainable mobility*, COM (92) 80.

Commission of the European Communities (1992f) *21st Report on Competition Policy 1991*, Office of Official Publications of the European Communities.

Commission of the European Communities (1992g) *The Future Development of the Common Transport Policy*, COM (92) 494.

Commission of the European Communities (1992h) *The European Maritime Industries*, COM (92) 490.

Commission of the European Communities (1992i) *Proposal for a Council Directive Concerning Common Rules for the Internal Market in Electricity*, COM (91) 548.

Commission of the European Communities (1992j) *A Community Strategy to Limit Carbon Dioxide Emissions and to Improve Energy Efficiency*, COM (92) 246.

Commission of the European Communities (1992k) 'A view to the future', in *Energy in Europe*, special edition.

Commission of the European Communities (1992l) *Report of the Committee of Independent Experts on Company Taxation.*

Commission of the European Communities (1992m) *Development Cooperation Policy in the Run-up to 2000*, Doc. SEC (92) 915.

Commission of the European Communities (1992n) *Green Paper on the Impact of Transport on the Environment: a Community Strategy for Sustainable Development*, COM (92) 46 final.

Commission of the European Communities (1992o) *The Future Development of the Common Transport Policy: a Global Approach to the Construction of a Community Framework for Sustainable Mobility*, COM (92) 494 final.

Commission of the European Communities (1993a) *European Economy: the European Community as a World Trade Partner.*

Commission of the European Communities (1993b) *Growth Competitiveness, Employment – the Challenges and Ways Forward into the 20th Century*, COM (93) 700 final.

Commission of the European Communities (1993c) *Towards Sustainability.*

Commission of the European Communities (1994a) *For a European Union Energy Policy – Green Paper*, COM (94) 659.

Commission of the European Communities (1994b) *The European Report on Science and Technology Indicators*, DG XII.

Commission of the European Communities (1995a) *A Common Policy on the Organisation of the Inland Waterway Transport Market and Supporting Measures*, COM (95) 199.

Commission of the European Communities (1995b) *Action Programme and Timetable for Implementation of the Action Announced in the Communication on an Industrial Competitiveness Policy for the European Union*, COM (95) 87.

Commission of the European Communities (1995c) *An Energy Policy for the European Union – White Paper of the European Commission*, COM (95) 682.

Commission of the European Communities (1995d) *Citizens Network*, COM (95) 601.

Commission of the European Communities (1995e) *Communication on a common policy on the Organisation of the Inland Waterway Transport Market and Supporting Measures*, COM (95) 199.

Commission of the European Communities (1995f) *Green Paper on Innovation*, COM (95) 688.

Commission of the European Communities (1995g) *High Speed Europe*.

Commission of the European Communities (1995h) *Short Sea Shipping*.

Commission of the European Communities (1995i) *The Citizens' Network Fulfilling the Potential of Public Passenger Transport in Europe, European Commission Green Paper*, COM (95) 601.

Commission of the European Communities (1995j) *The Common Transport Policy Action Programme 1995–2000*, COM (95) 302.

Commission of the European Communities (1995k) *The Development of Short Sea Shipping in Europe*, COM (95) 317.

Commission of the European Communities (1995l) *The Development of the Community's Railways*, COM (95) 337.

Commission of the European Communities (1995m) *Trans European Networks*.

Commission of the European Communities (1995n) *Green Paper Towards Fair and Efficient Pricing in Transport*, COM (95) 691.

Commission of the European Communities (1996a) *Benchmarking of the Competitiveness of European Industry*, COM (96) 463.

Commission of the European Communities (1996b) *Energy for the Future. Renewable Sources of Energy – Green Paper for a Community Strategy*, COM (96) 576.

Commission of the European Communities (1996c) *Impact of the Third Package of Air Transport Liberalisation Measures*, COM (96) 514.

Commission of the European Communities (1996d) *Proposal for a Council Decision Concerning the Organisation of Cooperation Around Agreed Community Energy Policy Objectives*, COM (96) 431.

Commission of the European Communities (1996e) *Report from the Commission on the Application of the Community Rules on Aid to the Coal Industry in 1994*, COM (96) 575.

Commission of the European Communities (1996f) *Services of General Interest in Europe*, COM (96) 443.

Commission of the European Communities (1996g) *The First Action Plan for Innovation in Europe*, COM (96) 589.

Commission of the European Communities (1996h) *The Situation of Oil Supply Refining and Markets in the European Community*, COM (96) 143.

Commission of the European Communities (1996i) *Towards a New Maritime Strategy*, COM (96) 81.

Commission of the European Communities (1996j) *Towards an International Framework of Competition Rules*, COM (96) 284.

Commission of the European Communities (1996k) *White Paper – a Strategy for Revitalising the Community's Railways*, COM (96) 421.

Commission of the European Communities (1996l) *Research and Technological Development Activities of the European Union Annual Report 1996*, COM (96) 437.

Commission of the European Communities (1997a) *An Overall View of Energy Policy and Actions*, COM (97) 167.

Commission of the European Communities (1997b) *Fifth Survey on State Aid in the European Union in the Manufacturing and Certain Other Sectors*, COM (97) 170.

Commission of the European Communities (1997c) *Towards the Fifth Framework Programme: Scientific and Technological Objectives*, COM (97) 47.

Commission of the European Communities (1997d) *Results of the Altener Programme*, COM (97) 122.

Commission of the European Union (1995a) *Competitiveness and Cohesion: Fifth periodic report on the social and economic situation in the regions of the community*, Office for Official Publications of the European Communities.

Commission of the European Union (1995b) *Towards Fair Efficient Pricing in Transport Policy: Policy Options for Internalizing the External Costs of Transport in the European Union*, Green Paper, COM (95) 691 final.

Commission of the European Union (1995c) *Communication from the Commission on the Development of the Community's Railways, Application of Directive 91/440/EEC: Future Measures to Develop the Railways*, COM (95) 337/I final.

Commission of the European Union (1995d) *Communication from the Commission to the European Parliament, the Council of the Economic and Social Committee and the Committee of the Regions, The Development of the Short Sea Shipping in Europe: Prospects and Challenges*, COM (95) 317 final.

Commission of the European Union (1995e) *Medium Term Action Programme Health and Safety at Work 1996–2000*, COM (95) 282 final.

Commission of the European Union (1995f) *White Paper – Teaching and Learning: Towards the Learning Society*, COM (95) 590 final.

Commission of the European Union (1996a) *First Cohesion Report*, COM (96) final, Brussels.

Commission of the European Union (1996b) *The Structural Funds and Cohesion Fund 1994–1999*, CEU, Brussels.

Commission of the European Union (1996c) 'The 1996 single market review', *Commission Staff Working Paper*, SEC (96) 2378, Brussels.

Commission of the European Union (1996d) 'Green paper on relations between the European Union and the ACP countries on the eve of the 21st century', CEU/DG VIII, Brussels.

Commission of the European Union (1996e) *XXVth Report on Competition Policy 1995*, CEU.

Commission of the European Union (1996f) *Lomé IV Revised: Changes and Challenges*, Doc. DE89.

Commission of the European Union (1996g) 'The Policies of the EU: Agriculture and Fisheries Policy', in *First Cohesion Report*.

Commission of the European Union (1996h) *The Impact of the Development of the Countries of Central and Eastern Europe on the Community Territories*, Office for Official Publications of the European Communities, Brussels/Luxembourg.

Commission of the European Union (1996i) 'The 1996 single market review', *Commission Staff Working Paper*, SEC (96) 2378.

Commission of the European Union (1996j) *Green Paper on Relations Between the European Union and the ACP Countries on the Eve of the 21st Century*, CEU/DG VIII.

Commission of the European Union (1996k) *Implementing Community Environmental Law*, COM (96) 500 final.

Commission of the European Union (1996l) *The Impact and Effectiveness of the Single Market*, COM (96) 520 final.

Commission of the European Union (1996m) *European Environmental Legislation*, Volumes 1–7, CEU DG XI.

Commission of the European Union (1996n) *Green Paper – Living and Working in the Information Society: People First*, EU Bulletin, Supplement 3/96.

Commission of the European Union (1996o) *Green Paper on vertical restraints in EC Competition Policy*, COM (96) 721.

Commission of the European Union (1997a) *Agenda 2000: For A Stronger and Wider Union*, Brussels, July.

Commission of the European Union (1997b) *XXVIth Report on Competition Policy 1996*, CEU.

Commission of the European Union (1997c) *Report on the Competitiveness of European Industry*, CEU.

Commission of the European Union (1997d) *Second European Report on S&T Indicators*, CEU/DG XII.

Commission of the European Union (1997e) *Sixteenth Annual Report to the European Parliament on the Community's Anti-Dumping and Anti-Subsidy Activities*, CEU/DG I, COM (97) 428. http:europa.eu.int/comm/dg01/16report.pdf

Commission of the European Union (1997f) *Green Paper on Relations Between the European Union and the ACP Countries on the Eve of the 21st Century*, Brussels.

Commission of the European Union (1997g) *Green Paper on Sea-ports and Maritime Infrastructure*, COM (97) 678 final.

Commission of the European Union (1997h) *Action Programme for the Free Movement of Workers*, COM (97) 586 final.

Commission of the European Union (1997i) *The European Report on Science and Technology Indicators*, DG XII.

Commission of the European Union (1997j) 'Notice on the definition of the relevant market for the purposes of Community competition law', OJ C372.

Commission of the European Union (1997k) 'Notice on agreements of minor importance', OJ C372.

Commission of the European Union (1997l) *Towards a Europe of Knowledge*, COM (97) 563 final.

Commission of the European Union (1998a) *General Report of the Activities of the European Union, 1998*.

Commission of the European Union (1998b) *Proposed Regulations and Explanatory Memorandum Covering the Reform of the Structural Funds 2000–2006*, Directorate-General for Regional Policy DG XVI.

Commission of the European Union (1998c) *European Economy*, no. 66, CEU/DGII.

Commission of the European Union (1998d) *Communication from the Commission to the Council and the European Parliament on Implementation and Impact of Directive 91/440/EEC on the Development of Community Railways and Access Rights for Rail Freight*, COM (98) 202 final.

Commission of the European Union (1998e) *Proposal for Council Regulation on the European Social Fund*, COM (98) 131 final.

Commission of the European Union (1998f) *Medium Term Social Action Programme 1998–2000*, COM (98) 251 final.

Commission of the European Union (1998g) *Consumer Policy Action Programme 1999–2000*, COM (98) 696 final.

Commission of the European Union (1999a) *Statement by Commissioner J.Pinheiro on the 'Challenges of the Post-Lomé Negotiation'*, DG8.

Commission of the European Union (1999b) *EU–ACP Negotiations: Information Memos No 8, 9*, DG8.

Commission of the European Union (1999c) *Sixteenth Annual Report on the Application of Community Law 1998*, COM (99) 301 final.

Commission of the European Union (1999d) *Mutual Recognition in the Context of the Follow-Up to the Action Plan for the Single Market*, COM (99).

Commission of the European Union (1999e) *Sixth Periodic Report on the Social and Economic Situation in the Regions in the Community*, Office for Official Publications of the European Communities, Luxembourg.

Commission of the European Union (1999f) *Annual Report on Equal Opportunities for Women and Men*, COM (99) 106 final.

Commission of the European Union (1999g) *The Amsterdam Treaty: a Comprehensive Guide.*

Commission of the European Union (1999h) *Institutional Implications of Enlargement.*

Commission of the European Union (1999i) 'Regulation 2790/1999 on the application of Article 81(3) of the Treaty to categories of vertical agreements and concerted practices', *OJ* L336.

Commission of the European Union (1999j) 'White Paper on modernisation of the rules implementing articles 85 and 86 of the EC Treaty', *OJ* C132

Commission of the European Union (1999k) *The Agricultural Situation in the European Union 1998.*

Commission of the European Union (2000) *EU–ACP Negotiations: Information Memo No. 10*, DG8.

Community of European Railways (1988) *Towards a European High Speed Rail Network*, Paris, CER.

Community of European Railways (1995) *High Speed Europe.*

Conant, L. (2000), 'Europeanization and the courts: Variable patterns of adaptation among national judiciaries', in J. Caparaso, M. Cowles and T. Risse (eds), *Europeanization and Domestic Structural Change*, Cornell University Press, Ithaca.

Congress of the United States, Office of Technology Assessment (1991) *Competing Economies America, Europe and the Pacific Rim.*

Congress of the United States, Office of Technology Assessment (1992) *Competing Economies*, USGPO.

Congressional Budget Office (USA) (1987) *The GATT Negotiations and US Trade Policy.*

Coombes, D. (1970) *Politics and Bureaucracy in the European Community*, Allen & Unwin.

Cooper, C. A. and Massell, B. F. (1965a) 'A new look at customs union theory', *Economic Journal*, vol. 75.

Cooper, C. A. and Massell, B. F. (1965b) 'Towards a general theory of customs unions in developing countries', *Journal of Political Economy*, vol. 73.

Corbett, H. (1979) 'Tokyo Round: twilight of a liberal era or a new dawn?', *National Westminster Bank Quarterly Review*, February.

Corden, W. M. (1965) 'Recent developments in the theory of international trade', *Special Papers in International Finance*, Princeton University Press.

Corden, W. M. (1972a) 'Economies of scale and customs union theory', *Journal of Political Economy*, vol. 80.

Corden, W. M. (1972b) 'Monetary integration', *Essays in International Finance*, no. 93, Princeton University.

Corden, W. M. (1973) 'The adjustment problem', in L. B. Krause and W. S. Salant (eds), *European Monetary Unification and Its Meaning for the United States*, The Brookings Institution, Washington.

Corden, W. M. (1974) *Trade Policy and Economic Welfare*, Oxford University Press.

Corden, W. M. (1976) 'Monetary union', *Trade Policy Research Centre Paper on International Issues*, no. 2, December.

Corden, W. M. (1977) *Inflation, Exchange Rates and the World Economy*, Oxford University Press.

Corden, W. M. (1988) 'Trade policy and macroeconomic balance in the world economy', *IMF Working Paper*, November.

Corden, W. M. (1997) *Trade Policy and Economic Welfare*, Oxford University Press, Oxford.

Cosgrave, C. A. (1969) 'The EEC and developing countries', in G. R. Denton (ed.), *Economic Integration in Europe*, Weidenfeld & Nicolson, London.

Cosgrove, C. (1994) 'Has the Lomé Convention Failed ACP Trade?', *Journal of International Affairs*, vol.48, no.1.

Cosgrove Twitchett, C. (1978) *Europe and Africa: From association to partnership*, Saxon House.

Cosgrove Twitchett, C. (ed.) (1981) *Harmonisation in the EEC*, Macmillan, Basingstoke.

Council of the European Communities (various years) *Review of the Council's Work.*

Council of the European Communities (1986) *Report by the Chairman of the Fiscal Borders Abolition ad hoc Group.*

Council of the European Communities (1990) *Council Directive of 28th October 1990 on the Transit of Electricity Through Transmission Grids* (90/547/EEC).

Council of the European Communities (1991) *Council Directive on the Development of the Community's Railways*, 91/440.

Court of Auditors (1982) *Annual Report Concerning the Financial Year 1981, Part II, The European Development Funds, OJ* C344 25, December.

Court of First Instance (1991) 'Reflections on the future development of the community judicial system', *European Law Review*, vol. 16.

Court of First Instance (1999) *Statistical Information of the Court of First Instance 1998*, Luxembourg.

Cowling, K. (1989) 'New directions for industrial policy', in Cowling, K. and Tomann, H., *Industrial Policy After 1992*, Anglo-German Foundation for the Study of Industrial Society.

Cowling, K. and Tomann, H. (1989) *Industrial Policy After 1992*, Anglo-German Foundation for the Study of Industrial Society.

Cox, A. and Chapman, J. (1999) *The European Community External Cooperation Programs*, ODI, London.

Cox, A. W. (ed.) (1982) *Politics, Policy and the European Recession*, Macmillan.

Craig, P. (1997) 'Democracy and rule-making within the EC: An empirical and normative assessment', *European Law Journal*, vol. 3.

Craig, P. and De Búrca, G. (eds) (1999) *The Evolution of EU Law*, Oxford University Press, Oxford.

Craig, P. and Dehousse, R. (1998) *The European Court of Justice*, Macmillan, Basingstoke.

Crouch, C. and Marquand, D. (1992) *Towards Greater Europe: A continent without an Iron Curtain*, Basil Blackwell, Oxford.

Crowley, J. (1992) 'Inland transport in the European Community following 1992', *The Antitrust Bulletin*, vol. 37, no. 2.

Cruickshank, A. and Walker, W. (1981) 'Energy research development and demonstration policy in the European Communities', *Journal of Common Market Studies*, vol. 20, no. 1.

Culem, C. G. (1988) 'The locational determinants of direct investment among industrialised countries', *European Economic Review*, vol. 32.

Cunningham, S. and Young, J. A. (1983) 'The EEC Fisheries Policy: retrospect and prospect', *National Westminster Bank Quarterly Review*, May.

Curzon, G. and Curzon, V. (1971) 'New-colonialism and the European Community', *Yearbook of World Affairs*, Institute of World Affairs, London.

Curzon, G. and Curzon Price, V. (1987) 'Follies in European trade relations with Japan', *World Economy*, June.

Curzon, G. and Curzon Price, V. (1989) 'The GATT, non-discrimination principles and the rise of "material reciprocity" in international trade', mimeo, Collège de Bruges.

Curzon Price, V. (1974) *The Essentials of Economic Integration*, Macmillan, Basingstoke.

Curzon Price, V. (1981) *Industrial Policies in the European Community*, Macmillan for the Trade Policy Research Centre.

Curzon Price, V. (1982) 'The European Free Trade Association', in A. M. El-Agraa (ed.), *International Economic Integration*, Macmillan, Basingstoke.

Curzon Price, V. (1988) '1992: Europe's last chance? From Common Market to single market', *Occasional Paper*, no. 81, Institute of Economic Affairs, London.

Cuthbertson, K. *et al.* (1980) 'Modelling and forecasting the capital account of the balance of payments: a critique of the "Reduced Form Approach" ' , *National Institute Discussion Paper*, no. 37.

Daintith, T. and Hancher, K. (eds) (1986) *Energy Strategy in Europe: The legal framework*, de Gruyter.

Dam, K. W. (1970) *The GATT: Law and international economic organization*, Chicago University Press.

Daniel, P. (1984) 'Interpreting mutual interest: non-fuel minerals in EEC–ACP relations', in C. Stevens (ed.), *EEC and the Third World: A survey. 4: Regenerating Lomé*, London.

Dauphin, R. (1978) *The Impact of Free Trade in Canada*, Economic Council of Canada, Ottawa.

Davenport, M. (1986) *Trade Policy, Protectionism and the Third World*, Croom Helm, Beckenham.

Davenport, M. (1992) 'Africa and the unimportance of being preferred', *Journal of Common Market Studies*, vol. 29.

Davenport, M., Hewitt, A. and Koning, A. (1995) *Europe's Preferred Partners*, Overseas Development Institute, London.

Davies, E. *et al.* (1989) *1992 Myths and Realities*, Centre for Business Strategy, London.

Davies, G. (1982) 'The EMS: its achievements and failures', *Special Analysis*, Simon & Coates.

Dayal, R. and Dayal, N. (1977) 'Trade creation and trade diversion: new concepts, new methods of measurement', *Weltwirtschaftliches Archiv*, vol. 113.

Deacon, D. (1982) 'Competition policy in the Common Market: its links with regional policy', *Regional Studies*, vol. 16, no. 1.

De Búrca, G. (1992), 'Giving effect to European Community directives' *Modern Law Review*, vol. 55.

De Grauwe, P. (1973) *Monetary Interdependence and International Monetary Reform*, Saxon House.

De Grauwe, P. (1975) 'Conditions for monetary integration: a geometric interpretation', *Weltwirtschaftliches Archiv*, vol. 111.

De Grauwe, P. and Peeters, T. (1978) 'The European Monetary System after Bremen: technical and conceptual problems', paper delivered to the International Economics Study Group at the London School of Economics and Political Science.

De Grauwe, P. and Peeters, T. (1979) 'The EMS, Europe and the Dollar', *The Banker*, April.

De la Mare, T. (1999) 'Article 177 in social and political perspective', in P. Craig and R. Dehousse (1998) *op. cit.*

De Vries, T. (1980) 'On the meaning and futures of the EMS', *Essays in International Finance*, no. 138, Princeton University.

Deaton, A. S. and Muellbauer, J. (1980a) 'An almost ideal demand system', *American Economic Review*, vol. 70.

Deaton, A. S. and Muellbauer, J. (1980b) *Economics and Consumer Behaviour*, Cambridge University Press.

Defrennes, M. (1996) 'The European nuclear industry in the context of the European Union', *Energy in Europe*, no. 27.

Degli Abbati, C. (1987) *Transport and European Integration*, Office for Official Publications of the European Community.

Dehousse, R. and Weiler, J. (1990) 'The legal dimension', in W. Wallace (ed.), *The Dynamics of European Integration*, RIIA, London.

Dell, E. and Mayes, D. G. (1989) *1992 and Environment for European Industry*, Centre for European Policy Studies.

Demekas, D. G. *et al.* (1988) 'The effects of the Common Agricultural Policy for the European Community: A survey of the literature', *Journal of Common Market Studies*, vol. 27, no. 2.

Denison, E. F. (1967) *Why Growth Rates Differ: Post-war experience in nine Western countries*, The Brookings Institution, Washington, DC.

Denison, E. F. (1974), *Accounting for United States Economic Growth 1929–1969*, Brookings Institution.

Dennis, G. E. J. (1979) 'German monetary policy and the EMS', mimeo, December.

Dennis, G. E. J. (1981) 'The United Kingdom's monetary interdependence and membership of the European Monetary System', in J. P. Abraham and M. Van den Abeele (eds), *The European Monetary System and International Monetary Reform*, College of Europe, Brussels.

Dent, C. M. (1997) *The European Economy: The global context*, Routledge.

Denton, G. R. (ed.) (1969) *Economic Integration in Europe*, Weidenfeld & Nicolson, London.

Denton, G. R. (ed.) (1974) *Economic and Monetary Union in Europe*, Croom Helm, Beckenham.

Denton, G. R. (1981) 'How can the EEC help to solve the energy problem?', *The Three Banks Review*, March.

Department of Industry (1982) *Inward Investment and the IIB 1977–82*.

Deringer, A. (1964) 'The interpretation of Article 90(2) of the EEC Treaty', *Common Market Law Review*, vol. 2, no. 2.

Deuchene, F. and Shepherd, G. (eds) (1987) *Managing Industrial Change in Western Europe*, Pinter.

Deutsche Bundesbank (1979) 'The European Monetary System', *Deutsche Bank Monthly Bulletin*, March.

Devroe, W. (1997) 'Privatization and Community law: neutrality versus policy', *Common Market Law Review*, vol. 34.

Dezalay, Y. (1992) *Marchands de droit. La réstructuration de l'ordre juridique internationale par les multinationals du droit*, Fayard, Paris.

Diebold, W. (1959) *The Schuman Plan: A study in economic cooperation, 1950–1959*, Praeger.

Diebold, W. (1980) *Industrial Policy as an International Issue*, McGraw-Hill.

Digby, C., Smith, M. A. M. and Venables, A. (1988) 'Counting the cost of voluntary export restrictions in the European car market', *Discussion Paper Series*, no. 249, Centre for Economic Policy Research.

Dixit, A. (1975) 'Welfare effects of tax and price changes', *Journal of Public Economics*, vol. 4.

Donges, J. B. *et al.* (1982) *The Second Enlargement of the Community: Adjustment requirements and challenges for policy reform*, Mohr.

Dore, R. and de Bauw (1995) *The European Energy Charter*, RIIA.

Dosser, D. (1966) 'The economic analysis of tax harmonisation', in C. S. Shoup (ed.), *Fiscal Harmonisation in Common Markets*, vol. 2, Columbia University Press.

Dosser, D. (1971) 'Taxation', in J. Pinder (ed.), *The Economics of Europe*, Knight.

Dosser, D. (1973) *British Taxation and the Common Market*, Knight.

Dosser, D. (1975) 'A federal budget for the Community', in B. Burrows et al. (eds), *Federal Solutions to European Issues*, Macmillan, Basingstoke.

Dosser, D. and Hans, S. S. (1968) *Taxes in the EEC and Britain – the Problem of Harmonisation*, PEP/Institute of International Affairs.

Doyle, M. F. (1989) 'Regional policy and European economic integration', in *Report on Economic and Monetary Union in the European Community* (Delors Report), Commission of the European Communities, Luxembourg.

Dreyer, P. (1980) 'The outlook for steel', in Helleiner, G. K. *et al.*, *Protectionism or International Adjustment*, Atlantic Institute for International Affairs.

Dunford, M. (1996) 'Disparities in employment, productivity and output in the EU: the roles of labour market governance and welfare regimes', *Regional Studies*, vol. 30.

Dunning, J. H. (1977) 'Trade, location of economic activity and the MNE: a search for an eclectic approach' in B. Ohlin et al. (eds), *The International Allocation of Economic Activity*, Macmillan, Basingstoke.

Dunning, J. H. (1982) 'Explaining the internal direct investment position of countries: towards a dynamic or developmental approach', in J. Black and J. H. Dunning (eds), *International Capital Movements*, Macmillan, Basingstoke.

Economic and Social Committee of the European Communities (1977) *EEC's Transport Problems with East European Countries*, EC Commission.

The Economist Intelligence Unit (1957) *Britain and Europe*, The Economist.

The Economist (1973) 'Europe and Britain's regions', *The Economist*, vol. 247, no. 6765, pp. 55–60.

Edward, D. (1995), 'How the ECJ works', *European Law Review*, vol. 20.

Edwards, G. and Wallace, H. (1977) *The Council of Ministers of the European Community and the President-in-Office*, Federal Trust, London.

Eeckhout, J. C. (1975) 'Towards a common Europe industrial policy', *Irish Banking Review*, December.

EFTA Secretariat (1968) *The Effects on Prices of Tariff Dismantling in EFTA.*

EFTA Secretariat (1969) *The Effects of the EFTA on the Economies of Member States.*

EFTA Secretariat (1972) *The Trade Effects of the EFTA and the EEC 1959–1967.*

Ehlermann, C. D. (1993) 'Managing monopolies: the role of the state in controlling market dominance in the European Community', *European Competition Law Review*, vol. 14, no. 2.

Ehlermann, C.-D. (1995) 'State aids under European Community competition law', 1994 *Annual Proceedings of the Fordham Corporate Law Institute*, vol. 21.

El-Agraa, A. M. (1978) 'On trade creation' and 'On trade diversion', *Leeds Discussion Papers*, nos 66 and 67, University of Leeds, School of Economic Studies.

El-Agraa, A. M. (1979a) 'Common markets in developing countries', in J. K. Bowers (ed.), *Inflation, Development and Integration: Essays in honour of A. J. Brown*, Leeds University Press.

El-Agraa, A. M. (1979b) 'On tariff bargaining', *Bulletin of Economic Research*, vol. 31.

El-Agraa, A. M. (1979c) 'On optimum tariffs, retaliation and international cooperation', *Bulletin of Economic Research*, vol. 31.

El-Agraa, A. M. (1981) 'Tariff bargaining: a correction', *Bulletin of Economic Research*, vol. 33.

El-Agraa, A. M. (1982a) 'Professor Godley's proposition: a theoretical appraisal', *Leeds Discussion Papers*, no. 105.

El-Agraa, A. M. (1982b) 'Professor Godley's proposition: a macroeconomic appraisal', *Leeds Discussion Papers*, no. 113.

El-Agraa, A. M. (ed.) (1982c) *International Economic Integration*, Macmillan, Basingstoke.

El-Agraa, A. M. (1982d) 'Comments on Rybczynski', in M. T. Sumner and G. Zis (eds), *European Monetary Union*, Macmillan, Basingstoke.

El-Agraa, A. M. (ed.) (1983a) *Britain within the European Community: The way forward*, Macmillan, Basingstoke.

El-Agraa, A. M. (1983b) *The Theory of International Trade*, Croom Helm, Beckenham.

El-Agraa, A. M. (1984a) 'Is membership of the EEC a disaster for the UK?', *Applied Economics*, vol. 17, no. 1.

El-Agraa, A. M. (1984b) *Trade Theory and Policy: Some topical issues*, Macmillan, Basingstoke.

El-Agraa, A. M. (ed.) (1987) *Conflict, Cooperation, Integration and Development: Essays in honour of Professor Hiroshi Kitamura*, Macmillan and St Martin's, New York.

El-Agraa, A. M. (1988a) *Japan's Trade Frictions: Realities or Misconceptions?*, Macmillan and St Martin's, New York.

El-Agraa, A. M. (ed.) (1988b) *International Economic Integration*, second edition, Macmillan and St Martin's, New York.

El-Agraa, A. M. (1989a) *The Theory and Measurement of International Economic Integration*, Macmillan and St Martin's, New York.

El-Agraa, A. M. (1989b) *International Trade*, Macmillan and St Martin's, New York.

El-Agraa, A. M. (1990) 'EC Budgetary politics: the rationality of the EC Commission being undermined by the irrationality of the member nations', *Review of Commercial Sciences*, vol. 38, no. 2.

El-Agraa, A. M. (1995) 'VERs as a prominent feature of Japanese trade policy: their rationale, costs and benefits', *The World Economy*, vol. 18.

El-Agraa, A. M. (1997) *Economic Integration Worldwide*, Macmillan and St Martin's, New York.

El-Agraa, A. M. (1999) *Regional Integration: Experience, Theory and Measurement*, Macmillan, London; Barnes and Noble, New York.

El-Agraa, A. M. and Goodrich, P. S. (1980) 'Factor mobility with specific reference to the accounting profession', in A. M. El-Agraa (ed.), *The Economics of the European Community*, first edition, Philip Allan, Chapter 16.

El-Agraa, A. M. and Hu, Y.-S. (1984) 'National versus supranational interests and the problem of establishing an effective EU energy policy', *Journal of Common Market Studies*, vol. 22.

El-Agraa, A. M. and Jones, A. J. (1981) *The Theory of Customs Unions*, Philip Allan.

El-Agraa, A. M. and Majocchi, A. (1983) 'Devising a proper fiscal stance for the EC', *Revista Di Diritto Finanziario E Scienza Delle Finanze*, vol. 17, no. 3.

Elbadawi. I. A. (1999) 'Can Africa Export Manufactures? The Role of Endowments, Exchange Rates and Transaction Costs', *World Bank Policy Research Working Paper*, No. 2120, Washington DC.

Eleftheriadis, P. (1998) 'Begging the constitutional question', *Journal of Common Market Studies*, vol. 36.

Ellis, F., Marsh, J. and Ritson, C. (1973) *Farmers and Foreigners – The impact of the Common Agricultural Policy on the associates and associables*, Overseas Development Institute, London.

Emerson, M. (1979) 'The European Monetary System in the broader setting of the Community's economic and political development', in P. H. Trezise (ed.), *The European Monetary System: Its promise and prospects*, Brookings Institution, Washington, DC.

Emerson, M. (1988) 'The economics of 1992', *European Economy*, no. 35.

Emerson, M., Anjean, M., Catinat, M., Goybet, P. and Jaquemin, A. (1988) *The Economics of 1992: The EC Commission's assessment of the economic effects of completing the internal market*, Oxford University Press. Oxford.

Emerson, M. and Dramais, A. (1988) *What Model for Europe?*, MIT Press, Cambridge, MA.

Emerson, M., Gros, D., Italianer, A., Pisani-Ferry, J. and Reichenbach, H. (1991), *One Market, One Money: An Evaluation of the Potential Benefits and Costs of Forming an Economic and Monetary Union*, Oxford University Press, Oxford.

Emmiger, O. (1979) 'The exchange rate as an instrument of policy', *Lloyds Bank Review*, July.

Erdmenger, J. (1983) *The European Community Transport Policy: Towards a common transport policy*, Gower, Aldershot.

Erdmenger, J. and Stasinopoulos, D. (1988) 'The shipping policy of the European Community', *Journal of Transport Economics and Policy*, vol. 22.

ESPRIT Review Board (1985) *The Mid-term Review of ESPRIT*, EC Commission.

Ethier, W. and Bloomfield, A. J. (1975) 'Managing the managed float', *Essays in International Finance*, no. 122, Princeton University.

European Council (1974) 'Resolution Concerning Financial Aid to Non-Associate Countries', *EU Bulletin*, 7/8.

European Council (1989) 'Regulation 4064/89 on the control of concentrations between undertakings', *OJ* L395.

European Council (1992), *Run-up to 2000: Declaration of the Council of 18 November*, Collection of Council Statements on Development Cooperation, vol. I, 05/92.

European Council (1995) *Resolution of the Council on Structural Adjustment*, 1 June.

European Council (1997) 'Regulation 1310/97 amending Regulation 4064/89 on the control of concentrations between undertakings', *OJ* L40.

European Council (1998) 'Regulation 994/98 on the application of Articles 92 and 93 of the Treaty to certain categories of horizontal state aid', *OJ* L142.

European Council (1999a) 'Regulation 659/1999 laying down detailed rules for the application of Article 93 of the EC Treaty', *OJ* L83.

European Council (1999b) *Presidency Conclusions: Berlin European Council*, 24–25 March.

European Court of Justice (1996) *Notes for Guidance on References by National Courts*, Proceedings of the Court 34/96, Luxembourg.

European Court of Justice (1999a) *Statistical Information of the ECJ*, Luxembourg.

European Court of Justice (1999b) *The Future of the Judicial System of the EU: Proposals and Reflections*, Luxembourg.

European Economy (1982) 'Documents relating to the European Monetary System', no. 12, July.

European Economy (1996) 'Economic evaluation of the internal market', *Reports and Studies*, no. 4.

European Environmental Agency (1996) *Environmental Taxes: Implementation and Environmental Effectiveness.*

European Investment Bank (1981) *Annual Report 1980*, Luxembourg.

European Investment Bank (1998), *Annual Report 1997*, Luxembourg.

European Parliament (1980) *European Taxation 1980/81*, Energy Commission.

European Parliament (1986) 'Report on the relations between the European Community and the Council for Mutual Economic Assistance', DOC AZ187/86, 19 December.

European Parliament (1993) 'The economic impact of dumping and the community's anti-dumping policy', *EP Directorate General for Research Working Papers*, Economic Series E-1, Luxembourg.

European Research Group (1997) *The Legal Agenda for a Free Europe*, London.

European Round Table (1985) *Missing Links*, ERT.

Eurostat (annual) *Basic Statistics of the Community.*

Eurostat (annual) *Statistical Review.*

Eurostat (1980) *Review 1970–1979*, EC Commission.

Eurostat (1982) *Farm Accountancy Data Network*, microfiche.

Eurostat (1995) *Panorama of EU Industry 1995/96*, Luxembourg.

Eurostat (1997) 'External and intra-EU trade', *Monthly Statistics*, Luxembourg.

Eurostat (1998) *External Trade EU 15-ACPs*, Luxembourg, European Commission.

Farrands, C. (1983) 'External relations: textile politics and the Multi-Fiber Arrangement', in H. Wallace, *et al.* (eds), *Policy Making in the European Community*, John Wiley, second edition.

Federal Reserve Bank of New York (1981) *Quarterly Review*, Summer.

Federal Trust (1974) *Economic Union in the EEC*, Federal Trust.

Fee, D. (1992) 'A new proposal in the framework of the Save Programme to limit carbon dioxide emissions by improving energy efficiency', *Energy in Europe*, no. 20.

Feldstein, M.B. (1997) 'The political economy of the European Econimic and Monetary Union: political sources of an economic liability', *Journal of Economic Perspectives*, vol. 11.

Fennell, R. (1979) *The Common Agricultural Policy of the European Community*, Granada (2nd edition, 1987).

Fielding, L. (1991) 'Europe as a global partner', *UACES Occasional Paper*, no. 7.

Finger, J. M. and Olechowski, A. (1987) *The Uruguay Round: A handbook on the multilateral trade negotiations*, World Bank.

Finon, D. (1990) 'Opening access to European grids in search of common ground', *Energy Policy*, vol. 18, no. 5.

Finon, D. and Surrey, J. (1996) 'Does energy policy have a future in the European Union?', in F. McGowan, *Energy Policy in a Changing Environment*, Physica Verlag.

Fitzmaurice, J. (1988) 'An analysis of the European Community's Co-operation Procedure', *Journal of Common Market Studies*, vol. 26, no. 4.

Fitzpatrick, P. (1997) 'New Europe and old stories: Mythology and legality in the EU', in P. Fitzpatrick and J. Bergeron (eds), *Europe's Other: European Law between Modernity and Postmodernity*, Ashgate, Aldershot.

Fleming, J. M. (1971) 'On exchange rate unification', *Economic Journal*, vol. 81.

Fligstein, N. (1997) 'Social skill and institutional theory', *American Behavioural Scientist*, vol. 40.

Flockton, C. (1970) *Community Regional Policy*, Chatham House.

Fogarty, M. (1975) *Work and Industrial Relations in the European Community*, Chatham House/PEP.

Foot, M. D. (1979) 'Monetary targets; nature and record in the major economies', in B. Griffiths and G. Wood, *Monetary Targets*, Macmillan, Basingstoke.

Forrester, I. and Norall, C. (1984) 'The laicization of Community: self-help and the rule of reason: how competition law is and could be applied', *Common Market Law Review*, vol. 22.

Forsyth, M. (1980) *Reservicing Britain*, Adam Smith Institute, London.

Forte, F. (1977) 'Principles for the assignment of public economic functions in a setting of multi-layer government', in Commission of the European Communities, *Report of the Study Group on the Role of Public Finance in European Integration*, vol. 2 (the MacDougall Report).

Francioni, F. (1992) *Italy and EC Membership Evaluated*, Pinter.

Franzmeyer, F. *et al.* (1991) *The Regional Impact of Community Policies*, Regional Policy and Transport Series 17, European Parliament.

Frazer, T. (1992) *Monopoly, Competition and the Law: the regulation of business activity in Britain, Europe and America*, Harvester/Wheatsheaf, Hemel Hempstead, second edition,.

Freeman, C. and Oldman, C. (1991) 'Introduction: beyond the Common Market', in C. Freeman, M. Sharp and W. Walker (eds), *Technology and the Future of Europe; Global competition and the environment in the 1990s*, Pinter.

Freeman, C., Sharp, M. and Walker, W. (eds) (1991) *Technology and the Future of Europe: Global competition and the environment in the 1990s*, Pinter.

Freeman, R. B. (1995) 'Are your wages set in Beijing?', *Journal of Economic Perspectives*, vol. 9.

Friedman, M. (1975) *Unemployment versus Inflation? An Evaluation of the Philips Curve*, Institute of International Affairs, London.

Fujita, M. and Thisse, J.-F. (1996) 'Economics of agglomeration', *Journal of the Japanese and International Economies*, vol. 10.

Gandia, D. M. (1981) *The EEC's Generalised System of Preferences and the Yaounde and Other Agreements*, Allenhead, Osmun & Co.

Garrett, G. (1992) 'International cooperation and institutional choice: the European Community's internal market', *International Organization*, vol. 46.

Garrett, G. (1995) 'The politics of legal integration', *International Organization*, vol. 49.

Garrett, G., Keleman, R. and Schulz, H. (1998) 'The European ECJ, national governments and legal integration in the EU', *International Organization*, vol. 52.

Garrett, G. and Tsebelis, G. (1999), 'The institutional foundations of supranationalism' at http://www.sscnet.ucla.edu/polisci/faculty/tsebelis/workpaper.html

Garrett, G. and Weingast, B. (1993) 'Ideas, interests and institutions: Constructing the European internal market', in J. Goldstein and R. Keohane (eds), *Ideas and Foreign Policy*, Cornell University Press, Ithaca.

Gatsios, K. and Seabright, P. (1989) 'Regulation in the European Community', *Oxford Review of Economic Policy*, vol. 5, no. 2.

GATT (1991) *Trade Policy Review: The European Communities*, vols I and II.

GATT (1993) *Trade Policy Review: The European Communities*, Geneva.

GATT (1994) *Market Access for Goods and Services: Overview of the Results*, Geneva.

Geddes, A. (1995) 'Immigrant and ethnic minorities and the EU's "Democratic Deficit" ', *Journal of Common Market Studies*, vol. 33.

Gehrels, F. (1956–7) 'Customs unions from a single country viewpoint', *Review of Economic Studies*, vol. 24.

George, K. (1990) 'UK competition policy: issues and institutions', in W. S. Comanor et al. (eds), *Competition Policy in Europe and North America: Economic issues and institutions*, Harwood Academic.

George, K. and Jacquemin, A. (1990) 'Competition policy in the European Community', in W. S. Comanor *et al.* (eds), *Competition Policy in Europe and North America: Economic issues and institutions*, Harwood Academic.

George, K. D. and Joll, C. (eds) (1975) *Competition Policy in the United Kingdom and the European Economic Community*, Cambridge University Press.

Gerber, D. J. (1998) *Law and Competition in Twentieth Century Europe: Protecting Prometheus*, Clarendon.

Geroski, P. A. (1989a) 'European industrial policy and industrial policy in Europe', *Oxford Review of Economic Policy*, vol. 5, no. 2.

Geroski, P. A. (1989b) 'The choice between diversity and scale', in E. Davis *et al.* (eds), *1992 Myths and Realities*, Centre for Business Strategy.

Geroski, P. A. (1990) 'Procurement policy as a tool of industrial policy', *International Review of Applied Economics*, vol. 4, no. 2.

Geroski, P. and Jacquemin, A. (1989) 'Industrial change, barriers to mobility and European industrial policy', in A. Jacquemin and A. Sapir (eds), *The European Internal Market: Trade and Competition*, Oxford University Press, Oxford.

Giavazzi, F. and Pagano, M. (1986) 'The advantage of tying one's hands: EMS discipline and central bank credibility', *European Economic Review*, vol. 28.

Giavazzi, F., Micossi, S. and Miller, M. (eds) (1988) *The European Monetary System*, Cambridge University Press.

Gibson, J. and Caldeira, G. (1995) 'The legitimacy of transnational legal institutions: compliance, support and the European Court of Justice', *American Journal of Political Science*, vol. 39 (2): 459–98.

Gibson, J. and Caldeira, G. (1998) 'Changes in the legitimacy of the European ECJ: A post-Maastricht analysis', *British Journal of Political Science*, vol. 28.

Giersch, H. *et al.* (1975) 'A currency for Europe', *The Economist*, 1 November.

Gilchrist, J. and Deacon, D. (1990) 'Curbing subsidies', in P. Montagnon (ed.), *European Competition Policy*, RIIA.

Gillingham, J. (1991) *Coal, Steel, and the Rebirth of Europe, 1945–1955: The Germans and French from Ruhr Conflict to Economic Community*, Cambridge University Press.

Godley, W. (1980a) 'Britain and Europe', *Cambridge Economic Policy Review*, vol. 6, no. 1.

Godley, W. (1980b) 'The United Kingdom and the Community Budget', in W. Wallace (ed.), *Britain in Europe*, Heinemann, Oxford, Chapter 4.

Godley, W. and Bacon, R. (1979) 'Policies of the EEC', *Cambridge Economic Policy Review*, vol. 1, no. 5.

Golub, J. (1996a) 'The politics of judicial discretion: Rethinking the interaction between national courts and the ECJ', *West European Politics*, vol. 19, 360.

Golub, J. (1996b) 'Sovereignty and Subsidiarity in EU environmental policy', *European University Institute Working Paper*, RSC no. 96/2.

Gormley, L. (1994) 'Reasoning renounced? The remarkable judgment in Reck and Mithouard' *European Business Law Review*, vol. 63.

Goulder, L. (1997) 'Environmental taxation and the "double dividend": a reader's guide', in L. Bovenberg and S. Cnossen (1997).

Gourevitch, P. (1986) *Politics in Hard Times*, Cornell University Press.

Goyder, D. (1999) *EC Competition Law*, Clarendon, Oxford.

Gramlich, E. (1994) 'Infrastructure investment', *Journal of Economic Literature*, vol. 32.

Granovetter, M. (1985) 'Economic action and social structure: The problem of embeddedness', *American Journal of Sociology*, vol. 91.

Grant, W. (1982) *The Political Economy of Industrial Policy*, Butterworths, London.

Grant, W. and Sargent, J. (1987) *Business and Politics in Britain*, Macmillan, Basingstoke.

Graubard, S. (ed.) (1964) *A New Europe?*, Oldbourne Press.

Greenaway, D. and Hindley, B. (1985) 'What Britain pays for voluntary export restraints', *Thames Essays*, no. 43, Trade Policy Research Centre.

Grilli, E. (1991) 'EC Development Policies and their Effects on Developing Countries: A Review', in A. B. Atkinson and R. Brunetta (eds), *Economics for the New Europe*, Macmillan, London.

Grilli, E. (1993) *The European Community and the Developing Countries*, Cambridge University Press.

Grilli, E. and Riedel, J. (1995) 'The East Asian Growth Model: How General is it?', in

R. Garnaut *et al.*, *Sustaining Export-Oriented Development: Ideas from East Asia*, Cambridge University Press, Cambridge.

Grilli, E. and Riess, M. (1992) 'EC Aid to Associated Countries: Distribution and Determinants', in *Weltwirtschaftliches Archiv*, vol. 128, no. 2.

Grilli, E. and Salvatore, D. (eds) (1994) *Economic Development*, Greenwood Press.

Grinols, E. L. (1984) 'A thorn in the lion's paw: has Britain paid too much for Common Market membership?', *Journal of International Economics*, vol. 16.

Gross, L. (1984) 'States as organs of international law and the problem of autointerpretation', in L. Gross (ed.), *Essays on International Law and Organisation*, Martinus Nijhoff.

Grossman, G. M. and Helpman, E. (1991) 'Trade, knowledge spillovers and growth', *European Economic Review*, vol. 35.

Guieu, P. and Bonnet, C. (1987) 'Completion of the internal market and indirect taxation', *Journal of Common Market Studies*, vol. 25, no. 3.

Guruswamy, I. D., Papps, I. and Storey, D. (1983) 'The development and impact of an EC directive: the control of discharges of mercury to the aquatic environment', *Journal of Common Market Studies*, vol. 22, no. 1.

Guy, K. *et al.* (1991) *Evaluation of the Alvey Programme for Advanced Information Technology*, HMSO.

Guzzetti, L. (1995), *A Brief History of European Union Research Policy*, Commission of the European Union, DG XII (Science, Research, Development).

Gwilliam, K. M. (1980) 'Realism and the common transport policy of the EEC', in J. B. Polak and J. B. van der Kemp (eds), *Changes in the Field of Transport Studies*, Martinus Nijhoff.

Gwilliam, K. M. (1985) 'The Transport Infrastructure Policy of the EEC', in S. Klatt (ed.), *Perspektwm verkehrswissenschaftlicher Forschüng: Festschrift für Fritz Voigt*, Berlin.

Gwilliam, K. M. and Allport, R. J. (1982) 'A medium term transport research strategy for the EEC – Part 1: context and issues', *Transport Review*, no. 3.

Gwilliam, K. M. and Mackie, P. J. (1975) *Economics of Transport Policy*, Allen & Unwin.

Gwilliam, K. M., Petriccione, S., Voigt, F. and Zighera, J. A. (1973) 'Criteria for the coordination of investments in transport infrastructure', *EEC Studies, Transport Series*, no. 3.

Haas, E. B. (1958 and 1968) *The Uniting of Europe*, Stevens.

Haas, E. B. (1967) 'The uniting of Europe and the uniting of Latin America', *Journal of Common Market Studies*, vol. 5.

Haberler, G. (1964) 'Integration and growth in the world economy in historical perspective', *American Economic Review*, vol. 54.

Habermas, J. (1996), *Between Facts and Norms*, Polity/Cambridge University Press, Cambridge.

Hager, W. (1982) 'Industrial policy, trade policy and European social democracy', in J. Pinder (ed.), *National Industrial Strategies and the World Economy*, Croom Helm, Beckenham.

Haigh, N. (1987) EEC *Environmental Policy and Britain*, Longman, Harlow, second edition.

Hall, R. and Van Der Wee, D. (1992) 'Community regional policy for the 1990s', *Regional Studies*, vol. 26.

Han, S. S. and Leisner, H. H. (1970) 'Britain and the Common Market', *Occasional Paper*, no. 27, Department of Applied Economics, University of Cambridge.

Hancher, L and van Slot, P. (1990) 'Article 90', *European Competition Law Review*, vol. 11, no. 1.

Hancher, L., Ottervanger, T. and Slot, P.-J. (1999), *EC state aids*, Sweet & Maxwell, London.

Hansard (1972), vol. 831, 15 February.

Hansen, N. M. (1977) 'Border regions: a critique of spatial theory and a European case study', *Annals of Regional Science*, vol. XI, no. 1.

Hardach, K. W. (1980*) The Political Economy of Germany in the Twentieth Century*, University of California Press.

Harding, C. (1992) 'Who goes to court in Europe? An analysis of litigation against the European Community', *European Law Review*, vol. 17.

Harlow, C. (1996) 'Francovich and the disobedient state', *European Law Journal*, vol. 2.

Hart, J. (1992) *Rival Capitalists*, Cornell University Press.

Hartley, T. (1996) 'The European Court, judicial objectivity and the constitution of the EU', *Law Quarterly Review*, vol. 112.

Hartley, T. (1999) *Constitutional Problems of the EU*, Hart, Oxford.

Hayek, F. A. (1945), 'The Use of Knowledge in Society', *American Economic Review*, vol. 35, no. 4.

Hayek, F. A. (1989) *The Fatal Conceit*, University of Chicago Press.

Hazlewood, A. (1967) *African Integration and Disintegration*, Oxford University Press.

Hazlewood, A. (1975) *Economic Integration: the East African Experience*, Heinemann, Oxford.

Hedemann-Robinson, M. (1996) 'Third country nationals, EU citizenship, and free movement of persons: a time for bridges rather than divisions', *Yearbook of European Law*, vol. 16.

Heidensohn, K. (1995) *Europe and World Trade*, Pinter, London.

Heidhues, T. *et al.* (1978) *Common Prices and Europe's Farm Policies*, Thames Essays, no. 14, Trade Policy Research Centre.

Heitger, B. and Stehn, J. (1990) 'Japanese direct investment in the EC: response to the internal market 1993?', *Journal of Common Market Studies*, vol. 29.

Helleiner, G. K. *et al.* (1980) *Protectionism or International Adjustment*, Atlantic Institute for International Affairs.

Hellman, R. (1977) *Gold, the Dollar and the European Currency System*, Praeger.

Helm, D. R. and McGowan, F. (1989) 'Electricity supply in Europe: lessons for the UK', in D. R. Helm, J. A. Kay and D. J. Thompson (eds), *The Market for Energy*, Oxford University Press.

Helm, D. R. and Smith, S. (1989) 'The assessment: integration and the role of the European Community', *Oxford Review of Economic Policy*, vol. 5, no. 2.

Helm, D. R., Kay, J. A. and Thompson, D. J. (eds) (1989) *The Market for Energy*, Oxford University Press.

Helpman, E. (1981) 'International trade in the presence of product differentiation, economies of scale and monopolistic competition', *Journal of International Economics*, vol. 11.

Henderson, D. (1989) *1992: The external dimension*, Group of Thirty, New York.

Henry, C. (1993) 'Public service and competition in the European Community approach to communications networks', *Oxford Review of Economic Policy*, vol. 9, no. 1.

Hervey, T. (1995) 'Migrant workers and their families in the EU: the pervasive market ideology of Community law', in J. Shaw and G. More (eds), *New Legal Dynamics of EU*, Clarendon, Oxford.

Heseltine, M. (1989) *The Challenge of Europe: Can Britain win?*, Weidenfeld & Nicolson, London.

Hewitt, A. (1983) 'Stabex: analysing the effectiveness of an institution', in C. Stevens (ed.), *EEC and the Third World: a survey, 3, The Atlantic Rift*, Hodder & Stoughton, London.

Hill, C. (1997) *Convergence, Divergence and Dialectics: National Foreign Policies and the CFSP*, RSC 97/66, EUI, Florence.

Hill, C. and Wallace, W. (1979) 'Diplomatic trends in the European Community', *International Affairs*, January.

Hindley, B. (1974) *Theory of International Trade*, Weidenfeld & Nicolson, London.

Hindley, B. (1984) 'Empty economics in the case for industrial policy', *The World Economy*, vol. 7, no. 3.

Hindley, R. (1992) 'Trade policy of the European Community', in P. Minford (ed.), *The Cost of Europe*, Manchester University Press.

Hine, R. C. (1985) *The Political Economy of European Trade*, Wheatsheaf.

HMSO (1967) *Treaty Setting up the European Economic Community*. The original was published in Rome in 1957 by the EDC, and Sweet & Maxwell publish a regularly updated comprehensive set on the *European Community Treaties*.

HMSO (1985) *Employment: the Challenge to the Nation*, Cmnd. 9474.

Hocking, R. D. (1980) 'Trade in motor cars between the major European producers', *Economic Journal*, vol. 90.

Hodges, M. (ed.) (1972) *European Integration*, Penguin, London.

Hodges, M. (1977) 'Industrial policy: a directorate general in search of a role', in H. Wallace, W. Wallace and C. Webb (eds*), Policy-making in the European Communities*, John Wiley.

Hodges, M. (1983) 'Industrial policy: from hard times to great expectations', in H. Wallace, W. Wallace and C. Webb (eds), *Policy Making in the European Communities*, John Wiley.

Hoekman, B. and Djankov, S. (1996a) 'Intra-industry trade, foreign direct investment and the reorientation of East European exports', *CEPR Discussion Paper*, no. 1377, Centre for Economic Policy Research, London.

Hoekman, B. and Djankov, S. (1996b) 'The European Union's Mediterranean Free Trade Initiative', *The World Economy*, vol. 19.

Hoekman, B. and Kostecki, M. (1995) *The Political Economy of the World Trading System*, Oxford University Press.

Hofstadter, R. (1965) *The Paranoid Style in American Politics, and Other Essays*, Knopf.

Holland, S. (1976a) *The Regional Problem*, Macmillan, Basingstoke.

Holland, S. (1976b) *Capital versus the Regions*, Macmillan, Basingstoke.

Holland, S. (1980) *Uncommon Market: Capital, class and power in the European Community*, Macmillan.

Holloway, J. (1981) *Social Policy Harmonisation in the European Community*, Gower, Aldershot.

Holmes, P. and Shepherd, G. (1983) 'Protectionist policies of the EEC', paper presented to the International Economics Study Group conference at Sussex University.

House of Commons (1985) *The European Monetary System*, Select Committee on the Treasury and Civil Service, report of a sub-committee.

House of Commons (1987) *Indirect Taxes: Harmonisation*, Select Committee on European Legislation, Eighth Report, HMSO.

House of Lords (1983) *European Monetary System*, report of the Select Committee on the European Communities, Fifth Report, 1983–4, HMSO.

House of Lords (1985–6) 'Single European Act and parliamentary scrutiny', in *12th Report of the House of Lords Select Committee on the European Communities*, no. 149.

House of Lords (1992) *Enlargement of the Community*, Select Committee on the European Communities, Session 1991–2, 10th Report, HL55, HMSO.

House of Lords Select Committee on the European Communities (1986) *European Maritime Transport Policy*, 9th Report, HL 106.

Hu, Y.-S. (1979) 'German agricultural power: the impact on France and Britain', *The World Today*, vol. 35.

Hufbauer, G. C. (1990) *Europe 1992: An American Perspective*, The Brookings Institution, Washington.

Hughes, M. (1982) 'The consequences of the removal of exchange controls on portfolios and the flow of funds in the UK', in D. C. Corner and D. G. Mayes (eds), *Modern Portfolio Theory and Financial Institutions*, Macmillan, Basingstoke, Chapter 9.

Hughes, T. P. (1983) *Networks of Power*, Johns Hopkins University Press.

Hull, C. (1979) 'The implication of direct elections for European Community regional policy', *Journal of Common Market Studies*, vol. 17, no. 4.

IFO (1990) *An Empirical Assessment of the Factors Shaping Regional Competitiveness in Problem Regions*, study carried out for the EC Commission.

Ingio, M. and Hathaway, D. (1996) 'Implementation of the Uruguay Round commitments in agriculture: issues and practice', paper presented to the fourth World Bank Conference on Environmentally Sustainable Development, Washington DC, 25–27 September.

Ingram, J. C. (1959) 'State and regional payments mechanisms', *Quarterly Journal of Economics*, vol. 73.

Ingram, J. C. (1962) 'A proposal for financial integration in the Atlantic Community', in *Factors Affecting the US Balance of Payments*, Joint Economic Committee Print, 87th Congress, 2nd Session, Washington.

Ingram, J. C. (1973) 'The case for European monetary integration', *Essays in International Finance*, no. 98, Princeton University.

International Coal Report, 1992.

International Energy Agency (1980) *Energy Policies and Programmes of IEA Countries*, 1979 Review, OECD.

International Energy Agency (1988a) *Coal Prospects and Policies in IEA Countries 1987*, IEA/OECD.

International Energy Agency (1988b) *Coal Information 1988*, IEA/OECD.

International Monetary Fund (various issues) *Balance of Payments Manual*.

International Monetary Fund (1974) *Guidelines for Floating Exchange Rates*, IMF, Washington.

International Monetary Fund (1979) 'The EMS', *IMF Survey*, Supplement.

International Monetary Fund (1989) *IMF Survey*.

International Monetary Fund (1991) *IMF Survey: The coming emergence of three giant trading blocks*, IMF, Washington, DC.

Inukai, I. (1987) 'Regional integration and development in Eastern and Southern Africa', in A. M. El-Agraa (ed.), *Protection, Cooperation, Integration and Development: Essays in honour of Professor Hiroshi Kitamura*, Macmillan and St Martin's.

Irving, R. W. and Fearne, H. A. (1975) *Green Money and the Common Agricultural Policy*, Centre for European Agricultural Studies, Wye College, Ashford, Kent.

Ishikawa, K. (1990) *Japan and the Challenge of Europe 1992*, Pinter Publishers.

Jacqué, J-P. and Weiler, J. (1990) 'On the road to EU – A new judicial architecture: An agenda for the intergovernmental conference', *Common Market Law Review*, vol. 27.

Jacquemin, A. P. (1974) 'Application to foreign firms of European rules on competition', *The Antitrust Bulletin*, vol. 19, no. 1, Spring.

Jacquemin, A. P. (1988) 'Cooperative agreements in R&D and European antitrust policy', *European Economic Review*, vol. 32.

Jacquemin, A. (1990) 'Discussion of Neven's chapter', *Economic Policy*, April.

Jacquemin, A. P. and de Jong, H. W. (1977) *European Industrial Organisation*, Macmillan, Basingstoke.

Jacquemin, A. and Sapir, A. (1991) 'Competition and imports in the European Market', in L. A. Winters and A. J. Venables (eds), *European Integration: Trade and Industry*, Cambridge University Press.

Janssen, L. H. (1961) *Free Trade, Protection and Customs Union*, Economisch Sociologisch Instituut, Leiden.

Jenkins, R. (1977) 'Europe's present challenge and future opportunity', *Bulletin of the European Communities*, vol. 10.

Jenkins, R. (1978) 'European Monetary Union', *Lloyds Bank Review*, January.

Jenkins, R. (ed.) (1983) *Britain and the EEC*, Macmillan, Basingstoke.

Jenny, F. (1990) 'French competition policy in perspective', in W. S. Comanor *et al.*, *Competition Policy in Europe and North America: Economic issues and institutions*, Harwood Academic.

Joerges, C. (1996) 'Taking the law seriously: On political science and the role of law in the integration process', *European Law Journal*, vol. 2.

Johnson, D. G. (1972) *World Agriculture in Disarray*, Macmillan, for the Trade Policy Research Centre.

Johnson, H. G. (1965a) 'Optimal trade intervention in the presence of domestic distortions', in R. E. Baldwin *et al.* (eds), *Trade, Growth and the Balance of Payments*, North-Holland.

Johnson, H. G. (1965b) 'An economic theory of protectionism, tariff bargaining and the formation of customs unions', *Journal of Political Economy*, vol. 73.

Johnson, H. G. (1971) *Aspects of the Theory of Tariffs*, Allen & Unwin.

Johnson, H. G. (1973) 'Problems of European Monetary Union', in M. B. Krauss (ed.), *The Economics of Integration*, Allen & Unwin.

Johnson, H. G. (1974) 'Trade diverting customs unions: a comment', *Economic Journal*, vol. 81.

Johnson, H. G. and Krauss, M. B. (1973) 'Border taxes, border tax adjustments, comparative advantage and the balance of payments', in M. B. Krauss (ed.), *The Economics of Integration*, Allen & Unwin, London.

Joilet, R. (1971) 'Resale price maintenance under EEC antitrust law', *The Antitrust Bulletin*, vol. 16, no. 3, Fall.

Jones, A. J. (1979) 'The theory of economic integration', in J. K. Bowers (ed.), *Inflation Development and Integration: Essays in honour of A. J. Brown*, Leeds University Press.

Jones, A. J. (1980) 'Domestic distortions and customs union theory', *Bulletin of Economic Research*, vol. 32.

Jones, A. J. (1982) 'A macroeconomic framework for customs union theory', *Leeds Discussion Papers*, no. 112.

Jones, A. J. (1983) 'Withdrawal from a customs union: a macroeconomic analysis', in A. M. El-Agraa (ed.), *Britain within the European Community: The way forward*, Macmillan, Chapter 5.

Jones, C. and Gonzalez-Diaz, F. E. (1992) *The EEC Merger Control Regulation*, Sweet & Maxwell, London.

Jones, K. (1983) 'Impasse and crisis in steel trade policy', *Thames Essays*, no. 35, Trade Policy Research Centre.

Jones, R. T. (1976) 'The relevance to the EEC of American experience with industrial property rights', *Journal of World Trade Law*, vol. 10, no. 6.

Jones, R. W. and Raune, F. (1990) 'Appraising the options for international trade in services', *Oxford Economic Papers*, vol. 42.

Jordan, A. (1999), 'European water standards: locked in or watered down?', *Journal of Common Market Studies*, vol. 37.

Josling, T. (1969) 'The Common Agricultural Policy of the European Economic Community', *Journal of Agricultural Economics*, May.

Josling, T. (1979a) 'Agricultural policy', in P. Coffey (ed.), *Economic Policies of the Common Market*, Macmillan, Chapter 1.

Josling, T. (1979b) 'Agricultural protection and stabilisation policies: analysis of current and neomercantilist practices', in J. S. Hillman and A. Schmitz (eds), *International Trade and Agriculture: Theory and policy*, Westview Press.

Josling, T. (1998) *Agricultural Trade Policy: Completing the Round*, Institute for International Economics, Washington DC.

Josling, T. and Harris, W. (1976) 'Europe's Green Money', *The Three Banks Review*, March.

Josling, T. *et al.* (1972) *Burdens and Benefits of Farm-support Policies*, Trade Policy Centre, London.

Kaldor, N. (1966) *Causes of the Slow Rate of Economic Growth of the United Kingdom*, Cambridge University Press.

Kaldor, N. (1971) 'The dynamic effects of the Common Market', in D. Evans (ed.), *Destiny or Delusion: Britain and the Common Market*, Gollancz.

Katz, M. and Ordover, J. (1990) 'R&D cooperation and competition', *Brookings Papers on Economic Activity*, special issue.

Katzenstein, P. (ed.) (1989) *Industry and Politics in West Germany*, Cornell University Press.

Kay, J. A. and Keen, M. (1987) 'Alcohol and tobacco taxes: criteria for harmonisation', in S. Cnossen (ed.), *Tax Coordination in the European Community*, Kluwer.

Kay, J. A. and King, M. A. (1996) *The British Tax System*, Oxford University Press.

Kay, J. and Silbertson, A. (1984) 'The new industrial policy: privatisation and competition', *Midland Bank Review*, Spring.

Kelly, M. *et al.* (1988) 'Issues and developments in international trade policy', *Occasional Papers*, no. 63, IMF.

Kelman, S. (1981) *What Price Incentives?*, Auburn House.

Kenen, P. (1988) *Managing Exchange Rates*, Routledge, London.

Kenny, S. (1998) 'The Members of the ECJ of the European Communities', *Columbia Journal of European Law*, vol. 5.

Kern, D. (1978) 'An international comparison of major economic trends, 1958–76', *National Westminster Bank Quarterly Review*, May.

Kierzkowski, H. (1987) 'Recent advances in international trade theory', *Oxford Review of Economic Policy*, vol. 3, no. 1.

Killick, T. (1991) 'The Development Effectiveness of Aid to Africa', in I. Husain and J. Underwood (eds), *African External Finance in the 1990s*, The World Bank, Washington DC.

Killick, T. And Stevens, C. (1989) *Development Cooperation and Structural Adjustment: The Issues of Lomé IV*, ODI, London.

Kirchner, E. (1982) 'The European Community and the economic recession: 1973–79', in A. Cox (ed.), *Politics, Policy and the European Recession*, Macmillan.

Klodt, H. (1989) 'European integration: how much scope for national industrial policy?', in K. Cowling and H.Tomann (eds), *Industrial Policy After 1992*, Anglo-German Foundation for the Study of Industrial Society.

Klom, A. (1996) 'Electricity deregulation in the European Union', *Energy in Europe*, no. 27, December.

Klou, F. and Mittlestädt (1986) 'Labour market flexibility', *OECD Economic Studies*.

Knox, F. (1972) *The Common Market and World Agriculture*, Praeger.

Koester, U. (1977) 'The redistributional effects of the Common Agricultural Financial System', *Economic Review of Agricultural Economics*, vol. 4, no. 4.

Kol, J. (1987) 'Exports from developing countries: some facts and scope', *European Economic Review*, vol. 29.

Korah, V. (1988) 'Research and development, joint ventures and the European Economic Community competition rules', *International Journal of Technology Management*, vol. 3, nos. 1/2.

Korah, V. (1990) *An Introductory Guide to EEC Competition Law and Practice*, ESC Publishing, fourth edition.

Korah, V. (1997a) *EEC Competition Law and Practice*, Hart, Oxford.

Korah, V. (1997b) *An Introductory Guide to EC Competition Law and Practice*, Hart, Oxford University Press, 6th edition.

Korah, V. (1998) 'The future of vertical agreements under EC competition law', *European Competition Law Review*, vol. 19.

Kouevi, A. F. (1965) 'Essai d'application prospective de la methode RAS au commerce international', *Bulletin du CEPREL*, vol. 5.

Kramer, L. (1998) *EC Treaty and Environmental Law*, Sweet & Maxwell, London, 3rd edition.

Krause, L. B. (1962) 'US imports, 1947–58', *Econometrica*, April.

Krause, L. B. (1968) *European Economic Integration and the United States*, The Brookings Institution, Washington, DC.

Krause, L. B. and Salant, W. S. (eds), (1973a) *European Economic Integration and the United States*, The Brookings Institution, Washington, DC.

Krause, L. B. and Salant, W. S. (eds), (1973b) *European Monetary Unification and Its Meaning for the United States*, The Brookings Institution, Washington, DC.

Krauss, M. B. (1972) 'Recent developments in customs union theory: an interpretative survey', *Journal of Economic Literature*, vol. 10.

Krauss, M. B. (ed.) (1973) *The Economics of Integration*, Allen & Unwin, London.

Kreinin, L. B. (1967) 'Trade arrangements among industrial countries', in B. Balassa (ed.), *Studies in Trade Liberalisation*, Johns Hopkins University Press.

Kreinin, M. E. (1961) 'The effects of tariff changes on the prices and volumes of imports', *American Economic Review*, vol. 51.

Kreinin, M. E. (1964) 'On the dynamic effects of a customs union', *Journal of Political Economy*, vol. 72.

Kreinin, M. E. (1969) 'Trade creation and diversion by the EEC and EFTA', *Economia Internazionale*, May.

Kreinin, M. E. (1972) 'Effects of the EEC on imports of manufactures', *Economic Journal*, vol. 82.

Kreinin, M. E. (1975) 'European integration and the developing countries', in B. Balassa (ed.), *European Economic Integration*, North-Holland.

Kreinin, M. E. (1979) *International Economics: A policy approach*, Harcourt Brace Jovanovich (also subsequent editions).

Kreis, H. W. R. (1992) 'EC competition law and maritime transport', *The Antitrust Bulletin*, vol. 37, no. 2.

Kreuger, A. O. (1974) 'The political economy of the rent-seeking society', *American Economic Review*, vol. 64.

Krugman, P. R. (1979) 'Increasing returns, monopolistic competition and international trade', *Journal of International Economics*, vol. 9.

Krugman, P. R. (1983) New theories of trade among industrial countries', *AER Papers and Proceedings*, May.

Krugman, P. R. (1986a) *Strategic Trade Policy and the New International Economics*, MIT Press.

Krugman, P. (1986b) 'Increasing returns, monopolistic competition and industrial trade', in Krugman (1986a).

Krugman, P. R. (1988) 'EFTA and 1992', *Occasional Papers*, no. 23, EFTA Secretariat.

Krugman, P. (1990) 'Policy problems of a monetary union', in P. de Grauwe and L. Papademos (eds), *The European Monetary System in the 1990s*, Longman, Harlow.

Krugman. P. (1994) *Re-Thinking International Trade*. MIT Press, Cambridge, MA.

Krugman, P. and Venables, A. (1993) 'Integration, specialisation and adjustment', CEPR Discussion Paper 886.

Kruse, D. C. (1980) *Monetary Integration in Western Europe: EMU, EMS and beyond*, Butterworth.

Kuhn, U., Seabright, P. and Smith, A. (1992) *Competition Policy Research*, CEPR.

Kumm, M. (1999) 'Who is the final arbiter of constitutionality in Europe?: three conceptions of the relationship between the German Federal Constitutional Court and the European ECJ', *Common Market Law Review*, vol 36.

Ladeur, K.-H. (1997) 'Towards a legal theory of supranationality – The viability of the network concept', *European Law Journal*, vol. 3.

Laidler, D. E. W. (1982) 'The case for flexible exchange rates in 1980', in M. T. Sumner and G. Zis (eds), *European Monetary Union: Progress and prospects*, Macmillan, Basingstoke.

Laird, S. (1997) 'Quantifying commercial policies', in J. F. Francois and K. Reinert, *Applied Trade Policy Modelling: A handbook*, Cambridge University Press.

Laird, S. and Yeats, A. (1990a) 'Trends in nontariff barriers of developed countries, 1966–1986', *Weltwirtschaftliches Archiv*, vol. 126.

Laird, S. and Yeats, A. (1990b) *Quantitative Methods for Trade-barrier Analysis*, Macmillan.

Lamfalussy, A. (1963) 'Intra-European trade and the competitive position of the EEC', *Manchester Statistical Society Transactions*, March.

Lancaster, K. (1980) 'Intra-industry trade under monopolistic competition', *Journal of International Economics*, vol. 10.

Lange, O. (1938) *On the Economic Theory of Socialism*, Minnesota University Press.

Langhammer, R. and Sapir, A. (1987) *Economic Impact of Generalized Tariff Preferences*, Gower (for the Trade Policy Research Center), Aldershot.

Lantzke, U. (1976) 'International cooperation in energy', *The World Today*, March.

Larre, B. (1995) 'The impact of trade on labour markets: an analysis by industry', *OECD Jobs Study Working Paper*, OECD, Paris.

Latour, B. (1993) *We Have Never Been Modern*, Harvester Wheatsheaf, London.

Laurent, P. (1996) 'Anti-dumping policies in a globalising world', European Commission DGI, Brussels.

Laury, J. S. E., Lewis, G. R. and Omerod, P. A. (1978) 'Properties of macroeconomic models of the UK economy: a comparative study', *National Institute Economic Review*, no. 83.

Layton, C. (1969) *European Advanced Technology: A programme for integration*, Allen & Unwin.

Leary, V. A. (1995) 'Workers' rights and international trade: the social clause', in J. Bhagwati and R. Hudec (eds), *Fair Trade and Harmonization: Prerequisites for free trade?*, MIT Press, Cambridge, MA.

Lehner, S. and Meiklejohn, R. (1990) 'Fair competition in the Internal Market: Community state and policy', *European Economy*, no. 48.

Leibfried, S. and Pierson, P. (eds) (1995) *European Social Policy*, Brookings Institution.

Lenior, R. (1974) *Les Exclus: un Français sur Dix*, Editions du Seuil.

Lévi-Sandri, L. (1968) 'Pour une politique sociale moderne dans la Communauté Européenne', reprint of speech to the European Parliament, March.

Lincoln, E. J. (1990) *Japan's Unequal Trade*, The Brookings Institution, Washington.

Lindberg, L. N. (1963) *The Political Dynamics of European Economic Integration*, Stanford University Press.

Lindberg, L. N. and Scheingold, S. A. (1970) *Europe's Would-be Policy Patterns of Change in the European Community*, Prentice Hall.

Linnemann, H. (1966) *An Econometric Study of International Trade Flows*, North-Holland.

Lipgens, W. (1968) *Europa-Föderationspäne der Widerstandsbewegungen 1940–45*, R. Oldenbourg Verlag for the Forschungsinstitut der Deutschen Gesellschaft für Auswärtige Politik.

Lipgens, W. (1982) *A History of European Integration*, vol. 1, *1945–47: The formation of the European Unity Movement*, Clarendon Press, Oxford.

Lippert, A. (1987) 'Independent generators and the public utilities', paper presented to the *Financial Times* World Electricity Conference.

Lippert, B. and Stevens-Strohmann, R. (1993) *German Unification and EC Integration*, RIIA.

Lipsey, R. G. (1957) 'The theory of customs unions, trade diversion and welfare', *Economica*, vol. 24.

Lipsey, R. G. (1960) 'The theory of customs unions: a general survey', *Economic Journal*, vol. 70.

Lipsey, R. G. (1975) *An Introduction to Positive Economics*, Weidenfeld & Nicolson, London.

Lipsey, R. G. (1977) 'Comments', in F. Machlup (ed.), *Economic Integration, Worldwide, Regional, Sectoral*, Macmillan, Basingstoke.

Lister, L. (1960) *Europe's Coal and Steel Community: an experiment in European union*, New York, Twentieth Century Fund.

Lister, M. (1988) *The European Community and the Developing World*, Gower, Aldershot.

Llewellyn, D. T. (1980) *International Financial Integration: The limits of sovereignty*, Macmillan, Basingstoke.

Llewellyn, D. T. (1982a) 'European monetary arrangements and the international monetary system', in M. T. Sumner and G. Zis (eds), *European Monetary Union*, Macmillan, Basingstoke.

Llewellyn, D. T. (1982b) in D. T. Llewellyn *et al.*, *The Framework of UK Monetary Policy*, Heinemann, Chapter 1.

Llewellyn, D. T. (1983) 'EC monetary arrangement: Britain's strategy', in A. M. El-Agraa (ed.), *Britain within the European Community: The way forward*, Macmillan.

Lloyd, P. L. (1992) 'Regionalism and World trade', OECD *Economic Studies*, Spring.

Loewenheim, U. (1976) 'Trademarks and free competition within the European Community', *The Antitrust Bulletin*, vol. 21, no. 4.

Lucas, N. J. D. (1977) *Energy and the European Communities*, Europa Publications for the David Davies Memorial Institute of International Studies, London.

Lucas, R. E. (1988) 'On the mechanics of economic development', *Journal of Monetary Economics*, vol. 22.

Ludlow, P. (1982) *The Making of the European Monetary System: A case study of the politics of the European Community*, Butterworths, London.

Lunn, J. L. (1983) 'Determinants of US direct investment in the EEC revisited again', *European Economic Review*, vol. 21.

McAleese, D. (1990) 'External trade policy', in A. M. El-Agraa (ed.), *The Economics of the European Community*, third edition, Phillip Allan.

McAleese, D. (1991) 'The EC internal market programme: implications for external trade', in N. Wagner (ed.), *ASEAN and the EC: The impact of 1992*, Institute of Southeast Asian Studies, Singapore.

McAleese, D. (1993) 'The Community's external trade policy', in D. G. Mayes (ed.), *The External Implications of European Integration*, Simon & Schuster, London.

McAleese, D. (1994) 'EC external trade policy', in A. M. El-Agraa (ed.) *The Economics of the European Community*, Harvester Wheatsheaf, Hemel Hempstead, 4th edition.

MacBean, A. I. (1988) 'The Uruguay Round and the developing countries', paper presented to the annual conference of the International Economics Study Group, Sussex University.

MacBean, A. I. and Snowden, P. N. (1981) *International Institutions in Trade and Finance*, Allen & Unwin, London.

MacCormick, N. (1993) 'Beyond the sovereign state', *Modern Law Review*, vol. 56.

MacCormick, N. (1996), 'Liberalism, nationalism and the post-sovereign state' in R. Bellamy and D. Castiglione (eds), *Constitutionalism in Transformation: European and Theoretical Perspectives*, Blackwell, Oxford.

MacCormick, N. (1999), *Questioning Sovereignty*, Oxford University Press, Oxford.

McCrone, G. (1969) *Regional Policy in Britain*, Allen & Unwin, London.

McCrone, G. (1971) 'Regional policy in the European Community', in G. R. Denton (ed.), *Economic Integration in Europe*, Weidenfeld & Nicolson, London.

MacDougall Report (1977) *see* Commission of the European Communities (1977c).

McFarquhar, A., Godley, W. and Silvey, D. (1977) 'The cost of food and Britain's membership of the EEC', *Cambridge Economic Policy Review*, vol. 3.

McGowan, F. (1990) 'Conflicting objectives in EC energy policy', *Political Quarterly*.

McGowan, F. (1993a) 'Utilities as infrastructures', *Utilities Policy*, vol. 3, no. 4.

McGowan, F. (1993b) *The Struggle for Power in Europe*, RIIA.

McGowan, F. (1994) 'The consequences of competition', *Revue des Affaires Européennes*, no. 2.

McGowan, F. (ed.) (1995) *European Energy Policy in a Changing Environment*, Physica.

McGowan, F. and Mansell, R. (1992) 'EC utilities; a regime in transition', *Futures*, vol. 16.

McGowan, F. and Seabright, P. (1989) 'Deregulating European airlines', *Economic Policy*, November.

McGowan, F. and Seabright, P. (1994) 'Regulation in the European Community', in M. Bishop, J. Kay and C. Mayer (eds), *Privatisation and Regulation in the UK*, Clarendon, Oxford, second edition.

McGowan, F. and Thomas, S. (1990) 'Restructuring the world power plant industry', *The World Economy*, vol. 12.

McGowan, F. and Trengove, C. (1986) *European Aviation: A Common Market?*, IFS.

McGowan, F. *et al.* (1989) 'A single European market for energy', *Chatham House Occasional Paper*, RIIA.

McGowan, F. *et al.* (1993) *UK Energy Policy*, SPRU, University of Sussex.

Machlup, F. (1977a) *A History of Thought on Economic Integration*, Macmillan, Basingstoke.

Machlup, F. (ed.) (1977b) *Economic Integration, Worldwide, Regional, Sectoral*, Macmillan, Basingstoke.

Mackel, G. (1978) 'Green Money and the Common Agricultural Policy', *National Westminster Bank Review*, February.

McKinnon, R. I. (1963) 'Optimum currency areas', *American Economic Review*, vol. 53.

McLachlan, D. L. and Swann, D. (1967) *Competition Policy in the European Community*, Oxford University Press.

MacLaren, D. (1981) 'Agricultural trade and the MCAs: a spatial equilibrium analysis', *Journal of Agricultural Economics*, vol. 32, no. 1.

MacLennan, M. C. (1979) 'Regional policy in a European framework', in D. MacLennan and J. B. Parr, *Regional Policy: Past experience and new directions*, Martin Robertson.

MacMahon, C. (1979) 'The long run implications of the EMS', in P. H. Trezise (ed.), *The European Monetary System: Its promise and prospects*, The Brookings Institution, Washington.

McManus, J. G. (1972) 'The theory of the international firm', in G. Paquet (ed.), *The Multinational Firm and the National State*, Collier Macmillan, New York.

McMillan, J. and McCann, E. (1981) 'Welfare effects in customs unions', *Economic Journal*, vol. 91.

McQueen, M. and Stevens, C. (1989) 'Trade preferences and Lomé IV: non-traditional ACP exports to the EC', *Development Policy Review*, September.

Magnifico, G. and Williamson, J. (1972) *European Monetary Integration*, Federal Trust, London.

Magrini, S. (1999) 'The evolution of income disparities among the regions of the European Union', *Regional Science and Urban Economics*, vol. 29.

Maher, I. (1995) 'Legislative review by the EC Commission: Revision without radicalism' in J. Shaw and G. More (eds), *New Legal Dynamics of EU*, Oxford University Press, Oxford.

Maher, I. (1998) 'Community law in the national legal order: A systems analysis', *Journal of Common Market Studies*, vol. 36.

Majone, G. (1991) 'Cross national sources of regulatory policy making in Europe and the United States', *Journal of Public Policy*, vol. 11, no. 1.

Majone, G. (1994) 'The rise of the regulatory state in Europe', *West European Politics*, vol. 17.

Majone, G. (1998) 'Europe's democracy deficit: The question of standards', *European Law Journal*, vol. 4.

Major, R. L. (1960) 'World trade in manufactures', *National Institute Economic Review*, July.

Major, R. L. (1962) 'The Common Market: production and trade', *National Institute Economic Review*, August.

Major, R. L. and Hays, S. (1963) 'Another look at the Common Market', in *The Market Economy in Western European Integration*, University of Louvain.

Malcor, R. (1970) 'Problèmes posés par l'application pratique d'une unification pour l'usage des infrastructures routières', *EEC Studies, Transport Series*, no. 2.

Maltby, N. (1993) 'Multimodal transport and EC competition law', *Lloyds Maritime and Commercial Law Quarterly*, no. 1.

Mancini, G. (1998) 'Europe: The case for statehood', *European Law Journal*, vol. 4.

Manners, G. (1976) 'Reinterpreting the regional problem', *Three Banks Review*, no. 3.

Mansholt, S. (1969) *Le Plan Mansholt*, EC Commission.

Marenco, G. (1983) 'Public sector and Community law', *Common Market Law Review*, vol. 20, no. 3.

Marer, P. and Montias, J. M. (1988) 'The Council for Mutual Economic Assistance', in A. M. El-Agraa (ed.), *International Economic Integration*, Macmillan and St Martin's, New York.

Marin, A. (1979) 'Pollution control: economists' views', *Three Banks Review*, no. 121.

Marjolin Report (1975) *see* Commission of the European Communities (1975c).

Marquand, D. (1982) 'EMU: the political implications', in M. T. Sumner and G. Zis (eds), *European Monetary Union: Progress and prospects*, Macmillan.

Marquand, J. (1980) 'Measuring the effects and costs of regional incentives', *Government Economic Service Working Paper*, no. 32, Department of Industry, London.

Marsh, J. and Ritson, C. (1971) *Agricultural Policy and the Common Market*, Chatham House, PEP European Series, no. 16.

Marsh, J. S. and Swanney, P. J. (1980) *Agriculture and the European Community*, Allen & Unwin (second edition, 1985).

Marshall. A. (1920) *Principles of Economics*, Macmillan.

Masera, R. (1981) 'The first two years of the EMS: the exchange rate experience', *Banca Nazionale del Lavoro Review*, September.

Mason, E. S. (1946) *Controlling World Trade: Cartels and commodity agreements*, McGraw-Hill.

Mathijsen, P. S. R. F. (1972) 'State aids, state monopolies, and public enterprises in the Common Market', *Law and Contemporary Problems*, vol. 37, no. 2, Spring.

Mathijsen, P. S. R. F. (1975) *A Guide to European Community Law*, Sweet & Maxwell/Matthew Bender.

Matthews, A. (1986) *The Common Agricultural Policy and the Less Developed Countries*, Gill & Macmillan.

Matthews, A. (1990) *The European Community's Trade Policy and the Third World: An Irish perspective*, Gill and Macmillan.

Matthews, J. D. (1977) *Association System of the European Community*, Praeger.

Matthews, M. and McGowan, F. (1992) 'Reconciling diversity and scale: some questions of method in the assessment of the costs and benefits of European integration', *Revue d'Economie Industrielle*, no. 59.

Mattli, W. and Slaughter, A.-M. (1998) 'Revisiting the European ECJ', *International Organization*, vol. 52.

Mayes, D. G. (1971) *The Effects of Alternative Trade Groupings on the United Kingdom*, PhD Thesis, University of Bristol.

Mayes, D. G. (1974) 'RASAT, a model for the estimation of commodity trade flows in EFTA', *European Economic Review*, vol. 5.

Mayes, D. G. (1978) 'The effects of economic integration on trade', *Journal of Common Market Studies*, vol. 17, no. 1.

Mayes, D. G. (1981) *Applications of Econometrics*, Prentice Hall.

Mayes, D. G. (1982) 'The problems of the quantitative estimation of integration effects', in A. M. El-Agraa (ed.), *International Economic Integration*, Macmillan.

Mayes, D. G. (1983a) 'EC trade effects and factor mobility', in A. M. El-Agraa (ed.), *Britain within the European Community: The way forward*, Macmillan, Chapter 6.

Mayes, D. G. (1983b) 'Memorandum of Evidence', in House of Lords Select Committee on the European Communities, *Trade Patterns: The United Kingdom's changing trade patterns subsequent to membership of the European Community*, HL (41), 7th Report, Session 1983–84, HMSO.

Mayes, D. G. (1988) Chapter Three, in A. Bollard and M. A. Thompson (eds), *Trans-Tasman Trade and Investment*, Institute for Policy Studies, Wellington, New Zealand.

Mayes, D. G. (ed.) (1990) 'The external implications of closer European Integration', *National Institute Economic Review*, November.

Mayes, D. G. (1993) *The External Implications of European Integration*, Harvester Wheatsheaf.

Mayes, D. G. (1996) 'The role of foreign direct investment in structural change: the lessons from the New Zealand experience', in G. Csaki, G. Foti and D. Mayes (eds), *Foreign Direct Investment and Transition: The case of the Visegrad countries*, Trends in World Economy, no. 78, Institute for World Economics, Budapest.

Mayes, D. G. (1997a) 'Competition and cohesion: lessons from New Zealand', in M. Fritsch and H. Hansen (eds), *Rules of Competition and East-West Integration*, Kluwer.

Mayes, D. G. (1997b) *The Evolution of the Single European Market*, Edward Elgar.

Mayes, D. G. (1997c) 'The New Zealand experiment: using economic theory to drive policy', *Policy Options*, vol. 18, no. 7.

Mayes, D. G. (1997d) 'The problems of the quantitative estimation of integration effects', in A. M. El-Agraa (ed.), *Economic Integration Worldwide*, Macmillan and St Martins, New York.

Mayes, D. G. and Britton, A. (1992) *Achieving Monetary Union*, Sage.

Mayes, D. G. and Chapple, B. (1995) 'The costs and benefits of disinflation: a critique of the sacrifice ratio', *Reserve Bank Bulletin*, vol. 34.

Mayes, D. G., Hager, W., Knight, A. and Streeck, W. (1993) *Public Interest and Market Pressures: Problems posed by Europe 1992*, Macmillan, London.

Maynard, G. (1978) 'Monetary interdependence and floating exchange rates', in G. Maynard et al., *Monetary Policies in Open Economics*, SUERF.

Mayne, R. (1970) *The Recovery of Europe*, Weidenfeld & Nicolson, London.

Meade, J. E. (1951) *The Balance of Payments*, Oxford University Press.

Meade, J. E. (1973) 'The balance-of-payments problems of a European free-trade area', in M. B. Krauss (ed.), *The Economics of Integration*, Allen & Unwin.

Meade, J. E. (1980) *The Theory of International Trade Policy*, Oxford University Press.

Meade, J. E., Liesner, H. H. and Wells, S. J. (1962) *Case Studies in European Economic Union: The mechanics of integration*, Oxford University Press.

Meadows, D. H. et al. (1972) *The Limits to Growth*, Earth Island.

Mehta, K. and Peeperkorn, L. (1999) 'The economics of competition', in J. Faull and A. Nikpay (eds), *The EC Law of Competition*, Clarendon, Oxford.

Memedovic, O., Kuyvenhoven, A. and Molle, W. (eds), (1999) *Multilateralism and Regionalism in the Post-Uruguay Round Era: What Role for the EU?*, Kluwer, Boston.

Merills, J. (1998) *International Dispute Settlement*, Cambridge University Press, Cambridge.

Messerlin, P. (1988) 'The Uruguay negotiations on dumping and subsidies', World Bank, mimeo.

Messerlin, P. (1989) 'The EC anti-dumping regulations: a first appraisal', *Weltwirtschaftliches Archiv*, vol. 125.

Messerlin, P. A. (1997) 'MFN-based freer trade and regional free trade: what role for the European Community?', mimeo, Institut d'Études Politiques, Paris.

Messerlin, P. A. (1999) 'MFN-based freer trade and regional free trade: what role for the EU?', in O. Memedovic et al. (eds) (1999).

Messerlin, P. A. (2000) *Measuring the Costs of Protection in Europe,* Institute for International Economics, Washington, DC.

Messerlin, P. A. and Reed, G. (1995) 'Anti-dumping policies in the United States and the European Community', *Economic Journal*, vol. 105.

Michalopoulos, G. T. (1991) *Macroeconomic Consequences of the US Dollar Exchange Rate Movements for the EC Economy: An empirical analysis*, unpublished doctoral thesis, University of Reading.

Midland Bank (1970) 'The dollar: an end to benign neglect?', *Midland Bank Review*, Autumn.

Mikesell, R. F. and Goldstein, H. N. (1975) 'Rules for a floating rate regime', *Essays in International Finance*, no. 109, Princeton University.

Millward, R. (1981) 'The performance of public and private ownership', in E. Roll (ed.), *The Mixed Economy*, Macmillan, Basingstoke.

Mingst, K. A. (1977/78) 'Regional sectoral economic integration: the case of OAPEC', *Journal of Common Market Studies*, vol. 16.

Mishan, E. J. (1967) *The Cost of Economic Growth*, Stables.

Molle, W. (1990) *Economics of European Integration: Theory, Practice, Policy*, Aldershot.

Molle, W. (1994) *The Economics of European Integration*, Dartmouth, Aldershot, 2nd edition.

Molle, W. and Morsink, R. (1990) 'Direct investment and European integration', *European Economy*, special issue.

Molle, W. et al. (1980) *Regional Disparity and Economic Development in the European Community*, Saxon House.

Monnet, J. (1995) *Les Etats-Unis d'Europe ont Commencé*, Robert Laffont.

Montagnon, P. (1990a) 'Regulating the utilities', in P. Montagnon, *European Competition Policy*, RIIA.

Montagnon, P. (1990b) *European Competition Policy*, RIIA.

Moore, B. and Rhodes, J. (1975) 'The economic and Exchequer implications of British regional economic policy', in J. Vaizey (ed.), *Economic Sovereignty and Regional Policy*, Gill & Macmillan.

Morgan, A. D. (1980) 'The balance of payments and British membership of the European Community', in W. Wallace (ed.), *Britain in Europe*, Heinemann, Oxford, Chapter 3.

Morgan, R. (1983) 'Political cooperation in Europe', in R. Jenkins (ed.), *Britain and the EEC*, Macmillan, Basingstoke, Chapter 12.

Morris, C. N. (1980a) 'The Common Agricultural Policy', *Fiscal Studies*, vol. 1, no. 2.

Morris, C. N. (1980b) 'The Common Agricultural Policy: sources and methods', *Institute of Fiscal Studies Working Paper*, no. 6.

Morris, C. N. and Dilnot, A. W. (1981) 'The distributional effects of the Common Agricultural Policy', *Institute of Fiscal Studies Working Paper*, no. 28.

Morris, V. (1979) *Britain and the EEC – the Economic Issues*, Labour, Economic, Finance and Taxation Association, London.

Mosley, P. and Hudson, J. (1995) 'Aid Effectiveness; a Study of the effectiveness of Overseas Aid in the Main Countries Receiving ODA Assistance', *Report to the UK Overseas Development Administration*, London.

Moss, J. and Ravenhill, J. (1982) 'Trade developments during the first Lomé Convention', *World Development*, vol. 10.

Moss, J. and Ravenhill, J. (1988) 'The evolution of trade under the Lomé Convention: the first ten years', in C. Stevens and J. V. van Themaat (eds), *EEC and the Third World: a survey, 6, Europe and the International Division of Labour*, Hodder & Stoughton, London.

Munby, D. L. (1962) 'Fallacies of the Community's transport policy', *Journal of Transport Economics and Policy*, vol. 1.

Mundell, R. A. (1961) 'A theory of optimum currency areas', *American Economic Review*, vol. 51.

Mundell, R. A. (1964) 'Tariff preferences and the terms of trade', *Manchester School*, vol. 32.

Munk, K. J. (1989) 'Price support to the EC agricultural sector: an optimal policy?', *Oxford Review of Economic Policy*, vol. 5, no. 2.

Musgrave, R. A. and Musgrave, P. B. (1976) *Public Finance in Theory and Practice*, McGraw-Hill, Maidenhead.

National Institute of Economic and Social Research (1971) 'Entry into the EEC: a comment on some of the economic issues', *National Institute Economic Review*, no. 57, August.

National Institute of Economic and Social Research (1983) 'The European Monetary System', *National Institute Economic Review*, February.

National Institute of Economic and Social Research (1991) *A New Strategy for Social and Economic Cohesion After 1992*, a study carried out for the European Parliament, Brussels/Luxembourg.

Nau, H. (1974) *National Politics and International Technology: Nuclear reactor development in Western Europe*, Johns Hopkins University Press.

Naur, C. and Reuter, J. (1992) *The Effect of 1992 and Associated Legislation on the Less Favoured Regions of the Community*, Office for Official Publications of the European Communities, Luxembourg.

Needleman, L. and Scott, B. (1964) 'Regional problems and the location of industry policy in Britain', *Urban Studies*, no. 12.

Neill, Sir P. (1996) *The European ECJ: A Case Study in Judicial Activism*, European Policy Forum/Frankfurter Institut, London/Frankfurt.

Nello, S. (1991) *The New Europe: Changing economic relations between East and West*, Harvester Wheatsheaf.

Neumark, F. (1963) *Report of the Fiscal and Financial Committee*, EC Commission; see Commission of the European Communities (1963).

Neven, D. and Wyplosz, C. (1999) 'Relative Prices, Trade and Restructuring in European Industry', in M. Dewatripont *et al.* (eds), *Trade and Jobs in Europe: Much Ado About Nothing?*, Oxford University Press, Oxford.

Neven, D., Nuttal, R. and Seabright, P. (1993a) *Competition and Merger Policy in the EC*, CEPR.

Neven, D., Nuttal, R. and Seabright, P. (1993b) *Merger in Daylight*, CEPR.

Neven, D., Papandropoulos, P. and Seabright, P. (1998) *Trawling for Minnows: European Competition Policy and Agreements Between Firms*, CEPR.

Neven, D. J. (1990) 'Gains and losses from 1992', *Economic Policy*, April.

Neven, E. T. (1988) 'VAT and the European Budget', *The Royal Bank of Scotland Review*, no. 157.

Nicolaides, P. (1990) 'Anti-dumping measures as safeguards: the case of the EC', *InterEconomics*, November/December.

NIESR (1991) *A New Strategy for Social and Economic Cohesion After 1992*, Study for the European Parliament, Brussels/Luxembourg.

Nijkamp, P., Reichman, S. and Wegener (eds), (1990) *Euromobile: Transport, Communications and Mobility in Europe: A cross national comparative overview*, Avebury.

Nkrumah, K. (1965) *Neo Colonialism: The last stage of imperialism*, Heinemann, Oxford.

Noel, E. (1975) *Working Together*, EC Commission.

Oates, W. E. (1972) *Fiscal Federalism*, Harcourt Brace.

O'Donnell, R. (1992) 'Policy requirements for regional balance in economic and monetary union', in A. Hannequart (ed.), *Economic and Social Cohesion in Europe: a New Objective for Integration*, Routledge, London.

O'Donnell, R. and Murphy, A. (1994) 'The relevance of the European Union and European integration to the world trade regime', *International Journal*, vol. 49.

OECD (various years) *Economic Survey of Europe*.

OECD (various issues) *Geographical Distribution of Financial Flows to Aid Recipients*.

OECD (1979) *The Case of Positive Adjustment Policies: A compendium of OECD documents 1978/79*, OECD.

OECD (1983) *The OECD Interlink Model*.

OECD (1985 and various years) *OECD Economic Outlook*, no. 38.

OECD (1985) *Costs and Benefits of Protection*.

OECD (1988) *The Newly Industrialising Countries: Challenges and opportunity for OECD industries*.

OECD (1990) *Competition Policy and the Deregulation of Road Transport*, OECD.

OECD (1992) *Regulatory Reform, Privatisation and Competition Policy*, OECD.

OECD (1994) *The OECD Jobs Study, Part I: Labour Market Trends and Underlying Forces of Change*, OECD, Paris.

OECD (1995) *Environmental Taxes in OECD Countries*, OECD, Paris.

OECD (1996a) *Employment Outlook, July 1996*, OECD, Paris.

OECD (1996b) *Indicators of Tariff and Non-tariff Trade Barriers*, OECD, Paris.

OECD (1997a) *Environmental Taxes and Green Reform*, OECD, Paris.

OECD (1997b) *Agricultural Policies in OECD Countries: Measurement of Support and Background Information*, OECD, Paris.

OECD (1998) *European Community Development Cooperation Review*, no. 3.

OECD (1999) *OECD in Figures*, supplement to *OECD Observer*.

O'Keeffe, D. (1998) 'Is the spirit of Article 177 under attack? Preliminary references and admissibility', *European Law Review*, vol. 23.

Oliver, H. (1960) 'German neoliberalism', *Quarterly Journal of Economics*, vol. 74.

Olson, M. (1982) *The Rise and Decline of Nations: Economic Growth, Stagnation and Social Rigidities*, Yale University Press, Yale.

Oort, C. J. (1975) *Study of Possible Solutions for Allocating the Deficits which may Occur in a System of Charging for the Use of Infrastructures aiming at Budgetary Equilibrium*, EC Commission.

Oort, C. J. and Maaskant, R. H. (1976) *Study of Possible Solutions for Allocating the Deficit which may Occur in a System of Charging for the Use of Infrastructure Aiming at Budgetary Equilibrium*, EEC.

Open University (1973) *The European Economic Community: History and institutions, national and international impact*, Open University Press.

Oppenheimer, P. M. (1981) 'The economics of the EMS', in J. R. Sargent (ed.), *Europe and the Dollar in World-wide Disequilibrium*, Sijthoff and Noordhoff.

Ordover, J. (1990) 'Economic foundations of competition policy', in W. S. Comanor *et al.* (eds), *Competition Policy in Europe and North America: Economic issues and institutions*, Harwood Academic.

Osborne, F. and Robinson, S. (1989) 'Oil', in F. McGowan *et al.*, *A Single European Market for Energy*, Chatham House Occasional Paper, RIIA.

Oughton, C. and Whittam, G. (1997) 'Competitiveness, EU industrial strategy and subsidiarity', in P. Devine, Y. Katsoulacos and R. Sugden (eds), *Competitiveness, Subsidiarity and Industrial Policy*.

Owens, S. and Hope, C. (1989) 'Energy and the environment – the challenge of integrating European policies', *Energy Policy*, vol. 17.

Owen-Smith, E. (1983) *The West German Economy*, Croom Helm, Beckenham.

Oxfam (1996) 'Protecting workers' rights: the case for a social clause', Oxfam Report, Dublin.

Oxford Review of Economic Policy (1987), vol. 3, no. 1.

PA Cambridge Economic Consultants (1989) *The Regional Consequences of the Completion of the Internal Market for Financial Services*, study carried out for the EC Commission.

Padoa-Schioppa, T. (1983) 'What the EMS has achieved', *The Banker*, August.

Padoa-Schioppa, T. (1985) 'Policy cooperation in the EMS experience', in W. H. Buiter and R. C. Marston (eds), *International Economic Policy Coordination*, Cambridge University Press.

Padoa-Schioppa, T. *et al.* (1987) *Efficiency, Stability and Equity: A strategy for the evolution of the economic system of the European Community*, report of a study group appointed by the EC Commission.

Page, S. A. B. (1979) 'The management of international trade', *National Institute Discussion Papers*, no. 29.

Page, S. A. B. (1981) 'The revival of protectionism and its consequences for Europe', *Journal of Common Market Studies*, vol. 20, no. 1.

Page, S. A. B. (1982) 'The development of the EMS', *National Institute Economic Review*, November.

Page, S. and Davenport, M. (1994) *World Trade Reform: Do developing countries gain or lose?*, Overseas Development Institute, London.

Palmer, M. and Lambert, J. (1968) *European Unity*, Allen & Unwin, London.

Panić, M. (1982) 'Some longer term effects of short-run adjustments policies: behaviours of UK direct investment since the 1960s', in J. Black and J. H. Dunning (eds), *International Capital Movements*, Macmillan, Basingstoke.

Papaconstantinou, H. (1988) *Free Trade and Competition in the EEC: Law, policy and practice*, Routledge, London.

Pappalardo, C. (1991) 'State measures and public undertakings: Article 90 of the EEC Treaty revised', *European Competition Law Review*, vol. 12, no. 1.

Parkin, J. M. (1976) 'Monetary union and stabilisation policy in the European Community', *Banca Nazionale del Lavoro Review*, September.

Parry, I. (1997) 'Revenue recycling and the costs of reducing carbon emissions', *Climate Issues Brief No. 2*, Resources for the Future.

Parry, I. and Oates, W. (1998) 'Policy analysis in a second-best world', *Discussion Paper 98-48*, Resources for the Future.

Pauly, M. V. (1973) 'Income redistribution as a local public good', *Journal of Public Economics*, vol. 2.

Paxton, J. (1976) *The Developing Common Market*, Macmillan, Basingstoke.

Peacock, A. T. (1972) *The Public Finance of Inter-allied Defence Provision: Essays in honour of Antonio de Vito de Marco*, Cacucci Editore.

Peacock, A. T. and Wiseman, J. (1967) *The Growth of Public Expenditure in the UK*, Allen & Unwin, London.

Pearce, D. W. (1976) 'The limits of cost–benefit analysis as a guide to environmental policy', *Kyklos*, vol. 29.

Pearce, D. W. and Westoby, R. (1983) 'Energy and the EC', in A. M. El-Agraa (ed.), *Britain within the European Community: The way forward*, Macmillan, Basingstoke, Chapter 10.

Pearce, J. and Sutton, J. (1985) *Protection and Industrial Policy in Europe*, Routledge & Kegan Paul, London.

Pearce, J. and Sutton, J. (1986) *Protection and Industrial Policy in Europe*, Routledge, London.

Pearson, M. and Smith, S. (1991) *The European Carbon Tax*, Institute for Fiscal Studies, London.

Peeperkorn, L. (1998) 'The economics of verticals', *EC Competition Policy Newsletter*, vol. 2.

Peeters, T. (1982) 'EMU: prospects and retrospect', in M. T. Sumner and G. Zis (eds), *European Monetary Union: Progress and prospects*, Macmillan, Basingstoke.

Pelkmans, J. (1984) *Market Integration in the European Community*, Martinus Nijhoff.

Pelkmans, J. (1987) 'The European Community's trade policy towards developing countries', in C. Stevens and J. V. van Themaat, *EEC and the Third World: a survey, 6, Europe and the International Division of Labour*, Hodder & Stoughton, London.

Pelkmans, J. (1991) 'Completing the EC internal market: an update and problems ahead', in N. Wagner (ed.), *ASEAN and the EC: The impact of 1992*, Institute of Southeast Asian Studies, Singapore.

Pelkmans, J. and Brenton, P. (1997) 'Free trade with the EU: driving forces and effects of "me-too"', mimeo, Centre for European Policy Studies, Brussels.

Pelkmans, J. and Brenton, P. (1999) 'Free trade with the EU: driving forces and effects of "me-too"', in O. Memedovic *et al.* (eds) (1999).

Pelkmans, J. and Carzaniga, A. G. (1996) 'The trade policy review of the European Union', *World Economy*, special edition on 'Global trade policy, 1996'.

Pelkmans, J. and Murphy, A. (1992) 'Strategies for the Uruguay Round', in P. Ludlow (ed.), *Europe and North America in the 1990s*, Centre for European Policy Studies, Brussels.

Pelkmans, J. and Robson, P. (1987) 'The aspirations of the White Paper', *Journal of Common Market Studies*, vol. 25, no. 3.

Pelkmans, J. and Winters, L. A. (1988) *Europe's Domestic Market*, Routledge, London.

Perman, R., Ma, Y., McGilvray, J. and Common, M. (1999) *Natural Resource and Environmental Economics*, Financial Times, Prentice Hall, Harlow, 2nd edition.

Peterson, J. (1991) 'Technology policy in Europe: explaining the framework programme and Eureka in theory and practice', *Journal of Common Market Studies*, vol. 29, no. 3.

Peterson, J. and Sharp, M. (1998) *Technology Policy in the European Union*, St Martin's Press, New York.

Petith, H. C. (1977) 'European integration and the terms of trade', *Economic Journal*, vol. 87.

Phelps, E. S. (1968) 'Money–wage dynamics and labour market equilibrium, *Journal of Political Economy*, vol. 76.

Philips, L. (1995) *Competition Policy: a Game Theoretical Perspective*, Cambridge University Press, Cambridge.

Phillips, A. W. (1958) 'The relation between unemployment and the rate of change of money wages in the United Kingdom', *Economica*, vol. 25.

Phinnemore, D. (1999) Association: *Stepping Stone or Alternative to EU Membership?*, Sheffield Academic Press, Sheffield.

Pinder, J. (1968) 'Positive integration and negative integration', *The World Today*, March.

Pinder, J. (1969) 'Problems of European integration', in G. R. Denton (ed.), *Economic Integration in Europe*, Weidenfeld & Nicolson, London.

Pinder, J. (ed.) (1971) *The Economics of Europe*, Knight.

Pinder, J. (1982) 'Industrial policy in Britain and the European Community', *Policy Studies*, vol. 2, part, 4, April.

Pinder, J. (1991) *European Community: The building of a union*, Oxford University Press.

Pintado, X. *et al*. (1988) 'Economic aspects of European economic space', *Occasional Papers*, no. 25, EFTA Secretariat.

Pisani, E. (1984) *La Main et l'Outil*, Editions Robert Laffont, Paris.

Platteau, K. (1991) 'Article 90 EEC Treaty after the court judgement in the telecommunications (1991) terminal equipment case', *European Community Law Review*, vol. 12, no. 3.

Plötner, J. (1998) 'Report on France' in A-M. Slaughter, A. Stone Sweet and J. Weiler (eds), *The European Courts and National Courts: Doctrine and Jurisprudence*, Hart, Oxford.

Political and Economic Planning (PEP) (1962) *Atlantic Tariffs and Trade*, Allen & Unwin.

Political and Economic Planning (PEP) (1963) 'An energy policy for the EEC', *Planning*, vol. 29.

Pollack, M. (1997) 'Delegation, agency, and agenda-setting in the European Community', *International Organization*, vol. 51.

Pomfret, R. (1986) *Mediterranean Policy of the European Community: Study of discrimination in trade*, Macmillan.

Porter, M. (1990) *The Competitive Advantage of Nations*, Macmillan.

Posner, R. (1976) *Antitrust Law: an Economic Perspective*, University of Chicago Press, Chicago.

Poyhonen, P. (1963a) 'Towards a general theory of international trade, *Ekonomista Samfundets Tidskrift*, no. 2.

Poyhonen, P. (1963b) 'A tentative model for the volume of trade between countries', *Ekonomista Samfundets Tidskrift*, no. 2.

Prais, S. J. (1982) *Productivity and Industrial Structure*, Cambridge University Press.

Presley, J. R. and Coffey, P. (1974) *European Monetary Integration*, Macmillan.

Press, A. and Taylor, C. (1990) *Europe and the Environment*, The Industrial Society.

Prest, A. R. (1972) 'Government revenue, the national income and all that', in R. M. Bird and J. G. Read, *Modern Fiscal Issues*, Toronto University Press.

Prest, A. R. (1975) *Public Finance in Theory and Practice*, Weidenfeld & Nicolson.

Prest, A. R. (1979) 'Fiscal policy', in P. Coffey (ed.), *Economic Policies of the Common Market*, Macmillan, Basingstoke, Chapter 4.

Prewo, W. E. (1974) 'Integration effects in the EEC', *European Economic Review*, vol. 5.

Primo Braga, C. A. (1995) 'Trade-related intellectual property issues: the Uruguay Round agreement and its economic implications', in W. Martin and L. A. Winters (eds), 'The Uruguay Round and the developing economics', *World Bank Discussion Papers*, no. 307, Washington, DC.

Pryce, R. (1962) *The Political Future of the European Community*, Marshbank.

Pryce, R. (1973) *The Politics of the European Community*, Butterworth.

Pryce, R. (ed.) (1987) *The Dynamics of European Union*, Croom Helm.

Pulliainen, K. (1963) 'A world trade study: an econometric model of the pattern of commodity flows in international trade 1948–1960', *Ekonomista Samfundets Tidskrift*, no. 2.

Quévit, M. (1992) 'The regional impact of the internal market: a comparative analysis of traditional industrial regions and lagging regions', *Regional Studies*, vol. 26.

Quévit, M. (1995) 'The regional impact of the internal market: a comparative analysis of traditional industrial regions and lagging regions', in S. Hardy, M. Hart, L. Albrechts and A. Katos (eds), *An Enlarged Europe: Regions in Competition?*, Jessica Kingsley.

Raisman Report (1961) *East Africa: Report of the Economic and Fiscal Commission*, Cmnd 1279, Colonial Office.

Rasmussen, H. (1986) *On Law and Policy in the European ECJ*, Martinus Nijhoff, Dordrecht.

Rasmussen, H. (1998) *European ECJ*, GadJura, Copenhagen.

Ravenhill, J. (1985a) 'Europe and Africa: an essential continuity', in R. Boardman *et al*., *Europe, Africa and Lomé III*, University Press of America.

Ravenhill, J. (1985b) *Collective Clientism: the Lomé Convention and North–South Relations*, Columbia University Press.

Rawlings, R. (1993) 'The Eurolaw game: Some deductions from a saga', *Journal of Law and Society*, vol. 20.

Rehg, W. (1996) 'Translators introduction' in J. Habermas, *Between Facts and Norms*, Polity, Cambridge University Press, Cambridge.

Reich, N. (1997) 'A European constitution for citizens: Reflections on the rethinking of union and community law', *European Law Journal*, vol. 3.

Resnick, S. A. and Truman, E. M. (1975) 'An empirical examination of bilateral trade in Western Europe', *Journal of International Economics*, vol. 3.

Richonnier, M. (1984) 'Europe's decline is not irreversible', *Journal of Common Market Studies*, vol. 22, no. 3.

Riezman, R. (1979) 'A 3 × 3 model of customs unions', *Journal of International Economics*, vol. 9.

Ritson, C. (1973) *The Common Agricultural Policy*, in *The European Economic Community: Economics and agriculture*, Open University Press.

Ritson, C. (1980) 'Self sufficiency and food security centre for agricultural strategy', *Discussion Paper*, no. 8, University of Reading.

Ritson, C. and Tangermann, S. (1979) 'The economics and politics of Monetary Compensatory Amounts', *European Review of Agricultural Economics*, vol. 6.

Ritter, L. and Overburg, C. (1977) 'An attempt at a practical approach to joint ventures under the EEC rules on competition', *Common Market Law Review*, vol. 14, no. 4.

Roarty, M. J. (1985) 'The EEC's Common Agricultural Policy and its effects on less developed countries', *National Westminster Bank Quarterly Review*, February.

Robinson, P. W., Webb, T. R. and Townsend, M. A. (1979) 'The influence of exchange rate changes on prices: a study of 18 industrial countries', *Economica*, February.

Robson, P. (1980 and 1985) *The Economics of International Integration*, Allen & Unwin.

Robson, P. (1983) *Integration, Development and Equity: Economic integration in West Africa*, Allen & Unwin.

Robson, P. (1987) 'Variable geometry and automaticity: strategies for experience of regional integration in West Africa', in A. M. El-Agraa (ed.), *Conflict, Cooperation, Integration and Development: Essays in honour of Professor Hiroshi Kitamura*, Macmillan and St Martin's.

Robson, P. (1997) 'Integration in Sub-Saharan Africa', in Ali M. El-Agraa (ed.), *Economic Integration Worldwide*, Macmillan and St Martin's Press, New York.

Rodger, B. (1999) 'The Commission's white paper on modernisation of the rules implementing articles 81 and 82 of the EC Treaty', *European Law Review*, vol. 24.

Rogers, S. T. and Davey, B. H. (eds) (1973) *The Common Agricultural Policy and Britain*, Saxon House.

Rollo, J. N. C. and Warwick, K. S. (1979) 'The CAP and resource flows among EEC member states', *Government Economic Service Working Paper*, no. 27, Ministry of Agriculture, Fisheries and Food, London.

Romer, P. (1994) 'New goods, old theory and the welfare of trade restrictions', *Journal of Development Economics*, vol. 43.

Roy, R. (1994) 'Investment in transport infrastructure: the recovery in Europe', *ECIS Report*.

Royal Institute of International Affairs (1953) *Documents on International Affairs, 1949–50*, RIIA.

Ruttan, V. W. (1998) 'The new growth theory and development economics: a survey', *Journal of Development Studies*, vol. 35.

Rybczynski, T. (1982) 'Fiscal Policy under EMU', in M. T. Sumner and G. Zis (eds), *European Monetary Union*, Macmillan.

Sachs, J. D. and Shatz, H. J. (1994) 'Trade and jobs in US manufacturing', *Brookings Papers on Economic Activity*, vol. 1.

Sachs, J. D. and Shatz, H. J. (1996) 'US trade with developing countries and wage inequality', *American Economic Review*, papers and proceedings, vol. 86.

Sala-i-Martin, X. (1996) 'Regional cohesion: evidence and theories of regional growth and convergence', *European Economic Review*, vol. 40.

Sand, I.-J. (1998) 'Understanding new forms of governance: Mutually interdependent, reflexive, destabilised and competing institutions', *European Law Journal*, vol. 4.

Sapir, A. (1996) 'The effects of Europe's internal market programme on production and trade: a first assessment', *Weltwirtschaftliches Archiv*, vol. 132.

Sapir, A. (1998) 'The Political Economy of EC Regionalism', *European Economic Review*, vol. 42.

Sapir, A. and Winter, C. (1994) 'Services trade', in D. Greenaway and L. A. Winters (eds), *Surveys in International Trade*, Blackwell, Oxford.

Sargent, T. J. and Wallace, N. (1976) 'Rational expectations and the theory of economic policy', *Journal of Monetary Economics*, April.

Sarna, A. J. (1985) 'The impact of a Canada–US free trade area', *Journal of Common Market Studies*, vol. 23, no. 4.

Sawyer, M. (1992) 'Reflections on the nature and role of industrial policy', *Metroeconomica*, vol. 43.

Sayigh, Y. (1982) *The Arab Economy*, Oxford University Press.

Scaperlanda, A. and Balough, R. S. (1983) 'Determinants of US direct investment in the EEC revisited', *European Economic Review*, vol. 21.

Schepel, H. (1997) 'Legal pluralism in Europe', in P. Fitzpatrick and J. Bergeron (eds), *Europe's Other: European Law between Modernity and Postmodernity*, Ashgate, Aldershot.

Schepel, H. and Wesseling, R. (1997) 'The legal community: Judges, lawyers, officials and clerks in the writing of Europe', *European Law Journal*, vol. 3.

Scherer, F. M. and Ross, D. (1990) *Industrial Market Structure and Economic Performance*, Houghton Mifflin.

Schilling, T. (1996) 'The autonomy of the community legal order – Through the looking glass', *Harvard Journal of International Law*, vol. 37.

Schindler, P. (1970) 'Public enterprises and the EEC Treaty', *Common Market Law Review*, vol. 7, no. 1.

Schmalensee, R. and Willig, R. D. (eds) (1989) *Handbook of Industrial Organization*, North-Holland.

Schuknecht, L. (1992) *Trade Protection in the European Community*, Harwood Academic.

Schumacher, D. and Mobius, U. (1991) 'Eastern Europe and the EC: trade relations and trade policy with regard to industrial products', paper presented to Joint Canada/Germany Symposium, November 1990, revised 1991, Berlin Deutsches Institüt fur Wirtschaftforschung (DIW).

Scitovsky, T. (1954) 'Two concepts of external economies', *Journal of Political Economy*, vol. 62.

Scitovsky, T. (1958) *Economic Theory and Western European Integration*, Allen & Unwin, London.

Scott, J. (1998) 'Law, legitimacy and EC governance: Prospects for "Partnership"' *Journal of Common Market Studies*, vol. 36.

Scully, R. (1997) 'The European Parliament and the co-decision procedure: A reassessment', *Journal of Legislative Studies*, vol. 3.

Secretariat of the European Parliament (1983) *The European Parliament, Its Powers*.

Sellekaerts, W. (1973) 'How meaningful are empirical studies on trade creation and diversion?', *Weltwirtschaftliches Archiv*, vol. 109.

Servan-Schreiber, J.-J. (1967) *Le Défi Américain*, Denoöl, Paris.

Shanks, M. (1977) *European Social Policy, Today and Tomorrow*, Pergamon Press, Oxford.

Shapiro, M. (1996) 'Codification of administrative law: The US and the EU', *European Law Journal*, vol. 2.

Sharp, M. L. (1987) 'Collaboration in the high technology sectors', *Oxford Review of Economic Policy*, vol. 3, no. 1.

Sharp, M. L. (1991) 'The single market and European technology policies', in C. Freeman, M. L. Sharp and W. Walker (eds), *Technology and the Future of Europe*, Pinter.

Sharp, M. L. and Pavitt, K. (1993) 'Technology policy in the 1990s: old trends and new realities', *Journal of Common Market Studies*, vol. 31, no. 2.

Sharp, M. L. and Shearman, C. (1987) *European Technological Collaboration*, RIIA.

Sharp, M. L. and Walker, W. B. (1991) 'The policy agenda – challenges for the new Europe', in C. Freeman, M. L. Sharp and W. Walker (eds), *Technology and the Future of Europe*, Pinter, London.

Shaw, J. (1996) 'EU legal studies in crisis? Towards a new dynamic', *Oxford Journal of Legal Studies*, vol. 16.

Shaw, J. (1999) 'Postnational constitutionalism in the EU', *Journal of European Public Policy*, vol. 7.

Shaw, J. and Wiener, A. (1999) 'The Paradox of the "European Polity"', *Harvard Jean Monnet Working Paper No 10/99*.

Shlaim, A. and Yannopoulos, G. N. (eds) (1976) *The EEC and the Mediterranean Countries*, Cambridge University Press.

Shonfield, A. (1965) *Modern Capitalism: The changing balance of public and private power*, Oxford University Press.

Short, J. (1978) 'The regional distribution of public expenditure in Great Britain, 1969/70–1973/74', *Regional Studies*, vol. 12, no. 5.

Short, J. (1981) *Public Expenditure and Taxation in the UK Regions*, Gower, Aldershot.

Shoup, C. S. (ed.) (1966) *Fiscal Harmonisation in Common Markets*, 2 vols, Columbia University Press.

Shoup, C. S. (1972) 'Taxation aspects of international integration', in P. Robson (ed.), *International Economic Integration*, Penguin, London.

Shourd, M. (1980) *The Theft of the Countryside*, Temple Smith.

Slaughter, A.-M. (1995) 'International law in a world of liberal states', *European Journal of International Law*, vol. 6.

Slaughter, A.-M. (1999) 'Globalisation and Wages', *Centre for Research on Globalisation and Labour Markets, research paper 99/5*.

Slaughter, A.-M., Stone Sweet, A. and Weiler, J. (1998) 'Prologue', in A.-M. Slaughter, A. Stone Sweet and J. Weiler (eds), *The European Courts and National Courts: Doctrine and Jurisprudence*, Hart, Oxford.

Smith, A. J. (1977) 'The Council of Mutual Economic Assistance in 1977: new economic power, new political perspectives and some old and new problems', in US Congress Joint Economic Committee, *East European Economics Post-Helsinki*.

Smith, S. (1988) 'Excise duties and the internal market', *Journal of Common Market Studies*, vol. 27, no. 2.

Snyder, F. (1999) *Global Economic Networks and Global Legal Pluralism*, EUI Working Paper Law, vol. 6, Badia Fiesolana, San Domenico.

Solow, R. M. (1957) 'Technical change and the aggregate production function', *Review of Economics and Statistics*, vol. 39.

Spaak Report (1987) *The Single European Act: a New Frontier – Programme of the Commission for 1987*. Supplement 1/87 of *EU Bulletin*.

SPRU–RIIA (1989) *A Single European Market for Energy*, RIIA.

Starkie, D. (1993) 'Train service coordination in a competitive market', *Fiscal Studies*, vol. 14, no. 2.

Steenbergen, J. (1980) 'The Common Commercial Policy', *Common Market Law Review*, May.

Stein, E. (1981) 'Lawyers, judges and the making of a transnational constitution', *American Journal of International Law*, vol. 75, no. 1.

Stern, J. (1989) 'Natural gas', in F. McGowan *et al.*, *A Single Market for Energy*, Chatham House Occasional Paper, RIIA.

Stern, J. (1992) *Third Party Access in European Gas Markets*, RIIA.

Stern, R., Francis, S. and Schumacker, B. (1976) *Price Elasticities in International Trade: An annotated bibliography*, Macmillan, Basingstoke.

Stevens, C. (1984) 'The new Lomé Convention: imperfections for Europe's Third World policy', Paper No. 16, Centre for European Policy Studies.

Stevens, C. (1992) 'The EC and the Third World', in D. A. Dyker (ed.), *The European Economy*, Longman, Harlow.

Stevens, C., McQueen, M. and Kennan, J. (1998) *After Lomé IV: a Strategy for ACP–EU Relations in the 21st Century*, Commonwealth Secretariat, London, December.

Stevens, C. and van Themaat, J. V. (eds) (1988) *EEC and the Third World: A Survey*, 6, *Europe and the International Division of Labour*, Hodder & Stoughton, London.

Stevens, C. and Watson, A. (1984) 'Trade diversification: has Lomé helped?', in C. Stevens (ed.)., *EEC and the Third World: a survey, 4, Renegotiating Lomé*, Hodder & Stoughton, London.

Stewart, J. A. and Begg, H. M. (1976) 'Towards a European regional policy', *National Westminster Bank Quarterly Review*, May.

Stigler, G. J. (1971) 'The theory of economic regulation', *Bell Journal of Economics and Management Science*, vol. 2.

Stoeckel, A. B. (1985) *Intersectoral Effects of the CAP: Growth, Trade and Unemployment*, Bureau of Agricultural Research, Canberra.

Stoffaes, C. (1986) 'Postscript', in W. Adams and C. Stoffaes (eds), *French Industrial Policy*, The Brookings Institution, Washington, DC.

Stokes, B. (1996) *Open for Business: Creating a transatlantic marketplace*, Council of Foreign Relations, New York.

Stone, J. K. N. and Brown, J. A. C. (1963) 'Input–output relationships', in *A Programme for Growth*, no. 3, Chapman & Hall, London.

Stone Sweet, A. and Brunell, T. (1997) 'The European Court and National Courts: A statistical analysis of preliminary references 1961–1995', *Journal of European Public Policy*, vol. 5.

Stone Sweet, A. and Brunell, T. (1998) 'Constructing a supranational constitution: Dispute resolution and governance in the European Community', *American Political Science Review*, vol. 92.

Stone Sweet, A. and Caporaso, J. (1998) 'From free trade to supranational polity: The European Court and integration', in W. Sandholtz and A. Stone Sweet (eds), *European Integration and Supranational Governance*, Oxford University Press, Oxford.

Stoneman, P. (1989) 'Technology policy in Europe', in Cowling, K. and Tomann, H., *Industrial Policy After 1992*, Anglo-German Foundation for the Study of Industrial Society.

Strange, S. and Tooze, R. (eds) (1981) *The International Politics of Surplus Capacity: Competition for market shares in the world recession*, Allen & Unwin, London.

Strasser, D. (1981) 'The finances of Europe', *The European Perspective Series*, EC Commission.

Strasser, S. (1995) *The Development of a Strategy of Docket Control for the European ECJ and the Question of Preliminary References*, Harvard Jean Monnet Working Paper, vol. 3.

Sturmey, S. G. (1962) *British Shipping and World Competition*, Athlone.

Sumner, M. T. and Zis, G. (eds) (1982) *European Monetary Union: Progress and prospects*, Macmillan, Basingstoke.

Sundelius, B. and Wiklund, C. (1979) 'The Nordic Community: the ugly duckling of regional cooperation', *Journal of Common Market Studies*, vol. 18, no. 1.

Swann, D. (1973) *The Economics of the Common Market*, Penguin, London.

Swann, D. (1978) *The Economics of the Common Market*, Penguin, London, second edition.

Swann, D. (1983) *Competition and Industrial Policy in the European Community*, Methuen, London.

Swann, D. (1988) *The Economics of the Common Market*, Penguin, London, fourth edition.

Swann, D. (1992) *The Economics of the Common Market*, Penguin, London, seventh edition.

Sweet & Maxwell (regularly updated) *European Community Treaties*.

Swinbank, A. and Ritson, C. (1988) 'The Common Agricultural Policy, customs unions and the Mediterranean basin', *Journal of Common Market Studies*, vol. 27, no. 2.

Swoboda, A. K. (1983) 'Exchange rate regimes and European–US policy interdependence', *International Monetary Fund Staff Papers*, March.

Symons, E. and Walker, I. (1989) 'The revenue and welfare effects of fiscal harmonisation for the UK', *Oxford Review of Economic Policy*, vol. 5, no. 2.

'**Symposium on SO$_2$ Trading**' (1998) *Journal of Economic Perspectives*, vol. 12, no. 3.

Szyszczak, E. (1996) 'Making Europe more relevant to its citizens: Effective judicial process', *European Law Review*, vol. 21.

Talbot, R. B. (1978) 'The European Community's regional fund', *Progress in Planning*, vol. 8, no. 3.

Tangermann, S. (1999) 'Europe's agricultural policies and the Millennium Round', *The World Economy*, vol. 22.

Temple Lang, J. (1998) 'Community Antitrust law and national regulatory prodedures', *1997 Annual Proceedings of Fordham Corporate Law Institute*, vol. 24.

Teubner, G. (1997) 'Breaking frames: The global interplay of legal and social systems', *American Journal of Comparative Law*, vol. 45.

Teubner, G. (1998) 'Legal irritants: Good faith in British law or how unifying law ends up in new divergences', *Modern Law Review*, vol. 61.

Tharakan, P. K. M. (ed.) (1991) *Policy Implications of Antidumping Measures*, North-Holland.

Tharakan, P. K. M. (1995) 'Political economy and contingent protection', *Economic Journal*, vol. 105.

Tharakan, P. K. M. (1999) 'Is anti-dumping here to stay?', *The World Economy*, vol. 22, no. 2.

Tharakan, P. K. M. and Waelbroeck, J. (1994) 'Anti-dumping and countervailing duty decisions in the EC and in the US', *European Economic Review*, vol. 38.

Thomas, S. D. (1984) *The Realities of Nuclear Power*, Cambridge University Press.

Thomas, S. D. (1988) 'Power plant life extension', *Energy the International Journal*.

Thomson, G. (1973) 'European regional policy in the 1970s', *CBI Review*, no. 10, Autumn.

Thomson, G. (1989) *Industrial Policy: USA and UK debates*, Routledge, London.

Thomson, K. J. (1983) 'CAP budget projections to 1988', *Discussion Paper*, no. 4, Department of Agricultural Economics and Department of Agricultural Marketing, University of Newcastle.

Thorbecke, E. and Pagoulatos, E. (1975) 'The effects of European economic integration on agriculture', in B. Balassa (ed.), *European Economic Integration*, North-Holland.

Thurow, L. C. (1971) 'The income distribution as a public good', *Quarterly Journal of Economics*, vol. 85.

Thygesen, N. (1979) 'EMS: precursors, first steps and policy options', in R. Triffin (ed.), *The EMS: the emerging European Monetary System*, National Bank of Belgium.

Thygesen, N. (1981a) 'Are monetary policies and performance converging?', *Banca Nazionale del Lavoro Quarterly Review*, September.

Thygesen, N. (1981b) 'The EMS: an approximate implementation of the Crawling Peg?', in J. Williamson (ed.), *Exchange Rate Rules*, Macmillan, Basingstoke.

Tiberi, U. and Cardoso, F. (1992) 'Specific actions towards greater penetration of renewable energy sources (ALTENER)', *Energy in Europe*, no. 20.

Timberg, S. (1972) 'Antitrust in the Common Market: innovation and surprise', *Law and Contemporary Problems*, vol. 37, no. 2.

Tinbergen, J. (1952) *On the Theory of Economic Policy*, North-Holland.

Tinbergen, J. (1953) *Report on Problems Raised by the Different Turnover Tax Systems Applied within the Common Market* (the Tinbergen Report), European Coal and Steel Community.

Tinbergen, J. (1954) *International Economic Integration*, Elsevier.

Tindemans, L. (1976) 'European Union', *Bulletin of the European Communities*, Supplement.

Toulemon, R. (1972) 'Etat d'avancement des travaux en matière de politique industrielle dans la Communauté', paper presented to the conference organized by the European Communities on 'Industrie et société dans la Communauté Européenne', Venice.

Trela, I. and Walley, J. (1990) 'Unraveling the threads of the MFA', in C. B. Hamilton (ed.), *Textiles Trade and the Developing Countries: Eliminating the Multi-Fibre Agreement in the 1990s*, World Bank.

Trezise, P. H. (ed.) (1979) *The European Monetary System: Promise and prospects*, The Brookings Institution, Washington.

Tridimas, T. (1996) 'The ECJ and judicial activism', *European Law Review*, vol. 19.

Trubek, D. *et al.* (1994) 'Global restructuring and the law: Studies of the internationalization of legal fields and the creation of transnational arenas', *Case Western Reserve Law Review*, vol. 44.

Truman, E. M. (1969) 'The European Economic Community: trade creation and trade diversion', *Yale Economic Essays*, Spring.

Truman, E. M. (1972) 'The production and trade of manufactured products in the EEC and EFTA: a comparison', *European Economic Review*, vol. 3.

Truman, E. M. (1975) 'The effects of European economic integration on the production and trade of manufactured products', in B. Balassa (ed.), *European Economic Integration*, North-Holland.

Tsebelis, G. (1994) 'The power of the EP as a conditional agenda-setter', *American Political Science Review*, vol. 88.

Tsebelis, G. and Garrett, G. (1997) 'Agenda setting, vetoes and the EU's co-decision procedure', *Journal of Legislative Studies*, vol. 3.

Tsebelis, G. and Kreppel, A. (1998) 'The history of conditional agenda-setting in European institutions', *European Journal of Political Research*, vol. 33.

Tsikata, T. M. (1998) 'Aid Effectiveness: a Survey of the Recent Empirical Literature', *IMF Working Paper on Policy Analysis and Assessment*, Washington, DC.

Tsoukalis, L. (1981) *The European Community and its Mediterranean Enlargement*, Allen & Unwin.

Tsoukalis, L. (ed.) (1982) *The European Community Past, Present and Future*, Basil Blackwell.

Tsoukalis, L. (1991) *The New European Economy: The politics and economics of integration*, Oxford University Press.

Tullock, G. (1967) 'The welfare costs of tariffs, monopolies and theft', *Western Economic Journal*, vol. 5.

Tyson, L. D. (1992) *Who's Bashing Whom?: Trade conflict in high technology industries*, IIE.

Ungerer, H., Evans, O. and Nyberg, P. (1983) 'The European Monetary System: The experience, 1979–82', *International Monetary Fund Occasional Papers*, no. 19, May.

Ungerer, H. *et al.* (1986) 'The European Monetary System – recent developments', *Occasional Papers*, no. 48, IMF.

Ungerer, W. (1993) 'EC: one step back, two steps forward', *Japan Update*, no. 17, February.

United Kingdom Civil Aviation Authority (1993) *Airline Competition in the Single European Market*, CAP 623, CAA.

United Kingdom Government (1996) *Memorandum by the British Government to the 1996 Intergovernmental Conference on the European ECJ*, Foreign and Commonwealth Office, London.

United Nations (1982) 'Standardised input–output tables of EEC countries for years around 1975', *Statistical Standards and Studies*, no. 34.

United Nations Economic Commission for Africa (1984) *Proposals for Strengthening Economic Integration in West Africa*, UNECA (Addis Ababa).

University of Louvain (1963) *The Market Economy in West European Integration*, Editions Nauwelaerts.

Uribe, P., Theil, H. and De Leeuw, C. G. (1966) 'The information approach to the prediction of interregional trade flows', *Review of Economic Studies*, July.

van der Linde, J. G. and Lefeber, R. (1988) 'IEA captures the development of European Community energy law', *Journal of World Trade*, vol. 22.

van Doorn, J. (1975) 'European regional policy: an evaluation of recent developments', *Journal of Common Market Studies*, vol. 13, no. 3.

van Gent, H. and Nijkamp, P. (1991) 'Devolution of transport policy in Europe', in K. Button and D. Pitfield (eds), *Transport Deregulation: An international movement*, Macmillan.

van Miert, K. (1996) 'The proposal for a European competition agency', *Competition Policy Newsletter*, vol. 2, no. 2.

van Themaat, J. V. and Stevens, C. (1987) 'The division of labour between competition and the Third World', in C. Stevens and J. V. Themaat, *EEC and the Third World: a survey*, 6, *Europe and the International Division of Labour*, Hodder & Stoughton, London.

Vanek, J. (1965) *General Equilibrium of International Discrimination: the Case of Customs Unions*, Harvard University Press.

Vanhalewyn, E. (1999) 'Trends and patterns in state aids', *European Economy Report and Studies: State Aid and the Single Market,* no. 3.

Vanhove, N. and Klaassen, H. (1987) *Regional Policy: a European approach*, Gower, Aldershot, second edition.

Vaubel, R. (1978) *Strategies for Currency Unification*, J. C. B. Mohr/Paul Siebeck.

Verdoorn, P. J. (1954) 'A customs union for Western Europe: advantages and feasibility', *World Politics*, vol. 6.

Verdoorn, P. J. and Schwartz, A. N. R. (1972) 'Two alternative estimates of the effects of EEC and EFTA on the pattern of trade', *European Economic Review*, vol. 3.

Verdoorn, P. J. and Meyer zu Schlochtern, F. J. M. (1964) 'Trade creation and trade diversion in the Common Market', in H. Brugmans (ed.), *Intégration Européenne et Réalité Économique*, Collège d'Europe, Bruges.

Vernon, R. (1966) 'International investment and international trade in the product cycle', *Quarterly Journal of Economics*, vol. 80.

Vickerman, R. W. (ed.) (1991) *Infrastructure and Regional Development*, Pion.

Vickerman, R. (1995) 'The regional impacts of trans-European networks', *Annals of Regional Science*, vol. 29.

Vickers, J. and Yarrow, G. (1988) *Privatization: An economic analysis*, MIT Press, Cambridge, MA.

Viegas, J. M. and Blum, U. (1993) 'High speed railways in Europe', in D. Banister and J. Berechman (eds), *Transport in a Unified Europe*, Elsevier, Oxford.

Viner, J. (1950) *The Customs Union Issue*, Carnegie Endowment for International Peace, New York.

Volcansek, M. (1986) *Judicial Politics in Europe*, Peter Lang, Frankfurt.

von Geusau, F. A. (1975) 'In search of a policy', in F. A. Geusau (ed.), *Energy Strategy in the European Communities*, Sijthoff.

Von Thünen, J. H. (1826) *Der isoliere Staat in Beziehung auf Landwirtschaft und Nationbalökonomie*, Perthes.

Vos, E. (1998) *Institutional Frameworks of Community Health and Safety Regulation: Committees, Agencies and Private Bodies*, Hart, Oxford.

Waelbroeck, J. (1964) 'Le commerce de la communauté Européenne avec les pays tiers', in H. Brugmans (ed.), *Intégration Européenne et Réalité Économique*, Collège d'Europe, Bruges.

Waelbroeck, J. (1977) 'Measuring the degree of progress of economic integration', in F. Machlup (ed.), *Economic Integration, Worldwide, Regional, Sectoral*, Macmillan, Basingstoke.

Waelbroeck, M. (1976) 'The effect of the Rome Treaty on the exercise of national industrial property rights', *The Antitrust Bulletin*, vol. 21, no. 1, Spring.

Waeterloos, C. (1991) 'Why a European energy charter?', *Energy in Europe*, no. 17.

Wagner, N. (1991) 'The EC internal market and ASEAN: an overview', in N. Wagner (ed.), *ASEAN and the EC: The impact of 1992*, Institute of Southeast Asian Studies, Singapore.

Wallace, H. and Ridley, A. (1985) 'Europe: the challenge of diversity', *Chatham House Papers*, no. 29, Routledge & Kegan Paul, London.

Wallace, H., Wallace, W. and Webb, C. (eds) (1977) *Policy-making in the European Communities*, John Wiley, Chichester.

Wallace, W. (ed.) (1980) *Britain in Europe*, Heinemann, Oxford.

Wallace, W. (ed.) (1990) *The Dynamics of European Integration*, Pinter, London.

Walter, I. (1967) *The European Common Market*, Praeger.

Walter, N. (1982) 'The EMS: performance and prospects', in M. T. Sumner and G. Zis (eds), *European Economic Union: Progress and prospects*, Macmillan, Basingstoke.

Walton, R. J. (1988) 'ECU financial activity', *Quarterly Bulletin*, Bank of England, November.

Ward, I. (1996), *A Critical Introduction to European Law*, Butterworths, London.

Weatherill, S. and Beaumont, P. (1999) *EU Law*, Penguin, Harmondsworth, 3rd edition.

Webb, C. (1977) 'Variations on a theoretical theme', in H. Wallace, W. Wallace and C. Webb (eds), *Policy-making in the European Communities*, Wiley, Chichester.

Weber, A. A. (1991) 'EMU and asymmetries and adjustment problems in the EMS – some empirical evidence', *European Economy*, special edition, no. 1.

Weck-Hannemann, H. and Frey, B. (1997) 'Are economic instruments as good as economists believe? Some new considerations', in Bovenberg and Cnossen (1997).

Weidemann, R. (1990) 'The anti-dumping policy of the European Communities', *Inter Economics*, January/February.

Weiler, J. (1993) 'Journey to an unknown destination: A retrospective and prospective of the European ECJ in the arena of political integration', *Journal of Common Market Studies*, vol. 31.

Weiler, J. (1994) 'A quiet revolution: The European ECJ and its interlocutors', *Comparative Political Studies*, vol. 26.

Weiler, J. (1997a) 'To be a European citizen: Eros and civilisation', *Journal of European Public Policy*, vol. 4.

Weiler, J. (1997b) 'The EU belongs to its citizens: Three immodest proposals', *European Law Review*, vol. 22.

Weiler, J. and Haltern, U. (1998) 'Constitutional or international? The foundations of the community legal order and the question of judicial Kompetenz-Kompetenz', in A.-M. Slaughter, A. Stone Sweet and J. Weiler (eds), *The European Courts and National Courts: Doctrine and Jurisprudence*, Hart, Oxford.

Weiss, F. D. (1988) 'A political economy of European trade policy against the less developed countries?', *European Economic Review*, vol. 30.

Weiss, F. D. (1992) 'Public procurement in the EC Internal Market, 1992: the second coming of the European champion', *The Antitrust Bulletin*, vol. 37, no. 2.

Wemelsfelder, J. (1960) 'The short term effects of lowering import duties in Germany', *Economic Journal*, vol. 70.

Wenban-Smith, G. C. (1981) 'A study of the movement of productivity in individual industries in the United Kingdom 1968–79', *National Institute Economic Review*, no. 3.

Werner Report (1970) *see* Commission of the European Communities (1970a).

Wesseling, R. (2000) *The Modernisation of EC Antitrust Policy*, Hart.

Wessels, W. (1997a) 'An ever closer fusion? A dynamic macropolitical view on integration processes', *Journal of Common Market Studies*, vol. 37.

Wessels, W. (1997b) 'The growth or differentiation of multilevel networks: A corporatist megabureaucracy or open city?', in H. Wallace and A. Young (eds), *Participation and Policy-Making in the EU*, Clarendon, Oxford.

West, E. G. (1973) '"Pure" versus "Operational" economics in regional policy', in G. Hallet (ed.), *Regional Policy for Ever?*, London, Institute of Economic Affairs.

Weyman Jones, T. (1986) *Energy in Europe*, Methuen, London.

Whalley, J. (1979) 'Uniform domestic tax rates, trade distortions and economic integration', *Journal of Public Economics*, vol. 11.

Whalley, J. (1985) *Trade Liberalisation among Major World Trading Areas*, MIT Press, Cambridge, MA.

Whitelegg, J. (1988) *Transport Policy in the EEC*, Routledge, London.

Whitney, S. N. (1958) *Antitrust Policies: American experience in twenty industries*, Twentieth Century Fund.

Wilhelmsson, T. (1995) 'Integration as disintegration of national law', in H. Zahle and H. Petersen (eds), *Legal Polycentricity: Consequences of Pluralism in Law*, Dartmouth, Aldershot.

Wilkinson, D. (1997), 'Towards sustainability in the EU? Steps within the European Commission towards integrating the environment into other EU policy sectors', *Environmental Politics*, vol. 6.

Williamson, J. and Bottrill, A. (1971) 'The impact of customs unions on trade in manufactures', *Oxford Economic Papers*, vol. 25, no. 3.

Williamson, O. E. (1987) 'Economies as an antitrust defense: the welfare trade-offs', in O. E. Williamson, *Antitrust Economics*, Blackwell, Oxford.

Wils, W. (1999) 'Notification, clearance and exemption in EC competition law: an economic analysis', *European Law Review*, vol. 24.

Winters, L. A. (1984a) 'British imports of manufactures and the Common Market', *Oxford Economic Papers*, vol. 36.

Winters, L. A. (1984b) 'Separability and the specification of foreign trade functions', *European Economic Review*, vol. 27.

Winters, L. A. (1987) 'Britain in Europe: a survey of quantitative trade studies', *Journal of Common Market Studies*, vol. 25.

Winters, L. A. (1988) 'Completing the European Internal Market: some notes on trade policy', *European Economic Review*, vol. 32.

Winters, L. A. (1991) 'International trade and 1992', *European Economic Review*, vol. 2.

Winters, L. A. (ed.) (1992) *Trade Flows and Trade Policy after 1992*, Cambridge University Press.

Winters, L. A. (1994a) 'The EC and protection: the political economy', *European Economic Review*, vol. 38.

Winters, L. A. (1994b) 'Intégration européenne et bien-être économique dans le Reste du Monde', *Économie Internationale*, vol. 65.

Wise, M. (1984) *The Common Fisheries Policy of the European Community*, Methuen.

Wolf, M. (1983) 'The European Community's trade policy', in R. Jenkins (ed.), *Britain in the EEC*, Macmillan, Basingstoke.

Wolf, M. (1987) 'An unholy alliance: the European Community and the developing countries in the international trading system', *Aussenwirtschaft*, vol. 1. Also in L. B. Mennes and J. Kol, *European Trade Policies and the Developing World*, Croom Helm, Beckenham.

Wolf, S. (1997) 'The Future Cooperation Between the EU and ACP Countries', in *Intereconomics*, vol.32.

Wonnacott, G. P. and Wonnacott, R. J. (1981) 'Is unilateral tariff reduction preferable to a customs union? The curious case of the missing foreign tariffs', *American Economic Review*, vol. 71.

Wood, A. (1994) *North–South Trade, Employment, and Inequality*, Oxford University Press.

Wood, A. (1995) 'How trade hurt unskilled workers', *Journal of Economic Perspectives*, vol. 9.

Woodland, A. D. (1982) *International Trade and Resource Allocation*, North-Holland.

Woolley, P. K. (1975) 'The European Investment Bank', *Three Banks Review*, no. 105, March.

World Bank (1981a*) World Development Report*, Oxford University Press.

World Bank (1981b) *Accelerated Development in Sub-Saharan Africa: An Agenda for Action*, Washington DC.

World Bank (1984) *Towards Sustained Development in Sub-Saharan Africa: A Joint Program of Action*, Washington DC.

World Bank (1988) *World Development Report*, 1987.

World Bank (1998) *Assessing Aid*, Oxford University Press, New York.

WTO (1995a) *Regionalism and the World Trading System*, Geneva.

WTO (1995b) *Trade Policy Review: European Union 1995*, vols I and II, Geneva.

WTO (1996) *Annual Report 1996*, Geneva.

WTO (1997) *Trade Policy Review: European Union 1997*, vols. I and II, Geneva.

WTO (1998), *Annual Report 1998*, Geneva.

Yannopoulos, G. N. (1985) 'EC external commercial policies and East–West trade in Europe', *Journal of Common Market Studies*, vol. 24, no. 1.

Yannopoulos, G. N. (1988) *Customs Unions and Trade Conflicts: The enlargement of the European Community*, Routledge.

Yannopoulos, G. N. (1990) 'The effects of the single market on the pattern of Japanese investment', *National Institute Economic Review*, November.

Yarrow, G. (1985) 'Strategic issues in industrial policy', *Oxford Review of Economic Policy*, vol. 1, no. 3.

Young, H. (1998) *This Blessed Plot: Britain and Europe from Churchill to Blair*, Macmillan.

Young, S. Z. (1973) *Terms of Entry: Britain's negotiations with the European Community, 1970–1972*, Heinemann.

Ypersele de Strihou, J. van. (1979) 'Operating principles and procedures of the European Monetary System', in P. H. Trezise (ed.), *The European Monetary System: Promise and prospects*, The Brookings Institution, Washington.

Yuill, D. and Allen, K. (1982) European Regional Incentives – 1981, Centre for the Study of Public Policy, University of Strathclyde Press.

Zürn, M. and Wolf, D. (1999) 'European Law and international regimes: The features of law beyond the nation state', *European Law Journal*, vol. 5

Author index

641

Subject index

Page numbers in italics indicate tables or figures. These are only shown separately when there is no textual reference on the page. A list of abbreviations used is given on pages xxv–xxxii.